TRANS HIRSTORY *IN* 99 OBJECTS

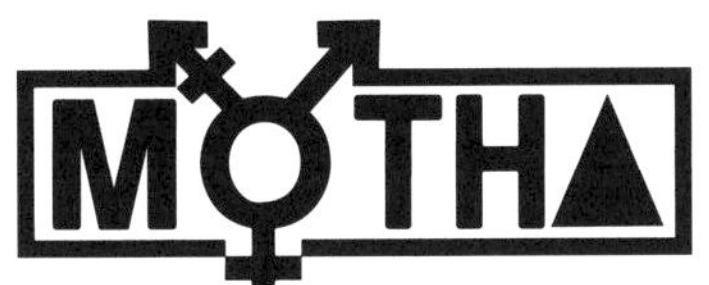

TRANS HIRSTORY *IN* 99 OBJECTS

EDITED BY

David Evans Frantz Christina Linden Chris E. Vargas

HIRMER

TABLE OF CONTENTS

DISCOVERY

RESTAGE

TRACES

SPACES

APPENDIX

* *Interior of Cover and Section Dividers: Edie Fake*

** *Cover and Drawings of Objects: Chris E. Vargas*

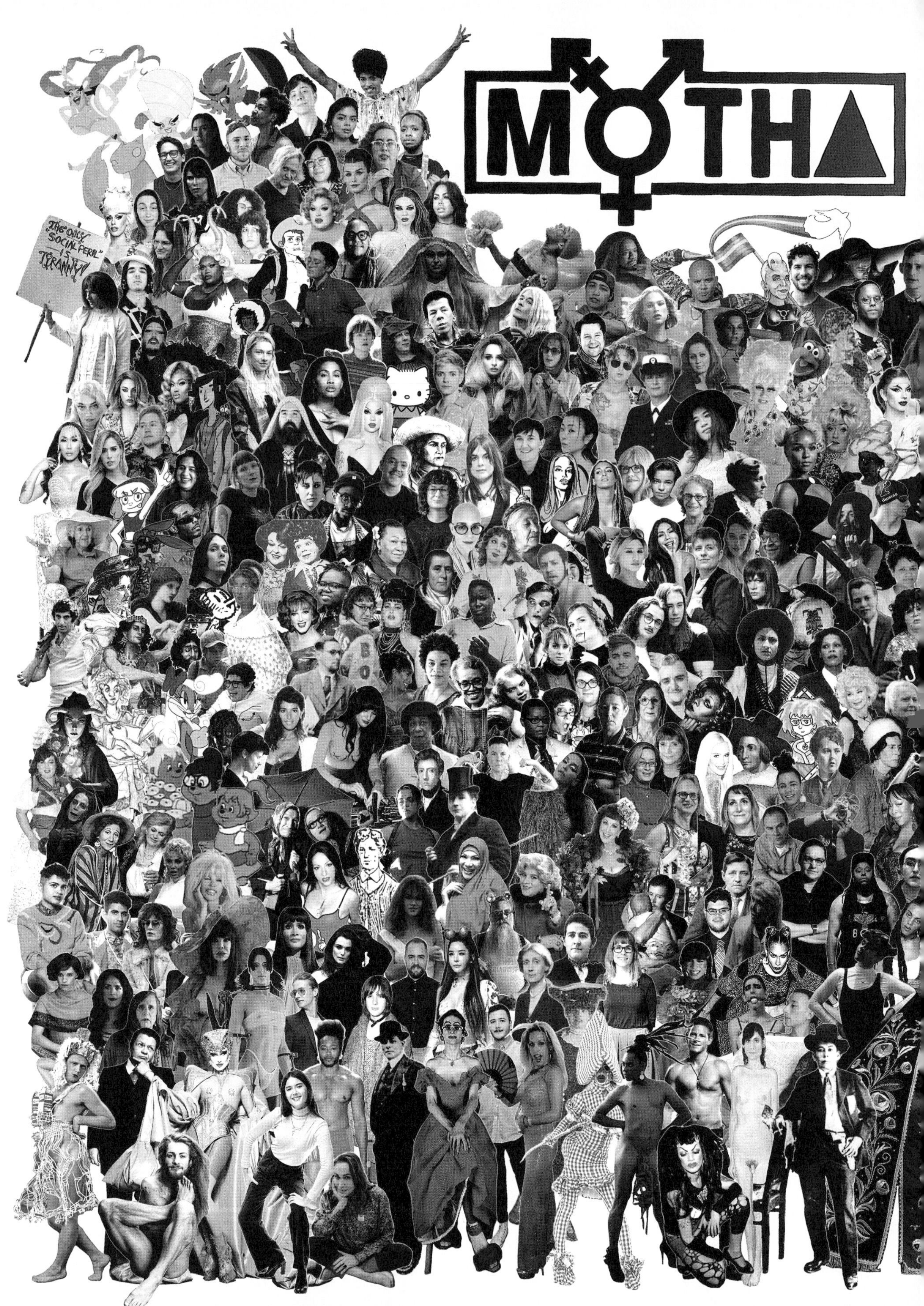
MOTHA
THE ONLY "SOCIAL PERIL" IS TYRANNY!

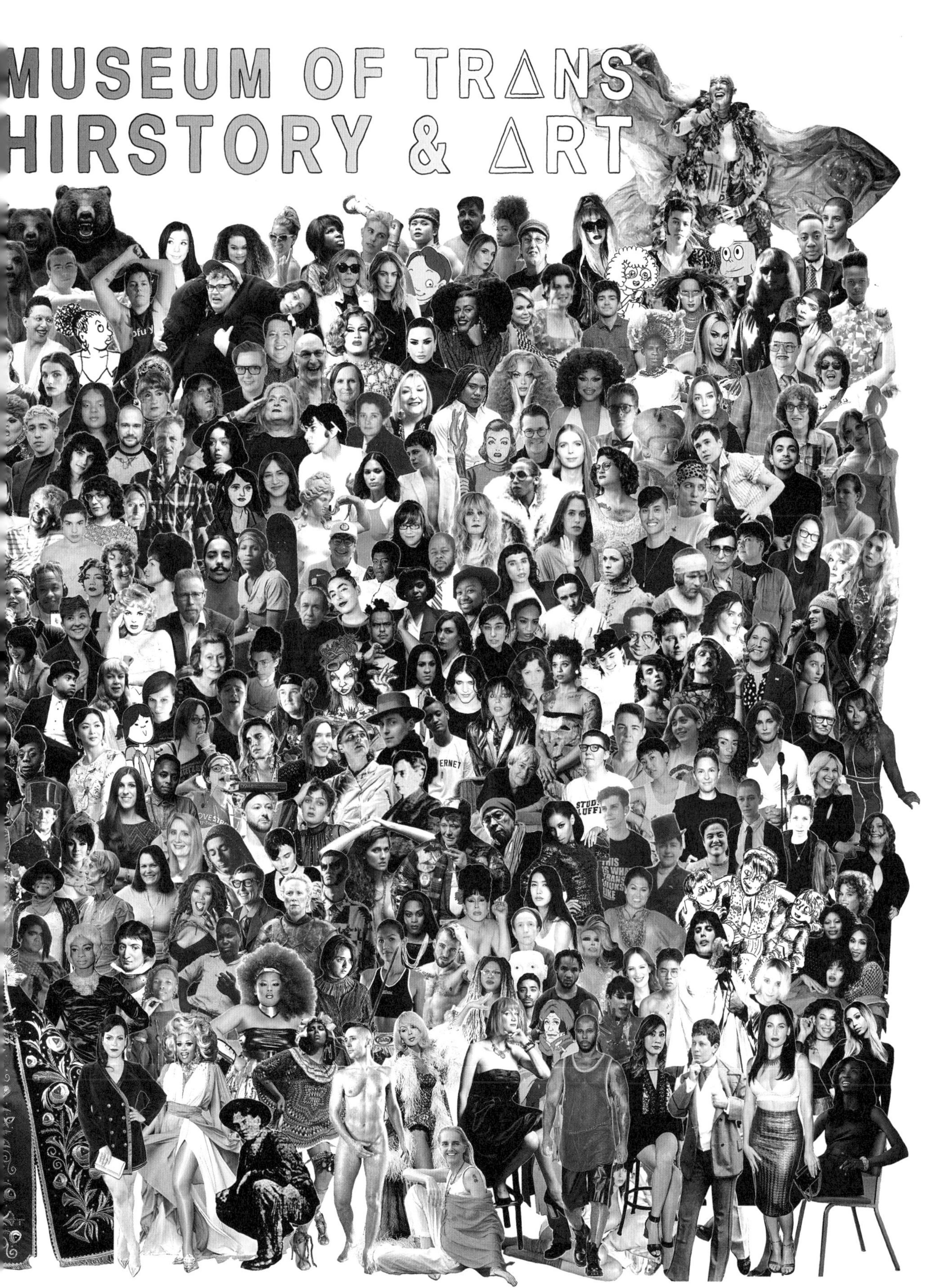
MUSEUM OF TRANS
HIRSTORY & ART

WELCOME TO MOTHA —Chris E. Vargas

Please allow me to introduce myself. My name is Chris E. Vargas, and I am an artist, as well as the founder and self-appointed Executive Director of the Museum of Trans Hirstory & Art, or MOTHA, an institution dedicated to highlighting the significance of trans art and *hirstory* to the current cultural and political landscape.[1] That's right. Not a patriarchal history, nor just a feminist herstory, but a gender-neutral, trans-centric art and activist *hir*story.

I founded MOTHA way back in June 2013, a year before *Time* magazine featured Laverne Cox on its cover and heralded the "Transgender Tipping Point," and two years before reality television and cable networks brought forth the Trans*Jenner* Tipping Point. This is to say that MOTHA surfed the early swell of our most recent wave of media fascination with all things trans—a wave that is either on the wane, has already waned, or is here to stay, depending on whom you ask. But no one would argue that it was definitely a wave that spurred a torrent of anti-trans legislation as well as an onslaught of related media hysteria in the United States.

MOTHA was an attempt to critically examine this heightened moment of visibility when trans art and culture found an entry for the first time into many institutions that had historically been closed off to us. Several trans artists were prominently featured in the 2014 Whitney Biennial, for instance, including Zackary Drucker, Rhys Ernst, and Yve Laris Cohen. Also in 2014, legendary trans historian and scholar Susan Stryker launched the first academic trans studies program, the Trans Studies Research Cluster (TSRC), at the University of Arizona in Tucson. That same year Stryker and Paisley Currah released *TSQ: Transgender Studies Quarterly*, the first non-medical academic journal on trans studies. And, of course, a year earlier in 2013, Cox appeared in a groundbreaking role on the hit Netflix show *Orange is the New Black*, a classic fish-out-of-water story about a privileged white cis woman going to jail.

TIME

THE TRANSJENNER TIPPING POINT

America's next media spectacle

Chris E. Vargas and MOTHA, *TransJenner Tipping Point*, 2015. Digital graphic

There was a widespread misconception that trans people's lives would become universally better as a result of this wave of media attention and visibility, and I'm certainly not the first to point out that this isn't the case. Foucault said it best in the oft-cited quote from his panopt-*iconic* theory: "Visibility is a trap."[2] More visibility brings more vulnerability to many, especially those of us whose lives are already precarious, those with less access to life-sustaining resources like jobs, housing, healthcare, and education. Because we live in a white supremacist, patriarchal, and ableist society, I am referring, in particular, to trans women of color, disabled, and mentally ill trans people. In the past few years, trans children have also been rendered more vulnerable by a moral panic targeting them with backlash bills that restrict their access to bathrooms, sports, educational resources, and gender-affirming medical care. This is all to say that for many of us, visibility is not only a trap but also a slap in the face.[3]

MOTHA was founded to investigate the drawbacks of hypervisibility while honoring trans people who have persevered in the many faces of adversity. Yes, of course, our history contains stories of those who've not only survived but thrived, but it also contains countless inflections of resistance, creativity, beauty, drama, scandal, and ordinariness—the full human experience. I started this museum because understanding my experience in a historical context made me feel connected to something bigger than myself. But I also wanted to examine what happens when marginalized histories get absorbed into mainstream institutions and exhibited on bigger platforms. History is never stable. We always have a stake in it, and it's always dependent on the teller's subjectivity and political aims in the present.

How do we investigate and imagine a history of trans people when the language and identity categories we use, or that are applied to us, are constantly shifting? The separation of sexuality and gender identity, for instance, is relatively new. And while the term "transgender" is not that old, it means something different today than it did a couple of decades ago. The term "nonbinary" now perhaps carries the expansiveness "transgender" once did.

◂ (previous spread) Chris E. Vargas and MOTHA, *Hiroes and Transcestors (Transgender Hiroes 2)*, 2023. Broadside, 33 × 22¾ in. (83.8 × 57.8 cm)

Considering so much flux, where do we look for our histories? Under what labels have they been filed away, and where? And ethically, what responsibility do we have when we apply our contemporary terms and understandings of trans experience to people in the past who had different frameworks to understand their gender and wouldn't recognize themselves within ours today? These questions apply not only when we look across time, but also across geography and culture. As a critical project, MOTHA is a way to explore and engage playfully with these issues and questions, while also acknowledging and honoring an expansively defined trans history and community.

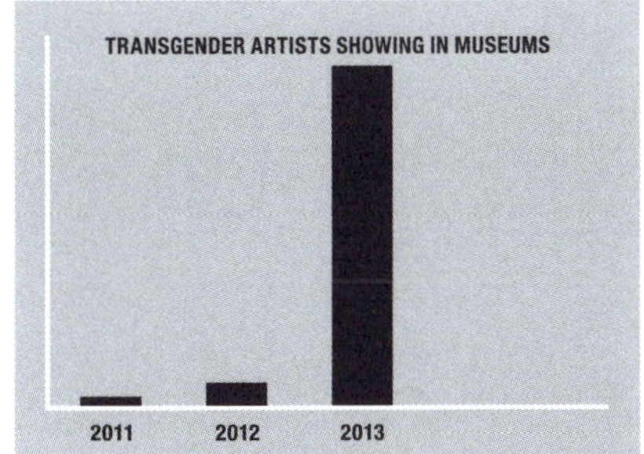

A BRIEF HIRSTORY OF MOTHA

Hirstory is written by the Victor/Victorias

—Anonymous

MOTHA began with a broadside poster. In 2012 I asked my social media networks (okay, Facebook) to name their gender *hiroes* and *transcestors*: the artists and activists and even fictional characters who made an impact or impression on them personally. I did so aware that everyone named would not necessarily call themselves "trans." I also disregarded the false binary of "positive" and "negative" images, recognizing that if I were to omit all negative representations I'd have no one to show from before the year 2014. (I joke.) I labored for nearly a year and compiled a collage of over 250 images of people—ranging from Christine Jorgensen to Sylvia Rivera to Reed Erickson to Peppermint Patty—which at the time felt like a lot, though of course, now it feels like merely a tiny sample of who's out there. Over the course of that year, I started to think about what MOTHA could and should look like, and if it's even possible to create a museum around an identity category that is slippery and unstable. I asked myself questions like, who might be included? And what would a trans art and history canon look like? Could I make that canon inclusive, which actually goes against the process of canonization? And what is the function of the museum anyhow? Who decides what's culturally important, what's worth preserving and exhibiting? What about the history of collecting and its relationship to colonialism? And how might I contribute to the legacy of artists critiquing the many inequities of museums? These questions only seemed to lead me to more questions, so I walked into that metaphorical burning building and just made a museum.

MOTHA was officially brought into this world in 2013 by way of a modest, symbolic ribbon-cutting ceremony at the Yerba Buena Center for the Arts in San Francisco. Symbolic, because even a decade later, I have yet to secure a plot of land on which to break ground for this exciting and still fairly young museum. Did I forget to mention that MOTHA is now and forever "under construction"? The lack of a brick-and-mortar institution has allowed the museum to be fluid

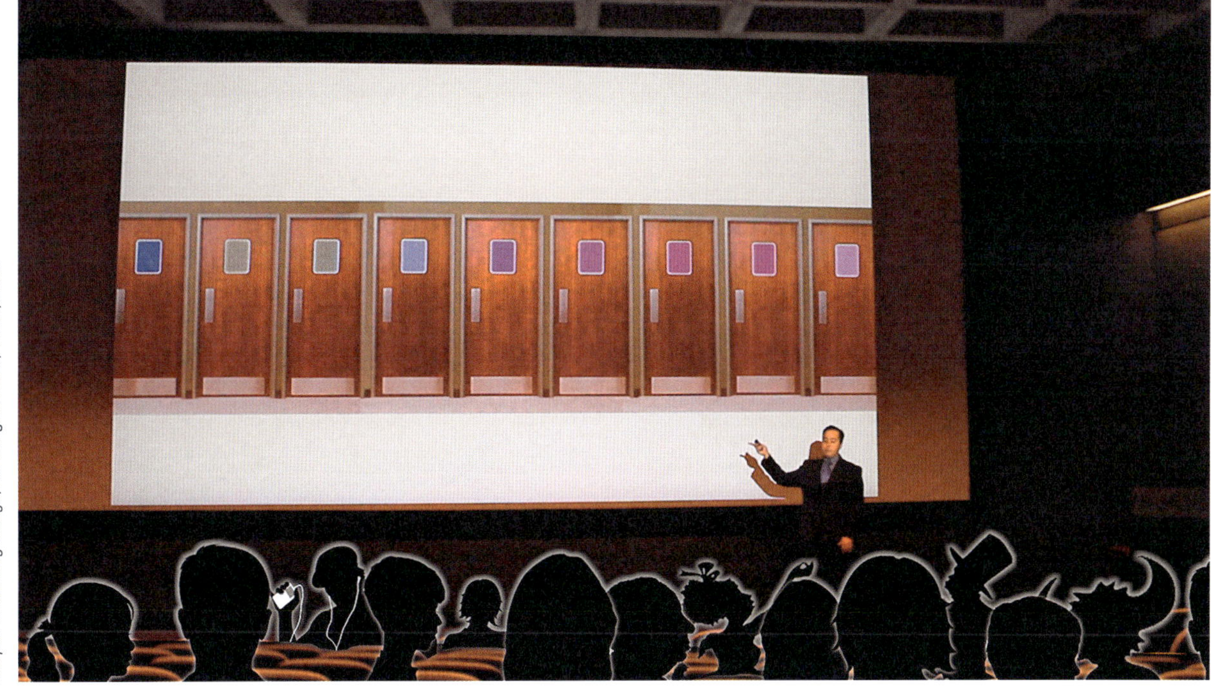

Chris E. Vargas and MOTHA, Stills from *MOTHA Executive Director Address, Chapter 2: Building Design*, 2014. Digital video, 4 min., 5 sec.

and take many forms. For example, in my role as executive director, I have given talks to packed houses around the country about potential design ideas for MOTHA's physical space, inviting audiences to imagine with me what a museum that actually centers trans people could and should look like.

Through MOTHA, I have been fortunate to be immersed in a community of fellow trans and nonbinary artists, activists, writers, scholars, historians, and other cultural producers, collaborators, and co-conspirators. Among them are the many people you will find in this book. I am indebted to this community. MOTHA has been a way for me to honor and support these networks of shared knowledge production and creative labor. MOTHA has also been a way to distribute opportunities. Until very recently, museums were not falling over themselves to extend resources to trans artists, so a goal of the project has always been to leverage the possibilities afforded to MOTHA by brick-and-mortar institutions to promote the work of other trans artists, collaborators, and exhibitors. I created the first (and thus far only) MOTHA Art Awards in 2013, which drummed up a good deal of attention about recent trans achievements (and was also the target of *much* criticism from people not content with the status of their art careers, which further proves my point about the impossibility of ever being wholly inclusive). MOTHA also developed two virtual residencies, one with Tuesday Smillie and another with Jamie Diaz, both of whom appear in this book (see entries 69 and 84). In 2014, Smillie approached me with a desire to create a line on her CV indicating she had attended an artistresidency, one marker of career success that galleries and collectors look for to confirm artistic legitimacy. MOTHA put out a press announcement establishing Smillie's "residency," which required the production of no new work nor time from the artist. In 2022, I was approached by Gabriel Joffe, a friend of the incarcerated artist Diaz, about creating a residency for her. Again, MOTHA announced the "residency," and the press release and an official-looking certificate will be used in Diaz's forthcoming parole appeal.

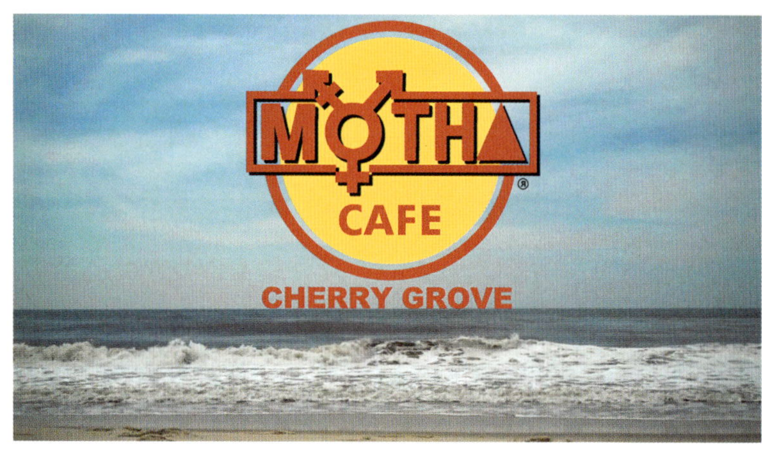

Chris E. Vargas and MOTHA, Still from *MOTHA Executive Director Address, Chapter 5: Cherry Grove*, 2014. Digital video, 4 min.

INSTITUTIONAL CRITIQUE

MOTHA has been a way for me to leverage my opportunities and share them with others, through commissions and collaborations, by exhibiting the work of other trans artists, and by calling attention to the scholarship that enlightens and sustains us. At the heart of the project is a spirit of generosity. It's been a way for me to wedge my foot in the door of institutional spaces and shoo in as many other trans and queer people as I can get away with.

But in addition to showcasing trans history and art, MOTHA has always been a project of institutional critique. Through it, I have playfully and critically interrogated the function and power of archives and museums, and I have also tried to expropriate and redistribute that power. MOTHA claims museum status because museums carry cultural weight and establish public trust. Through the project, I have managed to fool people when they first encounter it, not just for the sake of fooling them (because, you know, trans people are sneaky), but as a way to lure them into a critical stance.

To give some examples, in my presentations as executive director, I have proposed not only plans for MOTHA's new building but also for lucrative commercial tie-ins, including themed restaurants. Think Hard Rock Cafe or Planet Hollywood, except with important artifacts of trans history displayed behind Plexiglas while you dine. At the other end of the spectrum, when I was invited to contribute to SFMOMA's *Open Space* blog, I presented a press release stating that after weeks of careful negotiation, SFMOMA agreed to repatriate a number of significant trans-themed artworks from its permanent collection to MOTHA, where they rightfully belong.[4]

But even with this element of critique, from its inception MOTHA has been attractive to established institutions. Indeed, I have often been surprised (and dismayed) by the capacity museums have to absorb and diffuse critique. There are many amazing and visionary curators who invite artists and projects into museums to make interventions about institutional power in the hope of initiating dialogue. But the structural changes museums must make in order to have a real impact on the future—such as the reparation of colonial plunder, divestment from the fossil fuel industry, and taking an uncompromising look at the white supremacist, patriarchal, and transphobic roots of Western museum culture—don't come fast enough. Often it seems institutional critique only makes museums *more* powerful. They get to take credit for the radical ideas presented within their walls, and meanwhile, power structures remain the same. Independent curators who bring credibility and diversity to museums are freelance, which means they have no job security, and in general, museum labor is so underpaid that often the only people who can manage such careers are those blessed with trust funds. Let's face it, any capital trans artists are likely to receive from showing their work is non-material. If we want to leverage this exposure into sustainable lives, we'll have to do it ourselves.

TRANS HIRSTORY IN 99 OBJECTS

Most of my work as MOTHA has been focused on "Trans Hirstory in 99 Objects," a project that initially took the form of a series of six gallery exhibitions and now culminates in this book. This visual and material exploration of various objects that hold significance in narrating the history of trans communities includes artworks, archival documents, publications, films, videos, and other artifacts. Rather than try to outdo the British Museum's *A History of the World in 100 Objects* (2011) or the Smithsonian's very American act of one-upmanship, *History of America in 101 Objects* (2013), both of which were influences for the project, MOTHA's chosen number of 99 sought to acknowledge in advance the limitations that are inherent to this undertaking.

The first three exhibitions in this series were creative and critical explorations of LGBTQ archives and collecting in North America, largely focused on regional histories. The first show took place at the ONE National Gay & Lesbian Archives at the University of Southern California Libraries in Los Angeles in 2015. It was followed by a show at the Henry Art Gallery at the University of Washington in Seattle in 2016, and then an exhibition drawn from the Transgender Archives at the University of Victoria in British Columbia in 2018. Together, these exhibitions investigated the absences and distortions in queer archives. Which stories and biographies are included, and which aren't? What is present, and what else is missing, misread, or mislabeled? The shows were a mix of objects newly found and freshly excavated from the archives, and reconstructions and reimaginings of other objects lost to hirstory.

The fourth exhibition took place at the Portland Art Museum in 2018. For it, I moved away from an exploration of physical archives and instead focused on trans moving images. I made over the gallery to resemble a trans-centric Blockbuster Video store, with a wallpaper commemorating ninety notable titles as if they were displayed on the shelves. In this room was screened a program of nine short works by contemporary trans artists and filmmakers. The fifth exhibition, *MOTHA and Chris E. Vargas: Consciousness Razing —The Stonewall Re-Memorialization Project*, took place at the New Museum in New York City between late 2018 and early 2019 in the lead-up to the fiftieth anniversary of the Stonewall Uprising, which is often celebrated as the beginning of the modern LGBTQ movement. For the show, I explored how Stonewall remains a geographically, demographically, and historically contested site by inviting twelve artists to propose new memorials to the rebellion. We then presented these as maquettes within a 1:17

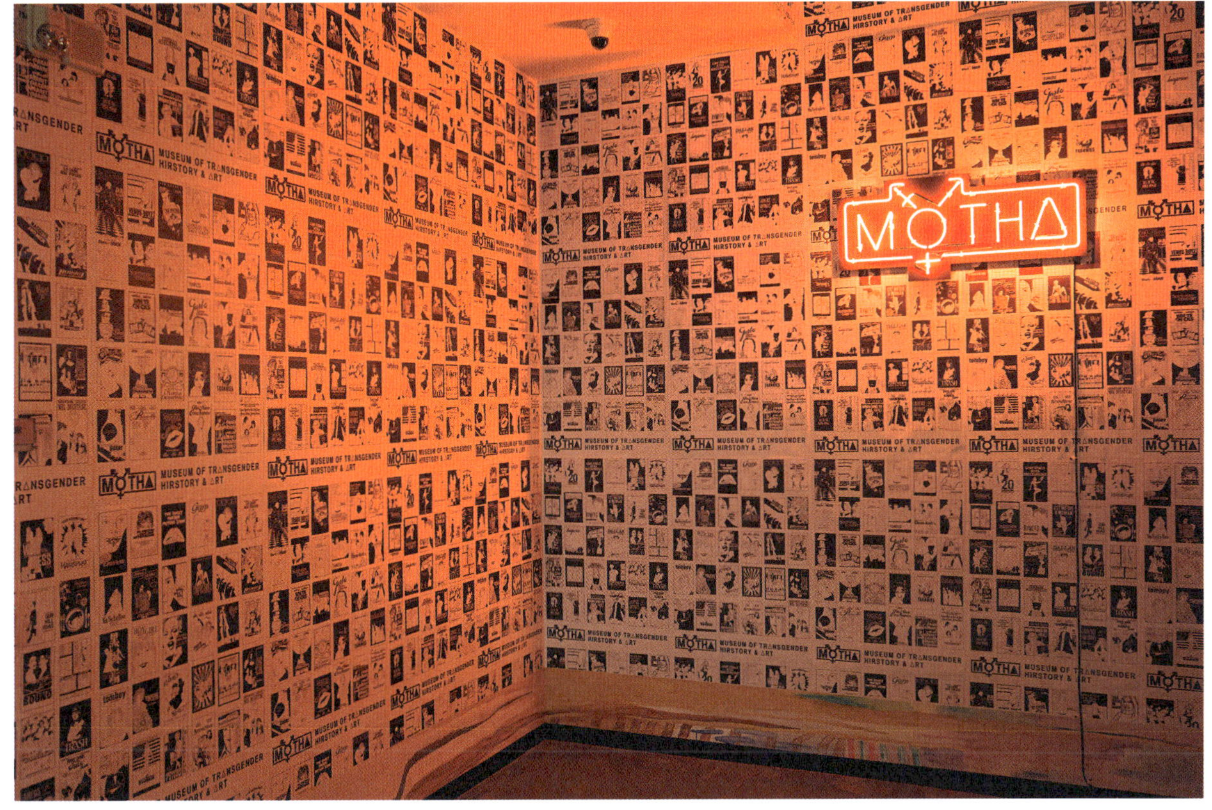

Installation of *Trans Video Store* in *Between.*, an iteration in the exhibition series *We. Construct. Marvels. Between. Monuments.* at the Portland Art Museum, 2018

scale model of Christopher Park, the small park across from the Stonewall Inn, known most prominently for the sculpture *Gay Liberation* (1981) by George Segal, a deficient monument to the rebellion on multiple levels.[5]

Finally, the sixth exhibition of the "Trans Hirstory in 99 Objects" series took place in the summer of 2019 at the Oakland Museum of California, as a MOTHA exhibition-within-an-exhibition in *Queer California: Untold Stories*, which itself commemorated the fiftieth anniversary of Stonewall by looking at histories of California. I designed a hand-drawn beaux-art style facade through which to enter the installation, along with an interior wallpaper behind the displayed objects that further commemorated people, places, organizations, books, and films of significance to the trans history of the San Francisco Bay Area.

THIS BOOK

The "Trans Hirstory in 99 Objects" exhibitions were always building toward this book, but the book you are holding is not a catalogue of those exhibitions. It's something entirely different. The exhibitions were limited geographically, and also, because galleries like to be filled, they were focused on physical, exhibitable objects. The format of the book allows for a more expansive approach, with alternative methods for including things lost to history, such as Charley Parkhurst's stagecoach (see entry 62) and Harry Allen's bowler hat (see entry 39), both of which are represented by my own illustrations, and even the inclusion of entirely non-material historical "objects," such as Crystal LaBeija's iconic read in *The Queen* (1968; see entry 11).

The nine sections of the book serve to pull out common threads among the objects, but they are porous and are by no means meant to deny the potential for objects to inhabit other sections just as easily. Approach the edges of each section as fluid. The first section highlights the **Refusal** of trans people to accept the unacceptable. **Transformation** is about physical, psychological, pharmacological, science fictional, and administrative changes to our bodies and lives. The next section looks at how some of those transformations, for better or for worse, become **Hypervisible** to the public. And when trans lives become visible, the inevitable cultural response has been **Sensation**. And if we're lucky, we become **Deities**; this section speaks to the spiritual, iconic, and transcendent within and among us. **Discovery** examines how we have been both the subject and perpetrator of invasive investigation. **Restage** reveals the impulse to reclaim various aspects of our history or reimagine shared cultural touchstones as trans-inclusive. **Traces** speaks to the clippings and fragments of trans lives and culture and the impulse to combat one's own erasure. **Spaces** is about the places we create and defiantly demand for ourselves.

The 99 objects are each paired with texts by a range of writers, from scholars to poets to activists to popular historians. Some of the texts are written by the artists themselves or are interview transcriptions. The book also contains another introductory essay by one of my co-editors, Christina Linden, examining MOTHA's historical trancestors and sibling projects. And finally, a chronology of MOTHA's activities was organized by former museum studies grad student and current disillusioned post-graduate, independent scholar, and musician Sage Ballard de la Bastida.

As I write this text in the spring of 2023, there is a spate of repressive legislation targeting healthcare for trans youths, as well as legislation purporting to prevent kids from being in contact with gender-transgressive adults, drag performers, and storybook readers. I'm referring to bills that seek to prevent trans kids' access to gender-affirming healthcare, as well as anti-drag bills. This backlash in response to heightened visibility is nothing new. Morgan M Page, who has multiple texts in this volume and is also the producer of the well-researched podcast, *One From the Vaults*, has reflected insightfully on this:

> As we move through continual cycles of visibility and violence that seem to have no end in sight, perhaps it is through control and access to our own narratives that we can begin to build a way out. Uncovering and sharing our histories is a powerful tool for helping us dream our way into futures we want to live.[6]

I couldn't have said it better myself. So I won't try. Thanks, Morgan.

As I stated earlier, the number 99 is inherently incomplete. Our history is still being written and will continue to be for every trans generation moving forward. History is dynamic and alive, and it absolutely should be. This book, like everything else that MOTHA has done, is a playful (and impossible) attempt to compile a cohesive history of trans art and culture, while also acknowledging its challenges. It is futile but essential work. The number also reminds me of a 99-cent store, and I hope this book pulls you in with the promise of a bargain. I think you'll find that it's a lot of trans hirstory and art bang for your buck. And I hope you'll use your savings to somehow contribute to that history, too.

Notes

1. The project was first called the Museum of Transgender Hirstory & Art, but Transgender was shortened to Trans for ease and inclusivity in 2016.
2. Michel Foucault, *Discipline and Punish: The Birth of the Prison*, trans. Alan Sheridan (New York: Vintage Books, 1995), 200.
3. For more critical writing on trans visibility and resistance, see *Trap Door: Trans Cultural Production and the Politics of Visibility*, eds. Johanna Burton, Eric A. Stanley, and Tourmaline [fka Reina Gossett] (Cambridge, MA: MIT Press, 2017).
4. Chris E. Vargas, "Disembodied States: Press Release," *Open Space* (SFMOMA blog), April 27, 2016, accessed April 6, 2023, https://openspace.sfmoma.org/2016/04/disembodied-states-press-release/.
5. Segal's monument has long been the subject of consternation for the queer community. For an overview of some controversies and information about MOTHA's New Museum installation, see Emily Colucci, "George Segal Sucks: Finding a Better Way to Memorialize Stonewall at the New Museum," *Filthy Dreams*, November 17, 2018, accessed April 6, 2023, https://filthydreams.org/2018/11/17/george-segal-sucks-finding-a-better-way-to-memorialize-stonewall-at-the-new-museum/.
6. Morgan M Page, "One From the Vaults: Gossip, Access, and Trans History-Telling," in Burton et al., *Trap Door*, 135–44.

▸
Chris E. Vargas and MOTHA, *PRONOUN SHOWDOWN*, 2015/19. 17 × 11 in. (43.2 × 27.9 cm)

AESTORY BEARSTORY
BISTORY BLACKSTORY
BROWNSTORY
GAYSTORY
EARTHSTORY EIRSTORY
FAWNSTORY
FAERSTORY FEYSTORY
ITSTORY HAYSTORY
HERSTORY
HIRSTORY
HISTORY HUSTORY
LEZSTORY
MEOWSTORY MYSTORY
NONSTORY NUNSTORY
ONESTORY OURSTORY
PAWSTORY PERSTORY
TERSTORY THEIRSTORY
TRANSTORY
VISTORY WITCHSTORY
XYRSTORY ZIRSTORY

MOTHA MUSEUM OF TRANSGENDER HIRSTORY & ART

MUSEUM/TRANS/HIRSTORY/ART —Christina Linden

99

Gender is multiple and changeable, and trans is multiple and changeable. The shape is hard to define, as is the correlating action. The act of refusal, the embrace of ambiguity, as well as the act of crossing over all come into play. For some there is the desire for a different destination and a complete abandonment of the point of origin. For some there is a desire to live in a more fluid and expansive space, to have the right to keep changing, and to hold multiple identities successively and/or concurrently.[1] Even with this basis in mutability, sometimes there is a need to be situated by pushing off against some*thing* and/or latching on to some*thing* else. How concrete does this thing need to be? How large? Are emotions good enough things? How unique or mundane should these things be? Does a website count? A diffusion of hormones in the air? This book counts on the idea that objects can be helpful touchstones or tools to this end, but also that we do not really need to have them in hand to be in dialogue with them. That they need not be contemporary but also that they might be lost to history. We hope this set of things provides an opportunity to develop a discourse that directs its gaze, at least in part, away from visibility, legibility, and bodily appearance and towards other forms of knowing and experience. This book, *Trans Hirstory in 99 Objects,* is part of artist Chris E. Vargas's decade-long project, the Museum of Trans Hirstory and Art (MOTHA). Both projects are implicated in open discussions about whether these objects need to be in museums or in archives, and whether these institutions need to be realized in real time and space. They follow an inquiry about what it means to be real—and realized.

The slipperiness of language is also in question. We might start there, with: "Language is both an entryway and a dead end," but a trans reading of language might be one in which the continuous process of transit, transition, and the right to changeability are central.[2] Let's try to use language to write these provisional *hir*stories at the same time we try to avoid a fixed or rigid reading of words and their possibilities, as with bodies and identities and their possibilities. Words can be more or less solid, more or less slippery, more or less misconstrued, misused, and contested. And sometimes a specific meaning doesn't last long. In 2018 (this feels so long ago), Jack Halberstam wrote that:

> Historical accounts of gender variance are crucial at a moment when change happens at a blistering pace. A student informed me recently that the term cisgender was so "old," it was, they suggested, "very two years ago" and no longer in use. ... For two years to represent a massive period of change (and nowadays it can) means that longer histories become almost irretrievable.[3]

Inevitably, the specific language used within this book will continue to shift after it is published. As you read this it will already be out of date. Nonetheless, as the specificity of each of the 99 objects allow us something to push up against, each of the words that make up the acronym MOTHA are also a productive starting point for this introduction. I'm setting out not so much to define these words, though, as to build out some context upon which these slippery objects might rest, temporarily. Catch them while you can.

MUSEUM

So, let's say the museum could also be an object, or at least a thing to push against.[4] Does *this* object have to be solid? Does it need a building, or can its infrastructure be utopian, be no place? Does it have to take physical form to be real? This is a moment in which there is widespread discussion about the need to reform or reimagine museums—with calls to bring them to a close entirely. Is it the essential character of the institution that it be solid, or is that the most problematic part?

If it is an object, the museum is also a system of classification for the objects it contains. As scholar Leah DeVun points out in *The Shape of Sex* (2021), "Classification always depends on boundaries, and boundaries always define who or what is included by deciding who or what is excluded,"[5] and at the same time, "... as soon as we imagine a binary, we tend to breach it in our thought, to imagine what lies between or beyond its contours."[6] So, let's say this museum is an instigation. I've heard MOTHA described as virtual, faux, fictional, and fake. In fact, I would say that it is none of these. Not a hoax but a possibility and a projection. It is, in fact, a small organization, sometimes just the size of one artist's imagination and action.

We can situate MOTHA within the legacy not only of trans representation, then, but also within the context of other museums and arts institutions by artists; museums as works of art and art

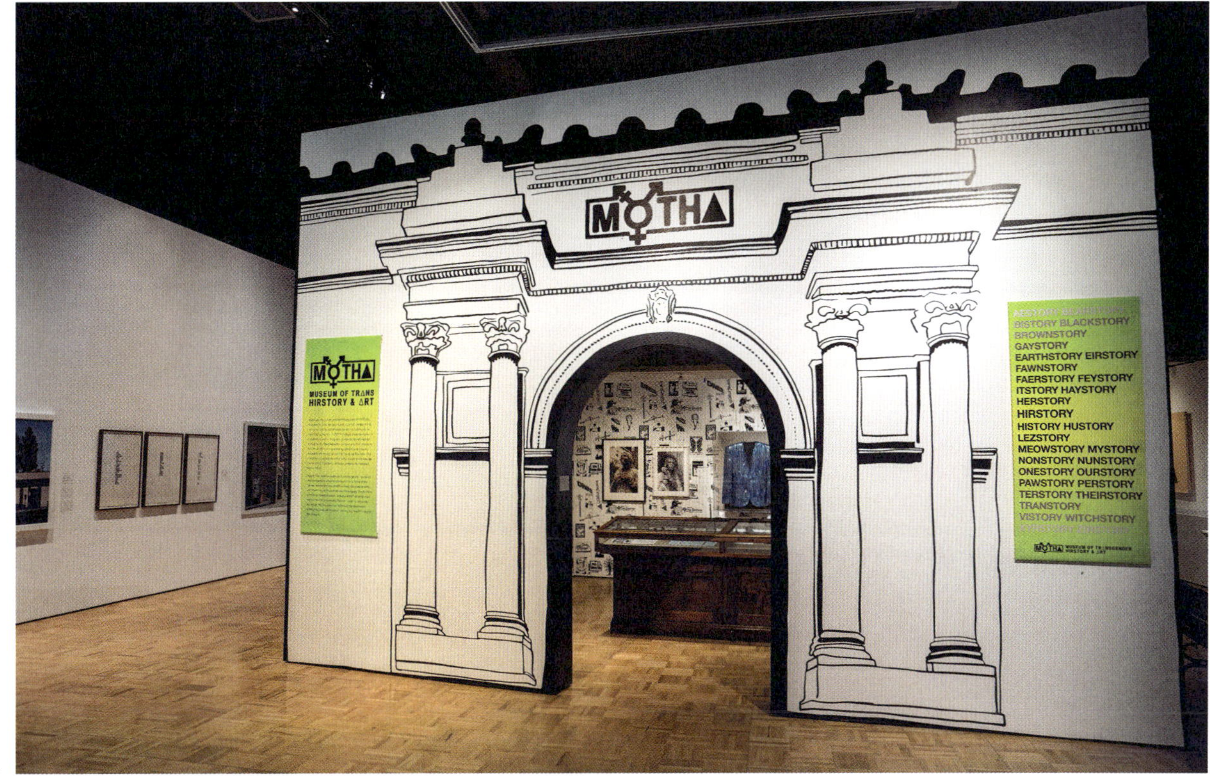

Chris E. Vargas and MOTHA, *Trans Hirstories of the Bay Area*, an installation of artworks and artifacts as part of the exhibition *Queer California: Untold Stories*, Oakland Museum of California, 2019

as critique of museums.[7] These are both conceptual and practical. Some of these have been extraordinarily well documented, theorized, and rehashed, and others much less so.

The most thoroughly historicized and discussed among these examples is also the work that is most often named as the progenitor of this form of institutional critique.[8] White cis male Belgian artist Marcel Broodthaers made himself the director of the "Musée d'Art Moderne, Département des Aigles" in 1968. The museum was a fiction and a work of art. We might think of some of Duchamp's work, such as the string installation he made for the 1942 *First Papers of Surrealism* exhibition, as a precedent for an artist's treatment of an exhibition as an occasion to bring attention to the form, structure, and function of the exhibition format. But Broodthaers' "Musée" took on many aspects of the institution of a museum, as subject for his artistic work, over the course of several connected projects. Between 1968 and 1972, Broodthaers, as the museum's director, inaugurated a number of divisions that were sometimes accompanied by exhibitions embedded within other arts institutions, including the Kunsthalle Düsseldorf and Documenta 5. The divisions, or sections, included a Cinema Section, a Literary Section, and an Eagle Section. Broodthaers parodied the form of collection display, as in his use of labels that declared each object in the Figure Section to NOT be a work of art. He also took aim at the entanglement of the art world in marketing interests and strategies as he mounted the Publicity Section. In Broodthaers' own words on the project:

> This Museum is a fictitious museum. It plays the role of, on the one hand, a political parody of art shows, and on the other hand an artistic parody of political events. Which is in fact what official museums and institutions like Documenta do. With the difference, however, that a work of fiction allows you to capture reality and at the same time what it conceals.[9]

MOTHA plays the role of a museum and provides political and artistic parodies of the structure of the museological, but it also, importantly, brings attention to the exclusion of work by trans artists, especially historically, within these institutions. While focused on women rather than trans artists, the use of humor to bring attention to the issue of exclusion based on gender identity is also central to the work of the Guerrilla Girls, a feminist collective of artists that formed in 1985 in the wake of a demonstration in response to the exhibition *An International Survey of Painting and Sculpture* at New York's Museum of Modern Art. As in much of their subsequent work, the protestors cited data about the disparity of representation for women artists and artists of color in the exhibition; there were only thirteen women included in the all-white exhibition of 161 artists and the curator made a statement that "any artist who wasn't in the show should rethink 'his' career."[10] The aesthetic and action of the Guerilla Girls makes reference to protest culture in its use of graphic-heavy posters and performances that protest the disproportionate underrepresentation of women artists in galleries, museums, and art museums, in particular.

Mining the Museum: An Installation by Fred Wilson, mounted in 1994 as a project of The Contemporary, Baltimore, took on museological activity under the umbrella of artistic practice, as did Broodthaers. But Wilson intervened within the collection, archives, and building of the Maryland Historical Society to do so, casting light on the fraught practices of acquisition, taxonomy, and representation within this particular institution and by extension, within museum practice at large.[11] Wilson's interventions were largely focused on histories of race and racism. Wilson called attention to both presence and absence within official histories: in one installation, three pedestals with carved marble busts of Henry Clay, Napoleon Bonaparte, and Andrew Jackson were shown alongside three empty pedestals labeled for Harriet Tubman, Frederick Douglass, and Benjamin Banneker.

Strategies for representing absence are especially important when it comes to individuals and communities that have been subject to neglect and erasure. MOTHA has similarly represented absence within its previous projects using a number of different strategies and continues to do so within this book. For *MOTHA and Chris E. Vargas: Consciousness Razing—The Stonewall Re-Memorialization Project* (2019), Vargas elevated mundane objects—like a brick, a shot glass, and fake dog poo—to the status of museum artifact by encasing them in a vitrine to stand in for the many alleged objects, all now lost to time, that sparked the Stonewall Riots (see entry 78). Drawing is another important strategy Vargas uses to represent objects that have been lost to, or obscured within, official history: in past exhibitions, including *Queer California: Untold Stories* (2019) at the Oakland Museum of California, he created a wallpaper with a repeated pattern of drawn motifs to represent icons, organizations, and places that he wanted to call out as having been important to trans hirstory in the San Francisco Bay Area. And in this volume, images which could not be photographed (for any of a number of reasons) are rendered by the artist for inclusion.[12]

While Vargas has thus far kept his clothes on when addressing audiences as the director of MOTHA, his performance of this role also begs some comparison to Andrea Fraser's embodiment of the museum director in her 2003 performance *Official Welcome*. Fraser lays bare the role and the implication of each player in the world of Fine Arts as carrying the institution within themselves. The artist disrobes while delivering the address, exploring the idea of becoming the art object at the same time she elaborates upon the "social conditions and relations" of the field of art, drawing on the work of a series of scholars and theoreticians as she does so. In a section of the performance for which she uses the writing of Benjamin H. D. Buchloh as a source, she states, "If visibility has become art's primary horizon of aspiration, then for any radical aesthetic practice to be historically convincing it must now define itself in opposition to that culture."[13]

Inarguably the most important precedent for Vargas's project of trans institutional critique and fabrication in MOTHA, though, is Museo Travesti del Perú (MTP) by Giuseppe Campuzano, also known as GiuCamp (see entry 95). The accompanying writing by curator and scholar Miguel A. López

THE ADVANTAGES OF BEING A WOMAN ARTIST:

Working without the pressure of success.
Not having to be in shows with men.
Having an escape from the art world in your 4 free-lance jobs.
Knowing your career might pick up after you're eighty.
Being reassured that whatever kind of art you make it will be labeled feminine.
Not being stuck in a tenured teaching position.
Seeing your ideas live on in the work of others.
Having the opportunity to choose between career and motherhood.
Not having to choke on those big cigars or paint in Italian suits.
Having more time to work after your mate dumps you for someone younger.
Being included in revised versions of art history.
Not having to undergo the embarrassment of being called a genius.
Getting your picture in the art magazines wearing a gorilla suit.

Please send $ and comments to: Box 1056 Cooper Sta. NY, NY 10276 **GUERRILLA GIRLS** CONSCIENCE OF THE ART WORLD

Guerrilla Girls, *The Advantages of Being a Woman Artist*, 1988. Offset lithograph, 17 × 22 in. (43.2 × 55.9 cm)

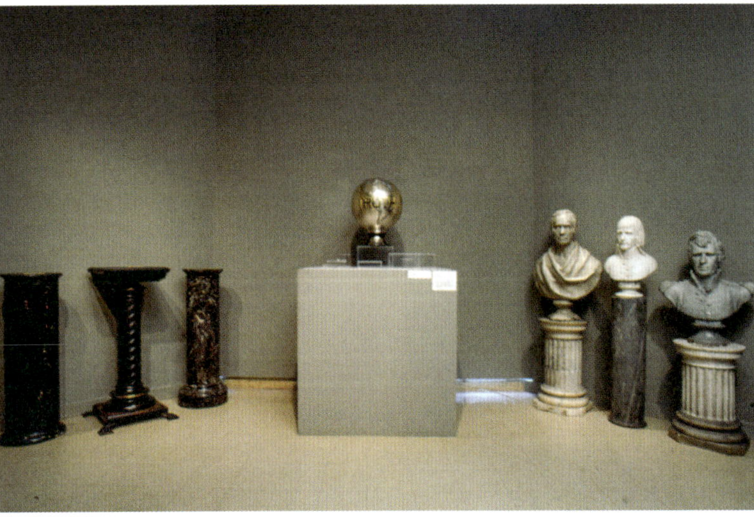

Fred Wilson, Installation in *Mining the Museum* at the Maryland Historical Society, Baltimore, 1992–93

presents a succinct summary of the project's importance, one that draws from the significant book he edited in 2013 on MTP together with GiuCamp as author, in the year of the artist's passing.[14] Vargas didn't yet know about MTP when MOTHA was founded, but it is an important sibling project, and there are even some strategic and aesthetic similarities in particular works created by GiuCamp and Vargas, as in the use of digital collage to assemble pertinent transcestors on a single plane of representation. This book aspires, like GiuCamp did, not just to collect "queer objects," but to set about "denaturaliz[ing] the expectations of scientific truth and legibility," as a means of "*queering* the historiographic methods ... and the systems of normative meanings that were passed on as truth."[15]

Ultimately, these works of institutional critique dig into the problematic nature of the systems that confine artifacts and artworks to vitrines, storage rooms, or archaeological labs, even as some also highlight those cases in which the careful protection of certain objects has allowed these artists to overturn long-held narratives. The clean, uncluttered interiors of a gallery with each cord carefully tucked and hidden away, a neat label to provide concise contextualization for every piece: each of these projects demonstrate the subversive possibility of turning this institutional language incrementally back on the repressive colonial systems from which it was born—even as it strains against the possible futility of the project.[16] Museum climate control standards were set after paintings stored in slate quarry caves in Wales during WWII were determined to have incurred minimum damage, as compared to paintings stored in underground rail tunnels during WWI.[18] The climate at large is clearly out of control, and so the project of trying to maintain climate control within galleries becomes an easy metaphor for the absurdity of the premise behind institutional collecting at its most basic. It is easy to forget about and lose things hidden in caves, but the advantage of a brick-and-mortar institution is that it creates the pretense of being set apart while still providing some ongoing access. It relates to the ritual function of a sanctuary in this way. We know, or we should know, that nothing really exists in isolation though. The interior is equally subject to the consequences of climate change and structural racism and shortsightedness and hyperbole and the desire to create clean narratives. Perhaps the porousness, ambivalence, and open-ended nature of the artist's institution is ultimately just more honest—not virtual, not fake, but shored up through the strength of imagination only an artist can bring, and through the flexibility made possible by informal collaboration.

The selection of objects for this book is not without restriction. Permissions, knowledge, records, bias, and omissions still dictate what we include here, even if we are infinitely grateful for the consultants and researchers who have contributed. Using illustration, insinuation, description, and fragment, this book can represent the missing objects in ways different from those that might be available in an exhibition. The between-the-lines becomes the clear subject; we can make much of this. Always under construction, never a complete collection, eccentric to its core, available to be mined and improved and transformed. Always in transformation.

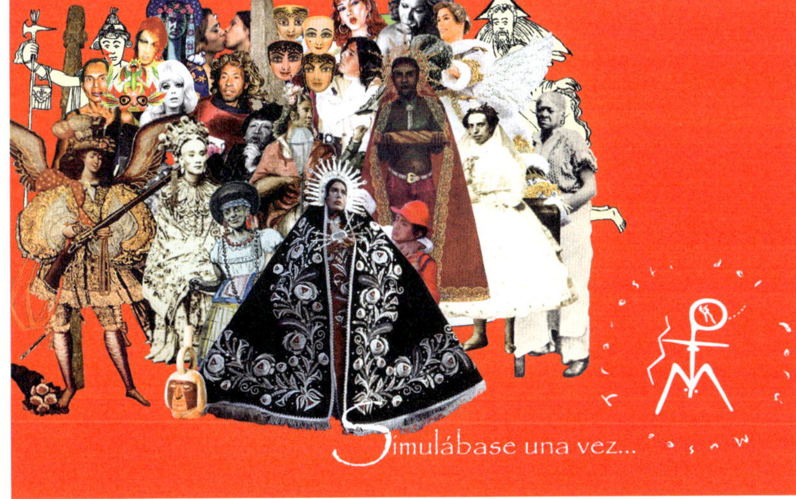

Giuseppe Campuzano, *Simulábase una vez...*, 2008. Digital collage

TRANS

This is almost certainly the most slippery word-object in this lot. Vargas has always been clear that he has aimed to create an inclusive project and considers any expression of gender transgression to be welcome within the purview of MOTHA. This comes not only from a place of generosity, but also from an insistence that it is important to seek out and honor transcestors, even those who might not have identified as such during their own lifetimes. It is helpful to think about scholar David J. Getsy's definition of trans capacity in this regard; one might think of the objects we will be including as some of the "things" Getsy refers to here:

> Transgender capacity is the ability or the potential for making visible, bringing into experience, or knowing genders as mutable, successive, and multiple. It can be located or discerned in texts, objects, cultural forms, situations, systems, and images that support an interpretation or recognition of proliferative modes of gender nonconformity, multiplicity, and temporality. In other words, transgender capacity is the trait of those many *things* that support or demand accounts of gender's dynamism, plurality, and expansiveness.[18]

This approach hasn't been without its complications. MOTHA had a large-scale installation within the exhibition *Queer California: Untold Stories* at the Oakland Museum of California, which included a sequined jacket that had been

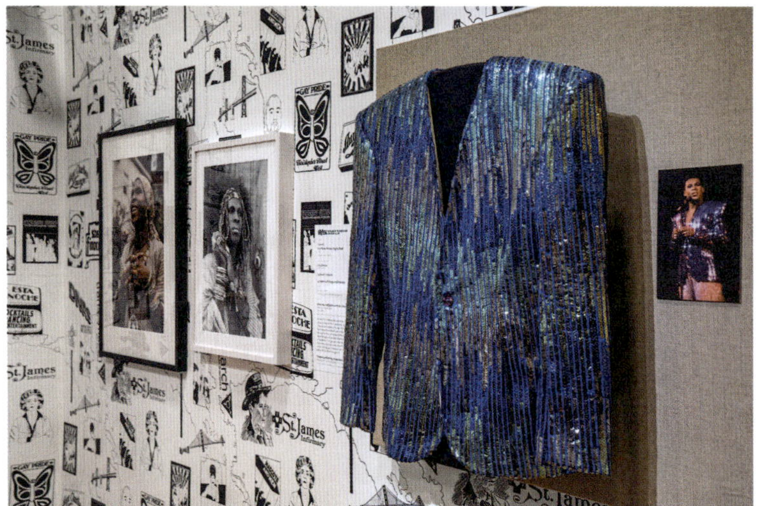

Materials related to Sylvester in the installation *Trans Hirstories of the Bay Area* as part of the exhibition *Queer California: Untold Stories*, Oakland Museum of California, 2019

worn by the performing artist Sylvester (see entry 50), and a photo of Sylvester on stage wearing it, and speakers that played a recording of Sylvester's 1978 hit song, "You Make Me Feel (Mighty Real)." A group of people who had been friends with Sylvester prior to his passing in 1988 were in attendance and took issue with his inclusion in MOTHA, declaring exuberantly at the door of the installation that "Girlfriend was not transgender; he was a gay man!" This assertion of the feeling that a friend was being misrepresented was itself *mighty real*, and not to be minimized. We know that Sylvester challenged the gender binary but also that he insisted on being simply Sylvester, opposing at times the application of labels like "drag queen." It is not possible to know how Sylvester himself might respond to the inclusion of his costumes in this book, just as we can't ask the unnamed individual represented in George Catlin's *Dance to the Berdash* (1835–37) how they felt about their representation in that painting, about the term "berdash," or about the painting's inclusion in this book along with Kent Monkman's 2020 counter-narrative as painting *Honour Dance* (see entry 72). The stakes around questions of representation, inclusion, and the right to self-define are elevated when we consider those historical figures who have been stigmatized over gender variance and also race, class, legal status, or other intersection factors, and certainly even more so for figures such as the Sac and Meskwaki (Fox) individual represented by the white cis colonizer-painter in 1835, for whom no means of self-representation remains on record. It cannot be overstated that the intention behind the inclusion of these objects in this volume is not to retroactively re-gender the dead nor is it to impose contemporary terms on historical figures, moments, and objects. Words have different meanings now than they might have had, in some cases, even months ago. Vargas uses "trans" in a sense that is in alignment with the way that activist and scholar Susan Stryker explains she chose to use the word "transgender" in her foundational book *Transgender History* (2008, revised and reprinted 2017): "to refer to people who move away from the gender they were assigned at birth, people who cross over (*trans-*) the boundaries constructed by their culture to define and contain that gender."[19]

The word *trans* in this title is thus meant as an umbrella term that encompasses any number of terms currently in common use that have important differences in meaning, including transgender, transmasculine, transfeminine, nonbinary, nonquaternary, genderqueer, genderfluid, Two-spirit, intersex, or Differences of Sexual Development (DSD). In some cases, it may also refer to the activities of drag and crossdressing. The text in this book also includes several terms which are no longer in common use, and which may in fact be not only offensive but also fully cancelable in the contemporary climate, including the term "berdash," which we've already mentioned as well as tranny, transvestite, sissy, hermaphrodite, and female husband, to name just a few. We ask readers to consider that where these are used it is in a historical sense and as a record of the changes that have taken place not only in language but in the way gender variance, transgression, identity, and expression have been considered at different points in time and in different cultures and subcultures. In DeVun's explanation of chosen terminology for *The Shape of Sex*, for instance she explains that in the premodern world,

> … a "hermaphrodite" was a concept that offered a highly flexible means to order the world. By drawing and crossing boundaries, the idea of a hermaphrodite enabled—and forced—communities to sort people, ideas, and situations into interrelated binaries and, moreover, to assign to them a positive or negative value. This idea could serve as a vector of fluidity and metamorphosis but also, at other times, as a hybrid that constricted and policed categories.[20]

This example not only insists on a suitably complex definition for the term at hand, but also the significant distance in time between the present day and the premodern is useful for throwing into clear contrast the shift in meaning over the course of time. This shift may be harder for contemporary readers to see when we turn to more recent changes, as with the use of the term "queer" over the course of the last half-century but both illustrate a related mutability.

HIRSTORY

A growing proportion of young people today identify as queer in some sense, and many of these as other than cis.[21] The framework for characterizing queer and trans culture shifts dramatically in this context and places a preponderance of weight on the present and the future. The project of finding transcestors takes on increased importance. In order to shift and queer that temporal weight on the present, it is important to understand that there were very different frameworks in the past and there will, in all certainty, be different ones in the future. How can we think through a trans framework of time and chronology? In assembling and editing the list of 99 objects for this book, my fellow editors and I have endeavored to include those missing objects and stories that won't have a place in the traditional museum, ever. After extended deliberation and consultation on the scope and organization of the history presented here, the editorial team decided to focus on the Americas, while acknowledging that the book, which emerged from MOTHA's regionally focused exhibitions in North America, will inevitably retain a North American bias.[22] We also decided not to arrange the objects chronologically—the typical default for most of the "History of X in X Objects" precedents—choosing thematic grouping and affective connections to create an order that provided some structure without resorting to linearity. Concise, neat narratives are often favored to make sense of a mess of shifting frameworks and identities and linguistic categories and names and lives. Can an aggregate approach hold more space and allow for the mutability and flexibility that are key to the project?

I turn again to DeVun in her apt articulation of the ways in which history can satisfy the contemporary's desire for both "a usable past and a more radically transformative future." Even at a less extreme remove from the present than the premodern period DeVun examines, the hirstories included in this book, I would argue, relate similarly to our contemporary consciousness: "Where we do find resonances between past and present, we are reminded that our own current controversies are far from unique. And where the premodern period stands as a world completely apart, it testifies to the simple fact that dramatic change has happened, and that it is indeed still possible."[23] On the other hand, scholar Howard Chiang asks, "If the past can be mobilized to serve the experience of the present, what are the stakes of counting on divides of culture—or race, ethnicity, nationality, and even language—for the purpose of bringing normative legibility and comfort to claims of alternate being?"[24] In the face of this challenge and this need for extreme care, we present not only one story, and certainly not only *his* story, but rather 99 texts in a variety of voices and styles. We hope that humor and poetry and activist declarations and personal perspectives together might help mobilize change and possibility but also do justice to each of these individual objects and the events and lives with which they intersected for their own sake and on their own terms.

ART

This book doesn't aim to be a comprehensive survey of anything. In particular, it is neither a complete survey of artistic projects that address trans identity—by artists who may or may not identify as trans—nor of art by trans artists.

Artists who examine, interrogate, and reveal historical aspects of trans capacity and expression in their work were prioritized when the list was assembled. Nicki Green's 2016 *Breaking Dishes at Gene Compton's* (see entry 14) is a clear example of this type of work. The work was made to commemorate the fiftieth anniversary of an uprising that took place in San Francisco's Tenderloin district at the popular Compton's Cafeteria. This spontaneous eruption was a response to persistent discrimination and harassment, usually at the hands of the police. By applying custom decals on mugs found in thrift stores in the Tenderloin in 2016, Green calls attention to the action which is purported to have set off the unrest in 1966: one queen throwing a cup of coffee in a cop's face. Tourmaline's film *Mary of Ill Fame* (2020–21; see entry 38), on the other hand, is a reimagining as well as a commemoration of the life of Mary Jones, a Black trans woman who came to "ill fame" in 1836 when she was arrested for stealing a man's wallet in Manhattan. She was mocked at the trial and imprisoned at Sing Sing Correctional Facility, but an alternate resolution for Jones is given form within Tourmaline's film, which is a work of speculative fiction.

Contemporary representation of historical figures, including those for whom no form of traditional portrait was ever made or preserved, are another important category in the book. Manuel Mathieu's painting *The Prophetess 2* (2020; see entry 5), which represents Romaine Rivière, a key figure in the Haitian Revolution also known as Romaine-la-Prophétesse, is perhaps the most beguiling. It uses a combination of abstraction and figuration as a means of giving meaningful form to Rivière's obscurity within traditional historical bodies of representation. The commissioned sculpture created by Keioui Keijaun Thomas for entry 79, *Memories on Cotton and Sugar Cane Receipts* (2022), is another example, and one which further complicates the notion of representation, especially when the official historical record is scant and written in a voice very far removed from that of the person whose own story one would wish to represent. The only official trace we can find in relation to Miss Betty Cooper is a fugitive slave announcement from 1771. Thomas created an assemblage out of materials, many of them ephemeral, used for their symbolic and not just their structural or formal properties. The assemblage could be described as figurative but not all elements lend to this effect. It could also be described as fugitive (black balloons, yellow yarn, and a delicately placed headscarf might slip away out of sight if the work were left on view for any length of time) and is reminiscent of a funerary memory jug (see entry 7 for another example of this type of object).

Notably, the book largely sidesteps the category of projects that assemble photographic portraits of individuals who transgress binary gender norms. In alignment with interest in visibility politics, which has waxed and waned over the course of decades, those projects have played an important role and have also received their due attention over time and continue to do so. Some of the photographers who have invested many years in these projects have individual images included in this book in relation to other represented objects. For instance, Del LaGrace Volcano, known for their photographic series including Visibly Intersex and the portraits created for *The Drag King Book* (1999), allowed us to include a campaign photograph (see entry 30) of Murray Hill taken in 1997 as part of Murray's run for the Mayor of New York. And Mariette Pathy Allen, who has also been working on portraiture projects including The Gender Frontier since the early 1990s, has contributed photographs that show the "CAMP TRANS: For Humyn-Born Humyns" banner that marked the 1994 Camp Trans gathering outside of the Michigan Womyn's Music Festival (see entry 90). Additionally, while Marcel Pardo Ariza's contemporary practice often includes portraits of intergenerational groups of trans-of-color individuals, they have created a series of commissioned photographs for this book which sometimes include partial images of people associated with objects that we are featuring. This is in line with a parallel practice where they often use cropping and unexpected angles that focus on skin and bodies rather than faces, in photographs that are integrated into colorful installations.

Beyond representation of individuals and events, contemporary artworks included in this volume also address the history of phenomena that have played a major role in changing trans experience over time. Works that address the possibilities for medicalized transition, for instance, fit this bill. We might think of *Hormonal Fog* (2016–22; see entry 17) by Candice Lin and P Staff in this category. Its subtle act of testosterone suppression for gallery visitors plays out as a nuanced and suggestive demonstration of the simultaneous prospect and threat of reliance on traditional herbal medicine for supporting transition. There are also works here that address the ways in which dramatic changes in technology have impacted trans experience and representation. For *Becoming Dragon* (2008; see entry 19), artist micha cárdenas created a performance that existed both on the multiplayer online platform Second Life and in physical space. Chelsea Thompto's *Landmarks* website (2021; see entry 67), on the other hand, illustrates the ramifications of the increasingly ubiquitous role that facial recognition software plays in our lives, with a look at its complicated role in reading and misreading trans faces.

Additionally, although a large number of films and video works by trans artists about trans experience could have added to the conversation fostered by this project, we also had to consider which works would lend themselves well to the format of a book. We ultimately (but reluctantly) had to cross a number of these off the list. Where we did include media works, it is in some cases because they were emblematic of a genre that has had a major impact on the perception of trans identity. Consider, for example, the popular films *Tootsie* (1982) and *Dressed to Kill* (1980) in relation to the representation of crossdressing and trans visibility in comedy and thriller, respectively. (see entries 44 and 42). And in these cases, we also found that there was something important to say about a prop or other object within the film upon which to focus the entry. As regards other moving image works that have been included, they address important issues related to the trans presence in official archives and historical records, as with Tourmaline's *Mary of Ill Fame* mentioned above, or Kiyan Williams' *Reflections / Refractions in BlaQ* (2017; see entry 68) which creates space for footage from filmmaker Marlon Riggs's archive that had previously been left on the cutting room floor.

The artworks created by Edie Fake for the endpapers and section dividers in this book suggest a kind of architecture or organizing structure within which representations of objects featured in each section are neatly presented. As in all of Fake's work, a vibrant set or setting for queer possibility, habitation, and sociability is suggested by each drawing. But, like in this essay, not every*thing* fits. A neat taxonomy was never our goal, and the sections are organized on affective links and loose associations rather than on strict themes. In determining the order, my coeditors and I found that the connections to be drawn across the section dividers are often as interesting as the juxtapositions that take place within the sections, resulting in a lovely kind of runniness.

As previously mentioned, the book also uses illustrations by Chris E. Vargas to represent objects that were never saved or documented in their own time, like the doughnut (see entry 1) that could have been one of those thrown in Los Angeles in May 1959 to kick off the Cooper Do-nuts Riot. Who is to say that doughnuts might not be the most important objects within the trans historical record? Imagine them sailing through the air, hurled at police officers and the systems of intolerance and oppression they represented. Imagine them ground into the pavement of downtown Los Angeles under the sharp heels of strong women, beaten down and fed up but emboldened by the solidarity of collective action. That which must have long since decomposed or disappeared becomes art within the book—with the distinction between art and mundane object also dissolved.

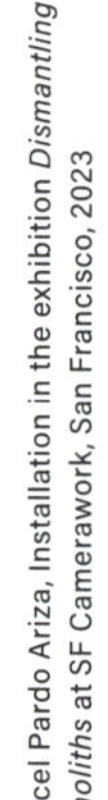

Marcel Pardo Ariza, Installation in the exhibition *Dismantling Monoliths* at SF Camerawork, San Francisco, 2023

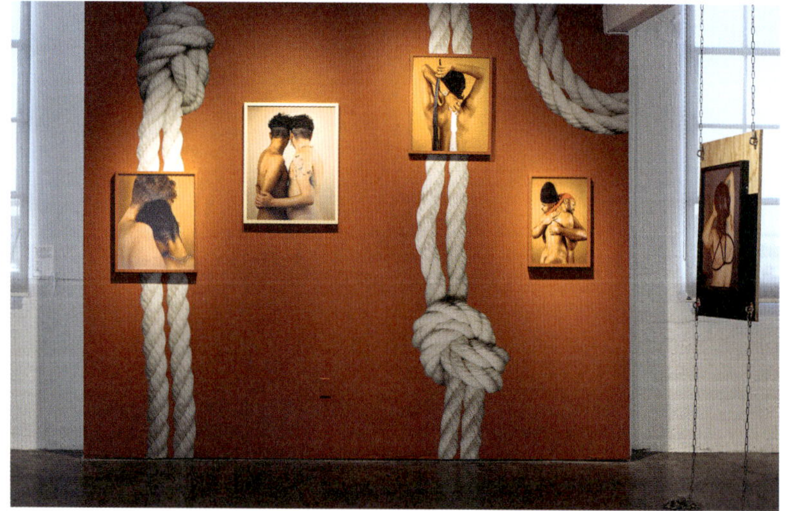

1. See Christina Elizabeth Sharpe, *In the Wake: On Blackness and Being* (Durham, NC: Duke University Press, 2016). Christina Sharpe—in recognizing wholly involuntary, forced transatlantic passage as one kind of trans* passage—evokes the irrevocable quality of displacement as one that renders the one who has moved or been moved away from a point of origin to another place of habitation as neither of one place nor another.
2. Michael Bronski, *A Queer History of the United States* (Boston: Beacon Press, 2011), xviii.
3. M. W. Bychowski, Howard Chiang, Jack Halberstam, Jacob Lau, Kathleen P. Long, Marcia Ochoa, C. Riley Snorton, Leah DeVun, and Zeb Tortorici, "Trans*historicities: A Roundtable Discussion," *TSQ: Transgender Studies Quarterly* 5, no. 4 (November 2018): 658.
4. Certainly, there are a couple of museums counted among the 99 objects in this book, see entry 29 for the Pritzker Military Museum and entry 95 for Museo Travesti del Perú.
5. Leah DeVun, *The Shape of Sex: Nonbinary Gender from Genesis to the Renaissance* (New York: Columbia University Press, 2021), 5.
6. DeVun, *The Shape of Sex*, 6.
7. We could trace several different and divergent paths through this lineage. Indeed, many have. See for example Elena Filipovic, *The Artist as Curator: An Anthology* (London; Milan: Mousse Publishing, 2017); James Putnam, *Art and Artifact: The Museum as Medium* (New York: Thames & Hudson, 2001 and 2009); Jeff Khonsary, Kristina Lee Podesva, and Pacific Association of Artist Run Centres, *Institutions by Artists*, vol. C. (Vancouver: Fillip Editions, 2012); and Julia Bryan-Wilson, "Impermanent Collections: Julia Bryan-Wilson on Queer and Trans Artists' Museums," *Artforum* 60, no. 1 (2021): 228; among many others.
8. Marcel Duchamp is sometimes named as a precedent even for Broodthaers, though, as George Baker points out, "Duchamp preceded Broodthaers here: having exposed through the use of the readymade the extent to which the forms of industry had penetrated those of art, Duchamp had similarly begun just before World War II to reflect on the extent to which art itself was becoming an industry, mediated through institutions like museums. He allegorized this situation when he reproduced his work in miniature or through photographs in the salesman's sample case that became the *Boîte-en-Valise* (Box in a Valise, 1941)." George Baker, "This is Not an Advertisement: Marcel Broodthaers' 'Section Publicité,'" *Artforum* 34, no. 9 (May 1996): 86–89, 124.
9. Marcel Broodthaers, "Musée d'Art Moderne, Département des Aigles, Section Art Moderne et Publicité" (1972), in *Marcel Broodthaers: Collected Writings*, ed. Gloria Moure (Barcelona: Ediciones Poligrafa, 2012), 354.
10. "The Guerilla Girls Archive," *The Getty Research Institute*, accessed January 21, 2023, https://www.getty.edu/research/special_collections/notable/guerrilla_girls.html.
11. See Lisa G. Corrin, ed., *Mining the Museum: An Installation by Fred Wilson* (New York: The New Press/The Contemporary, 1994).
12. For *Mining the Museum* (1994), Wilson included documents from the Manuscripts Division of the Maryland Historical Society Library as well, such as the 1812 estate inventory of a man named Nicholas Carroll, for whom slaves were listed on a ledger with accompanying values alongside livestock, crops, land, and a share of stock in the City of Baltimore. This book also turned to cruelly bureaucratic documents for evidence of the lives of those not recorded elsewhere in history, as in entry 80 on the registry of the Mission San José, in which the baptism and renaming of individuals recorded as male by the priests and designated as *joya* and/or effeminate indicates the presence of third gender or Two-spirit people among the Indigenous population of early California.
13. Andrea Fraser "Official Welcome," in *Museum Highlights: The Writings of Andrea Fraser*, ed. Alexander Alberro (Cambridge, MA: MIT Press, 2005), 215.
14. Giuseppe Campuzano and Miguel A. López, eds. *Saturday Night Thriller Y Otros Escritos, 1998–2013* (Lima: Estruendomudo, 2013).
15. Entry 95 in this publication, Miguel A. López, "Giuseppe Campuzano, Museo Travesti Del Perú, 2003–13," 276.
16. In a recent article that includes a discussion of MOTHA and Museo Travesti del Perú, art historian Julia Bryan-Wilson goes as far as saying that museums that exist as a queer artists' project are the only ones worth saving. See Bryan-Wilson, "Impermanent Collections," 228.
17. See Neil Prior, "How National Gallery's art was hidden from Hitler in WW2," *BBC News*, May 19, 2019, https://www.bbc.com/news/uk-wales-48308512.
18. David J. Getsy, "Capacity," *TSQ: Transgender Studies Quarterly* 1, nos. 1–2 (2014): 47–49.
19. Susan Stryker, *Transgender History: The Roots of Today's Revolution*, 2nd ed. (Berkeley: Seal Press, 2017), 1.
20. DeVun, *The Shape of Sex*, 6.
21. A number of articles in both mainstream and queer media platforms cite a 2021 Gallup survey to this effect. See for example Nico Lang, "Gen Z Is the Queerest Generation Ever, According to New Survey," *them*, February 24, 2021, https://www.them.us/story/gen-z-millennials-queerest-generation-gallup-poll; or Samantha Schmidt, "1 in 6 Gen Z Adults Are LGBT: And This Number Could Continue to Grow," *Washington Post*, February 24, 2021, https://www.washingtonpost.com/dc-md-va/2021/02/24/gen-z-lgbt/. Consider also a 2022 Pew Research Center survey on trans identity: Anna Brown, "About 5% of Young Adults in the U.S. Say Their Gender is Different from Their Sex Assigned at Birth," Pew Research Center, June 7, 2022, https://www.pewresearch.org/fact-tank/2022/06/07/about-5-of-young-adults-in-the-u-s-say-their-gender-is-different-from-their-sex-assigned-at-birth/.
22. Many thanks to the consultants who helped us interrogate and expand our focus in early stages of the project, including Qwo-Li Driskill, Che Gossett, Miguel A. López, Amos Mac, Cyle Metzger, Susan Stryker, and Jeannine Tang, among other friends and colleagues with which we had ongoing conversations throughout its development.
23. DeVun, *The Shape of Sex*, 14.
24. Bychowski et al., "Trans*historicities," 659.

▶
(following spread)
Chris E. Vargas and MOTHA, *Transgender Hiroes*, 2013. Broadside, 33 × 22¾ in. (83.8 × 57.8 cm)

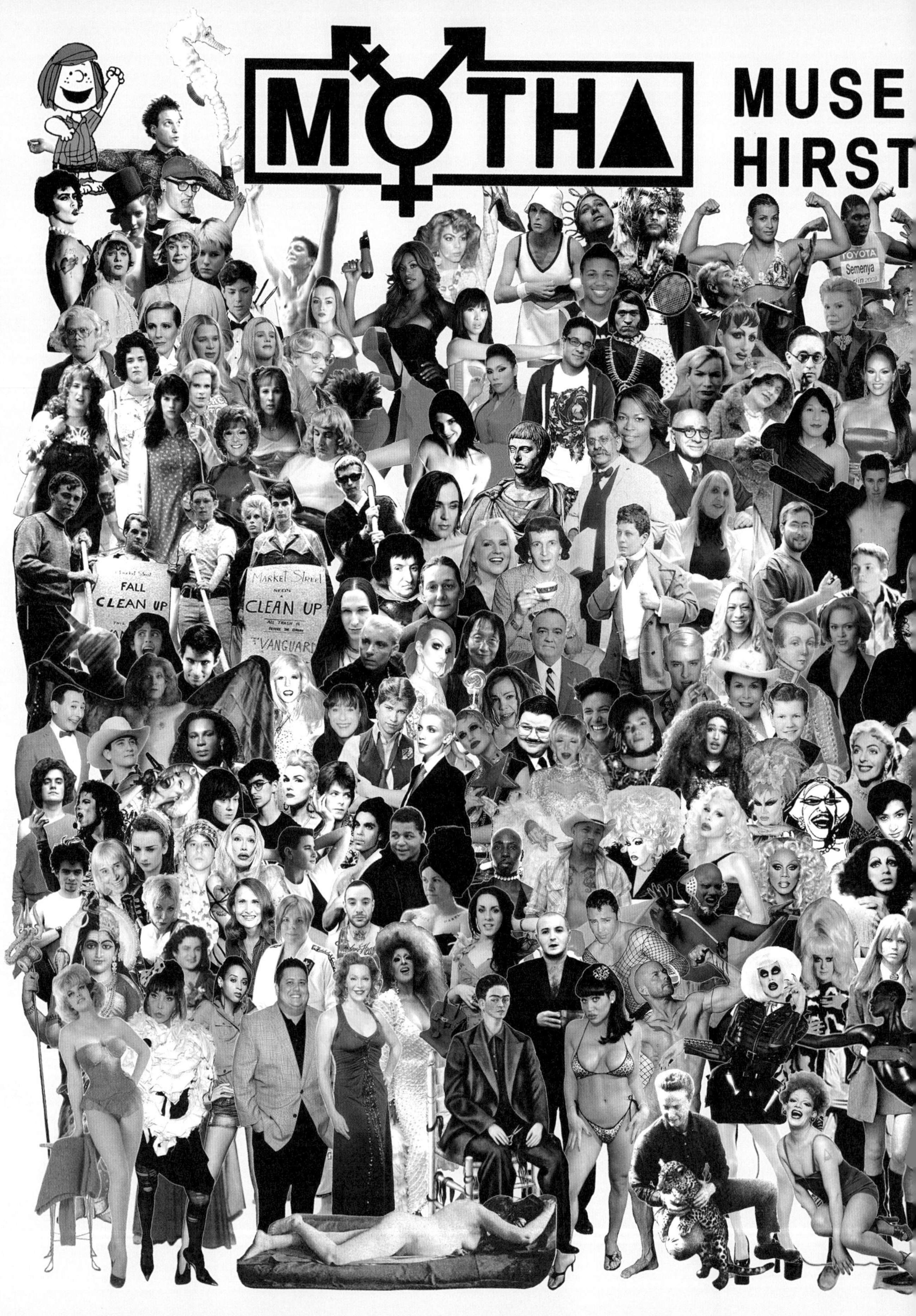
MOTHA
MUSE
HIRST
TOYOTA
Semenya
Market Street
FALL
CLEAN UP
Market Street
NEEDS
CLEAN UP
VANGUARD

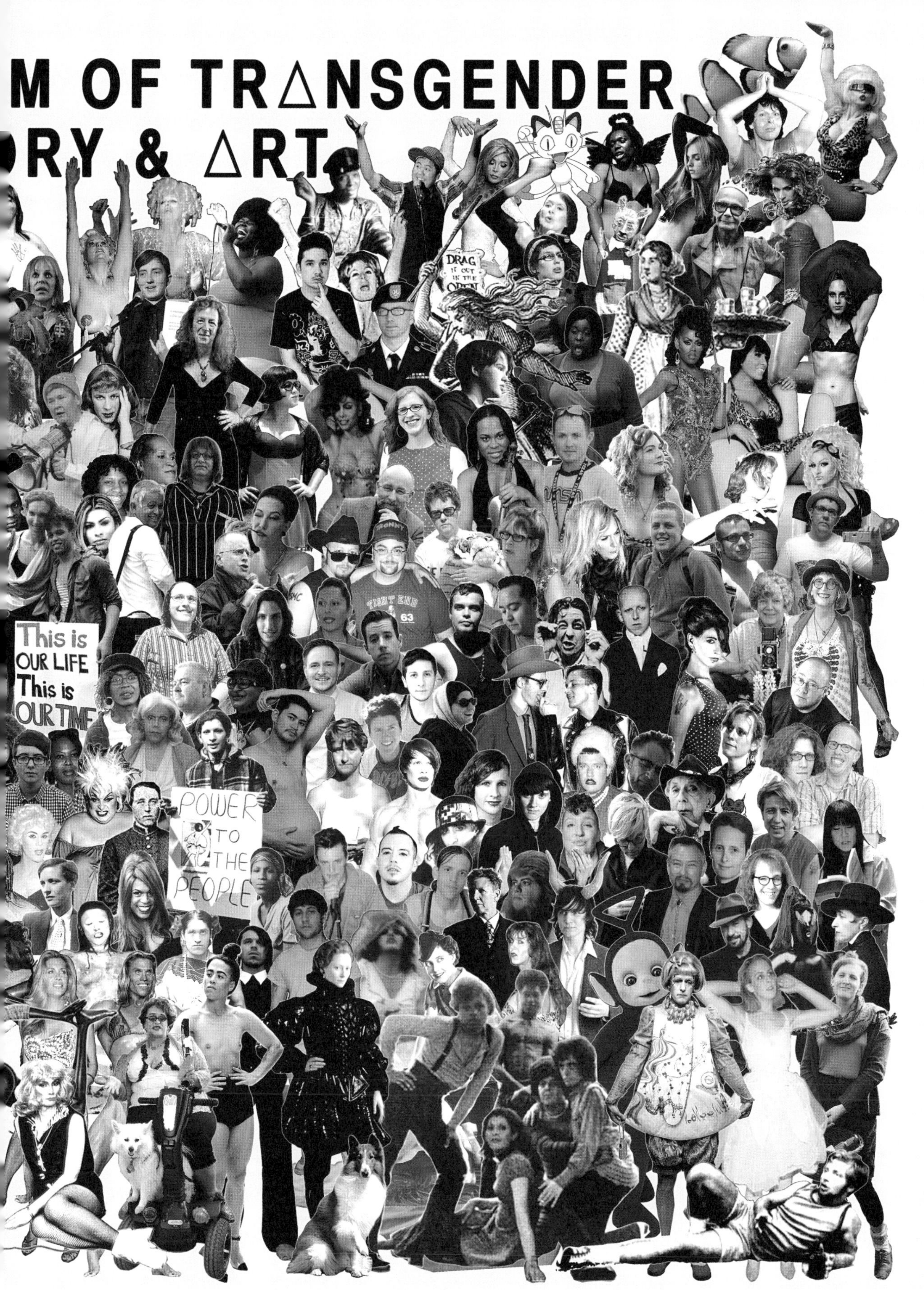
M OF TR∆NSGENDER
ORY & ∆RT
DRAG IT OUT IN THE OPEN
TIGHT END
63
This is OUR LIFE This is OUR TIME
POWER TO THE PEOPLE

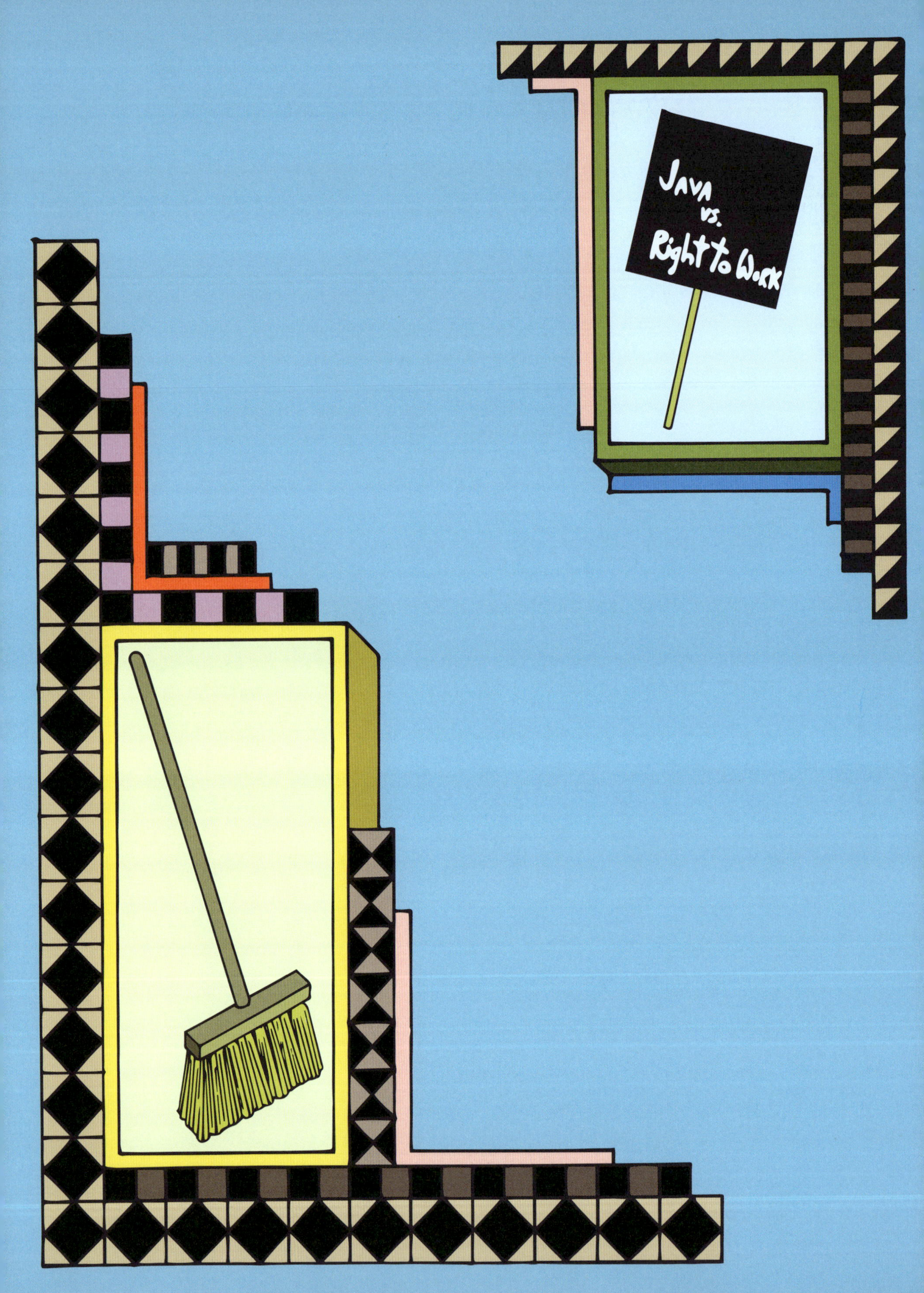
JAVA
vs.
Right to Work

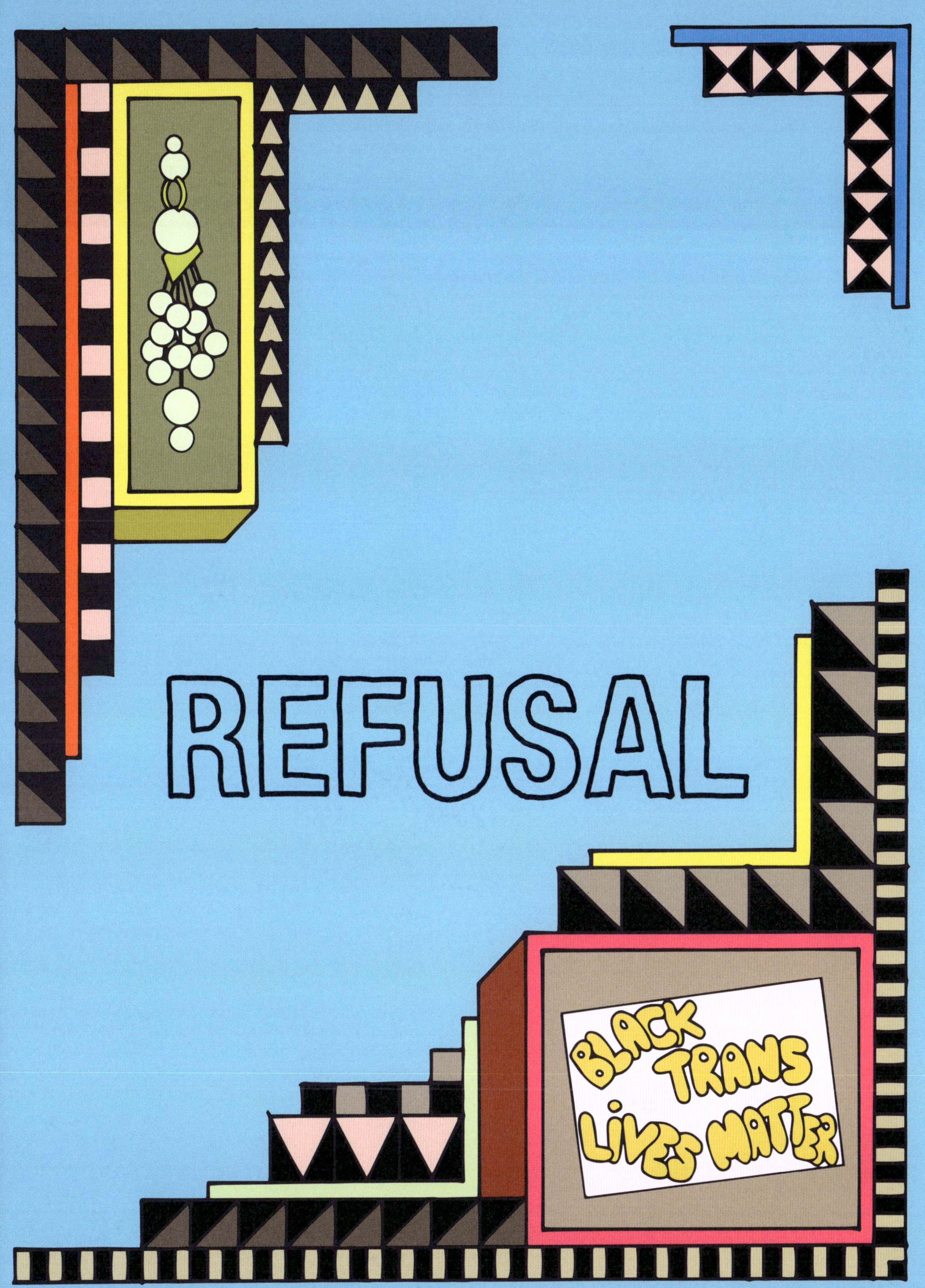
REFUSAL
BLACK TRANS
LIVES MATTER

1 DOUGHNUT THROWN IN THE RIOT AT COOPER DO-NUTS, MAY 1959

"It scrubs everything away," novelist and hustler icon John Rechy told *Los Angeles Magazine* in 2019.[1] The famous 1969 rebellion at the Stonewall Inn, now conceived as the moment upon which all of queer history hinges—a battleground where we collectively make "historical claims ... to wage contemporary struggles" as Susan Stryker puts it—blots out everything that came before.[2] The legend of Stonewall imposes a false divide, Rechy went on to explain, between the bad old days of repression and the bright future of liberal equality we are supposed to be living right now.

Rechy would certainly know. Ten years before the "shot glass heard around the world," the *youngman* hustler was at the center of another uprising.[3] On Main Street, Los Angeles's gay underground of the 1940s and 1950s, wedged between a male hustler bar called Harold's ("no queens allowed") and the queens' venue for picking up tricks, the Waldorf, was a twenty-four-hour cafeteria, Cooper Do-nuts. Lightly anonymized as "Hooper's" in Rechy's scandalous 1963 novel *City of Night*, this "Do-nut" joint served as neutral ground for the "scattered army" of young men and queens who poured out of the bars after closing. "It was very democratic," Rechy recalls.[4]

Police paid regular visits to the cafeteria, stalking up and down the long, rectangular bar. According to Lillian Faderman and Stuart Timmons's book *Gay L.A.*, to avoid arrest the queens dressed in half-drag—men's shirts worn over capri pants.[5] They would knot the shirts, transforming them into midriff tops, at least until the flashing lights of the police cruiser rolled up. But it was impossible to predict whom police would interrogate each night. They seemed to get a malicious thrill out of intimidating the patrons, letting the anxiety rise until they made that night's seemingly random choice.

One night, in or around May 1959, Rechy was one of the two or three people they took outside. Before the police could drive away with their captives, one—possibly drunk—patron exploded. "Take me, take me, see if you can take me!" they taunted the police. And within moments, chaos erupted. Stir sticks, paper cups, and, yes, doughnuts were pelted at the police with such force that the cops were forced to retreat. Rechy and the others managed to escape in the confusion, narrowly avoiding charges that could result—according to Rechy—in up to five years' imprisonment and being listed on the sex offender registry for three more.

The patrons of the Do-nut shop didn't stop. They poured out into the streets, joined by those leaving Harold's and the Waldorf at closing time. They surrounded the police, who locked themselves in their cruiser and called for backup. Queens, hustlers—most Black and Latine—shook the police car and attempted to flip it over. Additional police blocked off each end of the Main Street drag. The details are lost to time, but Rechy says, "It was quelled. It was quelled."[6]

No police records or newspaper coverage survives, only Rechy's account and a handful of vague recollections of other "friends of friends."[7] Did street queens, hustlers, and their associates really revolt against police a full decade before Stonewall? Maybe. But either way, it makes for a fabulous story!

—Morgan M Page

1. Jason McGahan, "Legendary Author John Rechy Recalls L.A.'s Oft-Forgotten Gay Uprising," *Los Angeles Magazine*, June 26, 2019, https://www.lamag.com/culturefiles/john-rechy-stonewall-cooper-do-nuts/.
2. Susan Stryker quoted in Ernesto Londoño, "Who Threw the First Brick at Stonewall?" *New York Times* blog, August 26, 2015, https://archive.nytimes.com/takingnote.blogs.nytimes.com/2015/08/26/who-threw-the-first-brick-at-stonewall/.
3. Rechy outlines "youngman" as a specific identity in his work, along with "fairyqueen," "malehustler," etcetera.
4. McGahan, "L.A.'s Oft-Forgotten Gay Uprising."
5. Lillian Faderman and Stuart Timmons, *Gay LA: A History of Sexual Outlaws, Power Politics, and Lipstick Lesbians* (Berkeley: University of California Press, 2009).
6. McGahan, "L.A.'s Oft-Forgotten Gay Uprising."
7. Even Rechy has revised his account of the event. See Erik Piepenburg, "A Gay Riot at a Doughnut Shop? The Legend Has Some Holes," *New York Times*, June 5, 2023, accessed June 18, 2023, https://www.nytimes.com/2023/06/05/dining/gay-riot-los-angeles-doughnut-shop.html.

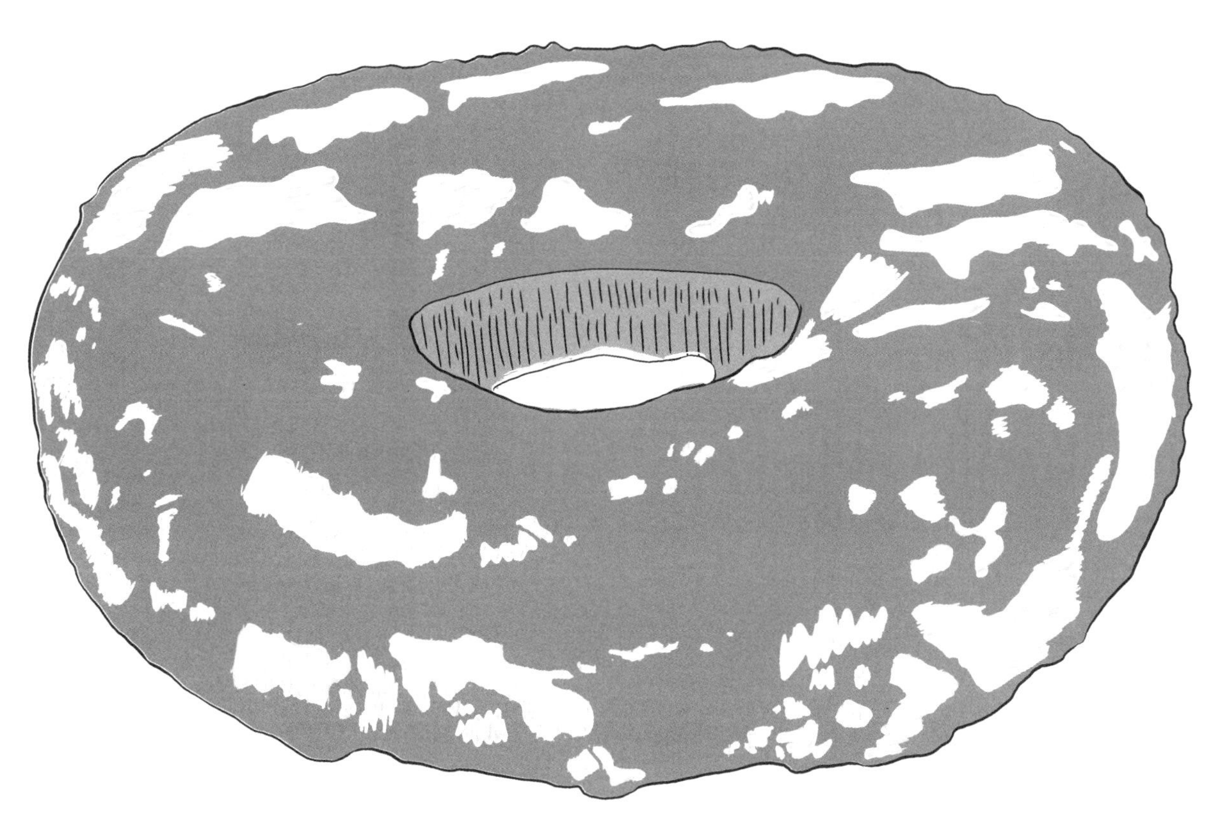

2 SIR LADY JAVA'S PROTEST SIGN, 1967

She was born in New Orleans's Ninth Ward as Archille P. DeVille in 1940 but was known privately as Sheila DuValle. At the age of seven her family moved to California and at fifteen she began attending underground gay parties where she adopted the name Java after a white friend told her, "You look like coffee—deep, dark and delicious. You're going to be my cup of Java."[1]

She met her future husband at sixteen, a minister she began living with before finishing high school. Once married, she added "Lady" to her name. After her high school graduation, she studied for a year at Riverside Junior College and completed a course in feminine charm as professional development for her future careers in modeling and dancing.

Lady Java began performing her nightclub act, inspired by her idol Josephine Baker, which included a mix of dance, comedy, and fashion, at Los Angeles clubs in the 1960s. In 1966, while working for Gertrude Gipson at the Club Nite Life, which showcased numerous rising African American performers at the time, she added "Sir" to her stage name and found freedom: "Sir Lady Java, I knew would tell it all. I was born at the Club Nite Life. People knew I wasn't hiding anymore."[2]

The following year she booked a two-week engagement at the Redd Foxx Club on La Cienega Boulevard, one of the few Black-owned clubs on LA's Westside, a revue that proved so successful she was invited back for an additional two weeks. Sir Lady Java's growing notoriety attracted attention from local police who threatened to pull the club's license based on the Los Angeles Police Commission's Rule No. 9, which stated, "No entertainment shall be conducted in which any performer impersonates by means of costume or dress, a person of the opposite sex, unless by special permit issued by the Board of Police Commissioners."[3] While California's anti-masquerading law regarding cross-dressing in public had previously been declared unconstitutional, it remained illegal to cross-dress on stage in Los Angeles.

On October 21, 1967, in spite of Foxx's pleadings, Java picketed the club protesting Rule No. 9 as an unconstitutional violation of her right to work. With supporters, including Jean H. Martin of the ACLU, the action received coverage from *Jet*, the *Los Angeles Sentinel*, and *The Los Angeles Advocate*, among other news media.

Elaborating on the Los Angeles Police Department (LAPD) targeting Foxx's club, Java shared, "We didn't know of any establishment that was white that they [the LAPD] were stopping [from employing impersonators], but they were definitely targeting me, because I was queen of the Black ones and they feel that they had more trouble out of the Black ones."[4]

While Java's legal action against Rule No. 9 was held up on a legal technicality, the ordinance was eventually struck down in 1969. Significantly, this moment occurred during a national trans movement against nightly police raids on gay bars and establishments frequented by femmes, specifically cross-dressers, drag queens, and trans people of color. Java's protest sign, immortalized in this photograph from *Jet*, serves as a portal for our collective remembering of Java's legacy of love and embrace of everything Black, Femme, and Beautiful.

—Kelly Besser

A version of this text previously appeared in the brochure accompanying the exhibition *Transgender Hirstory in 99 Objects: Legends & Mythologies* at ONE National Gay & Lesbian Archives at the USC Libraries, 2015.

1. Sir Lady Java quoted in "Sir Lady Java: America's Loveliest Female Impersonator," *Sepia* (March 1967): 20.
2. "Sir Lady Java: America's Loveliest Female Impersonator," 21.
3. "Sir Lady Java Fights Fuzz-y Rule Nine," *The Los Angeles Advocate*, no. 3 (November 1967): 1–2.
4. Sir Lady Java quoted in Treva Ellison, "The Labor of Werqing It: The Performance and Protest Strategies of Sir Lady Java," in *Trap Door: Trans Cultural Production and the Politics of Visibility*, eds. Johanna Burton, Eric A. Stanley, and Tourmaline [fka Reina Gossett] (Cambridge, MA: MIT Press, 2017), 10.

▸ (foreground) Page from *Jet*, vol. 33, no. 6 (November 16, 1967). ONE National Gay & Lesbian Archives at the USC Libraries; (background) Page from *Sepia* (March 1967). Black LGBT Project

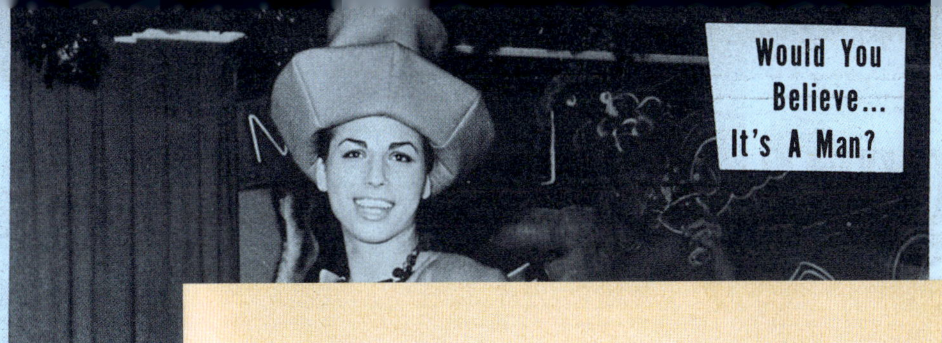

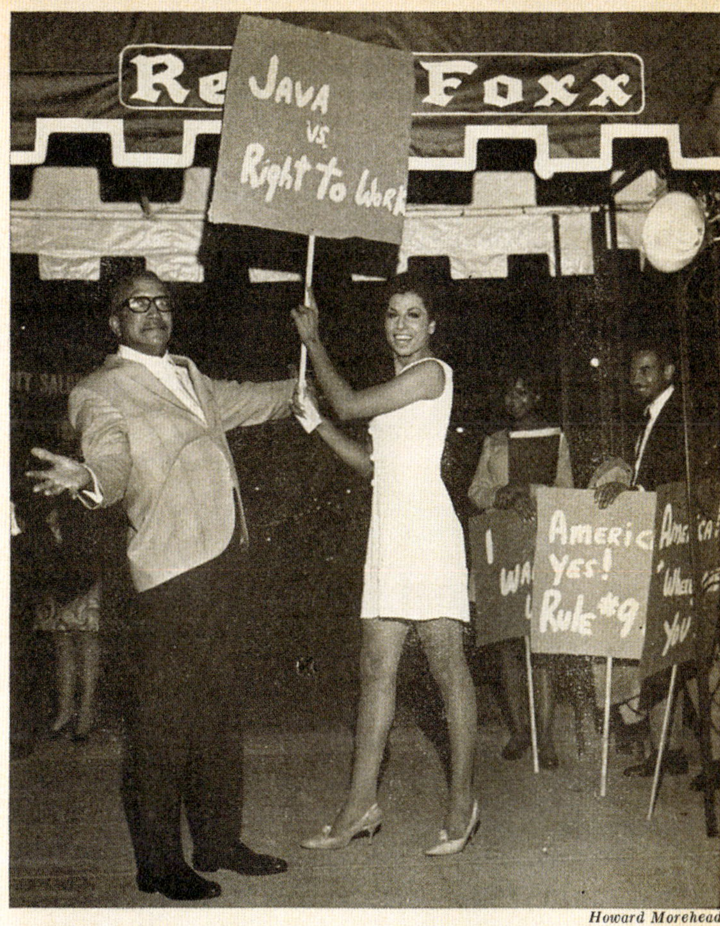

Howard Morehead

That's Life: After the Los Angeles Police Dept. closed out shapely dancer Sir Lady Java during an appearance at comic Redd Foxx's club, the female impersonator pickets place despite Foxx's pleadings. It appears there's a law against female impersonators in Hollywood.

AN... FEMALE IMPERSONATOR

...started changing as a child . . .
...minister took him into 'gay' life and they were 'married'

...Los Angeles night club audience waited in eager anticipation. ...he star was a few minutes late: His G-string had broken. ...the club lights went down low, the mistress of ceremonies took the bandstand microphone and announced, "Here she ... he ... is

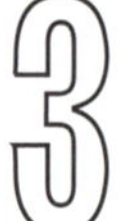

BROOKLYN LIBERATION, JUNE 14, 2020

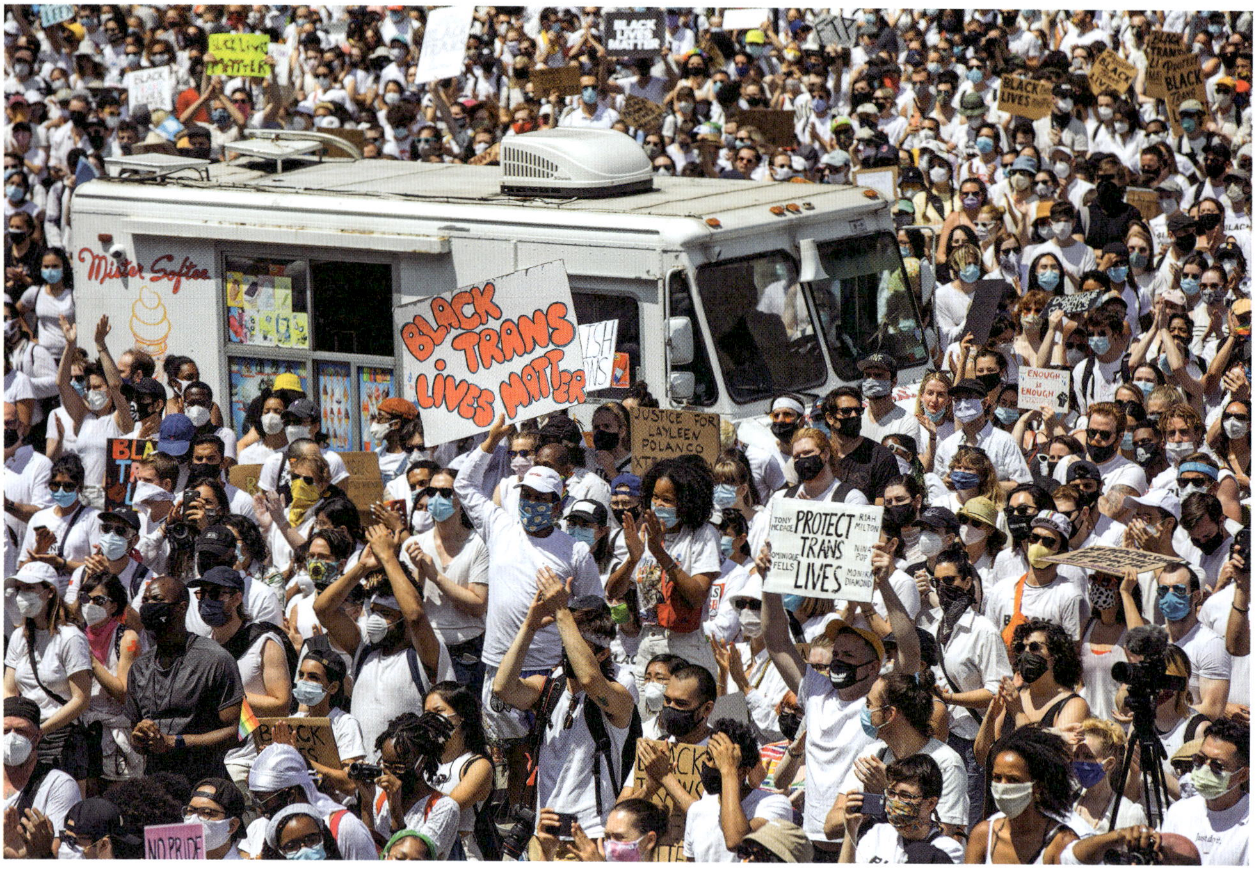

▲
Crowd gathered for Brooklyn Liberation, June 14, 2020. Photo by Demetrius Freeman

On June 14, 2020, more than 15,000 people, masked and dressed in all white, amassed outside the Brooklyn Museum in preparation for the Brooklyn Liberation march and rally. Only a few months into what was to be a multiyear global pandemic, a groundswell of activism in defense of Black lives was catalyzed by the circulation of video documentation of George Floyd's murder at the hands of Minneapolis Police Officer Derek Chauvin. In addition to Black Lives Matter and Black Trans Lives Matter movements, people gathered in solidarity with all trans people whose lives were, and continue to be, threatened by persistent state and federal bills targeting access to life saving and affirming resources.

I Believe in Our Power

I remember watching these strange New Year's Eve celebrations on December 31, 2020. Don Lemon and Brooke Baldwin were in their matching black silk PJs, getting drunk and making gumbo on CNN. My partner and I were sitting on the sofa, too, and although we don't drink alcohol, we had a nice charcuterie board, shrimp cocktail, popcorn, non-alcoholic champagne, and board games. We were ready, baby.

Then a new Google advertisement dropped, and it caught my attention. I said to my partner, "Hey, that's Raquel Willis." She was speaking through a megaphone, declaring, "I believe in your power. I believe in our power." She was addressing over fifteen thousand Transgender, gender-nonconforming, and gender-fluid folks, as well as their allies, as they marched to the steps of the Brooklyn Museum in New York. It was a sea of Black, Indigenous, People of Color. Most were dressed all in white, making the image all the more poignant and powerful.

"That's my girl. I interviewed her for the Trans Oral History Project," I said excitedly. It was one of the few moments of joy that I experienced that year, seeing a Black Transgender woman featured prominently in a Google ad. You see, my name is Andrea Jenkins. I am the first out Black Trans woman elected to public office in the United States, and I represent the very district in Minneapolis, Minnesota, where George Floyd was murdered. I literally live two blocks away from the infamous Cup Foods store where the racist cop held his knee on George Floyd's neck for nine minutes and twenty-nine seconds.

I paid attention to the march back in June 2020 when it initially happened. I was in the middle of trying to manage a city that had been set on fire. A city that was traumatized and terrorized by nefarious outside forces, and our own police department. One week before the second annual Trans Liberation March in Minneapolis, eight of my colleagues and I pledged to "defund the police" by reallocating resources to alternative means of keeping communities safe that don't involve police officers with guns. We were in Powderhorn Park, and it looked like there were thousands of people in front of us. With our pledge we sparked a national conversation.

So, when I saw the ad with Raquel on that New Year's Eve, I was delighted but not surprised to be reminded of the outpouring of Trans voices earlier that year demanding justice in Brooklyn, Minneapolis, and elsewhere. After all, Trans and gender-nonconforming people have always been at the forefront of social movements, starting with Gay Liberation, through the HIV/AIDS epidemic, the Black Lives Matter movement, right up to today as we join efforts for reproductive rights—because after all, we recognize that this fight is not about abortion, but rather who has control and agency over one's own body.

I believe, like Raquel, that Trans and gender-expansive people are beacons for what it means to be human, as possibility models for how to control your own life and not be shaped by the ideals and fantasies of others. We are living proof that change is possible.

On June 14, 2020, in Brooklyn, so many of my fearless, beautiful, and incredible friends were out there fighting for our lives. #BlackTransLivesMatter. In attendance were Ceyenne Doroshow, the founder of GLITS; Elle Moxley, the founder of the Marsha P. Johnson Institute; folks from The Okra Project and BLACK Trans Femmes in Arts; and thousands of others. We all continue to be committed to changing the world to be a place where Trans lives and all the lives of all marginalized people matter. Our movement is intersectional—it includes undocumented folks, disabled folks, women, POC, and low-income folks. Raquel Willis had considered calling her new memoir "I Believe in Our Power." Right on, Raquel, so do I.

—Andrea Jenkins

1. "Google – Year in Search 2020," December 8, 2020, advertisement, 3:00, https://www.youtube.com/watch?v=rokGy0huYEA. Raquel Willis appears at 1:38.

2. See Raquel Willis, interview by Andrea Jenkins, July 6, 2017, University of Minnesota Libraries, Jean-Nickolaus Tretter Collection in Gay, Lesbian, Bisexual and Transgender Studies, accessed January 16, 2023, https://umedia.lib.umn.edu/item/p16022coll97:172.

4 BETH ELLIOTT'S GUITAR, 1973–PRESENT

Hate is durable. Some people are more durable. Some musical instruments are more durable still.

Type and provenance are critical. Brazilian rosewood, rock maple, gunstock walnut, ebony, secreted away in warehouses scattered around the globe in anticipation of coming scarcity. Certain musicians, aware that greed is infinite and resources are limited, pool their money to gather as much of these precious resources as possible and preserve them for future use. Out of those stashes come some of the finest instruments.

Beth Elliott's is a Dreadnought, the design of which was first crafted by Christian F. Martin in the nineteenth century. Elliott's is somewhat newer, but still of the golden period of Martin guitars—hefty, sensitive, and precise, with a full, generous tone. There is a peculiar aura to Dreadnoughts; you can observe one nestled quietly in its case and feel that it's straining to leap out into someone's hands and sing.

A guitar can easily outlive its current owner, so one can just as easily talk about the person with whom the instrument is currently in a relationship. Guitars think long thoughts.

This guitar's person happens to be multitalented. She is active in humanitarian circles, nurturing organizations that promote freedom and equality, diversity, and inclusion.

The instrument registers this trauma as it does every single one. A convenient focus. A synecdoche for every wounding. Hundreds if not thousands of years of repression, ignorance, fear, and outright hatred come to ground in a scintilla of time. The wounded wounds.

Woody Guthrie's machine killed fascists. So did Pete Seeger's, but by then the fascists had a better handle on subtle repression. With Elliott's, "subtle" was an unknown language and, utterly consumed with hate, the fascists didn't even recognize themselves as fascists. The fell stroke comes from ones you trust.[1] How fucking Shakespearean.

Time doesn't stop. There will be other woundings, other healings. There is a next thing. A guitar can be more than a musical instrument. A guitar can be a companion, an emotional support animal, a love philter, a soothing elixir. With care, a guitar can be a faithful friend, someone who stays with you through bad times and good; it can be a light when all else is darkness, leading the way forward. Unlike flesh, wood endures; given the chance, a guitar remains vibrant, lacquer clear, bracing firm, action responsive. Its aura, if you will, is subtly changed with each encounter, but its constancy can also change you. Occasionally you can see the wear—the odd nick here, the scratch there, the blemish and repair that is visible only if you know precisely how and where to look—but for the greater part, if the joinery is true, it appears in the texture of the interaction, the time-weave of player and played. People come and go, empires rise and fall. The guitar still sings.

—Allucquére Rosanne (Sandy) Stone

Beth Elliott was one of the organizers of the 1973 West Coast Lesbian Conference in Los Angeles. As a well-respected lesbian feminist folk singer and guitar player, she was also invited by her co-organizers to perform at the conference. The Berkeley-based lesbian separatist Gutter Dykes Collective leafleted the conference to oppose Elliott's presence because she was trans; the question of whether she should perform was brought to a general vote. The vote came out three to one in favor of Elliott's performance. Shaking, she managed to play. Afterward, keynote speaker and poet Robin Morgan delivered a ninety-minute address in which she defamed Elliott and seeded polarity and division. From 1971 to 1972, Elliott served as vice president of the San Francisco chapter of the lesbian organization the Daughters of Bilitis (DOB) and worked on the chapter's newsletter Sisters. *While the controversy over her ejection from DOB splintered the group, Morgan also spread the untruth that it was Elliott, rather than this controversy, that caused the splintering.*

1. Beth Elliott notes that key trusted friends in San Francisco's Daughters of Bilitis chapter did not turn on her, even as others in the organization did. She also notes that none of her Los Angeles sisters denounced or abandoned her even as they later became targets for including her in the conference. In her view, the fell stroke came from some of those with whom she once had had a home, but not from all of the ones she had trusted.

▶ Beth Elliott with her guitar, 2022. Photo by Marcel Pardo Ariza

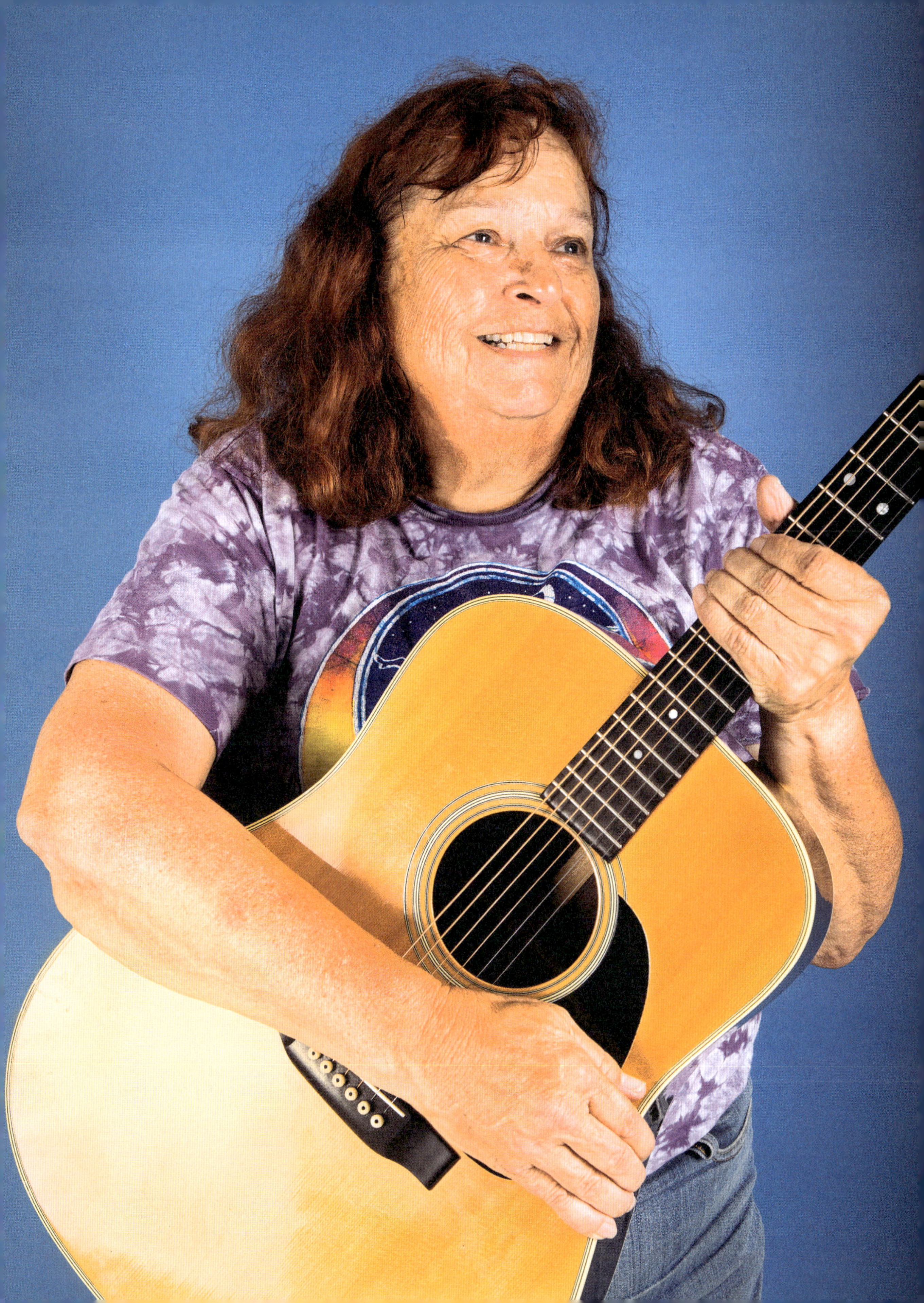

5 MANUEL MATHIEU, *THE PROPHETESS 2*, 2020

Romaine-la-Prophétesse was a free Black coffee plantation owner who led an early uprising in the Haitian Revolution and later controlled the cities of Léogâne and Jacmel. Like many marginalized figures of the Haitian Revolution, such as Sanité Bélair, Cécile Fatiman, and Catherine Flon, Romaine Rivière's revolutionary role is reconstructed from colonial archives and cultural memory. Romaine defied Catholic gender norms, identifying as *prophétesse* rather than *prophète*. They wore feminine clothing, ribbons, and rosaries. They spoke of being possessed by a female spirit; yet they also called themself "the godson of the Virgin Mary."[1] This transgressive behavior (which is not unusual in Afro-Diasporic religious practices, but is rarely condoned within Catholicism) explains why Rivière is often erased, excluded, and obscured from traditional histories of the Haitian Revolution. Moreover, there is a notable absence of the Prophétesse in Haitian visual culture, an invisibility that can be cautiously attributed to their aberrant religious beliefs and gender presentation.

As there are no surviving images of Romaine, artist Manuel Mathieu used his imagination to create two portraits, titled *The Prophetesse 1* and *The Prophetesse 2*. The paintings walk a line between abstraction and figuration, simultaneously revealing and complicating the Prophétesse's legacy. The works are large scale, measuring over nine feet in length. In each, the Prophétesse faces viewers head-on. By creating two portraits, Mathieu signals African and Afro-Diasporic spiritual beliefs in the multiplicity of the self as well as referencing Rivière's potential trans identity, i.e., the fact that the Prophétesse occupied two gendered societal roles. Mathieu expands the limits of portraiture; one can almost distinguish figures in the abstract use of acrylic, chalk, charcoal, and tape on the canvases.

Romaine-la-Prophétesse and Mathieu's representation of them transform and widen the potential of Black freedom by presenting alternative senses of self that were not defined by colonial discourses. "The best way to know yourself is to unlearn about who you think you are," says Mathieu in reference to the *Prophétesse* paintings.[2] The paintings' illegible and indecipherable artistic portrayals exemplify the fluid, mercurial, and ambivalent nature of the Prophétesse's self-fashioning, as well as their shifting position in revolutionary Haitian narratives.

Mathieu's work often references his Haitian heritage and depicts Haitian historical figures. In the *Prophétesse* paintings, he visualizes an enigmatic figure who challenged colonialism and slavery, forcing viewers to think about the relationships between identity, spirituality, and revolutionary politics. These artworks are an examination of the long-lasting repercussions of Haiti's pioneering revolt and its subsequent quest for self-determination. By focusing on the Prophétesse, Mathieu uncovers how Black gender-nonconforming subjectivity embodies the Haitian Revolution's full revolutionary potential.

—Jonathan Michael Square

1. Terry Rey, *Bourdieu on Religion: Imposing Faith and Legitimacy* (Abingdon, UK: Taylor & Francis, 2007), 119. I have opted to use nonbinary pronouns to respect the Prophétesse's nuanced gender identity.
2. Conversation with Manuel Mathieu, October 27, 2022.

▸ Manuel Mathieu, *The Prophetess 2*, 2020. Acrylic, chalk, charcoal, and tape on canvas, 110 × 90 in. (279.4 × 228.6 cm)

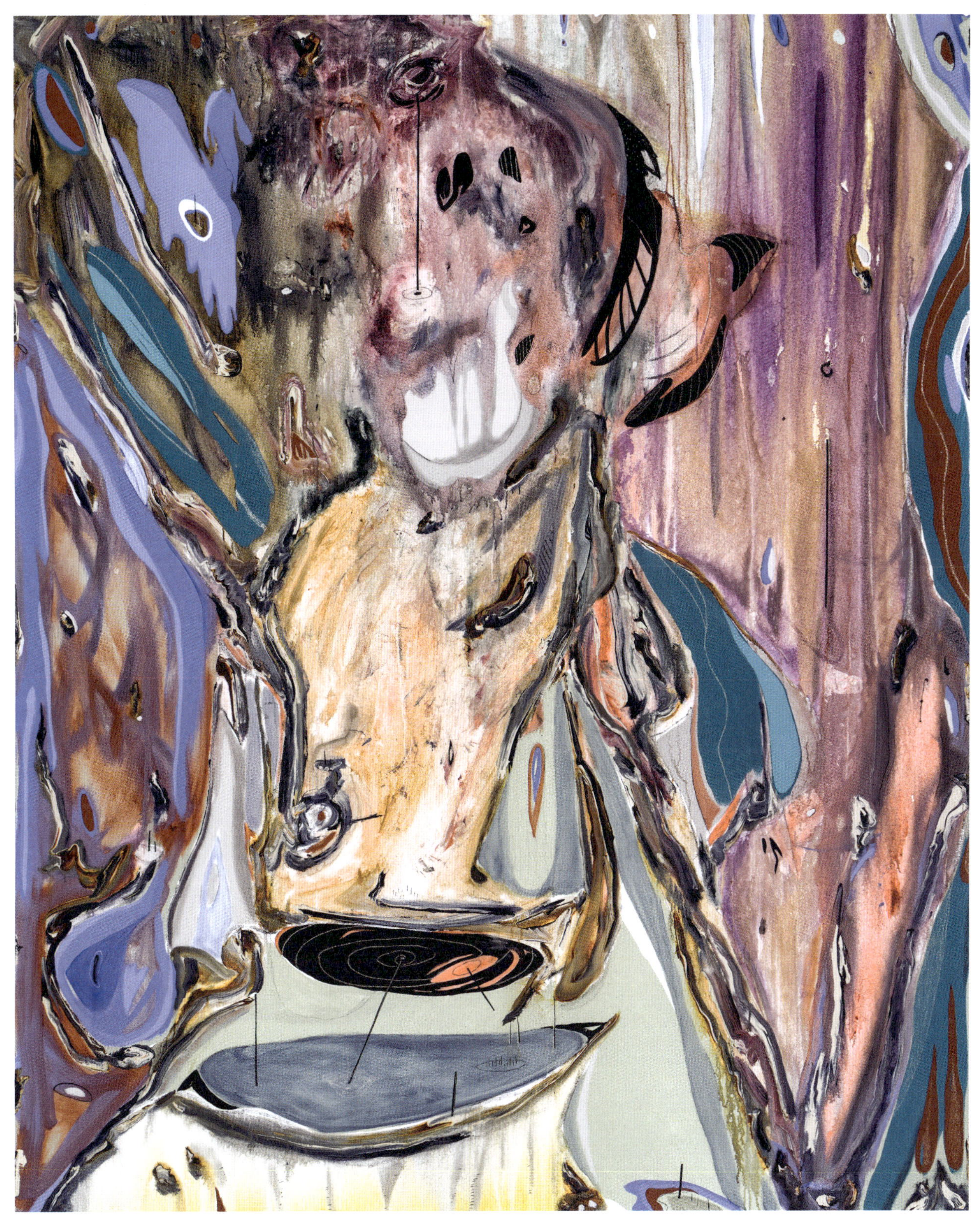

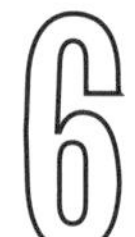

NANCY VALVERDE'S BARBER CHAIR, c. 1950s

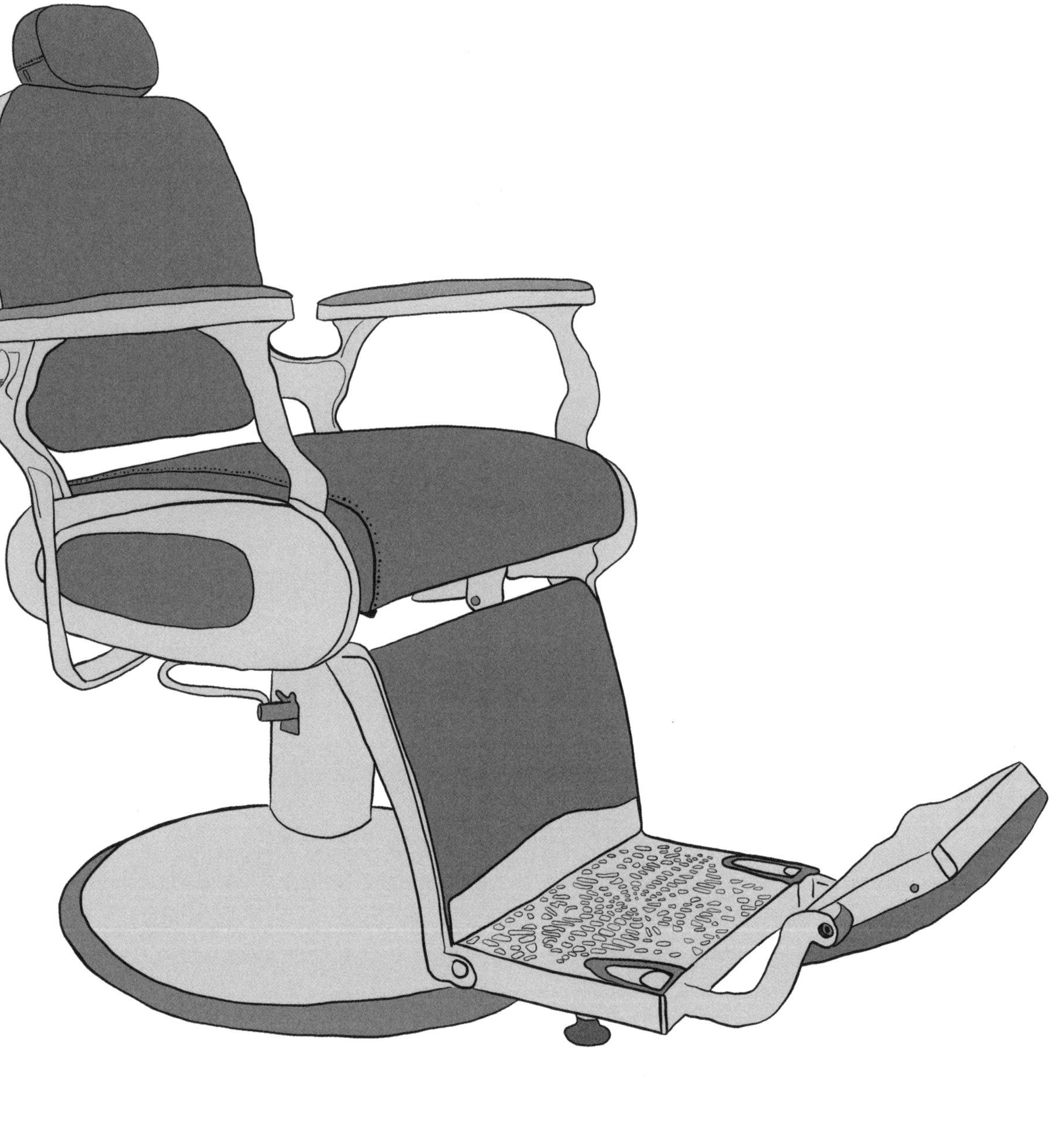

Nancy Valverde Stands Akimbo

Nancy Valverde stands akimbo. She knows the streets of East Los Angeles in ways we never will. She spent her adolescence driving sex workers around its various neighborhoods, a place she landed at nine years old when her parents spirited her away from Deming, New Mexico—not for the bright lights of the big city but for the bridges of East Los that carried the neighborhoods' working-class Chicanos into the city's various industrial workplaces. Valverde has been working since she was ten years old, she tells me in her old Montebello home, just a few years before she moves into Triangle Square, a complex of housing units for LGBT elders in Hollywood. Valverde narrates her introduction to the types of underground economies available to bulldaggers as a mysterious dancing lady in a revealing red dress hovers above this old butch's head. It's a velvet painting mounted on the wall of her home. I read it as an altar to the femme supremacy that has led Valverde valiantly down East Los Angeles's shadowy back alleys to revel in and defend.

Valverde stiffens to show how she stood in front of the door to listen for any rough stuff, arms folded over her chest, standing sentinel and keeping an eye out for cops looking for a reason. But she herself has had to look out for her own vulnerable state as well. I interview her as I am in the process of writing a play based on her life, *The Barber of East L.A.* First produced in 2008 by the queer Chicana performance group Butchlalis De Panochtitlan I cofounded in 2002, the play is about butch dykes surviving the hardest parts of the mid-twentieth century and the nascent trans masculine arrival that awaits us in the next century. I sit and listen to her narrate her experience in the Daddy Tank, the notorious holding cell for masculine AFABs at the Sybil Brand Institute for Women (a correctional facility run by the County Sheriff in Monterey Park outside Los Angeles). Valverde is proud of the ways she defended herself against other prisoners who had picked on her and saw her as competition for the jail's limited femme partners. But Valverde had bigger problems. Sybil Brand was considered a model prison with five sections: Maximum Security, Minimum Security, Mental Observation, Lock Up, and the Daddy Tank. The late Jeanne Córdova, in an issue of *The Lesbian Tide*, described the Daddy Tank as the worst section as it was Maximum Security for lesbians where prisoners were given the filthiest jobs and made examples of.[1] On Father's Day 1974, lesbians of Córdova's ilk protested the existence of the Daddy Tank. It would take damage from 1994's Northridge earthquake to eventually close the prison in 1997.

Valverde's main jailable offense was "masquerading in clothes not of her sex"—a law that had been on the California books since the Gold Rush and was intended to allow for the harassment of those deemed deviant or gender-bending. After conducting her own research at the Los Angeles County Law Library in 1951, Valverde was able to provide legal criteria to end her ongoing harassment and arrest (though masquerading laws in Los Angeles would continue to be enforced into the 1960s).

Through all this, Valverde remained a popular member of her community in both Lincoln and Boyle Heights. After receiving her diploma from the Moler Barber College in Downtown Los Angeles, she became a tax-paying citizen on the straight-and-narrow path. She opened a barbershop on the old Brooklyn Avenue corridor during the 1950s. It was there where she quietly established her reputation as a businessperson, a butch of few words but with a presence that commanded respect. The neighborhood itself was changing with the times too. Charlie, as Valverde tells me, was the owner of the bar that would eventually become Red's, where she would grab a beer between shifts. She remembers hitting the head in the small bar and coming out to find the bar owner standing in front of the bathroom door with his own arms folded firmly across his chest. Valverde never forgot that gesture of solidarity. And neither should you.

—Raquel Gutiérrez

1. Jeanne Córdova, "End the 'Daddy Tank' Now," *The Lesbian Tide* 4, no. 2 (September 1974): 11.

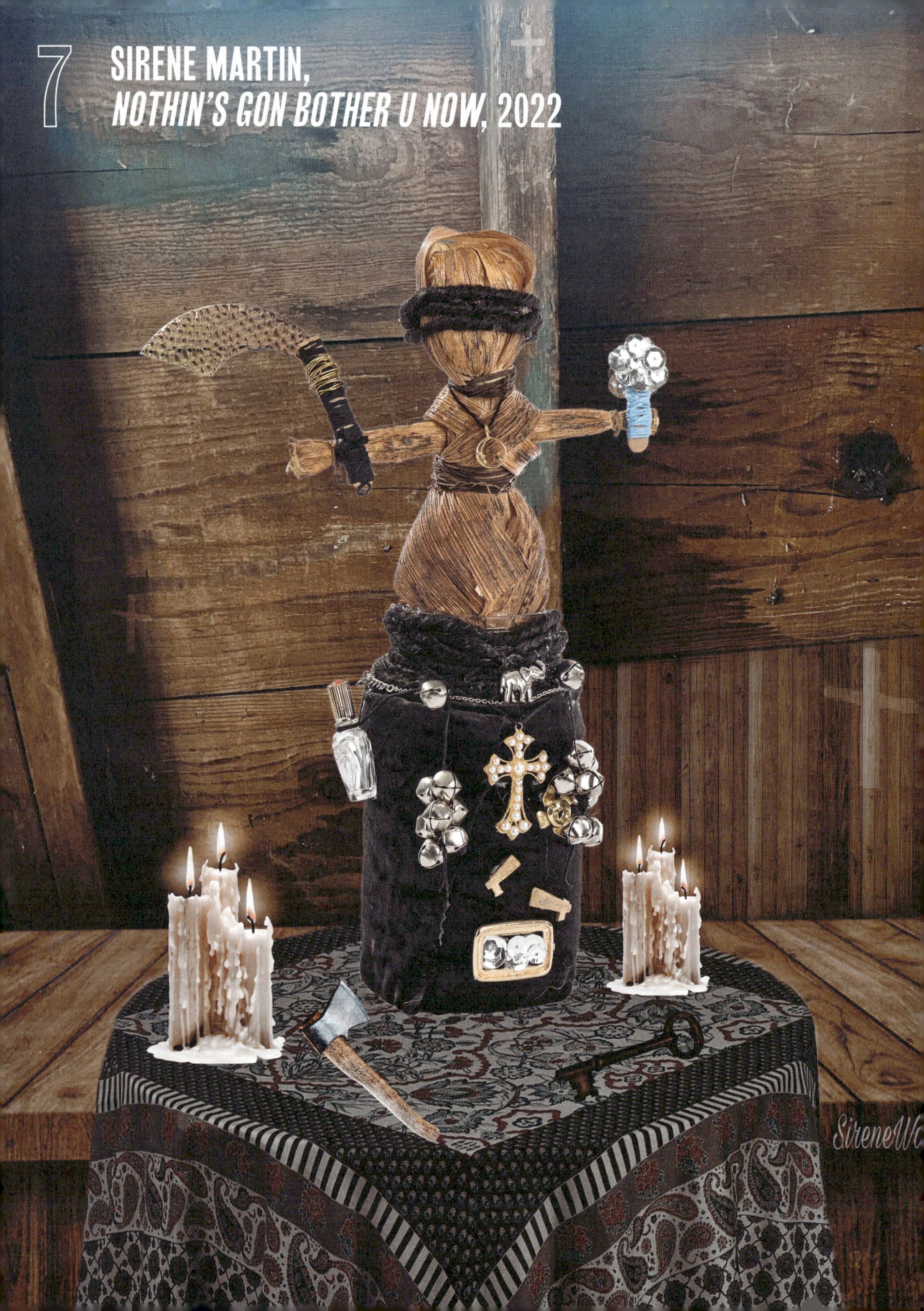

7 SIRENE MARTIN,
NOTHIN'S GON BOTHER U NOW, 2022

Last Rites for Frances

It should not be lost on anyone that Black lives—trans, nonbinary, and cisgendered alike—have always had to carve out their own mechanisms of survival in a world intent on doing them harm. Conjure, hoodoo, and rootwork traditions of the American South have consistently been applied as both salve and salvation; offering recipes, remedies, and rituals that have healed Black bodies and broken spirits. In a society where neither medicine nor justice have been equitably accessible to Black and transfolx, spirit work functions as the great equalizer. Imbued with the ability simultaneously to heal and to harm and all variations in between, the insurrectionary, nonbinary power of conjure and hoodoo levels the spiritual playing field. These African-derived cosmologies invoke the subversive power of the invisible world to privilege Black life and govern those in epistemic opposition to them accordingly.

Paying homage to TrAnscestor Frances Thompson, *Nothin's Gon Bother U Now* (2022) is a commissioned ritual object by artist Sirene Martin made in the tradition of African American "memory jugs" or "death jugs"—funerary objects traditionally placed as grave decor to appease and honor the dead. Thompson (1840–1876) was known as a local hoodoo lady and spiritualist in life, so it seems appropriate to invoke her memory with a ritual object from that tradition. The memory jug is an African retention heavily influenced by the Kongo who have a sustained culture of ancestor reverence and especially working with the dead. Cobbled together from shells, glass or porcelain shards, and items dear to the recently deceased, the central form is a literal "jug" or water vessel. In West African belief, water is the conduit through which the spirit of the deceased transitions from the plane of the living to that of the spirit realm, or afterlife. The jug is placed upside down on the grave, often chipped or broken in places to symbolize that it is in service of the dead.

When a person was said to have "died bad," under particularly violent or suspicious circumstances (homicide, racial violence, physical mutilation, or plain ol' American injustice), enslaved Africans and their descendants believed it critical to enact certain death rites to prevent the spirit of the deceased from seeking retribution or from lingering too long between worlds. Sirene Martin's object performs this rite on behalf of Thompson, a trans woman who survived rape during the Memphis race riot of 1866 and dared to testify against the white perpetrators before Congress. Her lifestyle then became the focus of white harassment, and she was later incarcerated for impersonating a woman after being subjected to a physical examination to determine her biological sex. The memory jug signifies the emblem of "Lady Justice." Here, Thompson's jug wields a spiritual justice of its own, with machete in one hand and what appears to be an ason—a percussive instrument consecrated for leading religious ceremony—notably painted in a shade of "haint blue" in the other. The message about Thompson in this conjured bottle is clear: In death we venerate her memory and send her spirit toward the light. But there is a message for the living as well. Imagining the death jug atop her grave with the queen of spades, joker, and dice neatly placed—the jug portends that all of Thompson's violators will feel the vengeance of a most powerful kind of hoodoo. Nothing and no one, on this plane or the next, is going to bother her now. Lady Justice, indeed.

—Kameelah L. Martin, PhD

◄
Sirene Martin, *Nothin's Gon Bother U Now*, 2022. Mixed-media sculpture, 12 × 4 × 3 in. (30.5 × 10.2 × 7.6 cm), reproduced with digital collage

1. Angel Serrano, Alvaro Toepke, and Vertamae Grosvenor, *The Language You Cry In* (San Francisco, CA: California Newsreel, 1998).
2. Margaret Washington, "Gullah Attitudes Towards Life and Death," in *Africanisms in American Culture*, ed. Joseph E. Holloway (Bloomington, IN: Indiana University Press, 1991), 69–97.
3. Daina Ramey Berry and Kali Nicole Gross, "Frances's Sex and the Dawning of Black Women's Era, 1876–1915," in *A Black Women's History of the United States* (Boston: Beacon Press, 2020), 104–22.
4. Thompson had established a life in Memphis in which she identified and moved about the world as a hoodoo woman. Her incarceration forced her to serve time on the male chain gang attired as such. Berry and Gross, 106.
5. Shoshi Parks, "What the Color 'Haint Blue' Means to the Descendants of Enslaved Africans," *Atlas Obscura*, January 14, 2020, accessed December 15, 2022, https://www.atlasobscura.com/articles/what-haint-blue-means-to-descendants-enslaved-africans.

8 CECE MCDONALD'S SCISSORS, 2011

Not CeCe's scissors in a Lucite box. This is a placeholder for the performance of abolition. Getting free doesn't fit in a box. Not enough faithful museum patrons are passionate about the faithful mundane routine of prisoner support. This won't be finding a way to be inert for suburban evaluation. If the millions who frequently visit expositions of Magritte bought a car and drove out to Atascadero, ten cars could knock over the first layer of fencing, the next ten could knock over the next, and so on until you had a critical mass of abolition consciousness focused on a goal that no amount of state violence could deny or control. To claim that we all consent to the continued existence of the prison industrial complex is only a fraction true. What's not encased for patron display is survival activity on the daily precarity perched above the jaws of cisheteronormative brutality. On this drive to outlive our murderers T. S. Madison's gun show is pedagogy. It's to show any curious who come by the chateau what you'll see. Which is to say that it doesn't and can never really matter what CeCe's scissors look like. You'll see them in their dynamic ingenious utility if and when the time comes. If necessary. A world continuing to fuck with the girls is a world waiting to be cut.

—Ralowe T. Ampu

Fashion design student CeCe McDonald was arrested in 2011 after defending herself when attacked verbally and physically by a group of men outside a bar in Minneapolis. Bleeding from a major cut caused by having a glass smashed into her face and with one of her assailants throwing bottles at her as she tried to escape, she pulled out the fabric scissors she had in her purse to defend herself. As he chased her, the assailant lunged at her and impaled himself on the shears. The district attorney refused to accept her self-defense claim, and rather than facing eighty years in prison for second-degree murder, McDonald accepted a plea deal for a reduced charge of second-degree manslaughter. She was sentenced to forty-one months in prison. After serving nineteen months of the sentence, at a men's facility, McDonald was released for good behavior in January of 2014. Through her ordeal and the attention the case generated, McDonald has become a vocal advocate for prison abolition.

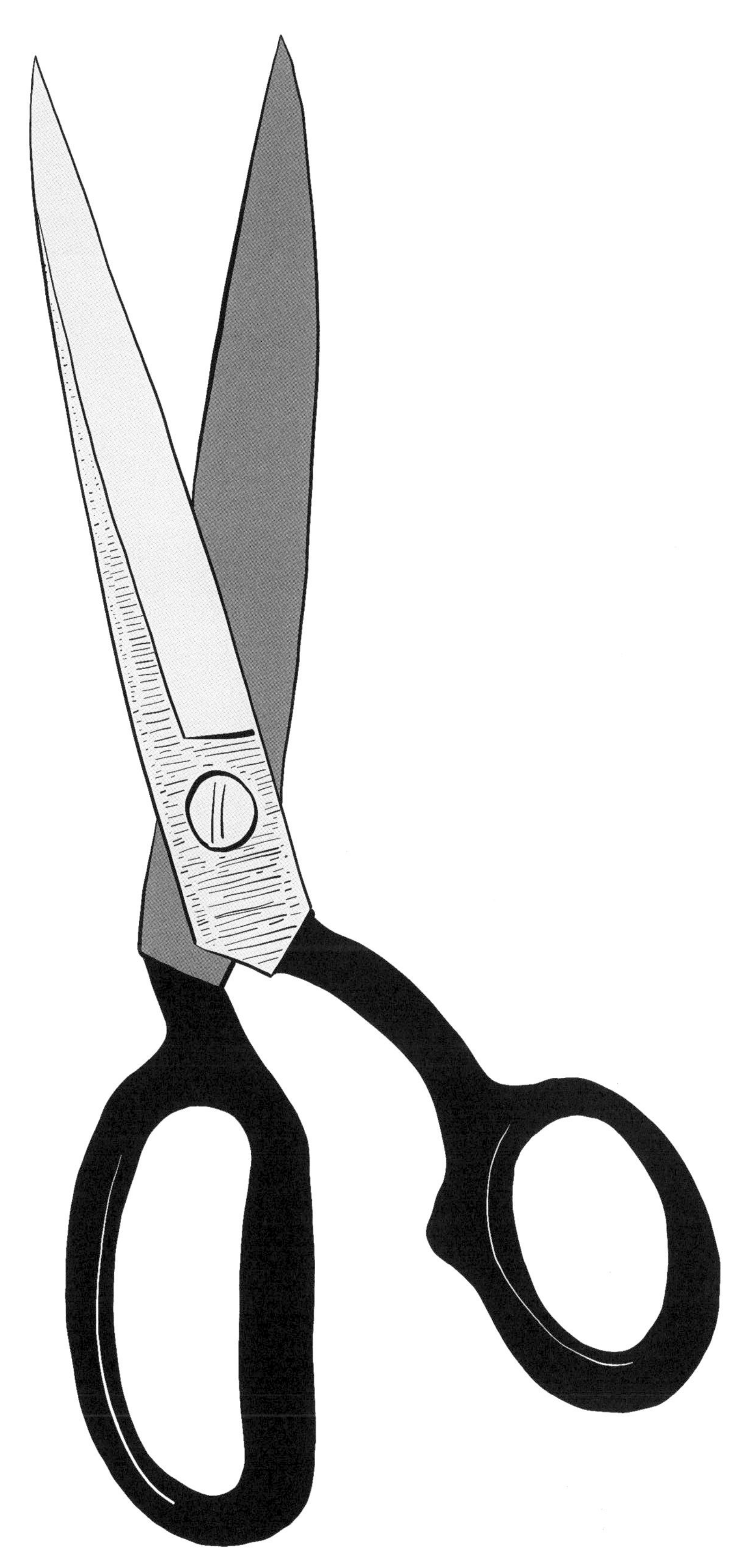

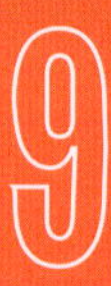

MISS MAJOR'S WHITE OPERA PUMPS, n.d.

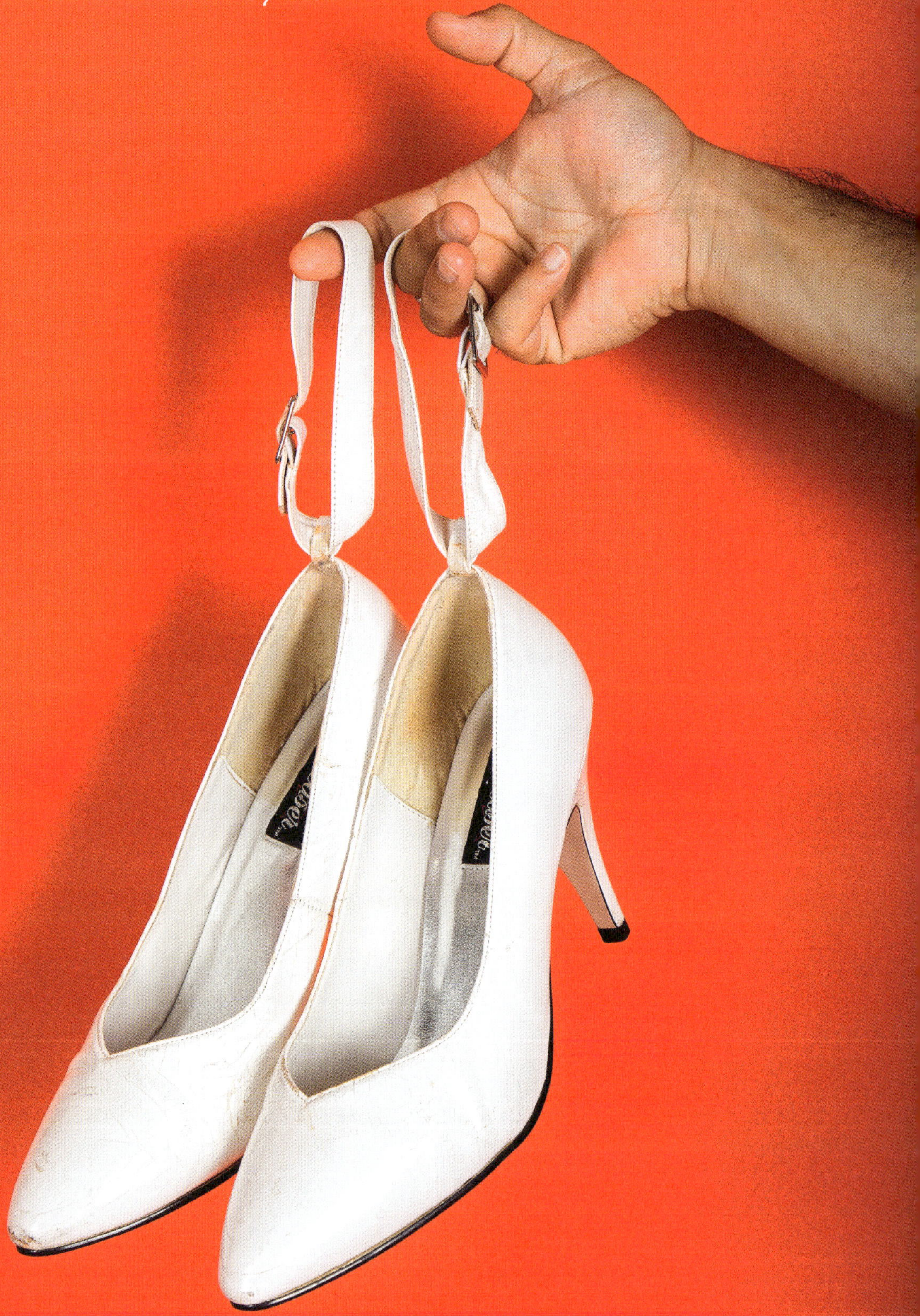

Miss Major
Interviewed by Toshio Meronek

Miss Major is a veteran of the Stonewall Riots, a former sex worker, and a survivor of Dannemora Prison and Bellevue Hospital's "queen tank." A grand/mother figure to trans people who never had one, Miss Major cared for people with HIV/AIDS in New York in the early 1980s, and later drove San Francisco's first mobile needle exchange. As director of the TGI Justice Project, she'd return to prisons as a mentor to her gurls inside. She now runs the retreat center TILIFI (Telling It Like It Fuckin' Is) in Little Rock, Arkansas (formerly House of GG). Her life and work are depicted in the documentary film *MAJOR!* (2015) and the book *Miss Major Speaks* (2023).

TOSHIO MERONEK (TM) So, we have this set of stilettos here…

MISS MAJOR (MM) Pair!

TM Ok, pair is what they call it. Why are they so significant to you?

MM Why the stilettos? Or the color or…?

TM All of it!

MM Ok, all of it. The very first time I got dressed up and felt good about who I was and how I looked was when this girl Kitty helped me get it together. Because my friends were painting me to look like Molly Moose, child. Ya know, eyebrows that connected in the middle, and hair—there were bangs that stuck out like saucers on my head. And then they would put me in these little flower print dresses. Since I was a big girl, I looked like a wall! And then flats. They always stuck my ass in flats.

So, Kitty convinced me, saying, "You're never going to appear to be 5' 6"—you're 6' 2". So, since you're 6' 2", wear the hair color you like." Well, blond was it for me. And then she said, "Dress like you want." She put me in a couple of shirtwaisted dresses with the big belts and the crinoline slips. And women at that time were wearing opera pumps twenty-four hours a day, so my opera pumps were white because she made me a yellow dress with a white belt. The white belt and a white hat and a white purse. Belt, shoes, purse had to be the same color.

TM Match. Match. Match. Ok.

MM That's right. And so, when I put on those shoes, it was just such a blessing. I mean, I felt tall and statuesque and beautiful and I could walk in them and spin and still dance, without that clumpy shit that a lot of people go through learning how to walk in them. It just came to me [snap] like that. And so, whenever something happened, like I went to jail, or when I would come out of the mental hospital, getting my nerves together to get back to being Major, the first thing I always bought was a pair of white pumps. Always. They didn't always have the ankle strap on them. That's a more current phase, but they were always white pumps. They were always at least two inches tall. And they're just nice to have around and look at. Because that's what being a girl is all about. You want to be yummy!

Originally conducted in 2017, this interview has been transcribed and edited for clarity from an audio recording made for MOTHA's installation in the exhibition *Queer California: Untold Stories* at the Oakland Museum of California, 2019.

◂
Miss Major's White Opera Pumps, n.d. Gift of Miss Major to MOTHA. Photo by Marcel Pardo Ariza

10 LEO BAKER'S CHEST BINDER, n.d.

A beige spandex chest binder worn by pro skateboarder Leo Baker, held in the Smithsonian.

Leo Baker made history in 2019 when he landed a coveted spot on the inaugural USA Skateboarding National Team for the 2020 Tokyo Olympics. Overshadowing this moment was Baker's iconic resignation from the team on his own terms, proving that living authentically was worth more than any gold medal.

Born in 1991 and raised in Covina, California, Baker gravitated towards skateboarding at a young age, captivated as his foster brothers tried to land tricks in their backyard. With a flair for the gritty sport and a supportive mom who saw Baker's spark, his talent was obvious early on. After winning a series of international competitions, his career took off. He nabbed his first sponsorship at age 11—getting free boards and T-shirts in exchange for repping a local skate shop. But as he reached his teen years, the stakes, and sponsorships, were greater. And not in a good way. Who Leo Baker was didn't match what big corporate skate brands wanted to represent to consumers. Billabong encouraged Baker to keep his blond hair long, and only gave him their "girl clothes" to wear in competitions. Fitted jeans and skintight T-shirts made Baker feel like a different person, forced to keep up appearances as some digestible all-American skater girl, far from how he felt inside. After coming out as queer, Baker shaved his head and only skated in clothes he loved—baggier and traditionally masculine, authentic to his unique style. When endorsements started to crack and drop away, life changed. He shifted his focus and pursued a career in graphic design as a professional backup, but he never stopped skating.

By the time Baker made the Olympic team, he was deeply in touch with his nonbinary trans identity and had already experienced the dip of what can happen to a career when your gender doesn't fit neatly into a box. The Olympics weighed heavy—how could he take part in this huge moment while also staying true to himself? Olympic teams are organized by sex assigned at birth, not gender identity, with no option for nonbinary or trans athletes. To skate on such a public stage and be referred to with incorrect pronouns, the wrong name, and to be represented as a gender he didn't identify with felt disingenuous and harmful. So, he made the decision to walk away. What's that saying, "When one door closes..."

Today, Leo Baker lives in New York City where he's combined his passion for gender inclusivity and LGBTQ+ rights with skateboarding. He's made a safe space for women, nonbinary, and trans skaters to learn. He's at no loss for major sponsorships, including Nike, who even put a Leo Baker shoe on the market. In 2020, Baker cofounded Glue Skateboards, an all-queer skate company that puts queer skaters at the forefront. He carved out the exact space he needed when he was younger, a gift that generations of young skaters will reap the benefits of. If you ask me, Leo Baker never needed the Olympics. They needed Leo Baker.

—Amos Mac

▸
Chest binder worn by professional skateboarder Leo Baker, n.d. Fabric (nylon and cotton), 12¼ × 13 in. (31.1 × 33 cm). National Museum of American History, Smithsonian Institution, 2018.0276.05

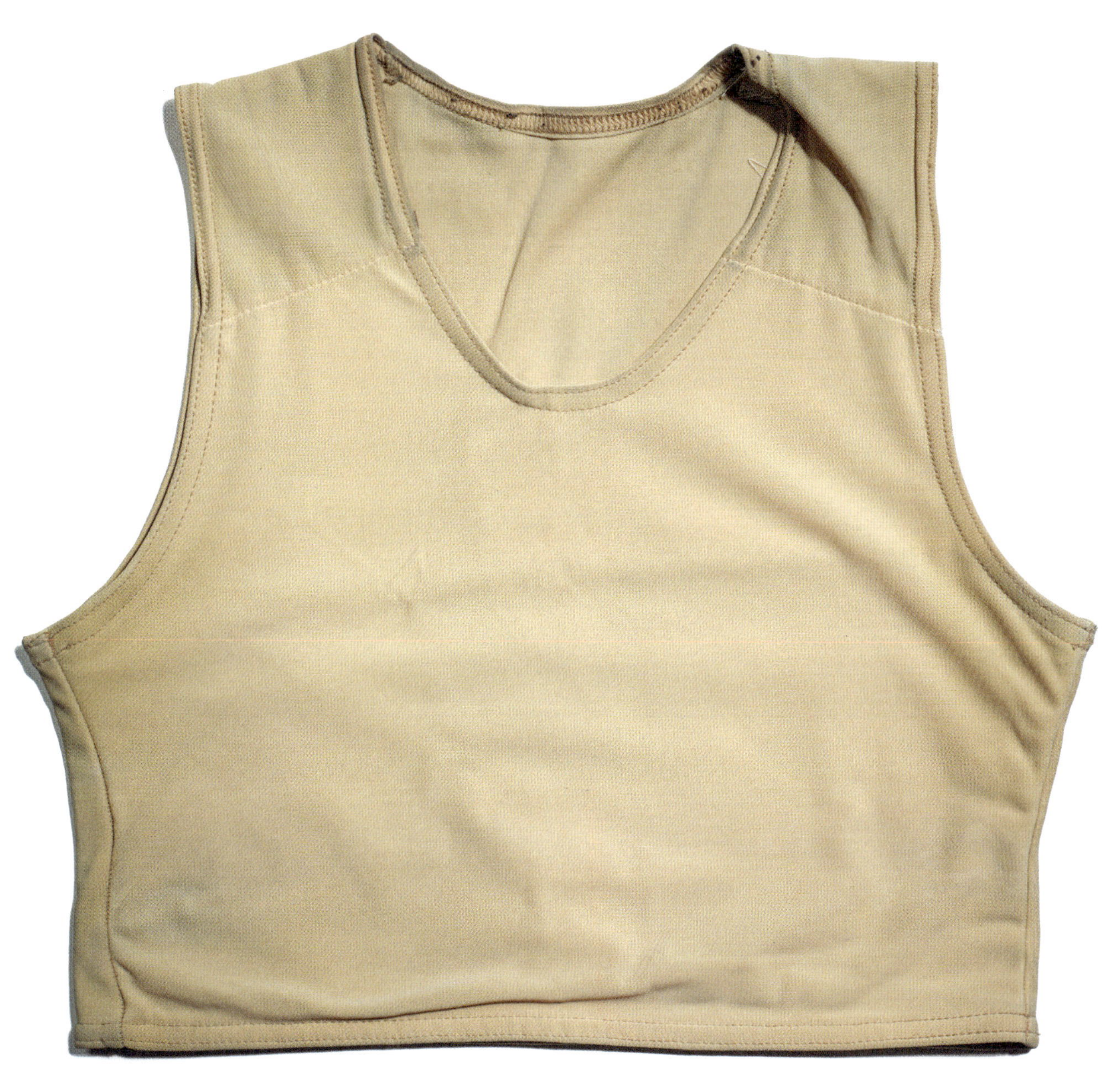

11 CRYSTAL LABEIJA'S ICONIC READ IN *THE QUEEN*, 1968

Your makeup looks nasty,
and you did not pay rent to own the stage.
Now, can we pump the beat?

—Honey Balenciaga

From 2020 to 2021 I co–executive produced the HBO Max show *Legendary*, a reality show where ballroom houses competed in themed balls to be the "superior house." Season one included a "smack talking" portion in the art of LGBTQ+ showdowns, for which we in the ballroom community have our own term: *reading*. Honey Balenciaga made TV gold with these words.

As any devotee of ballroom—or of the 1990 documentary about the ball community *Paris Is Burning*—knows, reading is a linguistic artform that the ballroom community popularized. It involves insulting one's adversary, whether on the runway or in life, with linguistic cunningness, humor, and wordplay. Reading is heavily associated with "throwing shade," which is a stealthier, more sophisticated, and subtler form of verbal attack. As Dorian Corey, one of the founding mothers and architects of the ballroom community, states in the famous documentary, "Shade comes from reading. Reading came first. Reading is the real artform of insult." Ms. Dorian goes on to explain how by extension "throwing shade" and "reading" are survival tools for Black and Brown LGBTQ+ people, as well as defensive or offensive tactics to use at a ball to win a category.

Prior to becoming a Balenciaga, Honey was in the House of LaBeija: the first house of the ballroom community, making them a direct descendant of Crystal LaBeija, ballroom's founding mother. As I watched Honey on set, I felt Crystal's presence. She is best remembered for her iconic read at the end of *The Queen* (1968), a documentary by Frank Simon chronicling the 1967 Miss All-America Camp Beauty Pageant held at Town Hall in New York, a female impersonation contest modeled after the Miss America pageant.

In *The Queen*, Crystal, already a major name in New York, was awarded third runner-up. She did not appreciate the consolation prize and stormed off stage. What followed next was the read of the century. Organized by the then Philadelphia-based female impersonator Flawless Sabrina—who also narrates the documentary—this ball was her first pageant in New York City. A cross-country pageant promoter, Flawless wanted to make an impression on the Big Apple. She rented out Town Hall and had a stellar judges panel that included Andy Warhol. One Miss Rachel Harlow, a young, white, waifish contestant also from Philadelphia, won Grand Prize. Flawless ruffled more than a few feathers as the film showed Flawless and her assistant unabashedly helping Harlow throughout the competition. When Crystal let Harlow have it in Town Hall's basement, her read woke up the building: "Miss Thing, I don't say she's not beautiful! But she doesn't look beautiful tonight! She doesn't equal me. Look at her makeup! It's terrible!" She goes on to read Harlow's lackluster presentation, highlighting the rigged nature of the night.

Some in the ballroom community see Crystal's iconic read as the genesis of ballroom. However, the evidence shows a more complex picture of a changing New York City in the late 1960s and '70s and the evolving nature of ballroom that would eventually distinguish female impersonation or drag performance from what we today know as ballroom culture. Nevertheless, the moment stands in our collective conscious for what it is, a read, an acknowledgement and a reckoning that withstands the test of time.

—Sydney Baloue

▸
Production still of Crystal LaBeija for *The Queen*, 1968. Directed by Frank Simon. Distributed by Grove Press

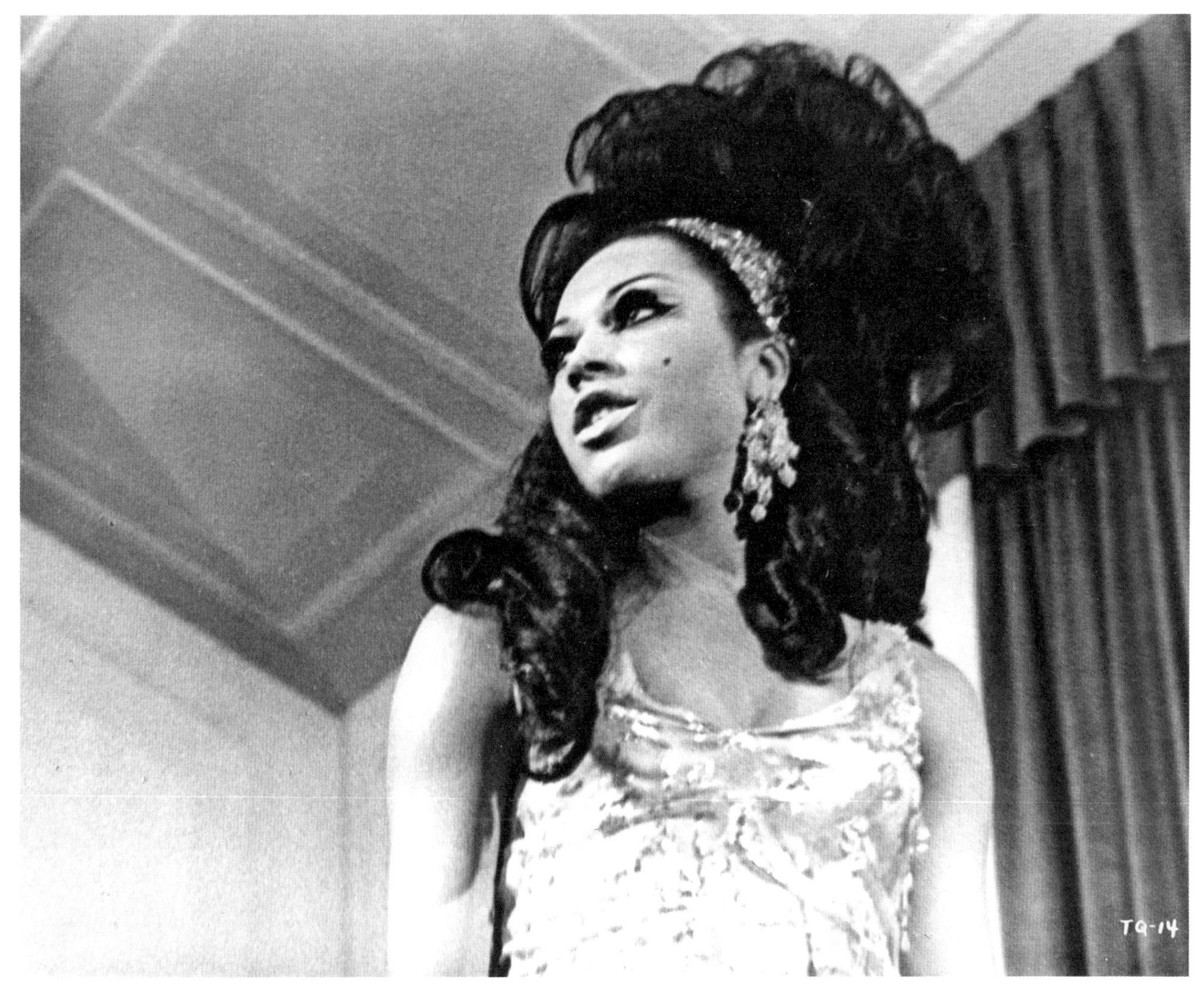
TQ-14

12 CONNIE NORMAN'S PUBLIC-ACCESS TELEVISION PROGRAM *GAY AND LESBIAN NEWSMAGAZINE*, 1992–95

"It has been a remarkably shitty couple of weeks. My T-cells took a big drop. I am now officially a person with AIDS. No longer am I just HIV positive. I have AIDS. I am going to die soon.

"I may have a couple of good years left, but I'm going to be a statistic and I'm not going to hold on to false hopes. Oh, I've had plenty of support and all that. My friends cried with me and worked hard to cheer me up. Sometimes it worked, but mostly it didn't. How can I be cheerful about losing my life? I'm pissed, pissed for life.

"We know how to prevent the spread of this virus. And yet this virus is spreading, to the women and the children and the teenagers and the gay men of color and our neighbors and our high school students and our high school teachers and our sons and our daughters and our brothers and our sisters and our fathers and our mothers and our aunts and our uncles and our priests and our preachers. And none of you yuppie scum, baby boomer, upward mobile, limousine-liberal, red-ribbon-wearing, death-cult assholes are doing enough to stop its spread.

"Is there no human compassion left in the world? Is the acceptance of this slaughter the best that the queer community can do? ... You disgust me.

"Till next time, I warned you it had been a really shitty week and I'm really pissed off. And my words are just musings and tribal writes."

Boy, that was a hard one to do. But you know, writing this column, if I really go to my space of truth, when I sit down to write the column, it does become somewhat cathartic for me and I'm able to shed some of it, you know. So thank you all for letting me dump.

—Connie Norman

Transcription of Norman reading her column Tribal Writes on the *Gay and Lesbian Newsmagazine*, June 21, 1993.

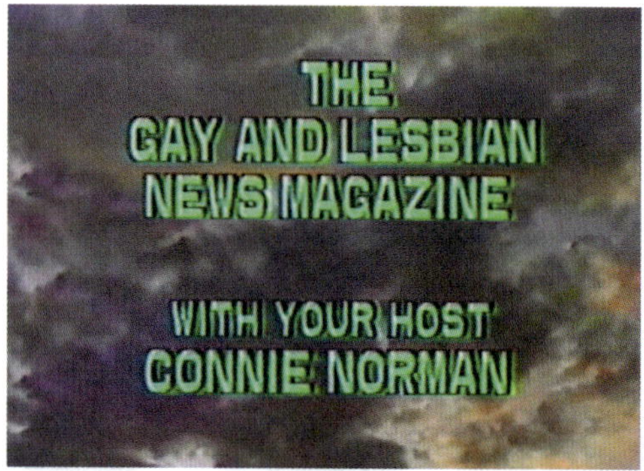

Connie Norman was an AIDS and trans activist, media spokesperson, and transgender policy advocate during the late 1980s and early 1990s in Los Angeles. Norman was a pivotal force within the Los Angeles chapter of ACT UP as the self-appointed "AIDS DIVA." In addition to her street activism, she wrote an opinion column, Tribal Writes, for Update, *an LGBTQ newspaper in Southern California, and co-hosted with Bob LaFont the public-access television program* Gay and Lesbian Newsmagazine *(1992–95). Norman was known widely for her unflinching honesty, her intersectional bridge-building politics, her soulful and salty rantings, her humor, and her piercing but compassionate voice.*

—Dante Alencastre and John Johnston

▸ Video stills of Connie Norman on *Gay and Lesbian Newsmagazine*, episode topic on "Women and AIDS," Los Angeles/Long Beach, June 21, 1993. From the documentary film *AIDS DIVA: The Legend of Connie Norman* (2021), directed by Dante Alencastre and John Johnston

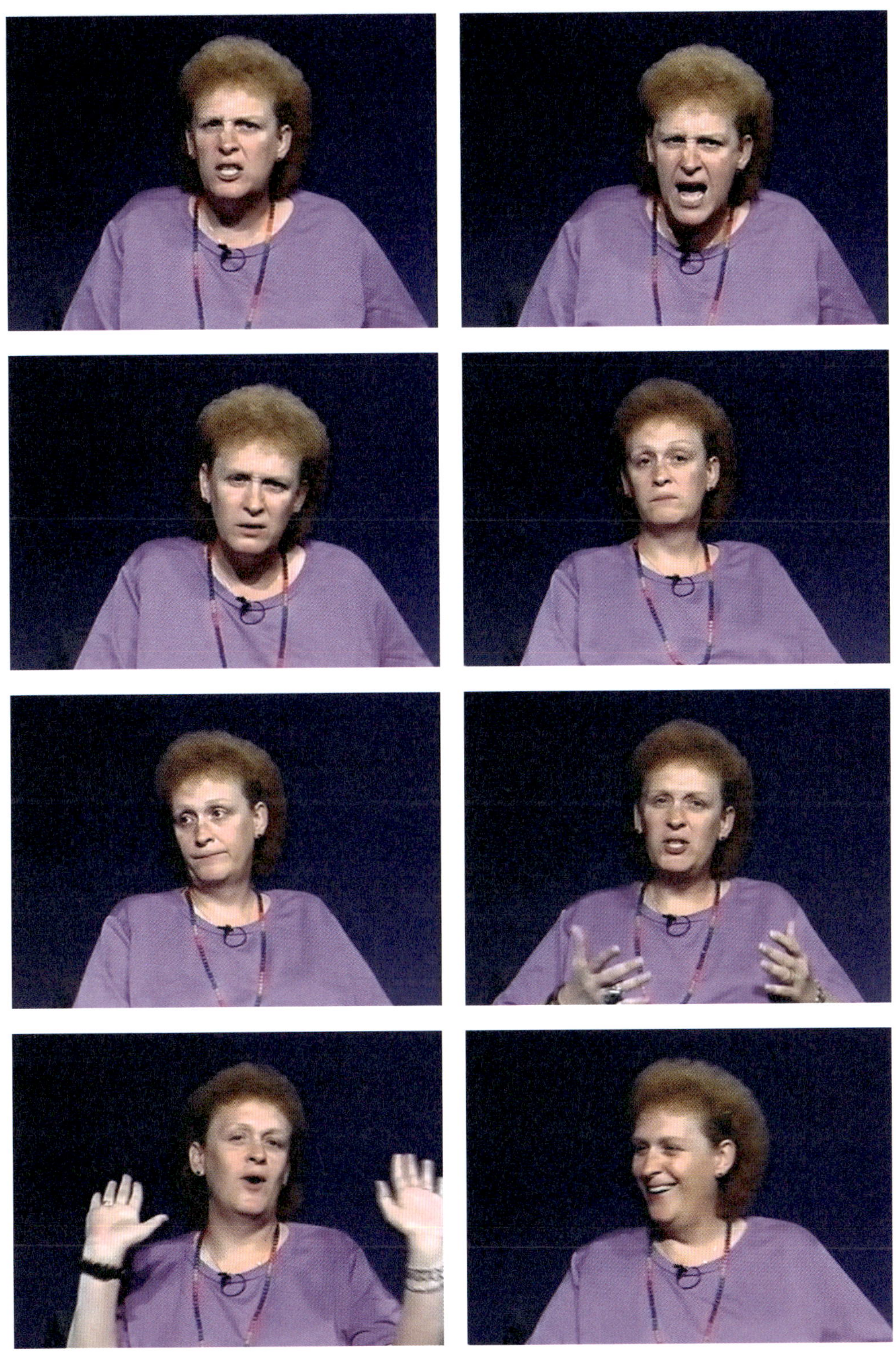

13 VANGUARD'S BROOMS, 1966

The chaos of night's end meets at Turk and Taylor. Everywhere, the police creep, and with them comes the possibility of harm's escalation and the search for shelter. For the lucky, tiny rooms fill with friends, service animals, lovers, and smoke. Trans/queer people on the run, refugees escaping CIA-funded wars, migrants searching for something more, Black families trying to stay in a city that continues to crush them, disabled people stranded by broken elevators, and those that know themselves in identity's braid fashion a pulsing geography at the edges of capital's totality. Precarity and possibility come at once as trans sociality takes the form of a confirming nod from a passing stranger. Under siege, San Francisco's Tenderloin remains.

The neighborhood's present echoes its past with such force they sometimes seem inseparable, but maybe that's just nostalgia. In 1966 it was "street people who are often the object of police harassment," who organized a "clean sweep"—with borrowed brooms and handmade signs—under the banner of Vanguard.[1] Their direct action restaged the daily attacks they survived, which were waged by the city under the guise of *cleaning up* the neighborhood. The idea of cleanliness, a signifier of white cis modernity, is always, according to its adjudicators, outside the grasp of the dispossessed. In other words, houseless people were blamed for the conditions of their lives, exonerating the over-housed, and understood as a problem in need of fixing. The solution then, as it is now, is always exile, never housing.

Thirty to forty members of Vanguard and their friends swept a section of Market Street, one of San Francisco's main arteries. Their action intended to position them as worthy of public life within a city that used all its tools to say otherwise. The brilliance of the group's action was also its limit. It was at once a counterattack against the logic of the state and its armed militias, but it also attempted to make a claim under a system that would never know them as anything more than refuse. This is not a critique of the action, but an attempt to sketch the antagonisms that held them hostage.

How, then, might the broom, a tool of the oppressor, be repurposed as a weapon ready for guerrilla warfare?

I ask this not only because of the "clean sweep" action, but because history's contradictions help us struggle differently now. The unlivable conditions that Tenderloin street youth were forced to survive in 1966 are perhaps more lethal today. Currently, trans nonprofits, youth service providers, and arts organizations join forces with the police to sweep away insurgent life so that only the blight of capital's triumph persists. But resistance too remains, led by groups like Gay Shame, whose thorny presence reminds us that "STREET SWEEPS KILL QUEERS." This is perhaps another way to say the one thing I really know: collective action is our only way out and, as Vanguard reminds us, this is "STREET POWER."

—Eric A. Stanley

1. *Vanguard: The Magazine of the Tenderloin* 1, no. 2 (October 1966).

▸
Page from *Vanguard*, vol. 1, no. 2 (October 1966). Gay, Lesbian, Bisexual, Transgender Historical Society

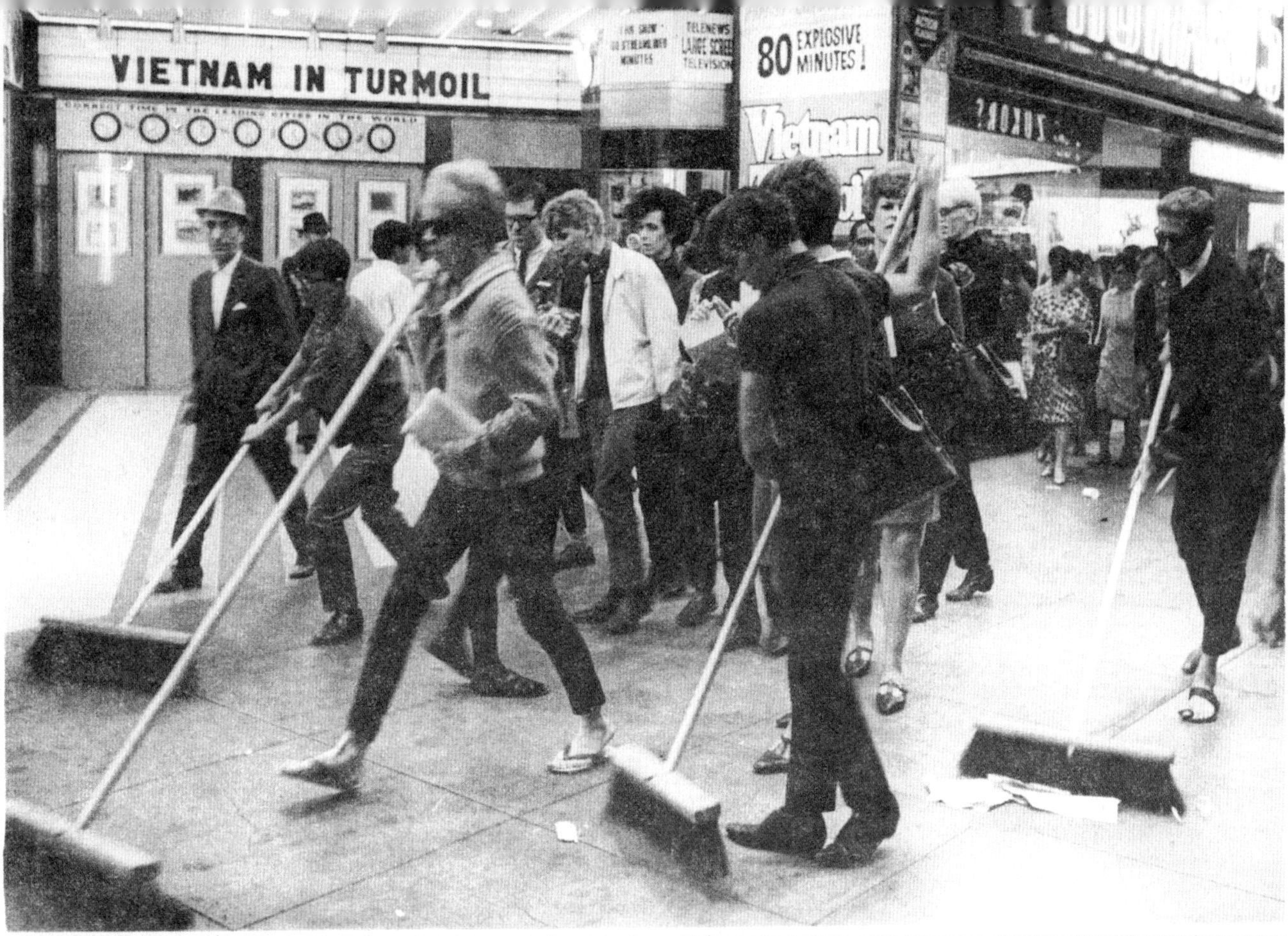

VIETNAM IN TURMOIL
80 EXPLOSIVE MINUTES!
Vietnam

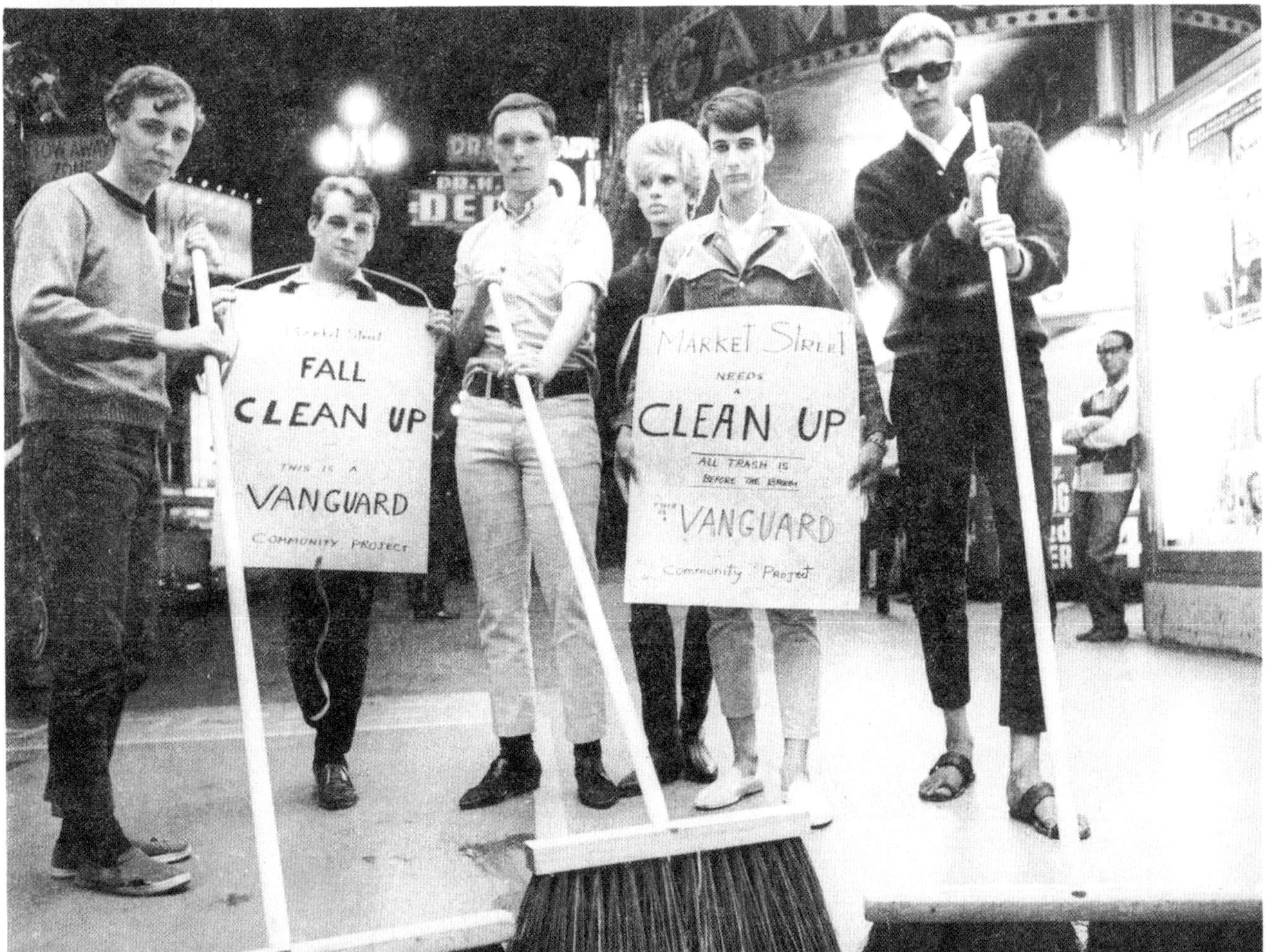

Market Street
FALL
CLEAN UP
THIS IS A
VANGUARD
COMMUNITY PROJECT
MARKET STREET
NEEDS
A
CLEAN UP
ALL TRASH IS
BEFORE THE BROOM
VANGUARD
Community Project

14 NICKI GREEN, *BREAKING DISHES AT GENE COMPTON'S*, 2016

"This is where there are other trans people in San Francisco"—this thought played like a record on repeat as Nicki Green biked to her artist studio in the Tenderloin. A self-described "object person," Green works in clay, sculpture, and ritual, generating a spatial poetics of trans embodiment. She cathected to the Tenderloin as both physical and psychic geography, a kind of transit point of bodies and hirstories making contact. In a world mostly absent of and destructive to trans life, Green sought out everyday spaces of trans gathering. Like all corners of San Francisco besieged by the relentless crisis of gentrification and homelessness, the story of the Tenderloin is erratic and ongoing. The 1966 riot at Gene Compton's Cafeteria—in which trans women, street queens, and hustlers fought back against police violence—was little known until historian Susan Stryker's archival excavation and community oral history amplified the intersectional abolitionist rebellion, giving voice to the specter of trans revolution in the Tenderloin that Green felt whispers of while navigating the city space. She began searching neighborhood thrift stores for any remaining signs of the all-night diner, imagining a coffee mug or breakfast plate in a ninety-nine-cent bin. Green had long been preoccupied with imbuing prosaic objects with the power of queer ritual. Dishware is so commonplace and integrated into everyday household use that Green considered it an especially potent object for "transing" (to borrow Stryker's formulation) the everyday.

Very little documentation of the riot at Compton's Cafeteria made it into the archive. What did exist told the story in print, but Green longed to touch and hold the trace of those revolutionary feelings and actions. The lack of any physical manifestation of the riot left open an opportunity for the artist to fabricate a surrogate for a now lost historical object. Balking at the fantasy of archival purity, Green designed commemorative dishware to mark the fiftieth anniversary of the riot at Compton's Cafeteria. Producing an edition of fifty diner mugs, she manipulated the logo of Gene Compton's, adding the word riot underneath cafeteria. In Green's iteration, dishware moves seamlessly from ordinary object to weapon, riot tool, ammunition. A mug is so commonplace, an object in regular contact with the body, the hand and the handle intertwined over the sometimes-utopic morning ritual of a first cup of coffee, imagining what the day could be. As an exploration of functional objects and functionality as conceptual container, Green has made an object for an archive that reimagines the archive as a conceptual and sculptural practice. In her meditation on the "stalls and turns in reference to spatial imaginaries," Stryker writes an architectural meandering of the Tenderloin that concludes, "a city space might generate an event."[1] The power of trans revolution has a materiality to it, one that, decades after the riots at Compton's Cafeteria, Green could feel cruising around on her bicycle. Perhaps, what is commemorated is the dream of another way of inhabiting space together.

—Jeanne Vaccaro

1. Susan Stryker, "On Stalling and Turning: A Wayward Genealogy for a Binary-Abolitionist Public Toilet Project," *Social Text* 39, no. 3 (September 2021): 37, 42.

▸
Nicki Green, *Breaking Dishes at Gene Compton's*, 2016. Custom decals and china paint on found mugs from thrift stores in San Francisco, edition 1 of 50, 4 in. × 3 in. dia. (10.2 cm × 7.6 cm dia.). Gay, Lesbian, Bisexual, and Transgender Historical Society. Photo by Marcel Pardo Ariza

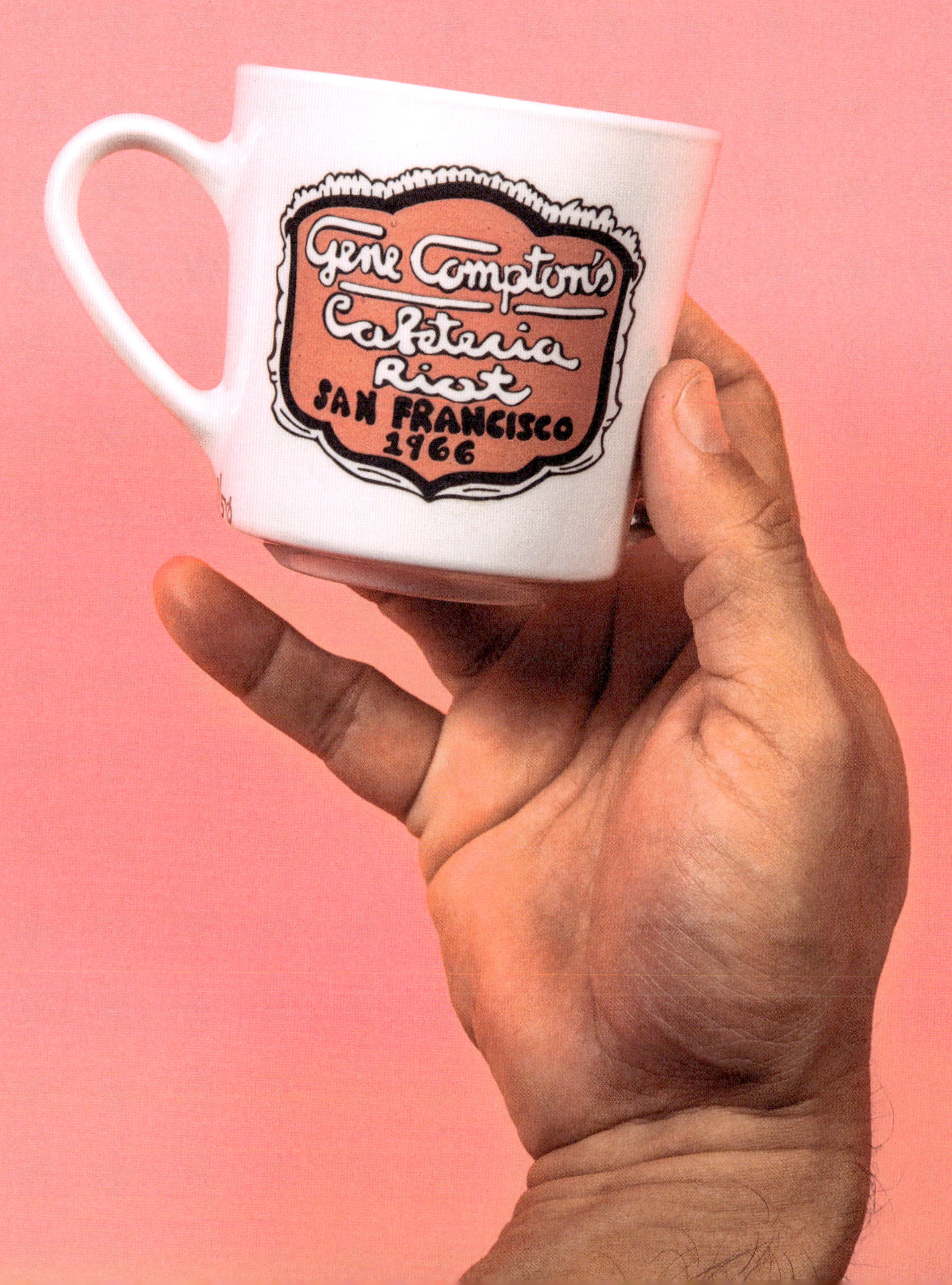
Gene Compton's
Cafeteria
Riot
SAN FRANCISCO
1966

TRANSFORMATION

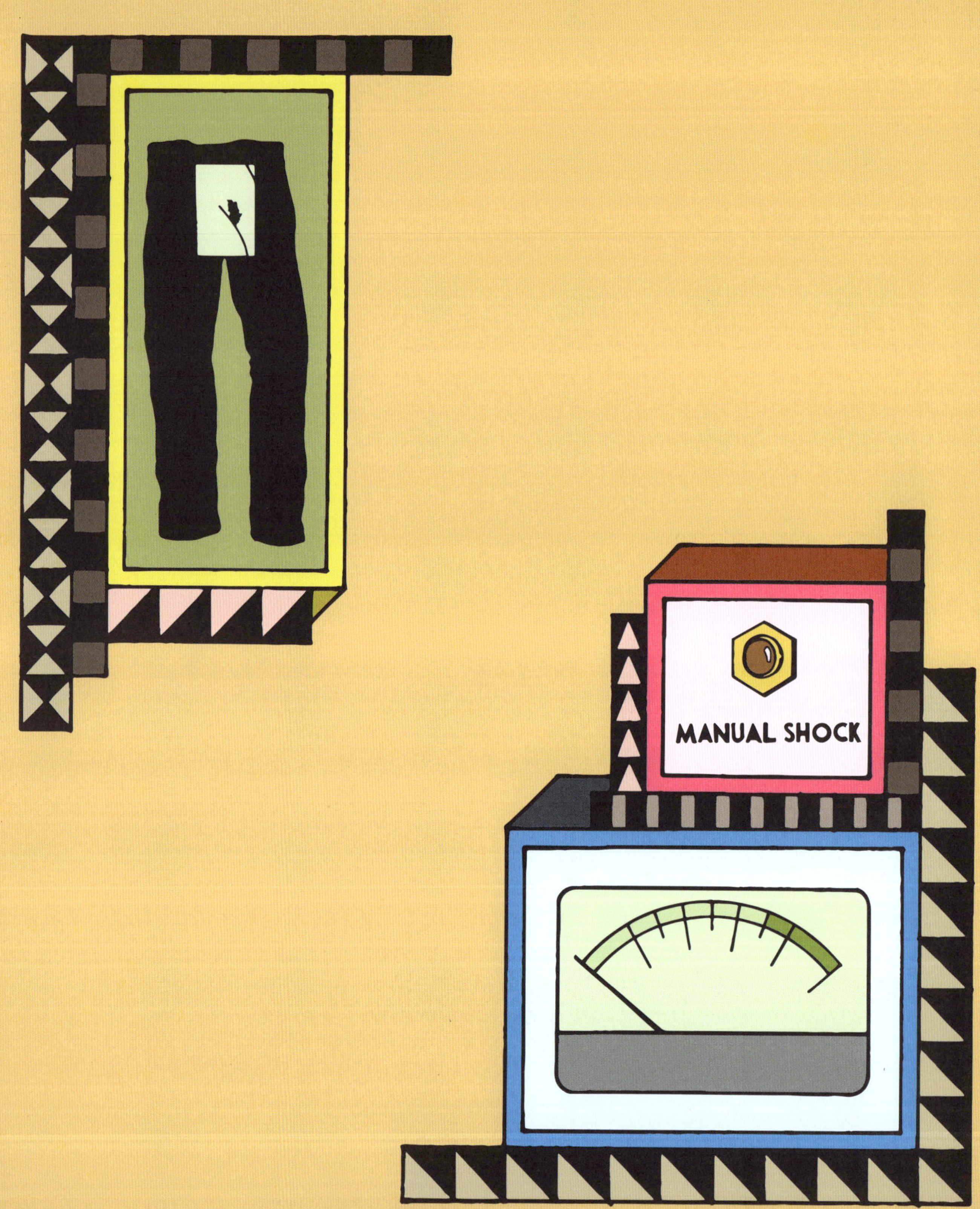

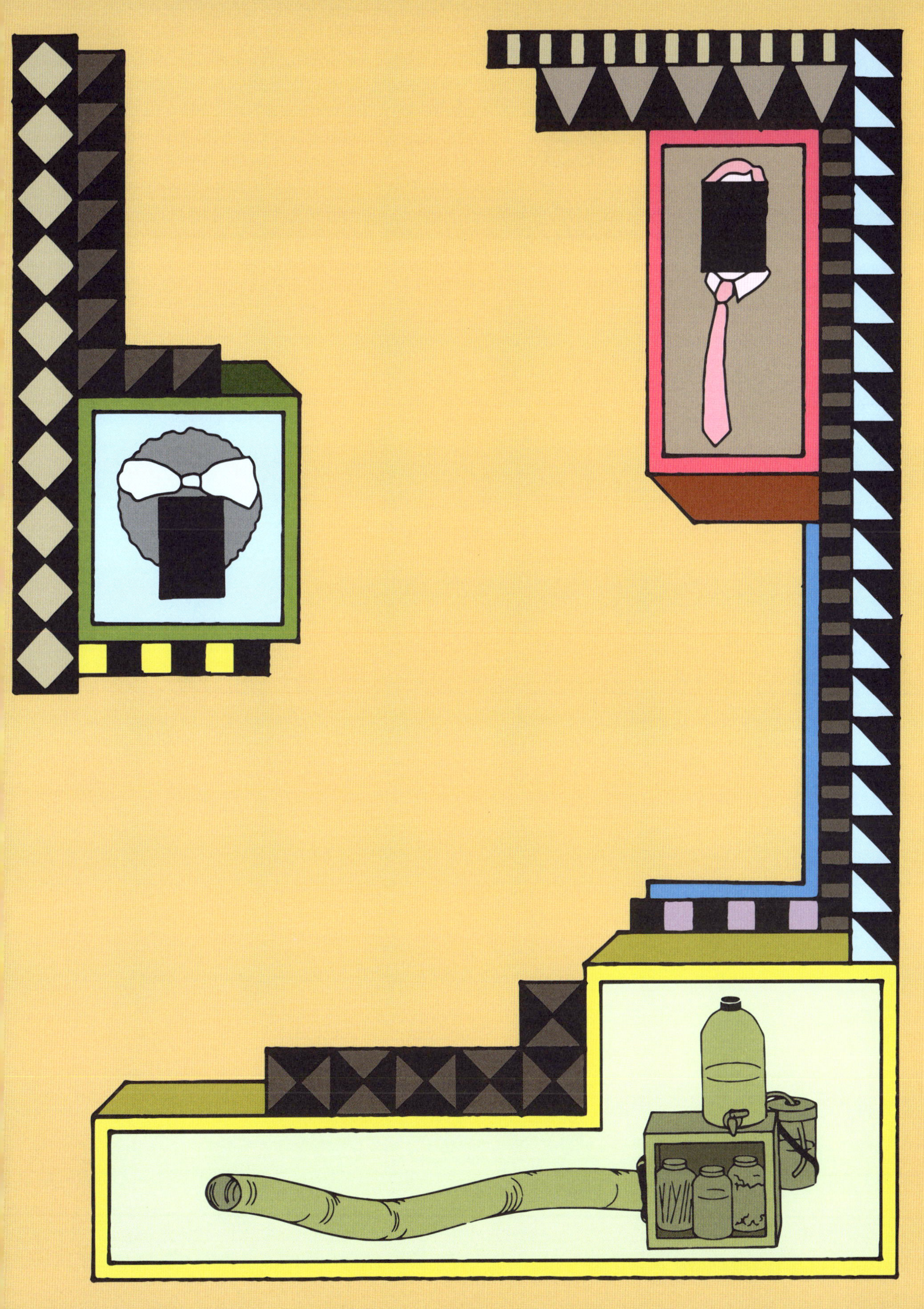

15 ULTRA-HUMANITE'S BRAIN, 1940

Superman, with a "sudden burst of intuition," recognizes that the "evil, blazing eyes" staring at him from movie star Dolores Winters's face are actually the windows to the soul of the Ultra-Humanite, his first recurring villain. A shriveled man whose powerful, mutated brain was consuming his own body, Ultra had kidnapped Winters and transplanted his brain inside her skull. Such a body would allow him to enact his plans for world domination without trouble from the authorities, who wouldn't imagine a woman capable of such dastardly deeds. How much pleasure Ultra might also have experienced being in Winters's "young, vibrant body" is not addressed, but tellingly his brain stays where it is for many subsequent storylines.

Superman's clocking of gender nonconformism (apparently yet another of his super senses) saves the day, ferreting out the villain seeking to pass in a fantastical trans body. This moment from DC Comics's *Action Comics* #20, published in 1940, is perhaps the first time that this sort of fictional gender play is used in the then newly minted superhero genre, but it certainly isn't the last.

Fifty-three years later, Rachel Pollack, an out trans writer, took over DC's *Doom Patrol*. In it, she created the character Kate Godwin, the first genuine trans superhero, named in part after trans performer and activist Kate Bornstein. Tellingly, Godwin is accidentally given her powers by one of the faux queer characters already occupying the pages of *Doom Patrol*; she has sex with Rebis, a divine amalgam of a man, a woman, and a sentient, radioactive spirit. Godwin's realistically portrayed transness then proceeds to profoundly destabilize the fantastical, faux queerness of the superheroes around her.

In one memorable exchange, Godwin is confronted by her Doom Patrol teammate Robot Man, who is a brain installed in a robot body. He has a crush on her, in part because of the genuine connection and empathy he's felt from her over his struggles with being in the "wrong body" and attempting to "pass" as a human. But when he discovers that Godwin is trans, he's dismayed that he's fallen for someone who has a penis and, in his mind, is therefore really a man.

Godwin responds, "Do you have a penis? What are you? ... Who's a man? Who's a woman?" She then turns to Doctor Caulder, the leader of the Doom Patrol, who is at that moment a talking, detached head lying in a bed of ice. Previously, he had inferred that she was simply a surgically altered man. She picks him up from the ice and asks, "What about you, Doctor Caulder? Are you a man or a woman? Which is it?"[1]

Pollack, like Superman creators Jerry Siegel and Joe Schuster before her, utilizes the fantastical elements of the superhero genre to explore the inherent power of gender transgression. Disconnecting bodies from gender identity terrifies, mystifies, and excites characters and readers alike. But Pollack uses a realistically portrayed trans woman to convey a real-world scenario of misunderstanding and prejudice, one which trans people face regularly.

In Godwin's first appearance in *Doom Patrol*, she tells a friend that, after receiving her powers, she attempted to join the Justice League. "They brushed me off. I suspect they liked my powers but couldn't handle me."[2] Perhaps Superman, founding member of the League and an alien who daily passes as a human male, had used his super senses to once again discover the queerness lurking in a woman's "young, vibrant body." Instead of "evil, blazing eyes," however, he had seen the reality of transness looking back at him, challenging him and the other superheroes to confront the obvious queerness inherent in their own fantastical bodies.

—Justin Hall

1. Rachel Pollack (writer) and Ted McKeever (penciler and inker), *Doom Patrol* 2, no. 76 (New York: DC Comics, 1994): 19.
2. Rachel Pollack (writer), Scot Eaton (penciler), and Tom Sutton (inker), *Doom Patrol* 2, no. 70 (New York: DC Comics, 1993): 9.

▶ Jerry Siegel (writer) and Paul Cassidy (penciler and inker), Page from *Action Comics*, vol. 1, no. 20 (January 1940)

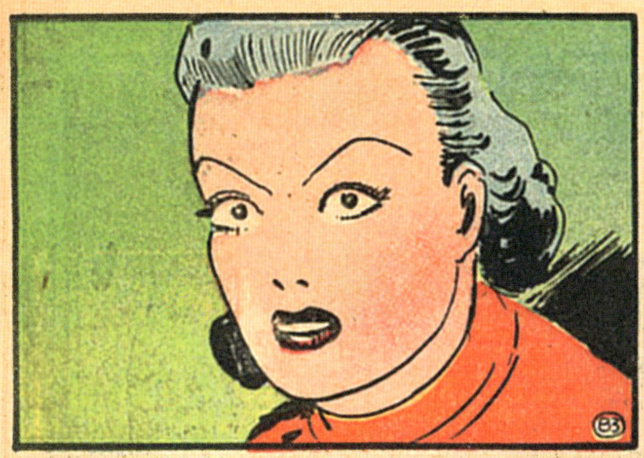

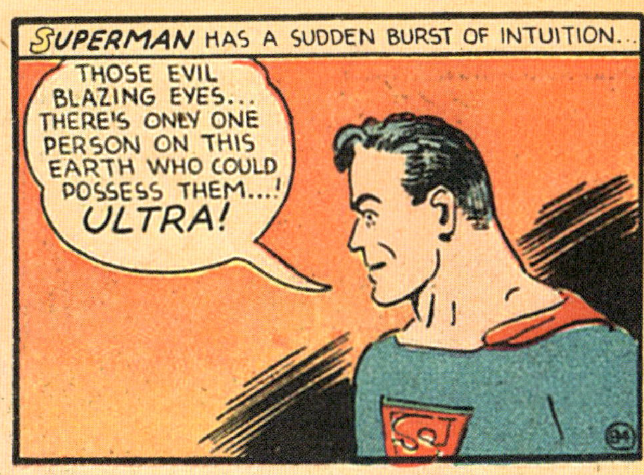
SUPERMAN HAS A SUDDEN BURST OF INTUITION...
THOSE EVIL BLAZING EYES... THERE'S ONLY ONE PERSON ON THIS EARTH WHO COULD POSSESS THEM...! ULTRA!

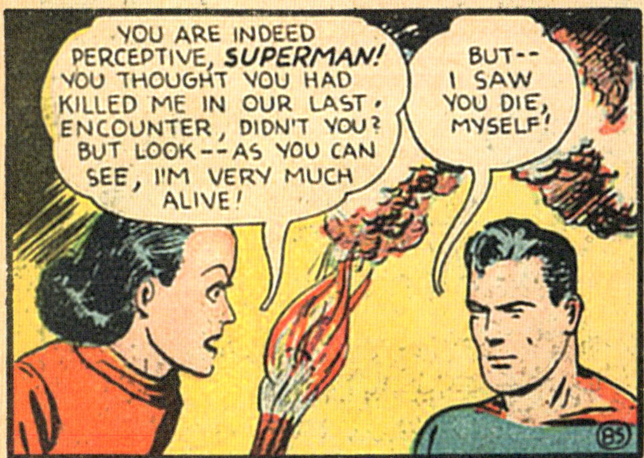
YOU ARE INDEED PERCEPTIVE, SUPERMAN! YOU THOUGHT YOU HAD KILLED ME IN OUR LAST ENCOUNTER, DIDN'T YOU? BUT LOOK--AS YOU CAN SEE, I'M VERY MUCH ALIVE!
BUT-- I SAW YOU DIE, MYSELF!

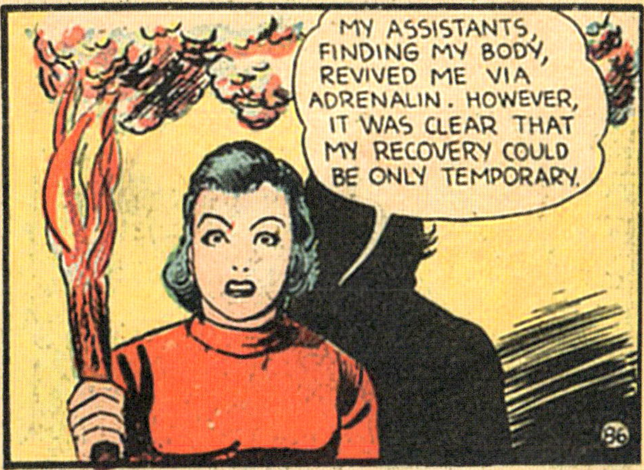
MY ASSISTANTS, FINDING MY BODY, REVIVED ME VIA ADRENALIN. HOWEVER, IT WAS CLEAR THAT MY RECOVERY COULD BE ONLY TEMPORARY.

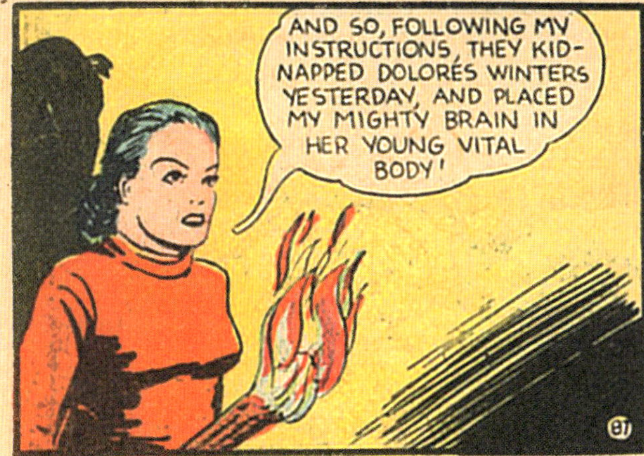
AND SO, FOLLOWING MY INSTRUCTIONS, THEY KID-NAPPED DOLORÉS WINTERS YESTERDAY, AND PLACED MY MIGHTY BRAIN IN HER YOUNG VITAL BODY!

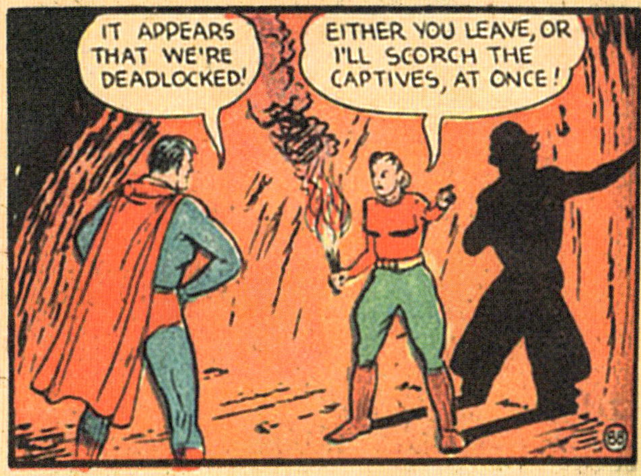
IT APPEARS THAT WE'RE DEADLOCKED!
EITHER YOU LEAVE, OR I'LL SCORCH THE CAPTIVES, AT ONCE!

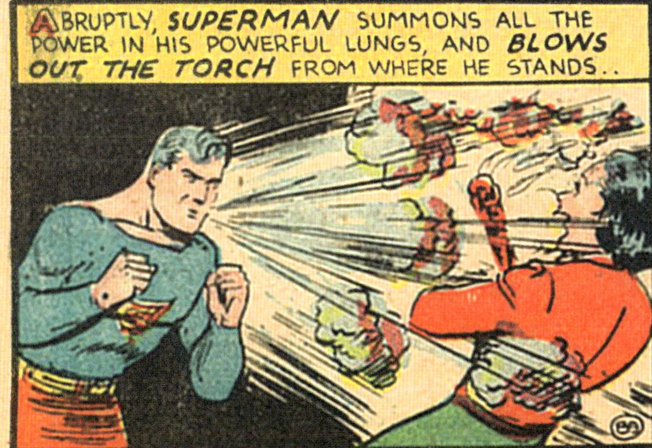
ABRUPTLY, SUPERMAN SUMMONS ALL THE POWER IN HIS POWERFUL LUNGS, AND BLOWS OUT THE TORCH FROM WHERE HE STANDS..

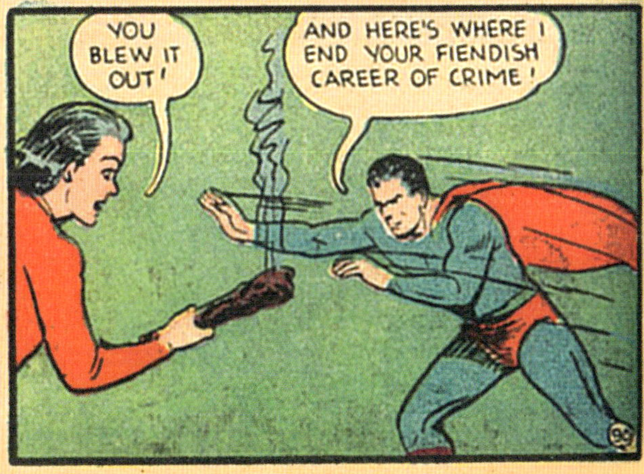
YOU BLEW IT OUT!
AND HERE'S WHERE I END YOUR FIENDISH CAREER OF CRIME!

16 HEATHER DEWEY-HAGBORG AND CHELSEA E. MANNING, *PROBABLY CHELSEA*, 2017

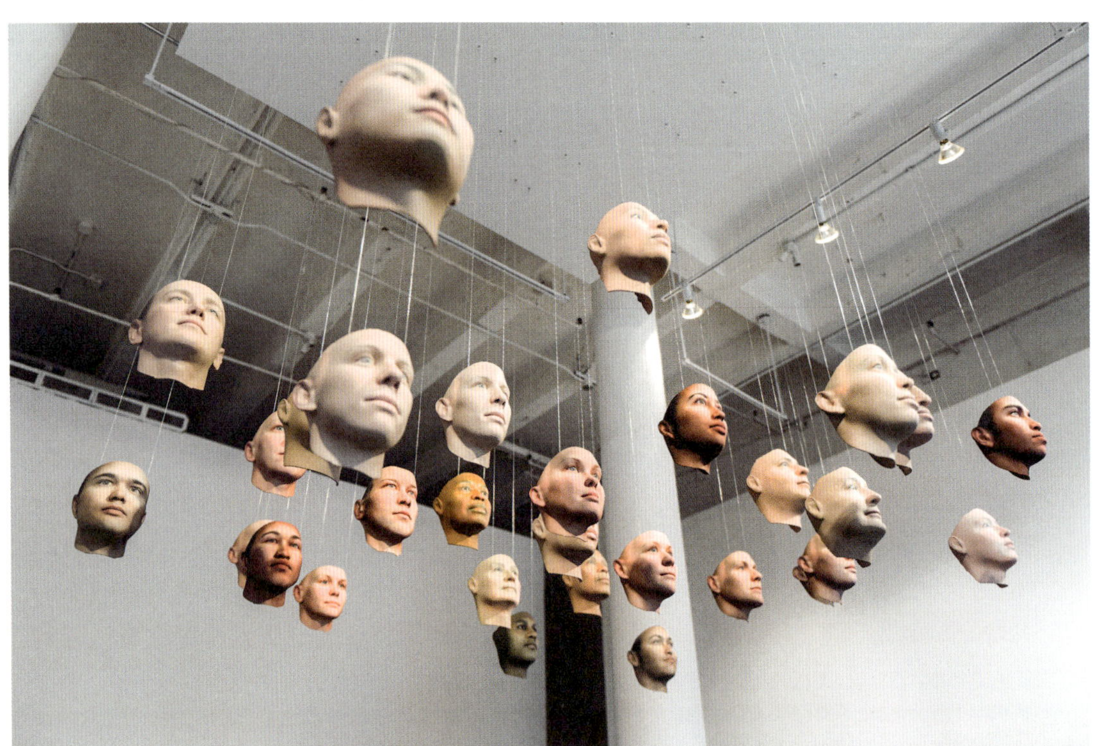

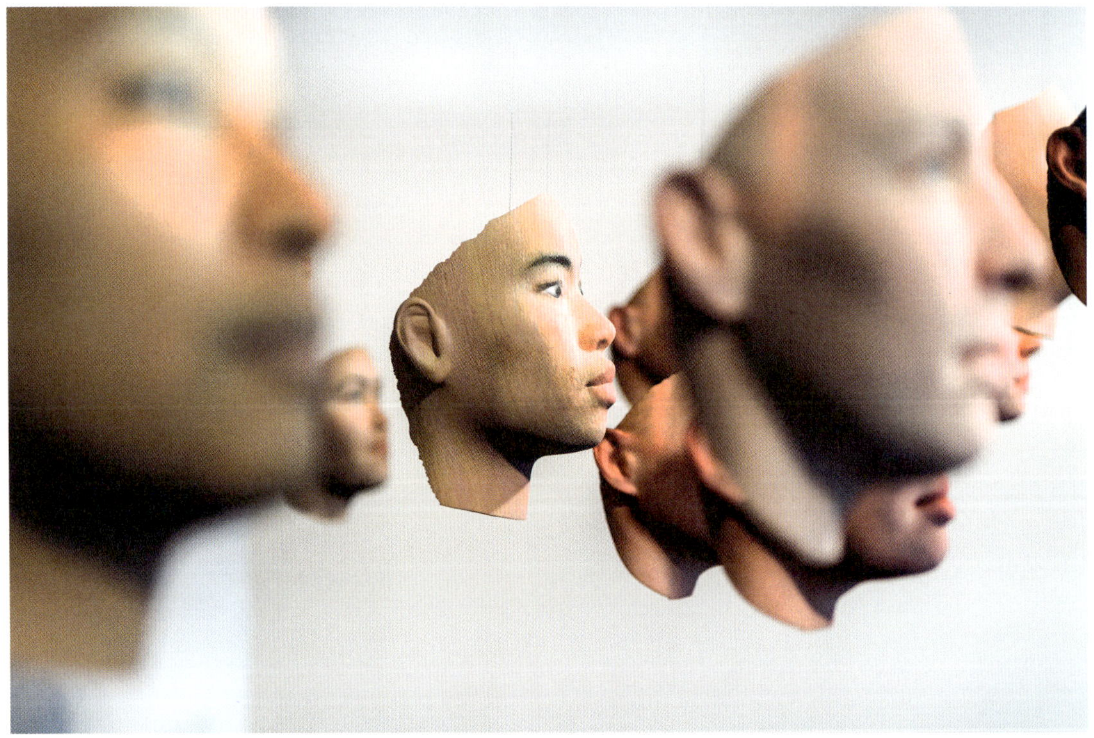

Chelsea's Face

Sometimes when I've been working online for a while, an ambient sense of sadness settles over me. So I search for pictures of Chelsea E. Manning. There are hundreds of them: She's smiling; she's thoughtful; she's wearing cute dresses or fetching sweaters with jeans, and her long blonde hair frames her face in a stylish waterfall. She's addressing a crowd, discussing her work, or she's posing for *Vogue* and DJing a glittering dance club in Berlin. Her face never fails to lift my spirits. I love to see her free.

Heather Dewey-Hagborg, an artist known for making portraits from samples of DNA, was working on the installation *Probably Chelsea* when the famed whistleblower was in prison. Somehow, she had managed to strike up a friendship with Chelsea, despite extremely restricted access. They exchanged letters, and eventually Chelsea sent the artist a cheek swab of DNA. Dewey-Hagborg sequenced it, ran it through a forensic DNA phenotyping algorithm, and created a collection of thirty life-sized, 3D-printed portraits representing what Chelsea might look like.

At that time, the only way we could see Chelsea's face was in a courtroom snapshot, where she'd been forced to wear a military uniform and a gender presentation that were not hers. I was working for a tech publication where we covered her case regularly. I had endless arguments with colleagues about why they needed to use female pronouns for Chelsea and absolutely should not put her deadname in a headline. I identified with Chelsea—I've had to argue with people about my own gender more times than I can count—and I worried about her. I wondered how she was really doing, behind the blank face I saw in pictures.

Dewey-Hagborg also wanted to see Chelsea's real face. *Probably Chelsea* is a kind of sequel to *Stranger Visions* (2012–13), a series of portraits generated from DNA samples collected from what the artist described as "hairs, chewed up gum, and cigarette butts from the streets, public bathrooms and waiting rooms of New York City."[1] Using what was at the time a nascent form of DNA analysis, she designed an algorithm to generate possible faces based on the genetic material she had collected. The results were startling, and made international news: Somehow, she was able to generate realistic portraits of people from DNA-saturated gum stuck to toilets.

Only two years after *Stranger Visions*, companies began offering forensic DNA phenotyping as a service to law enforcement, promising that investigators could create a perp sketch from a smear of DNA left at a crime scene. That promise is a lie. As *Probably Chelsea* makes clear in its wide array of faces—some pale, some dark brown, some male, some female—there is no easy relationship between how we look and the long strings of twisted polymers inside our cells.

You cannot recognize someone by reducing them to their constituent biological parts. In one sense, the message of *Probably Chelsea* is that her identity cannot be fathomed using the tools of a carceral state.

But there's another message too. When Dewey-Hagborg created delicate 3D molds of the many possible faces of Chelsea, she suspended them from the gallery ceiling at eye level. When you stare at them, they stare back. They are not easy to demonize; you cannot build a coherent stereotype around those faces because they are too different from one another.

Dewey-Hagborg crafted this installation to celebrate Chelsea's release in 2017, and I understand why. *Probably Chelsea* is about how our identities go far beyond the edges of our bodies. Our DNA contains endless probabilities, and our actions can replicate themselves far beyond the confines of our puny lives. *Probably Chelsea* is a warning to those who seek to reduce us to smears of genetic material. You can put Chelsea in prison, but you cannot constrain the possibilities she represents.

—Annalee Newitz

◄
Heather Dewey-Hagborg and Chelsea E. Manning, *Probably Chelsea*, 2017. Genetic materials, custom software, 3D prints; 30 portraits, each portrait 8 × 6 × 8 in. (20.3 × 15.2 × 20.3 cm), overall dimensions variable

1. Heather Dewey-Hagborg, "Stranger Visions," https://deweyhagborg.com/projects/stranger-visions.

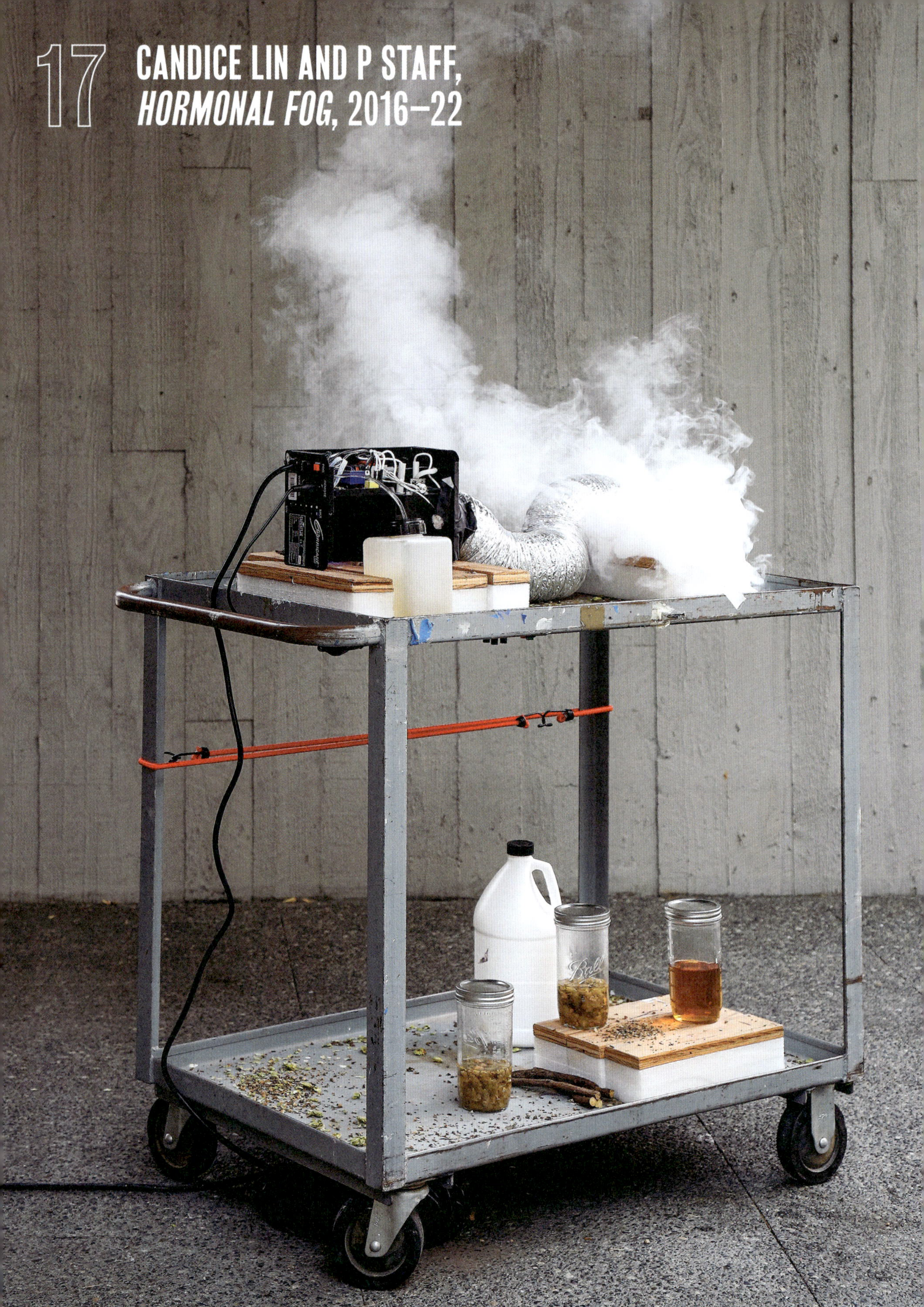
17
CANDICE LIN AND P STAFF,
HORMONAL FOG, 2016–22

Gallery visitors likely notice the somewhat improvised-looking contraption in the corner before they take note of the soft haze that it slowly emits into the room. These observations probably precede a consideration of the implications of breathing this testosterone-suppressing mist into the body. Re-created for a number of museums and other art spaces since 2016, *Hormonal Fog* is delivered by artists Candice Lin and P Staff for exhibition as a set of instructions. Dried licorice root, hops, black cohosh, and dong quai (當歸 or 당귀) need to be procured, combined, and brewed to create an herbal tincture. When the tincture is ready, it is diffused into the air, and eventually into exhibition visitors' lungs, by means of a hacked fog machine.

Each of these herbs has a long history in traditional herbal medicine and are used to serve a variety of needs. The year in which I'm writing this, 2022, has been a particularly bad year in legal terms for bodily autonomy and self-determination in the United States. In the wake of the repeal of the federal right of pregnant people to access safe surgical or pharmaceutical abortion, social media cast a spotlight on cohosh in particular as one potentially available abortifacient. In addition to ending pregnancy and bringing on childbirth at term, cohosh is often listed as a remedy for a number of maladies, including sore throat, depression, and snake bites.[1] Its ability to aid in the suppression of testosterone is less often cited in guides to traditional medicine where, as in every other archive, records of trans life and the methods and means for embodiment often need to be read between the lines.

Lin and Staff began developing this work towards the end of a brief period during which gender-affirming medical care was relatively accessible. We can map out this era as existing from 2012 to 2016, roughly speaking. It began with the American Psychiatric Association's 2012 update to its diagnostic manual to replace gender identity disorder with gender dysphoria, and Medicare's 2014 reversal of its thirty-three-year ban on coverage for "transsexual surgery," which had set a precedent largely followed by private insurance. Its end was heralded by a 2016 injunction by a Texas federal court judge challenging the U.S. Department of Health and Human Services Office for Civil Rights' rule prohibiting federally assisted insurance plans from wholesale exclusions of gender-affirming care. As of 2022, fifteen US states either have laws in effect restricting gender-affirming care, especially for minors, or are considering enacting this type of law as part of a broader spate of anti-LGBTQ+ bills that were introduced this year.

I am not suggesting that the testosterone-suppressing mist produced by Lin and Staff's *Hormonal Fog* is meant to directly address the decline of accessibility to legal and affordable gender-affirming care in this country, or that it presents a truly feasible large-scale alternative to the advanced techniques for transition developed by medical professionals over the past century. Its subversive presence does, however, suggest both the promise and the threat of a reliance on traditional plant-based medicine for everyone to whom mainstream medical treatment is neither attractive nor available. Moreover, the imposition of its suppression without the prior consent of those who enter the exhibition unawares rather mirrors the lack of choice presented to individuals (let's say, for instance, trans children raised in Texas or Florida) who find their bodies to be out of alignment with both their identity and with the cultural air they must breathe.

—Christina Linden

◄
Candice Lin and P Staff, *Hormonal Fog* (Study), 2016–22. Hacked fog machine, dried herbs, herbal tincture, wood, plastic, and miscellaneous hardware, approximately 24 × 12 × 20 in. (61 × 30.1 × 30.1 cm)

1. Siolo Thompson, *Hedgewitch's Field Guide* (Woodbury, MN: Llewellyn Publications, 2018), 51.

18 AV-6 VISUALLY KEYED SHOCKER, c. 1973

There is little joy to be had from an electric shock. Discombobulating enough when it happens by accident, when deliberately administered by another person with institutional medical power as a purported "corrective" technique it can have more debilitating effects (even for those who find pain exciting in certain self-determined contexts). It becomes a crude instrument for dehumanizing punishment.

During the 1960s, electric shock became a popular tool in a range of clinical psychological and therapeutic methods. One of these was a branch of psychology and psychiatry known as "aversion therapy"—a type of behavior therapy based on learning theory. Unlike other forms of therapy that focused either on talking (psychotherapy, psychoanalysis, etc.) or the body (brain surgery, psychopharmaceuticals, etc.), the goal of aversion therapy was to encourage patients to *unlearn* "undesirable" behaviors and *relearn* socially desirable ones. "Undesirable" behaviors included alcoholism, eating disorders, gambling, obsessive-compulsive symptoms, phobias, queer sexuality, and transgender.

"Treatment" of socially "undesirable" sexuality and gender typically involved hooking a queer or trans person up to an electric shock stimulator and issuing electric shocks while showing them pictures or text associated with their preferred gender, or in the case of trans people, having them dress in their preferred clothing, or listening to themselves describe the process of undressing. The use of electricity replaced an earlier, less precise method using nausea-inducing drugs such as apomorphine. Typically, shocks were administered to the fingers, arms, neck, thighs, or feet, but there are claims that genitals were sometimes involved. The purported goal was to establish a negative association with the "undesirable" behavior and thereby instill sexual and gender conformity.

Necessary equipment included not only electric stimulators but polygraphs, transducers, slide or film projectors, audio amplifiers and, of course, physical space. Most of these were available in whichever hospital, clinic, or university the practitioners worked in, provided by global medical instrument manufacturers such as Grass Technologies in Quincy, Massachusetts. Resourceful practitioners could and did DIY any parts that weren't.

The device pictured here—in its "attractive solid birch wood case," once owned by the University of Texas—was patented by William Farrall, head of Farrall Instruments of Grand Island, Nebraska, and appeared in a glossy sales catalog in 1973 along with a range of other aversion therapy instruments.[1] Aversion therapy was a global phenomenon, by no means confined to the United States. In fact, a majority of the published clinical experiments were conducted in the United Kingdom, as well as Australia, Canada, Czechoslovakia, and South Africa.[2] Yet the United States seems to be unique in the commercial marketing of aversion therapy technology.

The Farrall brochure included at least thirteen devices marketed towards practitioners of sexual and especially gender-aversion therapy, including compact versions for use by patients at home or even at work for "self-reinforcement." It offered a one-stop-aversion-therapy-shop, including a slide-printing service for practitioners who sent in a collection of images to be used in treatment, as well as voice recording and playback machines for use with trans people. There is also a list of eight articles from the medical literature, most of which proclaim the wonders of electrical machines for practicality and lasting reorientation effects—in truth the results are meager, describing "no genuine conversion," persistent depression, or based on improbable and coerced reports of "success" by subjects themselves in the aftermath of treatment.[3]

Farrall was evidently a savvy entrepreneur hoping to ride the aversion therapy wave. Yet due to its meager results and the rise of a movement for queer and trans rights, aversion therapy fell out of favor in the mid-1970s. Although Farrall continued as an evangelist for sexual and gender diagnostic and treatment technologies into the 1990s, these "attractive solid birch wood" devices quickly became obsolete and irrelevant, just like his views.

—Dr. Kate Davison

▸ (foreground) AV-6 Visually Keyed Shocker, c. 1973. Farrall Instruments Company. Previously owned by the medical school at The University of Texas at San Antonio. ONE National Gay & Lesbian Archives at the USC Libraries; (background) Page from Farrall Instruments's "Behavior Modification and Teaching Devices" catalog, 1973. ONE National Gay & Lesbian Archives at the USC Libraries

1. Farrall Instruments's "Behavior Modification and Teaching Devices" catalog, 1973. ONE Subject Files Collection (Coll2012.001), ONE National Gay & Lesbian Archives at the USC Libraries.
2. Kate Davison, "Cold War Pavlov: Homosexual Aversion Therapy in the 1960s," *History of the Human Sciences* 34, no. 1 (February 2021): 89–119.
3. Cited sources include: L. Solyom and S. Miller, "A Differential Conditioning Procedure as the Initial Phase of the Behaviour Therapy of Homosexuality," *Behaviour Research and Therapy* 3, no. 3 (November 1965): 147–60; Saul M. Levin, Irwin S. Hirsch, Gerald Shugar, and Robert Kapche, "Treatment of Homosexuality and Heterosexual Anxiety with Avoidance Conditioning and Systematic Desensitization," *Research and Practice* 5, no. 3 (Fall 1968): 160–68; B. H. Fookes, "Some Experiences in The Use of Aversion Therapy in Male Homosexuality, Exhibitionism and Fetishism-Transvestism," *British Journal of Psychiatry* 115, no. 520 (March 1969): 339–441; Isaac Marks, Michael Gelder, and John Bancroft with assistance from Maureen O'Neill, "Sexual Deviants Two Years after Electric Aversion," *British Journal of Psychiatry* 117, no. 537 (August 1970): 173–85; M. J. MacCulloch, C. J. Birtles, and M. P. Feldman, "Anticipatory Avoidance Learning for the Treatment of Homosexuality: Recent Developments and an Automatic Aversion Therapy System," *Behavior Therapy* 2, no. 2 (April 1971): 151–69.

AUTOMATED CONDITIONING

Both the projector and the shock unit are complete units and can be used either in combination or separately. Shock time can be variable or infinite. Delay between slide exposure and shock is adjustable. The shock intensity is variable and is indicated by a meter. Push buttons allow the clinician to override the shock program. Slides can be presented manually or automatically at preselected recycle intervals.

A special dual isolation circuit is used to connect the apparatus to the power line. This provides the necessary safety required in any line operated shocker.

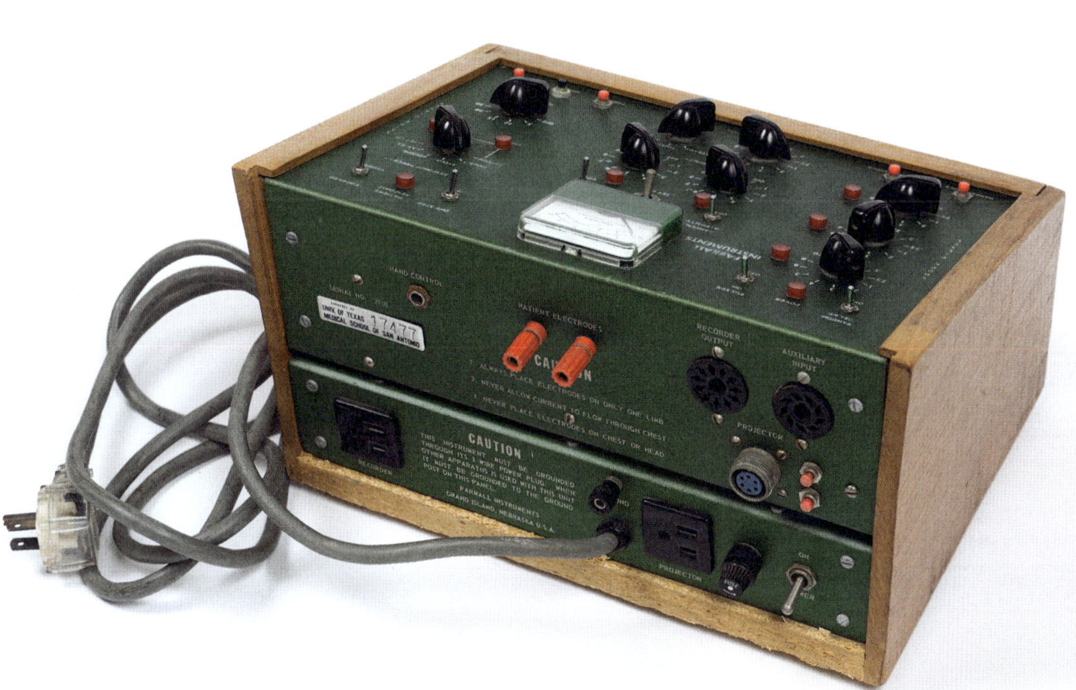

2. Marked slide gives shock after adjustable delay. Duration is adjustable. Patient can terminate shock by pressing button.
3. Marked slide gives shock after adjustable delay. Duration is adjustable. Patient can prevent shock by pressing button before a pre-shock delay period lapses.
4. Marked slide gives shock after adjustable delay. Duration is adjustable. Patient can terminate shock by pressing button or can also prevent shock by pressing before pre-shock delay has completed.
5. Systematic Desensitization with or without shock. Slide timer runs forward for increasing fear hierarchy. Patients hand press backs up projector to relax slide.

AV-5 SPECIFICATIONS

Model AV-5 Visually Keyed Shocker for automated behavior conditioning and systematic desensitization. Complete with 35MM E2 Ektagraphic slide projector f:3.5, 3'' lens, shock generator-control, patient response hand button, one slide magazine, silver electrode set and all connecting cables for operation from 117 volt 50-60 Hz power. Shock generator-control has the following features: Attractive solid birch wood case 8¼'' x 13¼'' x 9¼'' with high power shock source

and control circuits, with special square leg transformer core with metal shield between separate primary and secondary coils located on opposite sides of the square core, with transparent Woodhead three-wire safety plug (fits standard three-connection wall receptacle). Solid state with 26 transistors, 11 IC's, 12 diodes and 2 transient surge protectors.

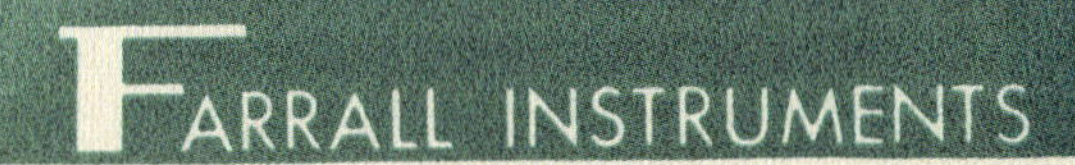

19 MOCK-UP FOR HARRY BENJAMIN'S *THE TRANSSEXUAL PHENOMENON*, 1966

It is hard to imagine today just how alone gender diverse people felt in the 1960s Western world. There were a few, very well hidden, private clubs where people might gather—if they were lucky enough to even know that such places existed, and brave enough to take themselves to them. Even so, most such places were behind unmarked doors, where entrance was only possible if you knew someone who could tell you the password that would get you past the tough guy at the door.

For everyone else, that is, almost all gender diverse people, there was only silence and shame. To speak aloud your inner thoughts and feelings that you were in the wrong body was to court beatings and beratings if you were a child. If you were an adult who tried to lay claim to a gender other than the one originally assigned to you, you were liable to be labeled as insane, criminal, a sinful abomination. Young or old, you could end up dead or incarcerated, drugged or electroshocked. Certainly, no one in their right mind would believe you. The accepted medical opinion was that claiming a gender other than the one assigned at birth was delusional, a sign of severe mental illness that should in no way be accommodated.

When Harry Benjamin (1885–1986) published *The Transsexual Phenomenon* in 1966, it was a game changer. Here was a respectable doctor making a compelling case for accommodating transsexual people's requests for medical and legal assistance in changing their gender. Other doctors and gatekeepers started to take Benjamin's arguments seriously and, as a result, started to take more transsexual people seriously. Many transsexual people read Benjamin's book like a bible and memorized it like scripture. When they sought treatment from doctors who had read Benjamin's book, they recited chapter and verse. As a result, doctors saw such people as "textbook cases" and approved them for treatment.

The book was illustrated with images meant to convince readers that it was, indeed, possible for people to successfully change from men into women, women into men. It being mid-twentieth century, gender and sex were thought of as synonymous. Thus, gender could not be convincingly changed without an equally convincing change of primary and secondary sex characteristics. To drive home the point that sex/gender changes could be convincingly accomplished, Benjamin illustrated his book with images such as these "before-and-after" photographs showing how an unremarkable, conservatively dressed, white middle-class young man could be transformed into an unremarkable, conservatively dressed, white middle-class young woman. However, to buttress the validity of the "sex change," images of provocatively exposed plump and perky breasts were also included. Curiously, in this pre-publication mock-up, held in the Transgender Archives at the University of Victoria, Canada, all faces have been blacked out. In the final publication, only the two photographs showing the woman's face were obscured, despite the captions clearly identifying that all photographs in this series are of the same person.

Today, we may well see these photographs as examples of demeaning objectification and exploitation. However, in addition to these mock-ups, we also have in the Transgender Archives the original signed model releases indicating that the people in the pictures gave their informed consent for these photographs to be published in *The Transsexual Phenomenon*. Both Benjamin and the people who posed for these photographs hoped to convince a skeptical public and medical establishment that transsexual people were entitled to treatment that would allow them to live more authentically. While the people who appeared in the photographs illustrating *The Transsexual Phenomenon* put themselves at considerable risk by showing themselves so openly, it was a gamble that paid off well for those of us who have come after. I, for one, am thankful to them for their bravery.

—Aaron H. Devor

▸ Harry Benjamin, *The Transsexual Phenomenon*, 1966. Published by The Julian Press. ONE National Gay & Lesbian Archives at the USC Libraries

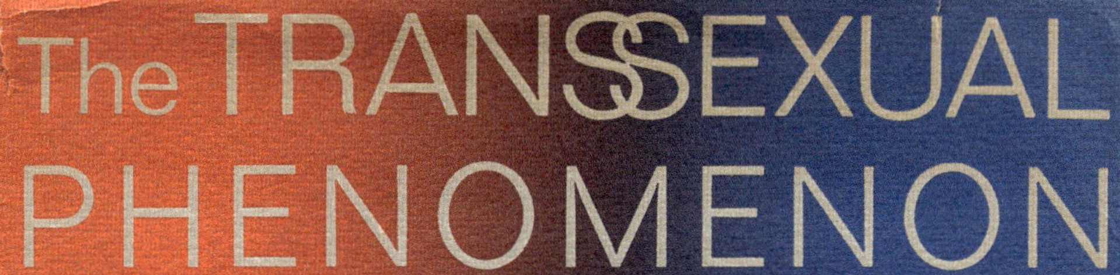

A scientific report on transsexualism and sex conversion in the human male and female. Harry Benjamin, MD

▸
Illustrations mock-up for Harry Benjamin, *The Transsexual Phenomenon*, 1966. Published by The Julian Press. Rikki Swin Collection (AR421), Transgender Archives, University of Victoria Libraries

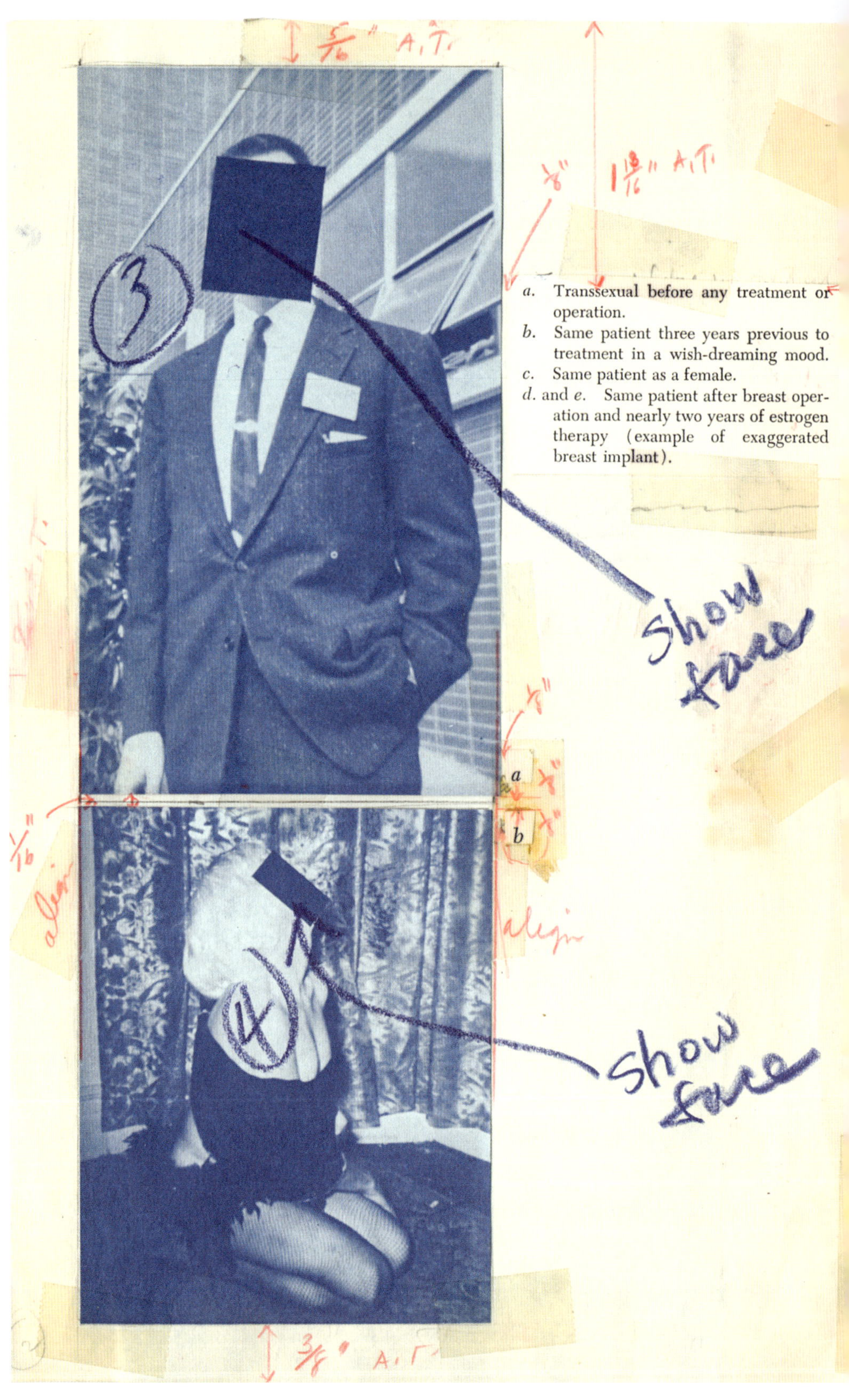

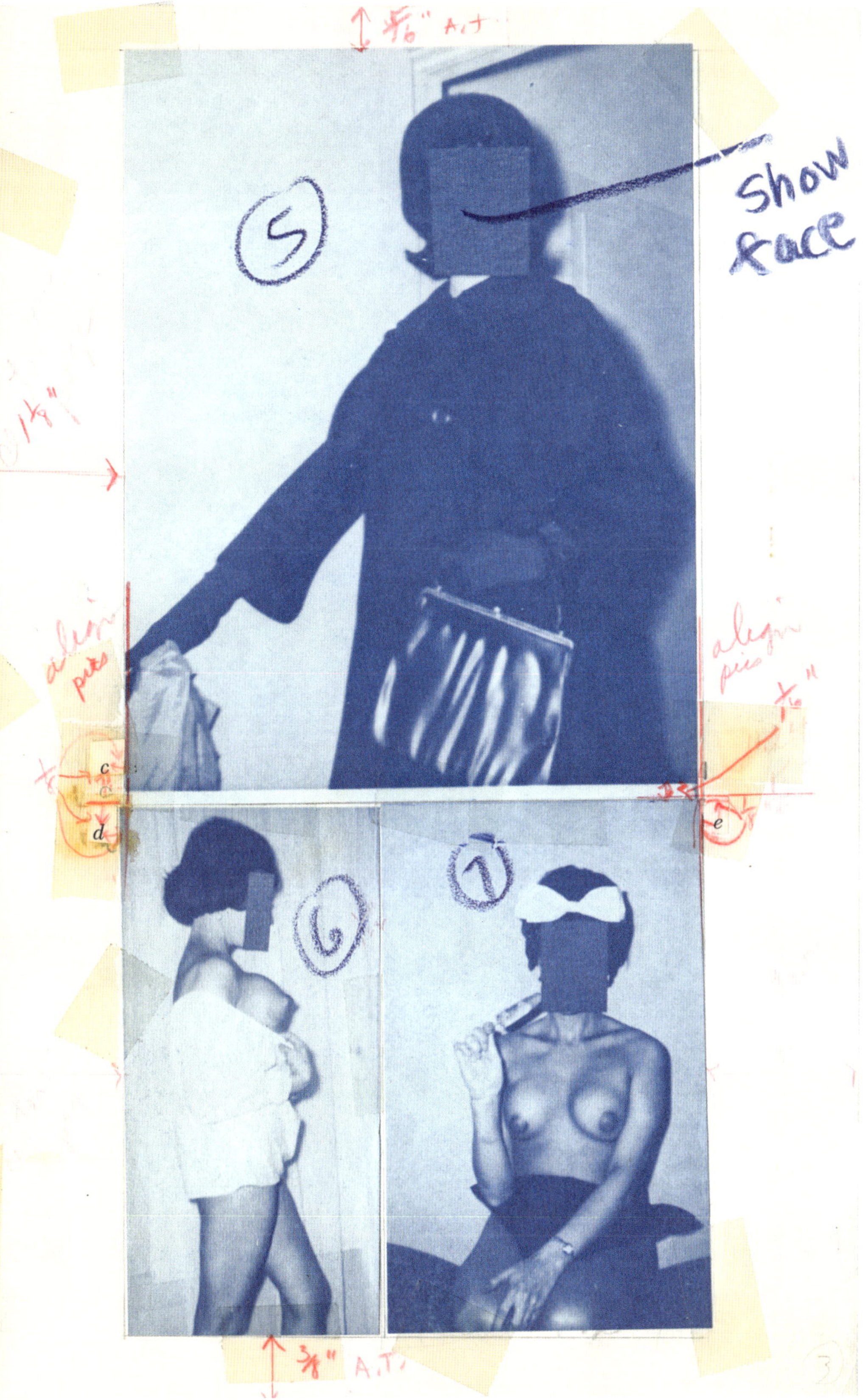
show face
5
6
7
c
d
e
align pics
align pics
A.T.
3/8" A.T.

20 MICHA CÁRDENAS, *BECOMING DRAGON*, 2008

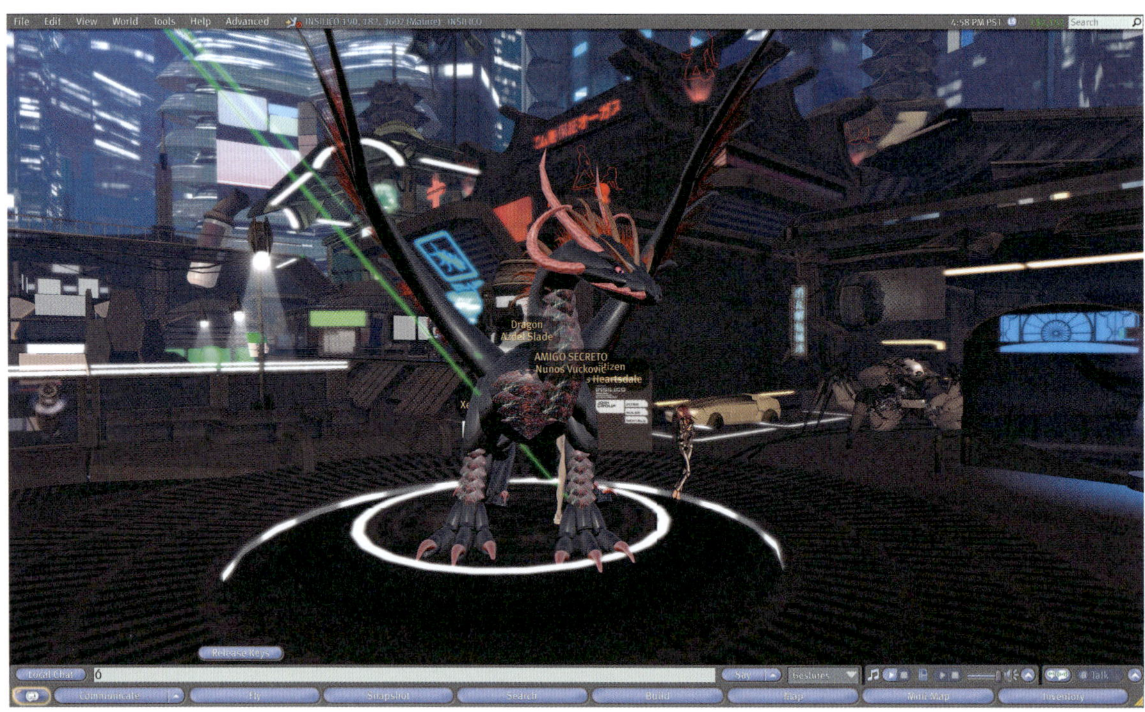

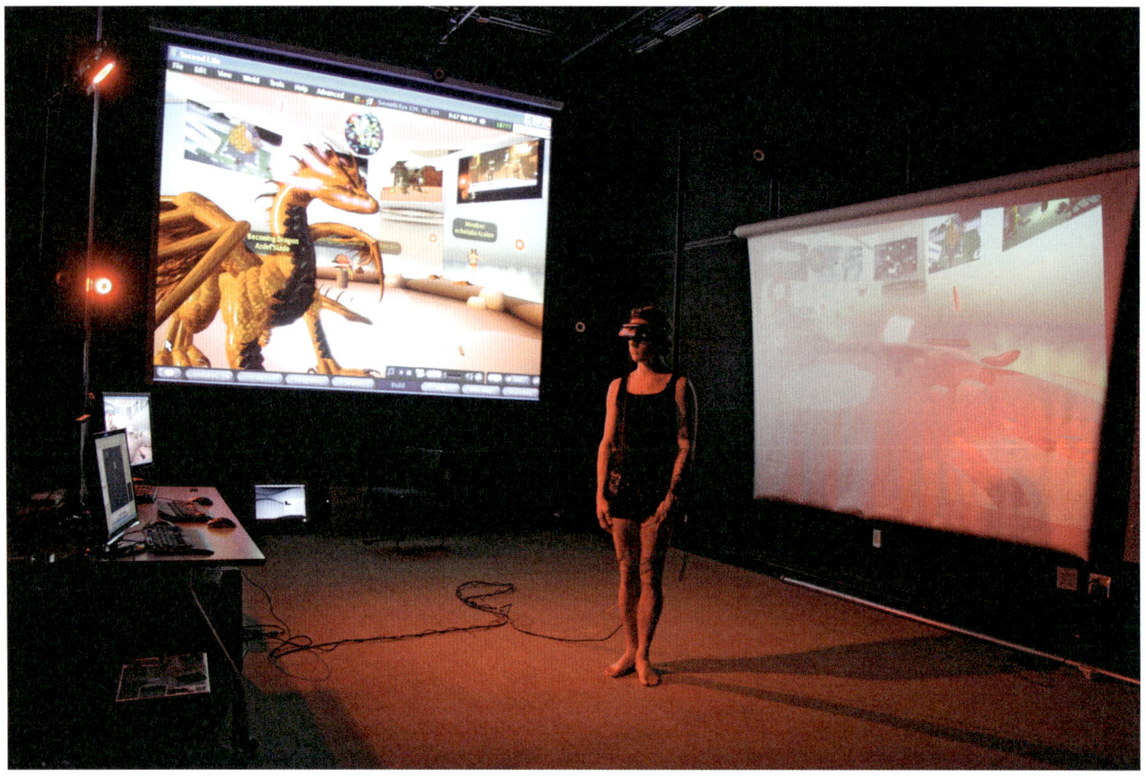

In December 2008 artist micha cárdenas lived as a dragon, Azdel Slade, for 365 hours on Second Life, an online multimedia platform inhabited and explored by self-fashioned avatars. Azdel Slade enjoyed the company of friends old and new, commingled with humans, dragons, cyborgs, and furries. Over the course of two weeks, this dragon enjoyed many enlivening conversations, received interesting gifts, and listened to anticapitalist poetry. Azdel Slade danced a great deal (sometimes naked), enthusiastically explored numerous spaces, including an S&M club, and got kicked out after pole dancing.

In order to inhabit and explore Second Life through a dragon's avatar, cárdenas wore a VR head-mounted display. This durational performance took place before a live audience who visited her at a black box installation within a room outfitted with computer terminals and large projection screens that visualized the virtual spaces of Second Life and the activities of Azdel Slade.[1] For *Becoming Dragon*, cárdenas and collaborators modified a motion-capture system to send her real-time physical movements and gestures into Second Life, while digital virtuality was reciprocally introduced into the gallery.[2] Her utterances were heard simultaneously in physical space and Second Life's chat, by way of a voice system whose modulated pitch troubled the gendered and presumably human legibility of a performer's voice.[3] cárdenas technically and symbolically prototyped alternate forms of identity and experience by connecting Second Life's virtual environment with IRL (in real life) encounters in a gallery, entwining the materiality of corporeal existence with the novel possibilities of online identity formation.

As cárdenas put it, "*Becoming Dragon* began with this question: given that transgender people have to fulfill one year of Real Life Experience as their chosen gender before getting Gender Confirmation Surgery (aka Sex Reassignment Surgery), could this be replaced by one year of Second Life Experience to lead to Species Reassignment Surgery?"[4] Since the 1960s, a year's "real life experience" or "real life test" of living in one's identified gender has often been medically required for gender-affirming surgical care or hormone replacement therapy (HRT). This requirement has been widely disputed for being an unnecessary, prohibitive, and gatekeeping barrier to accessing critical care, and criticized for its regulation of gender normativity and its pathologizing of gender variance. Or, as theorist and artist Sandy Stone once put it, "Under the binary phallocratic founding myth by which Western bodies and subjects are authorized, only one body per gendered subject is 'right.'"[5]

Appearing in 2008, *Becoming Dragon* is the progeny of both Critical Art Ensemble's tactical biopolitics and (trans)feminist gender insurgents, including Donna Haraway's cyborgs and Orlan's body art.[6] The project explicitly kept company with its foremothers: cárdenas twice read aloud poetry regarding transition and starting HRT, while lines of text behind her also paid homage to those such as playwright and performer Kate Bornstein—"in honor of experimentation and becoming a more frightening monster than they even expected."[7] Azdel Slade, in turn, was embraced by trancestors such as Stone, an artist and theorist of post-transexual and trans-species subjectivity who visited Azdel Slade in Second Life during a public conversation organized by cárdenas.[8] With these forbears, *Becoming Dragon* offered another line of flight, when cárdenas used her body as an experimental site for what she has since termed "transreal" identities: identities of multiplicitous realms and shimmering expressions beyond Enlightenment dualisms, troubling binaries between the organic and the machine, the human and non-human, male and female, virtual and real, on/offline, digital and analog.

—Jeannine Tang

◄ micha cárdenas, Views of *Becoming Dragon* in InSilico, a cyberpunk role playing region within *Second Life*, and at The Center for Research in Computing and the Arts (CRCA), University of California, San Diego, 2008

1. *Becoming Dragon* took place at The Center for Research in Computing and the Arts (CRCA) at the Visiting Artist Lab at Atkionison Hall, University of California, San Diego, and in Second Life at http://slurl.com/secondlife/Seventh%20Eye/186/12/35.
2. micha cárdenas, Christopher Head, Todd Margolis, and Kael Greco, "Becoming Dragon: a mixed reality durational performance in Second Life," in "The Engineering Reality of Virtual Reality 2009," ed. Ian E. McDowall and Margaret Dolinsky, *SPIE Proceedings* 7238 (January 26, 2009), https://doi.org/10.1117/12.806260. Also see micha cárdenas, "Motion Capture Second Life Script," *Second Loop* (December 16, 2008), second-loop.wordpress.com/2008/12/16/motion-capture-second-life-script/.
3. *Becoming Dragon* has been subsequently presented with different components, such as digital video, digital prints, and a VR headset, in the exhibitions *Beautiful New Worlds. Virtual Realities in Contemporary Art* (2017–18) at the Zeppelin Museum Friedrichshafen in Germany and *STILL I RISE: FEMINISMS, GENDER, RESISTANCE, ACT 2* (2019) at the De La Warr Pavilion, Bexhill-on-Sea, United Kingdom.
4. cárdenas et al., "Becoming Dragon."
5. Sandy Stone, "The Empire Strikes Back: The Posttranssexual Manifesto," 1987, accessed June 19, 2023, https://sandystone.com/empire-strikes-back.pdf.
6. See Claire Pentecost, "Outfitting the Laboratory of the Symbolic: Toward a Critical Inventory of Bioart," in *Tactical Biopolitics: Art, Activism, and Technology*, ed. Beatriz da Costa and Kavita Philip (Cambridge, MA: MIT Press, 2008); Donna Haraway, "A manifesto for cyborgs: Science, technology, and socialist feminism in the 1980s," *Socialist Review*, no. 80 (1985): 65–108; and Orlan, *Orlan: This Is My Body...This Is My Software = Ceci Est Mon Corps...Cesi Est Mon Logiciel* (London: Black Dog Publishing, 1996).
7. The poems are collected in micha cárdenas, *The Transreal: Political Aesthetics of Crossing Realities* (New York: Atroppos Press, 2012).
8. micha cárdenas, video documentation of *Becoming Dragon* (2008).
9. See micha cárdenas,"Becoming Dragon: A Transversal Technology Study," ctheory.net, issue *Code Drift: Essays in Critical Digital Studies*, April 29, 2010, https://journals.uvic.ca/index.php/ctheory/article/view/14680.

21 JEFFREY CATHERINE JONES, *LIGHT*, 1970

Jeffrey Catherine Jones (1944–2011) was a prominent American illustrator most recognized for her illustrations in the genres of horror, fantasy, and science fiction. Largely self-taught and known as simply Jeff Jones, in 1967 she moved to New York City from Atlanta, Georgia, to pursue a career in commercial illustration, arriving at a high point for the comic, pulp, and paperback publishing industry. Jones quickly found work and garnered attention for her distinct compositions and skillful use of light and shadow.

Twentieth-century fantasy and science fiction illustration traded in idealized bodies and stereotypical gender conventions to attract sales. The work of Frank Frazetta exemplifies a formula: a brutish, muscle-bound he-man fights off a monster while a voluptuous, bikini-clad damsel cowers seductively at his feet. Early in her career, Jones was often compared to Frazetta—both artists painted exaggerated action and gender archetypes with precision and expressive style—and Jones benefited professionally from the association. As her talent developed, Jones's work became increasingly recognized for its psychological complexity and imaginative interpretations.

This painting, retroactively titled *Light* by the artist, appeared on the cover of *Dark of the Woods* (1970), a science-fiction paperback by Dean R. Koontz.[1] In the novel, a man named Stauffer Davis visits a colonized alien planet, Demos. Davis begins a romantic relationship with his guide, Leah, one of the planet's few remaining native inhabitants belonging to a race of winged, human-like people. Miscegenation between humans and aliens is strictly forbidden, and when their affair is uncovered, Davis and Leah escape into the planet's wilderness, seeking refuge in an abandoned Demosian fortress. The military viciously hunts the couple in their flight, and Davis is mortally wounded. To save her beloved, Leah employs an artificial womb to transfer Davis's consciousness into the body of a fully grown, winged man. In Jones's cover, Leah appears perched on a rocky ledge, preparing to take flight over Demos. In the distance hovers the faint outline of another set of wings, presumably belonging to a reborn Davis.

The potential for queerness within science fiction goes without saying. Through this speculative genre, the accepted rigidity of roles can be demystified, what is presumed abnormal can be made commonplace, and the inequities of our world can be made visible through another. Contemplating the genesis of science fiction as a narrative genre, esteemed sci-fi writer Samuel R. Delany speculates on how both inspiration and improvement propelled authors in this relatively new literary field:

> One artist may find a work that seems to
> him [sic] to have an interesting kernel,
> but strikes him as so badly executed that he
> feels he can treat the same substance far
> more rewardingly. More frequently, I suspect,
> he finds an interesting technique employed
> to decorate a vapid center, and uses it to
> ornament his own central concerns.[2]

Koontz's tale is a rather unremarkable sci-fi re-telling of a white savior's awakening consciousness; however, it is appealing to imagine that for Jones, minor elements of Koontz's story might have provided a captivating departure for visual interpretation. Whereas the novel is told almost entirely from the perspective of Davis, Jones focused her cover on Leah, a figure who, while central to the storyline, receives scant character development beyond remarks on her significant beauty.

Dark of the Woods was just one of twenty-five paperbacks released in 1970 with a cover by Jones. By the late 1970s, Jones became more selective in her commercial jobs, opting instead to paint the subjects that most spellbound her and sell the works at fantasy and science fiction conventions. Of the limited resources available about the artist, much is made of the artist's battles with mental illness and alcoholism.[3] Jones publicly shared she was trans in 1998.

Asked in 1970 about how source material impacted her work, Jones candidly revealed there was often a discrepancy between what the author wrote and what she painted: "After I get an idea of the character, I go back to check what he really looks like in the book. But it really doesn't make a lot of difference ..."[4] Given the plot of escaping oppressive forces and bodily transformation in *Dark of the Woods*, one might want to imagine a chord was struck for a closeted trans artist; however, it is unknown if this work was particularly significant for Jones or if it was just one among many works produced throughout a prolific career.

—David Evans Frantz

1. Dean R. Koontz, *Dark of the Woods/Soft Comes the Dragons* (New York: Ace Books, 1970). *Light* is the title given to the work by Jones in 1993 in her series of trading cards.
2. Samuel R. Delany, "Critical Methods / Speculative Fiction," in *The Jewel-Hinged Jaw: Notes on the Language of Science Fiction* (Middletown, CT: Wesleyan University Press, 2009), 17.
3. Take for example the title of the chapter on Jones, "Tortured Genius," in Dian Hanson's *Masters of Fantasy Art* (Cologne, Germany: Taschen, 2020). Throughout this text I have used she/her pronouns following Jones's direction on her website archived on the Internet Archive: http://web.archive.org/web/20100424091223/http://www.jeffreyjones-art.com/autobiography.html.
4. Jeff Jones in an interview with Robert Gerstenhaber, *Reality*, no. 1 (November 1970): n.p.

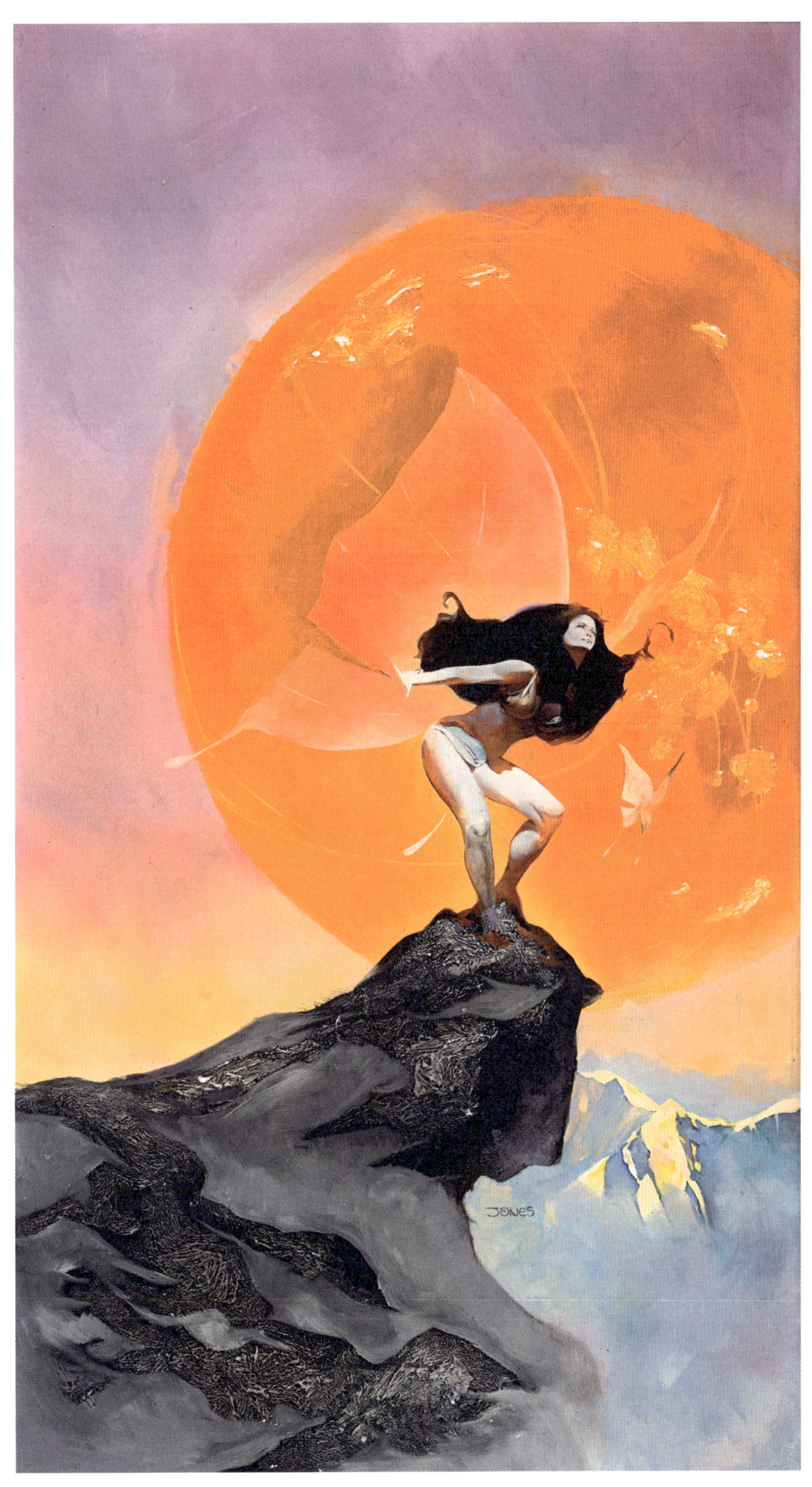

◄
Jeffrey Catherine Jones, *Light*, 1970.
Oil on paper, 22 × 12 in.
(55.9 × 30.5 cm)

22 PIPPA GARNER, *SUPER SHUFFLE*, 2018–PRESENT

Pippa Garner's long career in making things has always included a component of hacking existing mechanisms and structures to enhance or modify function—and comedic effect has long been one of the functions of which Pippa is most fond. *Super Shuffle* (2018–present) is Pippa's actual walker, but also sometimes a sculpture. The lines between high art and low art, sanctioned and self-taught are not relevant to Pippa, who finds both outsider art and insider art to be weird categories. The walker was included on a pedestal in the 2018 exhibition *Pippa Garner: Autonomy N' Stuff (Garnerrhea)*, at Redling Fine Art in Los Angeles, and then Pippa just brought it along to her opening for the 2021 exhibition *Immaculate Misconceptions* at JOAN Los Angeles and left it at the end of the night, so it stayed around for a while and ended up in the installation images. Super tricked out, the work is described in the press release for the Redling exhibition as demonstrating the "mantra—'everything is upgradable'—the homely, clinical-looking walker leaps from austerity (entry level) to audacity (high end) by selective accessorizing to complement the tastes and preferences of the individual shuffler."[1]

This is one of a series of conveyances Pippa has created throughout her life. She enrolled in the Car Design program at Art Center College of Design in Pasadena in the late 1960s, after serving in Vietnam. She was expelled for creating a half-human half-car sculpture; ultimately her quirky artistic vision didn't fit within the confines of that design world. She found a number of other outlets for her inventions, though, including *Car and Driver* magazine and the *Johnny Carson Show*. In 1973, she reconstructed a 1959 Chevy Biscayne sedan, mounting it backwards on its chassis so that the driver faced out through the rear window to drive. The project was supported by *Esquire* magazine; documentation shows the sedan in passage across the Golden Gate Bridge.

She crossed that same bridge frequently in the 1990s on a self-fabricated scooter; while living in Marin County completing the obligatory regime of visits with a psychiatrist in San Francisco who was evaluating her for "gender identity disorder," as it was known at the time. Forced to "prove" that she had been living publicly "as a woman" for a year, she would stop her scooter a block or so before reaching the office in the Mission district to put on a skirt and a scarf. Her own experiments with transition began outside of the sanctioned space of the medical office, where she began taking estrogen sourced from the black market which brought about a self-described revelation about the need for balance between male and female in culture. Her own interests in transition didn't fit neatly within the dictates of the American Psychiatric Association's definitions. As with all of the other kinds of apparatus in which Pippa saw a "not-quite-rightness" and a possibility for transformation and transgression, she considered her gender transition as a kind of "little experiment," and one she handled with a sense of humor.

Pippa has taken on the authority to tinker, change, and rework a vast array of things in her life, including her own body. She planned this change in advance and documented it as it progressed through notes, sketches, unorthodox DIY fashion hacks, photos, and more. I receive text messages from Pippa semi-regularly that demonstrate her ongoing sense of humor about the changes her body continues to experience as she ages. She models custom T-shirts in a lot of the texts: "Wet nurse: retired," one reads, and "I'm 80 but my [tits] are only 34," another quips. Turning her walker into a customized sculpture that doubles as a dashboard with all the comforts and flair of a well-loved car interior is, well, right in stride.

—Christina Linden

1. Press release for the 2018 exhibition *Pippa Garner: Autonomy N' Stuff (Garnerrhea)* at Redling Fine Art, Los Angeles, accessed December 28, 2022, https://web.archive.org/web/20190525001902/http://redlingfineart.com/content/2-exhibitions/1-autonomy-n-stuff-garnerrhea/pg_art-intro_2018_rfa-template-footer.pdf.

▸ (and following spread)
Pippa Garner, *Super Shuffle*, 2018–present. Mixed media, 42 × 42 × 21 in. (106.7 × 106.7 × 53.3 cm)

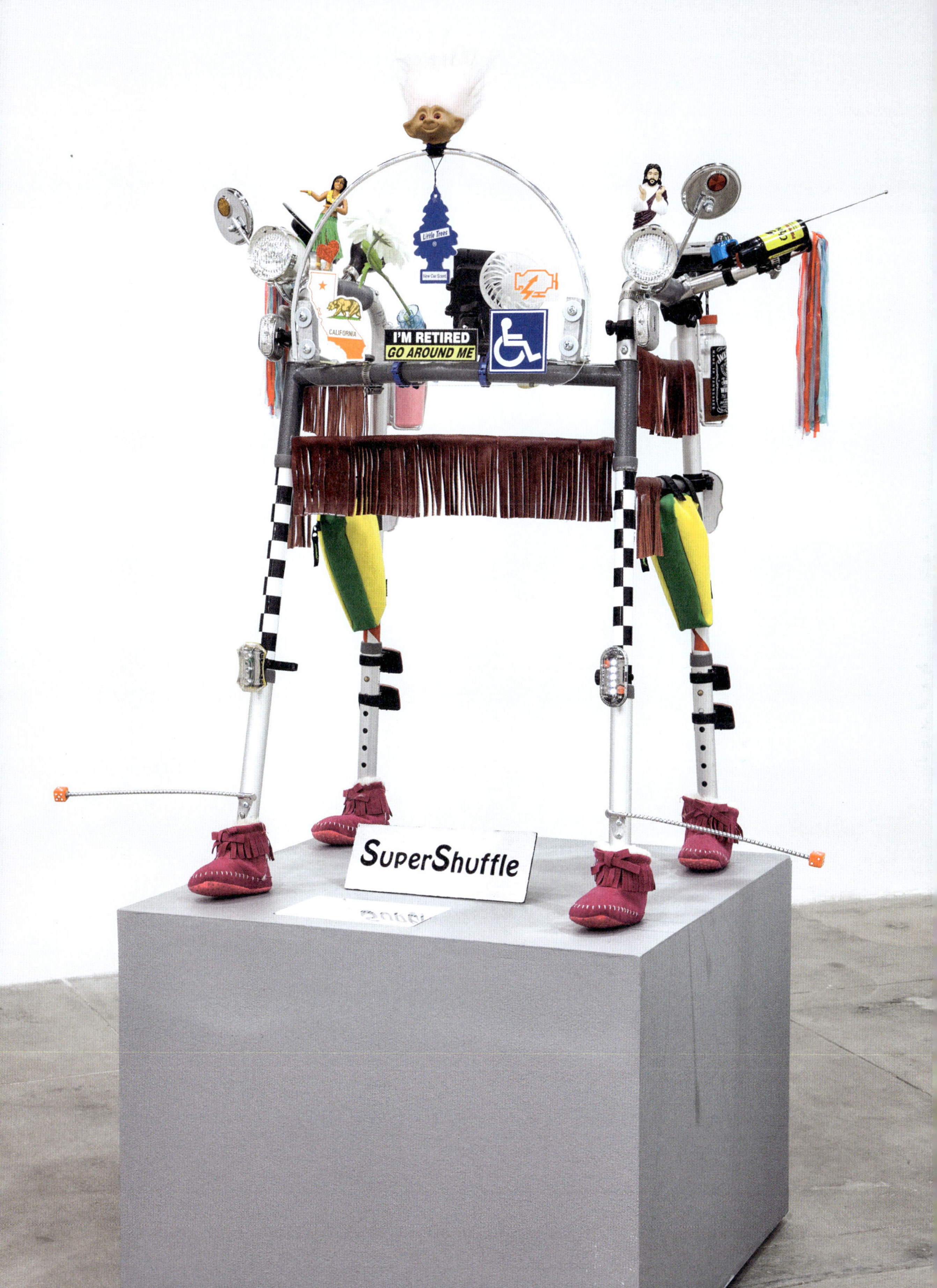

Little Trees
CALIFORNIA
I'M RETIRED
GO AROUND ME
SuperShuffle

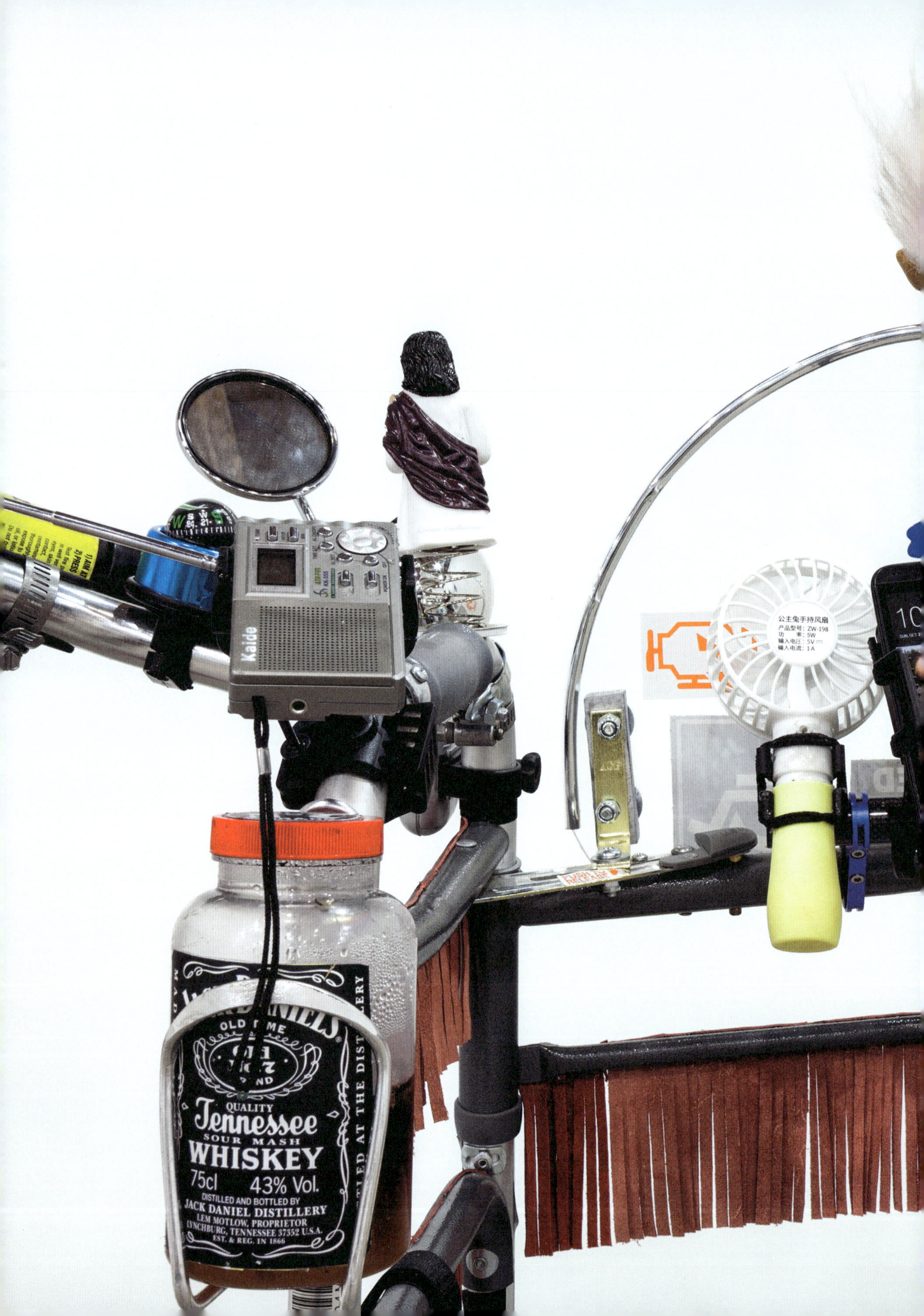
Kaide
公主兔手持风扇
产品型号：ZW-198
功　率：5W
输入电压：5V
输入电流：1A
OLD TIME
QUALITY
Tennessee
SOUR MASH
WHISKEY
75cl 43% Vol.
DISTILLED AND BOTTLED BY
JACK DANIEL DISTILLERY
LEM MOTLOW, PROPRIETOR
LYNCHBURG, TENNESSEE 37352 U.S.A.
EST. & REG. IN 1866

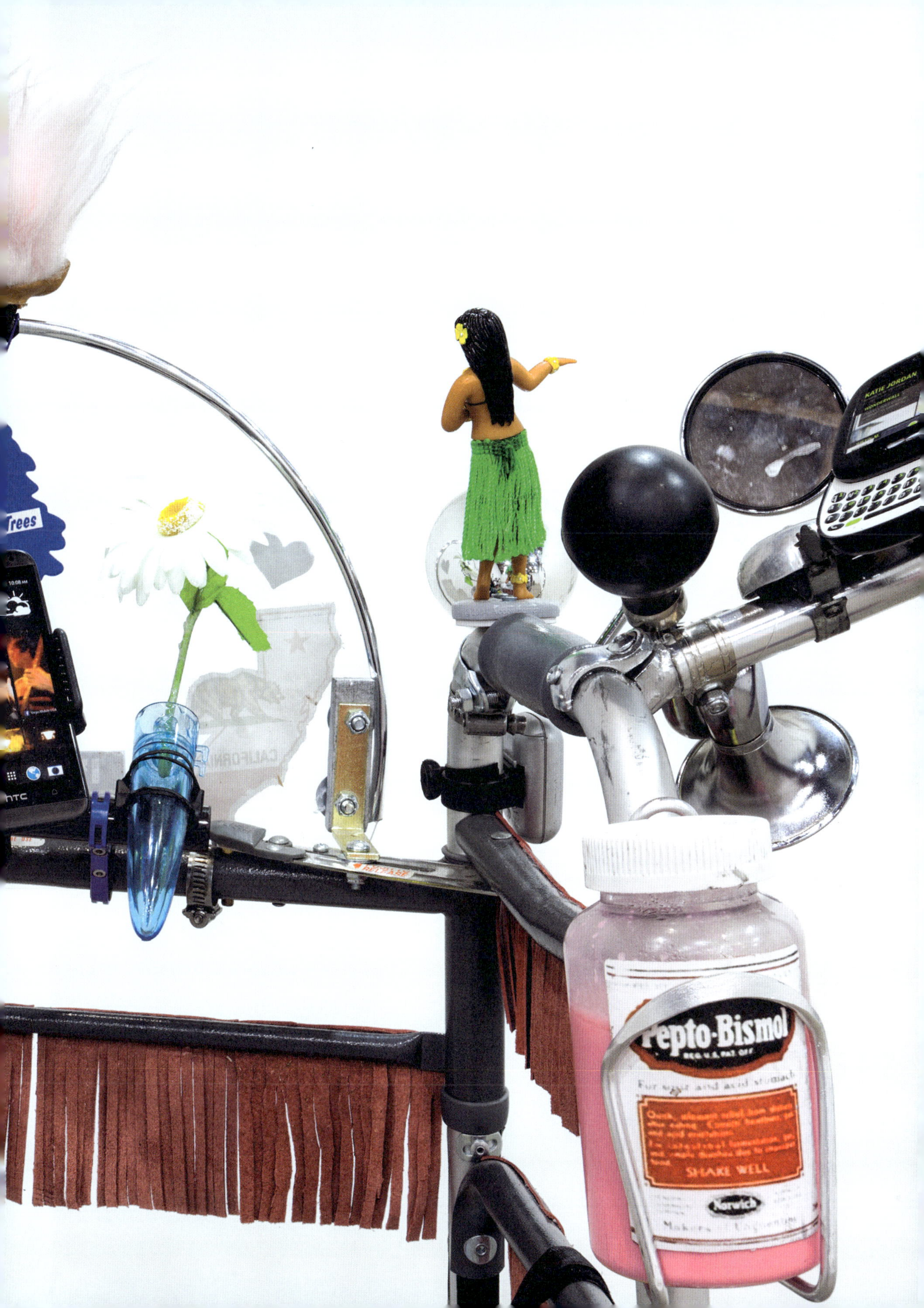
Trees
HTC
Pepto-Bismol
SHAKE WELL
Norwich

23 SANDY STONE, *PGP: THE PUBLIC GENITALS PROJECT*, 2000

Take a narrow bit of paper. It has two sides. Use the bit of paper to make a Möbius strip by turning it into a loop with a twist. Theoretically it is now a surface with only one side. Cut the Möbius strip in half lengthwise. It is now a single loop that is twice the length of the first one, with two, rather than just one, twists. Here's the fun part: cut it in half again. Now you have two separate Möbius strips, each with one twist, linked together.

I won't pretend to understand how this works. Just as I won't pretend to understand how gender works. Other than to say maybe gender is a Möbius strip which seems to be made of something with two sides, but isn't, that maybe has extra twists, or linked loops—depending on how you cut it.

Maybe one side of the Möbius strip of is the surface that is flesh (sex) and maybe the other side is the surface that is image (gender). Maybe they are two sides, or two twists, or two linked loops, or maybe they are one continuous surface. They're not separate but they're not *not* separate surfaces.

Transsexuality is only one place where the Möbius strip of flesh and image are a topological puzzle. A second is porn. A third is the vexed problem of what can be shown of the flesh in public and what has to be covered with clothing. Where clothing makes a sort of flattened image of the body, one that's not the body but not *not* the body. Not surprisingly, fascination/panic about the flesh/image strip latches onto all three of these instances, and often tries to connect or conflate them. It seems we've never not had moral panics about the Möbius strip of flesh/image. It's a cable news staple.

Sandy Stone's *PGP: The Public Genitals Project* (2000) braids all three flesh/image panics into one conceptual technology. I say conceptual because it seems not to have worked for very long. It was a hard thing to make with late 1990s media tech. So there's actually a fourth Möbius strip: the image/tech one. We know about the work through images of it that are the other side (the same side) as the tech.

There's always tech. Maybe tech is a third sex, or a third gender, or rather that which cuts sex and gender into shape. Only that shape is then the same Möbius strip, longer with an extra twist, or two strips, looped together. The cut that is tech isn't ever a clean cut.

A performer (originally Elana Logsdon) wears a screen over the genital area. (In one version the performer is naked, in another, clothed, but with cut outs over the genital area.) The screen shows images of genitals, crowdsourced from all over the world. Most are of humans, some are of other animals. The images get progressively abstracted the more the words "sex" and "violence" appear on news channels. That's it. That's the concept. An elegant idea, realized with great technical difficulty. To make a Möbius strip, to show the twists.

—McKenzie Wark

Allucquére Rosanne (Sandy) Stone is credited for founding the field of Transgender Studies with her landmark 1987 essay, "The Empire Strikes Back: A Posttranssexual Manifesto." This text responded to Janice Raymond's infamous attack on the legitimacy of trans identity in her book The Transsexual Empire: The Making of the She-Male *(1979). As a result of discord that Raymond's book fomented, Stone left her position at the collectively run lesbian label Olivia Records, where she was a recording engineer. In addition to working in music, Stone has been a computer coder and programmer, academic, and artist who is also recognized with establishing the field of New Media art.*

▸ Sandy Stone, *PGP: The Public Genitals Project*, 2000. Altered suit jacket and trousers, video broadcast receiver, battery pack, speaker, laptop computer, crowdsourced and digitally manipulated images, dimensions variable. Photo by Marcel Pardo Ariza

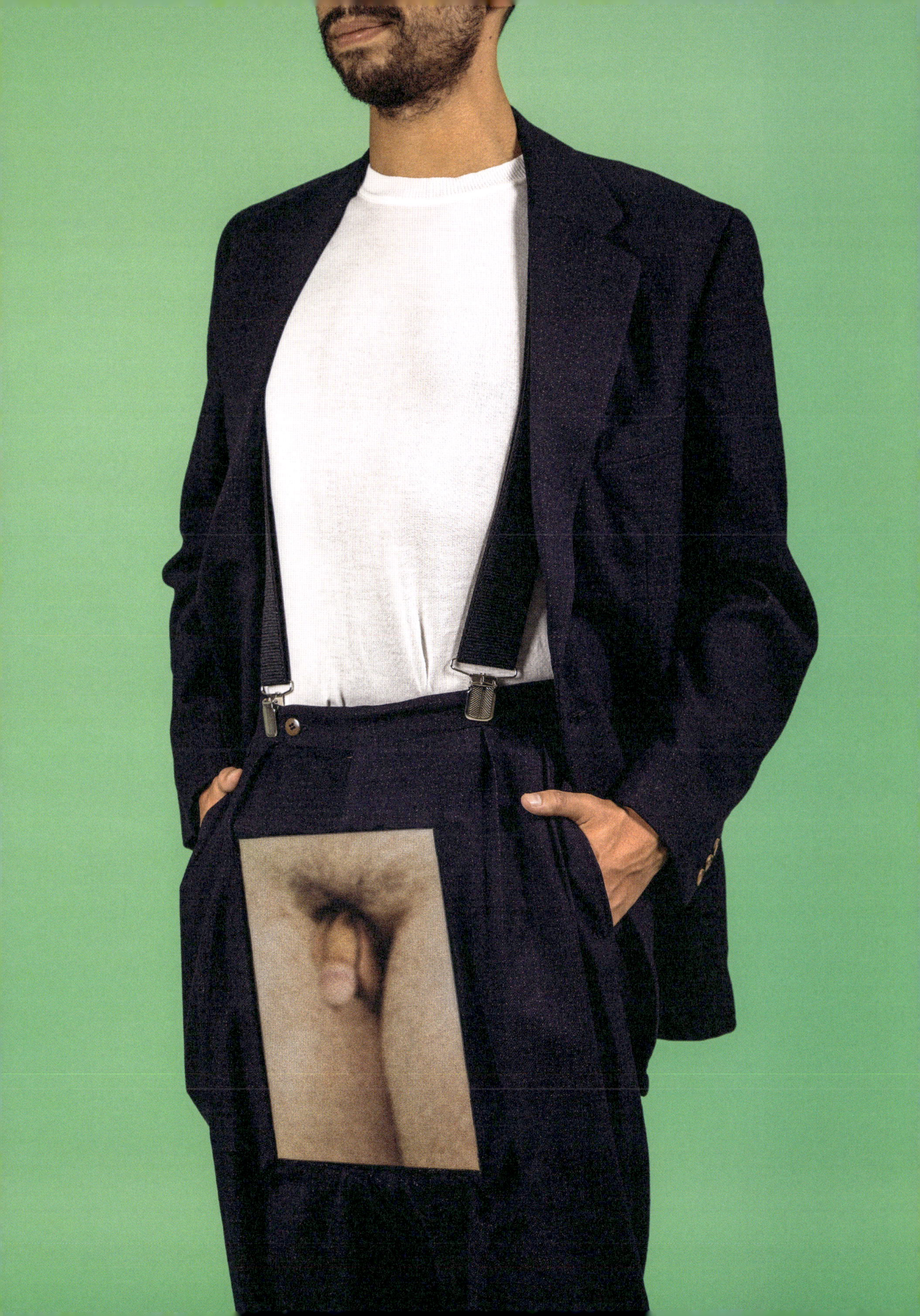

24 FORREST BESS, *THE HERMAPHRODITE*, 1957

Forrest Bess (1911–1977) was a painter who believed that the unification of both male and female genders in a single body was key to spiritual transformation, world peace, and perhaps even immortality. Though he showed at New York's prominent Betty Parsons Gallery from 1951 to 1967, he made paintings like *The Hermaphrodite* (1957) from his small, improvised home in Bay City, Texas, far from Parsons's gallery and the vibrant New York art scene that sprung up in the wake of World War II. Bess's theory and his art were inextricably linked. He asserted in a series of letters to Parsons and art historian Meyer Schapiro that the shapes and colors in his paintings came to him in dreams and visions and that he came to understand the meaning of these formal elements only after his paintings were finished. An avid reader, Bess came to assign meaning to these works based in ideas he found in literature on alchemy, Christianity, psychology, sexual science, anthropology, and art history.

The Hermaphrodite is perhaps the most overt expression of his theory and its roots in alchemy, psychoanalysis, and early twentieth-century anthropology. Here, a red-and-white capsule is caught between a pair of black cells that have fused together. In a letter to psychologist and sexologist John Money, Bess explained that the two dark shapes recalled the meeting place of the penis and the scrotum. This was a site on his own body that he had hoped to make penetrable like a vagina to produce the urethral orgasm that he theorized would lead to total liberation from human struggle and mortality. Bess also described that the color red in his paintings signified female, white signified male, and the union of the two signified "hermaphrodite." These chromatic associations seem to have derived from the alchemical manifesto *The Chymical Wedding of Christian Rosenkreutz* (1616), which equates red with masculinity and white with femininity. Though reversed, Bess appears to have deduced from this alchemical evidence that the red and white form at the center of *The Hermaphrodite* was itself a hermaphroditic form.

Elsewhere in his letters, Bess elaborated on the union of masculinity and femininity in this bicolored form by calling it a vagina dentata, or a vagina with teeth. This was a leitmotif that Freud used to represent the threat of castration. However, rather than recoiling at the threat of emasculation, Bess fully embraced this image as part of his broader quest for spiritual liberation. Bess may have also come to embrace the vagina dentata through anthropological literature from the early twentieth-century that described Maori peoples and their beliefs in the spiritual power of the genitals. In Maori mythology, 1 Hine-nui-te-po, guardian of the underworld, thwarted her own murder by the trickster demi-god Maui by crushing him with the obsidian teeth that lined her vagina. It appears that by interpreting the red and white form in *The Hermaphrodite* as a vagina dentata, Bess took both Freud's idea and this Maori legend as confirmation that the genitals are, indeed, the threshold between mortality and immortality.

—Cyle Metzger

▸
Forrest Bess,
The Hermaphrodite, 1957.
Oil on canvas, 7 15/16 ×
11 3/16 in. (20.2 × 28.4 cm).
Gift of John Wilcox,
in memory of Frank
Owen Wilson, 1992-06,
Menil Collection

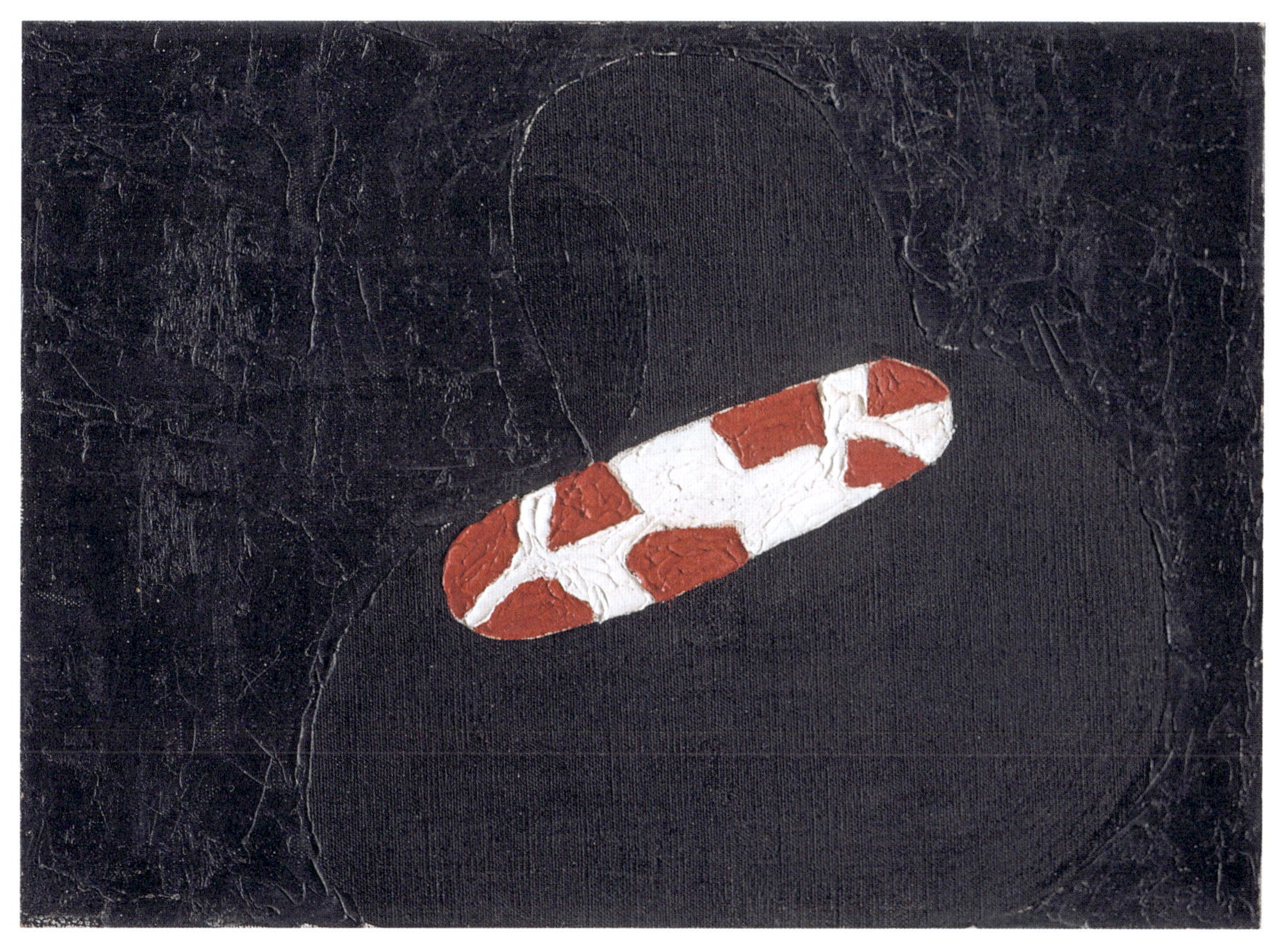

25 LOREN REX CAMERON'S SHUTTER RELEASE, c. 1990s

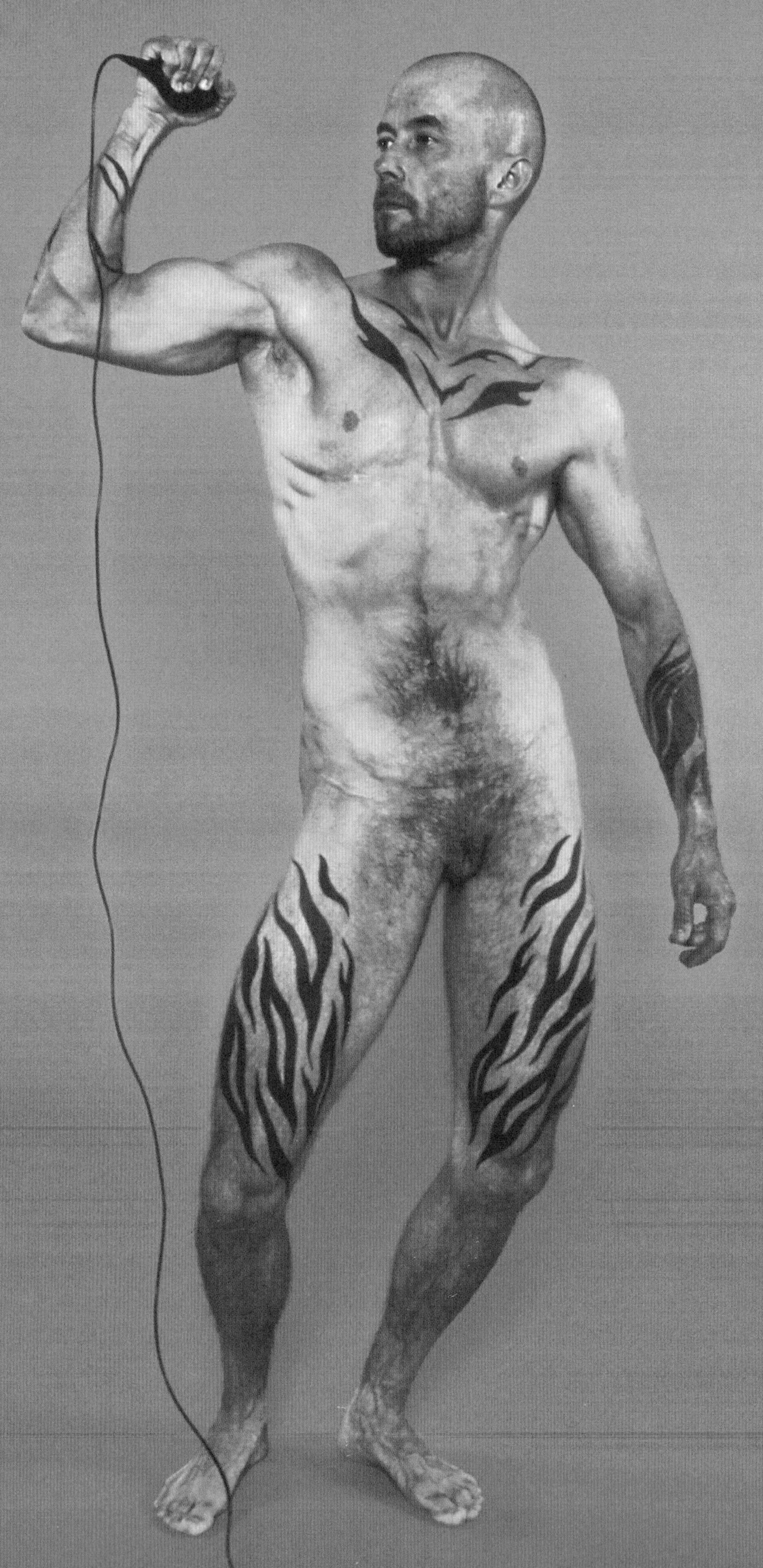

Loren Rex Cameron (1959–2022), self-taught American photographer and activist, turned to photography to document his experience as a transsexual man. With no formal training, he "began as a photographer the same way I became a man—by just taking my act to the streets and doing it and learning to pass in the process."[1] Cameron took a single course in the basics of photography, then began working with a Pentax K1000, experimenting with as many cameras and lenses as his fixed budget allowed. He printed his own images, and began documenting the trans people in his proximity, both locally and globally. He made exhibitions, the photo book *Body Alchemy: Transsexual Portraits* (1996), and a modest living touring a slide presentation and lecture that archived and brought into being a burgeoning transgender rights movement.

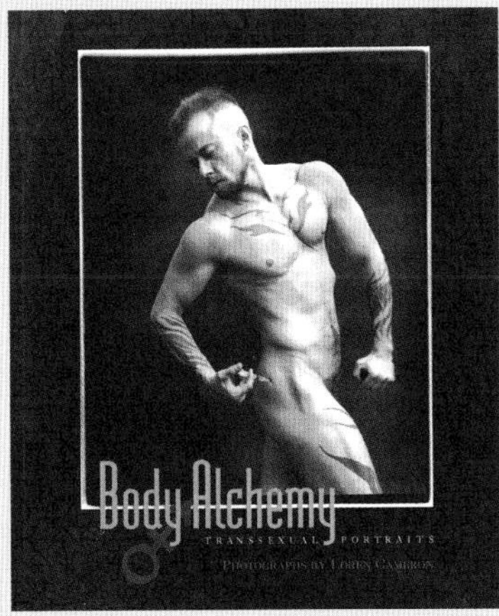

Loren Cameron, *Body Alchemy: Transsexual Portraits*, 1996. Published by Cleis Press

Cameron left rural Arkansas in 1979, buying a one-way bus ticket to San Francisco. He was active in the Bay Area lesbian scene until he began to identify as a transsexual man in 1985. Cameron was present for the first meetings of Female-to-Male International, the transmasculine social and activist network founded by self-taught archivist Lou Sullivan in 1986. In 1994, he marched in San Francisco Pride carrying a handmade banner that read: "FTM TRANS PRIDE," as part of what he identified as the first openly transmasculine contingent in the parade (he was joined by Susan Stryker, Matt Rice, David Harrison, Max Wolf Valerio, and others).

With photography, Cameron could track and share his self-actualizing identity, and put it into a social context. In the 1980s and 1990s, images of trans people *by* trans people were virtually nonexistent. In her review of Cameron's first photo exhibition, trans activist Kate Bornstein put it this way: "Andy Warhol, Robert Mapplethorpe, Diane Arbus among many others have all trained their lenses on the transgendered figure. Never have the transgendered seriously photographed their own. Not until Loren Cameron, that is."[2]

Although self-taught, he harnessed the camera to self-identify in new and nuanced ways, looking to self-portraiture as a means of self and collective understanding. Always made in direct address to the camera, in self-portraiture Cameron refuses to be the *object* of anyone else's gaze. An explicit refusal of the male and medical gazes that pathologize gender transformation, his photographs wrestle back control of the image. His nude self-portraits document the contours of his embodied transformation—both a physical and metaphysical process of self-actualization. Often made in the style of physique photography, his nude self-portraits capture the precision through which he sculpted his physical form as a body builder and with gender-affirming health care. Cameron's self-portraits injecting testosterone were made with a remote shutter-release bulb, a practical technique for someone who often worked alone, but as Cameron noted, "Its presence serves as a metaphor: I am creating my own image alone, an act that reflects the transsexual experience as well."[3] Making technology both visible and integral to the image, Cameron manifested something tangible that often eludes the camera's eye: the physical and metaphysical process of self-determination.

—Jeanne Vaccaro

◄ Loren Rex Cameron, Untitled, c. 1998. Color photograph, 8½ x 5¾ (21.6 x 14.6 cm). Loren Rex Cameron Papers (#7677), Division of Rare and Manuscript Collections, Cornell University Library

1. Quotation from materials in the Loren Rex Cameron Papers, Division of Rare and Manuscript Collections, Cornell University Library.
2. Promotional quote from Kate Bornstein on the back of Loren Cameron, *Body Alchemy: Transsexual Portraits* (Pittsburg, PA and San Francisco: Cleis Press, 1996).
3. Quotation from materials in the Loren Rex Cameron Papers.

26 PUPPIES PUPPIES (JADE GUANARO KURIKI-OLIVO), *ANDREW D. OLIVO 6.7.89–6.7.18*, 2018/21

Please listen to The Langley Schools Music Project's rendition of "God Only Knows" (2001) while reading this text: https://www.youtube.com/watch?v=P4UL1pLtexI

Hi Andrew

It feels weird to talk to you like this.
Pretending as if no one is listening to what I have to say to you.
It's about time I said these things.

I know at times you've felt there was never going to be anything good in life and that it will always just feel like managing to get through the days.
I know you felt deeply sad very early on and never knew what to make of it.
I know you wondered what life would be like if the fight or flight responses weren't always firing.

Andrew

I think you're beautiful. All those people who made you feel like there was nothing beautiful about you they were wrong.
All those people who made you feel that femininity in a perceived boy was worthy of hell were wrong
All those people who abused you verbally physically and sexually
they were wrong
all those people who made you feel less than in a moment's notice
they were wrong
All those people that said racist shit to you and your family growing up
they were wrong
All the times as a child where you blindly trusted people older than you and they let you down or hurt you or tried to brainwash you
you weren't in the wrong

I know at times you've prayed for a luckier life.
A life filled with less trauma and more relaxing.
A life void of having had a brain tumor.
An easier life in general.

I'm sorry I called you Andrew so much.
I just know many of your memories are associated with this name or I guess Drew once you hit a certain age.

Drew
as cheesy as this sounds please don't forget you're worthy of love

Don't let the world make you think otherwise.
Please know you'll eventually
see yourself as someone you can hug and kiss and say ily

Please know that life ahead won't be void of more pain but you'll feel joy you never thought existed…

Know that I love you
And that you're always with me
I see you I see your strength

Eternally yours
Jade

This text was previously presented as the press release for the exhibition *Andrew D. Olivo 6.7.89–6.7.18* at the artist-run space What Pipeline in Detroit, Michigan, 2018.

▸
Puppies Puppies (Jade Guanaro Kuriki-Olivo), *Andrew D. Olivo 6.7.89–6.7.18*, 2018/21. Installation at Kunsthaus Glarus, Switzerland, 2021. Grass, real human bones, and gravestone, dimensions variable

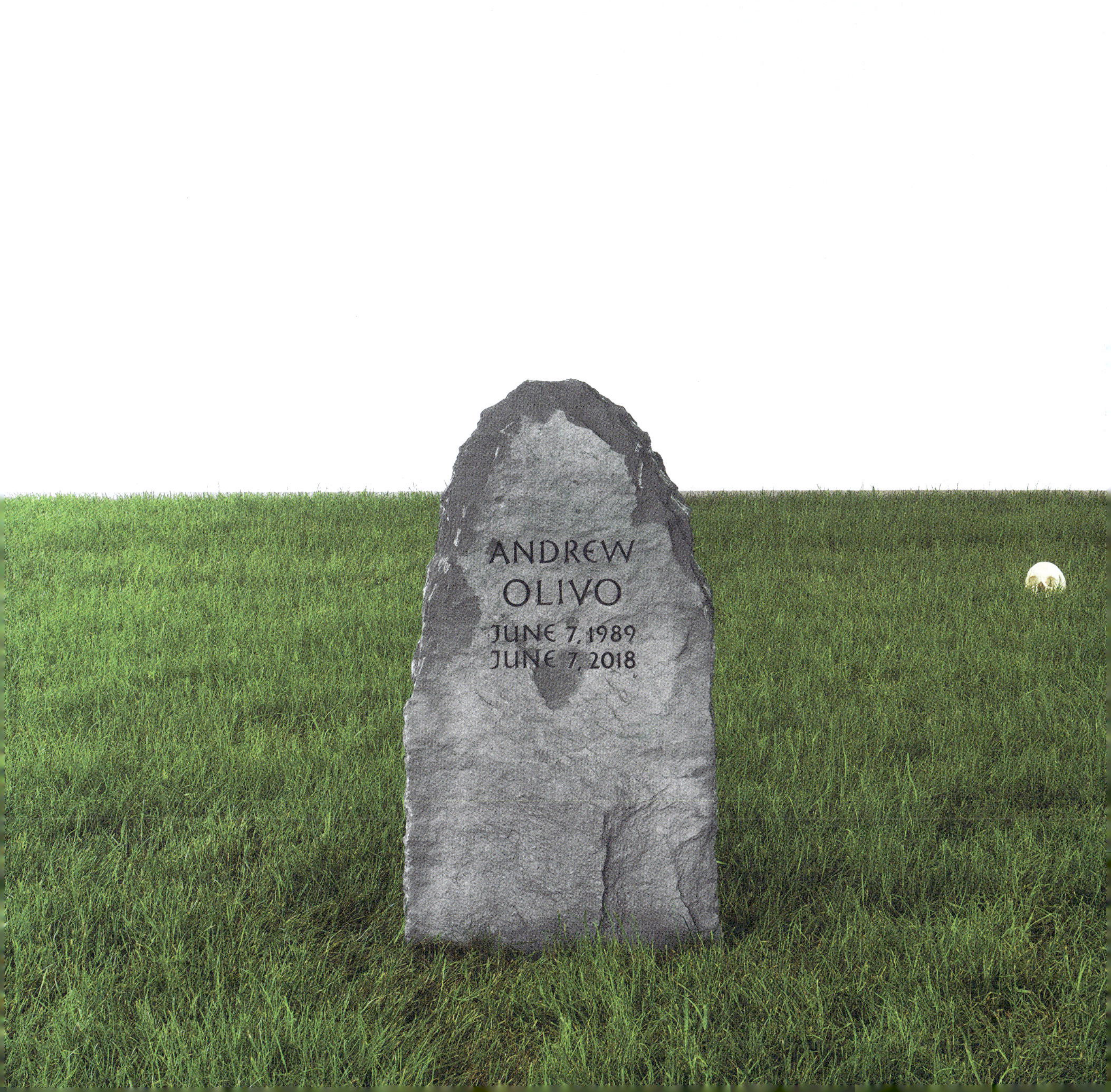
ANDREW
OLIVO
JUNE 7, 1989
JUNE 7, 2018

▼
Puppies Puppies (Jade Guanaro Kuriki-Olivo), *Andrew D. Olivo 6.7.89–6.7.18*, 2018/21. Installation at What Pipeline, Detroit, 2018. Grass, real human bones, and gravestone, dimensions variable

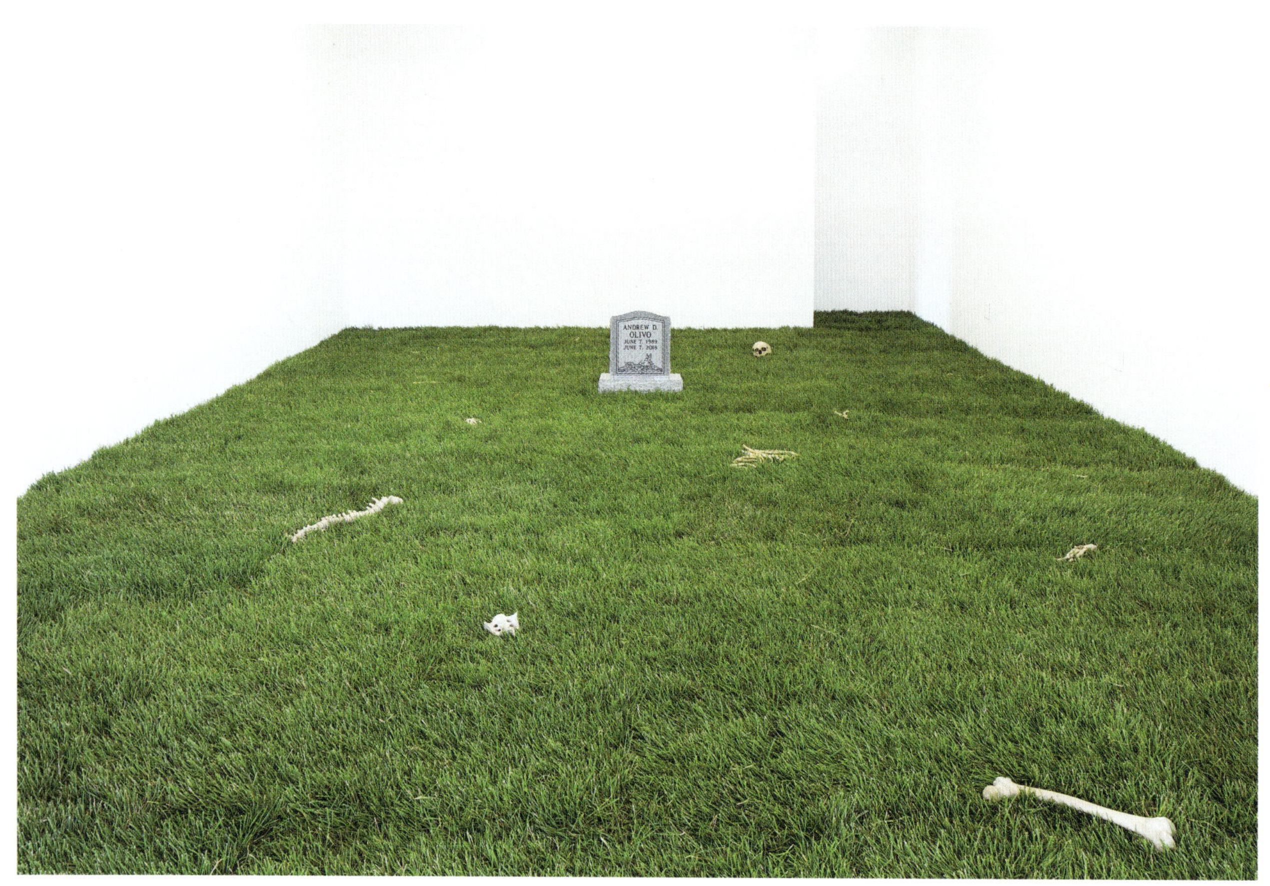

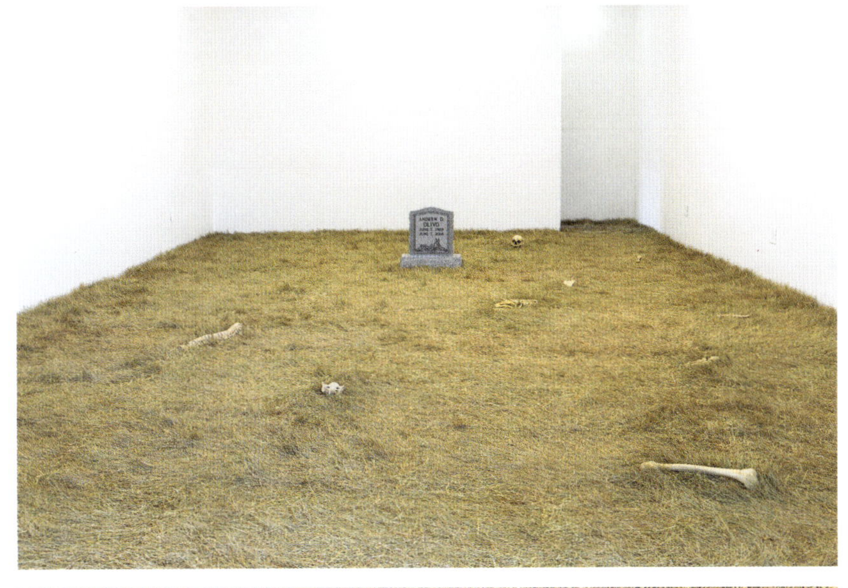

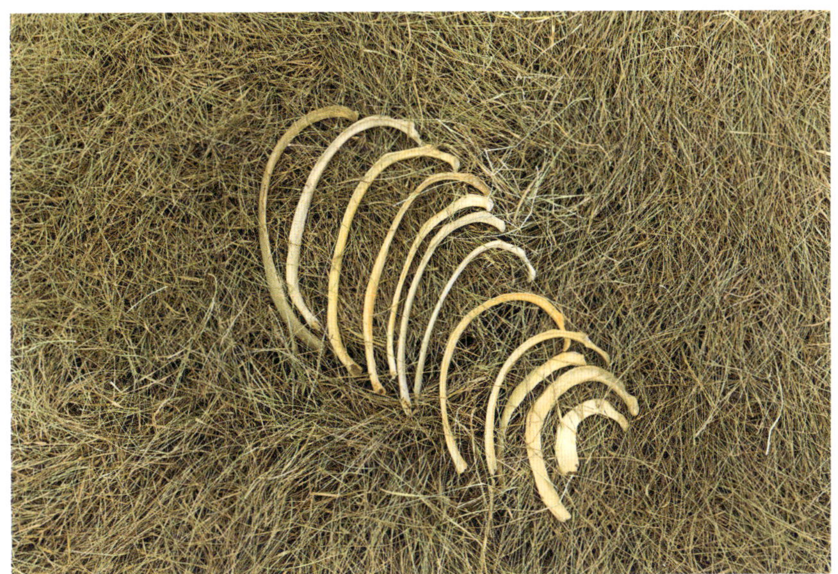

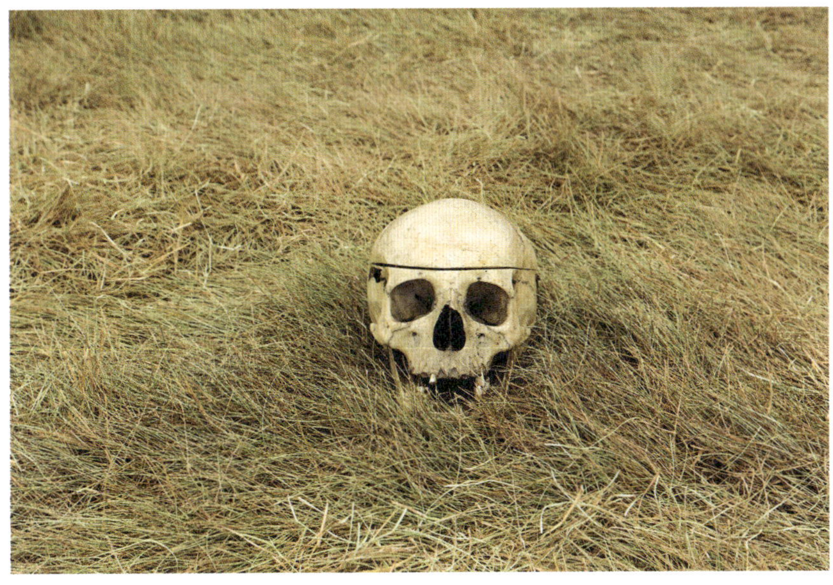

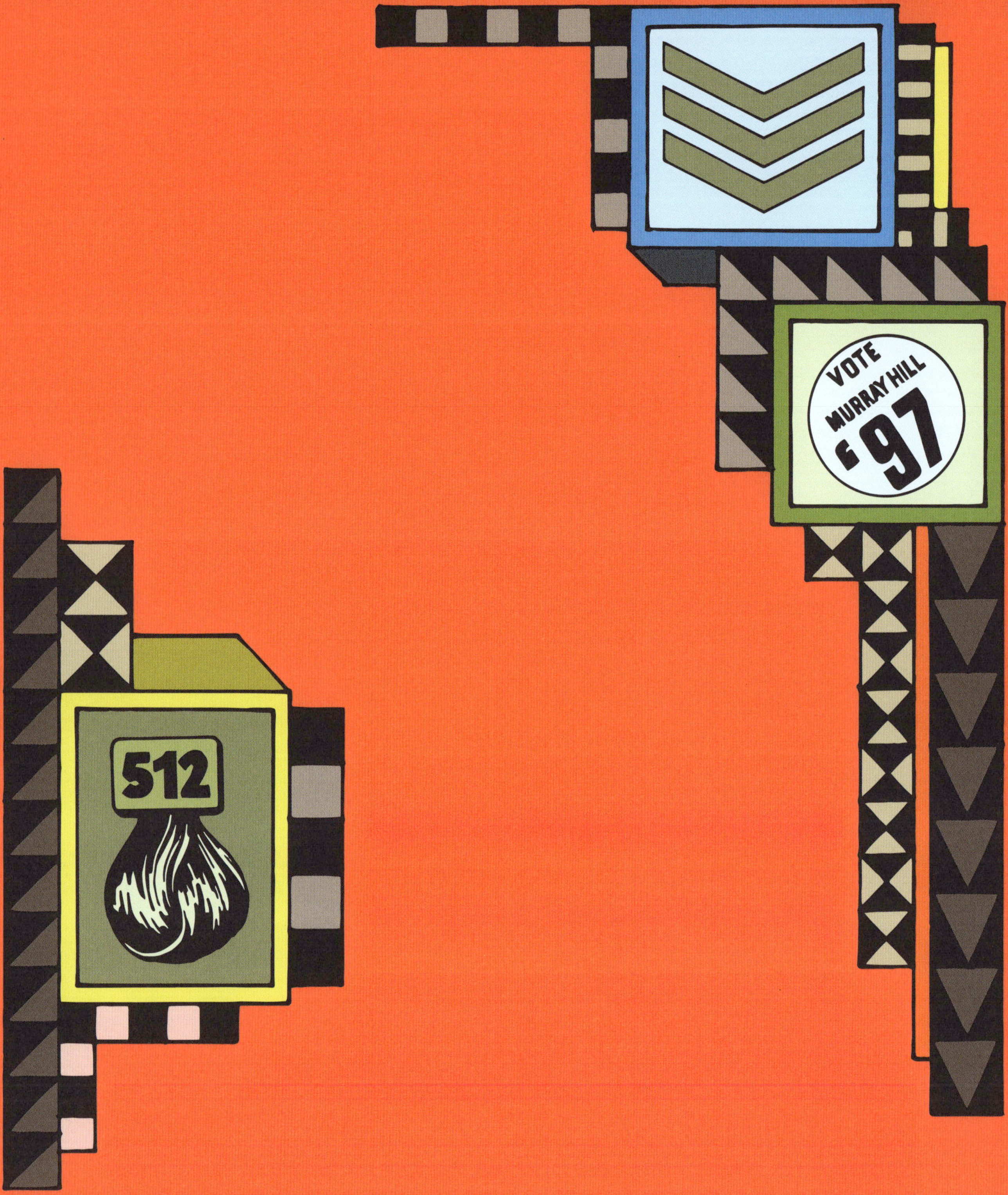

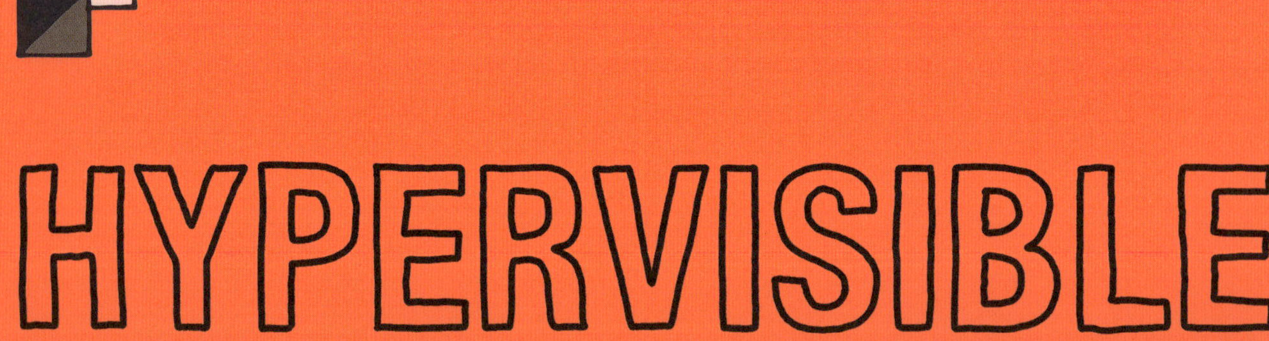
HYPERVISIBLE

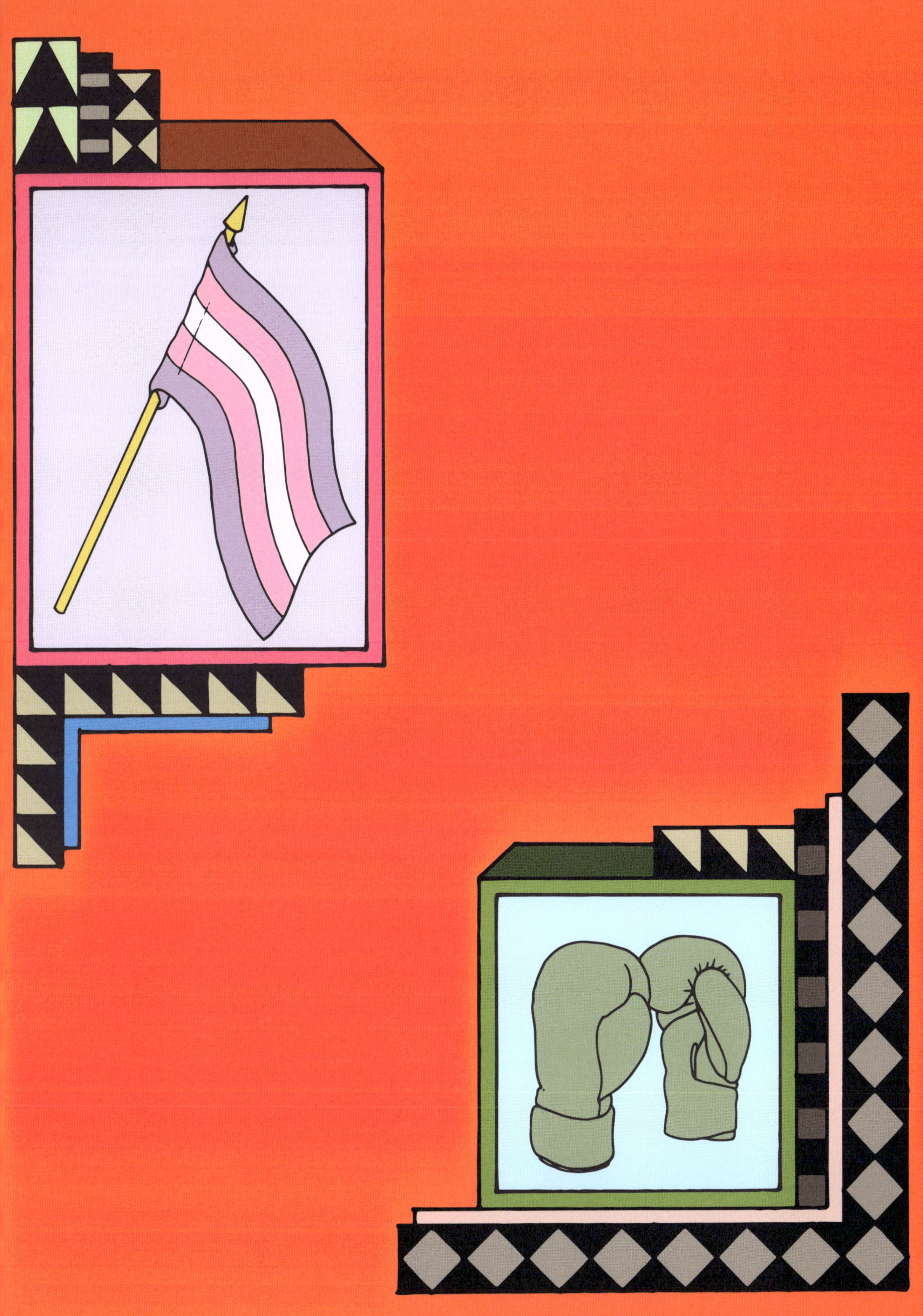

27 MONICA HELMS'S TRANSGENDER PRIDE FLAG, 1999

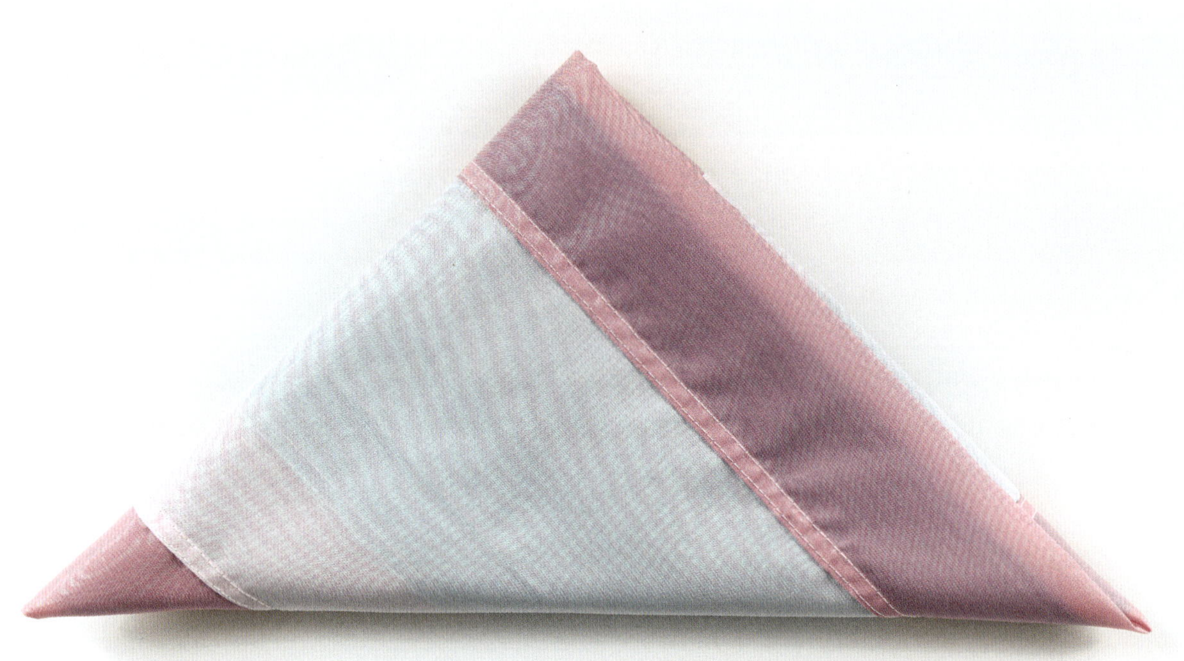

Monica Helms
Interviewed by Chris E. Vargas

CHRIS E. VARGAS (CV) First, please tell me a little bit about yourself.

MONICA HELMS (MH) Well, I currently live in Marietta, Georgia, but I'm originally from Phoenix, Arizona. I spent eight years in the Navy and served on two submarines. I have two sons and three grandsons. My transition started in 1997 and I quickly became an activist in Arizona. Then in Georgia, where I moved in 2000, I formed the Transgender American Veterans Association in 2003 and was its president until 2013. I worked for Sprint for twenty-five years and retired on January 23, 2015. My main hobby is building model rockets.

TM When did you design the transgender pride flag and where was it made?

MH The original flag was first made in August of 1999. I contacted the same company that made the bisexual pride flag because that individual [Michael Page] was the one who inspired me to do this. He said the trans community needed a flag. One day, I woke up and all of a sudden the design just appeared to me. So, I contacted the Freedom Flag & Banner in North Miami, Florida, and they sent me some swatches. I picked ones that I wanted. And a couple weeks later, I had the first flag for the transgender community.

CV Where did the flag make its first public appearance?

MH A month after I had the flag made for me, the local LGBT magazine, *Echo Magazine*, did an article on the flag. And that was the first time the public, anybody knew about it. The first time that it was seen in public for a large event was at the Arizona Pride Parade in 2000. I got to march up front in the color guard because I'm a veteran and I carried the flag for the first time.

CV What do the colors on the flag represent?

MH Light blue is for the traditional color for baby boys, and pink is traditional for baby girls. And the white in the middle is for everybody else, a neutral gender for anyone who doesn't fit into either side of the gender binary.

CV What do you think of some of the alternate designs of the transgender pride flag, specifically Jennifer Paladin's design, which represents gender as more like a continuum or a spectrum?

MH Over the years, I have seen at least six different transgender pride flag designs, including my own and Jennifer's. Jennifer's is the only one that has endured besides my own. I'm real proud of her for doing that. We're a very diverse community and we could use multiple flags.

CV Why is it important to have a separate pride flag for trans-identified individuals?

MH I think it's very important for us to have our own flag. There's many, many times when we need to be flying the rainbow flag, but there's a lot of times when we have to show our own individuality and the trans flag does that. It allows trans people to be able to show their individuality, to show that we are here as well. Thank you very much for all those who do fly it.

CV You donated the original flag to the Smithsonian's National Museum of American History in 2014. Did you have any hesitation about donating the flag?

MH Yeah. There was some hesitation. I mean, I contacted them, but it took me a little time before I finally got all the information together that they were looking for because I guess I just didn't want to give it up. It was something that was with me for a long time. At least I know it's going to be taken very good care of and people for generations will be able to see it.

CV Thank you very much, Monica.

Originally conducted in 2015, this interview has been transcribed and edited for clarity from a video by Chris E. Vargas made for inclusion in the exhibition *Transgender Hirstory in 99 Objects: Legends & Mythologies* at ONE National Gay & Lesbian Archives at the USC Libraries, 2015.

◂ Transgender Pride Flag purchased from Freedom Flag & Banner Company, North Miami, Florida, and folded in the military custom of the United States flag. Original flag in the collections of the National Museum of American History, Smithsonian Institution

28 AUTUMN SANDEEN'S NAVY UNIFORM, 2009

Uniforms have a lot to do with identity. For the military, the uniform can be a way to take identity away. The uniform is an external signal that the person is part of something larger than themself. Within the United States military, individuality is rarely important. People are a set of skills that can be replicated by the next person in line. When a person takes the uniform off for the final time, the line doesn't break. The next person steps up and the mission of the organization continues.

A uniform can also be about claiming an identity. Many who wear them are proud to do so because they are signifiers of accomplishment. They allow for recognition and affirmation of an individual's status. One glance can identify someone as a doctor, pilot, or sailor, and sometimes also reveal one's gender identity. Autumn Sandeen, a transgender woman who served in the United States Navy from 1980 to 2000, carried out her entire career in the wrong uniform. Like many who serve, Sandeen enlisted seeking education, career advancement, and financial independence. During her time in the Navy, Sandeen began to have a better understanding of herself as a woman. Yet in order to maintain the pay and benefits that she depended on, she had to hide her identity and wear the male uniform or risk being kicked out of the Navy and losing her pension.

Nine years after her military retirement, having already transitioned, Autumn's thoughts turned to how she'd be remembered. The standard photo at most veteran's funerals is of them in uniform, but Autumn's would be inauthentic. Knowing that there would never be a better time, Autumn acquired a women's uniform and had professional portraits taken to capture her as the version of a sailor she always meant to be.

In 2010 the "Don't Ask, Don't Tell" (DADT) policy that prevented lesbian, gay, and bisexual service members from serving openly was thrashing toward a conclusion. Sandeen saw an opportunity to use her authenticity, and her uniform, to make a difference. In an act of allyship and solidarity, despite trans rights often being left behind by LGB activist communities, Sandeen put on her dress uniform and handcuffed herself on two occasions to the White House fence alongside uniformed LGB service members. For her protest, Sandeen was arrested, mistreated, and misgendered in jail, but it made a difference. Later that year, DADT was repealed; however, it would take eight more years for trans individuals to serve openly in the United State military.

Sandeen petitioned the Department of Defense to formally recognize her gender identity, and in 2013 her military record was updated—this was the first time that the military used an administrative action to formally recognize a transgender veteran. By forcefully claiming her identity in legal terms, Sandeen paved the way for the estimated 200,000 transgender veterans to do the same.

Today, as thousands of transgender troops proudly serve wearing the military uniform of the United States, we recognize that the opportunities we now have did not come easily, nor are they secure. We thank the activists and advocates that came before us, and vow to continue working for everyone's opportunity to live as their true selves and be the next in line.

—Bree Fram

▸ Autumn Sandeen with her Service Dress Blue Uniform for the United States Navy, 2022. Lambda Archives of San Diego. Photo by Marcel Pardo Ariza

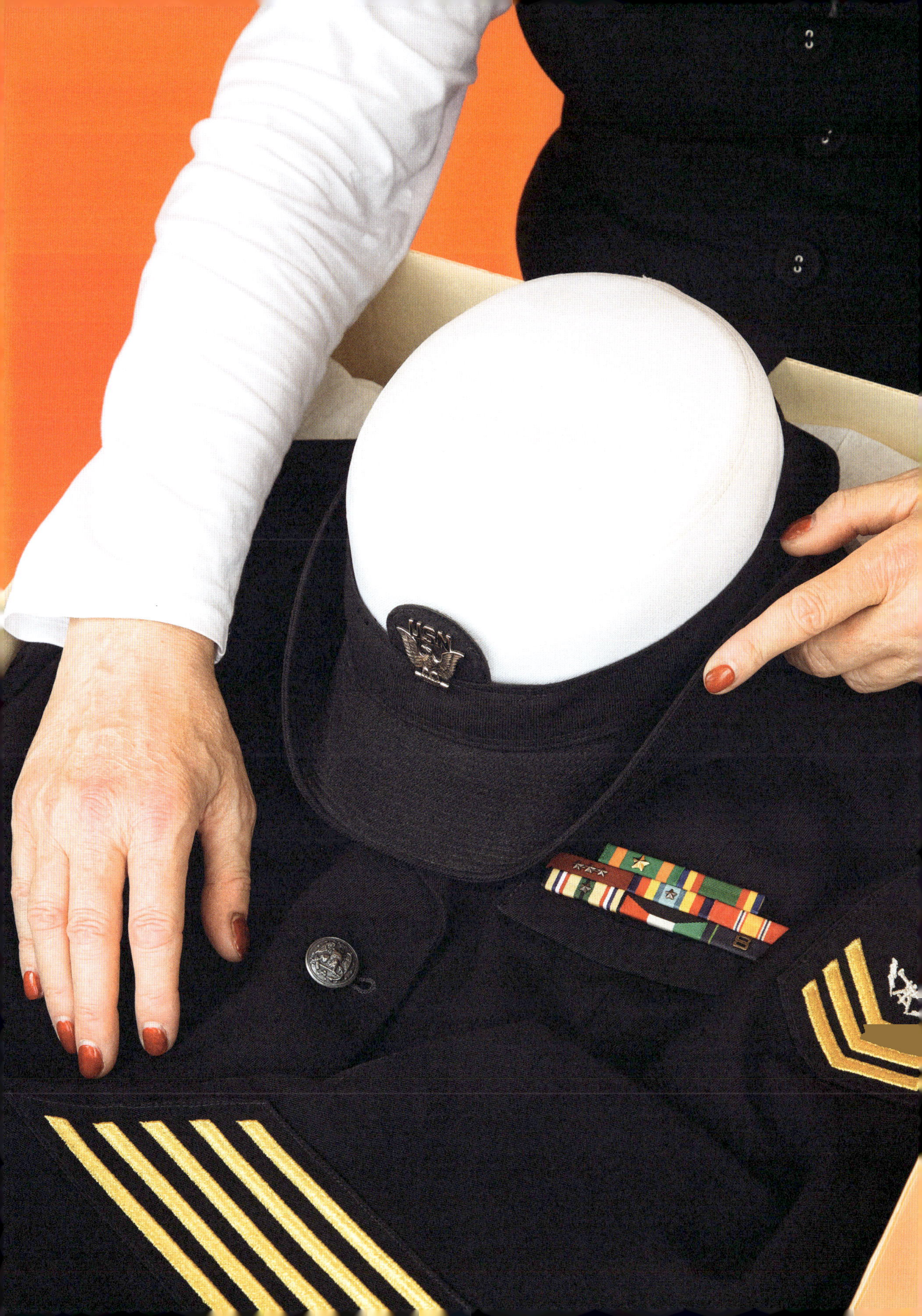
USN

29 PRITZKER MILITARY MUSEUM & LIBRARY, 2003–PRESENT

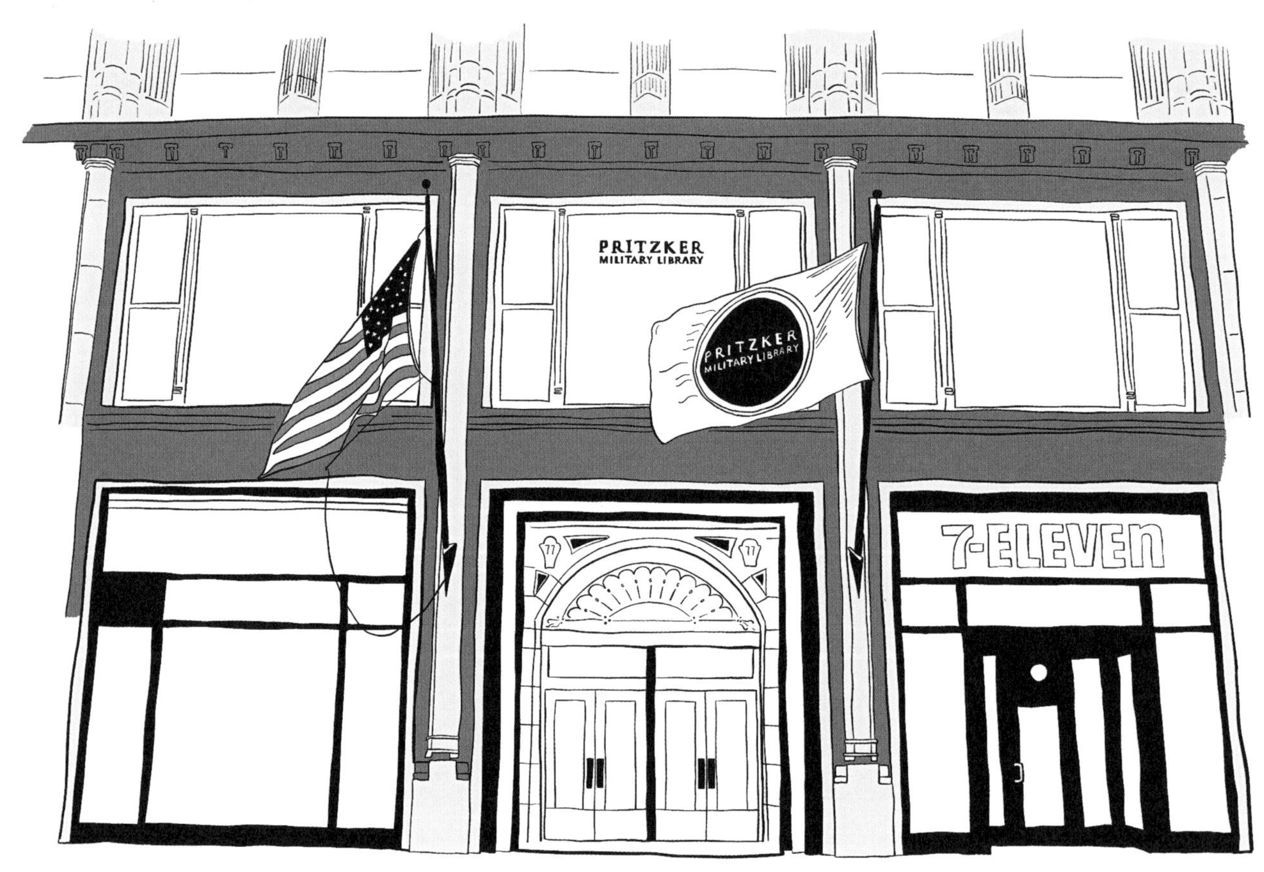

Col. Jennifer Pritzker is a transgender philanthropist and retired US Army Lieutenant Colonel.[1] She is renowned as the first transgender billionaire. Her family's fortune is wrapped up in exploitative and extractive industries, including hotels, tobacco, and credit reporting. Much of her philanthropy has been focused on celebrating US military imperialism and the military industrial complex under the guise of service and patriotism, demonstrated most prominently through her founding of the Pritzker Military Museum & Library in Chicago in 2003. Located across from the Art Institute of Chicago, the museum houses an expansive research library and presents rotating history exhibits, the majority of which focus on WWI and II. The museum is also working to open a new campus in Somers, Wisconsin, that will house the institution's archives, a memorial related to the Cold War, and a firearms education center and shooting range geared toward families.

Pritzker is, however, most known for her advocacy of LGBT inclusion in the US military, a topic that is largely unexplored in her namesake museum. In 2013, Pritzker's personal foundation, the Tawani Foundation, gave the largest grant ever given for trans advocacy: an award to the Palm Center for $1.35 million to advocate for the end of the US military's ban on transgender servicemembers. The Palm Center was credited as one of the organizations most responsible for the repeal of "Don't Ask, Don't Tell" (DADT) in 2011, and Pritzker provided the funds to enable the center to pursue the same strategies to end the ban on trans military service.

Since at least the 1970s, there have been important debates in US queer and trans communities about what queer and trans politics demands and how it envisions liberation. Legal equality advocates, especially gay rights nonprofit organizations, have focused on reforming key institutions that have defined white and heterosexual citizenship in the US—marriage, military participation, and law enforcement—to make them include gays and lesbians and more recently trans people. Racial and economic justice-centered queer and trans activists have argued that we should dismantle oppressive, colonial, racist institutions in order to win gender and sexual liberation. They have fought to separate the things people need to survive, like health care, immigration status, and parental rights, from the institution of marriage. Rather than trying to access marriage, racial and economic justice focused queer and trans organizers have argued for putting resources into fights like Medicare for all; opposing family law systems (including what is inaccurately called "child welfare") that tear apart the families of poor people, people of color, Indigenous people, and people with disabilities; and opposing immigration enforcement. They have also argued that rather than fighting for hate crime laws that give more money and resources to police and prosecutors, queer and trans politics should fight to defund and dismantle the racist systems of policing and imprisonment. They maintain that rather than celebrating the military as a job queer and trans people want, our movements should be allied with people around the world who stand against US military imperialism and with communities of color who are targeted for military recruitment in the US.

Gay and lesbian equality-focused legal organizations have supported inclusion strategies that take up a politics of respectability that says "we are good citizens like you, let us marry, call the cops on people, and join the military." For the first few decades of this wave of advocacy, these organizations explicitly excluded trans people. After years of trans advocacy, as trans politics has mainstreamed, more of these liberal LGBT rights organizations have begun to openly advocate on trans issues. However, they do it in a way that mirrors their general approach—pushing for trans people to be included in hate crime laws and military service. Trans organizers have criticized this approach, arguing that trans well-being would be better served by opposing policing and militarism and poverty. They have further argued that inclusion campaigns can "pinkwash" oppressive institutions, painting them as "LGBT friendly" when in fact prisons, jails, and US militarism hurt trans people.

Not surprisingly, advocacy work that aligns with dominant institutions is more popular with wealthy donors, corporations, and the corporate media than racial and economic justice-centered queer and trans work that seeks to dismantle those institutions. As a result, the gay and lesbian inclusion agenda is the one that most people today recognize as "LGBT rights" politics, and the trans equivalent has rapidly come to stand in for "trans rights." Meanwhile the grassroots antipoverty, antiracist, anti-imperialist queer and trans work has continued to develop over these decades and remains strong, albeit less visible and less resourced than its more conservative sibling.

Pritzker's gift to the Palm Center captures a common dynamic facing social movements in the twenty-first century, whereby conservative, wealthy people can help facilitate shifts that coopt the political work of marginalized groups for processes that recuperate violent institutions. Pritzker's influence on trans politics is out of proportion because her wealth lets her make a particular form of advocacy—promilitary trans advocacy—more prominent than advocacy done by more marginalized trans people for things trans people actually want and need, like housing, health care, and freedom from criminalization.

—Dean Spade

1. Some of the text included here previously appeared in Dean Spade and Aaron Belkin, "Queer Militarism?!: The Politics of Military Inclusion Advocacy in Authoritarian Times," *GLQ: A Journal of Gay and Lesbian Studies* 27, no. 2 (January 2021): 281–307.

30 MURRAY HILL FOR MAYOR CAMPAIGN FLYER, 1997

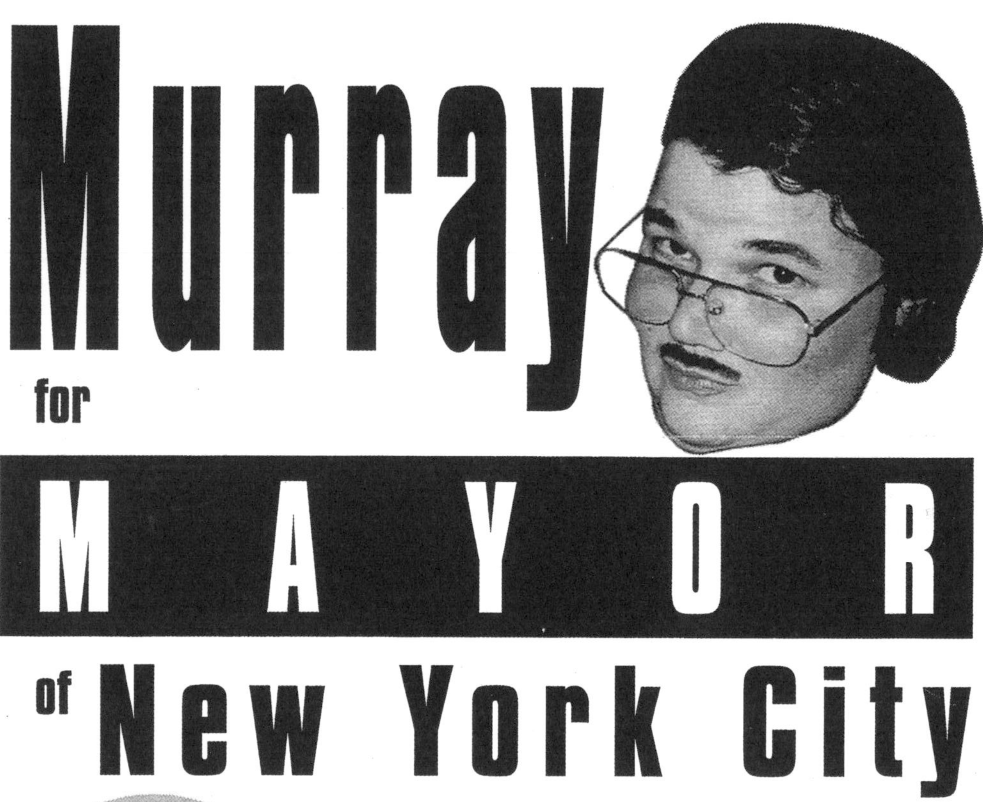

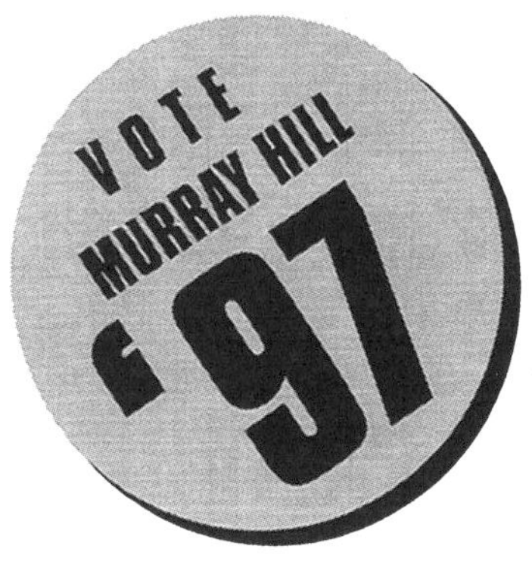

Murray Hill is running for Mayor and he *never* had a lobbyist. The city is governed by a bully, and what NewYork City needs is 'nice guy' politics. **Murray Hill** is the man to do it. **Murray** was born and raised in Manhattan. He earned a high school diploma from P.S. 134 where he made the honor roll two consecutive semesters and was an esteemed member of the student council. Since then, **Murray** has been working for the state of New York and serving the people of New York as a MTA subway token booth clerk. Most importantly, **Murray** is a *family man* with *family values.* He is married (25 years) to his beautiful wife, Pennelope, and they have two public school attending children. **Murray** is committed to the people of the city of New York.

A vote for **Murray** is a vote for *you.*
Vote MURRAY HILL for Mayor of the City of New York.

✓Murray for Mayor '97

Vote MURRAY HILL for Mayor in 1997. Please send election campaign contributions (check or money order) to: **Murray Hill**, P.O. Box 270, New York, NY 10156-0270. For more information or to be on the **Murray for Mayor** mailing list, please call 212.539.3197 or email MurrayHill@hotmail.com. Check local listings for upcoming campaign events and thank you for your support.

Mur-ray !! Mur-ray !! Mur-ray !!

These chants filled the air bringing hope and hilarity to the somber climate wafting through New York City's nightlife. On Sunday, April 20, 1997, Murray Hill threw his proverbial hat in the ring by announcing his candidacy for Mayor of New York City at Club Casanova, the premiere weekly drag king party in the East Village. The enthusiastic crowd cheered and chanted, but was Murray really serious?

Murray moved to NYC in the fall of 1995 to study photography and feminist performance art at the School of the Visual Arts. While photographing drag queens within a sea of maledom, he had an epiphany: "Where are the dykes?!?" The lack of visibility was palpable. Thus, his search began to find the other side of this spectrum, which led him to an early drag king contest at HerShe Bar. Murray began to photograph the "fellas" and was eventually inspired to give it a try himself.

Resembling a cherub-cheeked Benny Hill, Murray donned a men's suit to be a cigarette boy at a friend's new nightclub called the 999999's. Shortly after, he became a Club Casanova regular performing a variety of characters such as gymnastics coach Béla Károlyi, John Travolta in *Grease*, a hefty Elvis in his later years, and a handsy lounge singer, all the while taking photographs for school. He decided to drop his photographic pursuits to create a full-fledged drag king character as his master's thesis. He transformed his nightclub persona as a disreputable playboy into Mr. Murray Hill, the clean-cut family man running for political office. This wasn't mere folly but an active stance in response to the Prohibition-era Cabaret Law, which forbade musical entertainment, singing, dancing, or other form of amusement without a license. Murray came out in full force with his campaign slogan, "Let the Kids Dance."

As I was the proprietor of Club Casanova, Murray called me first to share he was running for mayor; we quickly scheduled show dates to roll out his campaign. I was privy to hilarious ideas, great talent, and a lot of fun. This party was the epicenter of everything drag king where photographers, filmmakers, and journalists covered our every move. Iconic photographer Del LaGrace Volcano was a frequent visitor because they were photographing us for *The Drag King Book*.[1] Del's photograph of Murray in a patriotic flag tie standing at the city's waterfront, the Statue of Liberty illuminated by a fading sunset behind him, captures him in all his glory. Little did he know then that he found his niche not just as a drag king but as a world-class entertainer.

As NYC's first drag king independent write-in mayoral candidate, Murray ran against Republican incumbent Rudy Giuliani (we called him "Ghouliani") whose campaign touted "Quality of Life." This so-called quality of life campaign brought an orchestrated crackdown from the various agencies that regulate the bar and nightclub industries. The crackdowns included raids, permit checks, and visits to issue citations for noise complaints, overcrowding, disorderly premises, or unlicensed sustained systematic dancing under the antiquated Cabaret Law. Bars and nightclubs, fearing their liquor licenses would be revoked changed to lounges with bottle service, which left a dearth in performance spaces for drag artists, rockstars, and all around freaks. Despite Club Casanova's immense popularity, I struggled to keep the party doors open due to the constant harassment.

Wearing his prerequisite snug-fitting navy blue polyester suit, patriotic tie, pinky ring, and painted on mustache, Murray was the nightlife candidate who stood for E-quality of Night-Life, His goal was to get kids in the clubs involved in politics and registered to vote. He campaigned at both mainstream clubs and downtown queer events such as Wigstock, Pervathon, and Lesbopalooza. As the nice-guy neighborhood politician, Murray urged partygoers to fight for your right to party in the city that never sleeps. His campaign slogan, "A Vote for Murray Is a Vote for You," made an impact on part of the electorate. Who knew the perpetually fifty-year old, short, stout, middle-aged, laid-off subway token booth clerk with a wife and two nonexistent kids would rake in 334 votes! If only more people took him seriously.

—Mo B. Dick

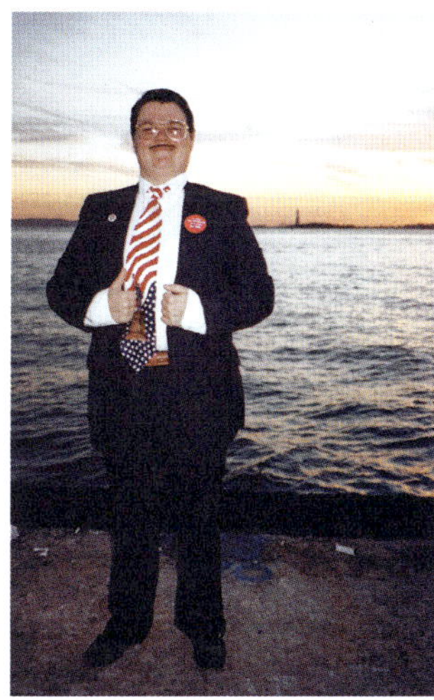

Del LaGrace Volcano, *Murray Hill Running for Mayor, NYC Docks*, 1997. Collection of Mo. B. Dick, co-creator of dragkinghistory.com

◄ "Murray for Mayor of New York City" campaign flyer, 1997. Collection of Mo B. Dick, co-creator of dragkinghistory.com

1. Del LaGrace Volcano and Jack Halberstam, *The Drag King Book* (London: Serpent's Tail, 1999).

31 **TRACEY AFRICA NORMAN ON CLAIROL BORN BEAUTIFUL BOX 512, 1975**

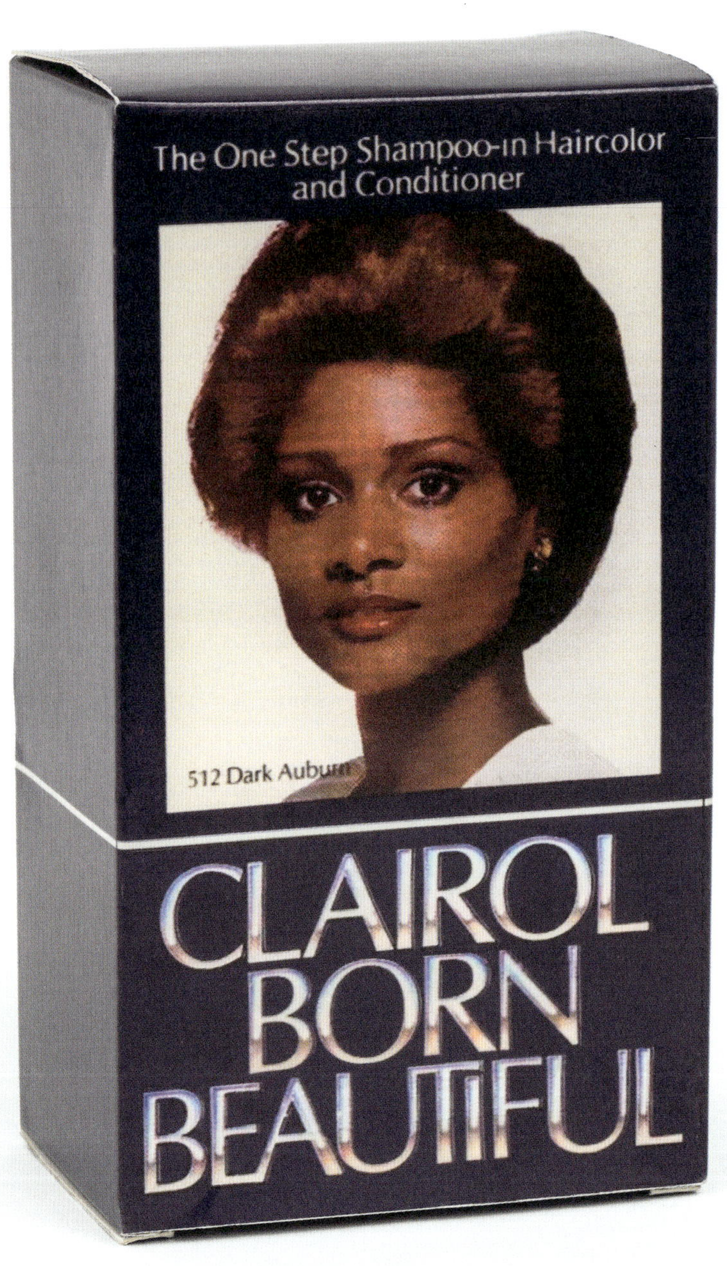

The dimensions of Clairol's "Born Beautiful" haircoloring Box 512 did not anticipate and could never contain the overwhelming beauty of Tracey Africa Norman. In 1975, the alluring, Black, transgender goddess from Newark, New Jersey, was featured on Clairol's product in an image with a history that has exceeded the box on which it was printed and the campaign of which it was a part.

Clairol's Box 512 features the graham cracker complexioned Norman, with a mane of hair as auburn as sunset, and a simple, sophisticated gold button earring. Norman's immaculately sculpted eyebrows, an angle of marvelous geometry above pools of arrestingly soulful eyes, are beset with delicate spider tentacle top and bottom lashes. Her lips, painted crimson, are slightly parted to a porcelain reveal, which give one the feeling that she has just greeted you at the door of her home in a manner that would make any etiquette queen proud.

Norman was invited to grace the cover of Clairol's then new campaign of haircoloring created specifically for women of color. The hair color for which Norman modeled did not exist in Clairol's pantheon. It was created to match Norman's own hair, which had become reddish-brown after she did a home perm, and her hair was lightened when the chemicals met the sunlight. Photographing Norman for the campaign, Clairol loved how what appeared to be dark brown hair turned auburn under the lights on set and created a new color they christened "Dark Auburn." The company signed Norman to a two-year contract to use the image. The color proved to be so popular that her contract was renewed two additional times—for a total of six years.[1]

To have only been a professional model a matter of months before being hired for the Clairol campaign was miraculous. She was discovered by storied photographer Irving Penn at a casting to which she snuck in as an aspiring model with no agent. Impressed, Penn booked her for an editorial in *Vogue Italia*, singing her praises as the next big thing. Overnight, Norman had a modeling agent and began booking gigs that only a week before would have gone to Black models she profoundly admired.[2] With the money she earned from Clairol and other jobs, Norman built the life she always wanted, moving into a lovely apartment with her poodle on New York's Upper West Side.[3] But she had done it all without ever revealing that she was trans, and working in constant fear that she would be outed.

In 1980, while on a photoshoot for *Essence*, Norman's fears were realized. Subsequently, she was dropped by her agency, and the bookings stopped coming. She went home to Newark to regroup before heading to Paris where she was able to find work as a house model for the historic fashion label Balenciaga. Returning to New York, she held the hope that she would no longer be discriminated against in the fashion industry for being transgender. Though she found some modeling work here and there, Norman's steadiest gig was in retail.[4]

Forty years would pass before Norman was back at the center of the beauty and fashion worlds. It wasn't until a 2015 feature article in *The Cut* that she was able to tell two acts of her story— the triumph and the pain—and ultimately jumpstart her third act. Serendipitously, it was Clairol who, in 2016, invited Norman to once again be a face of their product in a campaign for their latest hair color "Nice 'n Easy."[5] This time, however, Norman was seen fully as the stunning, unforgettable, Black woman she has always been; her identity and experience as a Black transgender woman amply noted and celebrated. A fictionalized version of Norman's 1975 work with Clairol was the basis for a story-arc for Angel Evangelista, an Afro-Latina trans woman character on the television drama *Pose*.[6] The series focuses on the ballroom community of which Norman, a member of the House of Africa, is also a part.[7]

Norman's twenty-first century rebirth put front and center the historic achievement of her modeling career. Clairol's Box 512 is a portrait of a Black trans woman as the exemplar of beauty, demonstrating how the normative markers of feminine beauty are not the divine provenance and property of people assigned female at birth. The image is of a Black trans woman as the epitome of born beautiful.

—Eric Darnell Pritchard

1. Jada Yuan and Aaron Wong, "The First Black Trans Model Had Her Face on a Box of Clairol," *The Cut*, December 14, 2015, accessed April 18, 2023, https://www.thecut.com/2015/12/tracey-africa-transgender-model-c-v-r.html.
2. Yuan and Wong, "The First Black Trans Model."
3. Jillian Eugenios, "Tracey 'Africa' Norman, the 1st Black Trans Model, Was Born before Her Time," *Today*, June 1, 2021, accessed April 18, 2023, https://www.today.com/style/tracey-africa-norman-1st-black-trans-model-was-born-her-t219674.
4. Yuan and Wong, "The First Black Trans Model."
5. "Real Color Stories with Tracey Norman Clairol Nice n Easy," *Pharmacy*, June 6, 2018, YouTube video, 3:20, https://www.youtube.com/watch?v=eA8LBWs9w9w.
6. Sonoma Serena, "Tracey Africa, Model *Pose*'s Angel Is Based On, Rejected by *Playboy*," *Out*, September 14, 2019, accessed April 20, 2023, https://www.out.com/transgender/2019/9/14/tracey-africa-model-poses-angel-based-rejected-playboy.
7. Jami Fletcher, Aaron Bryant, Darnell L. Moore, Tracey Africa Norman, and Eric Darnell Pritchard, "A Change Is Gonna Come: LGBTQIA+ Influences on Fashion," from Fashion, Culture, Futures: African American Ingenuity, Activism, and Storytelling Symposium, Smithsonian National Museum of African American History and Culture, October 21, 2021, YouTube video, 1:46:58, https://www.youtube.com/watch?v=McwbJNAAMTI.

◀ Recreation of Clairol Born Beautiful Box 512, 1975/2016

32 *TIME* FEATURING "THE TRANSGENDER TIPPING POINT," JUNE 9, 2014

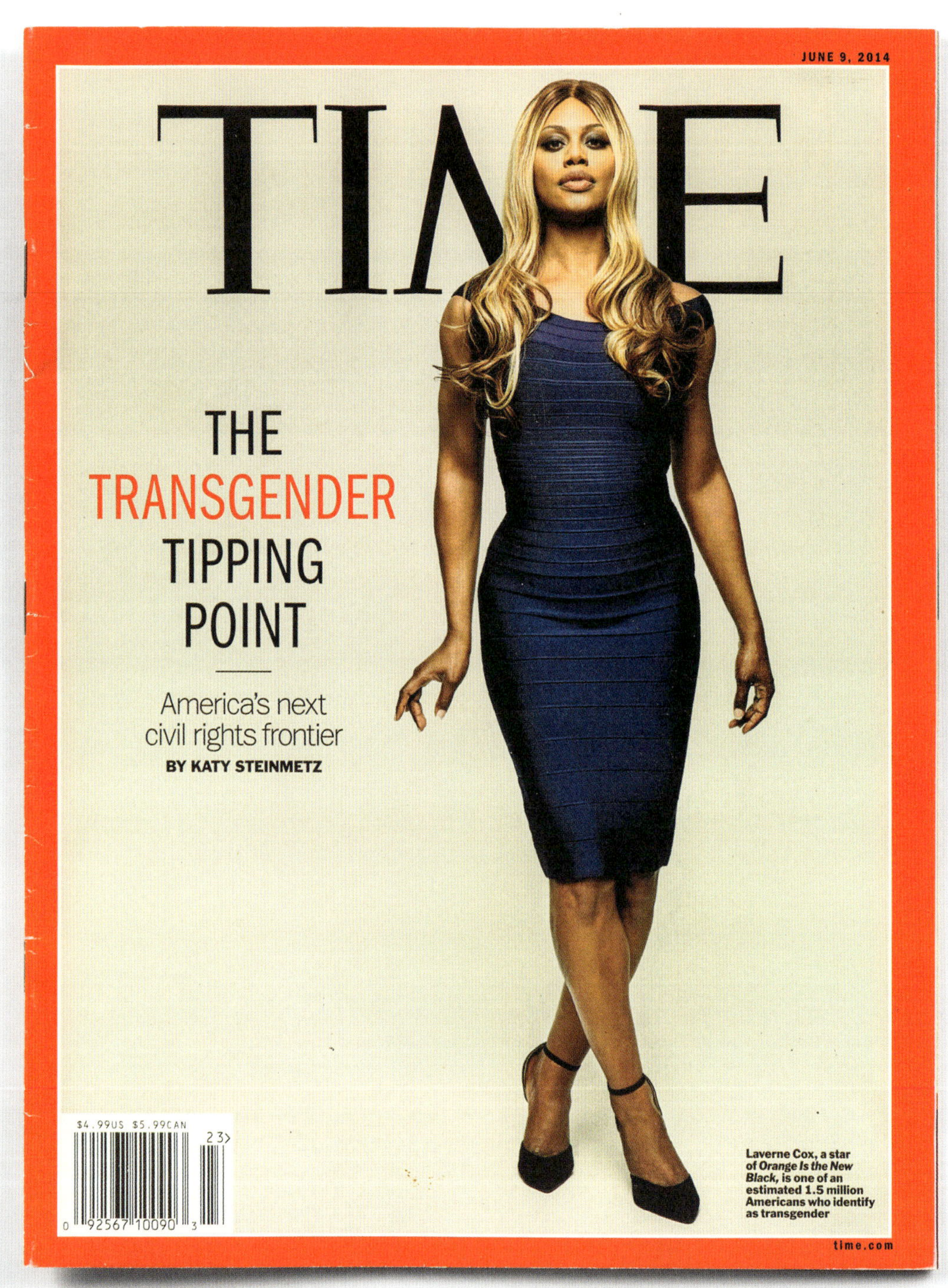

Who's Tipping Now?

Sex. For thousands of years, biological sex was the playing field—or the battleground—of humanity. Some aspect of bio sex has always been the basis of who's assigned male and who's assigned female. And it was an iron-clad law that once assigned a sex, you could never change, or so we have been told. Well, over time and here and there, some of us said no. Then more and more of us said NO, and gender identity was born: I am not what I've been assigned. I am what I know myself to be, and I alone define myself for me. Well, after a hundred or so years of gender in the world—in the blink of an eye, relatively—it was June 2014, our transgender tipping point. Mainstream America allowed an identity entirely new to American culture to cross over from the freak side of things into the reluctant embrace of the left to center-left wing of American culture. You let those of us in and this is what we taught you:

It's our tipping point and we say: trans men are men, trans women are women—no matter our genitals, the makeup of which is none of your business—not now, not at the time of our birth. It's our tipping point and we are embodying our authentic selves. It's our tipping point and we say: don't ask what my name used to be—and if you ever find out, don't ever use it cuz it's my dead name and I am alive and kicking. It's our tipping point and we say: ask for our pronoun, and use it. It's our tipping point, and trans men and trans women can get married too, even to each other. It's our tipping point and we say: keep your laws off my body. Biology is not destiny. So there, we've tipped—well, some of us have.

It's been nearly a decade and now there're more trans identities knocking on America's door. Our next tipping point will ask you to unleash your imagination. Male and female? Man and woman? What's coming is so much more than that and a whole lot less. Some of us are neither men nor women—we are nonbinary or genderqueer, agender, gender nonconforming, or gender fluid. And darling, we are tipping. My pronoun might be they or them, or hir, or ze, or zhem—I could be they and she or they and he. Hell, our pronouns might change every other day, and some of us don't give a flying fuck about pronouns. It's our new tipping point, and oh ... you still want to know about our genitals? Well you show us yours and if we really like you, we'll show you ours. Oh, and marriage? Well, can a polyamorous pod of four get married? No? Honey, we are the nightmare. It's the next transgender tipping point, and we are the ones shouting keep your transphobic laws off my body. Biology has never been and never will be destiny.

Oh, and there is so much more. Transgender, thy name is legion. With thanks to all who've come before us, and all yet to come. The third wave tipping point is gonna say that our genders and sexualities are simply ribbons of joy and possibility that begin with our birth and end with our death. Our pronouns are any, all, and none of them, depending on where and when we are. Our genitals? Oh darling, we fuck with every inch of our bodies. We are the queerest of the queer, we are tipping fast, and you are gonna fall head over heels in love with us.

—Kate Bornstein

◄
Laverne Cox on the cover of *Time*, June 9, 2014

33 MARTINE GUTIERREZ, *INDIGENOUS WOMAN*, 2018

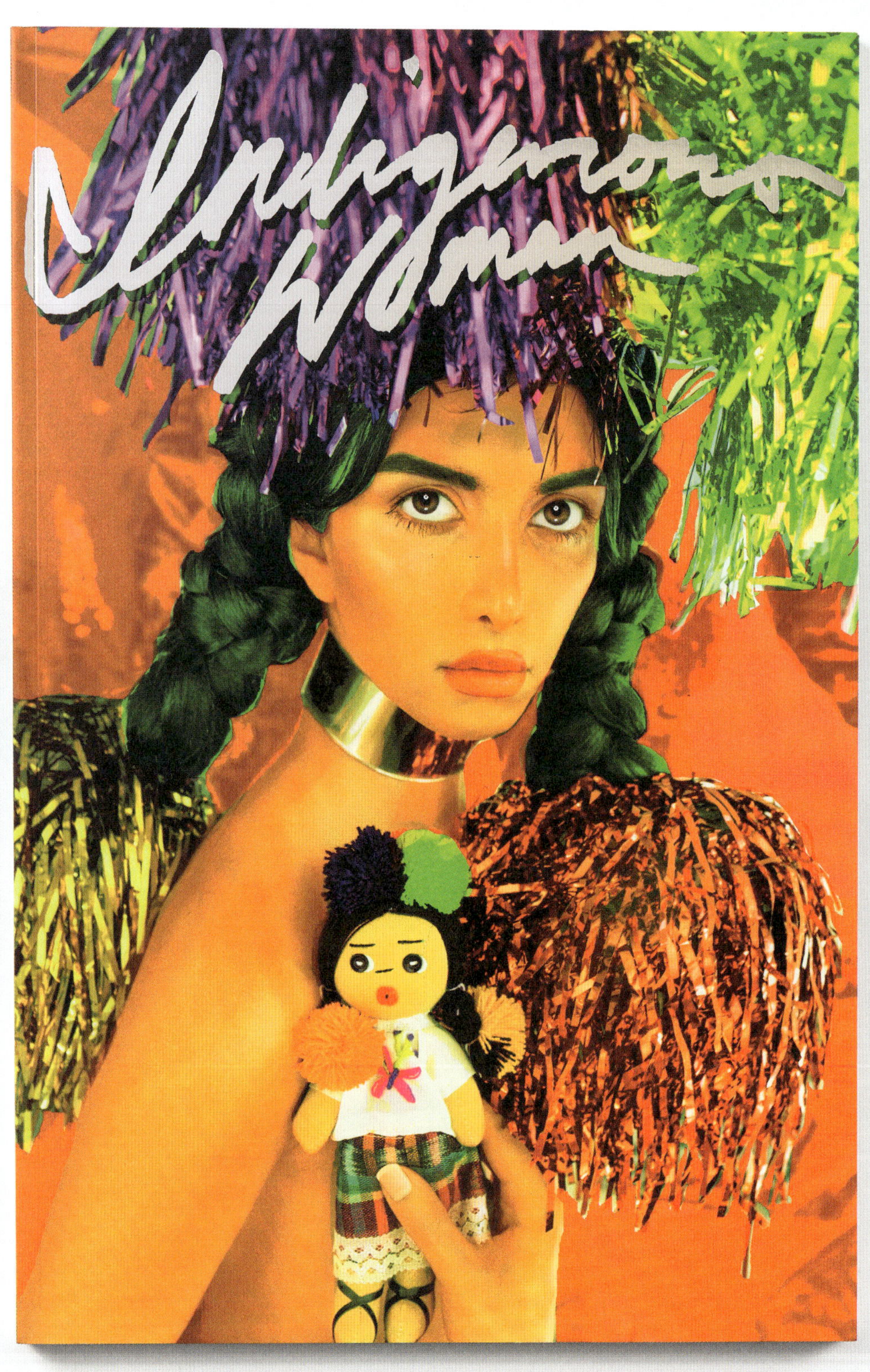

Letter from the Editor

This is not a magazine about fashion, lifestyle, or celebrity. *Indigenous Woman* is an independent art publication dedicated to the celebration of Mayan Indian heritage, the navigation of contemporary indigeneity, and the ever-evolving self-image. It is a vision, an overture, a provocation.

The word "Indigenous" here is used to refer to native cultures from a particular region, but also as a synonym for the natural and innate. It signifies a real, authentic, Native-born woman. There was a time when I believed there was no such title for me to claim. I was driven to question how identity is formed, expressed, valued, and weighed as a woman, as a trans woman, as a Latinx woman, as a woman of Indigenous descent, as a femme artist and maker. It is nearly impossible to arrive at any finite answers, but for me, this process of exploration is exquisitely life-affirming.

In working to convey my own fluid identity—an identity that bridges the binaries of gender and ethnicity—I aim in part to subvert cis, white, Western standards of beauty and raise questions about inclusivity, appropriation, and consumerism. From behind long lashes and lacquered lips, I use the fashion magazine's glossy framework to play with perception. I employ mannequins, advertorials, and Indigenous textiles to reassert control over my own image. Mine is a practice of full autonomy—all photography, modeling, styling, makeup, hair, lighting, graphic design, and product design I have executed myself.

Indigenous Woman marries the traditional to the contemporary, the Native to the postcolonial, and the marginalized to the mainstream in the pursuit of genuine selfhood, revealing cultural inequities along the way. This is a quest for identity. Of my own specifically, yes, but by digging my pretty, painted nails deeply into the dirt of my own image I am also probing the depths for some understanding of identity as a social construction.

It is also my ambition to forge a connection between the art world and my community. While it is my desire for *Indigenous Woman* to provide some sustenance for my fellow millennial nonbinary trans women of color, I sincerely hope that all audiences will find the work compelling and captivating. I believe it is possible to create an empathetic and supportive society, but it requires that we all educate ourselves, that we learn to be allies and activists who understand our own privilege. Mutual understanding has the power to change the world.

—Martine Gutierrez,
Editor-in-Chief

This text appears in the artist's magazine *Indigenous Woman*, 2018.

◄
(and following spread)
Martine Gutierrez,
Indigenous Woman, 2018.
Artist's magazine,
16½ × 11 in. (41.9 × 27.9 cm)

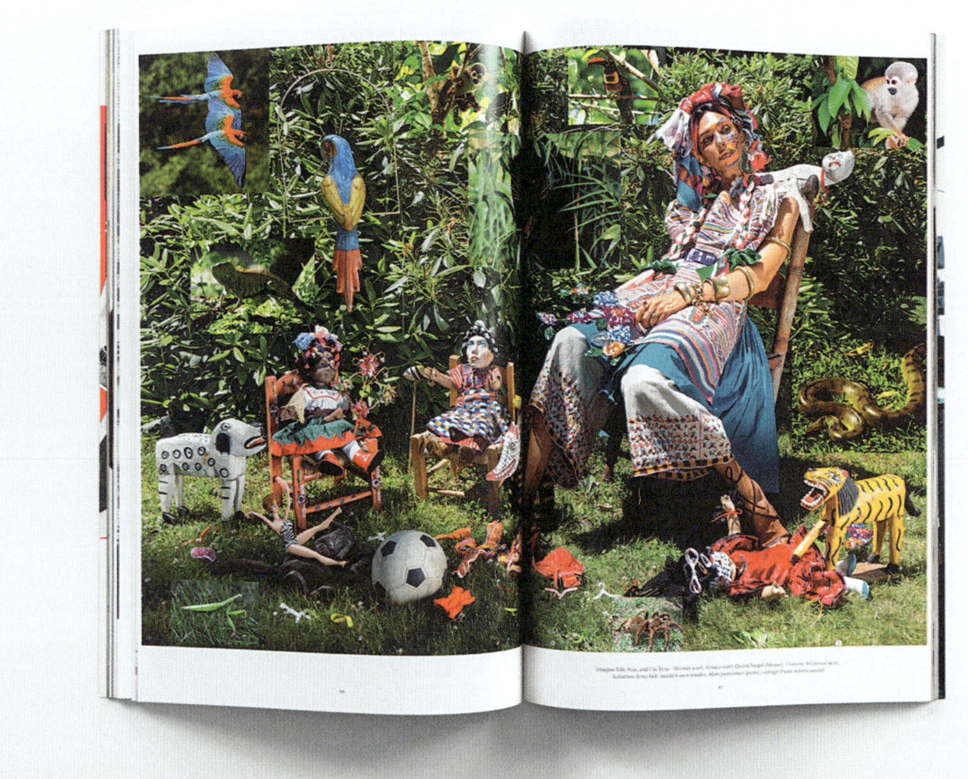

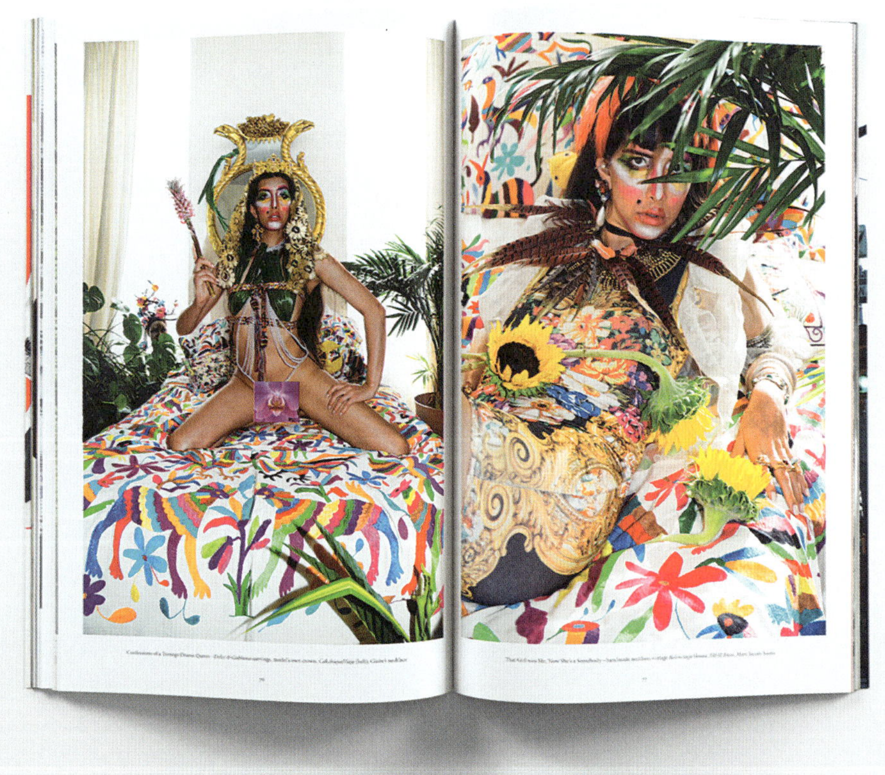

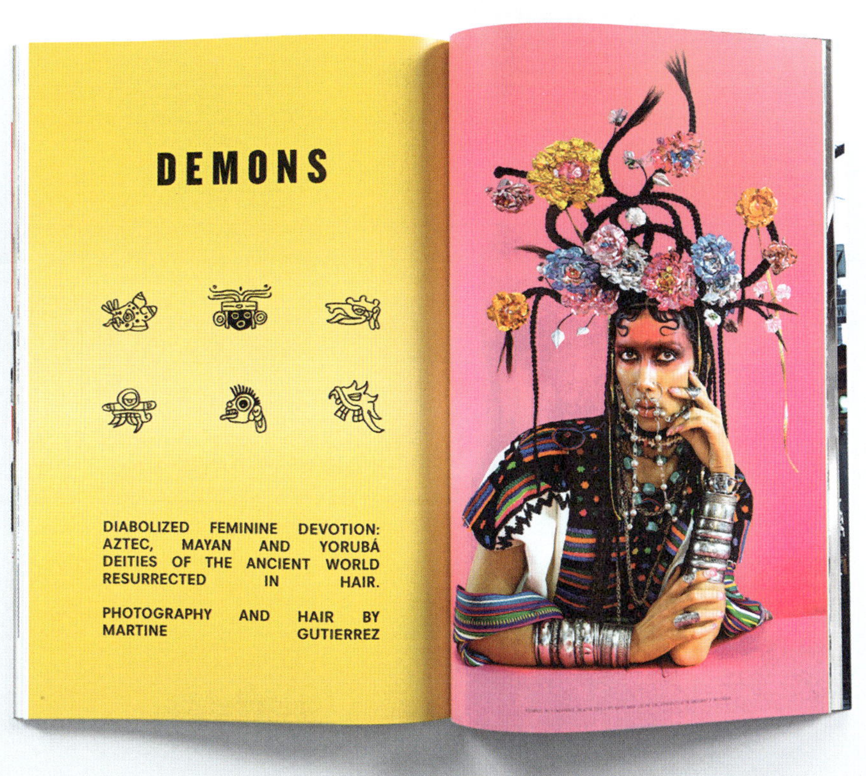
DEMONS
DIABOLIZED FEMININE DEVOTION: AZTEC, MAYAN AND YORUBÁ DEITIES OF THE ANCIENT WORLD RESURRECTED IN HAIR.
PHOTOGRAPHY AND HAIR BY MARTINE GUTIERREZ

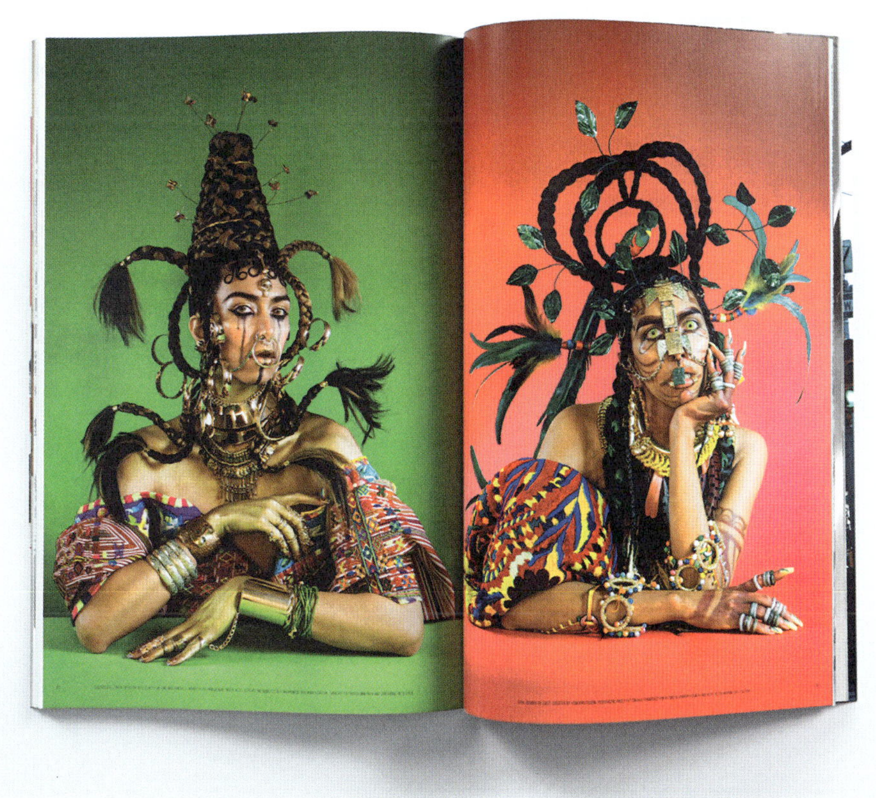

34 ARIANA AGUILAR IN *THE GAY ESSAY* AND *HOMEBOY BEAUTIFUL*, 1970/1978–79

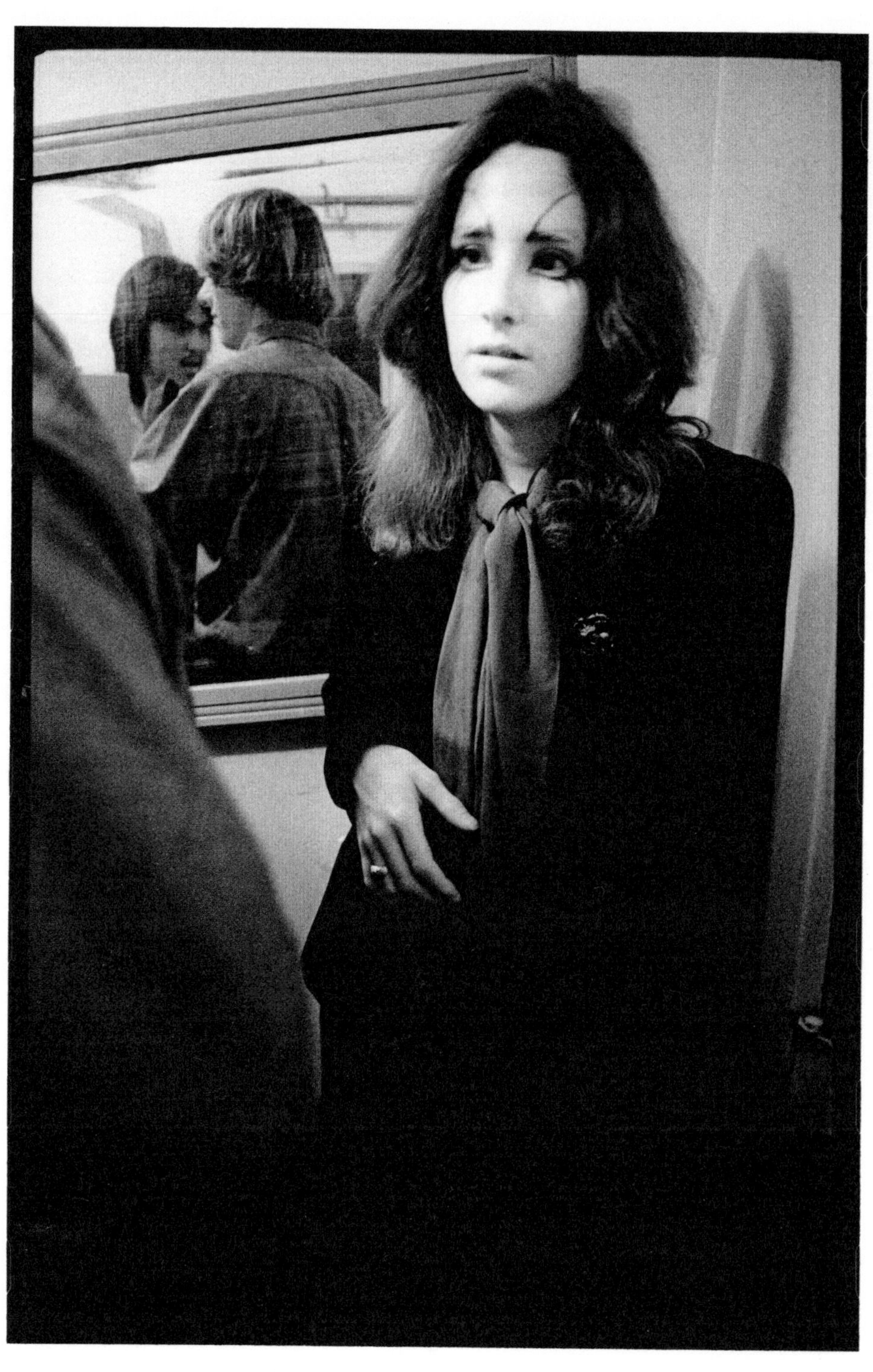

On the heels of New York's Stonewall riots, photographer Anthony Friedkin, himself just nineteen years old, set out to independently produce a photographic portrait of the gay community on the West Coast. At the invitation of gay liberation activist Morris Kight, Friedkin attended the Gay Funky Dances, a series of weekly, all-age dances at Troupers Hall in Hollywood.[1] There he met and photographed numerous young people, one of whom was known at the time as Jim Aguilar. Often referred to as "Pretty Jim" by friends, Aguilar was part of a tight-knit community of artists, performers, and other creatives, including Robert Legorreta (Cyclona), Mundo Meza, and Joey Terrill, in East Los Angeles's youth culture during the 1970s.[2]

Friedkin was immediately captivated by Aguilar's androgynous style and delicate features. In this photograph at Troupers, Aguilar's high-arched, Bette Davis-style eyebrows and rays of eye shadow reflect the gender-bending extravagance of LA's burgeoning glitter rock scene. Artist Joey Terrill recalls that the Gay Funky Dances were a space to explore identity and sexuality as well as fashion and style, and Aguilar is decidedly dressed up here—long slacks, wide-shouldered blazer, dangling scarf, and glistening brooch.[3]

Friedkin began a close friendship with Aguilar resulting in some of the series' most strikingly intimate photographs. *The Gay Essay* (1969–73) includes a handful of portraits of prominent community members, but countercultural young people like Aguilar, as well as drag queens and street hustlers, were Friedkin's most captivating subjects. This was both recognized and disparaged at the time by *Los Angeles Times* critic William Wilson: "Anyone hoping to find reassurance that homosexuals are just like everybody else is liable to find disappointment.... [Friedkin] was only able to photograph those who have little to lose by being identified as members of the subculture."[4]

Aguilar appears in eight of the fifty photographs Friedkin selected in 1973 for a book maquette of *The Gay Essay*. Aguilar was also the subject of a chapter in the unrealized publication, the only section dedicated to an individual.[5] A selection from Friedkin's photo essay was included in the October 1973 issue of *Gay Sunshine*, a countercultural gay liberation newspaper distributed nationally but particularly accessible in California. Printed as a tabloid, the interior centerfold of the magazine featured multiple images from the series, including a photograph of Aguilar and Meza together dressed in chic bohemian attire outside a hot dog stand in Montebello, California. When Friedkin first showed his series at the well-regarded Ohio Silver Gallery in Los Angeles, Aguilar, Meza, and others enthusiastically attended to be recognized alongside their portraits.

Sometime in the 1970s, Aguilar took the name Ariana. Terrill recalls that the two briefly worked together at Sears in Hollywood—Aguilar was in the women's shoes department—however, her trans identity remained undisclosed, and that job was short-lived. She continued to work odd jobs, primarily in fashion and retail. For a period, she assisted British ex-pat Simon Doonan with a scrappy T-shirt business. Around this time, Aguilar also featured in both issues of Terrill's zine *Homeboy Beautiful* (1978–79), a parody of women's lifestyle magazines mixed with camp and a biting satire of Chicano machismo. Aguilar appears in issue one as the stunning "homo-homeboy" named "Fred" who does a striptease at a party and performs in issue two as a no-nonsense chola within a fashion profile. In this "fashion spread," Aguilar (with teased hair) appears with her trans sisters Christina (in a short skirt) and Juanita Miller (in glasses and a hat). Together, this trio was known as the Mijas.

In the 1980s, friends recall Aguilar frequented Circus Disco in Hollywood, a queer nightclub founded as a safe space for Latinx and other people of color who were often denied entry to the predominately white discos. It is rumored that Aguilar moved in the 1980s or 1990s to Texas. The vulnerabilities of trans existence undoubtedly impacted Aguilar's life, but her friends are unclear on what became of her after the Circus Disco years. Aguilar's appearance in Friedkin's photo essay and Terrill's artist's magazines radiates the sensitivity and panache of queer youth and trans liberatory world-making at an earlier moment, when optimism was running high.

—David Evans Frantz

◂
Anthony Friedkin, Jim, *Restroom at Trouper's Hall, Hollywood*, 1970 (printed 2017). From *The Gay Essay*, 1969–73. Gelatin silver print, 14 × 11 in. (35.6 × 27.9 cm). Gift of Anthony Friedkin, ONE National Gay & Lesbian Archives at the USC Libraries

(following spread)
Joey Terrill, Pages from *Homeboy Beautiful*, no. 1 (1978) and no. 2 (1979). Photograph and mixed media on paper, 11 × 8½ in. (27.9 × 21.6 cm) each. Joey Terrill Papers, ONE National Gay & Lesbian Archives at the USC Libraries

1. Many sources identify the venue as Trouper's or Troopers Hall.
2. For more information on this period and community of artists, see C. Ondine Chavoya and David Evans Frantz, eds., *Axis Mundo: Queer Networks in Chicano L.A.* (Los Angeles: ONE National Gay & Lesbian Archives at the USC Libraries; New York: DelMonico Books/Prestel, 2017).
3. Oral history interview with Joey Terrill, interview by Stuart Timmons, 2005, audio-recording, ONE National Gay & Lesbian Archives at the USC Libraries.
4. William Wilson, "Gay World in Photos by Friedkin," *Los Angeles Times*, July 12, 1973, 8.
5. While Friedkin did not realize the book in 1973, decades later the catalogue accompanying a museum presentation of the series follows the format Friedkin originally planned: Julian Cox, ed., *Anthony Friedkin: The Gay Essay* (San Francisco: Fine Arts Museum of San Francisco; New Haven, CT: Yale University Press, 2014).

AS TWO O'CLOCK APPROACHED THE CROWD NUMBERED ABOUT 50! YES, 50! MOST OF THE HOMEBOYS HAD THEIR 'SIR-GUYS' AND T-SHIRTS OFF AND WERE SLOW DANCING CHEEK TO CHEEK! BOY I'VE HEARD OF VATO LOCOS BUT THIS WAS TOO MUCH. I WAS REALLY DISGUSTED. I PROMISED MYSELF, ONE MORE DANCE AND THEN I WAS LEAVING. I DON'T REMEMBER WHAT HAPPENED NEXT, IT'S ALL JUST A BIG BLUR, I REMEMBER A VATO TWISTING MY ARM TO FORCE ME TO KISS HIM ON THE LIPS AND GIVE HIM A HICKEY... I HAD NO CHOICE BUT TO SUBMIT! SEVERAL CHOLOS WERE ON ME ALL AT ONCE REMOVING MY CLOTHES CAMERA AND EYEGLASSES

I REMEMBER "FRED" STRIPPING...

I REMEMBER HAVING MY HANDS TIED BEHIND MY BACK...

I REMEMBER JUDY GARLAND RECORDS TILL 5 IN THE MORNING...

I REMEMBER THINKING URINE DOESNT TASTE THAT BAD AFTER ALL..

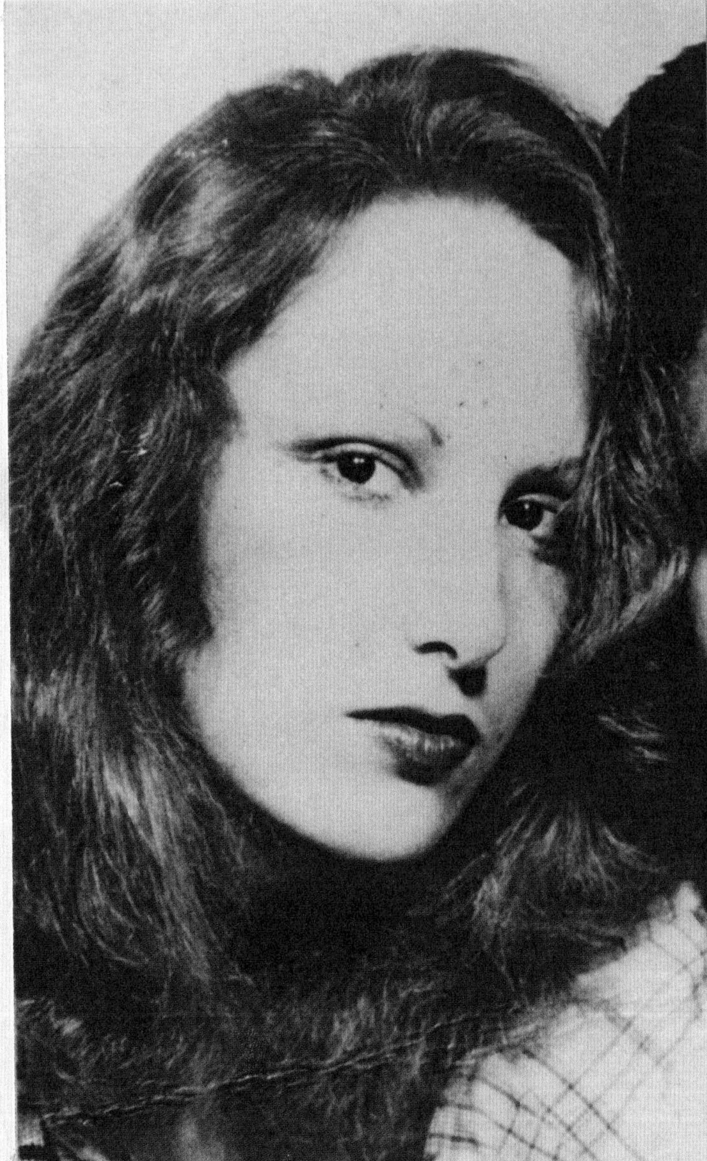

PHOTOGRAPH ABOVE IS "FRED," ONE OF THE HOMO HOMEBOYS. HE SERVED COOKIES AND DID A STRIPTEASE.

(16)

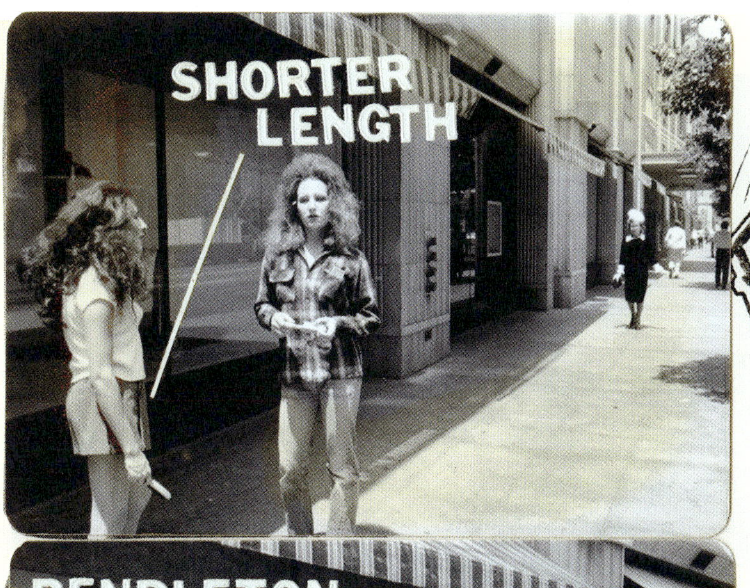

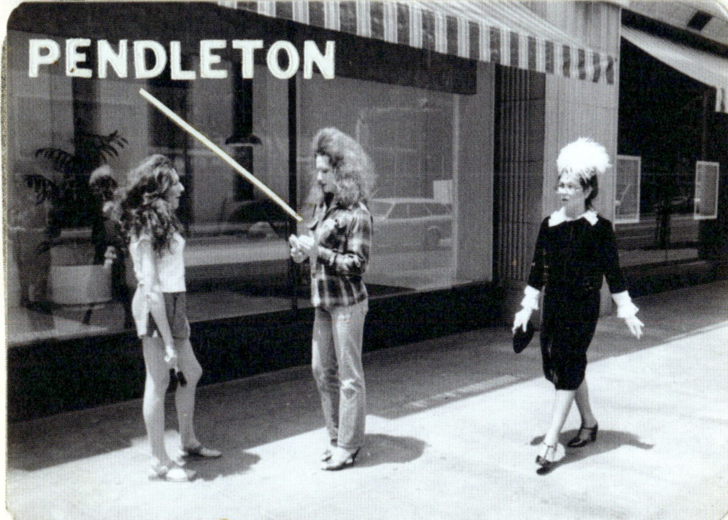

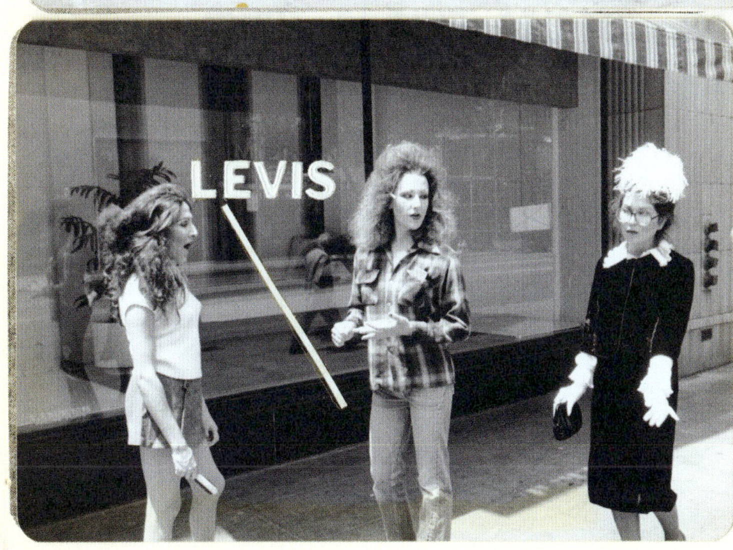

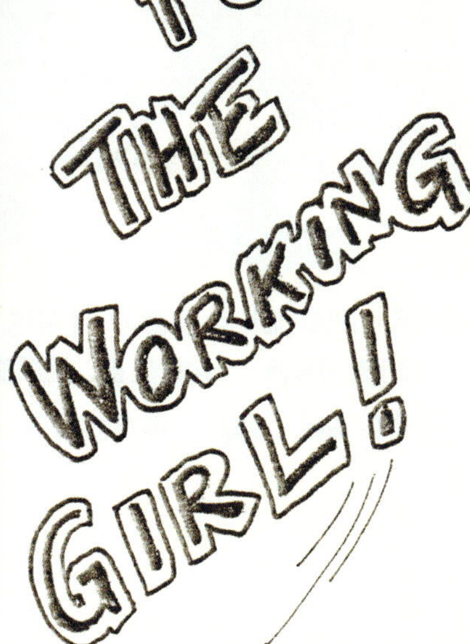

SHORTER SKIRTS FOR EASIER ACCESSABILITY AND RUNNING STARTS...

PENDLETON FOR A GOOD BODY PROTECTION...

AND OF COURSE THE EVER-POPULAR VERSATILE LEVIS.

THESE ARE "HOT ITEMS" FOR WORKING GIRLS ALL OVER DOWNTOWN LOS ANGELES.

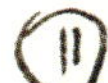

35 SHU LEA CHEANG, *BRANDON*, 1998–99

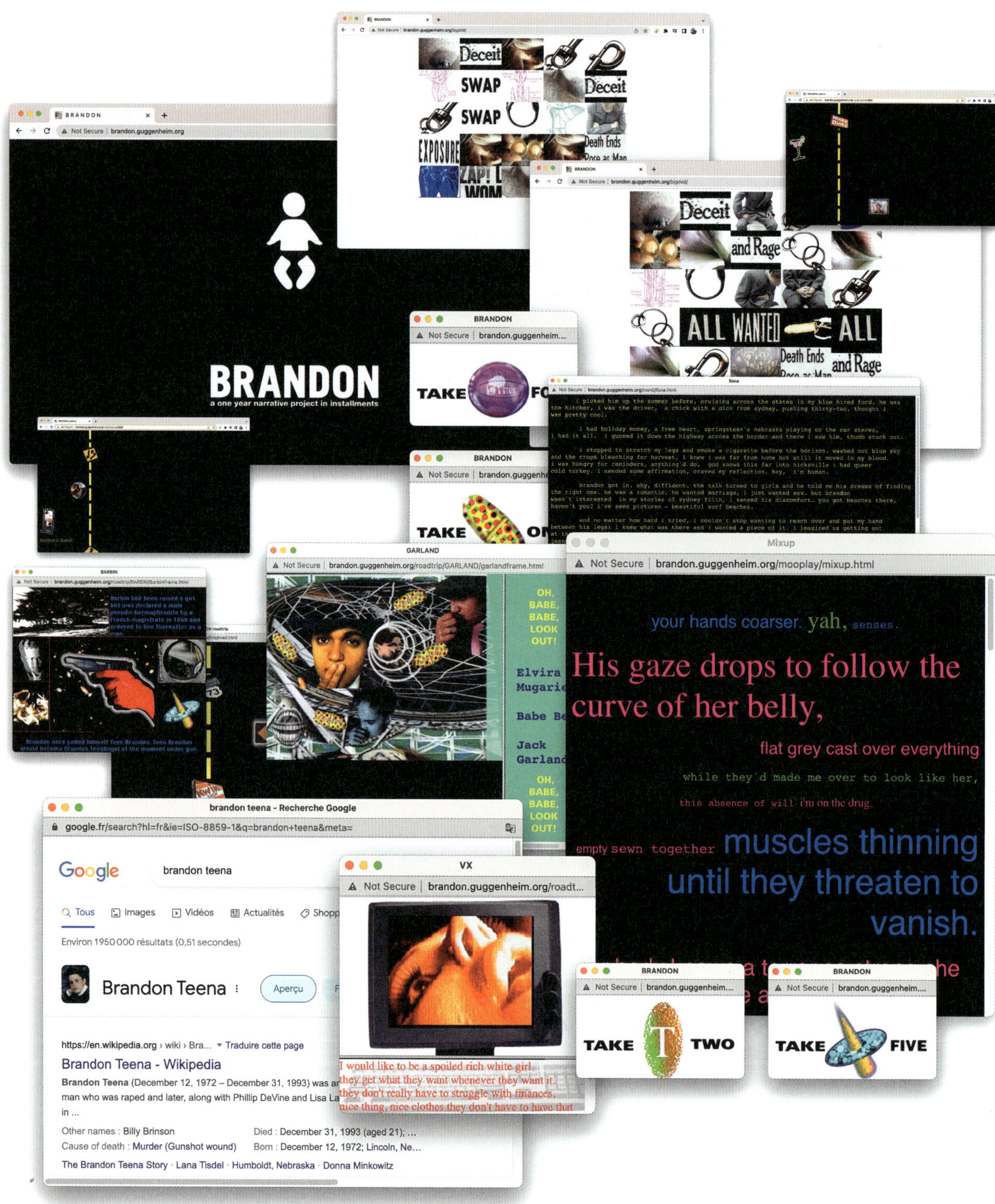

Hyper-Cruising in the Cyber-Erogenous Zone

In 1998, Taiwanese American artist Shu Lea Cheang conceived and executed *BRANDON*, the first net art commission by the Solomon R. Guggenheim Museum. Over the course of one year, Cheang created and orchestrated interfaces to probe the way transness interfaced with the history of sexuality, legality, and nascent web technologies. What initially began as research into the case of Brandon Teena, a Nebraska trans man who was sexually assaulted and killed in 1993, evolved into an expansive, multi-author project comprising five interactive web portals and public programming events.

Constructed like a click-based adventure game, *BRANDON* was a collaborative effort to map Teena's elusive trans body onto interlinked web pages and memorialize him. At a time when trans and nonbinary identities were far from visible in the public realm, it invited users to inhabit what Cheang calls the "digi-social body" by way of navigating institutionalized structures of knowledge as a form of game play while celebrating the eroticism imbued in gender and sexual nonconformity.

In the first of the five interfaces, the "bigdoll interface," the user moves the computer mouse to reveal and shuffle a grid of images. From anatomy diagrams to masculinity markers, sensationalizing media headlines to strap-on dildos, Brandon's trans-masculine body takes fluid, composite form. Completion of the bigdoll interface jumpstarts the "roadtrip interface," an animated highway decked with GIFs and hyperlinked popup windows. In this fantasy of a trans*ient queer hyper-cruising Nebraska's Route 75, the user's mouse click activates imagined flirtatious encounters with American and European trans icons, including Herculine Barbin, Jim McHarris, and Venus Xtravaganza, delivered through texts, imagery, and erotic mapping. Morphing with each user interaction, the body literally escapes legibility.

In addition to uploading Brandon to fantastical cyber-erogenous zones, the roadtrip interface functions as a central spine for *BRANDON*, further linking out to the "mooplay," "panopticon," and "Theatrum Anatomicum" interfaces. Popular in the 1990s, mooplay refers to Lambdamoo, a text-based virtual community where users could construct fictive avatars and explore gender variability. Narratives written by commissioned writers are scrambled and displayed in various colors and font sizes. Clicking on hyperlinked unknown genders—such as don-monster, Snakeboy, junkie—launches a chatbox that simulates gender-coded chat environments in online communities like Lambdamoo.

Throughout the navigation of *BRANDON*, pop-up windows featuring neon-colored pills continuously interrupt: "Take one." "Take two." Each corresponding to the five interwoven interfaces, these "sugar-coated theory pills" take the user on a dizzying, revelatory high.[1] While previous interfaces employ random sampling and poetics to explore the recombinant social body in cyberspace, "panopticon" and "Theatrum Anatomicum" deploy social-architectural metaphors to illustrate how institutions manage and control perceived sexual deviancy and gender nonconformity. Borrowing from the eighteenth-century prison designs of Jeremy Bentham and tiling them into GIF art, the "panopticon interface" instantiates virtual prison cells that measure 390 by 315 pixels. Links embedded in each window trigger a new window, forming an archaic loop of discipline and punish.

Queer theorist Jack Halberstam writes that "transgender bodies have come to represent new frontiers for state recognition, social tolerance, and flexible norms."[2] As a prefix in gendered contexts, the term "trans" attaches itself to whatever that follows, breaks open categories, and opens alternative conditions and possibilities for living. Cheang's complex vision for *BRANDON* precisely understands the trans body as a frontier that is always shifting, one that is always subjected to technical, juridical, and discursive forces. Looking at *BRANDON* now, the sugar-coated pills are time capsules, revealing a socio-techno cross-section surrounding the trans body; they are also hallucinogenics for the present and future: take a few and dive into the cyber-erogenous zone.

—Banyi Huang

◄
Shu Lea Cheang, Screenshots of *BRANDON*, 1998–99. Interactive networked code (html, Java, Javascript, and server database), Solomon R. Guggenheim Museum, New York, 2005.44

1. See http://brandon.guggenheim.org/gifts/.
2. Jack Halberstam, *Tran*: A Quick and Quirky Account of Gender Variability* (Oakland: University of California Press, 2018), 49.

36 PATRICIO MANUEL’S BOXING GLOVES, 2014–19

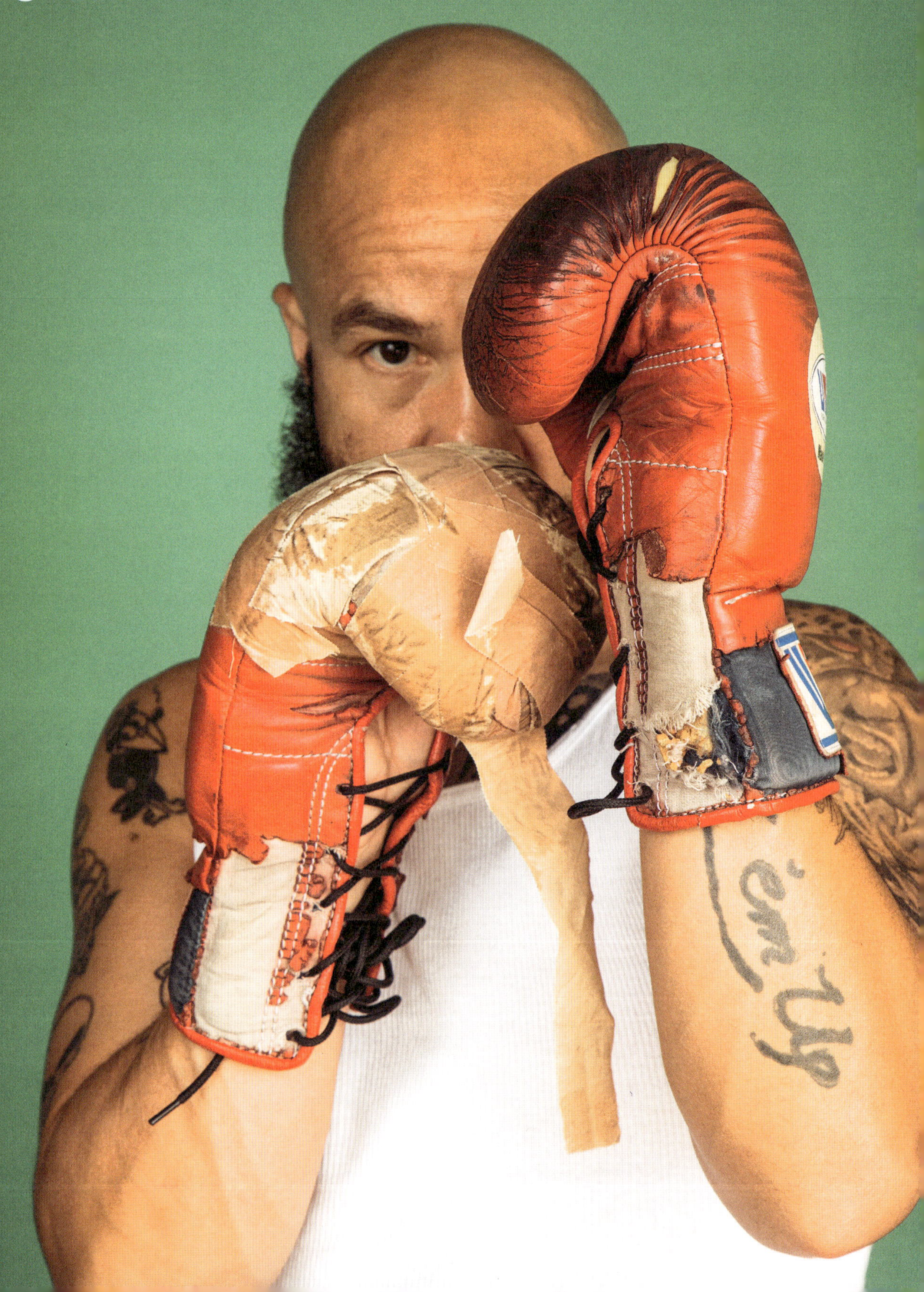

A Pair of Tools that Helped Build a New Path

For a boxer, all the training and the work to prepare for a bout comes down to what is at the end of a fighter's reach: a pair of gloves designed to protect the hands while inflicting damage on the opponent. Patricio Manuel's journey to being the first transgender man to compete and win a professional boxing match in the US began with a pair of boxing gloves that show the scars of a long voyage toward competition, respect, and acceptance.

"I'm proud that this, the sport I'm a part of, and that so many men have said 'you deserve to be here,'" Manuel said. "What continues to bring me into this sport is the affirmation. I walk through the gym, and I spend the most time not being a trans man, but just another man to people."[1]

Those gloves came into his possession at the first steps of the climb in 2014. Manuel was living in Long Beach, California then. He worked as a youth mentor at a local LGBTQ center teaching the sport that he loves while working through his transition. "I was pretty broke, and those gloves were pretty expensive," he remembered. "They [the center] helped me to get those gloves. They were with me and were part of the things I used day in and day out to get me to the point of being the first in 2018."

Those gloves helped build a new dream in place of the dream that crumbled before his transition. He was a five-time women's amateur champion. The 2012 Olympic Games in Beijing were a goal, but a defeat at the US Olympic Boxing Trials, while fighting with an injured shoulder, derailed that ambition. The next year, he started masculinizing hormone replacement therapy.

Those gloves went on a ride with him through the turbulence of being displaced from one gym because a coach "did not approve" of his gender transition. They traveled on the seventy-mile-both-ways-roundtrip drives to train in a new affirming space. They helped as Patricio Manuel pushed through the slow-but-certain process of building support and community while dealing with the physical and mental changes he was going through. "I can't look at who I am as a person today without acknowledging that the training in boxing has been a core foundation in who I am as a person," Manuel said. "I was pulled into not only the particular kind of masculinity that comes with fighters but also the toughness."

"I really just wanted to be tough," he continued. "I always appreciated the drag-out fights when people would just have wars with each other and a particular kind of grit and toughness. That became a cornerstone of who I am as a person and because of that cornerstone and my own pride of being that tough fighter when getting in the ring, it allowed me to be tough when I was growing and forming who I would be as a man." That growth and formation motivated his return to the ring as an amateur, as a man. In some of those fights, even though he was sanctioned to fight, the opponent refused to recognize this man as a man and refused to enter the ring.

Manuel trained on and pressed on to a night at Fantasy Springs Resort Casino in Indio, California. It was December 8, 2018, and Patricio Manuel was on the fight card against a seasoned pro in Hugo Aguilar. Manuel controlled the pace of the four-round bout en route to a unanimous decision, and a small pocket of derision from some hecklers in the crowd. Smiling in the post-fight interview, the winning fighter had a quick answer. "I hear some fans aren't happy," Manuel quipped. "It's OK. I'll be back. I'll make you happy then."

Today, those gloves are tired and worn, but far from forlorn. They were retired when Patricio Manuel signed an endorsement deal with boxing equipment giant Everlast in 2019. They received a deserved rest, and a place of honor because of what they mean to his personal history, and his love for the inner workings of what is known as "the sweet science."

"I don't think people really understand the level of dedication and perseverance that got to that point," he continued. "That's why those gloves mean so much to me, because they symbolize that work and all that grit that I had to endure."

—Karleigh Webb

◀
Patricio Manuel with his boxing gloves, 2022. Photo by Marcel Pardo Ariza

1. All quotes in this text are from an interview with Patricio Manuel conducted by the author for the episode "Patricio Manuel: He's Getting Ready to Rumble!" of the Outsports podcast *The Trans Sporter Room*, November 16, 2022, accessed January 21, 2023, https://podcasts.apple.com/us/podcast/the-trans-sporter-room-patricio-manuel-hes-getting/id1455161872?i=1000586402273.

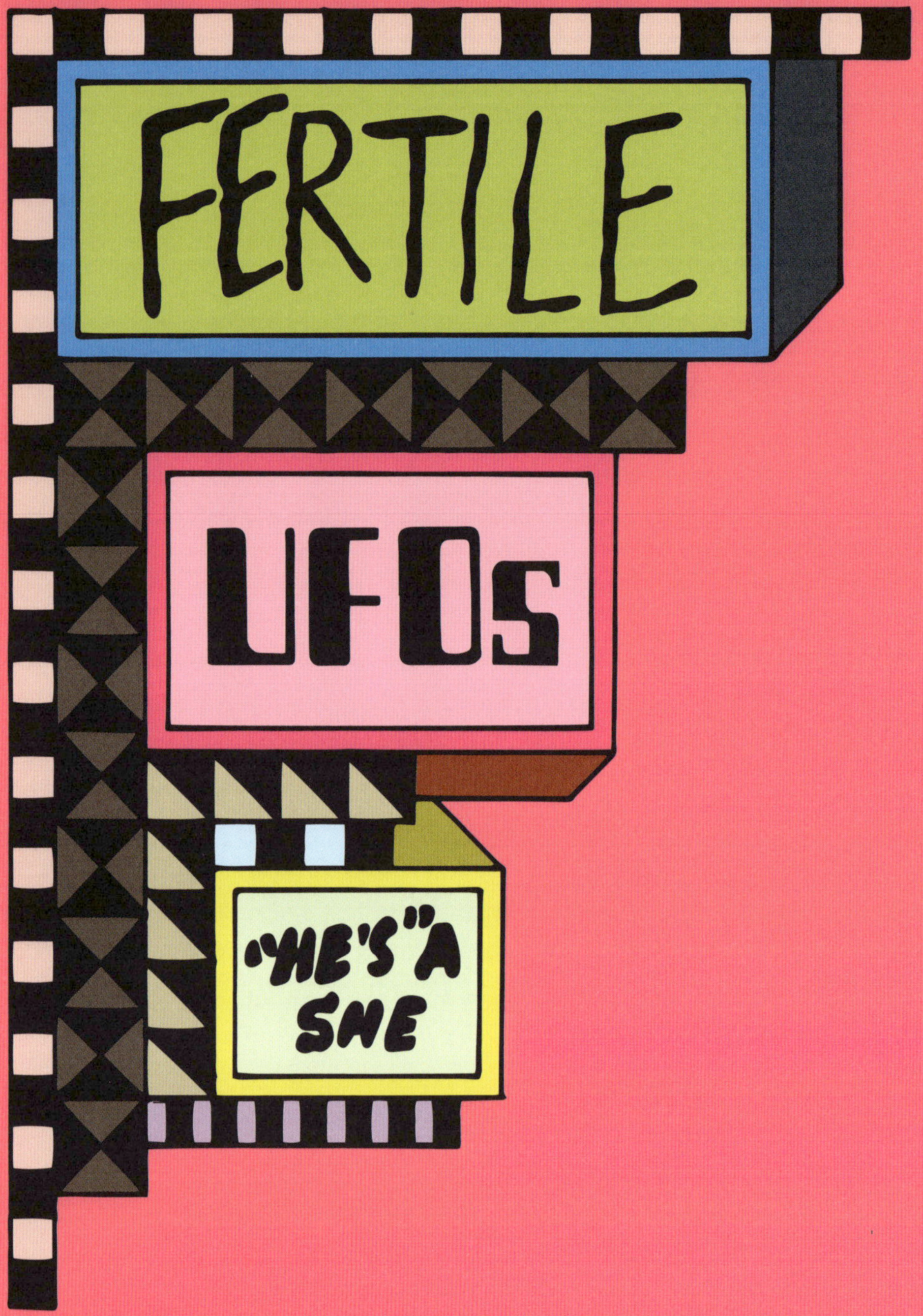
FERTILE
UFOs
"HE'S" A SHE

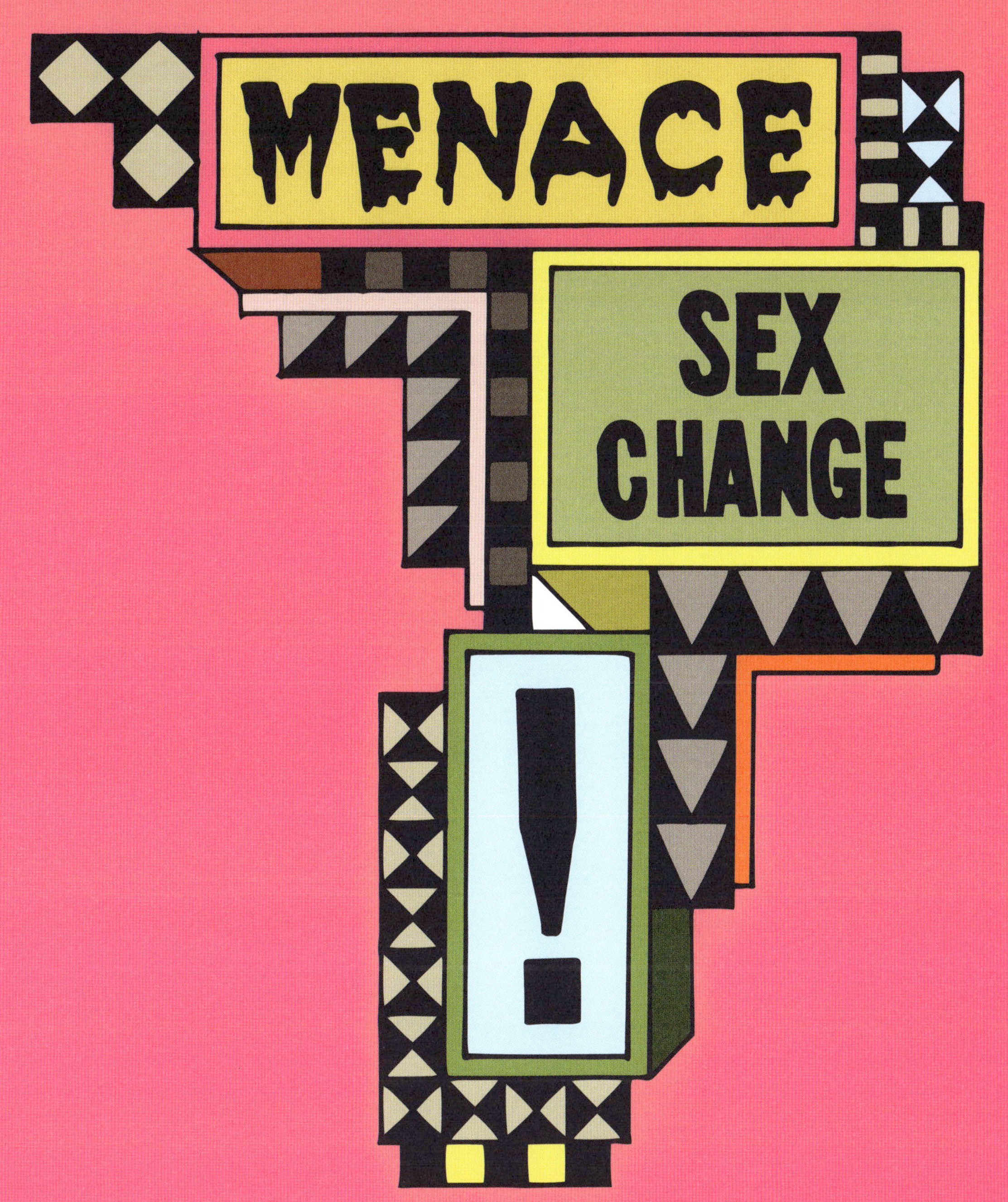

SENSATION

37 MUJERCITOS IN *ALARMA!*, 1963–86

Mujercitos is a term used first in the Mexican magazine *Alarma! Únicamente la Verdad* to designate "effeminate men." The term in Spanish plays with gender through a grammatical feminization of the male subject by masculinizing the noun used only to name females. Mujercitos, however, is feminizing not the grammatical subject, but the subject that has been assigned "male" sex at birth. *Alarma!* was the exemplary of a *nota roja* periodical, a genre of journalism that focuses on violence and is characterized by its gruesome photographs of dead bodies. Yet mujercitos are not pictured dead, burned, or mutilated, like the bodies in other photographs in *Alarma!* or in accordance with the crude reality of trans subjects in Mexico, which ranks second in the world for the most hate crimes. Instead, every month for twenty-three consecutive years (1963–86) with a print run of half a million copies (at its highest), *Alarma!* featured photographs of mujercitos posing for the camera at their own will or that of the photographer.

Their poses are elegant, sophisticated, and dignified. Mujercitos pose as fashion models, brides, or housewives. For example, the cover of an *Alarma!* from 1970 shows Lorena modeling as if it was for a high-end fashion magazine, performing a very sexualized femininity, in poses that are "flirting, suggestive and daring," according to the captions. An issue of *Alarma!* from 1979 portrays Claudia as the wife of a high-class man who belongs to the cultural elite in Mexico; she entertains the upper classes in exclusive parties at her mansion. Paulette becomes, like Dolores del Río, one of the few Latin American movie stars to succeed in Hollywood, the greatest beauty of her time. Importantly, all of these aspirational identities are linked to perceptions related to class and skin tone.

Since Spanish colonization, the perception of skin color has been a marker of class in the pigmentocratic sociocultural system of Mexico: lighter skin tonalities are associated with the ruling European upper and middle classes, while darker tones are associated with indigenousness, with lower socioeconomic status, and with exposure to racism and labor discrimination.[1] Whiteness marks the space of privilege and is a widely desired subject position. The gender performance of mujercitos in these photographs reflects their desire to access a privileged class/skin tonality position.[2] The names mujercitos adopt for themselves underscore this desire: names like Odette and Paulette sound French, allowing them to lay claim to a Europeanness that makes them sound better, whiter, and more distinguished than would Spanish names.

In the photographs of *Alarma!*, mujercitos provide for themselves an identity not of what they are but of what they might want to become. The photographs work as a site of resistance and subversion to the many forms of violence in Mexico.

—Susana Vargas Cervantes

1. For more on the pigmentocratic system in Mexico see Susana Vargas Cervantes, "Pigmentocracy and the performance of whiteness in contemporary photography: Yvonne Venegas's San Pedro Garza and Dana Lixenberg's United States," *Feminist Media Studies*, July 14, 2022, https://www.tandfonline.com/doi/full/10.1080/14680777.2022.2098795.
2. Mónica G. Moreno Figueroa, "Distributed intensities: Whiteness, mestizaje and the logics of Mexican racism," *Ethnicities* 10, no. 3 (2010): 387–401.

▸ Page from *Alarma!*, March 23, 1977. Text and photos by Francisco Rámirez Flores

"MUJERCITOS" BLASFEMOS Y CINICOS!

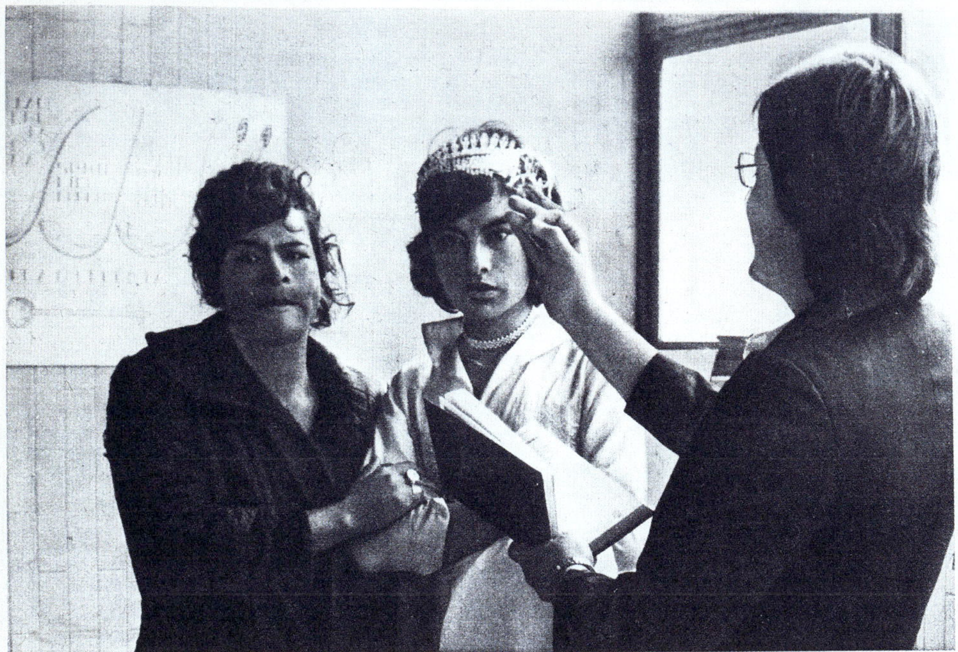

MUY SERIOS RECIBIAN LA BENDICION QUE LOS UNIA... EN LA PRISION!

CASAMIENTO DE DOS HOMOSEXUALES!

FELICES ERAN EN LA ORGIA!

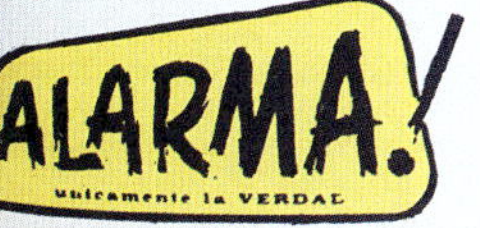

$4.00 EN TODO EL PAIS

LA AMOROSA PAREJITA DE LOS HORRIBLES

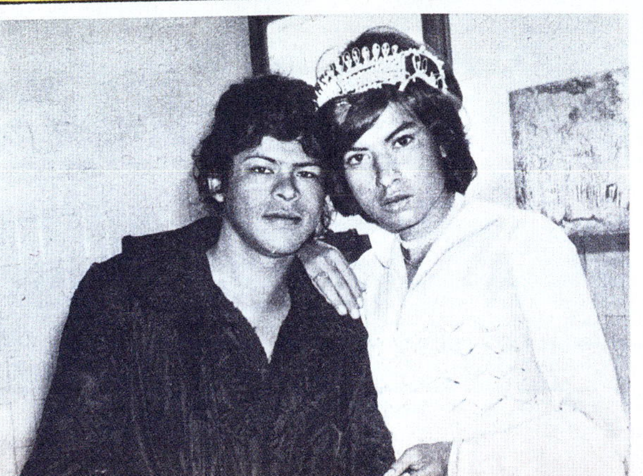

LUNA DE MIEL SUSPENDIDA!

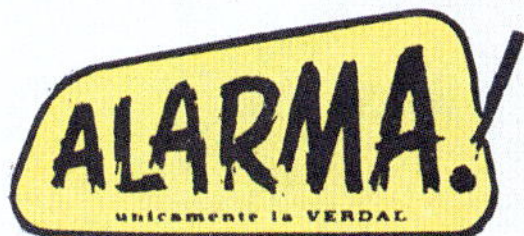

NUMERO 725

...ADEMAS DE TODO, SON "UNAS CINICOTAS!"

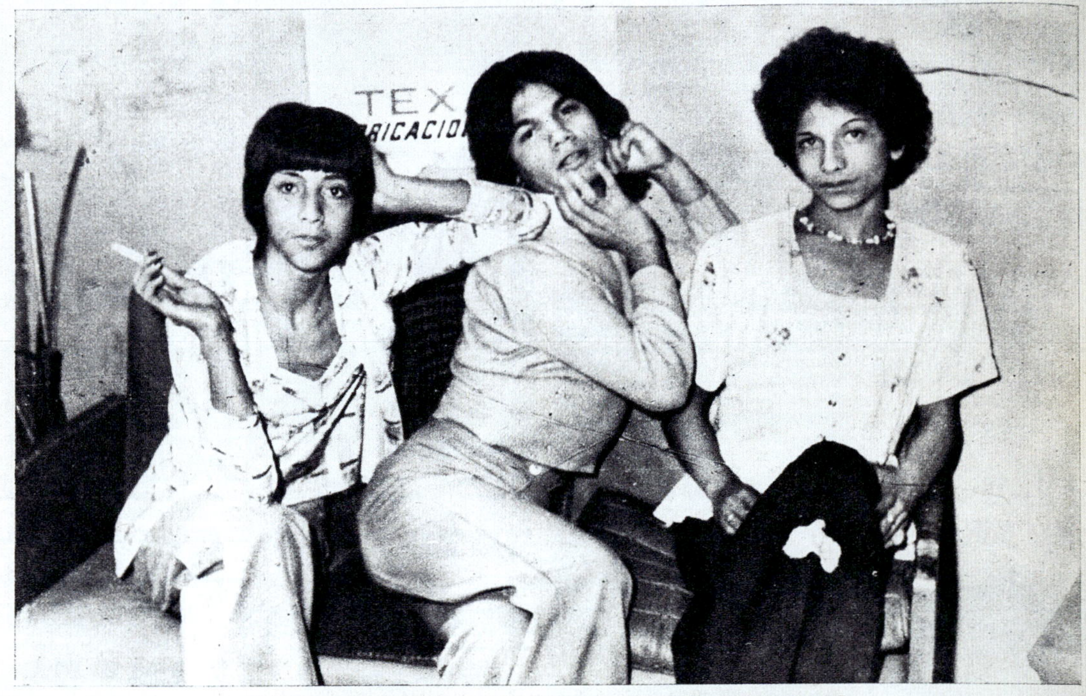

"LA YIRAN DONEY", "LA NAYELLI", "LA RAROTONGA"

Este trío de "lilos" ya está en prisión, en donde esperamos se les dé severo castigo, para evitar continúen con su inmoral actividad. Sus sobrenombres son: "Yirán Doney", "Nayelli" y "La Rarotonga".

FICHABAN EN CABARETS LOS MUJERCITOS!

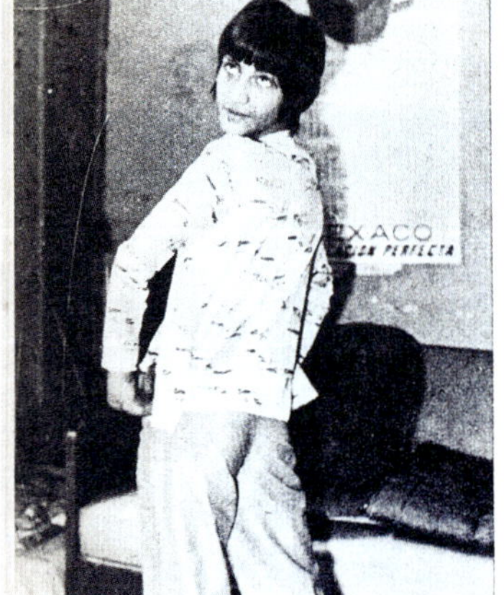

NADA DE VERGUENZA

Miguel Angel Moreno, "Yirán Doney", se siente "hermoso". Dice que no tiene cuerpo, pero "sí linda cara" (?). Ahora está tras las rejas por sus inmorales actividades.

ZAMORA, Mich.— Las autoridades policiacas iniciaron una campaña tendiente a erradicar a los sujetos que reniegan de su sexo y que se visten como mujeres, a fin de engañar a clientes que se dan cita en los distintos antros de vicio de la zona de tolerancia de esta población.

En la primera "razzia" efectuada por la policía local, se logró la captura de varios de estos invertidos, como son: Miguel Angel Moreno (a) "Yirán Doney", Raúl Sánchez (a) "Nayelli", J. Jesús Vázquez Pérez (a) "La Rarotonga" y otro que dijo llamarse Gonzalo Fernández.

Cabe mencionarse que a "Yirán Doney" y a "Nayelli" se les capturó cuando "fichaban" en el prostíbulo de Ignacio García Alfaro, conocido como "Nacho el Terrible". Precisamente, el agente segundo del Ministerio Público giró orden de aprehensión en contra de este último, acusado de lenón, pues se supo también que los "lilos" que "trabajan" en su antro de vicio, son menores de edad.

Los detenidos, por su parte, informaron al corresponsal de ALARMA! que Miguel Angel Moreno ("Yirán Doney"), es originario de San Luis Río Colorado, Sonora; Raúl Ramírez Sánchez, ("Nayelli") de Apatzingán, Michoacán; y Rarotonga" es de esta ciudad.

Todos ellos se encuentran tra rejas, pero con cinismo dijeron esta situación no les preocup pues "tan luego logremos sal libertad, volveremos a ej nuestra 'profesión' ".

Indudablemente la intenció las autoridades es sumamente tiva, pero consideramos que campaña se debe intensificar y más dictar severos castigos c los degenerados, a fin de que se ga coto a sus inmorales activid (Escribió: Guillermo Váz Razo).

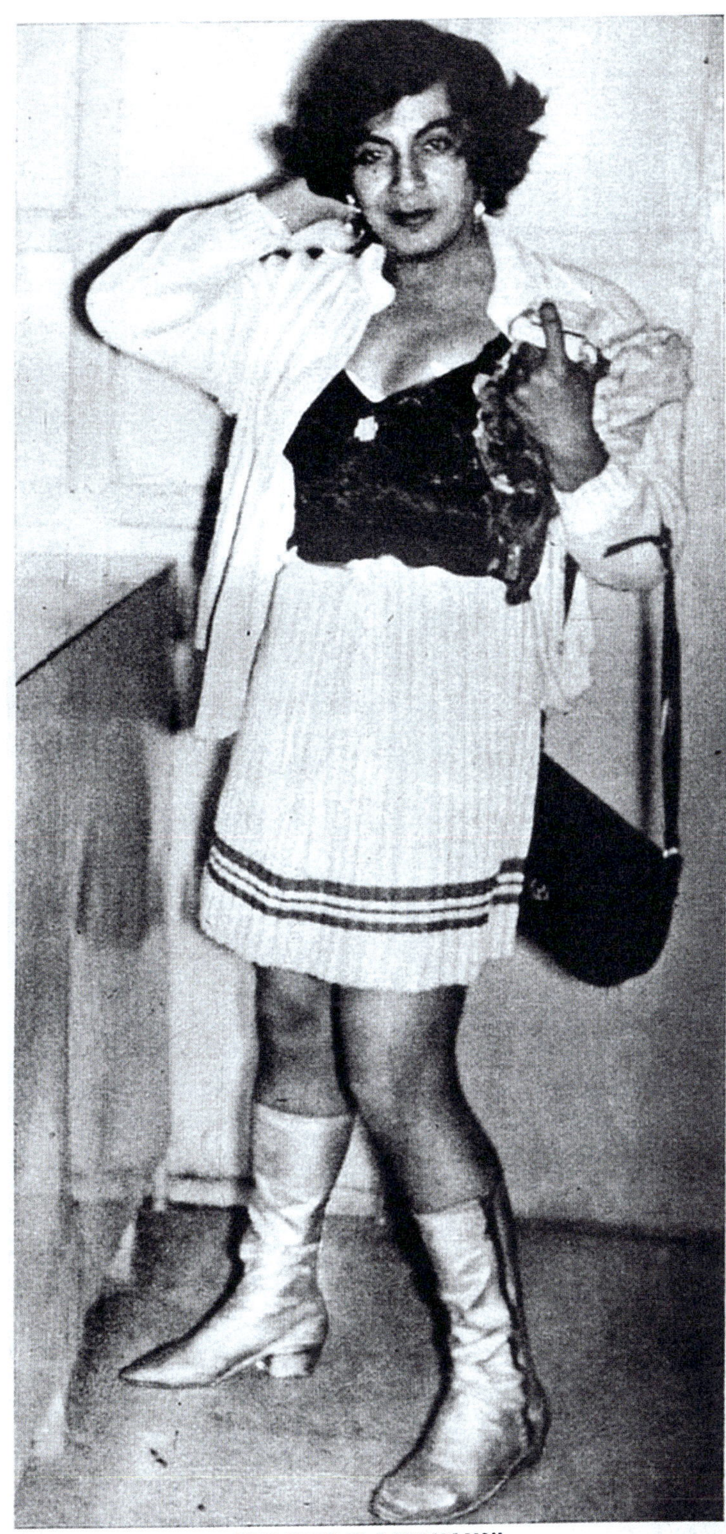

◀
Page from *Alarma!*, June 2, 1976. Text and photos by Guillermo Vázquez Razo

▶
Detail from *Alarma!*, April 28, 1971. Text and photo by David Medrano Gómez

LE DICEN "LA WANANI"

Le pusieron el nombre de Armando Martínez del Valle cuando nació y fue llevado a la pila bautismal porque vieron que era hombre. No sabían que con el correr del tiempo preferiría considerarse una "mujercita" a la que conocen como "La Wanani". (Información completa en la página No. 34).

38 TOURMALINE, *MARY OF ILL FAME*, 2020–21

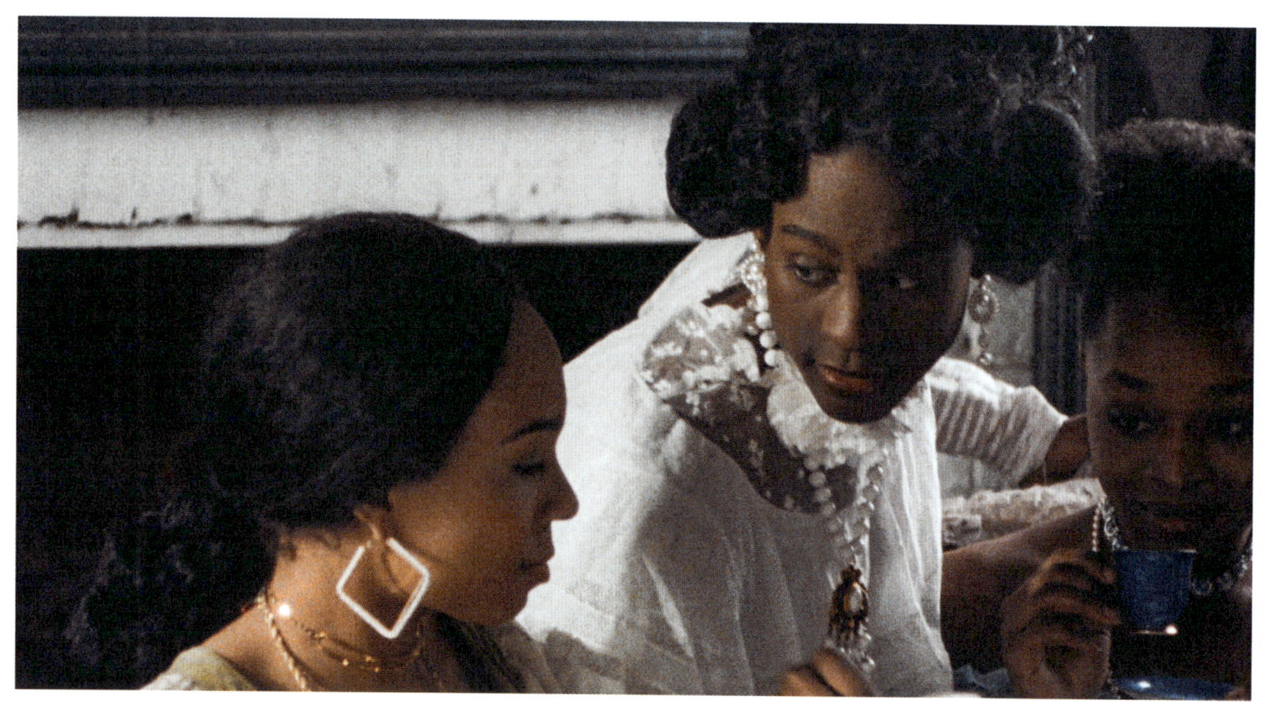

▲
(and following spread) Tourmaline, Stills from *Mary of Ill Fame*, 2020–21. 16 mm, sound, 17 min., 14 sec. Edition of 5 plus II AP.

Anything We Want to Be

In the short film *Mary of Ill Fame* (2020–21) by Tourmaline, set in the 1830s, Mary Jones (1830–unknown) is transported from downtown Manhattan where she lived before being tried for stealing a man's wallet, to Seneca Village, a community of free Black and Irish immigrant landowners located in what we now call Central Park.[1] When the city destroyed the village through eminent domain, all traces of the settlement were lost to history. Tourmaline's choice to set the film in Seneca Village was not only a feat of imagination—as Jones is not known to have found refuge there—but a political feat of class solidarity: then, as now, women accused of thieving and making their money through sex were not always welcome by landowners, whatever their race.

During a dreamlike sequence in which Jones (played by Rowin Amone) is seen behind bars, the film moves forward in time. A shot of the water that surrounds Castle Williams—just south of Manhattan, where Jones was imprisoned—transitions to the lapping banks of Manhattan's West Side. Through archival footage, we witness Sylvia Rivera, who once stayed at the Christopher Street Piers, a refuge for queer and trans homeless folks before gentrification and displacement, laughing and gossiping with friends as she reflects on the Hudson River. She says, "Every time you look at that damn river and meditate on the river you got to keep fighting, girly, 'cause it's not time for you to cross the River Jordan." As Rivera analogizes the Hudson to the Jordan, evoking the Biblical journey to freedom and resurrection, the video returns to Jones and those who remain warehoused with her, as if Rivera were speaking backward in time, across the river to her foresister.

Just as historical time moves without linear progression, the narrative time of *Mary of Ill Fame* ebbs and flows so that the words with which Jones begins seem to touch her last utterances. The film opens with a refrain from *The People Could Fly*, a collection of African American folktales for children retold by Virginia Hamilton and illustrated by Leo and Diane Dillon. "They say the people could fly. Say that long ago in Africa, some of the people knew magic. And they would walk up on the air like climbin up on a gate."[2] Belief overwhelms circumstance.

Jones made what Tourmaline has called "a way out of no way," an evocation that at once recalls the language of spirit and belief as well as what cultural historian Saidiya Hartman describes as "critical fabulation"—an approach to narration in which the building blocks of a story are broken down.[3] In *Mary*, Tourmaline juxtaposes divergent viewpoints in a variety of ways: split screens; montages that flow from the documentary grain of archival video to the lush purples and oranges of period narrative; layered images of waterscapes, the face of the moon, and the sun's flashes; and captions that sync in and out of describing the visuals with which they are paired. Incommensurable textures and asymmetrical scales rub up against one another to create a sense of friction that reanimates the past in the present to tell the story of one impossible woman.

—Thomas (T.) Jean Lax

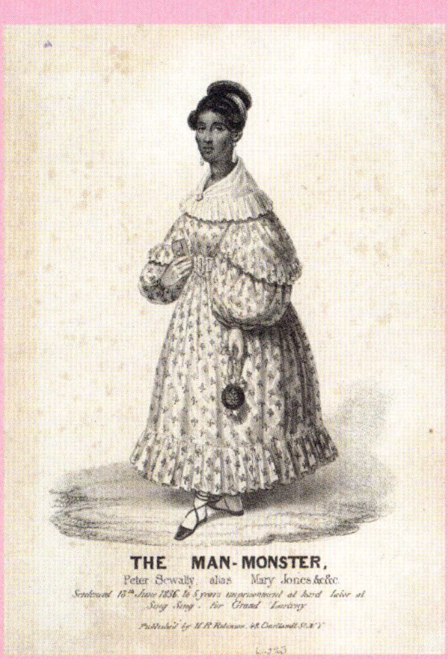

Henry R. Robinson, *The Man-Monster*, 1936. Lithograph, 15½ × 11½ in. (39.4 × 29.2 cm). Harry T. Peters "America on Stone" Lithography Collection, National Museum of American History, Smithsonian Institution, 60.2363

1. Tourmaline produced an earlier version of this work titled *Salacia* (2019).
2. Virginia Hamilton, "The People Could Fly," in *The People Could Fly: American Black Folktales* (New York: Alfred A. Knopf, 1985), 166.
3. Saidiya Hartman, "Venus in Two Acts," *Small Axe* 12, no. 2 (June 2008): 1–14.

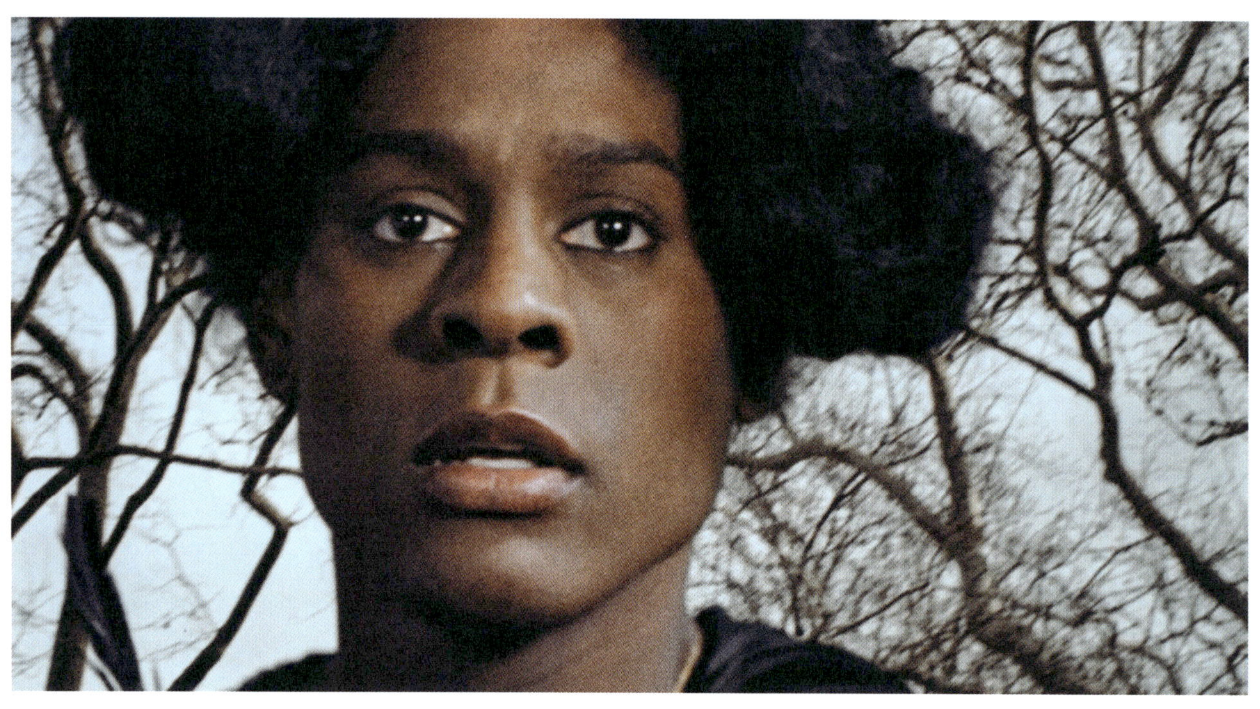

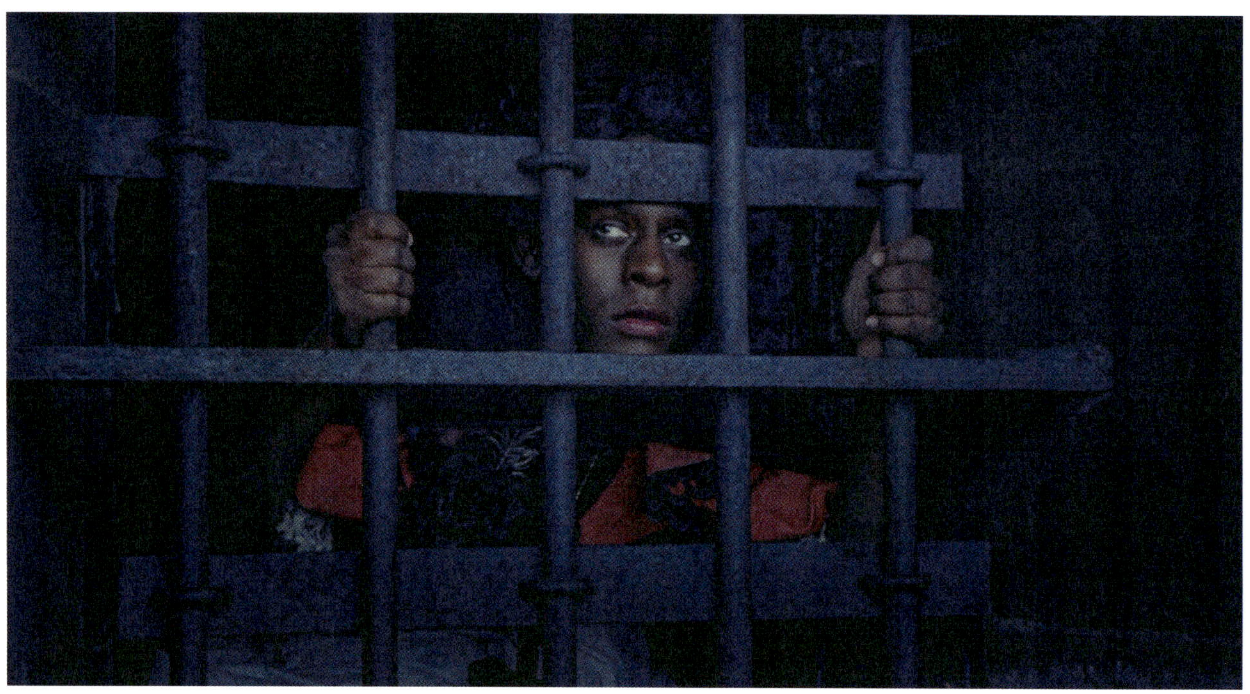

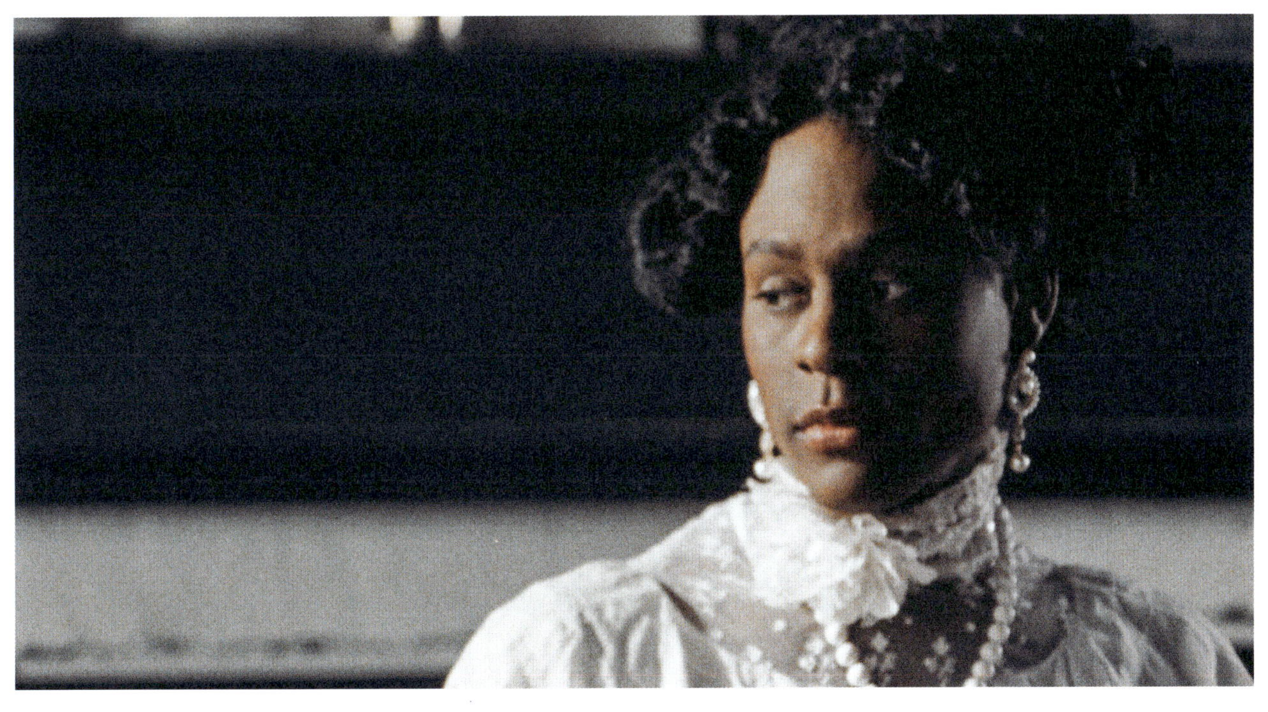

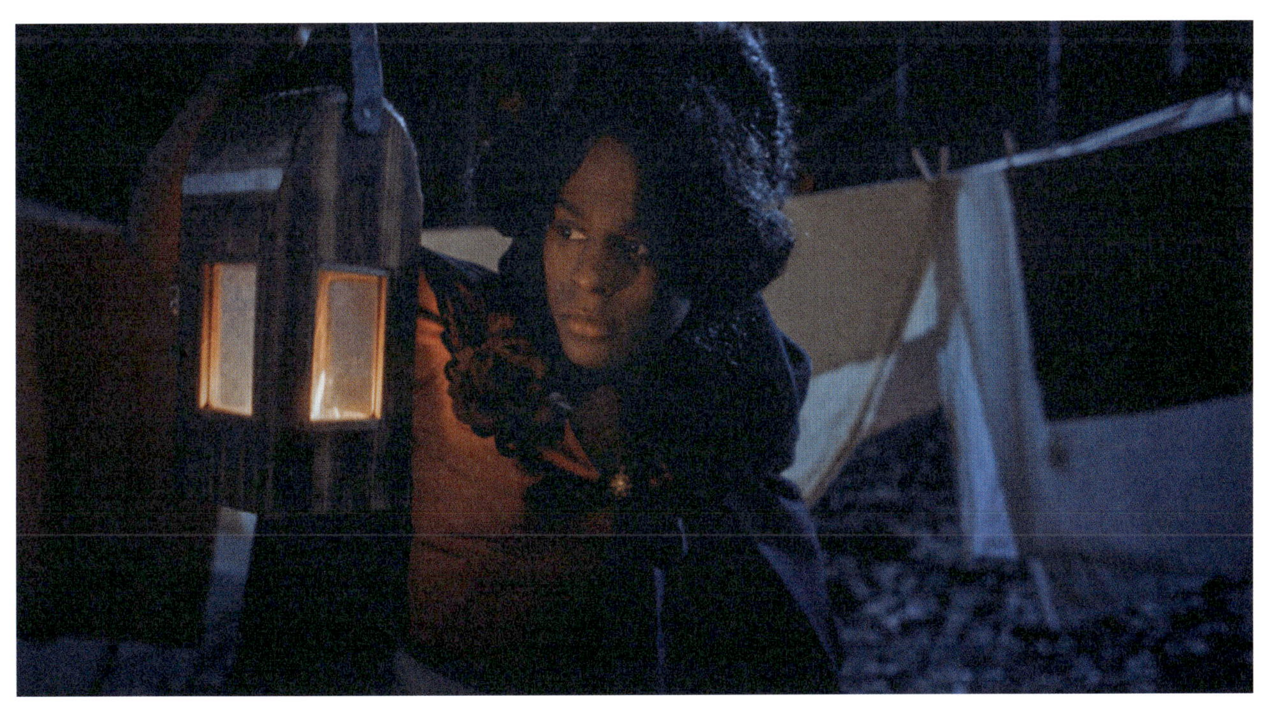

39 HARRY ALLEN'S BOWLER HAT, c. 1900

Most men in the late nineteenth- and early twentieth centuries did not attract the attention of newspapers unless they were very wealthy or very powerful. Harry Allen was neither. Born in Indiana—probably South Bend—in 1882, Allen, who also went by Harry Livingstone, came from humble beginnings and led a short but retrospectively very noteworthy life. Allen was trans, but this only accounted for a small part of why newspapers all over the country reported on his escapades between sometime around 1900 and his death in 1922.

I. THE LATEST-STYLE DERBY HAT

Unlike many trans people who lived during the nineteenth century in happy, or sometimes not-so-happy, obscurity, Allen left a robust public record of his life. Between 1900 and 1911, stories about Allen's life appeared in newspapers in more than fifteen different states, from Allen's domicile of Washington state to Philadelphia, where Allen himself, as far as we know, had never visited. To read these reports is to simultaneously experience what was newsworthy in early twentieth-century United States and glimpse what reporters found newsworthy about Harry Allen in particular. Contrary to what we might expect the fact that Harry Allen had intentionally elected to live as a man was really only a small portion of what seemed to interest reporters. No, it was *the kind of man* that Harry was that fascinated journalists and readers. Importantly, Harry's style received the lion's share of attention in news reports. According to an article reprinted in *The Buffalo Evening News* in 1900, Harry "... always dresses fashionably, wears the latest style Derby hat, alternates between a sack and a cutaway coat and is careful to have a pronounced crease in [his] trousers."[1] Even a police officer who would later arrest Allen remarked on his style, telling reporters that Allen was "a sporty gentleman."[2]

II. FISTIC ENCOUNTERS

Boxing was a popular sport in the late 1800s and early 1900s in major urban areas, but just because it was popular did not mean it was legal. Indeed, prizefighting tended to sit on the edge of behaviors that, then and now, are gathered under the umbrella of *vice*: gambling, sex work, prizefighting. That prizefighting, as a behavior, was exclusively available to men during this time probably doesn't need to be said, and Harry Allen had enjoyed a number of successes in the Seattle prizefighting scene; "very agile and wiry," he distinguished himself as a force to be reckoned with in the ring.[3] Allen however, was not only a participant; he was also a boxing enthusiast. According to newspapers, Allen "attends all the prize fights and *fistic encounters* in Seattle."[4]

III. PAPER BALLS

Despite his style in and out of the ring, Allen could not escape the criminalization to which trans people have always been subject in the United States. He spent much of his adulthood in and out of jails, frequently being arrested, if not also charged, for wearing "male attire," despite the lack of any laws in Washington state that prohibited the wearing of clothes understood to be proper to the "opposite" sex. Harry had "repeatedly been arrested, ostensibly for creating a disturbance of the peace, but really for wearing the wrong clothes," but attracted later scrutiny from police after a series of romantic affairs he conducted with local socialites that apparently ended in either suicide or suicide attempts by his spurned paramours.[5] While reports by scholars and trans history enthusiasts tend to make much out of these stories, titillating as they appear to our modern-day eyes, a closer look at the record of Allen's life is difficult to romanticize. Allen, known for his jack-of-all-trades

1. "Odd Occupations for Young Woman [*sic*], Nellie Pickerell of Indiana Discards Feminine Pursuits and Takes to Occupations of Men," *Buffalo Evening News*, June 6, 1900.
2. "Odd Occupations."
3. "In Boy's Apparel, Nellie Pickerell Makes Masquerade," *The Washington Standard*, July 6, 1900.
4. "In Boy's Apparel" 1. Emphasis added by the author.
5. "Odd Occupations."
6. "Odd Occupations."
7. "Odd Occupations."

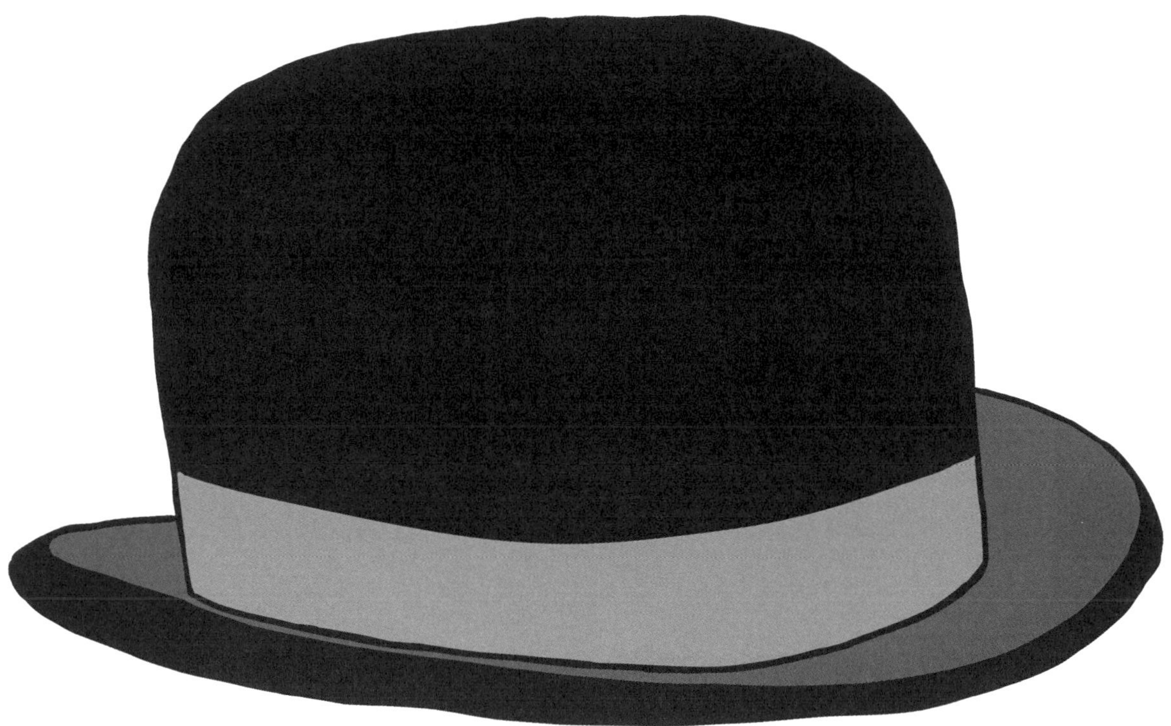

career trajectory—he was a ranch hand, then a bartender, then a tailor, then a night watchman, and probably had many other jobs—was repeatedly fired or refused work when his employers learned that he had been assigned female at birth. And Allen's hobbies—prizefighting, bike racing, and hanging out in barbershops, "joshing the barber," all understood to be the pastimes of working-class white men of his era—were all criminalized or only marginally legal, leaving him vulnerable to arrest.[6] According to the newspapers that followed his exploits with such avidity, however, Allen still eluded capture here and there. One report, for example, details the story of yet another close brush with the law, wherein one "Policeman Cameron" tried to capture and arrest Allen. Allen got away, and the policeman "fired two shots in [his] direction." The story ends triumphantly, detailing that Allen, with roguish bravery, "took no more notice of the bullets than if they had been paper balls."[7]

—Greta LaFleur

40 BILLY TIPTON, *BILLY TIPTON PLAYS HI-FI ON PIANO*, 1957

Two leaning modelesque women flank a suited fellow sitting behind piano keys. The man gazes upward, hands at the ready, pocket square detail peeking out to say hello, school picture-day smirk barely touching on his forty-three years.

Billy Tipton has been in the ether for as long as I can remember. I first saw the cover of *Billy Tipton Plays Hi-Fi on Piano* (1957) during a particularly desperate moment in ye olden days of trans-Googling. Actually, since it was the early 2000s, I was probably Asking Jeeves. What I queried Jeeves for specifically were websites that showed me a cache of "famous trans men," or proved that "trans guys in history," existed. *Anything* to link my experience to some sort of historical radar blip in pop culture, darling. My memory from this moment, which is not at all reliable, starts with a GeoCities website. Up popped a string of gyrating, low-resolution musical notes. Billy Tipton's name blinked front and center, with an oversaturated scan of a record album cover. Below it, facts lie next to bullet points: *Stealth trans man. Father of three adopted sons. Married five times. Successful jazz musician active in the 1940s and 1950s. Died from an untreated stomach ulcer. Outed after death.*

What happened to Billy Tipton after he died in 1989, penniless and in the arms of his youngest son, is nothing short of a wild reimagination of his career. With his posthumous outing by the coroner to the local press—or was it the EMT, or his most recent ex-wife?—Tipton's story blew up on a national scale and became fodder for talk show circuits and *Star* magazine exposés, using language we've left in the 1990s for good reason. But with this grand exposure on his life after death, Tipton went from regional, working-class jazz musician to larger-than-life artist, a touchstone for some queer and trans people. While he was alive Tipton never got too famous (some argue by choice), but he worked hard, rose out of Depression-era Oklahoma City, and toured doing what he loved. He eventually became a bandleader, founded the Billy Tipton Trio, and played until arthritis forced him to transition to a quiet desk job in Spokane, Washington. He aged in solitude, ephemera from his heyday kept in scrapbooks alongside stacks of black-and-white promotional glossies.

What physically remains of Billy Tipton is this record, one of two he recorded for Tops Records. While Tipton wrote and performed the occasional original song, the songs on these albums are exclusively covers. In the 1950s, Tops released popular hits covered by relatively unknown session musicians to sell at gas stations and five-and-dimes. Priced at only 39 cents, a Tops record was a deal compared to 79 cents for an album by a major label. My favorite part of this album, besides the biography on the back (rumored to have been written by Tipton himself and where he shaves five years off his age) is the cover photo! I imagine Billy Tipton played art director at this moment, requesting not one model but two. He looks up to one of the women with adoration, a willing audience. While the album cover image may look like camp today, Billy Tipton felt he was serving the highest levels of masculinity and class—exactly how he wanted to be seen, and how he hoped to be remembered.

—Amos Mac

▸
Billy Tipton, *Billy Tipton Plays Hi-Fi on Piano*, 1957. Released by Tops Records, Los Angeles

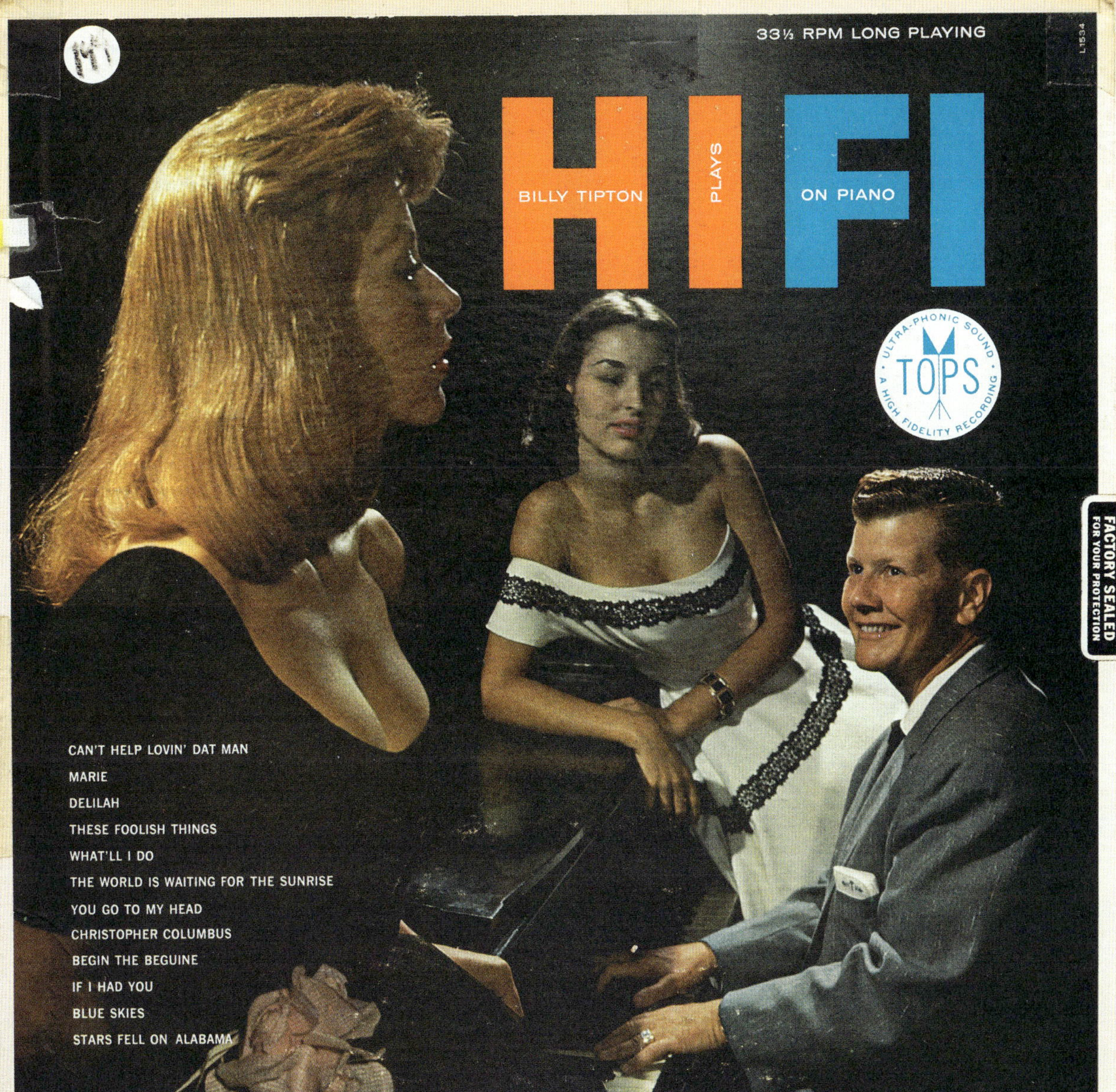
33⅓ RPM LONG PLAYING
L1534
HI FI
BILLY TIPTON
PLAYS
ON PIANO
ULTRA-PHONIC SOUND
TOPS
A HIGH FIDELITY RECORDING
FACTORY SEALED
FOR YOUR PROTECTION
CAN'T HELP LOVIN' DAT MAN
MARIE
DELILAH
THESE FOOLISH THINGS
WHAT'LL I DO
THE WORLD IS WAITING FOR THE SUNRISE
YOU GO TO MY HEAD
CHRISTOPHER COLUMBUS
BEGIN THE BEGUINE
IF I HAD YOU
BLUE SKIES
STARS FELL ON ALABAMA

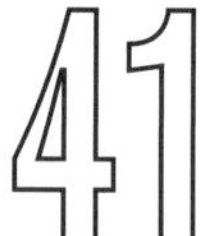

CHRIS E. VARGAS, *TRANSVESTISM IN THE NEWS*, 2015

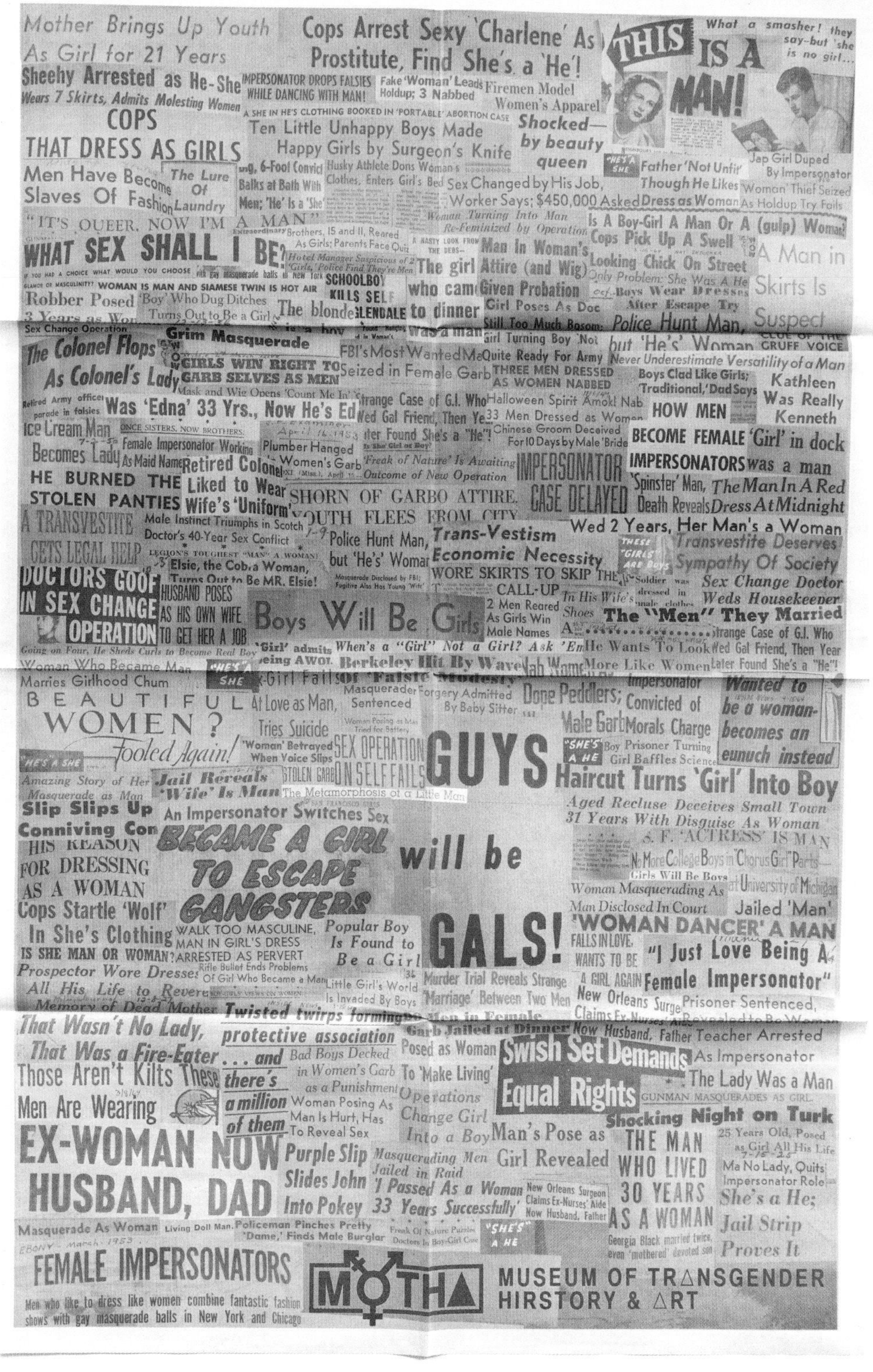

Mother Brings Up Youth As Girl for 21 Years
Cops Arrest Sexy 'Charlene' As Prostitute, Find She's a 'He'!
THIS IS A MAN!
What a smasher! they say–but 'she is no girl...
Sheehy Arrested as He-She
Wears 7 Skirts, Admits Molesting Women
IMPERSONATOR DROPS FALSIES WHILE DANCING WITH MAN!
Fake 'Woman' Leads Holdup; 3 Nabbed
Firemen Model Women's Apparel
A SHE IN HE'S CLOTHING BOOKED IN 'PORTABLE' ABORTION CASE
COPS THAT DRESS AS GIRLS
Ten Little Unhappy Boys Made Happy Girls by Surgeon's Knife
Shocked—by beauty queen
Men Have Become Slaves Of Fashion
The Lure Of Laundry
Husky Athlete Dons Woman's Clothes, Enters Girl's Bed
Father 'Not Unfit' Though He Likes Dress as Woman
Jap Girl Duped By Impersonator
Sex Changed by His Job, Worker Says; $450,000 Asked
'Woman' Thief Seized As Holdup Try Fails
"IT'S QUEER, NOW I'M A MAN"
Woman Turning Into Man Re-Feminized by Operation
Is A Boy-Girl A Man Or A (gulp) Woman
WHAT SEX SHALL I BE?
Brothers, 15 and 11, Reared As Girls; Parents Face Quiz
Hotel Manager Suspicious of 2 'Girls,' Police Find They're Men
Cops Pick Up A Swell Looking Chick On Street
A Man in Skirts Is Suspect
WOMAN IS MAN AND SIAMESE TWIN IS HOT AIR
SCHOOLBOY KILLS SELF
The girl who came to dinner
Man In Woman's Attire (and Wig) Given Probation
Only Problem: She Was A He
Robber Posed
'Boy' Who Dug Ditches Turns Out to Be a Girl
The blonde
Boys Wear Dresses After Escape Try
Girl Poses As Doc
Still Too Much Bosom: Girl Turning Boy 'Not Quite Ready For Army
Police Hunt Man, but 'He's' Woman
CLUE OF THE GRUFF VOICE
Grim Masquerade
The Colonel Flops As Colonel's Lady
GIRLS WIN RIGHT TO GARB SELVES AS MEN
FBI's Most Wanted Man Seized in Female Garb
Never Underestimate Versatility of a Man
THREE MEN DRESSED AS WOMEN NABBED
Boys Clad Like Girls; 'Traditional,' Dad Says
Kathleen Was Really Kenneth
Mask and Wig Opens 'Count Me In'
Was 'Edna' 33 Yrs., Now He's Ed
Strange Case of G.I. Who Wed Gal Friend, Then Years Later Found She's a "He"!
Halloween Spirit Amok! Nab 33 Men Dressed as Women
HOW MEN BECOME FEMALE IMPERSONATORS
Ice Cream Man Becomes Lady
ONCE SISTERS, NOW BROTHERS
Female Impersonator Working As Maid Named
Plumber Hanged Women's Garb
Chinese Groom Deceived For 10 Days by Male 'Bride'
'Girl' in dock was a man
Retired Colonel Liked to Wear Wife's 'Uniform'
'Freak of Nature' Is Awaiting Outcome of New Operation
IMPERSONATOR CASE DELAYED
'Spinster' Man, Death Reveals
The Man In A Red Dress At Midnight
HE BURNED THE STOLEN PANTIES
SHORN OF GARBO ATTIRE, YOUTH FLEES FROM CITY
A TRANSVESTITE GETS LEGAL HELP
Male Instinct Triumphs in Scotch Doctor's 40-Year Sex Conflict
Police Hunt Man, but 'He's' Woman
Trans-Vestism Economic Necessity
Wed 2 Years, Her Man's a Woman
Transvestite Deserves Sympathy Of Society
Elsie, the Cobra Woman, Turns Out to Be MR. Elsie!
WORE SKIRTS TO SKIP THE CALL-UP
DOCTORS GOOF IN SEX CHANGE OPERATION
HUSBAND POSES AS HIS OWN WIFE TO GET HER A JOB
Boys Will Be Girls
2 Men Reared As Girls Win Male Names
Soldier was dressed in female clothes
Sex Change Doctor Weds Housekeeper
The "Men" They Married
Strange Case of G.I. Who Wed Gal Friend, Then Year Later Found She's a "He"!
Going on Four, He Sheds Curls to Become Real Boy
'Girl' admits being AWOL
When's a "Girl" Not a Girl? Ask 'Em
He Wants To Look More Like Women
Berkeley Hit By Wave of 'False' Modesty
Woman Who Became Man Marries Girlhood Chum
Girl Fails At Love as Man, Tries Suicide
Masquerader Sentenced
Forgery Admitted By Baby Sitter
Dope Peddlers; Male Garb
Impersonator Convicted of Morals Charge
Wanted to be a woman–becomes an eunuch instead
BEAUTIFUL WOMEN? Fooled Again!
'Woman' Betrayed When Voice Slips
SEX OPERATION ON SELF FAILS
GUYS
Boy Prisoner Turning Girl Baffles Science
Amazing Story of Her Masquerade as Man
Jail Reveals 'Wife' Is Man
STOLEN GARB
The Metamorphosis of a Little Man
Haircut Turns 'Girl' Into Boy
Slip Slips Up
Aged Recluse Deceives Small Town 31 Years With Disguise As Woman
Conniving Con
An Impersonator Switches Sex
HIS REASON FOR DRESSING AS A WOMAN
BECAME A GIRL TO ESCAPE GANGSTERS
will be
S. F. 'ACTRESS' IS MAN
No More College Boys in 'Chorus Girl' Parts
Girls Will Be Boys
Woman Masquerading As Man Disclosed In Court
at University of Michigan
Jailed 'Man'
Cops Startle 'Wolf' In She's Clothing
WALK TOO MASCULINE, MAN IN GIRL'S DRESS ARRESTED AS PERVERT
Popular Boy Is Found to Be a Girl
GALS!
'WOMAN DANCER' A MAN
FALLS IN LOVE, WANTS TO BE A GIRL AGAIN
"I Just Love Being A Female Impersonator"
IS SHE MAN OR WOMAN?
Rifle Bullet Ends Problems Of Girl Who Became a Man
Prospector Wore Dresses All His Life to Revere Memory of Dead Mother
Little Girl's World Is Invaded By Boys
Murder Trial Reveals Strange 'Marriage' Between Two Men
New Orleans Surgeon Claims Ex-Nurses' Aide Now Husband, Father
Prisoner Sentenced, Revealed to Be Woman
That Wasn't No Lady, That Was a Fire-Eater
Twisted twirps forming protective association ... and there's a million of them
Men in Female Garb Jailed at Dinner
Teacher Arrested As Impersonator
Those Aren't Kilts These Men Are Wearing
Bad Boys Decked in Women's Garb as a Punishment
Posed as Woman To 'Make Living'
Swish Set Demands Equal Rights
The Lady Was a Man
GUNMAN MASQUERADES AS GIRL
Woman Posing As Man Is Hurt, Has To Reveal Sex
Operations Change Girl Into a Boy
Shocking Night on Turk
EX-WOMAN NOW HUSBAND, DAD
Purple Slip Slides John Into Pokey
Masquerading Men Jailed in Raid
'I Passed As a Woman 33 Years Successfully'
Man's Pose as Girl Revealed
THE MAN WHO LIVED 30 YEARS AS A WOMAN
25 Years Old, Posed as Girl All His Life
Ma No Lady, Quits Impersonator Role
She's a He; Jail Strip Proves It
Georgia Black married twice, even 'mothered' devoted son
Masquerade As Woman
Living Doll Man
Policeman Pinches Pretty 'Dame,' Finds Male Burglar
Freak Of Nature Puzzles Doctors In Boy-Girl Case
'SHE'S A HE'
EBONY March 1953
FEMALE IMPERSONATORS
Men who like to dress like women combine fantastic fashion shows with gay masquerade balls in New York and Chicago
MOTHA
MUSEUM OF TRANSGENDER HIRSTORY & ART

Reading Between the Headlines

This poster by Chris E. Vargas of collaged headlines provides a panorama of how transgender people were portrayed in the trashy tabloids of the mid-twentieth century sensationalist press. And even if the stories are exaggerated fictions, they represent what mainstream culture was titillated by or willing to believe about people whose gender identity or presentation did not conform to their anatomy:

They are deceitful...
Amazing Story of Her Masquerade as Man
The Man Who Lived 30 Years as a Woman

Even in marriage.
Wed 2 Years, Her Man's a Woman
Strange Case of G.I. Who Wed Gal Friend,
Then Years later Found She's a "He"!

They are criminal...
Cops Arrest Sexy 'Charlene' As Prostitute,
Find She's a 'He'!
Jail Reveals 'Wife' Is Man

Unpatriotic...
Wore Skirts To Skip The Call-Up
'Girl' Admits Being AWOL

Unstable...
Rifle Bullet Ends Problems Of Girl
Who Became a Man Found Hanging in
Women's (Clothes)

Pushy...
Swish Set Demands Equal Rights
Twisted twirps forming protective
association ... and there's a million of them

And they could be anywhere.
Aged Recluse Deceives Small Town 31
Years With Disguise As Woman
'Boy' Who Dug Ditches Turns Out to
Be a Girl

◀
Chris E. Vargas, *Transvestism in the News*, 2015. Newsprint poster, 35 × 23 in. (88.9 × 58.4 cm). Collage composed from mid-twentieth-century newspaper clippings collected by Louise Lawrence in the scrapbook "Transvestism in the News." Kinsey Institute, Indiana University

This was society's view of transgender people when Lew Lawrence began living as Louise in the 1940s. She called herself a "permanent transvestite" and helped lay the foundation for today's transgender community. An avid correspondent, Louise's address book became the initial subscription list for the first iteration of the magazine *Transvestia* in 1952.

In the mid-1940s Louise began lecturing to scientists and medical authorities about transvestites and transsexuals at the University of California's Langley Porter Clinic in San Francisco. Sometime around 1945 Arnold Lowman, a post-doctoral student in pharmacology and life-long crossdresser, attended one of Louise's lectures. He obtained her address, possibly surreptitiously and, using the name Charles Prince, visited Louise at her home in Berkeley. Louise was the first transgender person Arnold/Charles had ever met. Louise introduced him to psychiatrist Karl Bowman, the Langely Porter Psychiatric Institute's director. Arnold/Charles started therapy with Bowman, who counseled him to accept his crossdressing. Eventually, Arnold/Charles took this advice to heart and in 1968 began living full-time as Virginia Prince.

Louise and Virginia were what Virginia would later call transgenderists, not transsexuals, because, though they had changed their gender, they had not changed their sex. They lived as women largely without major medical intervention. Virginia did take hormones for a time but discontinued them when her breasts reached an agreeable size.

Because of Louise's work at Langley Porter, Bowman introduced her to famous sexologist Alfred Kinsey, who in turn introduced her to endocrinologist Harry Benjamin. Louise became one of Kinsey's and Benjamin's primary sources for things transgender. She introduced Kinsey to transexuals, transvestites, and female impersonators, many of whom he interviewed. She transcribed Kinsey's interviews, for which she was eventually paid. She sent Kinsey trans-related books and compiled scrapbooks of clippings and photographs. These materials, including her diary for 1944, the year she transitioned, are now at the Kinsey Institute, Indiana University Bloomington.

Louise introduced Harry Benjamin to David O. Caldwell's work with transvestites and transsexuals. An editor of the magazine *Sexology*, Dr. Caldwell's writing contrasts dramatically with the headlines in the collage. He sees the study of transgender as part of an intellectual tradition. The title of his article "Psychopathia Transexualis" (December 1949) is a reference to early sexologist Richard von Krafft-Ebing's 1886 classic *Psychopathia Sexualis.* Caldwell's writing is fact-based and scientific. His book, *Transvestism: Men in Female Dress* (1956), includes autobiographical chapters by eleven male cross-dressers and a chapter by Benjamin. And, most importantly, both Caldwell and Benjamin are much more supportive of transgender people than the popular press of their era, as can be seen in Caldwell's pamphlet *What's Wrong with Transvestism? A Compilation of the Diaries of Transvestites as Revealed to the Author, with Letters and Day-By-Day Events from the Lives of Those Who Prefer to Wear the Clothing of the Opposite Sex* (1949).

Louise's commitment to teaching the medical community about transvestites and transsexuals helped shape medical providers' perception of transgender people and their behavior. The materials she sent to Kinsey became the data that future researchers used to create their theories and inform their practices. Louise wanted doctors to know more about transgender people than they were being taught in medical school and more than they could ever learn from the articles represented in this collage.

—Ms. Bob Davis

Sources

Joanne Meyerowitz, *How Sex Changed: A History of Transsexuality in the United States* (Cambridge, MA: Harvard University Press, 2002).

Susan Stryker, *Transgender History: The Roots of Today's Revolution*, rev. ed. (New York: Seal Press, 2017).

Zagria, *Louise Lawrence (1912–1976): Activist, Building Manager, Artist*, May 8, 2009, rev. June 2016, https://zagria.blogspot.com/search?q=Louise+Lawrence#.YruBBuzMKUk.

▸ Chris E. Vargas, Detail of *Transvestism in the News*, 2015

As Colonel's Lady

Army officer
de in falsies

GIRLS WIN RIGHT TO
GARB SELVES AS MEN

Mask and Wig Opens 'Count Me In'

Was 'Edna' 33 Yrs., Now He's Ed

ONCE SISTERS, NOW BROTHERS.

Seized in Female Garb

THREE MEN DRESSED
AS WOMEN NABBED

Strange Case of G.I. Who
Wed Gal Friend, Then Yea
ater Found She's a "He"!

Halloween Spirit Amok! Nab
33 Men Dressed as Women

Chinese Groom Deceived
For 10 Days by Male 'Bride'

Cream Man
Becomes Lady

Female Impersonator Working
As Maid Named

S.F. Examiner
April 16. 1953

Plumber Hanged
In Women's Garb

OXI (Miss.), April 15

Is 'She' Girl or Boy?

'Freak of Nature' Is Awaiting
Outcome of New Operation

IMPERSONATOR
CASE DELAYED

E BURNED THE
STOLEN PANTIES

Retired Colonel
Liked to Wear
Wife's 'Uniform'

SHORN OF GARBO ATTIRE,
YOUTH FLEES FROM CITY

TRANSVESTITE
SEEKS LEGAL HELP

Male Instinct Triumphs in Scotch
Doctor's 40-Year Sex Conflict

Wed 2 Ye

Police Hunt Man,
but 'He's' Woman

Masquerade Disclosed by FBI;
Fugitive Also Has Young 'Wife'

Trans-Vestism
Economic Necessity

LEGION'S TOUGHEST "MAN" A WOMAN!

Elsie, the Cobra Woman,
Turns Out to Be MR. Elsie!

WORE SKIRTS TO SKIP THE
CALL-UP

DOCTORS GOOF
SEX CHANGE
OPERATION

HUSBAND POSES
AS HIS OWN WIFE
TO GET HER A JOB

Boys Will Be Girls

2 Men Reared
As Girls Win
Male Names

In His Wife's
Shoes

The

on Four, He Sheds Curls to Become Real Boy

'Girl' admits
being AWOL

When's a "Girl" Not a Girl? Ask 'Em

He Wan

Woman Who Became Man
Marries Girlhood Chum

"HE'S" A
SHE

Ex-Girl Fails
At Love as Man,
Tries Suicide

Berkeley Hit By Wave
Of 'Falsie' Modesty

Masquerader
Sentenced

Forgery Admitted
By Baby Sitter

Dope Peddlers;

Male Garb

BEAUTIFUL
WOMEN?
Fooled Again!

Woman Posing as Man
Tried for Battery

'Woman' Betrayed
When Voice Slips

SEX OPERATION
ON SELF FAILS

STOLEN GARB

GUYS

"SHE'S"
A HE

Boy Pri
Girl B

Haircut T

"A SHE"

Amazing Story of Her
Masquerade as Man

Jail Reveals
'Wife' Is Man

The Metamorphosis of a Little Man

Aged Rec
31 Years

p Slips Up

nniving Con

S REASON
R DRESSING
A WOMAN

SAN FRANCISCO GIRLS

An Impersonator Switches Sex

BECAME A GIRL
TO ESCAPE
GANGSTERS

will be

GALS!

Dear Sir: How did they get Elvis Presley to dress up like a girl in his new movie, "Girl Happy"? —Ellen Cordrey, Tacoma, Wash.

Dear Ellen: By paying him $50,000 a week.

Woman Ma

Man Disclos

'WOM
FALLS IN LOVE,
WANTS TO BE
A GIRL AGAI

os Startle 'Wolf'

She's Clothing

HE MAN OR WOMAN?

WALK TOO MASCULINE,
MAN IN GIRL'S DRESS
ARRESTED AS PERVERT

Popular Boy
Is Found to
Be a Girl

Inspector Wore Dresses
All His Life to Revere
Memory of Dead Mother

Rifle Bullet Ends Problems
Of Girl Who Became a Man

BOY-GIRLS' VIEWS ON WOMEN.

Little Girl's World
Is Invaded By Boys

Murder Trial Reveals Strange
'Marriage' Between Two Men

New Orlea
Claims Ex-N
Now Husba

Twisted twirps forming
protective association

... and
there's
a million
of them

30 Men in Female
Garb Jailed at Dinner

That Wasn't No Lady,
That Was a Fire-Eater

Bad Boys Decked
in Women's Garb
as a Punishment

Posed as Woman
To 'Make Living'

Swish Set De
Equal Rights

Those Aren't Kilts These
Men Are Wearing

Woman Posing As
Man Is Hurt, Has
To Reveal Sex

Operations
Change Girl
Into a Boy

Man's Pose as
Girl Revealed

EX-WOMAN NOW
HUSBAND, DAD

Purple Slip
Slides John
Into Pokey

Masquerading Men
Jailed in Raid

'I Passed As a Woman
33 Years Successfully'

New Orleans Surgeon
Claims Ex-Nurses' Aide
Now Husband

42 REFLECTIVE SURFACES IN *DRESSED TO KILL*, 1980

For those concerned with the politics of transgender representation and respectability, Brian De Palma's *Dressed to Kill* (1980) is a notoriously offensive entry. After escort Liz (Nancy Allen) witnesses the brutal murder of a woman in an elevator (Angie Dickinson), she teams up with the victim's son (Keith Gordon) to exonerate herself and catch the real killer. As the film reaches its climax, it is revealed that the victim's psychiatrist, Dr. Robert Elliott (Michael Caine), is indeed the murderer. But *twist!* the psychiatrist—the gatekeeper of certifiable sanity—is, in fact, Bobby, a trans woman who must kill to repress her/Elliott's sexual attraction towards women. An overt fan-boy reimagining of Alfred Hitchock's *Psycho* (1960), which replaces the former's psychoanalytic musings with pathologizing psycho-medical diagnostics of "transgenderism," De Palma's *Dressed to Kill* is a winning bingo card of transphobic visual and narrative rhetoric.

However, what can clearly be deemed a *bad object* of transgender media history, to borrow from Cáel Keegan, is not necessarily the same as an *invaluable object*. Bad objects such as *Dressed to Kill*, can and do offer entry points for critique and discussion that may not be available elsewhere. We should take seriously the legacy of *Dressed to Kill* as we examine how larger themes of visibility, legibility, and authenticity ebb and flow throughout the set design, costuming, and cinematography of the film.

One telling example is the psychiatrist's office: situated on the ground-level of a New York brownstone, Dr. Robert Elliott's office features an iron wrought gate protecting the front entrance and two street-facing windows with iron bars on the outside. Once inside, the office is tellingly split into a salmon-colored waiting room/administrative space and a larger room for Elliott to meet with patients, decorated in darker, more masculine earthen tones. When De Palma's camera enters the office, it is careful to frame characters with reflective or luminous sources in the background, placing emphasis on literal surface-level appearances. Indeed, visuality, and the assumed (dis)trust in the image, is a key motif: diopter shots break down the depth of field into two seemingly distinct images, split screens contrast action, elevator doors and concave mirrors distort the reflection of their users, a hidden 8mm camera surveils Dr. Elliott's office, and sunglasses protect a murderer's identity. Likewise, the use of windows in other sets betray a biased link between transparency and legitimacy: locations like the police station feature clear glass with characters in full view; Dr. Elliott's curtained windows, while visible to passersby obscure or keep private the identity of those inside, including Bobby; and the setting of the mental institution contains no windows at all, creating a darkened amphitheatre of madness and revolt. What is first blueprinted in the set design of Elliot's office is magnified throughout the film, returning viewers to the question, "How much do you trust what you see?"

Yet, visuality, or the emphasis between what is seen and what is known, is often weaponized against the trans community. Trans persons are forced to conform to colonial, white supremacist, cis-heteronormative, and classist codes of legibility, with failure to do so resulting in violent retribution or death. Why then not find pleasure in Bobby's use of the hyper-reflective razorblade as her weapon of choice? If we treat the body count in this film as metaphoric (since it is narrative fiction), Bobby's attacks can be read as ones against systems of legibility and the very ignorance of cis-heteronormative society, to suggest they are simply beyond the boundaries of judgement.

—Dan Vena

▸ Still from *Dressed to Kill*, 1980. Directed by Brian De Palma. Distributed by Filmways Pictures

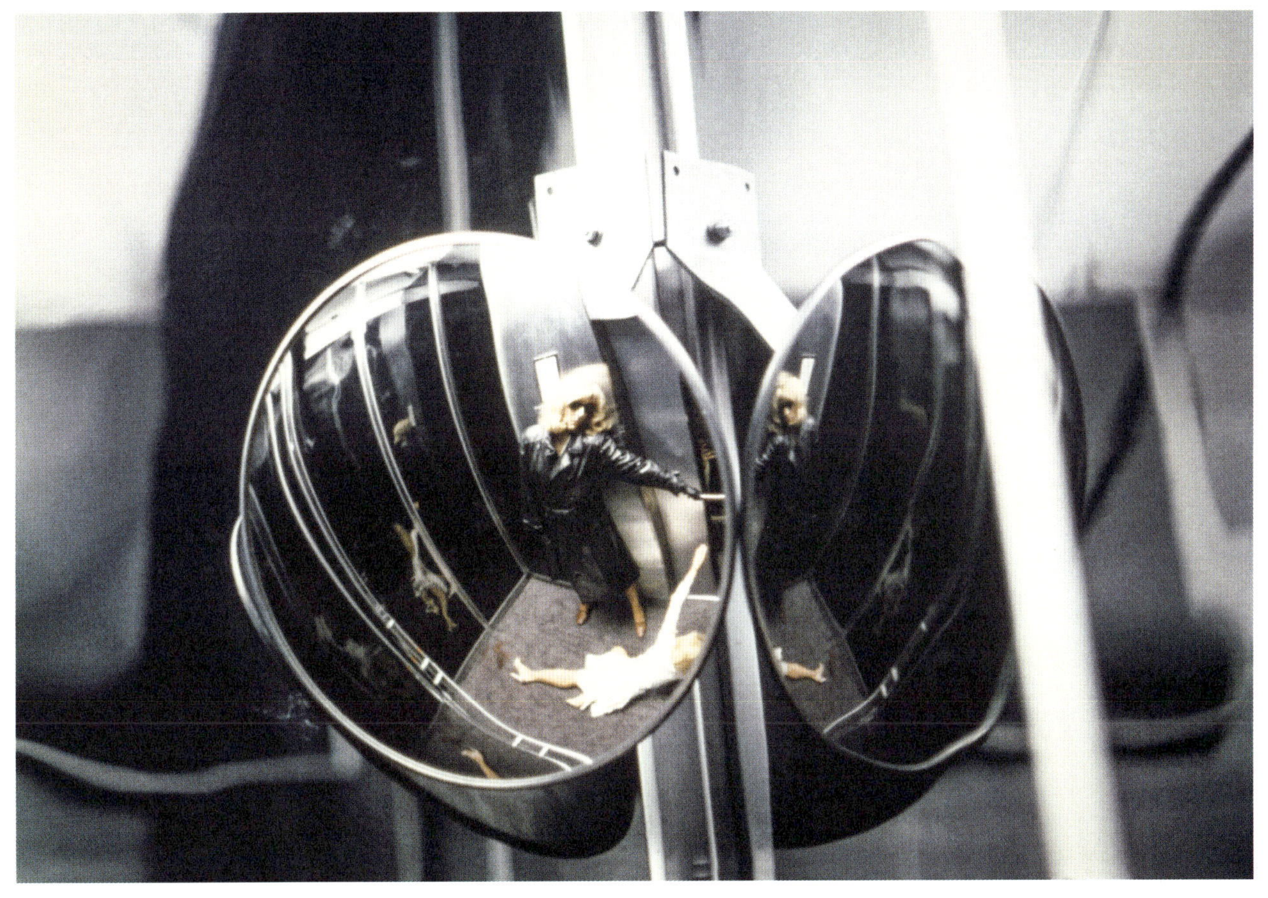

43 THE TRANSEXUAL MENACE T-SHIRT, 1993

In 1993, there had been anger about leaving the "T" out of LGB Pride marches in New York City. The June 1994 march was to be the twenty-fifth anniversary of the Stonewall riots and a number of activists vowed to fight for recognition and inclusion.

NYC activist Denise Norris and a friend reached out to me about doing a local action to put additional pressure on organizers of the march. I wasn't enthusiastic. I'd never attended the march and I'd never seen myself as an activist—in fact my life and career were finally settling down into something approximating normal.

But they were persuasive. We decided we needed something that would make us and the other troops we sincerely hoped would show up visible, and at the same time mock organizers for their fears of being inclusive of transgender people.

In 1968, lesbian and bisexual women were purged from the National Organization for Women (NOW). According to reports, NOW cofounder Betty Friedan personally accused writer Rita Mae Brown of being the "Lavender Menace." The following year Rita and her friends stormed the podium at the Second Congress to Unite Women wearing T-shirts that read... "Lavender Menace."

We thought that was a dandy example. We cheekily called our group "The Transexual Menace" (I'd always preferred the British spelling—with one "s"—which seemed to at least make a single word out of "trans-sexual"). Luckily my partner at the time, Montine Jordan, was a gifted graphic designer. I told her we wanted to channel *The Rocky Horror Picture Show* (a huge underground hit at the time) with its blood-dripping red letters.

She came up with a killer logo, one of those inspired designs that just "clicks" visually the first time you see it. We had three dozen T-shirts with the logo printed up and started giving them out to anyone who promised to attend and protest the march.

It was wild putting one on. It's hard to explain now, but this was a time when *passing* as cisgender was everything. My surgeons had even told me that I would be successful *as* a transsexual to the degree to which no one suspected me of being one. Acceptance by passing and blending in were important goals for many transgender women.

There really wasn't such a thing as "genderqueer" even within the community. Certainly Leslie Feinberg had been doing something that tripped the boundaries between butch lesbian and FTM. And Kate Bornstein was always exploring gender beyond the binary.

But, in the main, most of us thought in terms of binary men and women and wanted very much to fit into one or the other. For me this meant being accepted as a "real woman," by looking like one. It was all very cisgender-oriented. And of course you wanted to be safe. That was a big unspoken part of passing. If you passed, you were safe.

But pulling on the T-shirt screwed all of that forever.

—Riki Wilchins

A version of this text previously appeared in Riki Wilchins's memoir *TRANS/gressive: How Transgender Activists Took on Gay Rights, Feminism, the Media & Congress... and Won!* (Riverdale, NY: Riverdale Avenue Books, 2017), 78–80.

▸ Model wearing The Transexual Menace T-Shirt, 2022. Photo by Marcel Pardo Ariza

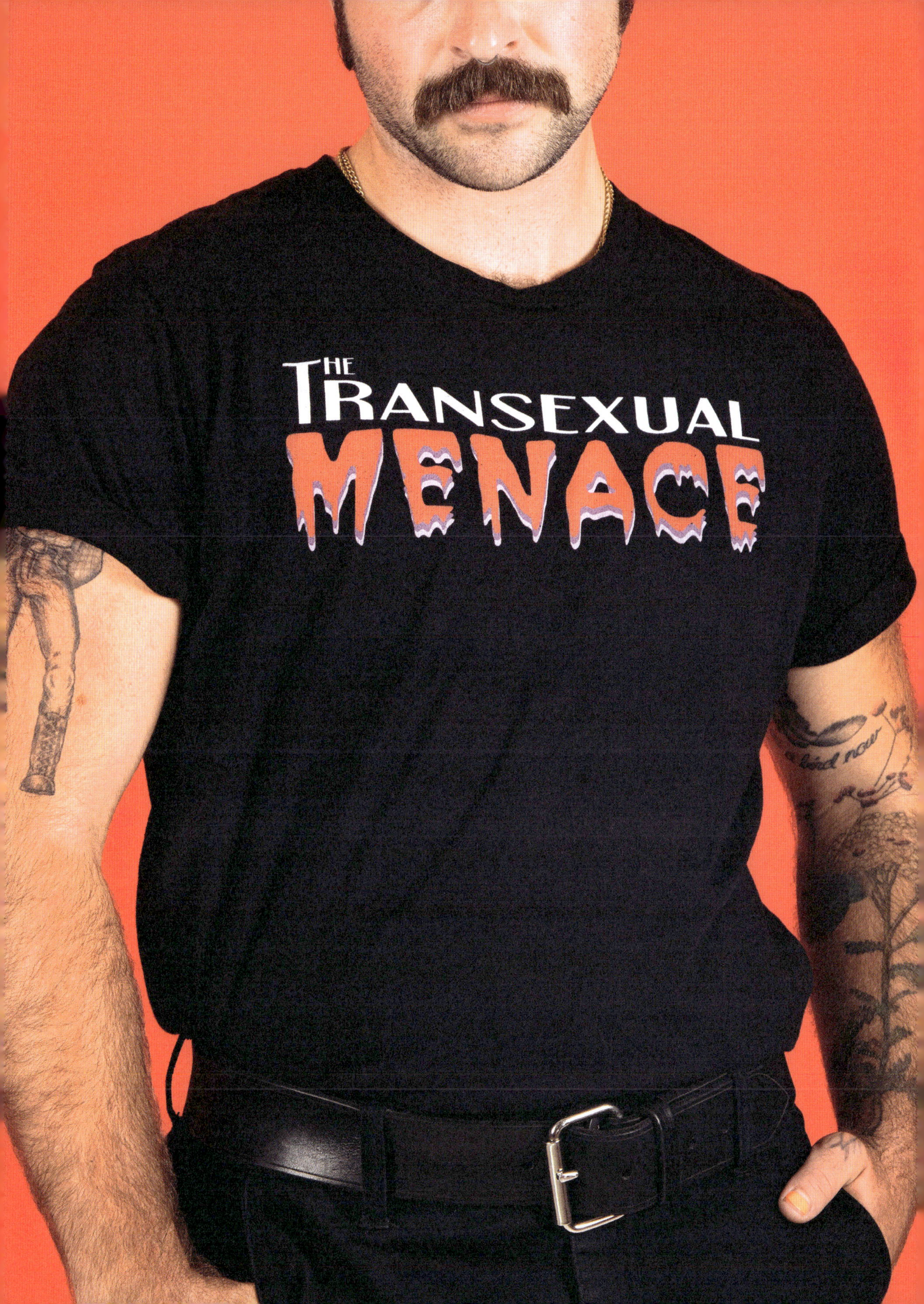
THE
TRANSEXUAL
MENACE

44 DUSTIN HOFFMAN'S DRESS IN *TOOTSIE*, 1982

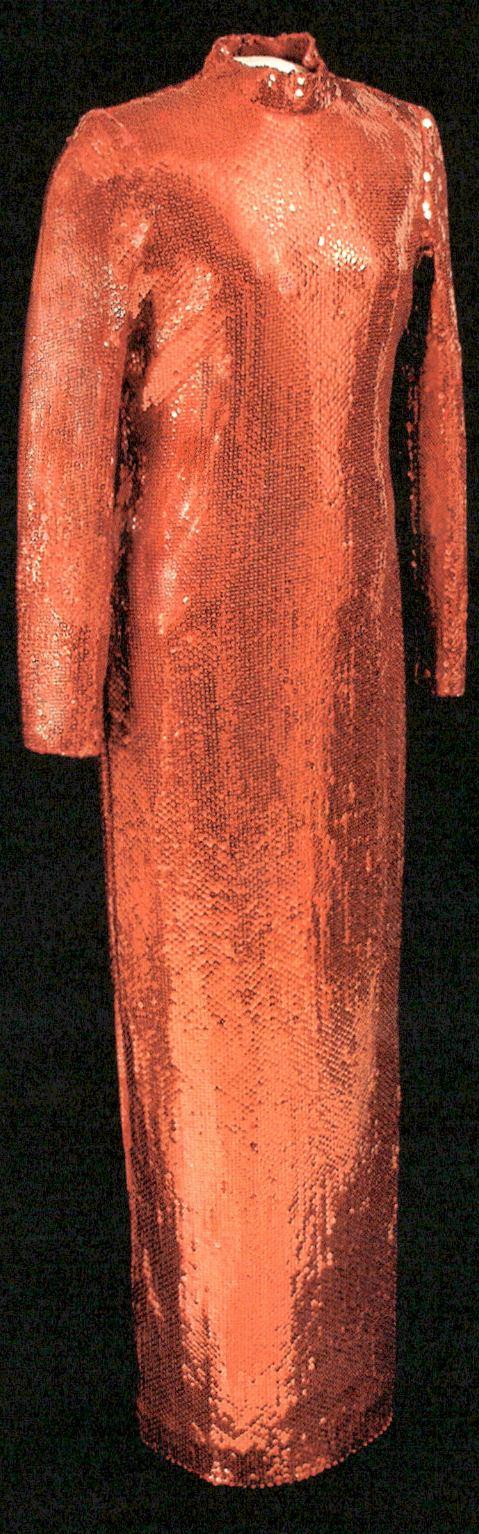

Tootsie's Transvestite Was Temporary, but the Dress Lives On!

The red sequin dress that Dorothy Michaels models for the cover of New York magazine during the joyful photo shoot montage in Sydney Pollack's 1982 film *Tootsie* is now an official object in the Smithsonian Institution's National Museum of American History, "Dress worn by Dustin Hoffman in the Film *Tootsie*"—ID Number 1984.0549.01. When Hoffman, care of Punch Productions Inc., donated the dress, along with Dorothy's bra, panty girdle, waist cincher, eyeglasses, rings, and earrings, Hoffman's personal assistant Frank Piazza included an accompanying letter that wistfully states, "Enclosed you'll find the remains of Dorothy Michaels. I hope you enjoy her as much as I have." (Accession file 1984.0549). Hoffman's character in the film, Michael Dorsey, like other temporary transvestites in the movies, gave up the dress. But the dress lives on!

"Lives on," first in the sense of embalmed by the Textile Conservation Laboratory, which not only provides an environment of gentle temperature, humidity, and lighting but also constructs display forms. According to Senior Costume Conservator Sunae Park Evans, it is necessary to fully support a garment to avoid deformation or stress during exhibition. Perhaps a display form accurate to Dorothy's red sequin dress, which was designed for Hoffman's body, will enable it to someday stand beside Benjamin Franklin's Three-Piece Silk Suit—ID number 2012.0187.001.

"Lives on," also in the sense of embodying new life, shaping desire, resurrecting transvestism.

Designed by Ruth Morley and constructed by Mignon, *Tootsie*'s red sequin dress was undoubtedly also inspired by New York City's vibrant drag, ballroom, and crossdressing cultures, including Lee's Mardi Gras Boutique at 400 West 14th Street, which, beginning in 1969, sold gowns, high heels, corsets, etc. to crossdressers of all persuasions. According to Susan Dworkin's book *Making Tootsie*, Morley was advised by an unnamed woman who was known for supplying clothing to the transvestite community. This is almost certainly Muriel Olive. Olive not only advertised lingerie and dresses "'maid' to measurement" alongside "coaching, analysis, instruction, counseling, and training" in the newsletter *Our Sorority*, but also was herself a participant at the Provincetown crossdressing event Fantasia Fair that began in 1975 and continues today.[1]

One advantage of a conceptual art project like Chris E. Vargas's Museum of Trans Hirstory & Art (MOTHA) is that conservation is a mental activity and, as such, promotes spatial and temporal fluidity. Whereas the Smithsonian relies on immobility to ensure a garment's longevity, a virtual archive relies on mobility. *Trans Hirstory in 99 Objects* rescues, propels, appropriates, morphs, remembers, and instantiates. It thrusts transgender hirstory not only backwards but also forwards. It opens our minds to a wearable dress.

Ruth Morley knew, as Dustin Hoffman knew, as crossdressers knew and know, how a dress can make a woman. Dorothy Michaels grew into this red sequin dress. So why shouldn't others? How many girls would have lined up to model this dress for the cover of *Tapestry* magazine? Imagine Dorothy's dress now hanging at Michael Salem Boutique on the East Side of Manhattan. Someone falls in love with it and wears it through today's trendy meatpacking district into the West Village piers of the 1980s. Then back another decade and someone wears it in Harlem for the House of LaBeija Ball at Up the Downstairs Case. Won't this red sequin dress be the envy at next month's CDINYC dinner party? Wouldn't it make a gorgeous prize at Lady Bunny's Wigstock? Let's ask Veronica Vera to throw in a body sculpting and comportment workshop at Miss Vera's Finishing School. When the red sequin dress becomes wearable, you can slip it onto Antony, stretch it out for Divine, and let it rip on Lil Nas X. Can I dare it onto a drag king?

And the wonderful thing is that during all this wearing and all this sharing, as the sequins are virtually popping off in the name of gender euphoria, we can rest assured that *Tootsie*'s red sequin dress will remain intact at the Smithsonian Institution, alluding to a history of crossdressing for centuries to come.

—Chris Straayer

◄
Red sequin dress worn by Dustin Hoffman in the film *Tootsie*, 1982. Polyester, sequins, and metal, 60½ × 19 in. (153.7 × 48.3 cm). National Museum of American History, Smithsonian Institution, 1984.0549.01

1. Muriel Olive's listing in "Our Sorority Shoppers Guide," *Our Sorority*, no. 3 (June 1981): 9.

45 GREER LANKTON, *CANDY DARLING*, 1995

Candy Darling (1944–1974) has been an icon of transgender history for decades. Her prominence in transgender culture was forged through her work with Andy Warhol and Paul Morrisey in the late 1960s and early 1970s. She aspired to be a famous Hollywood actress, but she was consistently denied roles in mainstream films because of her gender—even the title role in *Myra Breckenridge,* which chronicled the life of the film's transsexual namesake. Warhol was "fascinated by boys who spend their lives trying to be complete girls because they have to work so hard—double time—getting rid of all the telltale male signs and drawing in all the female signs."[1] Warhol rightly pointed out that "Candy didn't want to be a perfect woman.... What she wanted was to be a woman with all the little problems that a woman has to deal with—runs in her stocking, runny mascara, men that left her. She would even ask to borrow Tampaxes, explaining that she had a terrible emergency."[2] Warhol appreciated Darling for her astute awareness of the very subtle visual and behavioral signifiers that produced female gender in the 1960s and the skill with which she made them her own.

Greer Lankton (1958–1996) appreciated this, too. She idolized Darling for her astute manipulation of feminine signifiers. A central artist of the early 1980s East Village art scene, Lankton showed most frequently at the emblematically indulgent Civilian Warfare gallery. Her dolls, sculptures, drawings, and artist's books often addressed her experience with what was then called transsexual medicine in ways that blended glamorous (and even glamorously grotesque) ideals of womanhood with the gritty realities of surgery, hormone treatments, and her day-to-day experience as a transsexual woman.

Lankton also paid homage to her heroes in her work. She made a plush rendition of Darling in 1985 that was complete with a changeable wardrobe. In 1995 she made this dioramic bust of Darling for that year's Whitney Biennial, and it became part of Lankton's installation *It's All About ME, not you*, which debuted at the Mattress Factory museum in Pittsburgh in 1996, just after the artist's death. Here Lankton rendered Darling with supple red lips and an Adam's apple. She gave the doll pectoral muscles instead of breasts and between them cut out a heart-shaped window revealing a diorama. In this diorama, Lankton placed a miniature woman's dressing table next to an anatomical heart, as if to parody the idea of being a woman trapped in a man's body—the trope that defined public discourse on gender transformation through the end of the twentieth century. Lankton also cast Darling's eyes askance, making it is easy to imagine this bust as a material confidante with whom Lankton could share a knowing glance, full of all the joys and pains that continue to come with being a transgender woman in the United States.

—Cyle Metzger

1. Alexis Bard Johnson, "The Work of Being Sexed: Andy Warhol on Drag," in *Contact Warhol: Photography Without End* (Stanford, CA: Iris & Gerald Cantor Center for the Visual Arts at Stanford University; Cambridge, MA: MIT Press, 2018), 169.
2. Andy Warhol and Pat Hackett, *POPism: The Warhol Sixties* (Boston: Mariner Books, 2006), 285–86.

▸ Greer Lankton, *Candy Darling*, 1995. Mixed media, 27 × 17 × 10 in. (68.6 × 43.2 × 25.4 cm). Part of the installation *It's All About ME, not you* (1996) at the Mattress Factory, Pittsburgh

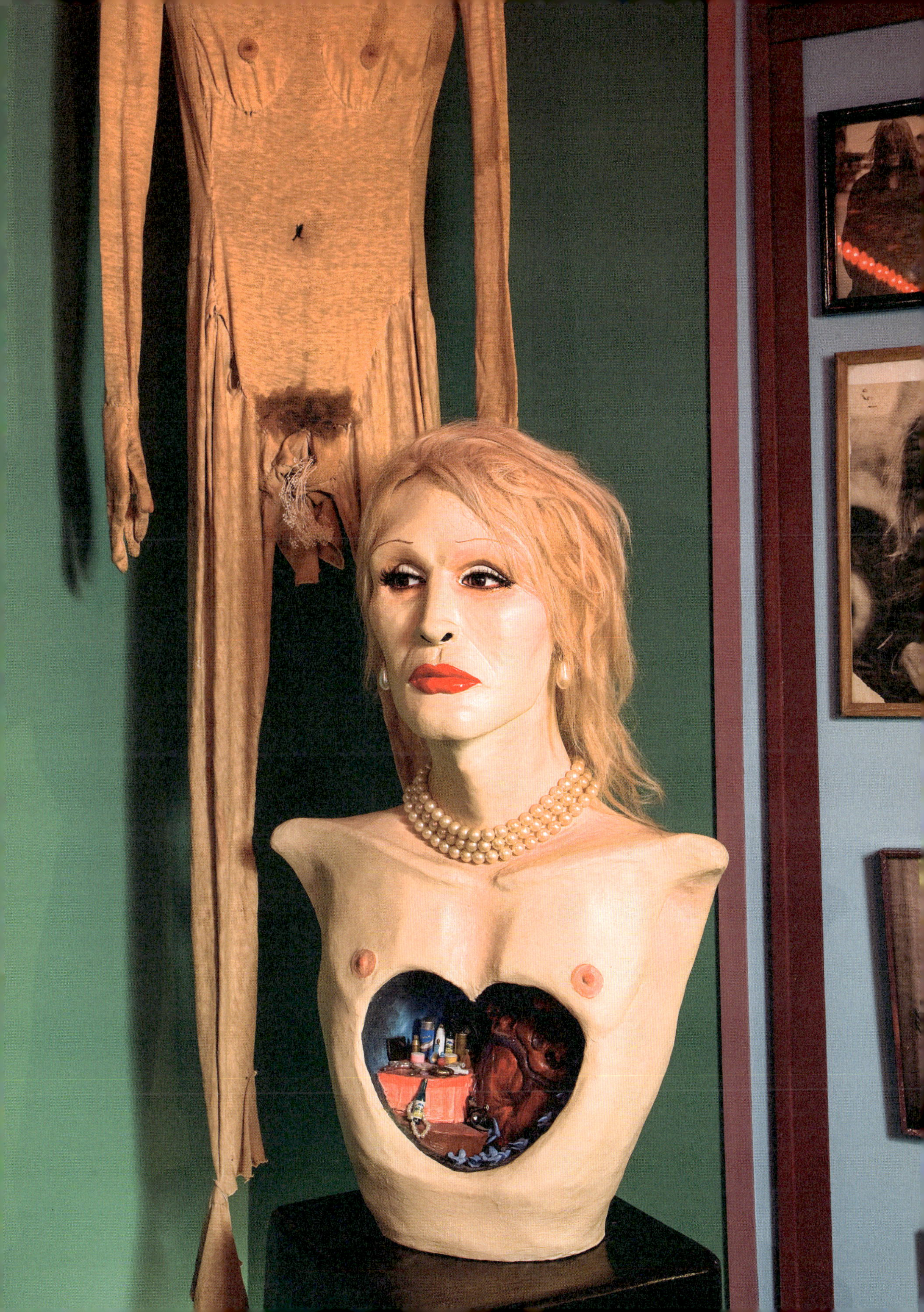

46 CRAIG CALDERWOOD, *THIS WORLD WILL SOON BE OURS*, 2015

Few figures capture the complexities and contradictions of transgender history as strongly as Angela Keyes Douglas (1943–2007). In 1970, after an early career as a rock musician, Douglas founded one of the first post-Stonewall trans activist groups: the Transexual Action Organization (TAO). In Susan Stryker's words, TAO would prove "the first truly international grassroots transgender community organization," with chapters forming across North America and in the UK.[1] In 1972, Douglas relocated to Miami Beach, Florida, where she helped build a multiracial, feminist collective that prioritized the needs of low-income trans sex workers and immigrants. Douglas became an outspoken advocate for "transsexual liberation" nationally, writing prolifically in left-wing media and building ties with numerous gay and trans organizations. She gained particular notoriety for her clashes with radical feminists after her (possibly satirical) critique of cis-womanhood was published in the lesbian feminist newspaper *Sister* and later quoted in Janice Raymond's *Transsexual Empire* (1979).

Douglas's commitment to traditional activist work, however, is but one piece of a more fraught biography. Douglas cleaved to the countercultural and iconoclastic. She seemed most at home in psychedelic and underground music scenes and had a lifelong fascination with the occult. Under Douglas's leadership, TAO used occult rites to protect its community from police brutality and hostile feminists. References to UFOs permeate Douglas's writings and TAO's publications, *Mirage* and *Moonshadow*, and she was deeply affected to learn that her friend and fellow activist, Randy Towers, was apparently a "reptilian, transsexual ET" that had come to earth "to aid human transsexuals."[2] Despite her progressive political work, Douglas claimed to have been an FBI informant and even professed brief affiliation with the Nazi party—although she later attributed this to brainwashing. Douglas gradually alienated her friends with accusations and aspersions and became increasingly obsessed with celebrity plots to plagiarize her work. Her material conditions also worsened as she aged, and when she died, she was homeless and mostly alone. Douglas's eventual decline, however, should not eclipse her inventive and fantastic views on transgender liberation—in particular, she staunchly held that otherworldly forces offered crucial resources for building community self-defense and self-determination.

Against the temptation to relegate Douglas's unorthodoxies to the margins of trans history, Craig Calderwood's drawing instead centers them. Calderwood's portrait, in which the reptilian Randy Towers stands over Douglas, their fingers interlaced, offers what some speculative philosophers might call a "flat ontology." Refusing to qualify Douglas's extraordinary friend as a mere projection of her mind, or a strictly subjective truth, here, Douglas and Towers are equally present and real, consubstantial. Depicted late in her life, Douglas finds in Towers, potentially, a gesture of comfort, an affirmation of the trans-extraterrestrial solidarity that she long envisioned. In its rendering of this unearthly alliance, the piece also conjures a transgender imaginary that is at once expansive, chimerical, and strange, gazing at us sternly—but also, perhaps, protectively—from Towers's coal-black eyes.

—Abram J. Lewis

▸ Craig Calderwood, *This world will soon be ours*, 2015. Pen on cotton paper, 24 x 18 in. (61 x 45.7 cm)

(following spread) Issues of TAO's publications *Mirage* and *Moodshadow*, written by Angela Keyes Douglas and illustrated by Suzun David and Vanessa Wolfe, c. 1970s. ONE National Gay & Lesbian Archives at the USC Libraries

1. Susan Stryker, *Transgender History* (Berkeley, CA: Seal Press, 2008), 88.
2. Angela Douglas, *Triple Jeopardy: The Autobiography of Angela Lynn Douglas* (n.p., Angela Douglas, 1983), 55, 72; copies on file with the Gay, Lesbian, Bisexual, Transgender Historical Society and ONE National Gay & Lesbian Archives at the USC Libraries.

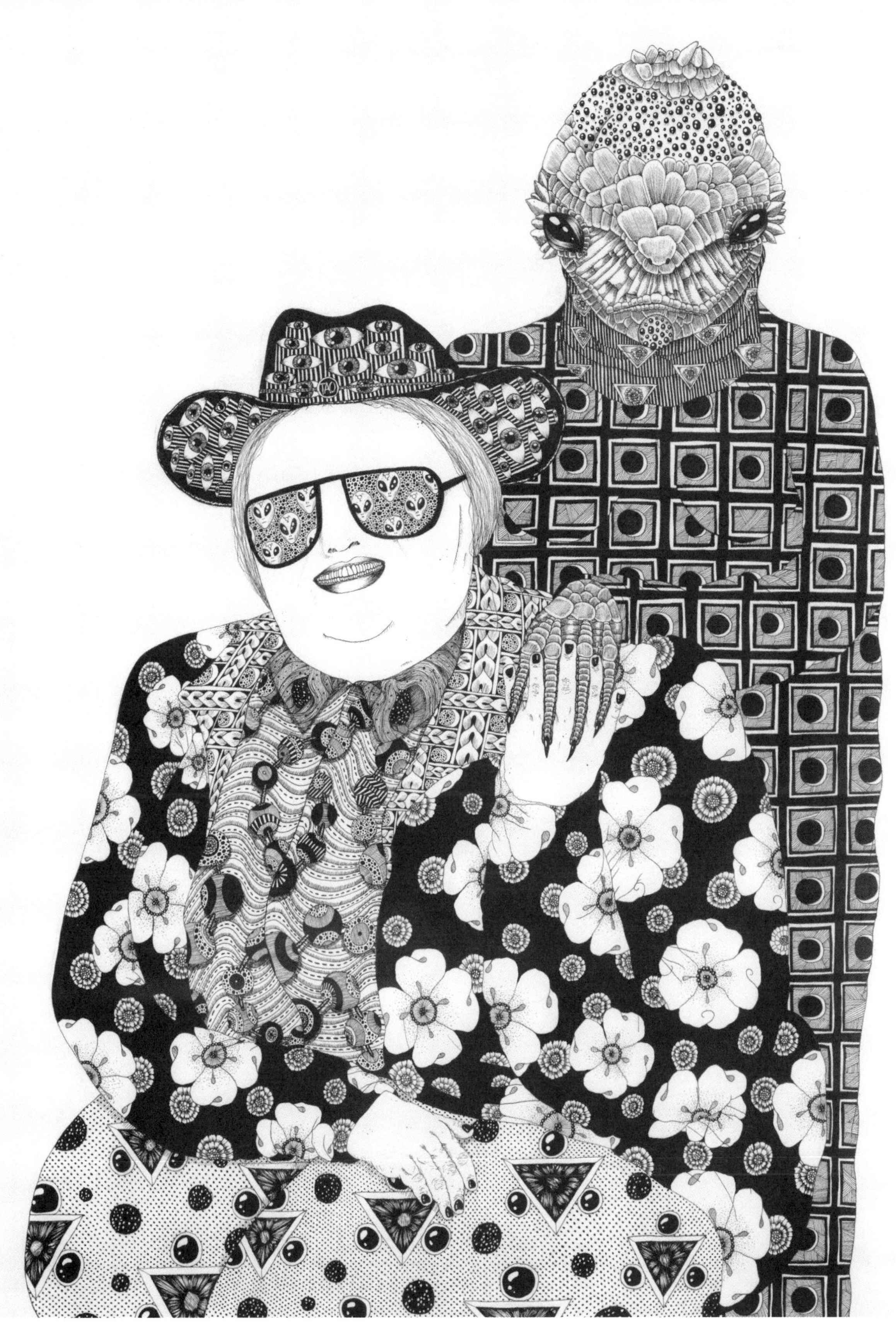

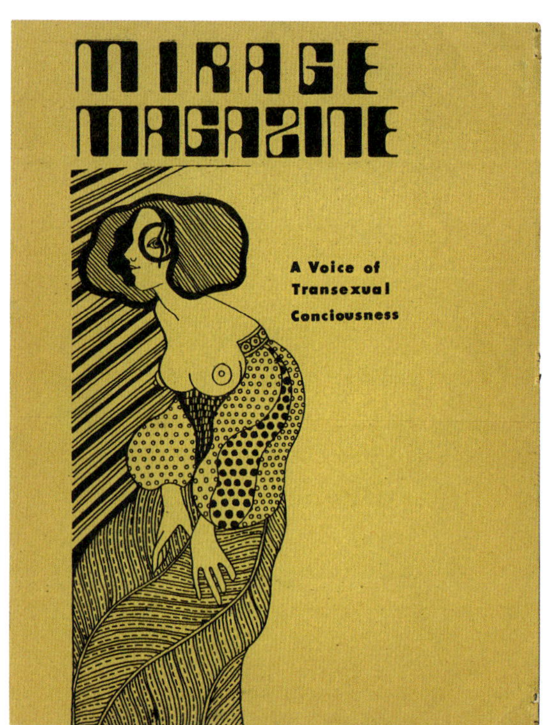

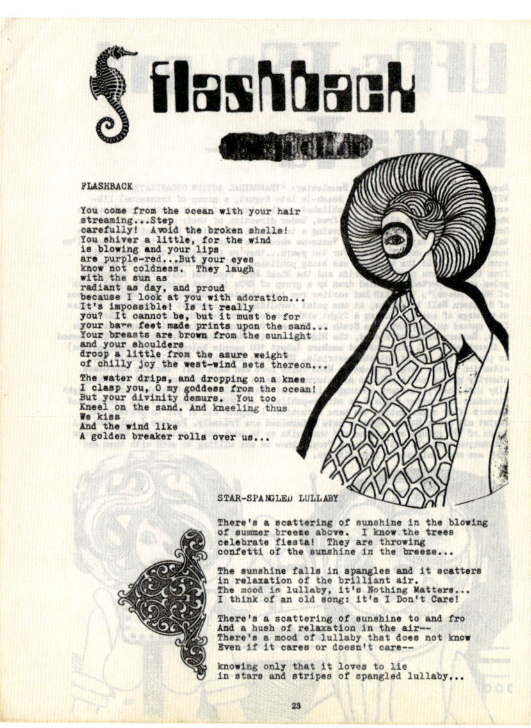

flashback

FLASHBACK

You come from the ocean with your hair
streaming...Step
carefully! Avoid the broken shells!
You shiver a little, for the wind
is blowing and your lips
are purple-red...But your eyes
know not coldness. They laugh
with the sun as
radiant as day, and proud
because I look at you with adoration...
It's impossible! Is it really
you? It cannot be, but it must be for
your bare feet made prints upon the sand...
Your breasts are brown from the sunlight
and your shoulders
droop a little from the azure weight
of chilly joy the west-wind sets thereon...

The water drips, and dropping on a knee
I clasp you, O my goddess from the ocean!
But your divinity demurs. You too
Kneel on the sand. And kneeling thus
We kiss
And the wind like
A golden breaker rolls over us...

STAR-SPANGLED LULLABY

There's a scattering of sunshine in the blowing
of summer breeze above. I know the trees
celebrate fiesta! They are throwing
confetti of the sunshine in the breeze...

The sunshine falls in spangles and it scatters
in relaxation of the brilliant air.
The mood is lullaby, it's Nothing Matters...
I think of an old song: it's I Don't Care!

There's a scattering of sunshine to and fro
And a hush of relaxation in the air--
There's a mood of lullaby that does not know
Even if it cares or doesn't care--

knowing only that it loves to lie
in stars and stripes of spangled lullaby...

23

UFOs, TSs, and Extra-Ts—

Excerpt from the UFO Sightings Newsletter: "TRANSEXUAL ACTION ORGANIZATION ALLIES WITH EXTRA-TERRESTRIALS". Miami Beach-In late August, a group of transexual liberationists headquartered here published another issue of their monthly publication Moonshadow, which is distributed free. Under direction of their president Angela K. Douglas, a cartoon was drawn depicting a transexual contacting Venus with a walkie-talkie with the caption "come in Venus-we should have no trouble taking over here-I've been living with one of "them" for two years...they're pathetic...this planet will soon be ours." As the magazine was being published, UFO sightings began to come in from the northern part of Florida and the Miami News reported that "five telephone poles were reportedly knocked down by a group of UFOs in Fort Lauderdale (just north of Miami Beach)". (The TAO had earlier run into physical confrontation with employees of Southern Bell telephone, at one point resulting in the arrest of President Douglas on a charge of assault during a fight with two Southern Bell truckdrivers.) The UFO flap spread quickly thru the South to Alabama, Georgia, Mississippi, Tennessee, then Ohio, Eastern Seaboard states, the Midwest and the West Coast. Meanwhile the TAO issued a directive to all officers and members (about 500 people belong to the organization) to protect and assist extraterrestrials, UFO crews and their vehicles should the situation arise. Douglas spoke on WBUS radio here and said that "certain oppressed minority groups would welcome extraterrestrials as liberators" and would "probably ally with them", contrary to suggestions that the people of Earth might unite to fight "invaders from outer space." As editor-publisher of UFOSN I also give all readers and members of my organization the same directive. I expect all of you to protect and assist all Space Beings whom we have determined are friendly. Further I ask that all heads of UFO groups contact me and work with me to work out a nationwide UFO friends network;we must all let the Space People know we are willing to work with them and they are most welcome to live with us.

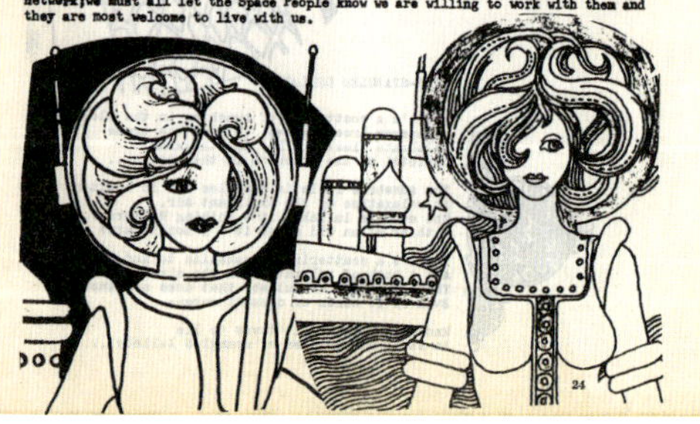

24

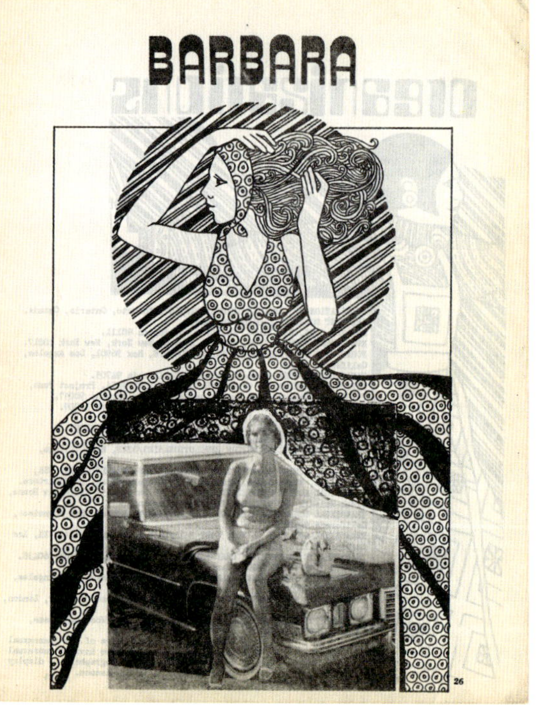

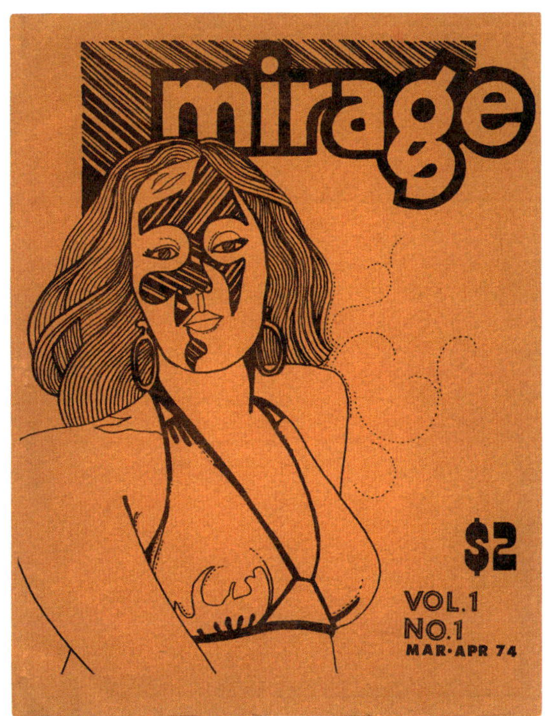

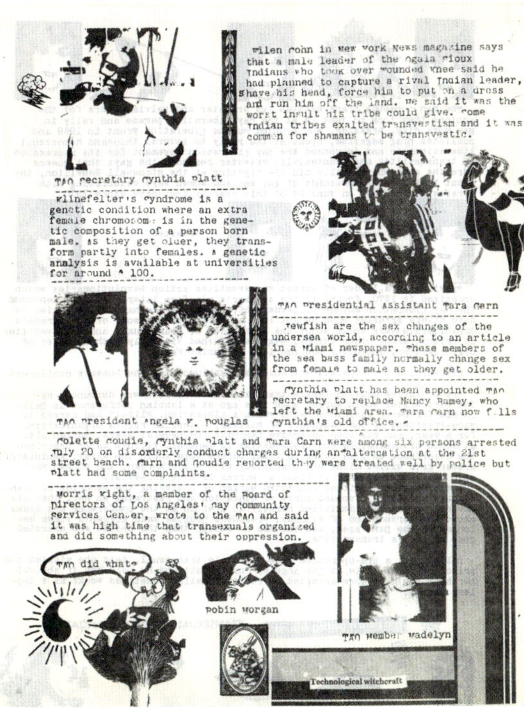

Ellen Cohn in New York News magazine says that a male leader of the Ogala Sioux Indians who took over Wounded Knee said he had planned to capture a rival Indian leader, shave his head, force him to put on a dress and run him off the land. He said it was the worst insult his tribe could give. Some Indian tribes exalted transvestism and it was common for shamans to be transvestic.

TAO secretary Cynthia Platt

Klinefelter's syndrome is a genetic condition where an extra female chromosome is in the genetic composition of a person born male. As they get older, they transform partly into females. A genetic anmlysis is available at universities for around $ 100.

TAO presidential assistant Tara Carn

Jewfish are the sex changes of the undersea world, according to an article in a Miami newspaper. These members of the sea bass family normally change sex from female to male as they get older.

Cynthia Platt has been appointed TAO secretary to replace Nancy Ramey, who left the Miami area. Tara Carn now fills Cynthia's old office.

TAO president Angela K. Douglas

Colette Goudie, Cynthia Platt and Tara Carn were among six persons arrested July 20 on disorderly conduct charges during an altercation at the 21st street beach. Carn and Goudie reported they were treated well by police but Platt had some complaints.

Morris Kight, a member of the Board of Directors of Los Angeles' Gay Community Services Center, wrote to the TAO and said it was high time that transexuals organized and did something about their oppression.

TAO did what?

Robin Morgan

TAO member Madelyn

Technological witchcraft

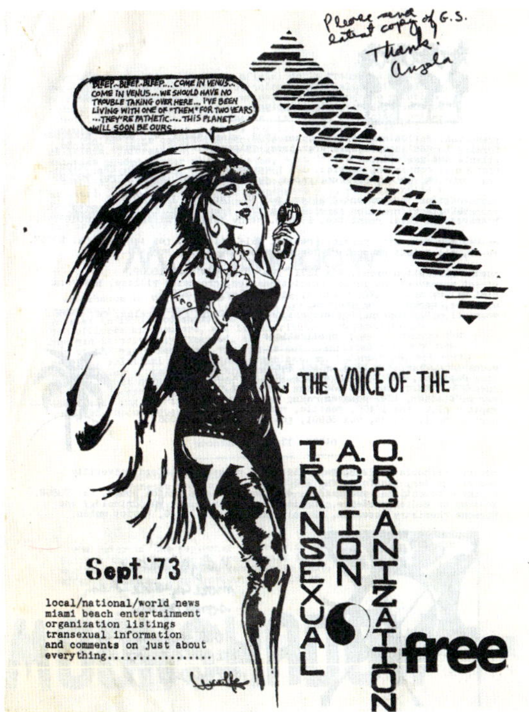

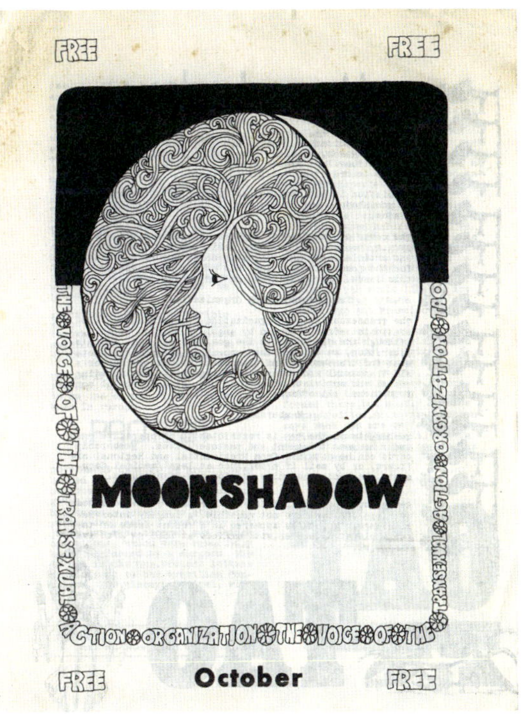

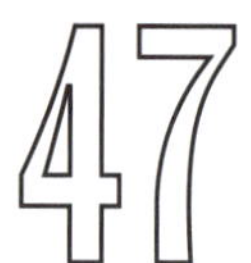

47 VAGINAL DAVIS, *FERTILE LA TOYAH JACKSON MAGAZINE*, 1987–91

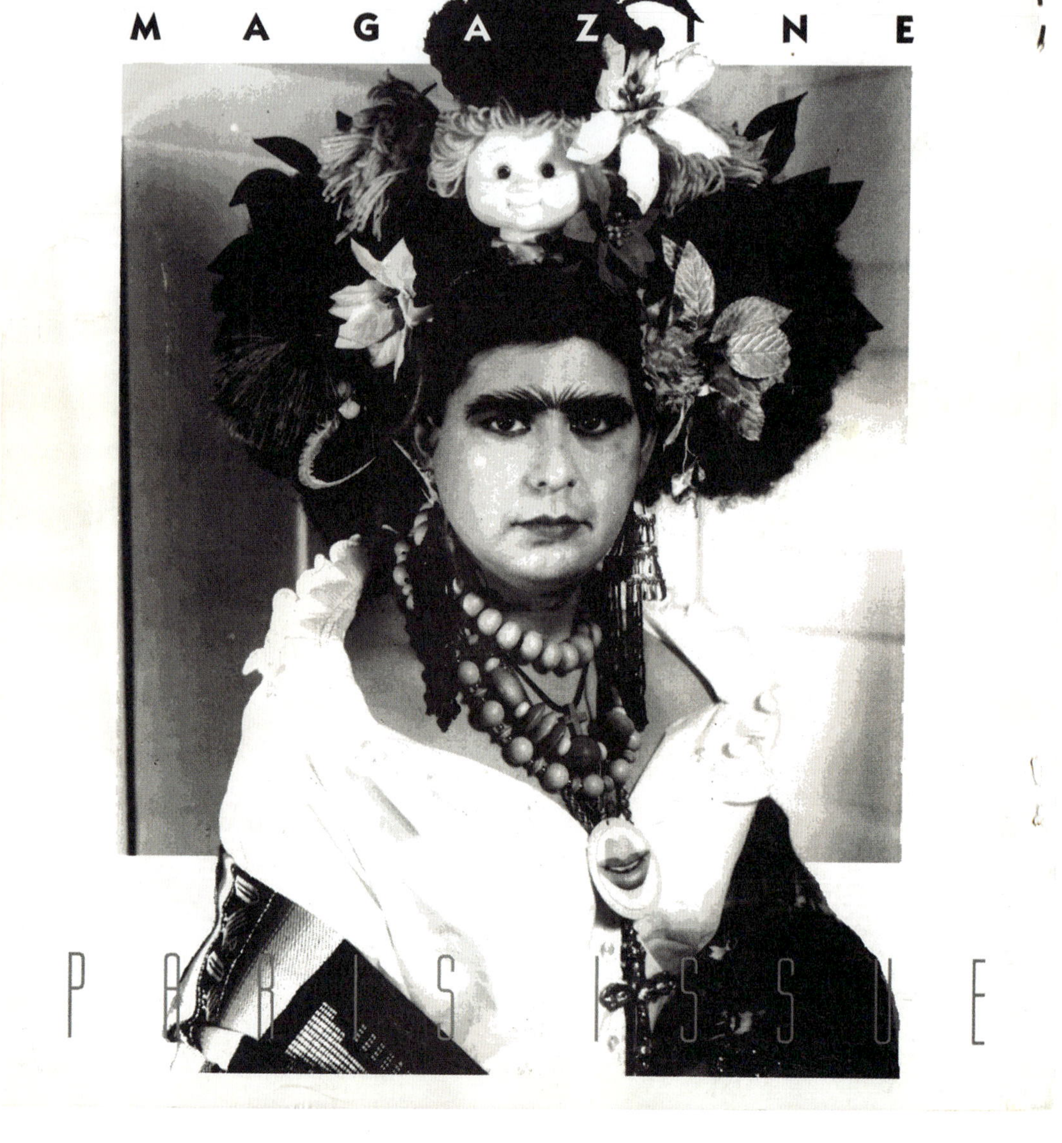

Mother Vaginal Davis Interviewed by Brontez Purnell

Vaginal Davis is an icon of the punk and queercore movements. Born and raised in Los Angeles, Davis founded and performed in numerous bands, including the Afro Sisters, Black Fag, ¡Cholita!, and Pedro, Muriel, and Esther (PME), as part of the city's alternative music scene between the late 1970s and 1990s. As a zinemaker, Davis gained attention for her self-published *Fertile La Toyah Jackson Magazine* (1987–91), which purported to compile the often hilarious and sometimes raunchy views, gossip, and exploits of the zine's namesake, Fertile La Toyah Jackson, alongside articles attributed to Davis. Played by a friend of Davis, Fertile appeared on the cover of each issue and was the subject of entries such as "Things That Make Fertile Mad." Renowned for her visual and performance art, Davis has lived in Berlin since 2006.

BRONTEZ PURNELL (BP) So, there's this image I have of you that's very celestial, though I have to say it lives in a sort of mixtape of my memory—formed through old photos and flyers of LA gay scenesters, photographs in old underground rags, and fragments of your zine *Fertile La Toyah Jackson*.

VAGINAL DAVIS (VD) When it comes to the first wave of queercore and my zines *Fertile La Toyah Jackson* and *Shrimp: The Magazine for Licking and Sucking Bigger and Better Feet* (1993), I am so surprised that people are still fascinated by that period. I would just make something and then move on to the next project. I am bad at archiving my own work. I am thankful to hungthrobs like Larry Bob Roberts of *Holy Titclamps* who had the foresight to save copies of my zines. I never thought I would live beyond my twenties and here I am almost 600 years old. It's great being an elder stateswoman.

I just watched your twerking dance recitation and was mesmerized by the way you hold your gaze at the camera like a challenge—the giddy abandon of the gang bang.

BP Who are some of the queers who were part of the punk scene in LA that deserve greater recognition?

VD Oh, you know Miss Tequila Mockingbird? I love her—she is the ultimate grifter. You have to grift to survive in this world and she does it with such stylish panache.

The late great Sean DeLear: I always felt she would live forever, surviving a broken neck, hep C, and HIV. She partied with everyone! The late Matt Dyke [aka Matt Dike] of Delicious Vinyl records wanted me for the video of Tone Loc's "Funky Cold Medina" song. I hate being in videos, so they hired Sean D instead. She was the better fit for that sort of thing.

Mrs. Michael Glass, who contributed extensively to the *Amok Dispatches* and graduated with an MFA from CalArts—so brilliant. He came out of Watts and his father was a Baptist minister. Mrs. Glass was such a talented artist and wasn't a careerist, or as Jack Smith put it an "Uncle Fishhook." He wound up homeless and destitute and died in 2015. So sad, LA destroyed him—it's a hard-knock town.

BP How did you get involved in the punk scene?

VD I would have never been involved in punk if it hadn't been for my cousin Karla DuPlantier of The Controllers. Karla and Alice Bag were one of LA's first 100 punks. Before the advent of hardcore, the early scene was led by women, queers, and people of color. It was very art-based and urban. The white boys from the beachy suburbs didn't infiltrate 'til late 1978, followed by Orange County meatheads. Since I was younger than Karla and Alice, I never considered myself punk. I wrote songs that I felt were more like show tunes and operetta but with my flat, bad singing voice people took it for punk.

BP What about your background?

VD My father was born in Mexico City, but he and my mother were never married. She was twenty years his senior. My mother was a lesbian and only wound up getting pregnant when she would get really drunk. I didn't start to explore the Mexican part of my heritage until the mid 1980s when I formed the band ¡Cholita!, "The Female Menudo," with Alice Bag. At that point in time, I was sick of post-punk and so-called alternative music and was only listening to Spanish language radio like K Radio Amor.

Being of a mixed racial background is no big deal. Every Black person in America is mixed with either American Indian or white because of slavery. My mother is a Black Creole from Louisiana on her father's side and her mother is Choctaw Indian born on the reservation. That's where I get my high cheekbones.

◂ (and following sparead) Covers of and pages from *Fertile La Toyah Jackson Magazine*, 1987–91. ONE National Gay & Lesbian Archives at the USC Libraries

2 THINGS THAT MAKE FERTILE MAD

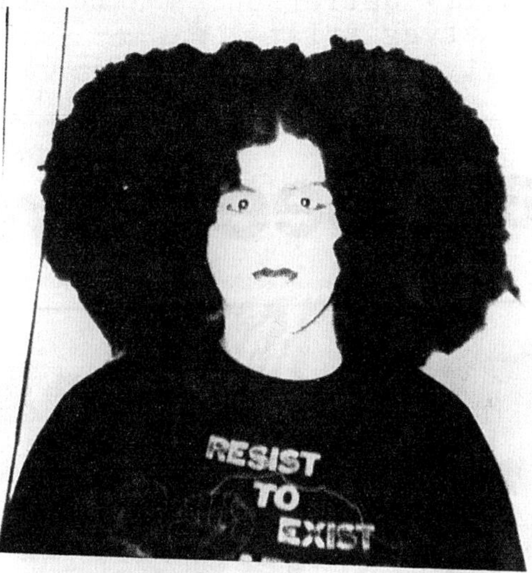

unk rock type trendies rom the suburbs that re narrow minded and igoted that think they re cool because they ress all in black and even dye their air black. Well these ype of people have rusty butt's and I ate them and when I ee them I tell them o.

People who drive fancy expensive cars like BM and the like that wher they are stopped at a light and they look ov and see a third-world person they immediatel lock their door.

reprinted by Permission from "The Five Days of Fertile", copyright © 1986 Big Binocer Press.

photo by Jacqueline Diverse

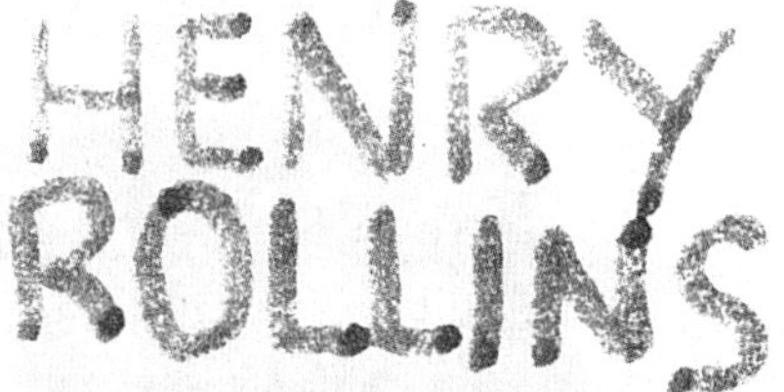

unnatural desires

By Vag Davis

I heard that Henry Rollins moved to Silverlake in some house where he produces his writings. Well honey thats the house that I'd sure like to live in. Yes indeed. I've had the extreme hots for that pile of tatoos and muscles ever since he took Dez Cadena's place in Black Flag. Now dez was another saucy cutee, but back to Henry. The reason I feel he is so angry looking all the time because he doesn't have a beautiful black women to have sex with, well Henry just give me a call and I'll satisfy your natural and unnatural desires.

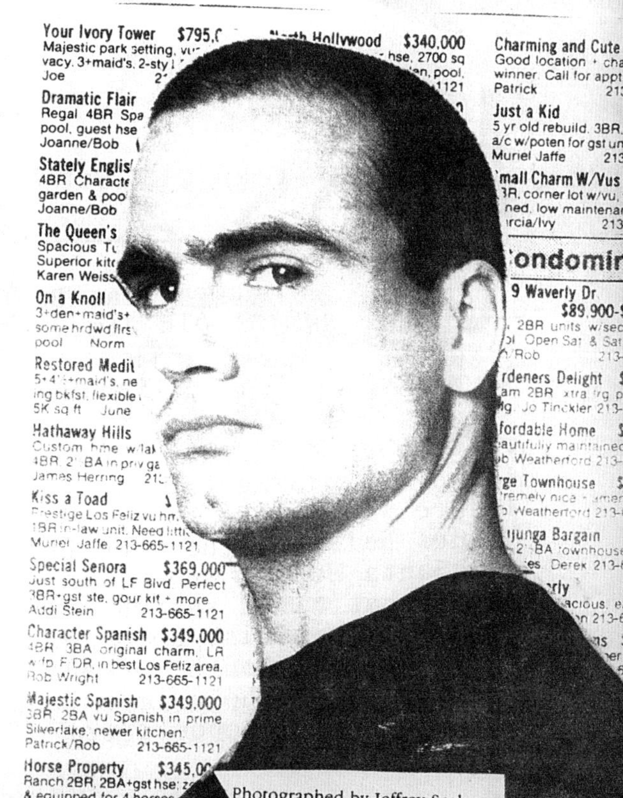

Photographed by Jeffrey Scales

Photo By JACQUELINE IVERSE

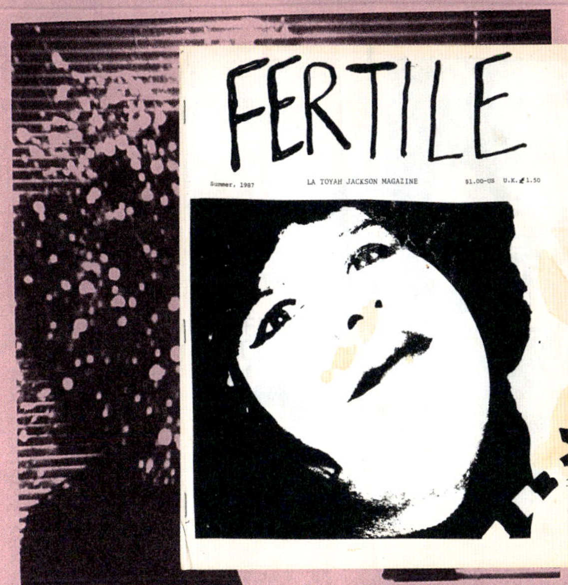

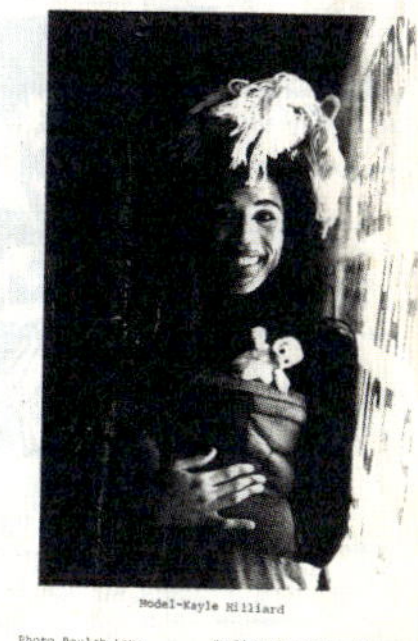

Fertile LaToyah Jackson,The Magazine
...ncept in perio-
...ertile The
...Music com-
... Editorials
...try whatever
...d interesting
...kson.
...n Jackson?
...not in the
... one of
... internationally
...g sensation.
... other and
...om you can
...remiere issue
...one is talking

FERTILE LATOYAH JACKSON—STAR!

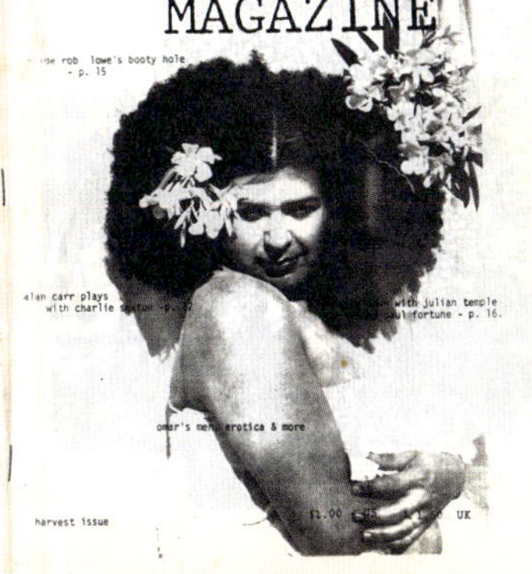

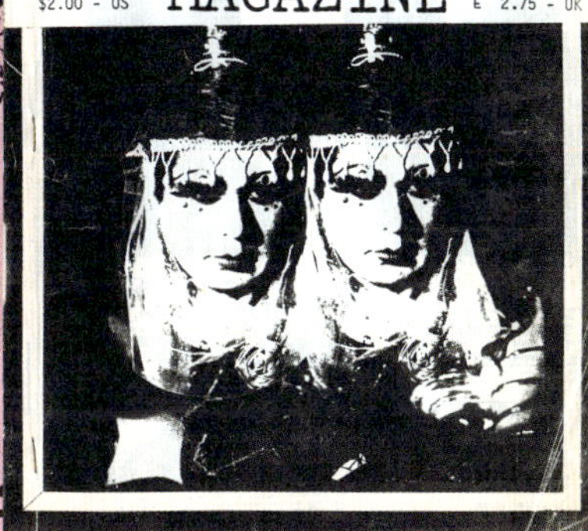

...SON MAGAZINE
... Sunset Blvd
...s, 90046
...quiries to
...ll (213) 851-

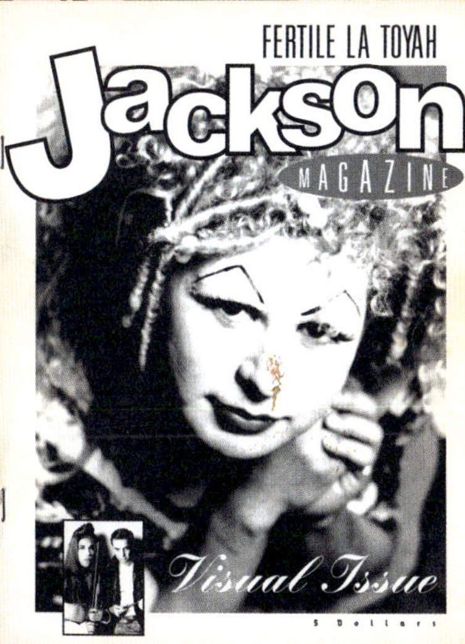

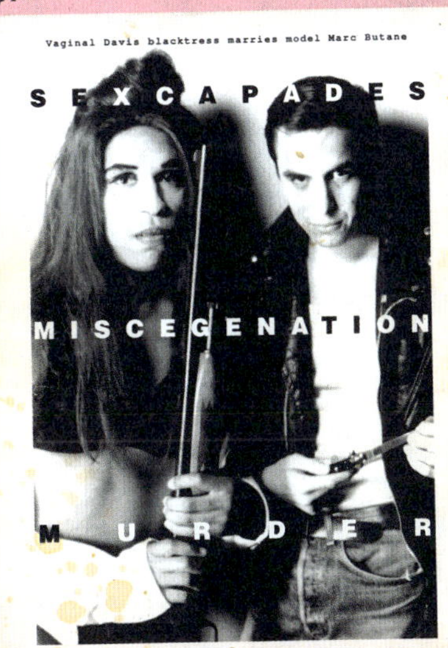

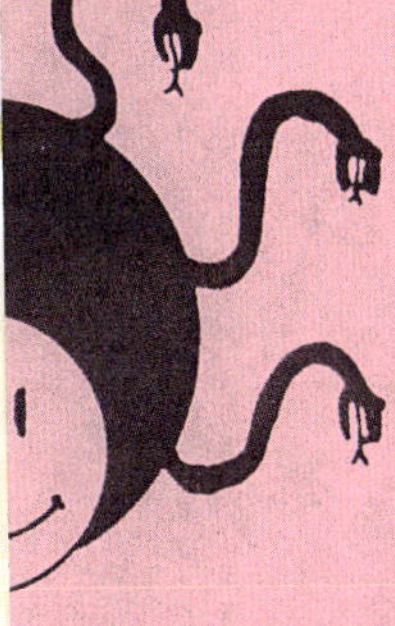

...hoto by
...no

Sexual-Eaze Liberation Front
Design By Mark Maxwell

I Love Ricky/Cloutier

Photo By Beulah Love

48 REED ERICKSON'S PSYCHEDELIC SELF-PORTRAITS, c. 1977

Reed Erickson (1917–1992) occupies a place in trans history equal parts prominent and fraught. The notoriously eccentric transsexual millionaire began providing crucial early funding for Harry Benjamin's gender identity research in the late 1960s—before Stonewall—following Erickson's own transition under Benjamin's care. He founded his philanthropy group, the Erickson Educational Foundation (EEF), in 1964, which would provide ongoing support and resources to trans communities—including referrals, direct services, and educational material—throughout most of the 1970s. The EEF also joined a national network of aligned groups agitating for trans liberation in the years of post-Stonewall radicalism. But while Erickson has been well recognized by historians for what now stands as his more "traditional" work on trans politics, less has been said about Erickson's expansive and idiosyncratic interests that lay, by appearances, far beyond matters of gender or sexuality. Erickson was a longtime enthusiast for psychedelics, New Age initiatives, animal communication, parapsychology, techniques for inducing altered states of consciousness, and a panoply of other countercultural pursuits. Erickson integrated these interests into the EEF's work, which supported them under its nebulous commitment to "provide assistance and support in areas where human potential was limited by adverse physical, mental or social conditions."[1]

Although historical accounts have tended to partition Erickson's more unorthodox proclivities as mere footnotes to his work on transsexualism, both the EEF and Erickson's personal life recurrently intertwined them. In this respect, Erickson arguably saw trans justice as part and parcel of a far more expansive imaginary that located trans communities within an interconnected, cosmopolitical ecology of the human and nonhuman, secular and enchanted, rational and oneiric. Erickson himself clearly incorporated these dualities into his own life; indeed, historians have often linked his growing investments in practices like psychotropic consumption and communion with animals to an overarching narrative arc of his decline.[2]

Erickson's use of ketamine deepened as the 1970s progressed, and he became increasingly distrustful and antagonistic toward gay activist groups with which he had allied previously; accordingly, he gradually slackened his efforts to advance gay and trans liberation in favor of his more "far out" (yet longstanding) investments. During these years, Erickson's personal writings also become more prolific on the matter of his own uncanny capabilities and achievements. Erickson claimed he could sense energies (for instance, discerning whether an electrical appliance was plugged in just by touching it); he also attested to his ability to lift thousands of pounds of weight; and claimed to enjoy an IQ of 5,000 and hold doctoral degrees in several fields.[3] Understandably, then, much less attention has been paid to Erickson's activities of the latter half of the 1970s, marked as they are by the specter of madness and declension. Yet his psychedelic paintings, likely produced under the influence of ketamine in the late 1970s, reveal Erickson's ongoing contributions to trans cultural production during this period.

In Erickson's self-portrait, *I am fire, I am wind, I AM BEING ALL that YOU IS SEEING* (c. 1977), he depicts himself with demonic pointed ears, suggesting super-human characteristics; likewise, auras emanating above his head and the inscription "Love / Joy," within a cross form demarcating a third eye, elicit powers of perception that extend beyond the ordinary sense channels. A similar painting, *La Curacion del Hombre* (c. 1977), depicting the outline of a humanoid head—likely another self-rendering by Erickson—features a rotated symbol of eternity overlaid on the head's featureless contours, evoking the infinite, untapped potential of the human mind that the EEF strove to actualize. The psychedelic color palette and its patterning are reminiscent of the visual disturbances occasioned by ketamine, just as the infinity sign gestures at the advanced dissociative state of the "K-hole" and its vast stretches of time dilation. And underpinning both works is a presentation of transfiguration, of the alchemical transubstantiation of the worldly human plane into something beyond. If these, in sum, are the visual imprints of Erickson's decline, perhaps today we may locate within this madness not just beauty but also a vision of the preternatural capabilities of trans insight, agency, and power.

—Abram J. Lewis

1. Erickson Educational Foundation brochure, n.d., Box 1, Folder 14, Reed Erickson Fonds, Transgender Archives (AR417), Transgender Archives, University of Victoria Libraries, British Columbia.
2. See, for example, Aaron Devor and Nicholas Matte, "ONE Inc. and Reed Erickson: The Uneasy Collaboration of Gay and Trans Activism, 1964–2003," *GLQ: A Journal of Gay and Lesbian Studies* 10, no. 2 (November 2, 2004); Joanne Meyerowitz, *How Sex Changed: A History of Transsexuality in the United States* (Cambridge, MA: Harvard University Press, 2002), 258; and Susan Stryker, *Transgender History* (Berkeley: Seal Press, 2008), 106.
3. See, for example, Personal notes, Reed Erickson, n.d., n.p., and Reed Erickson to unknown recipient, September 26, 1983, Box 34, Folder 7, "Awards / Mental Health & Personal / Miscellaneous, Pinecrest Hospital," Reed Erickson Fonds (AR417), Transgender Archives, University of Victoria Libraries, British Columbia.

▸ Reed Erickson, *I am fire, I am wind, I AM BEING ALL that YOU IS SEEING*, c. 1977. Acrylic on canvas, 24 × 36 in. (61 × 91 cm). Reed Erickson Fonds (AR417), Transgender Archives, University of Victoria Libraries, British Columbia

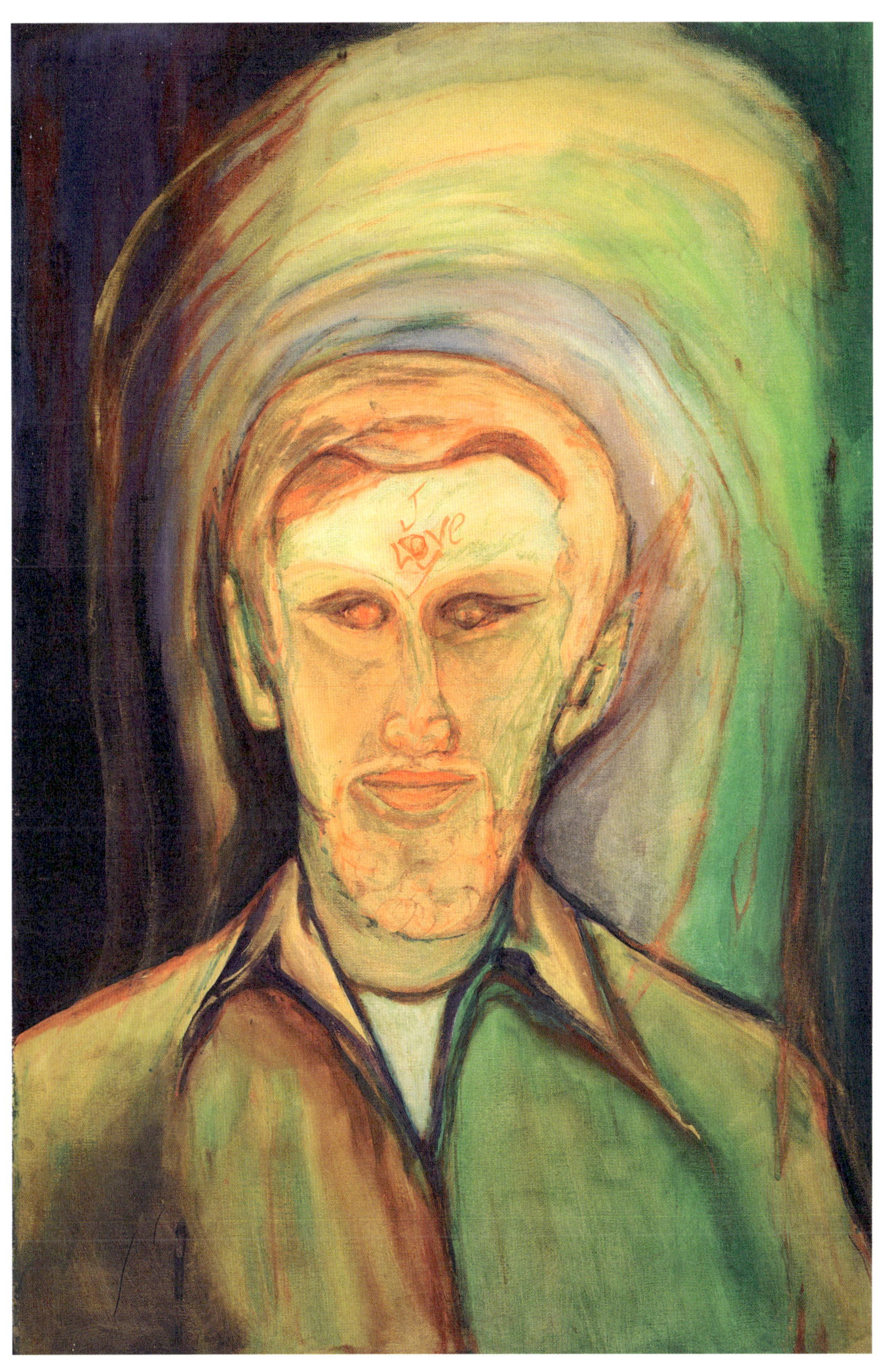
I Love

▼
Erickson Educational Foundation (EEF) educational pamplets, c. 1970s. Reed L. Erickson Papers, ONE National Gay & Lesbian Archives at the USC Libraries

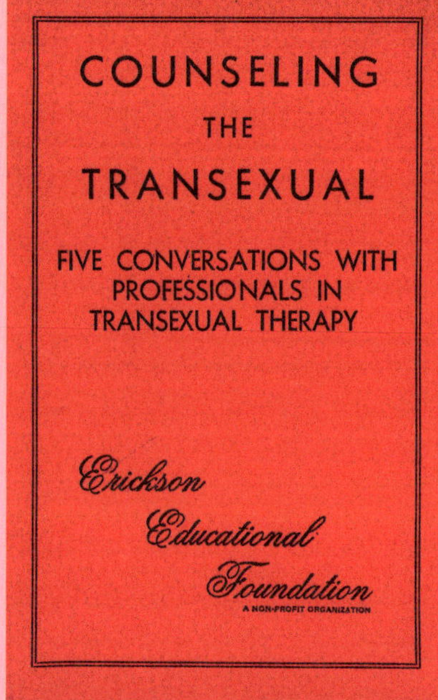

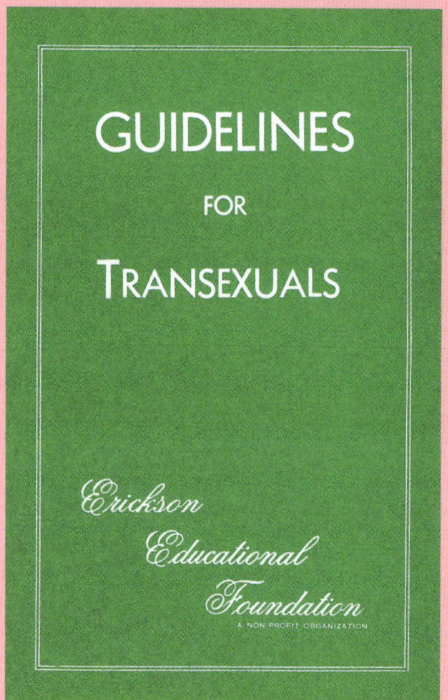

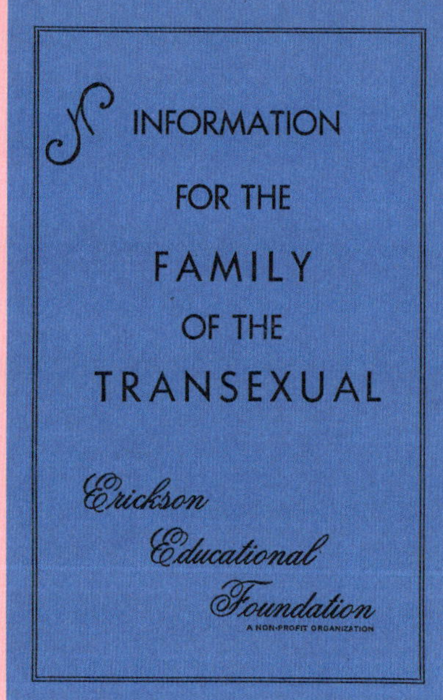

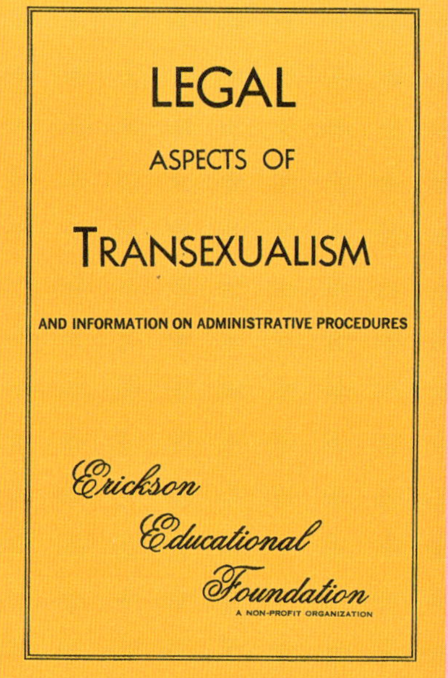

▶
Reed Erickson, *La Curacion del Hombre*, 1977. Acrylic on canvas, 24 × 36 in. (61 × 91 cm). Reed Erickson Fonds (AR417), Transgender Archives, University of Victoria Libraries, British Columbia

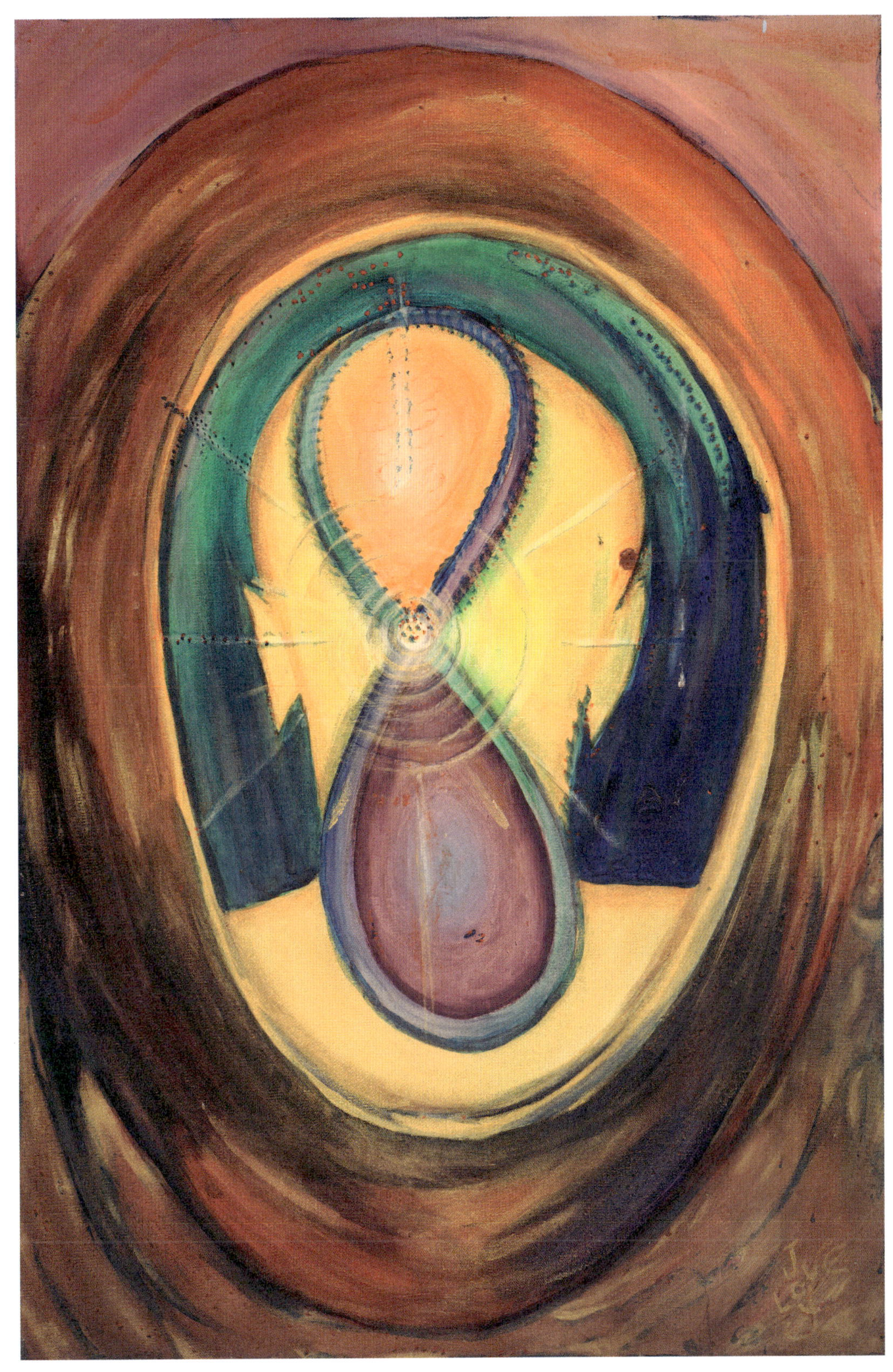

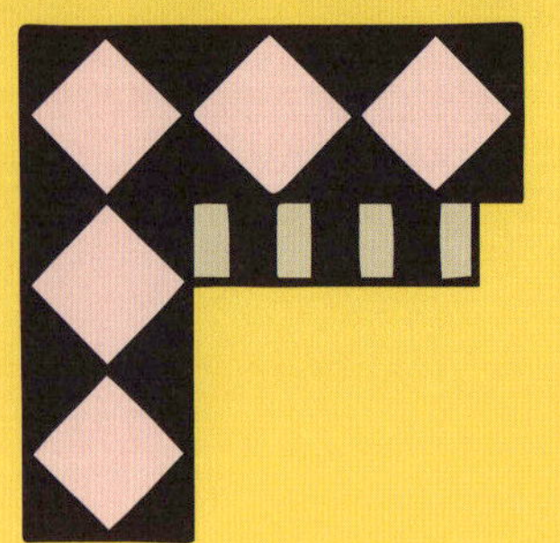
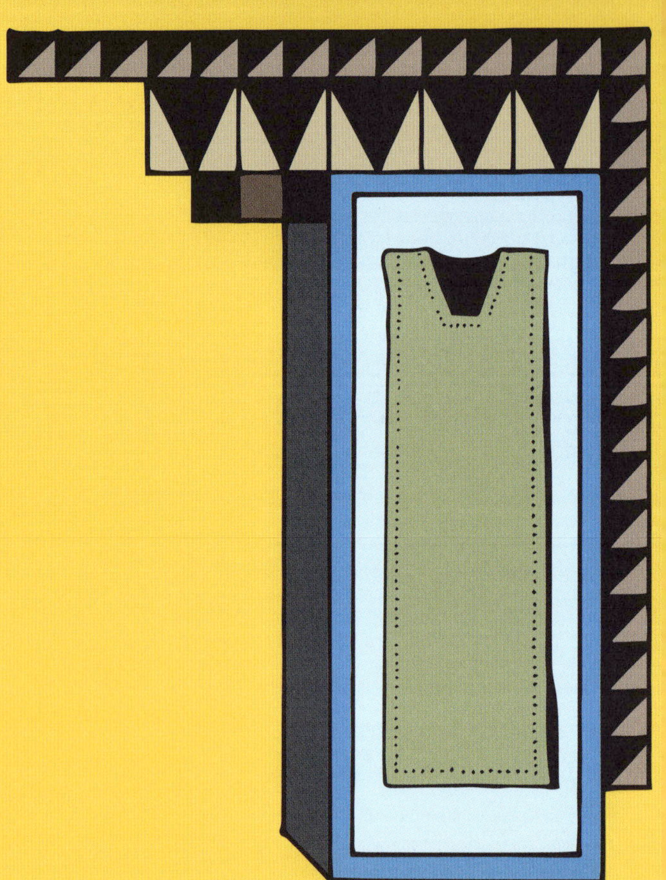
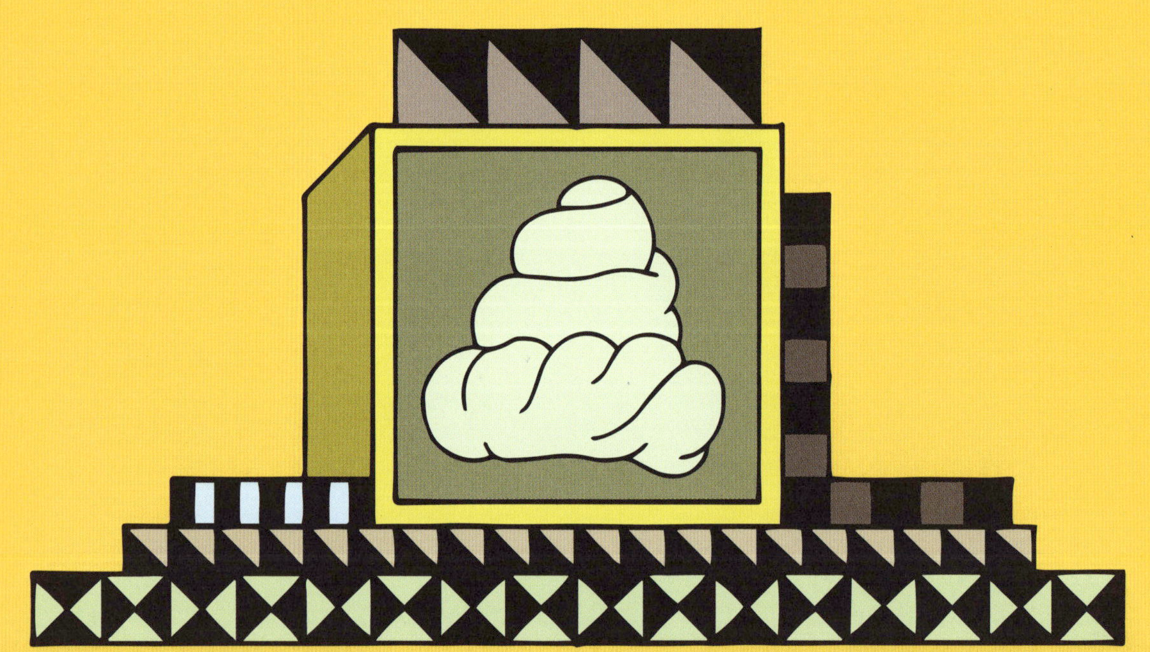

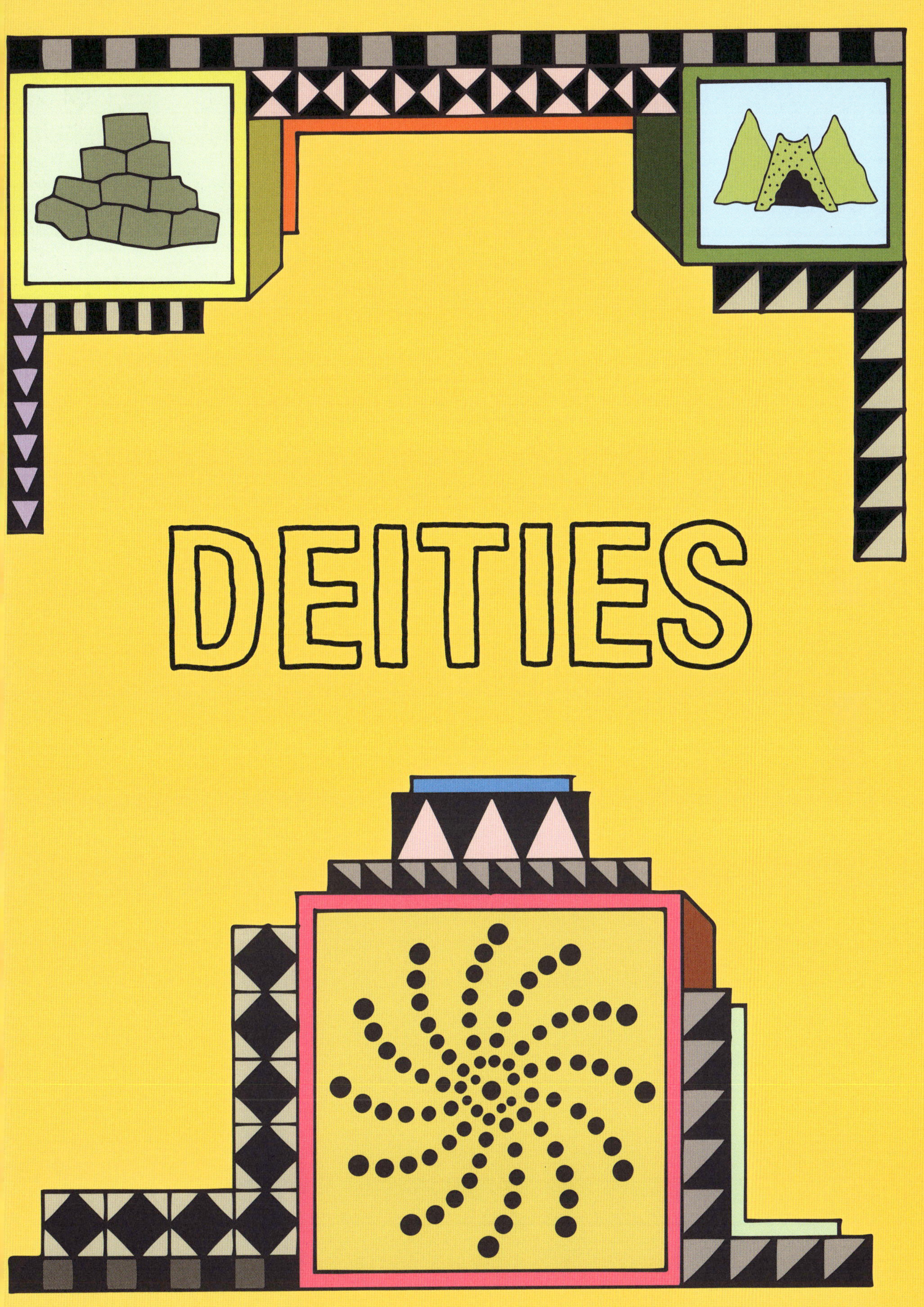
DEITIES

49 VINCENT CHONG, *TEAL AT 98.6° F*, 2022

Kwun Yum (Cantonese for Guan Yin) is an ancient protector, and her sight transcends time, space, gender, sexuality, and race. In my youth, she could see that my soft heart was in danger. She projected herself to me in the form of a pendant to offer a small amount of protection.

My life as a queer, gender-nonconforming, mixed-race Chinese American was engineered to make me feel invisible, ashamed, and disgusting beneath the American flag. Wearing my pendant could not protect me from the totality of this oppressive force, but it pierced the small hole in this narrative that allowed me to begin deconstructing and discarding this insidious lie, piece by piece.

"I pledge allegiance, to the flag, of the United States of America, and to the republic, for which it stands, one nation, *my lips shut tight*, indivisible, with liberty and justice for ALL."

I stood with my white classmates, eyes fixed on the flag tacked up in our classroom—the great symbol of genocide, imperialism, slavery, transphobia, queerphobia, and white supremacy. As I stared at the flag, my awareness focused on the small object around my neck, deflecting the flag's evil away from my body.

"Don't show that to people," my white mom had told me when I extended my eight-year-old palm, displaying the back side of the brassy oval pendant. A small Buddhist swastika sat at its center, encircled by two rings of smaller swastikas, all a deep crimson hue. In Buddhism, swastikas are ancient sacred symbols whose spiraling forms represent the circular nature of existence and the footprint of the Buddha—my mom's eyes could only recognize their adoption by Nazis. As I retracted my hand, I felt sad.

And so I never showed my classmates. The pendant hung around my neck on a crimson string. It must have been a gift from my Chinese uncles. No one made me wear it, but it felt like a secret that only I could understand, which made me feel safe—so I kept it around my neck.

On the pendant's face was Kwun Yum atop a lotus, draped in a flowing white gown, pouring out the contents of a Coke-bottle-shaped vessel with a hand emerging from beneath her sleeve. She stood against a backdrop of deep brown ochre.

As the heat from my body seeped into the pendant, the brown would gently brighten to gold-brown before transitioning to a delicate sea-mist teal with touches of pale pink around the edges. I learned that if I held the pendant tightly in my palm—or better yet, in my armpit—the pink would fill the pendant. It felt as though it might turn fuchsia if my body could just produce a bit more heat.

"Kwun Yum is like the female Buddha," explained my dad. And so it seemed fitting that she hung around my neck in her sea of changing colors. I knew my heart was different. Inside my chest, I always felt, was a girl's heart. I hid Kwun Yum inside my T-shirt, and beneath her I hid my girl's heart.

When I stood to pledge my allegiance, Kwun Yum and her swastikas created a barrier in front of my sternum and blocked the poisonous words from entering my body. My mouth formed the sounds, but wearing my pendant was like crossing my fingers behind my back.

—Vincent Chong

The embodiment of compassion, Kwun Yum or Guan Yin (觀音), a bodhisattva also known as Avalokitesvara, is known as the one "who hears the cries of the world." Transcending gender identity, Kwun Yum appears in whatever form is necessary to help people in need: sometimes female, sometimes male, sometimes androgynous. According to scholar Hsiao-Lan Hu, "Identity-shifting is done not to avoid certain identities, but to serve the need at the moment."

▸
Vincent Chong,
teal at 98.6° F, 2022.
Oil on canvas, 24 × 20 in.
(61 × 50.8 cm)

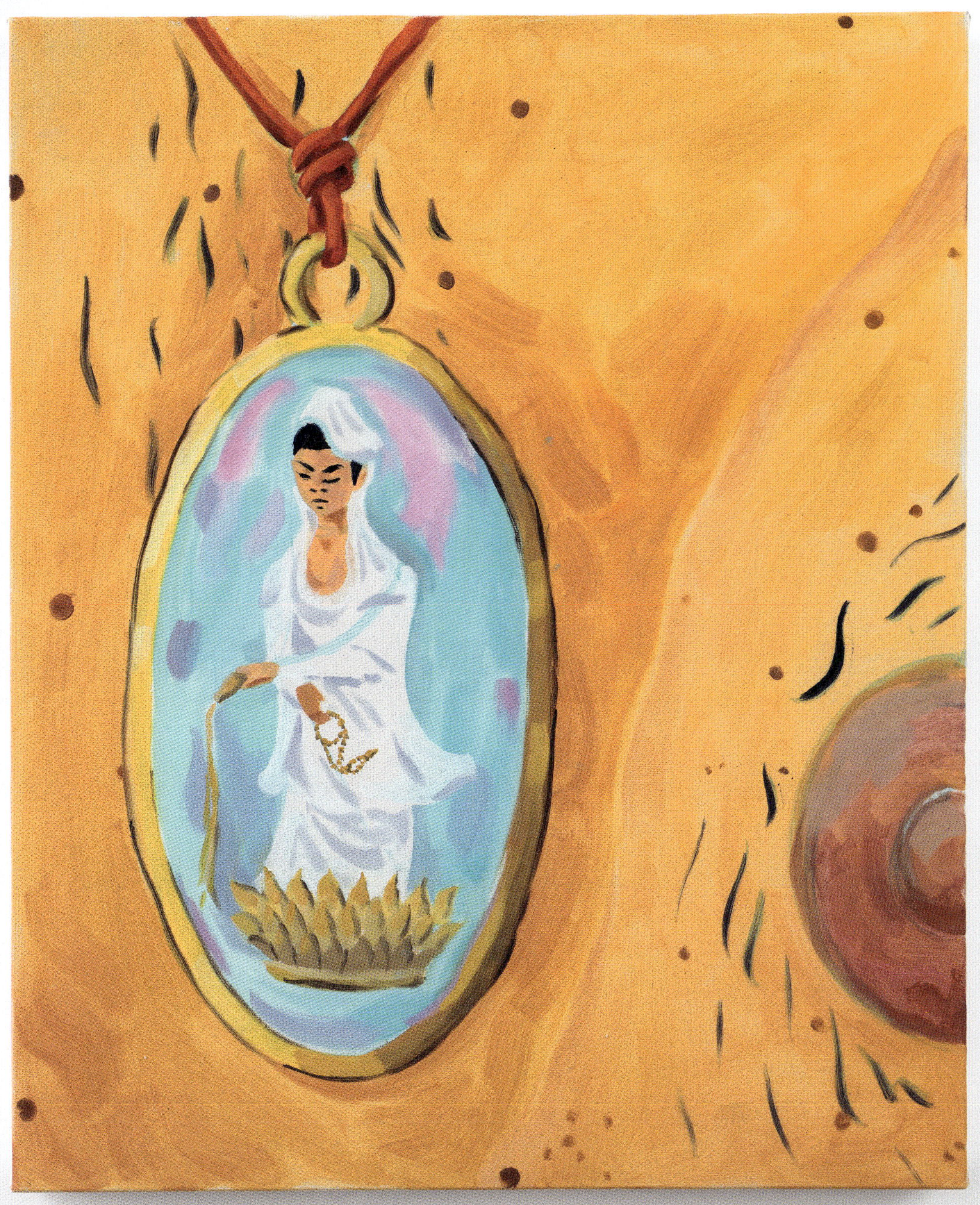

50 SYLVESTER'S SEQUINED BLAZERS, c. 1985

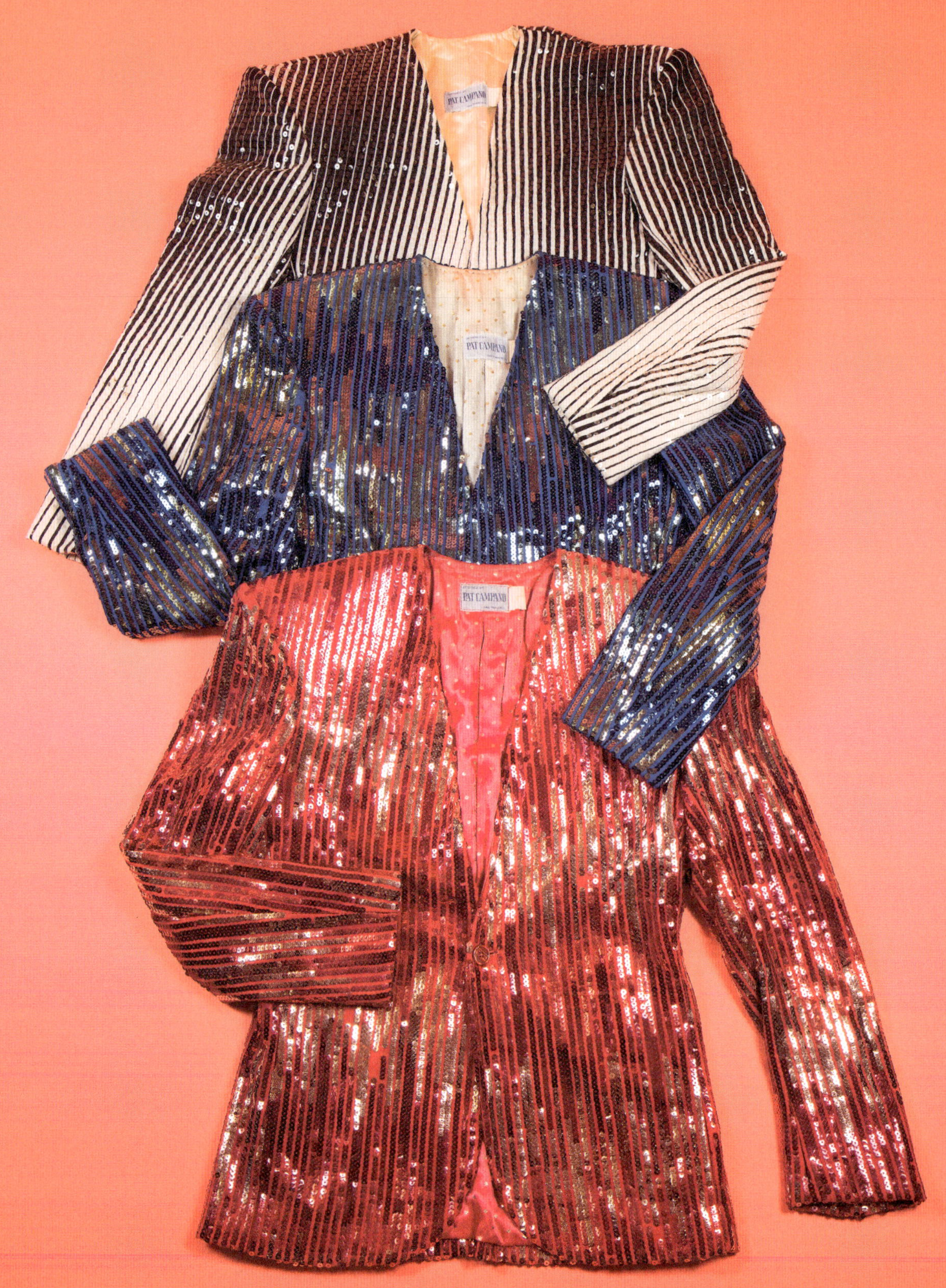

All that Shimmers

If sequined clothing came with a soundtrack, this audible accompaniment would, in my mind, be the music of Sylvester (1947–1988). When I hear the intro to Sylvester's classic 1982 disco/ Hi-NRG song "Do You Wanna Funk?"—a collaborative effort between "the Queen of Disco" and music producer Patrick Cowley—the succession of shimmering synthesized sounds that entwine with the song's opening tempo cannot help but conjure visuals of Sylvester draped in his widely recognizable and deeply admired attire. Indeed, these shimmering sounds allow us, paraphrasing cultural theorist Tina Campt, to "listen to the image" of Sylvester, whose wardrobe facilitated a way to recognize alternative formations of gender, sexuality, and race.[1] Extrapolating from Roland Barthes's assessment of the variable meaning of the textile's shimmering surface, trans studies scholar Eliza Steinbock argues that shimmering images "describe [a] persistent vision of trans as change, and as a force that continues to achieve change through varying means and ways."[2] Sylvester's cultivated look, predicated upon the inseparability of music and image, appeared as a shimmering vision that refused sex and gender norms as they fiercely served as a catalyst for ideological transformation.

According to Joshua Gamson, the "diva persona" of Sylvester (né Sylvester James Jr.) "symbolized, more broadly, the 1970s subcultures of glittery, druggy, self-celebrating fantasy worlds where gender was something you could try on and race was an exploding costume, where your body's sex and desires and color would not matter if you wore them imaginatively, where flaming was neither a stigma nor a joke but an art form."[3] But Sylvester's fashion sense also captured a something new to "try on" just as it was "an exploding costume" that refused to play by the rules of gender. As the Los Angeles-born singer adopted a falsetto singing style that indexes, in the words of Black queer theorist Francesca T. Royster, "one part blues woman, one part space age funkster," Sylvester drew "from a vocabulary of images of black female sexuality and black male soulfulness that might be familiar to his audience, while switching codes, rewiring the circuits."[4] The sequined blazers designed by Pat Campano—who also lent his fashion hand to the Supremes—simultaneously served to accentuate Sylvester's aim to switch codes and rewire circuits while charging the twin sonic and visual currents underscoring his iconic persona. In an interview with Campano, Paul-Francis Hartmann registers the association of Campano's apparel "with the spectacular," affixed "with personality and possibilities" and "designed to enhance the entertainer provided the performer takes advantage of what the costume can do."[5] Campano's multicolored blazers therefore played a dual role in enhancing the shimmer of Sylvester's self-presentation and amplifying the shimmering music providing the vehicle through which to showcase an unparalleled vocal capacity.

Sylvester passed on December 16, 1988, yet his memory lives on. A paragon of flair whose gender defiance boldly guided his life's work, Sylvester's iridescent example continues to influence and inspire. And riveted by the shimmering lure of his music and those elegantly adorned sequined blazers, how could anyone resist the desire to funk with Sylvester?

—Richard T. Rodríguez

◂
Sequined blazers designed by Pat Campano for Sylvester, c. 1985. Gay, Lesbian, Bisexual, Transgender Historical Society. Photo by Marcel Pardo Ariza

1. Tina Campt, *Listening to Images* (Durham, NC: Duke University Press, 2017).
2. Eliza Steinbock, *Shimmering Images: Trans Cinema, Embodiment, and the Aesthetics of Change* (Durham, NC: Duke University Press, 2019), ix.
3. Joshua Gamson, "Sylvester," *Camera Obscura* 65, vol. 22, no. 2 (September 2007): 140.
4. Francesca T. Royster, *Sounding Like a No-No: Queer Sounds and Eccentric Acts in the Post-Soul Era* (Ann Arbor, MI: University of Michigan Press, 2013), 26.
5. Paul-Francis Hartmann, "Pat Campano Designer Extraordinaire," *Bay Area Reporter*, July 31, 1980, 27.

51 LORRAINE MERRITT, PORTRAIT OF CHRISTINE JORGENSEN, 1954

Dear Christine,

My mother was a toddler in 1953 when you came home from Europe with a fresh pussy between your legs. Not to essentialize you, but the global clamor that occurred after you famously stepped off the plane from Denmark was catalyzed by that man-made vagina. Having learned about your life then as I have lived my life today, it seems to me that you were genuinely surprised by such a calamitous reception, stunned by overnight celebrity, yet still somehow prepared and dignified.

Christine, your grace touched the world as the first transsexual superstar. You were a messenger, out of time with the Cleavers and John Wayne, but every bit in sync with Marilyn and Grace. With gumption, glamour, and panache, you established a precedent of white woman respectability that transcends time. Your legacy is indelible. Eternal.

In 1954, you sat for a painted portrait, perhaps to commemorate the height of your fame, an age-old symbol of social prominence, forever sealing your status as *somebody*. You posed for photographs over and over again in front of this painting as a measure of time and, like most objects, it outlived your mortal body.

What it must have meant to you, to be created with care, through hours of attentive witness. To memorialize one's own significance by the alchemical process of artmaking is to bestow a part of one's soul into a world inherently alien to our inner realities. No one's inner world is ever truly known by another. But it seems a most human project to externalize the unseen, that though we may be destined to live alone within, there is still a home in the body and the art here, a window.

I see the meaning that this image must have had for you in the public record of your life. Throughout the years, this portrait made appearances in photographs that were taken of you, it clearly occupied a place of prominence in your home in Laguna Niguel, Orange County, California. But it is in your death where I find evidence of its profound meaning to you, and its own immortal destiny. In your will, you bequeathed many things to the Royal Danish Library (Det Kgl. Bibliotek) in Copenhagen, including personal papers and, of course, that portrait. So the window remains open, and you are known by others who are separated from you not only by the boundaries of the body, but by time.

Christine, you jumped through hoops of fire to appear on television and stand upon the stages where you were nothing if not beheld in the mind by an audience of others. We cannot control what they see when we stand before them, but we are still seen. On stage, you performed as a headlining chanteuse in order to personify a trans experience. Audiences came to witness an oddity, but they got a bona fide star, darling, and a charming ingénue. Did you feel at all like yourself beneath the stage lights, home at last in a world where transgender people have no place? Was it how you felt when you were made by brushstrokes?

My mother was a teenager when she read your autobiography in high school. That text surely held significance for you. How could it not? Did you know it would be another window into a human soul, and that through it your life would be ongoing in its impact on others? I am grateful it was written. Your autobiography was one of the precedents that my mother had for understanding me as a trans woman, decades later.

Flawless Sabrina once said to me, "Pioneers seldom live to walk in the paths they cut." We walk in your path, Christine. We walk in the kaleidoscopic ephemeral glitter of your wake. We honor your sacrifices and we honor your grace, intelligence, and wit. We celebrate you, we mourn you, we see your luminosity through the windows you left open despite the haze of time, with love.

xo Z

—Zackary Drucker

On December 1, 1952, Christine Jorgensen (1926–1989) made a public splash when she was outed by the New York Daily News *with the headline "Ex-GI Becomes Blonde Beauty." Jorgensen had been receiving gender-affirming medical treatment in Denmark when her shocking "sex change" story was taken up by the paper. A trans media spectacle ensued. Unable to live the private life she had hoped for, she leveraged this sensational publicity and launched a nightclub act, made many television appearances, lectured at universities, and published* Christine Jorgensen: A Personal Autobiography *(1967), all of which chronicled her own experience in her own words. In 1954 she commissioned this portrait by Lorraine Merritt.*

▸ Lorraine Merritt, Portrait of Christine Jorgensen, 1954. Oil on canvas, 46 × 38⅝ in. (117 × 98 cm). Royal Danish Library

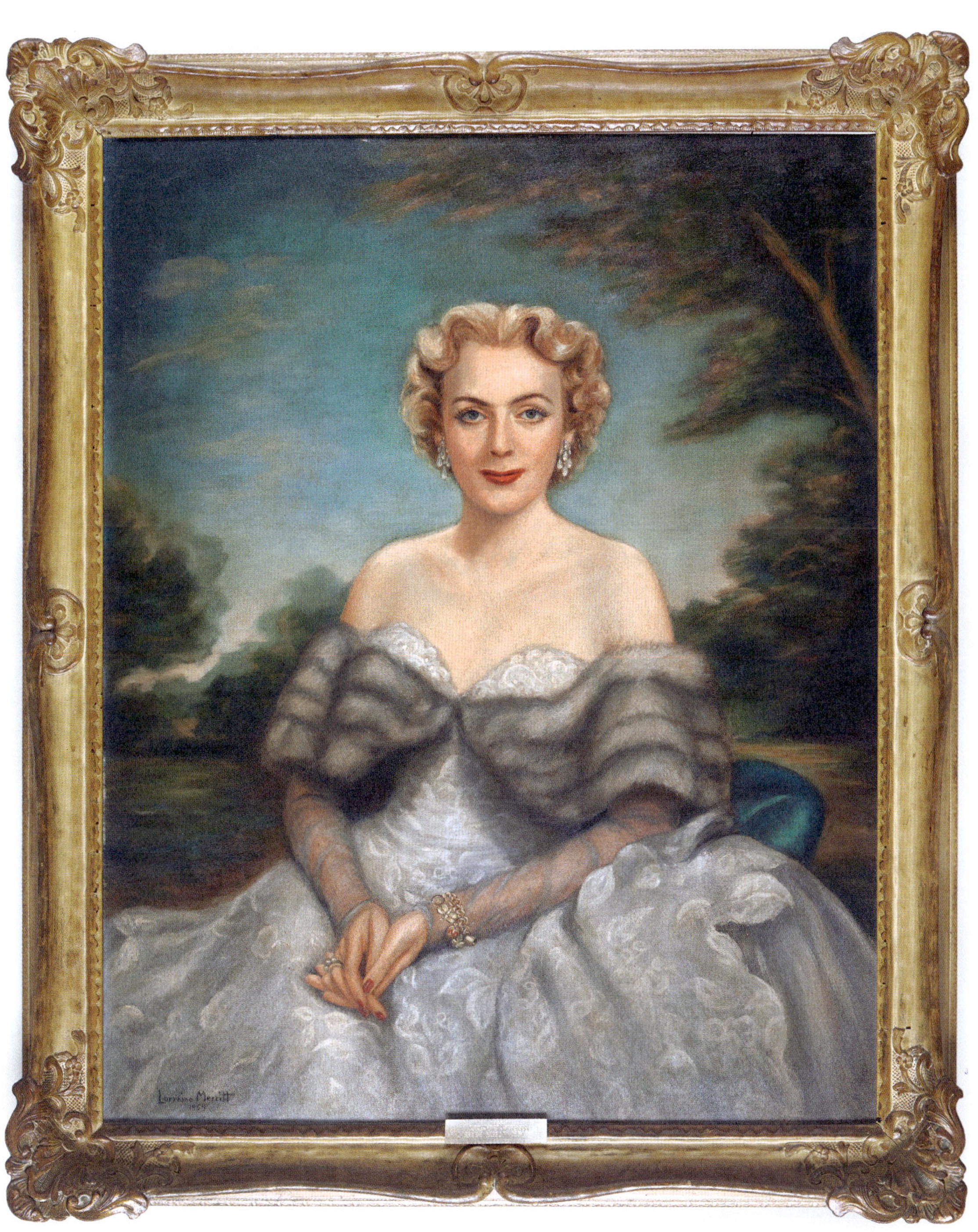
Lorraine Merritt

52 JEROME CAJA, *ASCENSION OF THE DRAG QUEEN*, 1994

Jerome Caja (1958–1995) was a central figure in the radical queer art and performance scene in San Francisco in the late 1980s and early 1990s. He was also one of eleven children born into a devoutly Catholic household in Cleveland, Ohio, and Saint Jerome—known for spreading the gospel of Christian morality to those living in dense city centers—was a fitting namesake. After graduating with a master's degree from the iconic (and sadly shuttered as of July 15, 2022) San Francisco Art Institute, Caja spread his own gospel through stage performances around San Francisco. One of his most iconic performances was a reenactment of the crucifixion and resurrection of Christ that he did in drag at Club Uranus in honor of Easter. Caja died of AIDS in 1995, and his own resurrection continues through the work of the Jerome Project.

Founded by Anthony Cianciolo, the Jerome Project is working to preserve Caja's legacy, which includes the vibrant, pocket-sized paintings that Caja made entirely out of nail polish. A lover of Catholic statuary and painters El Greco and Egon Schiele, Caja's painted figures loom large within their miniature scenes. In *Bozo Venus Peeing on a Burning Bush* (1987), the body of a drag queen clown stretches across a tiny floral surface like a figure distorted in a funhouse mirror. The crew of sinister figures in *New Eyes for Saint Lucy* (1994) meets our gaze like precocious playmates eager for us to climb through our bedroom windows and join them in the night. The angular jawlines, craggy cheekbones, and knobby joints of *Venus in Cleveland* (1995) make this figure resemble a tiny, demented tree standing tall and steady as violent winds swirl around her. Rendered on plastic tip trays, old picture frames, and scraps of paper, these works deliberately pervert Western art history and Christian theology.

In *Ascension of the Drag Queen* (1994), Caja casts Christ as a drag queen guided to heaven, not by the golden light of the divine, but by a tiny egg, cooked sunny side up. The drag queen's blonde hair falls long along the side of her face, itself painted a clownish white with bright blue eyeshadow and rich red lips. Her body is sheathed in an emerald ensemble. Fingerless gloves climb to her shoulders, thigh-high stiletto boots meet the straps of an almost-hidden garter belt, and a floor-length dress falls open, exposing her navel and genitals. A matching handbag hangs from the crook of her right elbow while a long-stem pink rose stands erect in her left hand. Two winged clowns float below her, naked except for their oversized red shoes. These perverse angels grip her heels as they usher her upward toward the ovum above. A plucked and spatchcocked chicken floats below this central arrangement, as if to ask which came first, the chicken or the egg? Heaven or Earth? Meanwhile, the mammy figure clutching her chest below calls our attention to the clownishness, and even devilishness, implied in this racist trope. The pale-faced devil across from her also holds his hand to his heart, but his gaze falls blank, bored, and beyond the rough edges of this tiny painting. If Christ is a drag queen, what's left to corrupt?

—Cyle Metzger

▸
Jerome Caja, *Ascension of the Drag Queen*, 1994. Nail polish on paper with hair, 21¼ × 13¼ in. (53.98 × 33.66 cm). San Francisco Museum of Modern Art, Gift of the artist

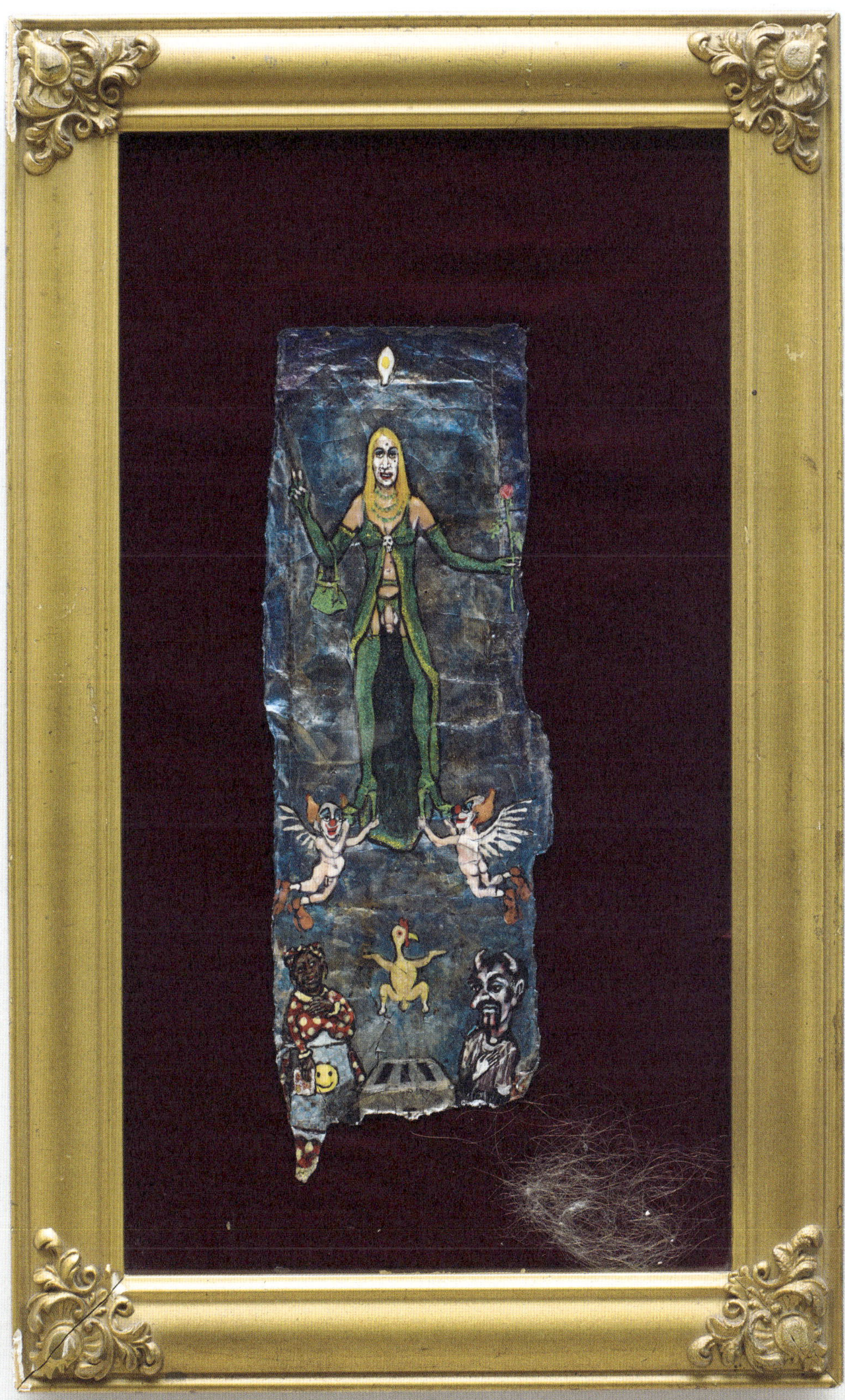

53 RACHEL POLLACK, *THE SHINING TRIBE TAROT*, 2001

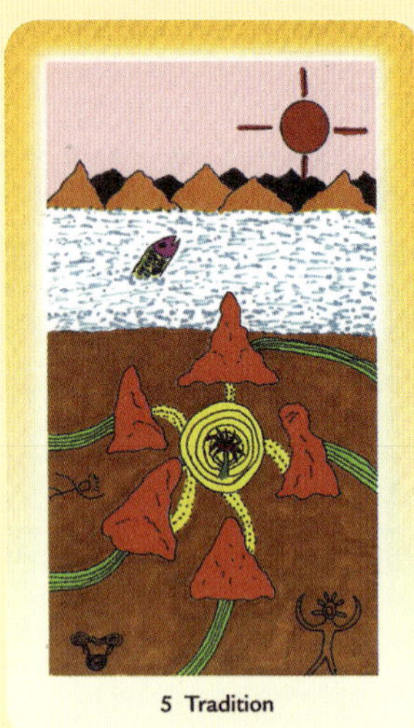

5 TRADITION

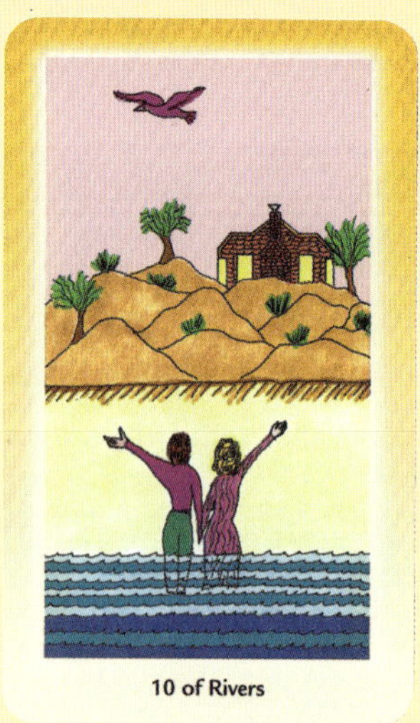

10 OF RIVERS

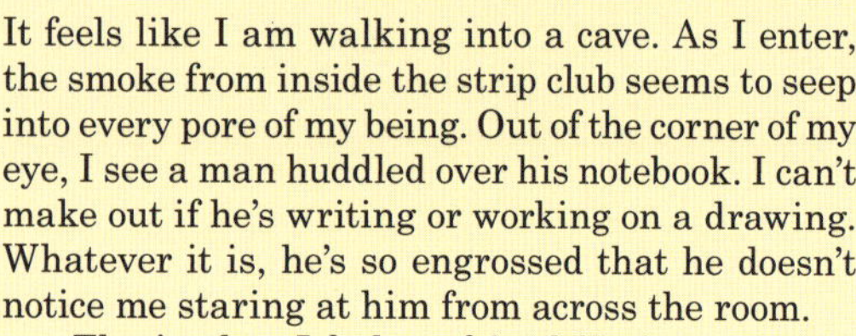

It feels like I am walking into a cave. As I enter, the smoke from inside the strip club seems to seep into every pore of my being. Out of the corner of my eye, I see a man huddled over his notebook. I can't make out if he's writing or working on a drawing. Whatever it is, he's so engrossed that he doesn't notice me staring at him from across the room.

That's when I feel my friend Kevin tap me on the shoulder.

"You can't do that, Edgar! You and your straight men…," he comments with a look of concern and judgment spread across his face.

Annoyed, I roll my eyes and head straight to the bar.

"Fuck that," I think in my head as I order a $2 PBR. I get a stack of dollar bills and stuff them into my pocket as I take a desperate chug of my beer. I look over at the man in the corner of the room, still gazing with intensity into his notebook. I notice he's drinking whiskey and has a pack of cigarettes on the table next to his drink. A stripper tries, unsuccessfully, to get his attention as I notice Kevin waving at me from another table.

I had multiple dreams about going on a hike with my partner, Thaddeus, and finding a crystal. The dreams felt eerily real and compelling. I remember smelling the dirt and feeling the moistness in the air. I could see my partner running up and down mountain paths, excited about finding something.

To my surprise, Thaddeus was really into the idea of crystal hunting in the mountains near my parents' home in Bloomington, California. It turns out that he has an uncanny ability to feel crystals when they are nearby. I lost count of the times he veered off a hiking trail, following what seemed to be a call from an old friend. A few minutes later, he'd come back, beaming, and with a crystal in his hand.

Published in 2001, The Shining Tribe Tarot *deck was created by Rachel Pollack (1945–2023) and revisits some of the themes and motifs of her 1992* Shining Woman Tarot. *In addition to being considered one of the foremost experts on divinatory tarot, Pollack was an author of science fiction and comic books. As the writer for DC Comic's* Doom Patrol *between 1993 and 1995, Pollack introduced the character Kate Godwin, also known as Coagula, the first transgender superhero in mainstream comics.*

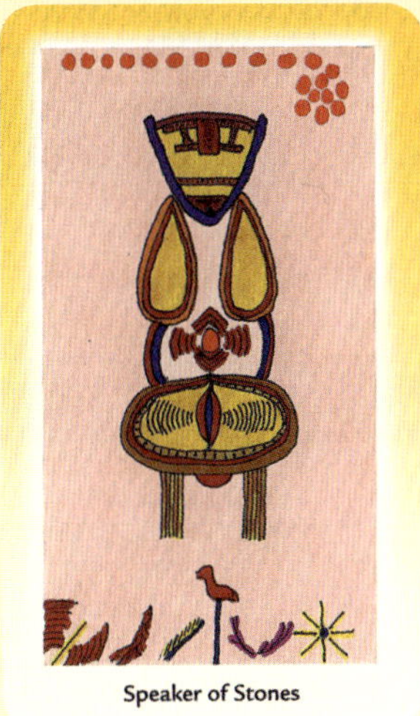

SPEAKER OF STONES

Sandy asked me during the session:
"Edgar, what do you think is wrong with you?"

I paused and thought about it for a while. At first I said nothing... but then I remembered something.

I remembered the day I tracked tar into the Gonzalez's home. They had invited us over to celebrate the extensive renovation they had just done on the house, which included brand-new carpet.

I shared this with Sandy and, for some strange reason, she smiled.

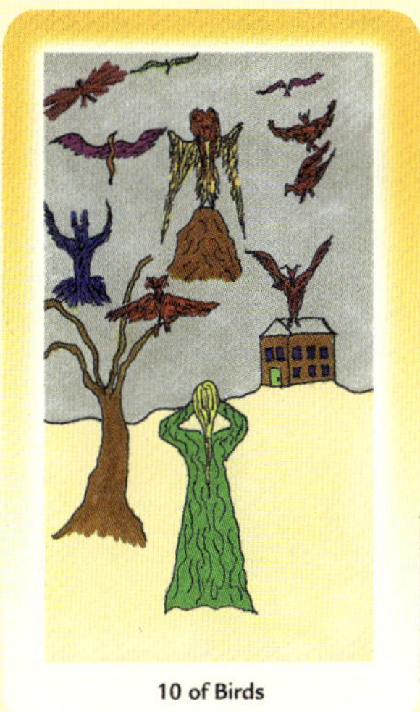

10 OF BIRDS

Here's a tip, witches. Sometimes when you gaze into obsidian, you might notice the eyes of a disembodied spirit peering back at you. Do not be afraid. You are powerful.

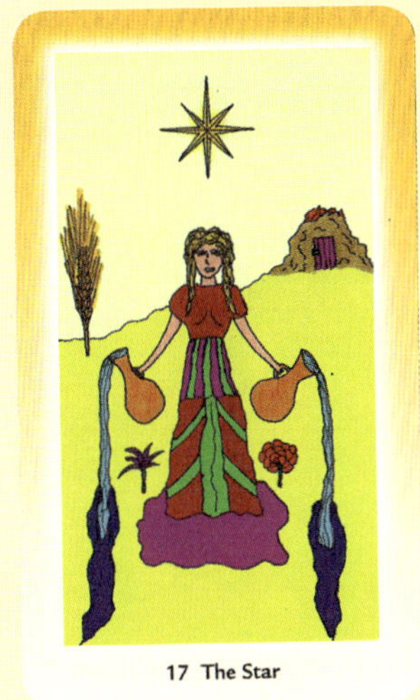

THE STAR

When I finished my graduate degree in clinical mental health counseling, I decided that I needed to have a self-initiation. I collected a whole lot of fruits: oranges, apples, plums, peaches, and grapes. I diligently washed and cleaned them and prepared them by cutting them and removing anything that could later be considered an obstacle. Who has time for that during an initiation?

It was my first time communing with psilocybin. I ate two mushrooms and settled into my room. I closed my eyes and offered a prayer and an energetic offering to the mushrooms. After a few minutes, I started to feel giddy and energized. It almost felt like that short window of time while drinking when you feel like everything is possible and that you are an unstoppable force of nature.

Then the walls melted. That's when I knew.

—Edgar Fabián Frías

▲
(and following spread) Cards from Rachel Pollack, *The Shining Tribe Tarot*, 2001. Published by Llewellyn Publications

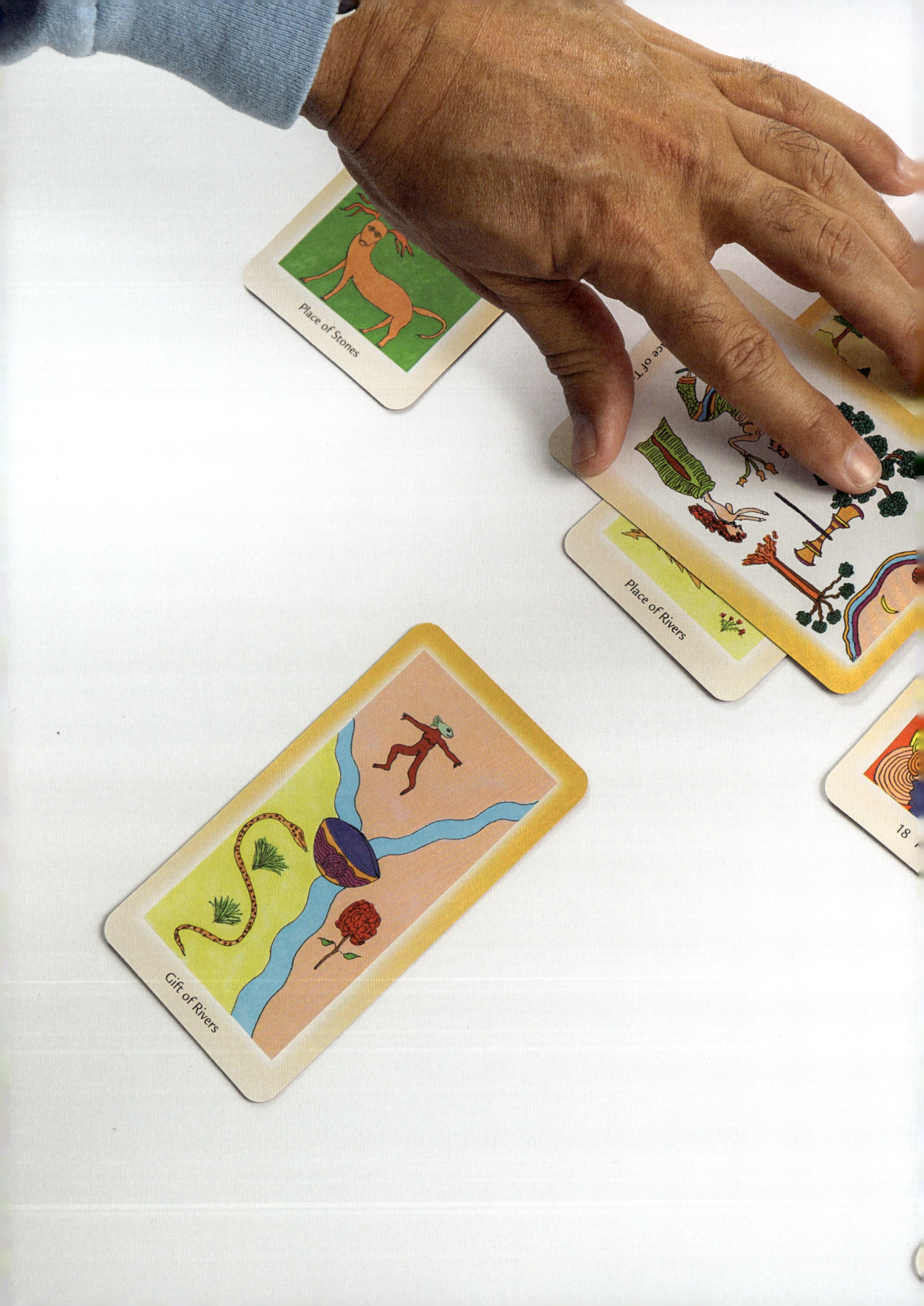
Place of Stones
Place of Rivers
Gift of Rivers
18

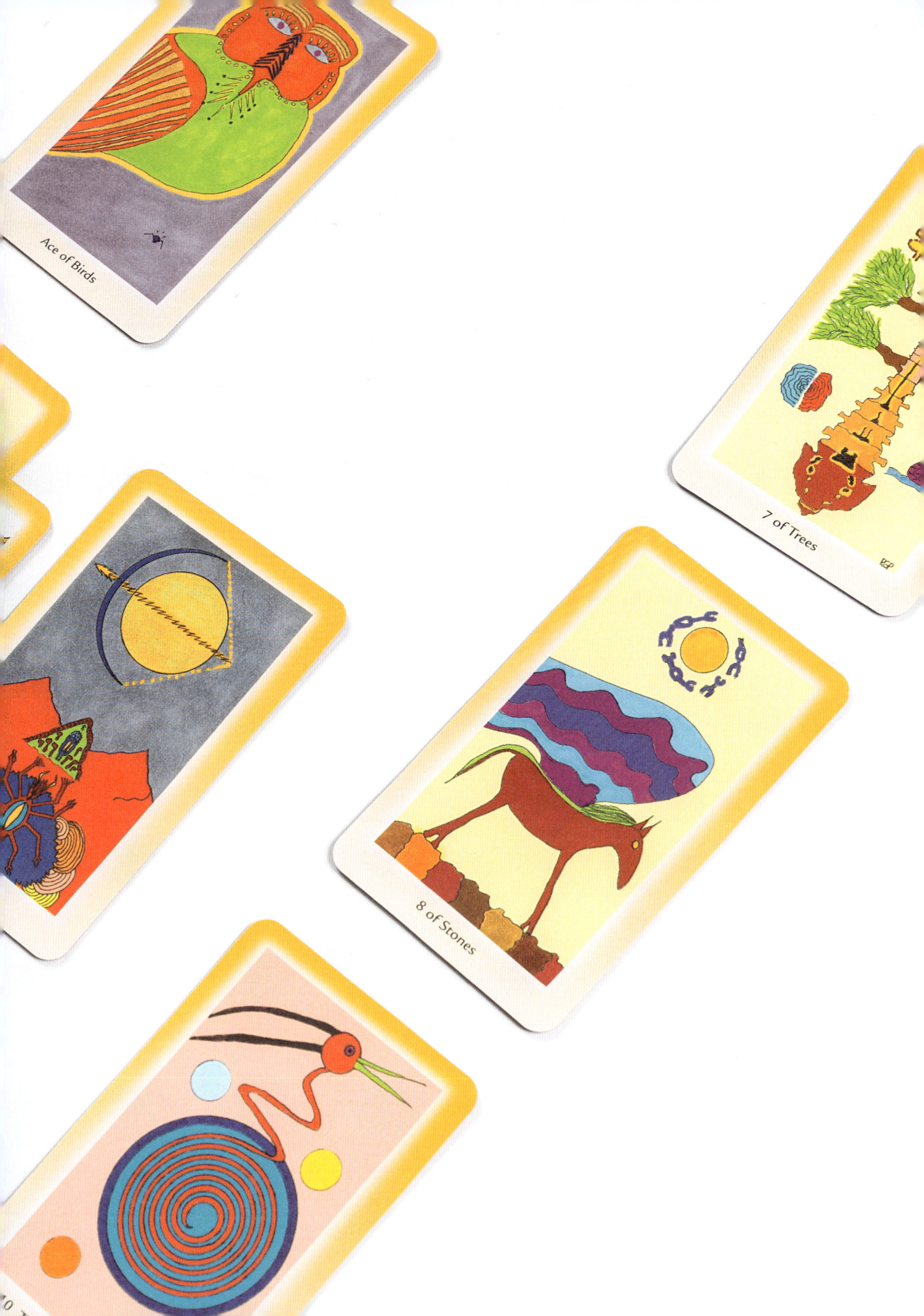
Ace of Birds
7 of Trees
8 of Stones

54 JAYNE COUNTY'S PAINTINGS OF BASTET, THE GODDESS OF WET DREAMS, c. 2019

My art seems to actually call me, as if to say "come finish me" or "come create me." I will be upstairs lying on my couch and my art that I keep and work on downstairs seems to be drawing me to it. I can feel it when I am driving my car or when I am out shopping. It beckons me to come home and finish it. The way that it calls me is very strange. Sometimes I will be doing something else, like feeding Miss Kitty in the basement where I do my art, and I will have to sit down at my table, even for a few seconds, and add something to the piece I am working on. It demands to be finished.

Art is that spark of human creation that links us with something that is larger than ourselves. That is why it is satisfying and meaningful to each artist. Artists create because we inherit that spark of creation. Even if there were no God, there would still be creative energy, but I would rather believe that I was created by some fabulous superior being that exists in some far away galaxy than to believe that I came from a monkey. Evolution is also a creative process, so where did that energy come from? Out of nowhere? An accident? I would rather feel special and believe that it is a gift from a superior being, an ARTIST that lives in another universe.

Bastet is an important figure to me both historically and spiritually. The Cat Goddess of Ancient Egypt has always been fascinating to me, ever since I was a small child. I am a cat freak and have had many cats throughout my life. Bastet is the epitome of cat worship and concentration. She protects me and my cats from harm and hostility from ignorant humans, so it is my privilege to present Bastet. She comes in dreams and has sexual inclinations, as she once did in Ancient Egypt, thus, she is the Goddess of Wet Dreams. The Ancient Greeks referred to incubus and succubus, creatures that visited mortals in their dreams in order to have sex with them. I have depicted her as a fertility goddess with multiple breasts and huge snake-like penises, a representation of the fertility of both sexes, male and female, as one. Bastet, the Goddess of Wet Dreams!

—Jayne County

Excerpts from the zine *Paranoia Paradise: Interviews with Jayne County, Volume One* (New York: Michael Fox, 2018), an accompaniment to Jayne County's retrospective exhibition *Paranoia Paradise* curated by Michael Fox at Participant, Inc., New York, 2018; and the gallery statement accompanying her exhibition *BASTET, Goddess of Wet Dreams* at Marlborough Gallery, New York, 2020.

While her artistic career began through her participation in New York's experimental theater scene during the late 1960s and 1970s, Jayne County is most recognized as the frontwoman for punk bands. Then known as Wayne County, during the 1970s she founded multiple groups including Wayne County & the Electric Chairs. County's foul-mouthed, glam-meets-punk persona and songs such as "Toilet Love," "Fuck Off," and "Man Enough to Be a Woman," garnered her notoriety within both the US and Europe. County has produced artworks that examine spirituality, sexuality, and multi-gendered bodily formations throughout her life. She lives in Atlanta, Georgia, where she continues to produce art and music, as well as rescue lost or abandoned cats.

▼
Jayne County, *Untitled*, c. 2019. Acrylic and ink on canvas, 30 × 40 in. (76.2 × 101.6 cm)

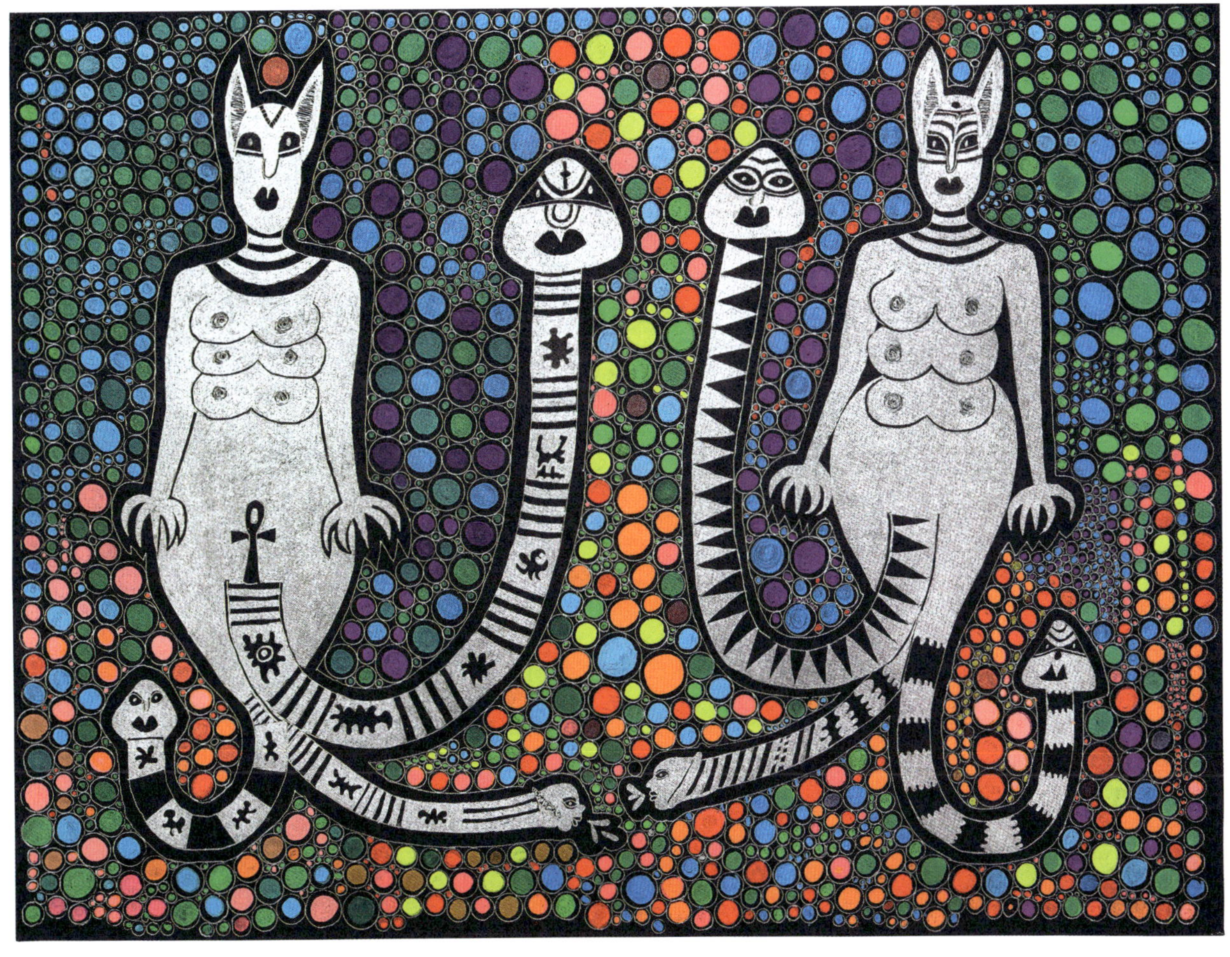

▼
Jayne County, *Bastet White Dot 22*, 2019. Acrylic and ink on canvas, 16 x 20 in. (40.6 x 50.8 cm)

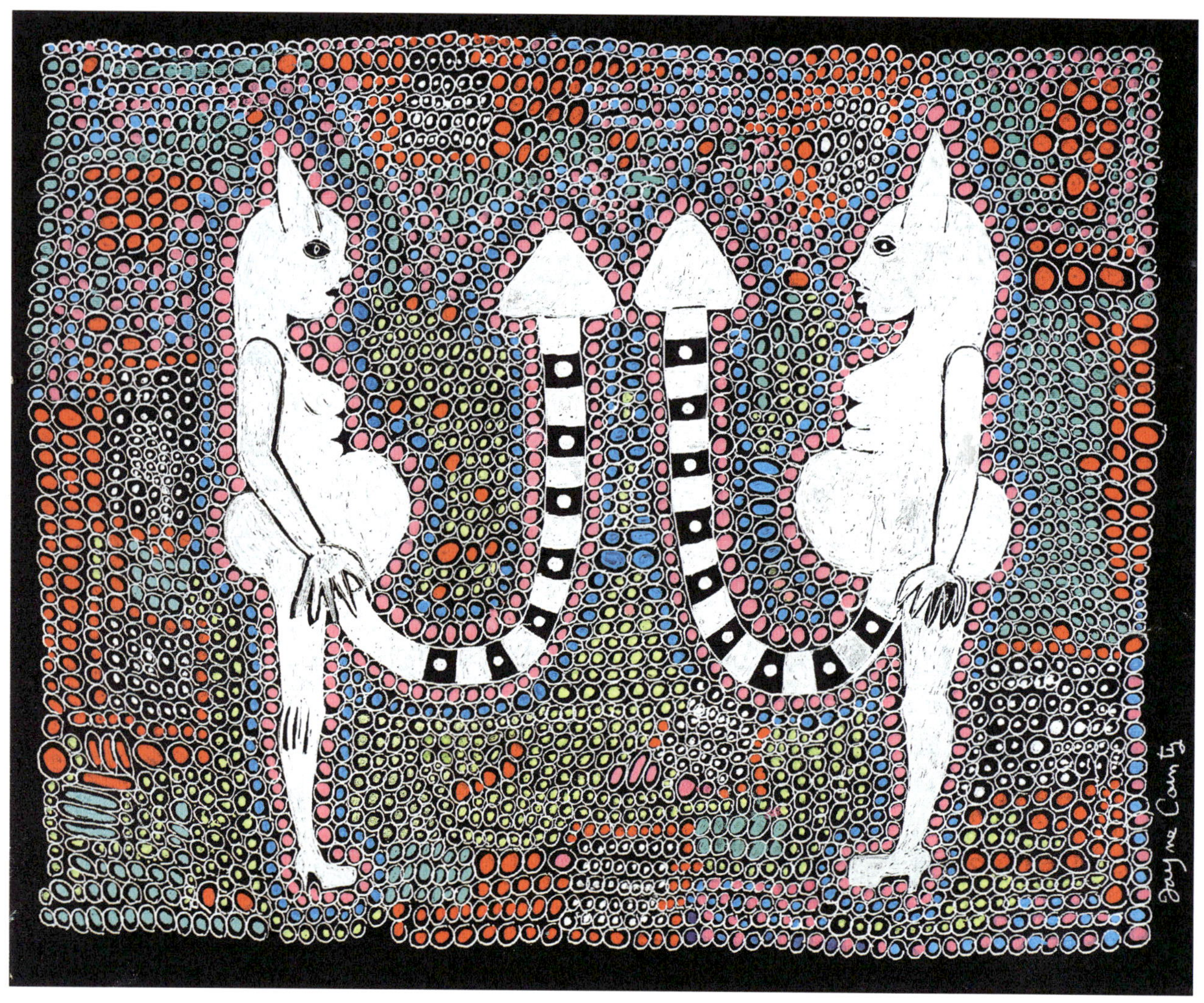

▼
Jayne County, *Praise Bastet*, 2019. Acrylic and ink on canvas, 16 x 20 in. (40.6 x 50.8 cm)

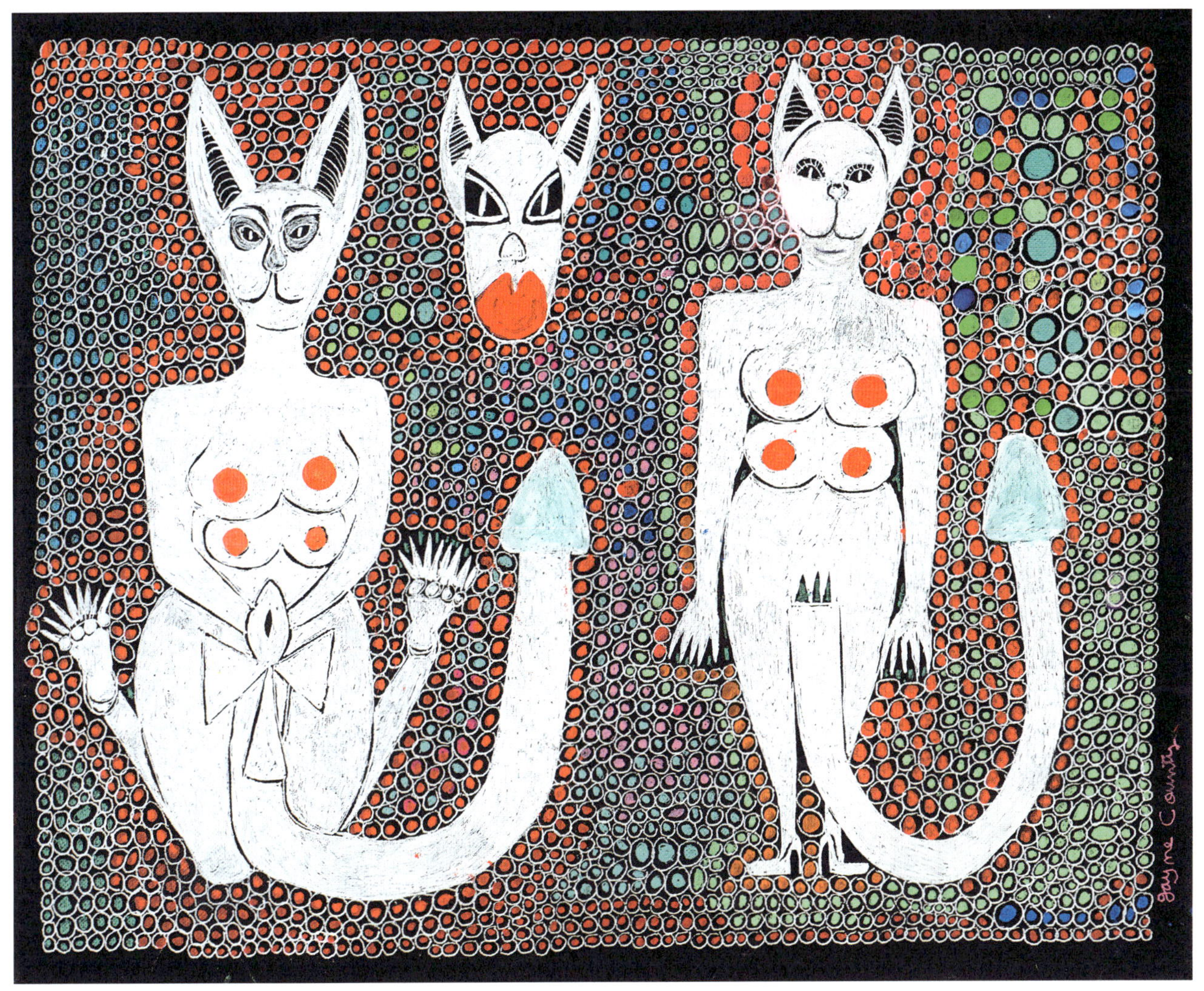

55 RIA BRODELL, *JEANNE OR JEAN BONNET 1849–1876 UNITED STATES*, 2012

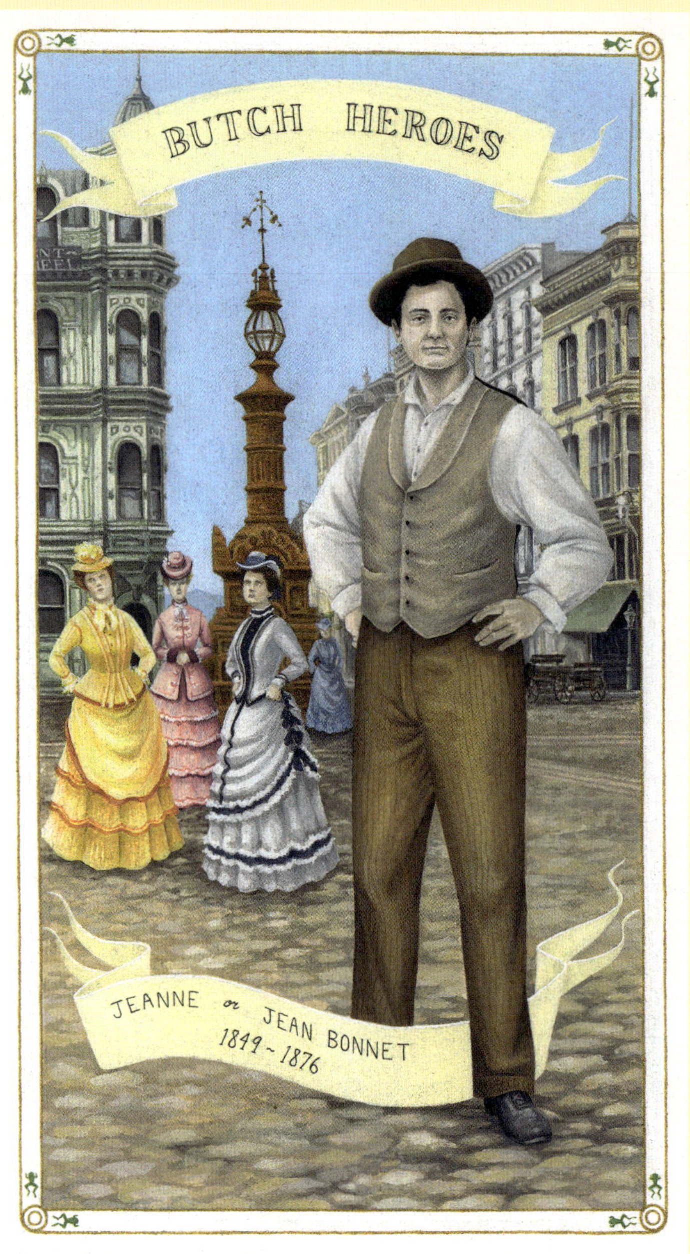

▲
Ria Brodell, *Jeanne or Jean Bonnet 1849–1876 United States*, 2012. Gouache on paper, 11 × 7 in. (27.9 × 17.8 cm). Henry Art Gallery, University of Washington, Seattle, Purchased with funds from the Ambrose M. and Viola H. Patterson Endowment Fund, FA 2017.477

Jeanne or Jean Bonnet was born in Paris but moved to San Francisco with their family as part of a French theatrical troupe. By the time Bonnet was fifteen, he was in trouble for fighting and petty thievery, and was placed in the Industrial School, San Francisco's first reform school.

As an adult, Bonnet was arrested dozens of times for wearing male clothing, an illegal act that got him mentioned frequently in the press. Bonnet "cursed the day she was born a female instead of a male," according to one newspaper account. He was quoted as declaring, "The police might arrest me as often as they wish—I will never discard male attire as long as I live."

Bonnet spent much of his time on Kearny Street and made a fairly good living by catching frogs and selling them to French restaurants in downtown San Francisco. In 1875 he began visiting brothels, convincing the women to leave prostitution and form an all-female gang. Together they supported themselves by shoplifting. One of these gang members was Blanche Buneau or Beunon, who had just arrived from Paris.

Bonnet and Blanche moved into McNamara's Hotel in San Miguel, just outside of San Francisco, to keep Blanche safe from a threatening ex-lover. On the evening of September 14, 1876, Bonnet was lying in bed waiting for Blanche when a shotgun blast came through the window, killing him instantly. It was eventually determined that the shot was meant for Blanche and was the act of either a jealous lover or a pimp wanting to kill Blanche as "an example to the other girls." Unfortunately, neither theory was ever proven. The women of San Francisco's red-light district came out en masse for Bonnet's funeral.

—Ria Brodell

Brodell's ongoing series Butch Heroes, *begun in 2010, honors figures from history who were most likely designated female at birth but who inhabited a more masculine gender during their lives. Modeled after Catholic holy cards, each portrait is carefully researched and painted with visual details about the individual's life, and an accompanying text written by the artist provides biographical information about the historical figure. "Butch," in this project, is used as an expansive term to refer to those who were defiant in the way they challenged their time and place's rigid gender expectations.*

Sources

Peter Boag, *Re-Dressing America's Frontier Past* (Berkeley: University of California Press, 2011).

"Brevities," *Daily Alta California*, December 17, 1875.

"By State Telegraph," *Sacramento Daily Union*, September 16, 1876.

Kevin J Mullen, "The Little Frog Catcher," *The Toughest Gang in Town: Police Stories from Old San Francisco* (San Francisco: Noir Publications, 2005).

Leila J. Rupp, *A Desired Past: A Short History of Same-Sex Love in America* (Chicago: University of Chicago Press, 1999).

The San Francisco Lesbian and Gay History Project, "'She Even Chewed Tobacco': A Pictorial Narrative of Passing Women in America," slide show based on primary research by Allan Bérubé. Edited and reprinted in *Hidden from History: Reclaiming the Gay and Lesbian Past*, eds. Martin B. Duberman, Martha Vicinus, and George Chauncey (New York: New American Library, 1989).

Zagria, "Jean Bonnet (1849–1876), Frog Catcher," *A Gender Variance Who's Who: Essays on Trans, Intersex, Cis and Other Persons and Topics from a Trans Perspective*, January 9, 2012, accessed January 26, 2023, https://zagria.blogspot.com/2012/01/jean-bonnet-1849-1876-frogcatcher.html#.Y9LYMuzML0s.

56 ASSUNTA FEMIA'S SCAPULAR, n.d.

Assunta Femia (1947–2006), or Saint "Species of Crow," was a deeply spiritual visionary poet, activist, and a difficult personality. While residing in rural Oregon, she came to be known as the "Nun with a Gun" for the Catholic religious garb she wore and the piece she carried—an outcome of her home being previously firebombed. Her friend Jacob Breedlove, who knew Assunta in the last years of her life, describes her affectionately as "a trailblazer who took a lot of shit," who wasn't invested in masculine or feminine pronouns but preferred "she" in a gay way. Breedlove believed she had conceptualized her gender beyond a binary. Here's Assunta Femia's self-written bio from the book *Sex and Spirit: Exploring Gay Men's Spirituality* (1995):

> **Sister species of crow**, o.c. (Assunta maria Femia), guinea bitch, ex-convict, drag queen nun. Born 1947. Raised in a traditional 19th century Calabrese morality. My family, the men, worked in the coal mines in West Virginia. The year I turned thirteen we moved to south Philly. I came out at the age of 21 in a federal prison in Kentucky. I live in Oakland, California, and southern Oregon.[1]

Assunta Femia arrived in San Francisco in 1975 after serving time for breaking into a military office in Boston and pouring black paint on draft files to protest the Vietnam War. In the Bay Area she became associated with several queer groups including the Butterfly Brigade—a 1970s-era Castro Street safety patrol—and was said to have inspired the iconic international nun drag group the Sisters of Perpetual Indulgence. Despite her radical political leanings, she had a cop fetish, and humorously collected pig figurines. She especially liked pig figurines dressed as cops.

Assunta was also an early resident of what is now known as the Wolf Creek Radical Faerie Sanctuary in rural southern Oregon. She resided there for a while and had a good relationship with the landowner George Jalbert. At the end of 1986, on his deathbed, Jalbert intended for the property to be transferred to Assunta. Due to her felony conviction, the transfer couldn't be processed. A deal was reached where Nomenus, the organization now associated with the sanctuary, took ownership of the land and accepted Assunta's ongoing residency indefinitely.

In general, Assunta wasn't fond of the patriarchal focus of the Catholic Church, but she loved nuns and the Catholic rituals she learned in childhood. She kept canonical hours, set times for prayer throughout the day, and would hike up her habit and wade into the nearby spring that fed into Wolf Creek with her breviary—a Catholic book of daily spiritual readings. The water where she would pray was named Quan Yin Spring, for the genderfluid Buddhist deity. According to Breedlove, she might have gone into a spiritual order if her challenging nature hadn't been likely to cause the same problems she encountered in her other collective endeavors. Thus, she was a solo practitioner. A visionary spiritual trailblazer unassimilated into a group.

The relationship between Assunta and other residents on the land at Wolf Creek eventually soured. Harry Hay, a gay activist, Communist, and cofounder of the Mattachine Society and the Radical Faeries, didn't appreciate the Catholic idolatry Assunta brought to the sanctuary. His distaste was supported by others that came up from San Francisco. As a result of mounting tensions, an angry Assunta smashed all the phallus statues newly erected on the land. This legendary story is recounted in her poem "I smashed the phalloi."[2]

This scapular came to Breedlove along with some other materials from Assunta after her death, but he says she might have never worn it. Breedlove noticed the name "Oscar" embroidered on it, the name of another caretaker on the land. He described Oscar as "a weirdo monastic," living on the opposite end of the land from Assunta, her archnemesis. He had died before she did. But she held onto it. Perhaps she did so to honor Oscar's eternal spirit and her own, despite their disagreements on the mortal plane. Or with a knowledge that our cherished objects carry meaning but aren't ever truly ours alone. Either way, the certainty and connection that we hope objects will give us about the past is always dubious.

—Chris E. Vargas

1. Author's entry on Sister species of crow (Assunta Femia) in *Sex and Spirit: Exploring Gay Men's Spirituality*, ed. Robert Barzan (San Francisco: White Crane Newsletter, 1995), 140.
2. Sister species of crow, "I smashed the phalloi," *Sex and Spirit: Exploring Gay Men's Spirituality*, 62.

▸ Scapular that belonged to (or was cared for by) Assunta Femina, n.d. Photo by Marcel Pardo Ariza

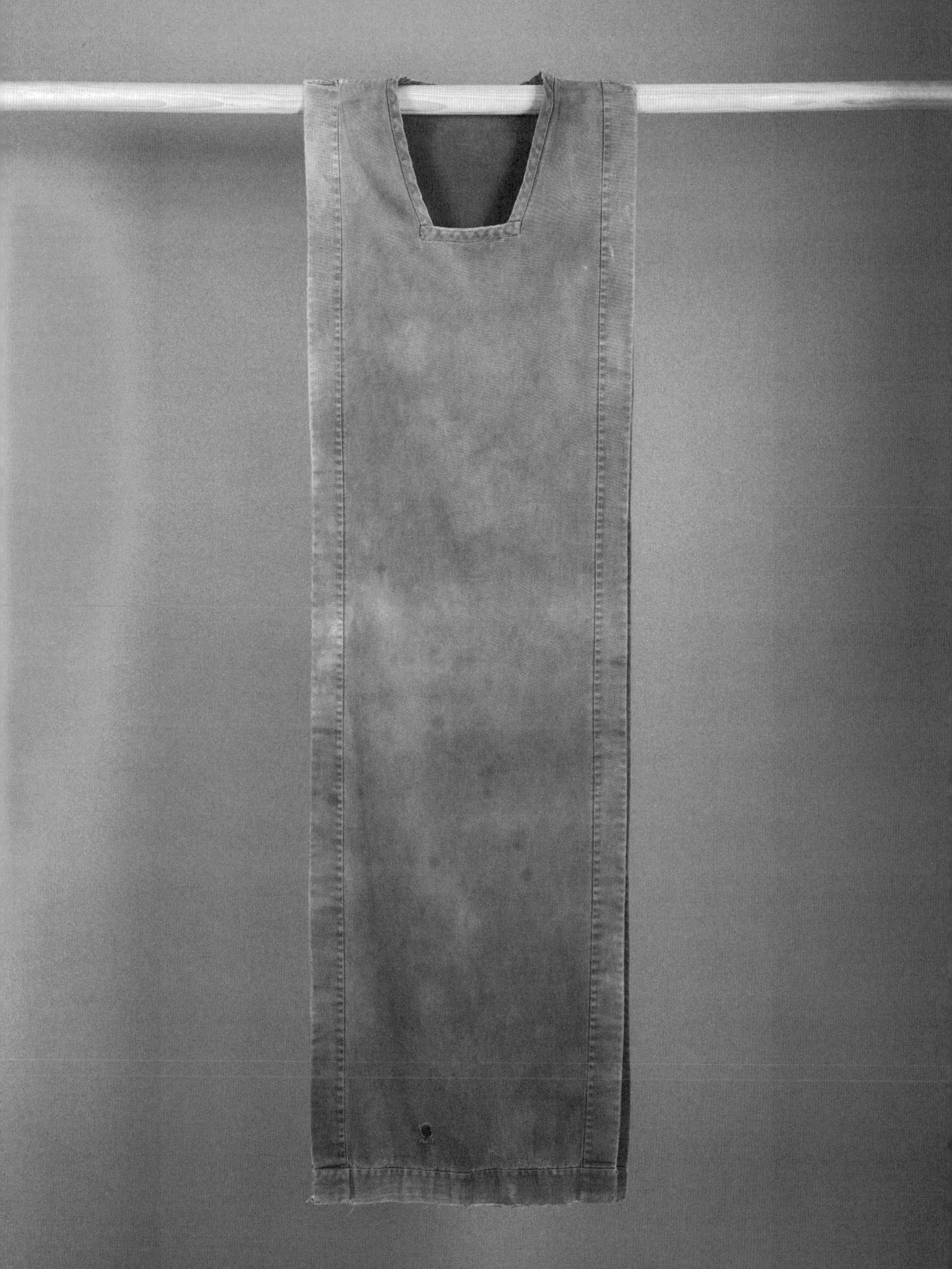

57 GIOVANNI ANTONIO CAVAZZI, DEPICTION OF A JINBANDAA, c. 1665–68

Behold the figure of the *jinbandaa,* striding forth in an ink-and-watercolor drawing from the manuscript *Missione Evangelica al Regno del Congo* (c. 1665–68) by the Italian missionary Giovanni Antonio Cavazzi.[1] Depicted as a solitary dark-skinned figure walking amid the Angolan hills, they are wearing clothing that we've come to identify as feminized—a light blue loincloth folded in the stylings of a skirt—and overtly feminine—a bright yellow blouse and matching headscarf styled as a turban, the latter traditionally considered in that region to be women's clothing. Cavazzi shows the figure in the center of the image, holding a forward gaze perpendicular to the manuscript page. They wear a subtle smile, their body in motion, a wooden staff suggesting momentum.

Unlike the other images in Cavazzi's series, which depict scenes of African collectivity and sociality directly framed in relation to Christian conversion, enslavement, and labor, this *jinbandaa* is rendered alone. And in this solitude, they seem temporarily satisfied and self-possessed. Like caterpillars, which are born with everything they need to metamorphose into butterflies, the *jinbandaa* has everything they need to be(come) themself. Moreover, they appear content and undefined by the various normative (e.g., religious or other cultural) elements that might have impeded their becoming for generations.

We know that depending on the context, the various and entangled fields of perception, the term *jinbandaa* had multiple meanings: either defined as a "passive and sinful sodomite" by the Christian West and/or "a medicine man and healer" with the capacity for undergoing spiritual possession by their West and Central kin. Historians and elders have warned us about the perils of ahistoricizing the past by seeking to reconcile it to contemporary comprehension. As modern systems of gender are themselves byproducts and afterlives of colonial regimes, we should relinquish the imposition of those totalizing and antagonistic logics. We might instead speak of capacities and affinities. There is an affinity here to the Black trans and nonbinary realities that took shape generations after the *jinbandaa* strolled amid those fields. We can note a shared habitus, an ecology of embodiment that flouts the linear maxims of colonial determination while simultaneously embracing the experiences and practices of individual and ancestral pasts—pasts that reflect something familiar from the *jinbandaa* to today. This is not least because mainstream contemporary articulations of the rapidly developing category of nonbinary translate into both the "not-binary" and "in between the binary," in the middle space along the spectrum of gender as "not-man" and "not-woman." But just as the *jinbandaa* inhabited a "third" space, we are also moved to acknowledge the Black nonbinary as a space and set of practices for otherwise possibility: that is, of not "between" but disruptively beyond, self-capacitating with everything it needs to become, forging a chrysalis despite the confines of coloniality.

The *jinbandaa*'s presence was similarly disruptive of colonial realities. Sexual practices were collapsed into Western social categories like "sodomite," "homosexual," and "pederast," which disarticulated their spiritual capacities and social categories from collective and kin. Still, we remember the *jinbandaa*, lingering here in a solitary rendering in this colonial archive, for their capacity for collective healing, proud upright signal of possibility and self-possession. We will never know the heights or depths of the *jinbandaa*'s role in our present, untouched by the ideological confines of natal alienation. Yet, in the wake of that colonial violence and dispossession, remembering is our legacy too.

This image is the only known representation of the figure of the *jinbandaa* in their own time. In our era of unfathomable death and loss

1. Giovanni Antonio Cavazzi, *Missione Evangelica al Regno del Congo* (the Araldi manuscript), vol. C, c. 1665–68. Collection of Gallerie Estensi, Biblioteca Estense Universitaria. Digitally reproduced on the Material Objects Archive, Center for the Study of Material & Visual Studies of Religion, Yale University. See other pages from this manuscript here: https://mavcor.yale.edu/material-objects/giovanni-antonio-cavazzi-missione-evangelica-al-regno-del-congo-araldi-manuscript.

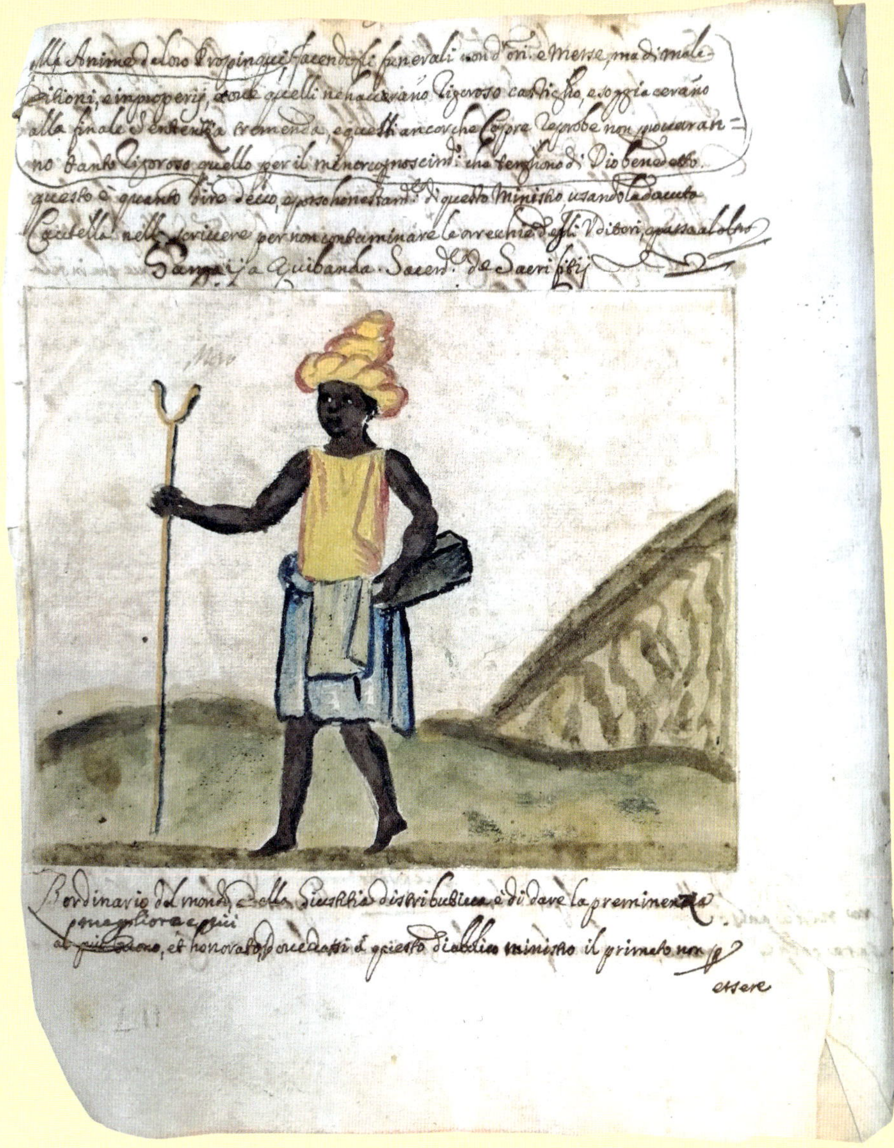

▸ Giovanni Antonio Cavazzi, Depiction of a Jinbandaa in the *Missione Evangelica al Regno del Congo* (the Araldi manuscript), vol. A, c. 1665–68. Collection of Gallerie Estensi, Biblioteca Estense Universitaria

due to racialized pandemics, abuses, and ecological disasters, all exacerbated by capitalist greed and human disregard, what does it really mean to reckon with remembrance? Rote recollection and enumeration of our persistent absenting from the annals of history continues to be insufficient for us. When faced with such insurmountable loss, we hold fast and humanize our historical work of remembering. Those of us inhabiting shared ecologies of multiplicity, transgression, deviance, and divinity have been counted, but most of us are counted out—unthought and unthinkable through the ages. So, without collapsing our historicities and translating the dead into further unrecognizable terms, we continue to humanize and breathe life into that task.

In that spirit, we might regard with delight the *jinbandaa* and name this figure and others like them who continue to be treated as unnameable as we slip through the matrix of binary gender. We reckon with their slight smile and purposeful walk alongside the capacity of trans people to bring and steal joy to one another, to heal our communities. We remember and imagine and hold our ephemeral stories and keep an indelible mark on this world that tries to wipe us from its collective memory. We behold and regard this solitary force of nature and the divine healing multitudes they carried and thus teach us to carry—all with a generosity of spirit that persists into our present and emerging futures.

—SA Smythe

58 FREDDIE MERCADO, *CARIÁTIDE CARIBEÑA*, 2020

Cariátide caribeña: a Caribbean caryatid that holds up the universe, standing straight as an arrow. Tropical exuberance (Bacchus with fruit) in a concrete house in Puerto Rico that would catch on fire months later due to an electrical mishap caused by Hurricane Isaias. Precarious baskets held by a tropical princess, no, a baroque queen, an architectural motif, Freddie Mercado, who stares at us regally, perhaps with disdain or anger or contempt, like the poet Luis Palés Matos's Tembandumba de la Quimbamba, walking down *por la encendida calle antillana*. An exposed leg and very straight back. Excessive ornamentation or perhaps the right amount in this domestic kingdom marked by the profusion of plastic and foam. A beautifully lit photo by Javier Romero of a light-skinned African princess, transculturated, transformed, embodied as if a sacred divinity, possessed in the body of a man or a woman who self-identifies as androgynous.

For Freddie Mercado, mother of us all, is all about confusion, transgression, and upsetting people and making them shake their fists demanding clarity. What are you? How dare you! The opaqueness of the visual challenging the imperative for categorical definition. Here, the baroque excess, which becomes neo-Baroque in the Caribbean and *neobarroso* in the Southern Cone, becomes tropicamp and *transloca* in Country Club, a *comarca* or lower-middle class subdivision in San Juan, the epitome of 1950s urban development and suburbanization, where countryside folk became large-city residents but still live in a space in between. But the signs of the feminine and of agricultural bounty are unmistakable, as is their fiction, made out of plastic and cosmetics, as that brilliant green spray of plantains made out of foam in the background or that third eye on Freddie's forehead. For she sees it all, like Medusa, and in her infinite wisdom blesses us and curses us at the same time with her hidden snakes, in a religious ectasis conjured by beaded accoutrements and tiger-print fabrics that mesh and clash with the leopard-print upholstered sofas. *Ecléctico total.*

What do I see? Beauty in chaos as a cosmic tropical movement, invoking the Cuban writer Severo Sarduy's conceptions of transvestism and the Brazilian artist Hélio Oiticica's tropicamp. Freddie Mercado's *transloca* performance is the result of a precarious life well lived, of training in the visual arts and a personal history marked by playing with dolls, becoming a doll, making do with scraps to engender themselves in an authentic way. Mercado transmogrifies the visual in translocal ways, mixing varied referents, insisting on multiplicity and potential confusion. I am not Carmen Miranda, but I could be. I am not Myrta Silva, that extraordinary and fearful lesbian Puerto Rican singer who became Madame Chencha, the terrifying overweight fortune teller and gossip monger on 1960s television in Puerto Rico and New York. I am not a vendor at the market, at least not yet. Who am I, and why does everything sparkle when I walk into a room? What are the histories of these textiles draped across my body and of all these beads? Why am I standing and not lounging on pillows as Manet's Olympia or Goya's maja? Why do I live in poverty in the abandoned tropical colony of Puerto Rico? What do these closed lips have to say?

—Lawrence La Fountain-Stokes

▸ Freddie Mercado,
Cariátide caribeña, 2020.
Photo by Javier Romero

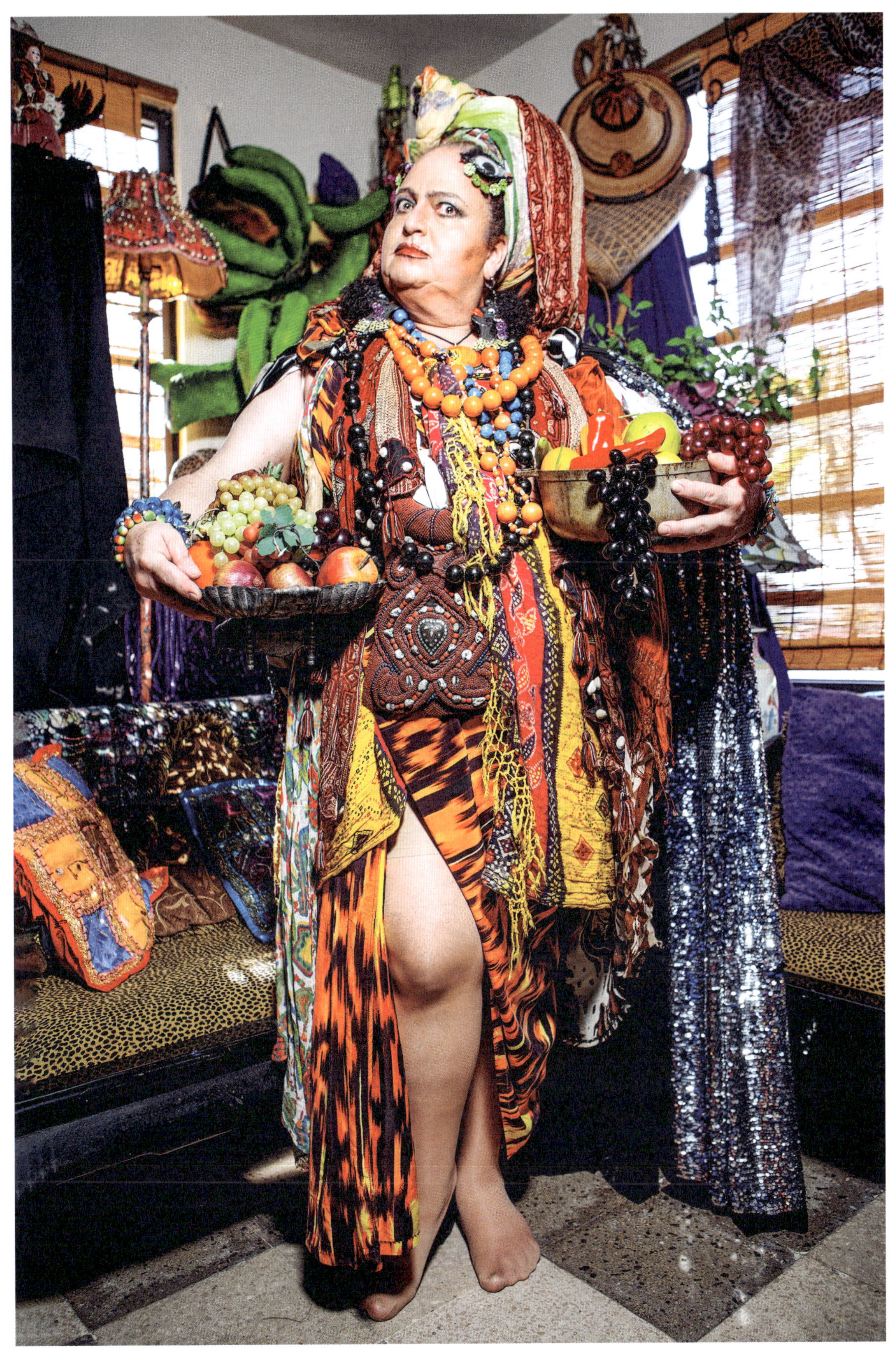

59 **CORABONELLI STATUETTE, n.d.**

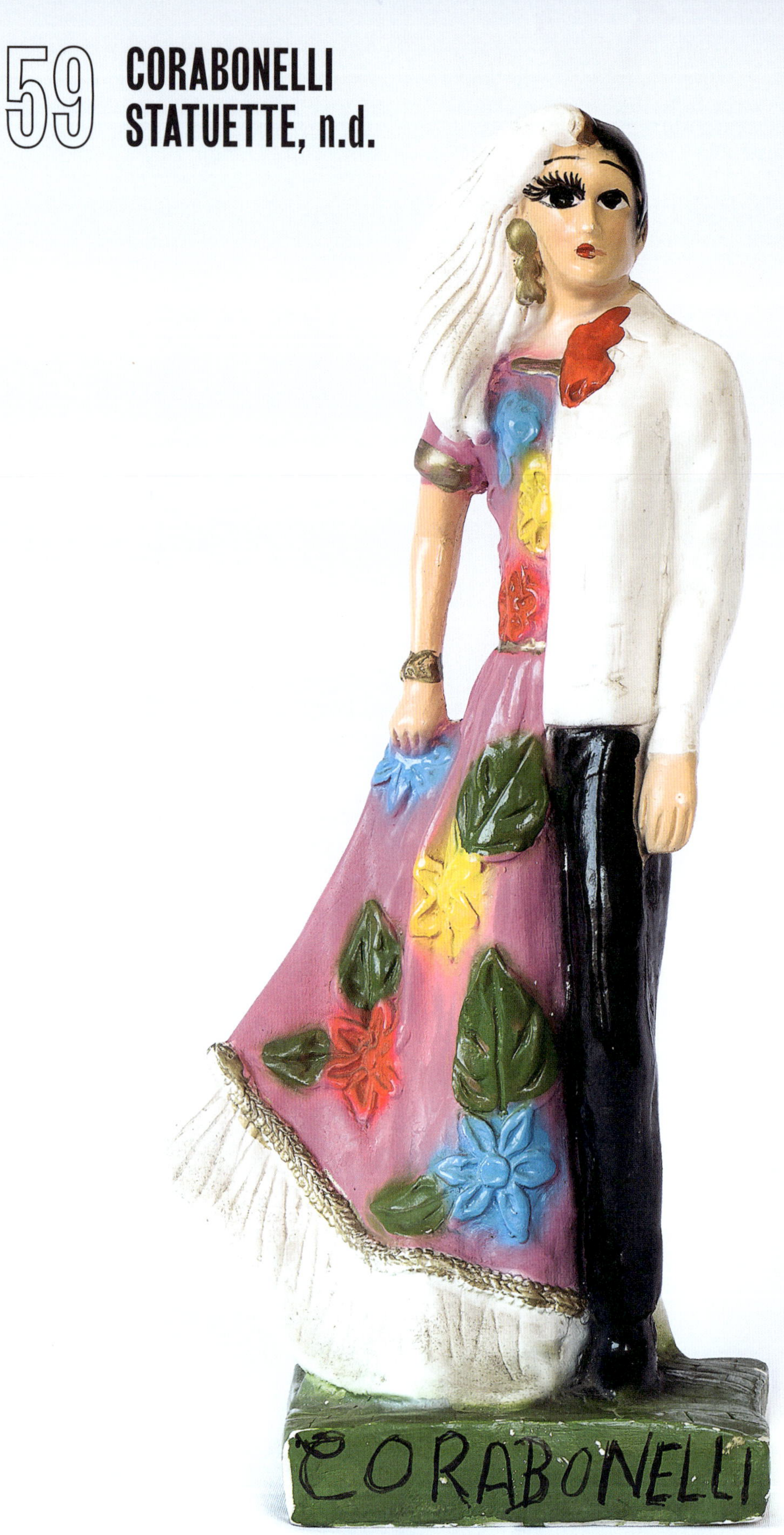

Fernanda Coral García Ortega (1963–2019), better known as Coral Bonelli, was a trans actress whose career began when she was still a child in Mexico City. As a performer, she worked in both theater and film. She was also a dancer and a contestant in various drag revues and choreographed countless *quinceañera* celebrations. With her mother, Mrs. Lilia Ortega, she starred in the Roberto Fiesco–directed documentary *Quebranto* (2013), which received the Ariel Award for best documentary feature in 2014. When touring Oaxaca, Bonelli adopted as her personal symbol a type of figurine that had a long history in the region and was associated with the *muxe*, an Indigenous, third-gender identity. Like the award bestowed by the Mexican Academy of Cinematographic Arts and Sciences, the "Corabonelli" statuette can also be considered a trophy of sorts, acknowledging how Bonelli forged her own path as a trans actress within an industry and wider society that was hostile to trans individuals.

This statuette, now in the collection of the Archivo Memoria Trans México, is divided down the middle, with one half depicting a feminine appearance with long hair and makeup wearing a pink floral dress, while the other half is a masculine figure with short hair wearing black trousers and a white shirt. Fused together like this, they suggest the creation of a third gender: the *muxe* identity originating in Zapotec culture that today exists primarily in the city of Juchitán in the state of Oaxaca. *Muxe* artist and activist Karla Rey sees the statuette as issuing from an amalgam of the female doll Basayú and the male doll Tanguyú—traditional children's toys made of clay in the Oaxacan cities of Tehuantepec and San Blas Tempa.

Bonelli acquired this figurine during the annual celebration of *muxes* in Juchitán, Vela Muxe, where copies of the *muxe* statuette are given to the attendees, personalized with their names. The festivities also include the singing of a folksong entitled "Tanguyú" from the Isthmus of Tehuantepec. The statuette's origin thus reflects a cultural history of *muxe* identity, while mirroring Bonelli's own trans identity, allowing her to establish ties with a geographically distant but emotionally familiar community.

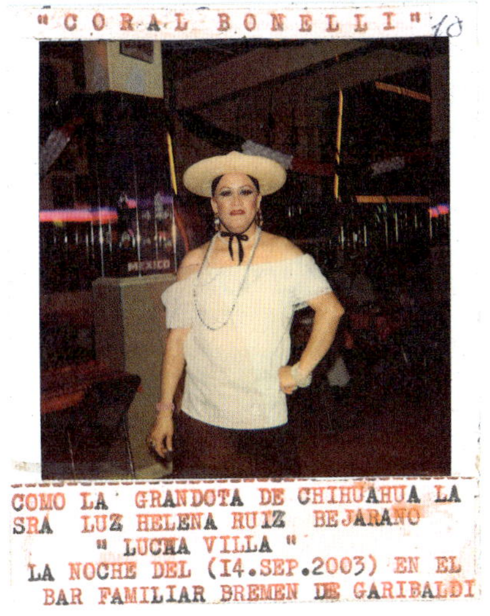

Coral Bonelli as Lucha Villa, Bar Bremen, Mexico City, 2003. Polaroid, 4 × 3½ in. (10.2 × 8.9 cm). Courtesy of Archivo Memoria Trans México

Antonella Rubens and Emma Yesica Duvali, members of the Archivo Memoria Trans México, recall having shared the stage with Coral Bonelli at various venues in Mexico City as well as in other towns around the country. They believe that she may have first encountered the dual-gender figurine while touring the Isthmus of Tehuantepec. A photograph where Bonelli is impersonating the famous ranchera singer and actress Lucha Villa—who Bonelli affectionately called "The Grande Dame of Chihuahua"—shows her in a pose quite similar to that of the figurine, standing proud and staring straight at the viewer. The figurine's two faces evince Bonelli's performative character, but also resonates with a history composed of multiple folktales, voices, and identities.

—César González-Aguirre

◂ Corabonelli Statuette, n.d. Molded and painted plaster, 16 × 7 × 5 in. (40.6 × 17.8 × 12.7 cm). Courtesy of Archivo Memoria Trans México

60 SUNNY A. SMITH, *UNQUIET COMFORTER*, 2022

In 1776, a new entity was announced into the world in Cumberland, Rhode Island. The Public Universal Friend came to inhabit the "tabernacle of flesh" left behind by the dying Jemima Wilkinson. The Friend was—according to their written testimony—a genderless spirit sent by God as a prophet to warn the world of impending doom. The fleshly body of the Friend had been born as Jemima Wilkinson in 1752 to a Quaker family in the Rhode Island Colony but was now a new being, and one beyond human gender categories of male or female.

Following this transformation, the Public Universal Friend embarked on a preaching tour of New England and Pennsylvania, attracting disciples, critics, and curious observers. In the 1790s, a group of followers bought a parcel of land in upstate New York previously belonging to the Iroquois Confederacy. Over 200 people moved to this "New Jerusalem," where they imagined they would live a holy life away from critics and the "wicked world." The community was led by the Public Universal Friend along with women and men of the society who acted as social, economic, and spiritual leaders. Despite their hopes and initial farming successes, the community fought over land ownership and was torn by family conflicts; it largely disbanded after the Friend "left time" for good in 1819.

The Friend signified their state as a spiritual being who was "neither male nor female" through dress and preaching style. Observers routinely noted either that the Friend wore male attire or used a combination of men's and women's clothing to signify their genderless state. They wore a combination of robes similar to those worn by preachers in the Church of England and a beaver hat in a style associated with the Society of Friends (the inspiration for this contemporary reimagining by Sunny A. Smith). Ezra Stiles, then president of Yale College, recorded the Friend's use of men's clothing: "Wears light cloth Cloke with a Cape like a Man's—Purple Gown, long sleeves to Wristbands—Mans shirt down to the Hands with Neckband—purple handkerchief or Neckcloth tied around the neck like a man's."[1] Philadelphia Quaker William Savery noted the Friend's attempts to present a genderless figure, even as he used gendered pronouns to do so: "As she [*sic*] is not to be supposed of either sex, so this neutrality is

To invoke the Public Universal Friend (1752–1819), who was also referred to as The Comforter, Sunny A. Smith made the hat they wear in this photograph by Marcel Pardo Ariza. One of the Friend's biographies was titled The Unquiet World *(2010) by Frances Dumas, and indeed the Friend's identity transformed during a time of upheaval, crisis, and pandemic, as did Smith's. The Friend had a very sad end of life, and as a softening gesture this recreation, made by working with milliner DeAnna Gibbons, was crafted to be a little more supple and a little rounder than the Friend's actual hat, now held at the Yates County History Center. Smith, who can trace their blood lineage to the Friend and considers them a transcestor, added a subtle ribbon to make it their own version of an agender accessory rather than a copy of a man's hat, striving for something perfectly in-between.*

▸ Sunny A. Smith, *Unquiet Comforter*, 2022. Wool and silk, 4¾ in. × 17¾ in. dia. (12.1 cm × 45.1 cm dia.) Photo of the artist wearing *Unquiet Comforter* by Marcel Pardo Ariza

1. Ezra Stiles, *The Literary Diary of Ezra Stiles*, vol. 3, January 1, 1782–May 6, 1795, ed. Franklin Dexter (New York: Charles Scribner's Sons, 1901), 290.
2. Jacob Hiltzheimer, *Extracts from the Diary of Jacob Hiltzheimer, of Philadelphia, 1765–1798*, ed. Jacob Cox Parsons (Philadelphia: W. F. Fell, 1893), 66.

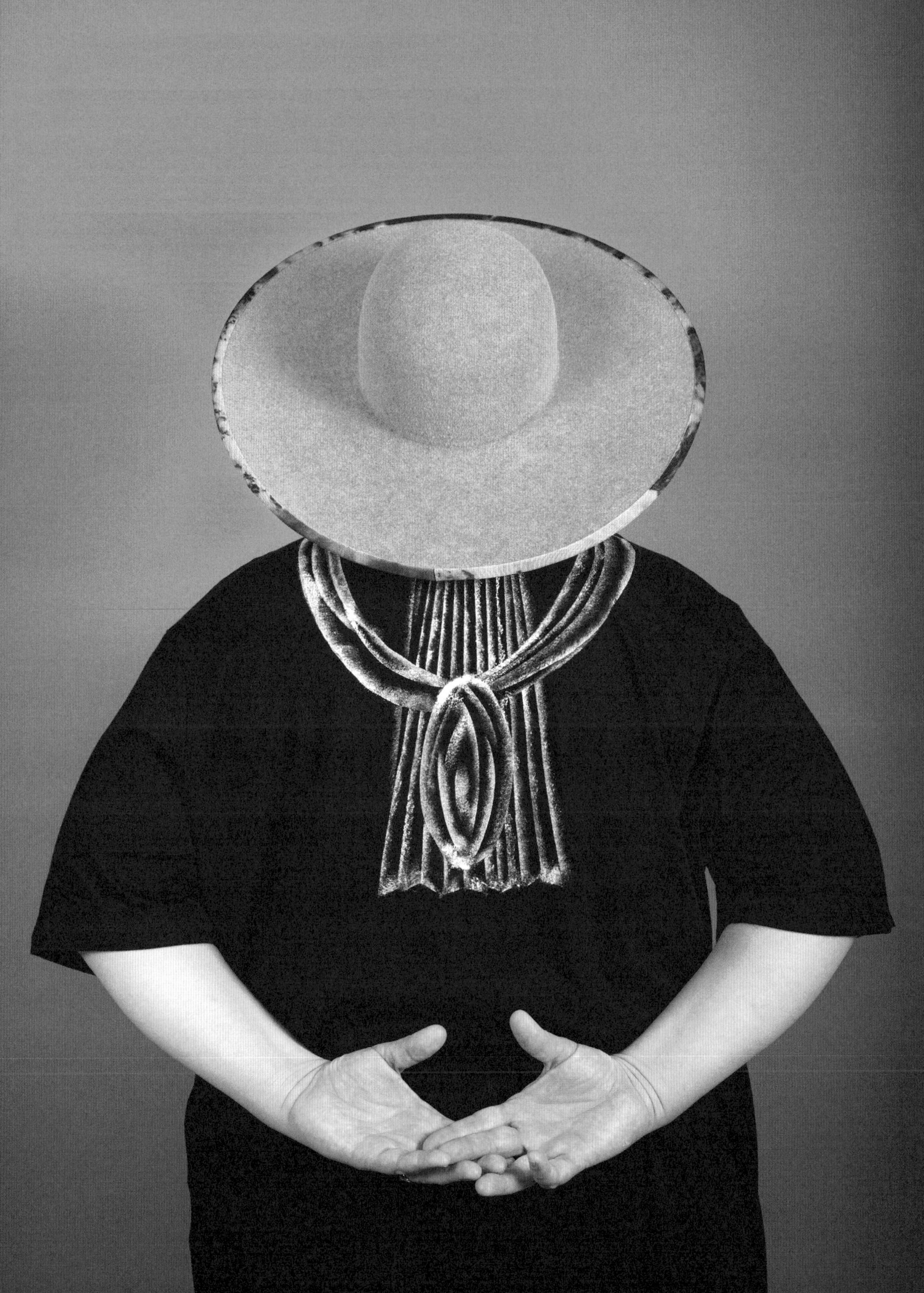

manifest in her [*sic*] personal appearance."[2] These clothing signifiers combined with a preaching style that defied gender conventions. One follower-turned-apostate considered the Friend's voice to be at once low- and high-pitched, "very grum and shrill."[3] While critics derided the Friend's vocal ambiguity, other hearers considered their sermons remarkable, striking, and even divine.

The Friend's resurrection story and preaching tours drew international attention. Newspapers in Europe and the American colonies printed stories of the Friend, often with salacious criticism accusing the Friend and their followers of sexual impropriety, fraud, and even murder. International tourists visited the Friend's society in New Jerusalem, and one critic even published a defamatory biography of the Friend. While most attention paid to the Friend was critical, this rich archive reveals a world that encountered, critiqued, and occasionally saw divinity in a self-proclaimed genderless spirit.

The Public Universal Friend offers a remarkable example of a figure who "transed" gender and openly lived outside of the gender binary in early America.[4] The Friend did this specifically through religious claims and practices, insisting that as a spirit, they were "no longer male or female," as human distinctions such as these were to be eliminated after death according to Biblical promises found in Galatians 3:28. This way of understanding gender and genderlessness is distinct in many respects from contemporary frameworks of transgender and nonbinary identities, but the Friend nevertheless offers a remarkable case of how the Friend and their followers imagined possibilities and even divinity beyond the gender binary.

—Scott Larson

The Eyes that seldom could close;
With Sorrow forbiden to sleep;
Seal'd up in eternal repose,
Have strangely forgotten to weep!
The Friend said, Precious in the sight of
the Lord are the death of his Saints:—
1. of the 4th Sabath Day, The Friends Text was these
words, Better is the Poor that walketh in the
integrity of his heart, than he that is pere-
-verse in his way, tho' he be rich:——
2. First D. These were the words of the Text,
They Come before me as my People, &
they sit before me as my People; and
they hear my words, but they will not
do them; And lo! Thou art unto them
as one the song of that hath a pleasant voice; & more
was added: for they hear Thy words
but they will not do them!——
8. Sabath D. The Friend said With the heart man
believeth unto Righteousness, & with
the mouth confession is made unto
Salvation.
9. First Day, The Friends Text was in St.
John's: Writings —— He that hath
2008.017.185

3. Abner Brownell, *Enthusiastical Errors, Transpired and Detected in a Letter to His Father, Benjamin Brownell* (New London, Conn., 1783), 5.
4. I use "transed" as a verb here following the use of this term by scholars like Jen Manion; see Manion, *Female Husbands: A Trans History* (London: Cambridge University Press, 2021).

▲
Handwritten letter from the Friend to Ruth Pritchard, 1793. Wilkinson Collection, Yates County History Center, Penn Yan, New York

▶
John Mathies, *Portrait of the Public Universal Friend*, 1816. Oil on canvas, 24⅞ × 29¾ in. (63.2 × 73.7 cm). Wilkinson Collection, Yates County History Center, Penn Yan, New York

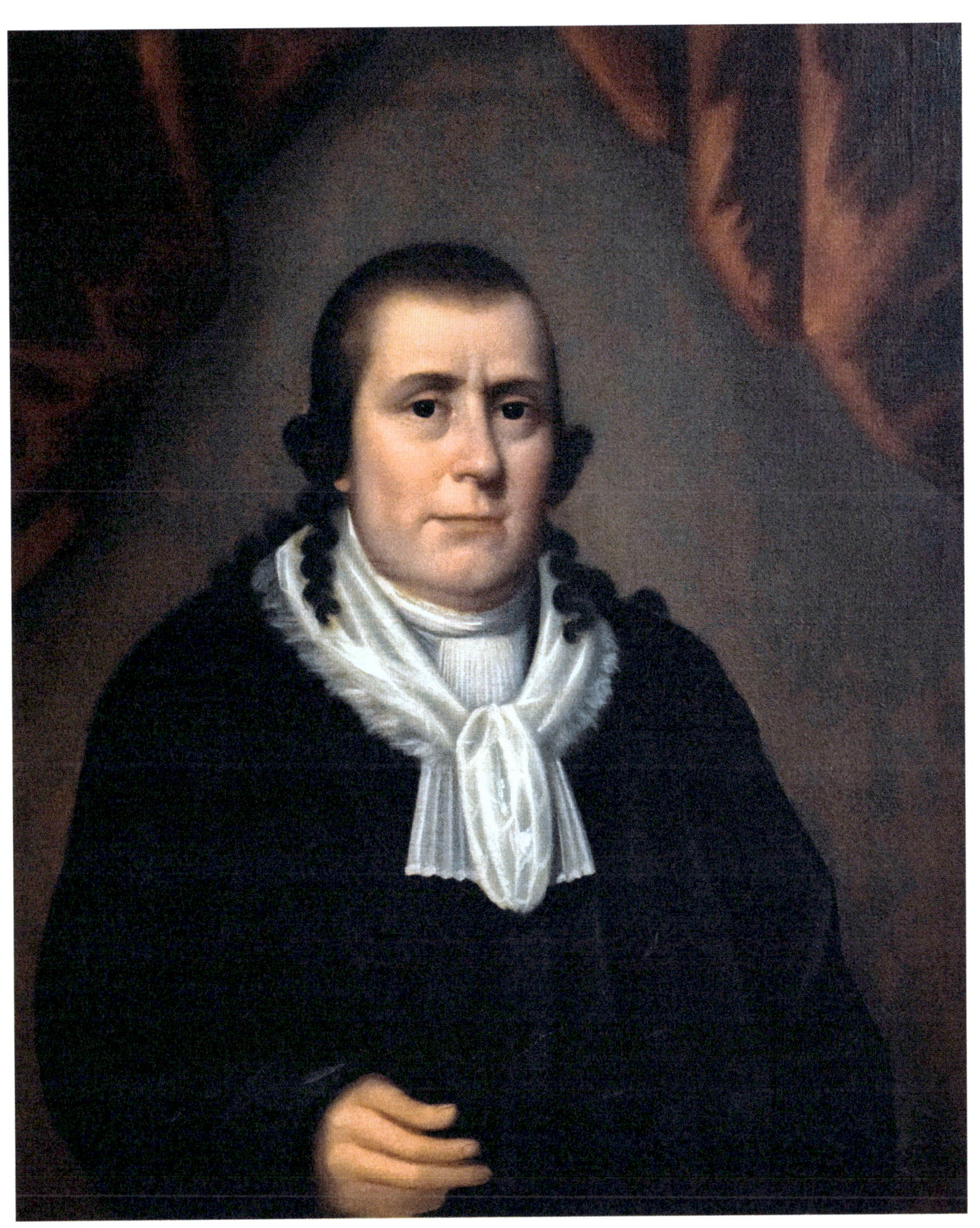

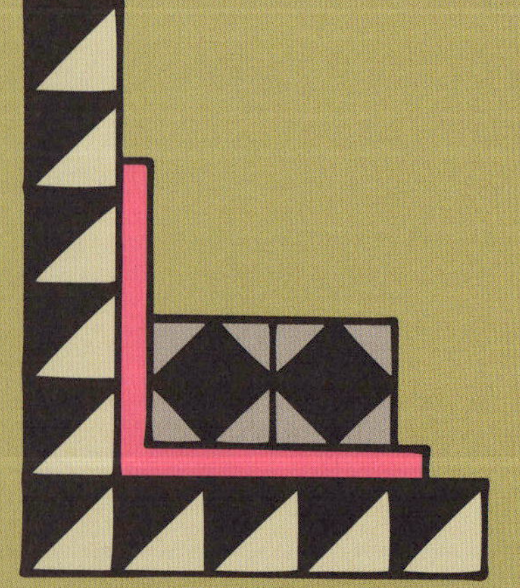
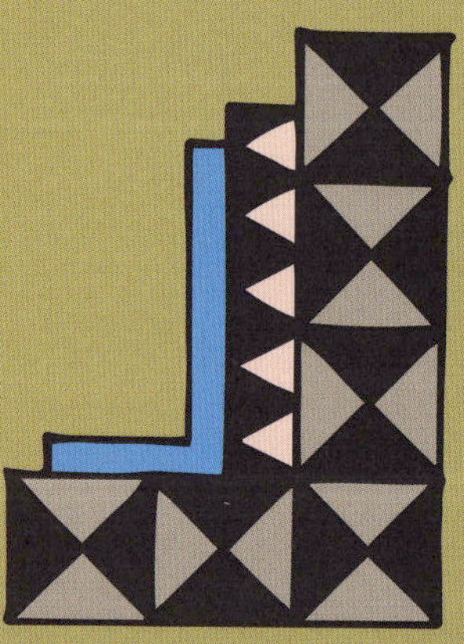

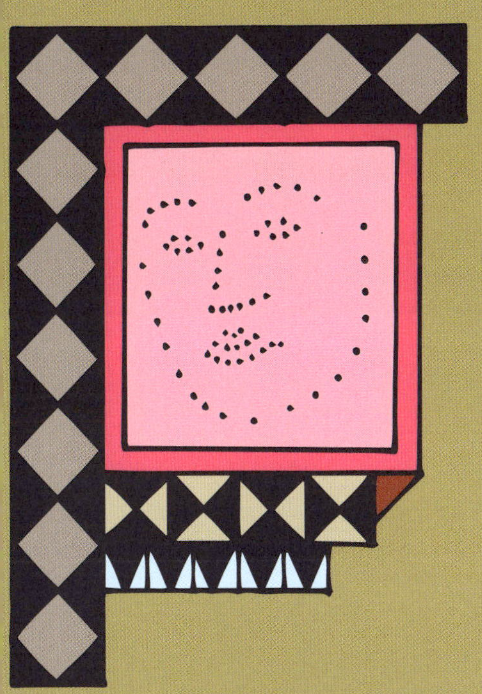
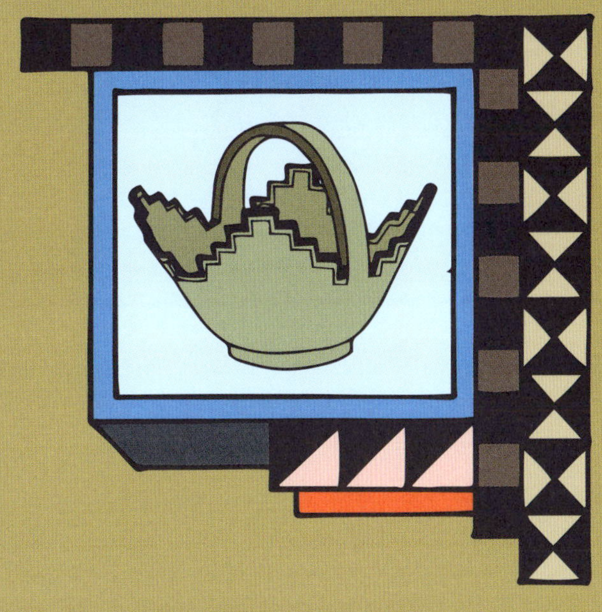

DISCOVERY

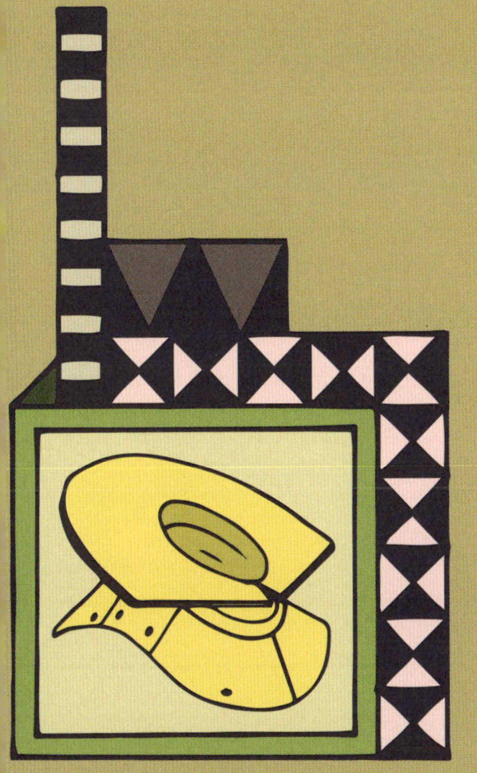
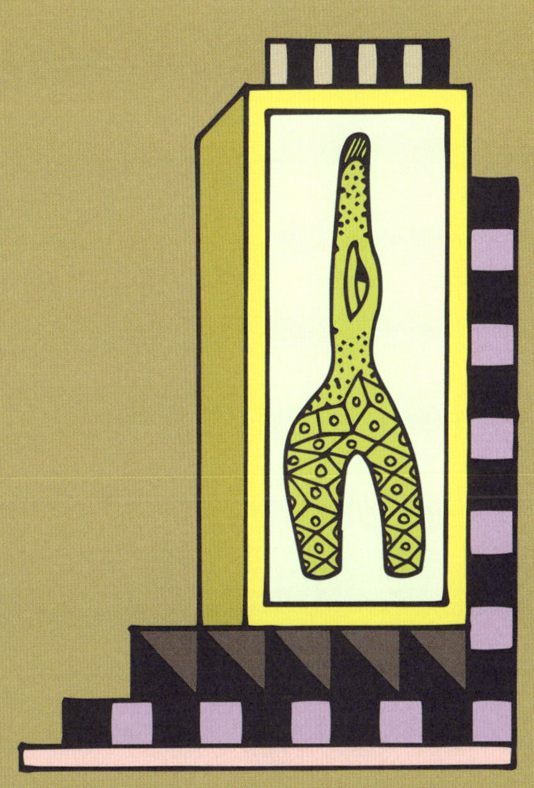

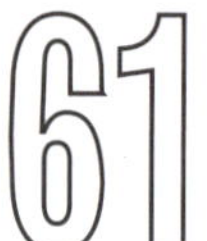

JUAN VAN DER HAMEN, *PORTRAIT OF ERAUSO*, c. 1626

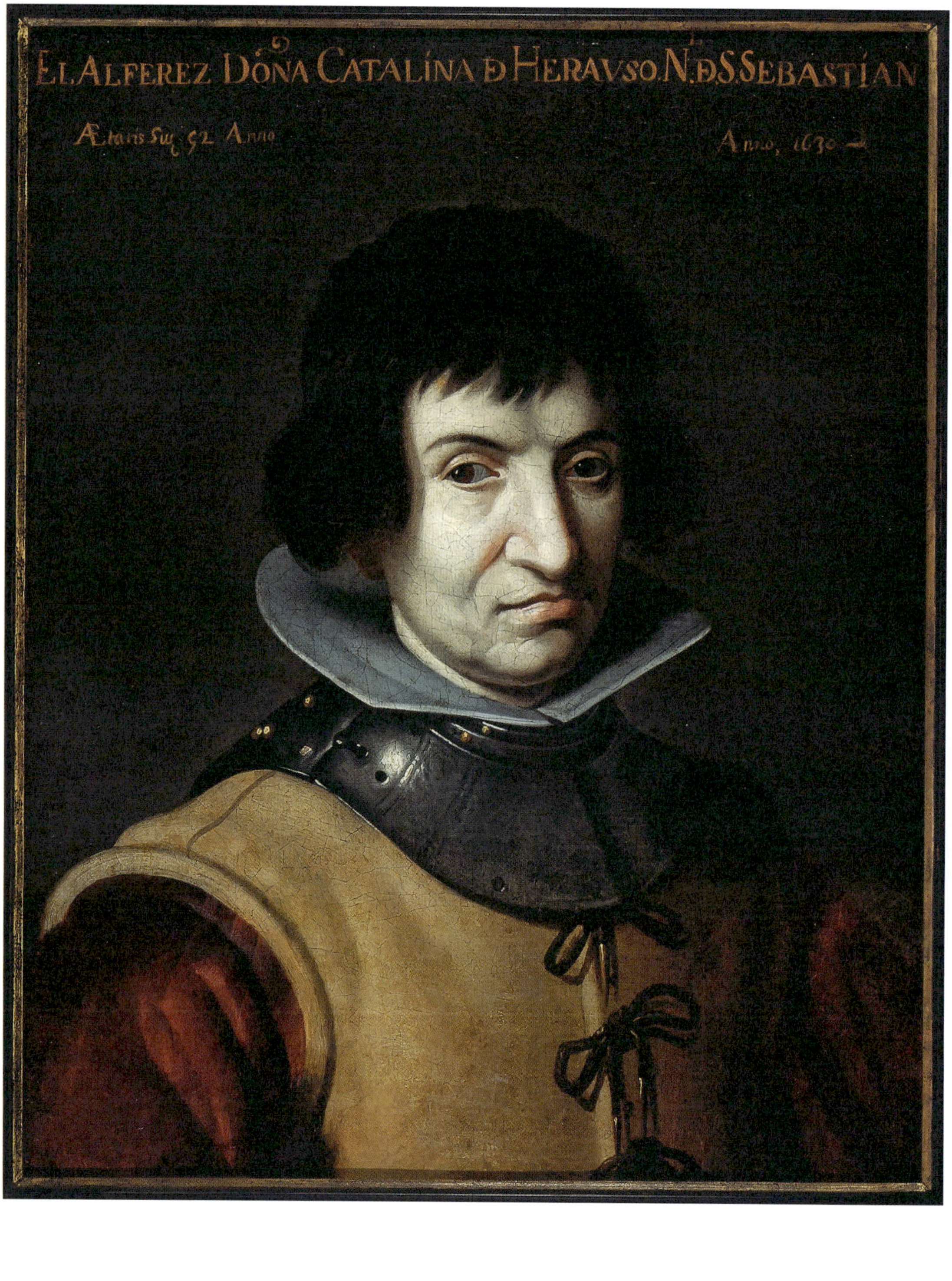

Erauso Looks at Us, Erauso Poses (Chronopolitics of a portrait)

2021/22: The exhibition *Cabello/Carceller: A Voice for Erauso. Epilogue for a Trans Time* opened in March 2022. Although the gestation of the work began in 2019, its presentation was delayed by the COVID-19 pandemic. In the audiovisual component of the work, three characters portraying different contemporary dissident sexual identities interrogate the historical figure Erauso, as depicted in this painting. The three characters question Erauso's violent participation in the colonial period while identifying with Erauso's gender-transgressive adventure. The painting responds by singing but eludes justification of Erauso's actions. "I lived against everyone," Erauso tells us in one of the verses.

While developing the project, curated by Paul B. Preciado, we realized that we were probably in front of the first realistic, posed, and identified portrait of a trans person made in the West.[1]

c. 1626: Erauso poses. The Madrid-based painter Juan van der Hamen y León paints a portrait of the person then known at court as Catalina de Erauso. The painting was faithful to the physical and mental reality of the sitter. A posthumous inventory of the possessions in the painter's studio after his death records the painting having become part of a gallery of portraits of illustrious men/characters, mostly writers. This suggests that Erauso was not placed in the context of buffoons, marvels, and/or monsters, unlike other contextualization to which Erauso has historically and contemporarily been subjected.

1620: Public mockery takes the form of verse written on paper, thrown through the window of writer Lope de Vega, a friend of the painter. The sonnet expressed an opinion about the quality of the painting and called Erauso's place among the literati inappropriate. The following was ultimately directed at Van der Hamen:

> Oh fart-colored Lieutenant Nun!
> Who enrolled you with that gang
> by Gongora Satan, Boreas Quevedo?[2]

1626: Erauso asks King Philip IV of Spain for a life pension for having served in the colonial army and for permission to wear the habit of a man. In March 1626, Erauso is granted the former but not the latter. Faced with this refusal, Erauso travels that same year to Rome where Pope Urban VIII issues a decree authorizing them to wear the male habit for life. From a contemporary perspective this would indicate the recognition by the Catholic Church of Erauso's identity, if not as trans then at least as nonbinary. Catalina de Erauso thus becomes Antonio de Erauso—using their different names as bureaucratic needs require. In search of greater freedom, they move to Mexico where they would reside until the end of their life.

NO DATE DETERMINED: A caption, which is considered apocryphal, is added to the painting and reads: "*EL ALFÉREZ DOÑA CATALINA DE HERAVSO N. DE S. SEBASTIAN. A Etatis Suae 52 anno. anno 1630.*" Whoever made this later annotation did so in ignorance of Erauso's date of birth (without possible confirmation for the moment). Whoever made this later annotation also obviated the other identities used by Erauso during their lifetime.

1829: A manuscript written in autobiographical style is published for the first time, entitled: *Historia de la Monja Alférez, Doña Catalina de Erauso*, later translated into English as *Lieutenant Nun: Memoir of a Basque Transvestite in the New World*. The diplomat Joaquín María de Ferrer adds a prologue and edits this first version of Erauso's history. Compelled by their story, it was also Ferrer who searched for possible portraits of Erauso and located the painting by Van der Hamen in Germany. Ferrer later commissioned Jean Claude Auguste Fauchery to make an engraving from the original portrait to illustrate the book, linking Erauso's image unequivocally with his writings.

◄
Juan van der Hamen,
Portrait of Erauso,
c. 1626. Oil on canvas,
22½ × 18 in. (57 × 46 cm).
Kutxa Fundazioa
Collection

1. For more information about the project, see Cabello/Carceller and Paul B. Preciado, eds., *Cabello/Carceller: Una voz para Erauso. Epílogo para un tiempo trans* (Bilbao, Spain: Azkuna Zentroa–Alhóndiga Bilbao, 2022).
2. Lope de Vega, *Cartas (1604–1633)*, ed. Antonio Carreño (Madrid: Cátedra, 2018).

1900: Luis Gómez de Arteche makes an oil copy of the painting, which is kept in the San Telmo Museum in San Sebastian. This copy was used on stage during the filming of our project *A Voice for Erauso. Epilogue for a Trans Time*. The two paintings, original and copy, appear with similar prominence in both the video production and the installation, replicating a queer critique of the concepts of original and copy.

1970: Van der Hamen's portrait is acquired by the collection of the Caja de Ahorros Municipal de Donostia/San Sebastián, Erauso's former hometown. This municipal collection becomes part of the Kutxa Fundazioa collection.

1971: Fire at the headquarters of the Caja de Ahorros Municipal. An electrician rescues the painting as the wooden frame was already beginning to burn.

2012: We see the painting for the first time: face to face with Erauso. It is part of the exhibition *No fueron solos. Mujeres en la conquista y colonización de América* (They Were Not Alone. Women in the Conquest and Colonization of America), exhibited in Madrid at the Naval Museum. The title is very explicit, no need to comment.

2021_06_16: We visit the San Telmo Museum. Luis Gómez de Arteche's copy of the painting is exhibited there, not in the section of the museum dedicated to art but in the "Navigators" section. That same day we visited Gordailua (Irun), the archive where a large part of the collections of Guipuzcoa are kept, including the original portrait by Van der Hamen. The conservators showed us the painting in the storage racks. Erauso looks back at us.

—Cabello/Carceller

▸
Cabello/Carceller,
Stills from *Erauso Looks at Us, Erauso Poses (Chronopolitics of a portrait)*, 2021–22. Synchronized double projection, 4k video transferred to HD, color, sound, 16:9, 28 min., 15 sec.

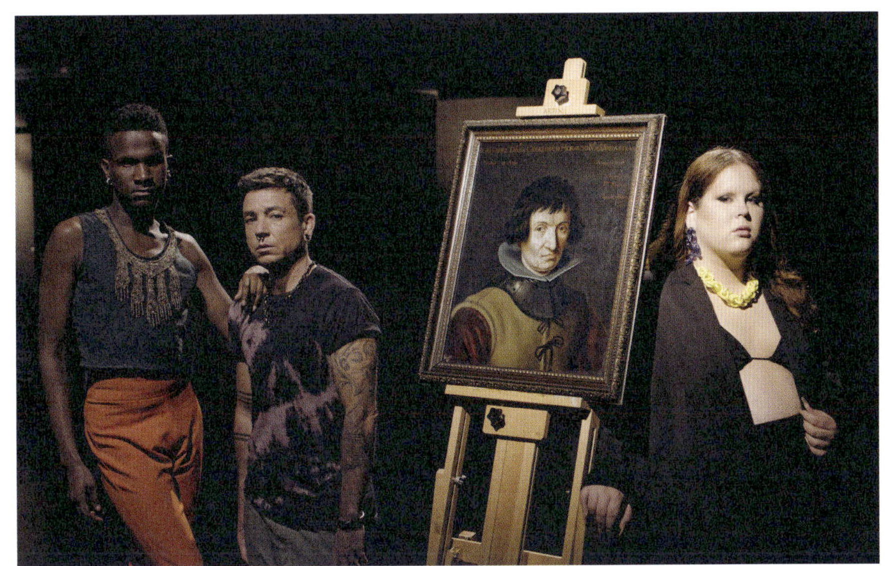

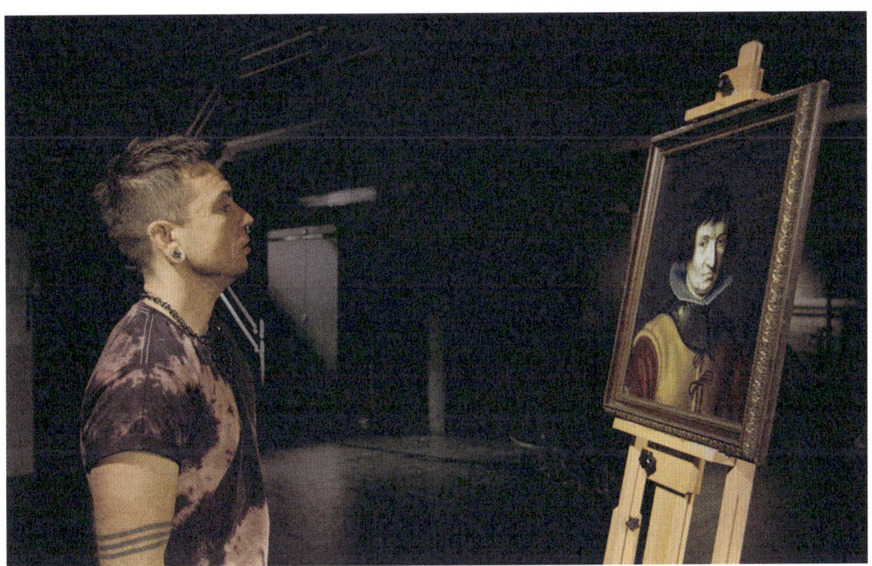

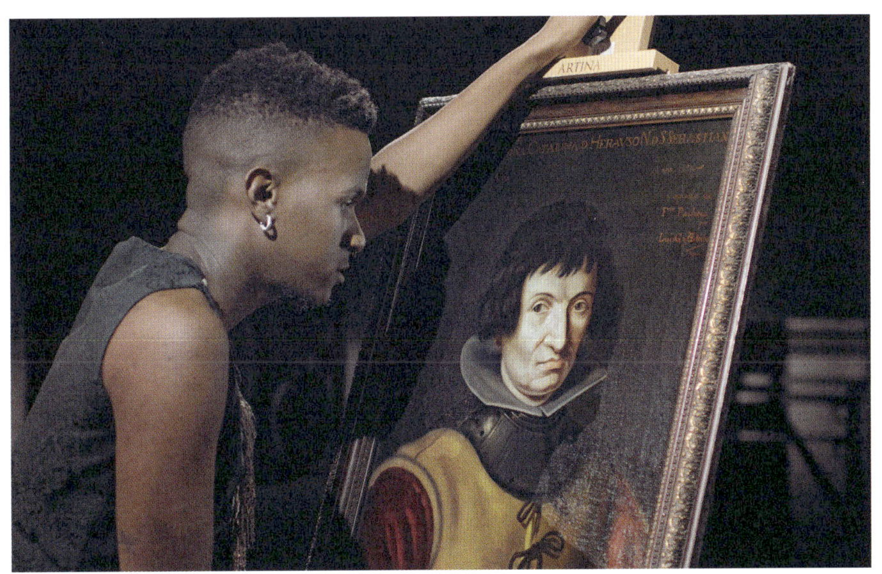
ARTINA

62 CHARLEY PARKHURST'S STAGECOACH, c. 1849

On display at the Autry Museum of the American West in Los Angeles is one of the few remaining authentic stagecoaches from the California gold rush era. The restored, ornately painted Concord Mail stagecoach (c. 1855) is not the one Charley Parkhurst drove, but it bears all the features we might imagine Charley's coach to have had: a seat for the dexterous and fearless driver in the front, a leather trunk in the rear to hold supplies and goods, and passenger/cargo space inside and atop the coach. I pay a visit to the museum, trying to channel Charley's ghost. I imagine him expertly leaping up into the driver's seat shortly after his arrival in California in 1849, fresh off a steamboat and ready to put his years of horse-handling experience to work on the new frontier. I watch as he tucks a chaw of tobacco into his lip and pulls his fringed leather gloves onto his hands. He clenches one hand around the reins guiding six horses at the front of the coach, while the other hand rests gently on the butt of his gun holstered at his hip. He turns and winks at me with his one good eye as he cracks the whip.

Lost in my reverie, I step back and bump into a display case. When I turn and examine the case, I find it features the "dapper" fashion of stagecoach drivers. So revered were the inimitable drivers that they were known to play to the admiration of crowds by dressing with flare. The exhibit includes a pair of bejeweled fringed leather gloves, much like the ones I imagine Charley wearing. As I read the placards, I am suddenly surprised to find Charley there in the glass case. One small note explains that the drivers "adopted flashy dress and colorful nicknames," further noting that "one venerated driver, Charlie [*sic*] Parkhurst, turned out to be a woman in disguise."

Too many stories about Charley end this way, suggesting that he led a life of disguise, that the "truth" of his womanhood was revealed upon death (allegedly shocking some of his closest friends), that he was the first woman to vote in California long before women were granted the right to vote (he voted as a man). I want to imagine otherwise. I want to remember Charley as he was known in life—as one of the baddest whips west of the Sierra Nevada. Charley was an orphan on the run from New Hampshire who eventually gained legendary status in the Wild West as "One-Eyed Charley" or "Cockeyed Charley" (he is said to have lost one eye to the kick of a horse). He outdrank and outdrove some of the toughest coachmen of the era.

But he is not a perfect hero of trans hirstory. He participated in the colonial project of westward expansion; he drove for prospectors who thought nothing of taking life and land. How do we reconcile that history with the story of how he carved a life for himself in a world that would have otherwise left someone like him for dead? Maybe we can't. Many of the details of Charley's life are uncertain and disputable, as he left behind little more than legend and lore. But we can at least account for his role as a settler even as we tell his story as one of trans possibility. While Charley may not have had the language to describe himself as "trans," we do know that he lived much of his life as a man, whatever that may have meant to him. I look again at the stagecoach. There Charley sits, both eager and terrified for what this life holds for him. He tips his hat and smiles at me just before he rides off into the sunset. And this is how I remember him, Charley Parkhurst, 1812–1879.

—KJ Cerankowski

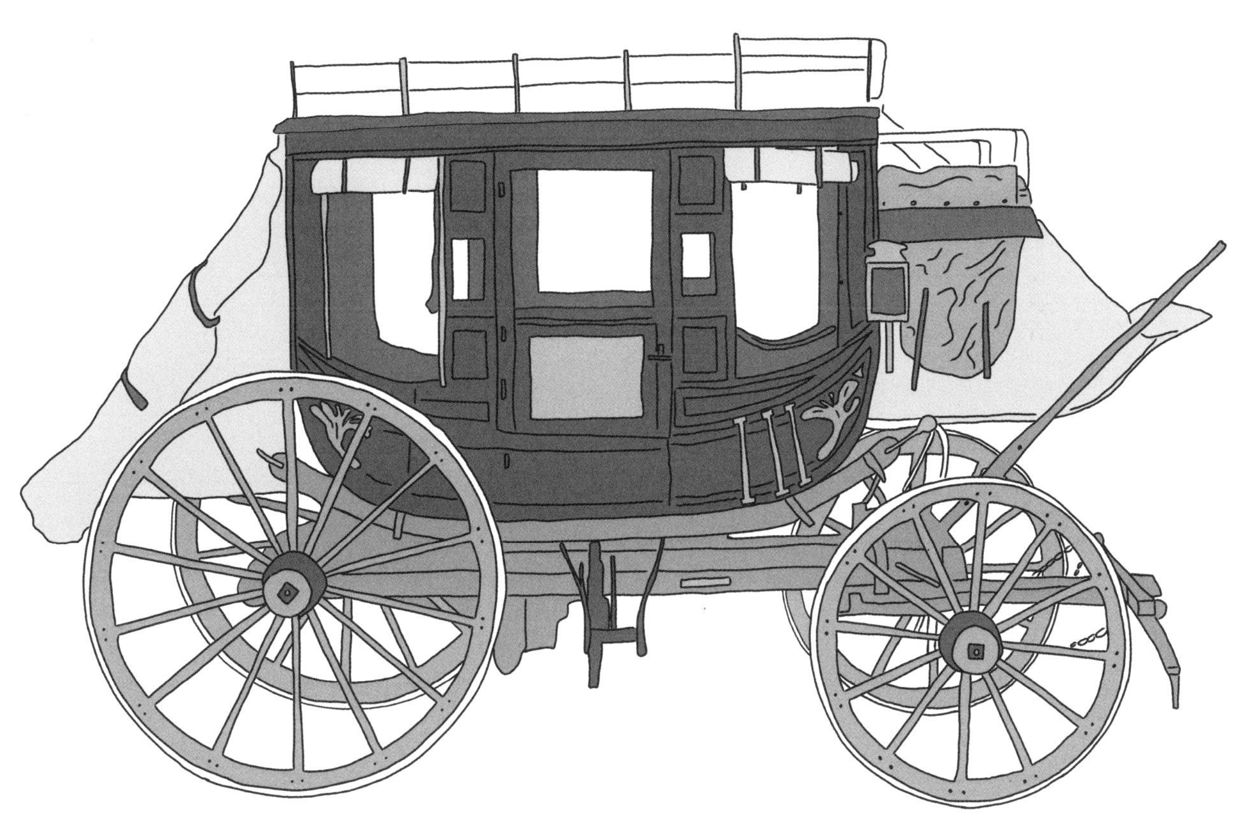

63 ANTHROPOMORPHIC FIGURE, CHORRERA, c. 500 BCE–500 CE

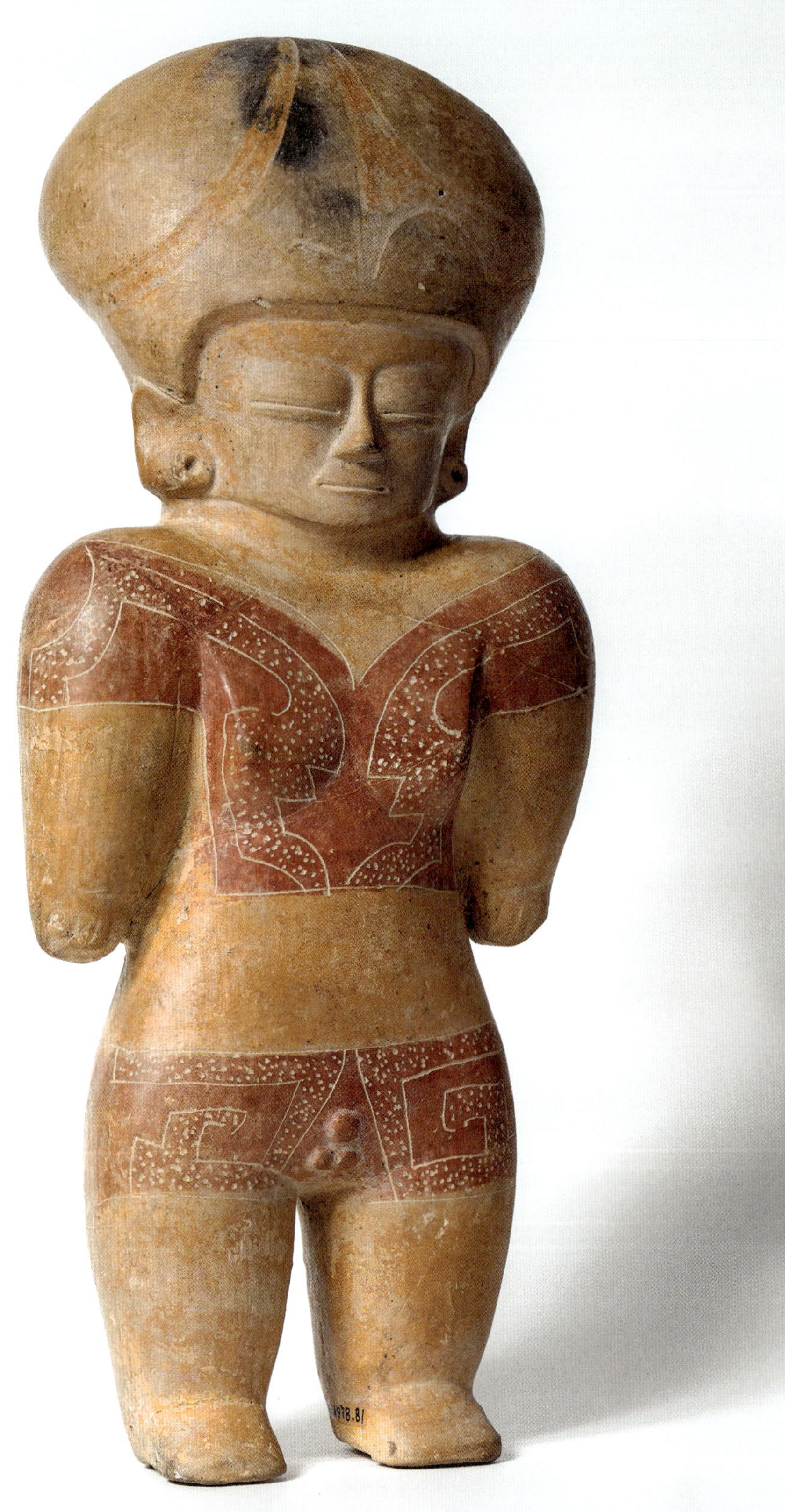

Oneiric encounter with a two-thousand-year-old Indigenous clay being

Once upon a time, I had this dream about you. You, a small and old being made of clay. You are older than me, older than the oldest of my elders. You came into material existence at a time none of us can recall. About 2,500 years ago, you were molded by the hands, mind, spirit, and technology of a human being in the land caressed by the Pacific Ocean that is now called Ecuador. You are now called a figurine from the Tolita culture. Today, you and thousands of others like you are observed, studied, analyzed, scrutinized, measured, photographed, exposed to the eyes of other humans like me. (Are they really like me?) Some of us spend years trying to understand you, trying to reveal the stories you tell about these times we can't recall. I am an archaeologist. This is what we do. We ask mute objects to tell us stories about past times in order for us to make sense of the times we live and the futures we want to live.

In my dream, you were not silent. You appeared to me accompanied by a loud laughter. Like you were already mocking the rules governing this strange future of yours I live in. I could see your shapes and colors, the bumps and lines running on your body made of clay, drawing patterns and carrying unknown meanings about those who made you and their society. Did you already know that this appearance and these clothes of yours are at the center of ontological disputes in my time? You see, in the time span separating you and me, colonial violence has established that only two possibilities of bodily and social existence are possible: man and woman. Now and here, in parts of the world forcefully impacted by modern Western understandings of the world, masculinity and femininity are exclusively attributed according to body formats, and are used to define who holds power and who doesn't.

And archaeologists have been desperately trying to make you fit into one of these two gender categories. Is it your loincloth, this masculine adornment, that matters most, or is it your curvy hips and breasts, that define your story the most? An archaeologist from your land, María Fernanda Ugalde, has been one of the very few who dared affirm the legitimacy of your existence beyond modern Western understandings of gender.[1] You know, the fact that you display characteristics that are both understood as masculine and feminine in this time and place not only confuses them, it scares them. It reminds them of the ancientness of people like me. It reminds them that in other times and places, people who lived in the border of what is now called gender were not denied the right to exist. It reminds them that the existence of those of us called transgender, nonbinary, queer, gender nonconforming is older than the violence now directed to us.

After a silent prayer thanking you for your existence, I gathered courage and asked you: what are you, after all? Behind your tiny ceramic eyelids, I thought I saw a spark. I heard a whisper in my ear made of flesh: "I am like you. Timeless. Untranslatable. Ancestral. An ancient reminder of your eternal existence."

—Gabby Omoni Hartemann

◀
Anthropomorphic figure, Chorrera, c. 500 BCE–500 CE. Ceramic, 15 × 6 7/16 × 3 7/8 in. (38.5 × 16.3 × 9.8 cm). Museo Nacional del Ecuador

1. María Fernanda Ugalde and O. Hugo Benavides, "Queer Histories and Identities on the Ecuadorian Coast: The Personal, the Political, and the Transnational," *Whatever: A Transdisciplinary Journal of Queer Theories and Studies* 1, no. 1 (2018): 157–82.

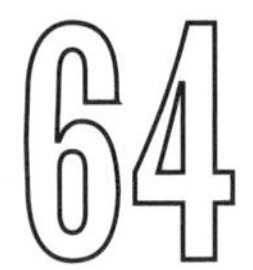

JOHN MONEY'S "DISTRACTION DOODLES," 1974

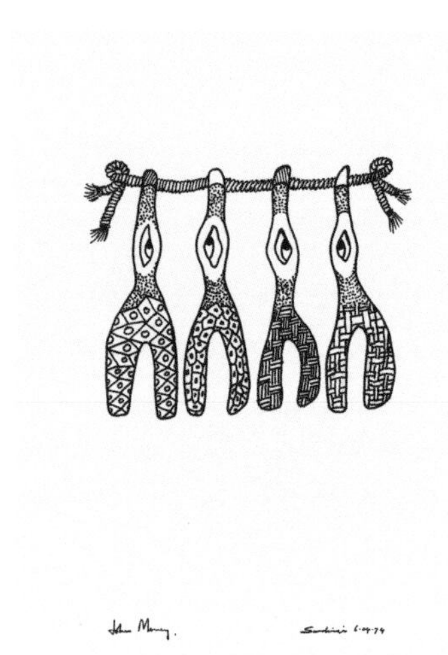

John Money, *Untitled*, 1974. Ink on paper, 7¾ × 10¾ in. (19.7 × 27.3 cm). Kinsey Institute, Indiana University Bloomington, IN

The eccentric sex researcher John Money (1921–2006), a maximalist, wrote forty-some-odd books and more than five hundred articles, and invented hundreds of neologisms: *lovemap, mindbrain, behavioron,* and *normophilia.* He wrote of sex as *deriviative, adjunctive, arbitrary,* and *adventitious.* He theorized "gender identity errors" and "gender transposition," though stated definitively that there is "no proven cause of gender identity disorder." He called the quasi-empiricism of sexology *fuckology*—a queer-sounding science. Money was not a physician, psychologist, or psychiatrist, but he did manage and administer diagnosis through the Johns Hopkins Gender Identity Clinic, which after being cofounded by Money in 1967, became the first clinic in the United States to perform sex-related surgeries on children and adults. Money is perhaps most infamous for the nonconsensual treatment of David Reimer, and the diagnostic frameworks tested at the clinic through encounters with vulnerable populations continue to reverberate in the suppressing of gender-affirming healthcare and self-determination.[1]

In a 1955 memo, "Hermaphroditism, Gender and Precocity in Hyperadrenocortism: Pychologic Findings" printed in the Johns Hopkins bulletin, Money parsed the concept of gender along the axes of "role" and "identity," anticipating the feminist analytic of gender as a social construct and of sex and gender as interlocking yet distinct categories. His formulation of gender as accumulative and as a "role" is affirmed in his writings again and again; in *Gay, Straight, and In-Between* (1988), he explains, "gender is more inclusive than sex," and goes on to describe gender as "an umbrella under which are sheltered all the different components of sex difference, including the sex-genital, sex-erotic, and sex-procreative components."[2]

Money self-styled as an artist and made countless drawings in pencil and marker. Redundantly called "distraction doodles," his scribbles were often made on scraps of paper close at hand—pathology slides, hotel stationary—tracking his comings and goings in the colonial network and knowledge project of sexology, a scientific apparatus that formally theorizes race and sex as part of a hierarchy of the human. Money's aesthetic practice—of doodles, photocollages, and self-portraits—constitutes an important and overlooked component of his archive and legacy, existing in parallel production to both his theorizing and management of sex and gender on the page and in the clinic. His groovy doodles of forensic criminology and sexed anatomy function as experimental diagrams of diagnosis, and the captions to his neon drawings of human and animal embodiments record his movements in and through the global sexological apparatus. An ink drawing *Garden of Eden* (1974) depicts an apple whose core is a multi-sexed organ containing a clitoris, penis, labial folds, and testicles. Made in Sardinia at the Symposium of Pharmacology and Sexual Behavior, the drawing imagines the sexed body as multiply outfitted for sensory pleasure—not confined by a binary rendering of sex or gender—emphasizing a tension in Money's practice between a utopian longing for bodily autonomy and the material constraints of the empirical sciences.

What do we do with the mess and incoherence of the archive? With the flawed figure of history? How are we to come to terms with Money's legacy, taking into consideration the known and unknown violences he committed against material and psychic embodiments? What place does he have in feminist, queer, and transgender histories and movements?

—Jeanne Vaccaro

1. For more information, see Iain Morland, "Gender, Genitals, and the Meaning of Being Human," in *Fuckology: Critical Essays on John Money's Diagnostic Concepts*, eds. Lisa Downing, Iain Morland, and Nikki Sullivan (Chicago: University of Chicago Press, 2014), 69–100.
2. John Money, *Gay, Straight, and In-Between: The Sexology of Erotic Orientation* (New York: Oxford University Press, 1988), 53.

▶ John Money, *Garden of Eden*, 1974. Ink on paper, 7¾ × 10¾ in. (19.7 × 27.3 cm). Kinsey Institute, Indiana University Bloomington, IN

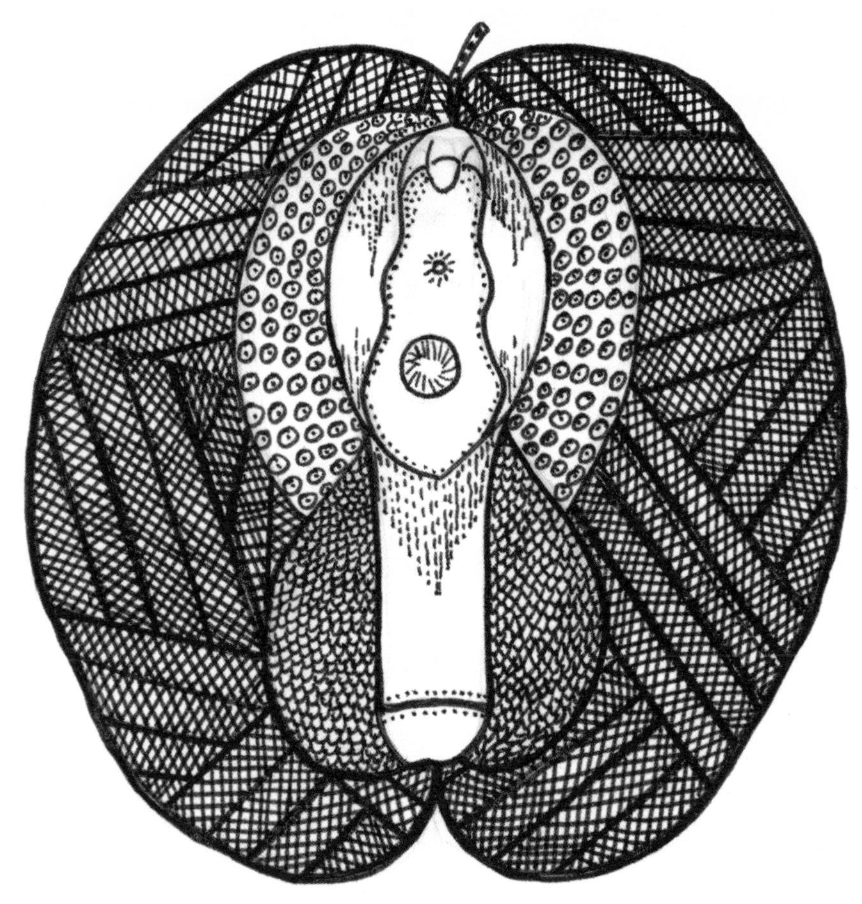

GARDEN OF EDEN

Symposium on Pharmacology and Sexual
. . . . . Behavior . . . . .
John Money 6.07.74 . . . . Sardinia

65 LUCY HICKS ANDERSON'S CLUTCH, c. 1945

This iconic photo of Ms. Lucy Hicks Anderson, pictured between a uniformed police officer and, more than likely, another officer of the court, is as enigmatic as it is descriptive. Impeccably dressed in a light-colored skirt suit with dark hat and matching leather gloves, Ms. Hicks Anderson was a sought-after chef, socialite, philanthropist, and madam in Oxnard, California. She was also a woman of trans experience, which became national news in 1945 after she was charged and tried for perjury in Ventura County.

In the foreground of the image are three pristine leather bags for shoes, garments, and toiletries, and in her hands she clasps a leather clutch—all further evidence of what she told reporters outside of the courtroom: "I have lived, dressed, and acted just what I am, a woman."[1] With humor and wit, Hicks Anderson tried to convey to the Ventura County courtroom how everyone's gender came with baggage. In response to a question from the prosecutor about her first husband's gender and whether he was a man, she reportedly replied, "Well, he's supposed to be." As her response indicates, other people's genders are often assumed rather than known. We are all trying to dress the part.

During the weeklong trial the prosecutors compelled five doctors to give testimony about her sex, to which Hicks Anderson responded on the stand, "I defy any doctor in the world to prove that I am not a woman."[2] For Ms. Hicks Anderson, gender was not something that could be determined in a medical clinic, even as researchers Robert Stoller and Harold Garfinkel would pursue a series of studies to determine whether gender could be transformed in their clinic at the University of California, Los Angeles some years later. The jury returned a verdict of guilty and a week later, approximately the length of time for which she'd packed, Lucy Hicks Anderson was sentenced to ten years of probation without custody.

News of the trial incited further investigation. Federal prosecutors filed felony fraud charges against her second husband, Reuben Anderson, who had returned to New York from military service overseas, and against Hicks Anderson in Los Angeles. A photograph of her entering the New York federal courthouse for Reuben's trial shows her in another suit with a mink stole over her shoulder.

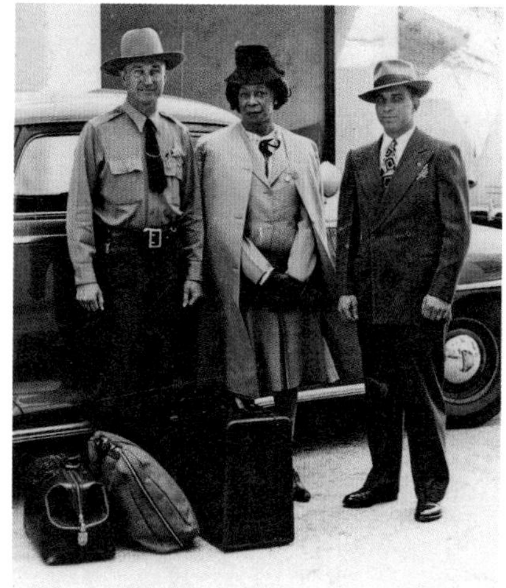

Lucy Hicks Anderson with law enforcement officers, Ventura, California, c. 1945. Museum of Ventura County Research Library and Archives

One wonders if she brought those same pieces of luggage with her for her cross-country trip. And of course, one cannot help but to imagine what might have happened had she taken them somewhere far away, where she would have not been charged, sentenced, and compelled to serve time at a federal penitentiary.

In this second trail, both Reuben and Lucy were founded guilty and sentenced to ten years at separate men's prisons. After serving time, Reuben and Lucy relocated to Los Angeles, having been told by the town's police chief that they would not be welcomed back in Oxnard for another ten years. She would die before being able to return from exile. While most reports describe her as dying in relative obscurity, it might be truer to say that she sought to lessen the burden the nation handed her and travel light.

—C. Riley Snorton

1. David Minier, "Before Caitlyn Jenner, there was Lucy Hicks," *VC Star*, November 7, 2015, accessed January 24, 2023, https://archive.vcstar.com/news/local/oxnard/before-caitlyn-jenner-there-was-lucy-hicks-ep-1356699260-347835751.html/.

2. Ebony Adams and Anita Sarkeesian, *History vs Women: The Defiant Lives that They Don't Want You to Know* (New York: Feiwel & Friends, 2018), 31.

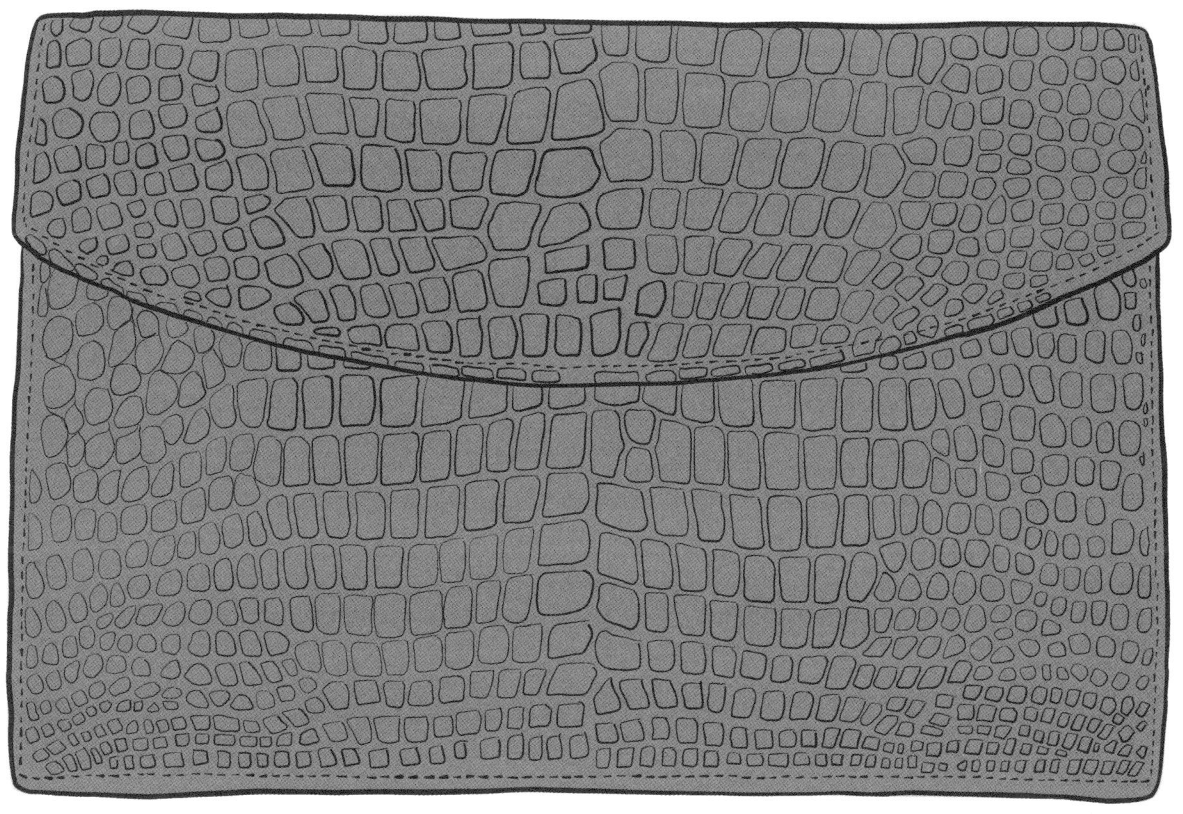

66 MAGNUS HIRSCHFELD'S DEATH MASK IN LI SHIU TONG'S SUITCASE, 1935

Magnus Hirschfeld (1868–1935) was instrumental in supporting the rights of homosexuals, transsexuals (a term he coined in 1923), and others who practiced and embodied sexual and gender variance in Germany from the 1890s through the end of the Weimar era. He founded the Institut für Sexualwissenschaft (Institute for Sexual Science) in 1919. Through this organization he focused on research and counseling for a community of which he was an integral part and fought for public education and the repeal of anti-homosexual laws.

Hirschfeld departed for an extended speaking and research tour abroad in 1930 and met Li Shiu Tong (1907–1993) in Shanghai in 1931. They subsequently traveled together in several countries, collecting books and other materials related to sex and gender to be added to the Institute's library. They were in Paris together when Nazis raided the Institute in Berlin and burned most of its collection, including around 20,000 books and a larger number of photographs and objects.

Hirschfeld died in exile in Nice in 1935. After his passing, Li moved frequently, studying in Zurich and at Harvard, and visiting his family in Hong Kong. He transported this case and its materials, including a plaster cast death mask of Hirschfled, with him. Sometime between 1958 and 1975, Li moved to Vancouver, Canada, where he spent the last part of his life. When he died in 1993, his younger brother cleared out his apartment and discarded the case. It was discovered in a dumpster by someone unfamiliar with Hirschfeld, who thought its contents interesting enough to post about online. Hirschfeld historian Ralf Dose came across the post, and eventually brought the suitcase back to Berlin, where it is now housed in the archives at the Magnus-Hirschfeld-Gesellschaft (Magnus Hirschfeld Society).

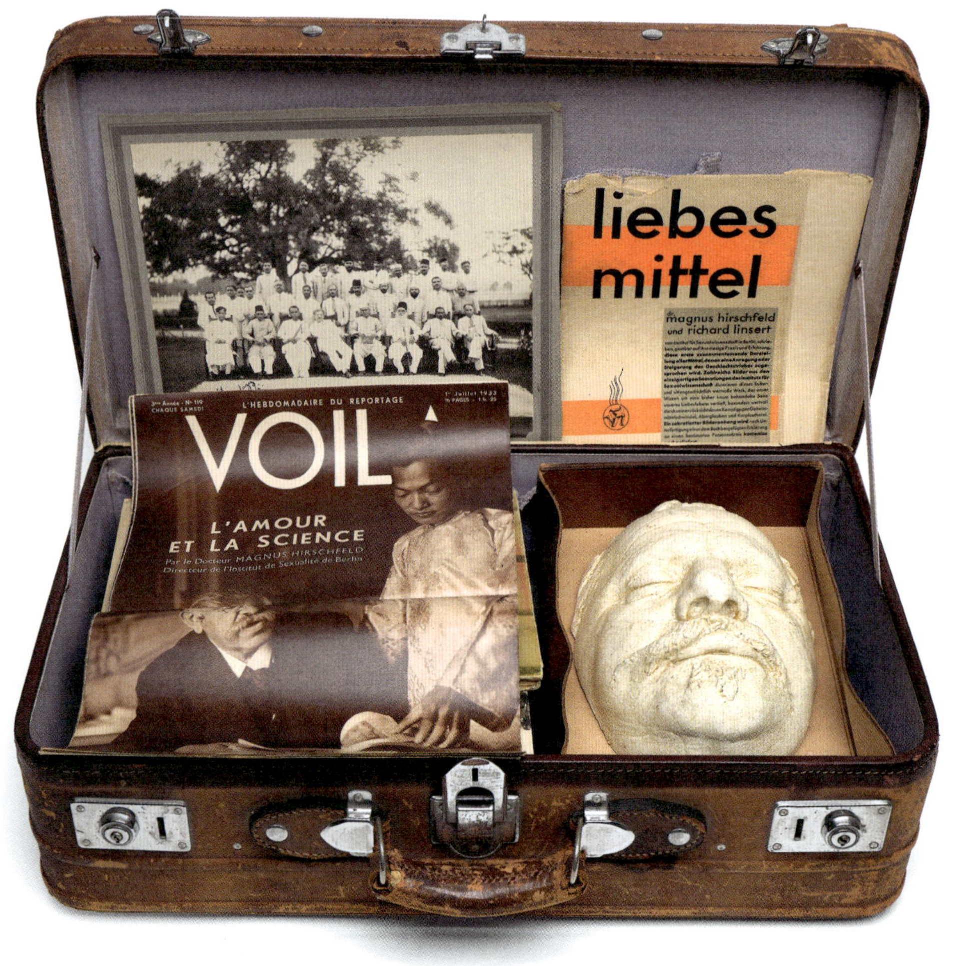

Mask4Mask

HORNED UP DADDY MASK

ISO/IRL/OL/FLESH/DIGITAL/SEXTING/VOICE/VBL/NVBL

CRUISY NB OTTER PIG BEAR UNICORN GOLD STAR VERS JOCK BOTTM THICC TWINK BRUTAL TOP BB BHM BBW DTE DWM/F/NB/T/NG FFA FEMME GC GF GSH SSBBW SSBBH VGL W/E DF 420 AL CD D D2F GCWOK GU K LD LD MBA MBL MM MNC NBM N/K NM N/S OR SD B&D @N4L BB BDSM BI CD COB D/S DFK DOM DOMME G GG GGG LE$BEAN LE DOLLAR BEAN LE DOLLAR SIGN BEAN LGBTQIA+++++++++ LACE LEATHER LIPSTICK LINGERIE

HAIRY BALD INBETWEEN ALL M4M M4T T4T FEMME4FEMME DILFS MILFS PILFS OPFYP OWO PEGGING PSE RO ROUGH TRADE SM SUB SWITCH TG TRADE TS TV WSAFF ASL ACCA AF AFF THEy/THEMS/HE/HIM SHE/HER VE/XE ZE/ZIE PER/PERS (F)AE/(F)AER E/EY XE/XEM XYR/XYRS ZIRAKA BACKSLIDE BAE BFWB BREADCRUMBING C2C CATFISH CILF CMIYC CORN NOCONUCOPIA CPL COTD CU CUFFED EDGING F2F F9 FAG FTA FTTB FYI NOGHOST H/O HUMMER A MUST JBY KARY BAE LDA DLH LDR LFG LDA LTR MLTR MM MTAF NETFLIX AND CHILL NIP NOPS NON DATE- DATE NSA OAT POF OTH ONS OSO OTH PEACOCKING Q RTS SECKS SEGGS SI SLAY A OF DATES MAYBE SLOW-FADING SPOON W/ SPICY EGGPLANT STR SWS THIRST TRAP TLC WILLING TO POSSIBLY UNCUFF AND WAA WLTM FOR WATERMELLON SUGAR X-FACTOR ?Y/O

ME: German/Jewish Groucho Marx meets Deep Throat Harry Reems thick Selleck Stash. Exiled in France, until transported to Vancouver. Kept in a leather suitcase since 1935, painfully hard and ready to be used. Rock solid/smooth plaster to touch, ride, stroke, lick, and suck. Haven't felt a warm intentional touch since the early 90s, however am forever non-monog/poly and up for any kind of creative configuration. Open to suggestions. Useful for breath play, water sports, D/D, sensory depravation, cos play, Daddy/Switch, groups, couples, deep submission, bondage, autoerotic edging, celebrity dress-up and more propositions. Patient and Ready. All holes accessible accept mouth, eyes, and ears. Easy to clean. Hefty, however not indestructible. Not into shattering and/ or being repaired. If you break me, you break me.

YOU: All of the above with a deep need to dismantle and have fun. All materials okay, except latex (sorry, allergy! Sad I know!!) All genders, (most) sexualities, proclivities and identifications welcome. Consensual, caring and not afraid to be mean AF!

NO TERFS NO SWERFS NO NAZIS NO RACISTS NO KARENS NO REPS NO DEMS NO HETEROFLEXIBLES NO MASC4MASC NO FEMME HATERS NO BODY SHAMERS

Daddy(ies) says/said/say: "Love is a Conflict Between Reflexes and Reflections."

What do you think?

CUM AND USE ME!

—Liz Rosenfeld

◂ Suitcase left by Magnus Hirschfeld to Li Shiu Tong, containing Hirschfeld's plaster death mask, documents, two diaries, photographs, and other materials, c. 1935. Magnus-Hirschfeld-Gesellschaft, Berlin

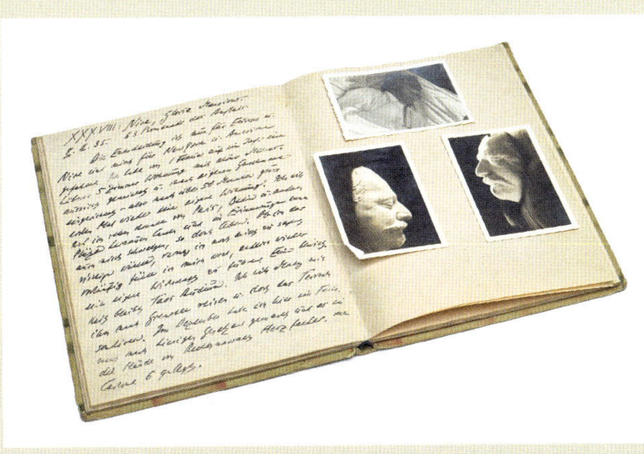

▸ Photo album from the suitcase with pictures of Hirschfeld's death mask, c. 1935. Magnus Hirschfeld-Gesellschaft, Berlin

67 CHELSEA THOMPTO, *LANDMARKS*, 2021

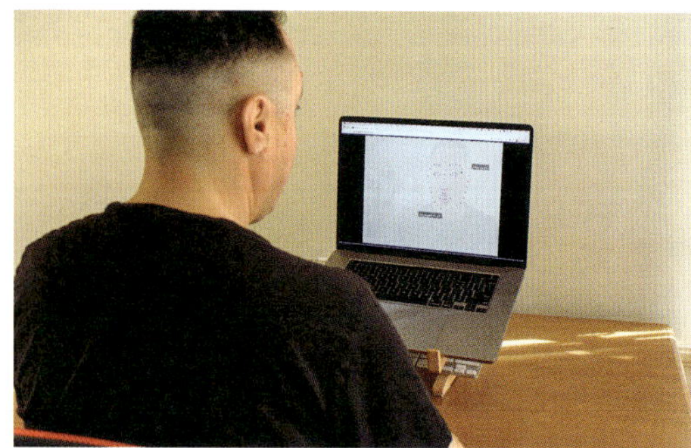

Chris E. Vargas using the facial recognition elements of *Landmarks*, 2023

Human measurement has served as a method of categorization, classification, and a way of disciplining human bodies. There has been a rampant proliferation of machine learning models generating fictitious pictures such as OpenAI's DALL-E or Runway's generative moving images and filmmaking platform. These tools and many like them cannot prevent the erasure of the multitude of human morphologies, body types, and phenotypes. Facial recognition and AI systems are built on specific datasets, which inherently make them biased. While these systems allege to work towards an ethics to reduce, if not mitigate, harm, these programs continue to raise questions related to visibility, perceptibility, and recognition. In Chelsea Thompto's web-based work *Landmarks* (2021), she explores the various types of actions that facial recognition technology performs and disrupts these actions through poetic gestures. She prompts us to question these technologies, especially their creators, who promote their supposed magical features and capabilities. Thompto's research and creative intervention asks us to think through questions and concerns not commonly asked within the development of these software programs.

The artist includes five investigations within the work: Rote, Stages, Empire, Machine, and Landmarks. Within each, she writes and enacts new ways of seeing and understanding how facial recognition software is programmed to read, perceive, and process. How might a minute rote task become insidious? How does the machine recognize AI-generated faces yet not a real transgender person? How might we gain greater awareness of the relationship between the human body as a vessel for data extraction and a mapping of specific facial landmarks for recognition?

Thompto dissects the various functions of facial recognition software by the way they have been coded to see her face through various facial landmark rules. The software misgenders her and assumes expressions and emotions through misrecognition. She asks, "How can I convince this machine of my gender?" and "How can I communicate something that is the sum of so many little moments, gestures, and decisions?"[1] Within the Stages section, the artist shows the viewer four screens: Discover, Map, Define, and Exploit. As the viewer scrolls through each frame, the machine's level of confidence in recognizing its subject is measured as a percentage, then mapped by codified facial landmarks dependent upon the subject's brows, eyes, nose, lips, and jaw. Depending upon how the facial features are measured by the machine, it makes assumptions of possible emotions. The program has been written to execute a subtle fading effect of the viewer's face, which serves as a metaphor and visual marker of its inability to truly see and know what it is looking at. Yet what I found most compelling and provocative about the work is Thompto's deconstruction of how facial recognition software charts the human face with what has been codified in accordance with a binary system. *Landmarks* forces the viewer to ponder not only AI's ability to recognize imaginary and non-existent faces, as produced by a generative adversarial network or machine learning framework, but also its inability to identify people of color and trans bodies and faces.

—Dorothy R. Santos

1. Chelsea Thompto, *Landmarks*, accessed November 15, 2022, https://landmarks.cloud/.

▸ Chelsea Thompto, Screenshot of *Landmarks*, 2021. Website, https://landmarks.cloud/

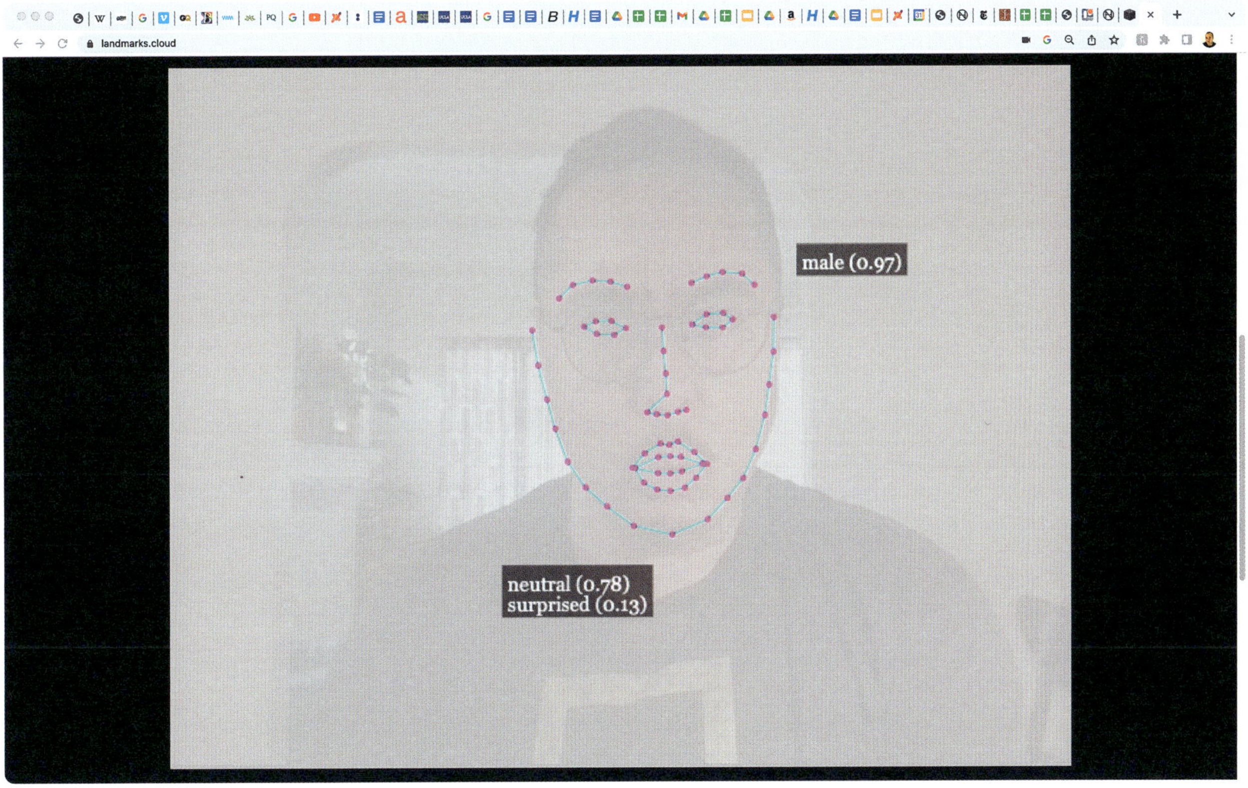

landmarks.cloud

male (0.97)

neutral (0.78)
surprised (0.13)

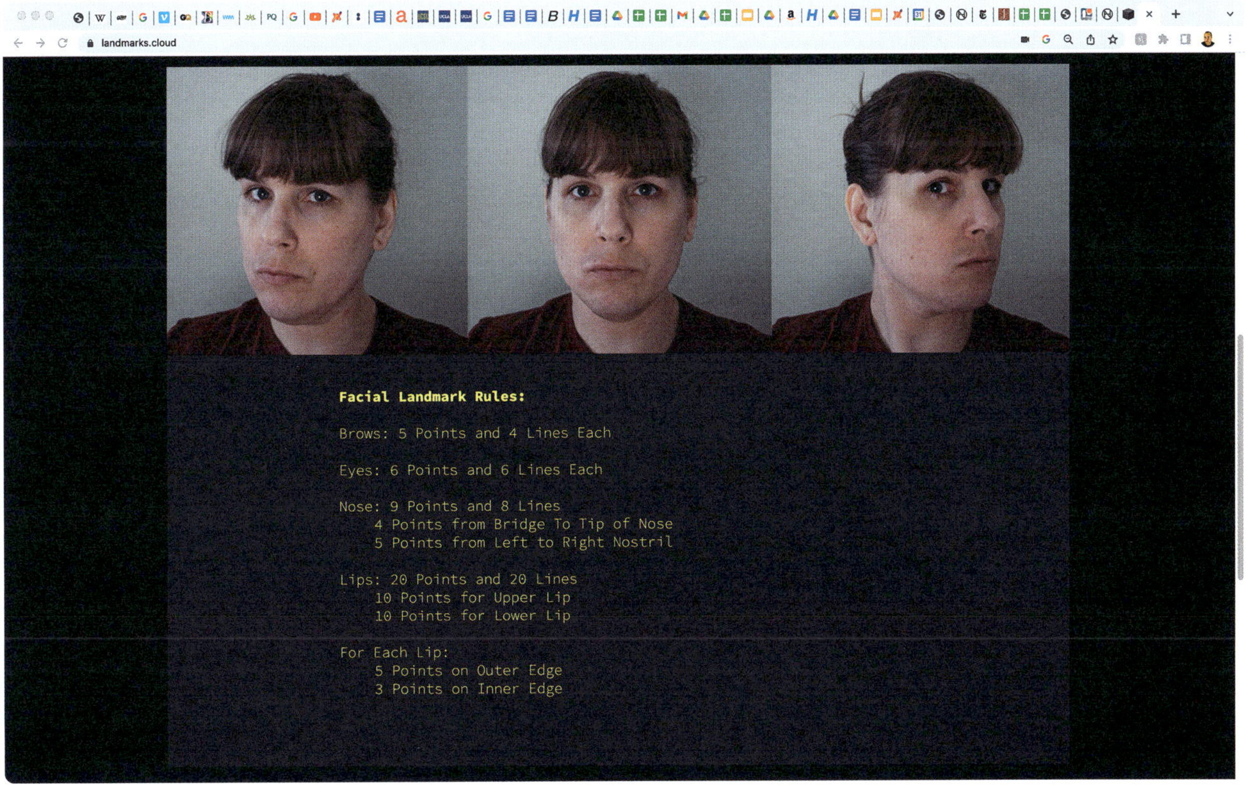

landmarks.cloud

Facial Landmark Rules:

Brows: 5 Points and 4 Lines Each

Eyes: 6 Points and 6 Lines Each

Nose: 9 Points and 8 Lines
    4 Points from Bridge To Tip of Nose
    5 Points from Left to Right Nostril

Lips: 20 Points and 20 Lines
    10 Points for Upper Lip
    10 Points for Lower Lip

For Each Lip:
    5 Points on Outer Edge
    3 Points on Inner Edge

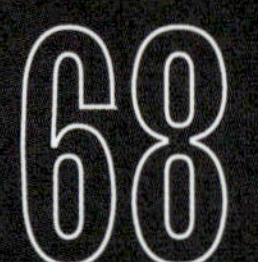

KIYAN WILLIAMS, *REFLECTIONS / REFRACTIONS IN BLAQ*, 2017

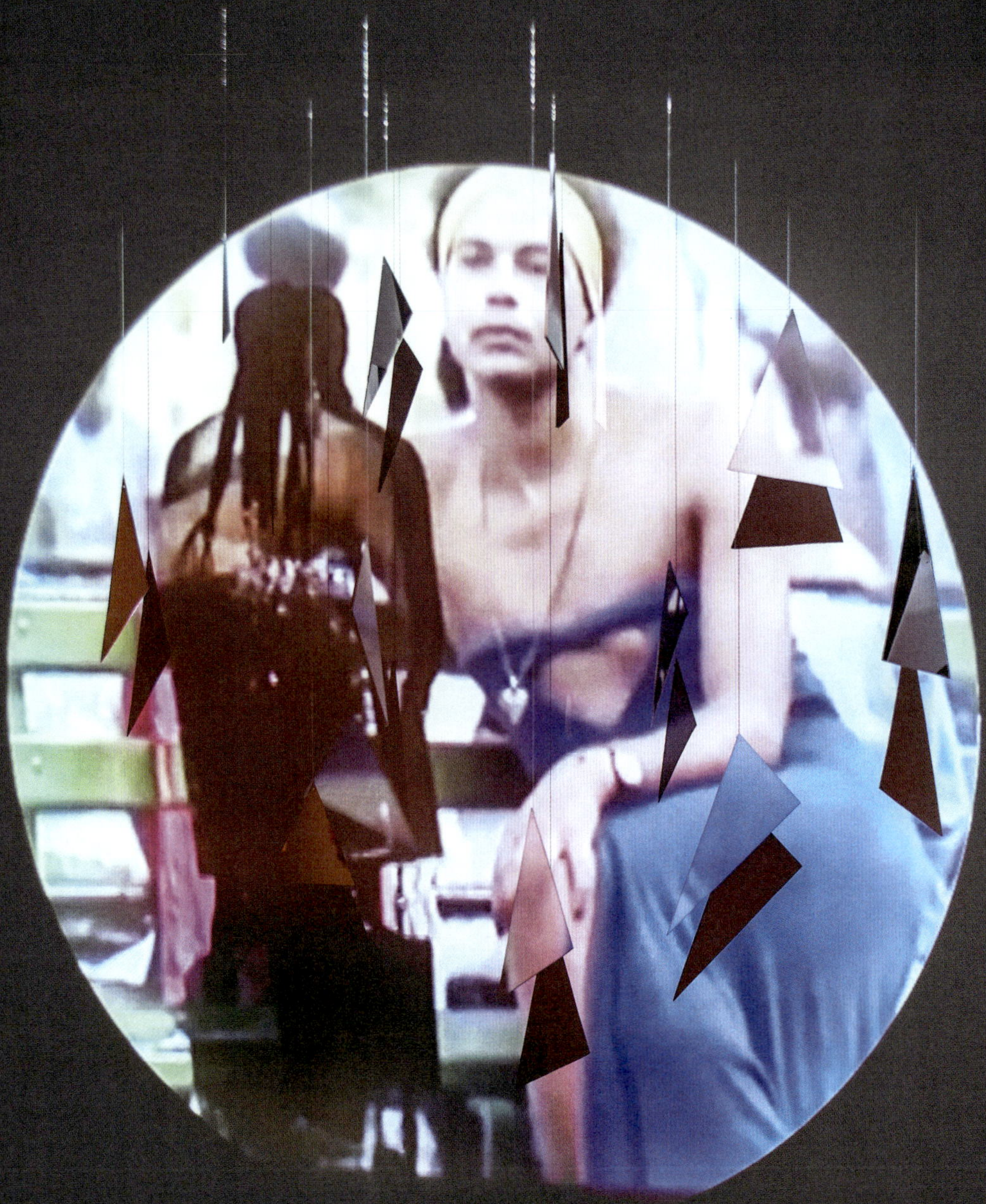

A Corridor of Becoming

There isn't a single document, nor record nor report. There is no pattern. No map. No diagram. No blueprint. But still I search for something, a manual, a historical document, a collection of elders and ancestors, an archive of voices that point me in a direction—or reflect back to me a familiarity or parallel existence. A reflection which might restore a sense of wonder in the body that I see but do not feel. I search José Esteban Muñoz's textual imagining of the *collective political becoming* to speculate what may come of the gendered body.[1] I'm searching for the set of conditions in a space that gives us a way to see and a direction to move—to see ourselves through movement. To "cultivate space to live, to become-as-being, in this movement."[2] A movement both structural and fluid in principle. A movement that differentiates being from the body, the body from flesh, and flesh from pleasure. A movement that prioritizes the sensorial. There's a passageway, a corridor of perception, through which I journey daily. Discovering at each end a different dimension of existence. On one end there's the way the other sees me and on the other end, there's the way I see myself. Each passage through gives another dimension to my understanding of self, my own movement as an intermediary. Both ends, I imagine, have reflective properties, bouncing material back and forth—like glitter dancing about in a shaken jar, hitting the top and cascading slowly back down and settling at the bottom. The cascade proffers a series of fragmented evanescent reflections that make the back and forth of self-discovery less exhaustive, shiny even. Between these poles of existence, of being seen, I become glitter shuffling between, dancing down the long stretch of *being* and *becoming*. The space between the perceived self and the felt self disappears through the movement. A movement for which to sublimate phobia to philia—*phil*, feel. A movement that stretches the elastic experience of being a body past the tenancy of flesh and figure. The movement builds a collection of voices—my movement, our movement, is a changing to and toward and into the archive for which I search. The mass of bodies in the mess of becoming is both collective and political. The reflection of flesh.

"To become flesh is to enter the world and engage with it so fully that the distinction between one's body and the world ceases to have meaning."[3]

—Leila Weefur

Engaging with the seminal work Tongues Untied *(1989) by filmmaker and activist Marlon Riggs, Williams created the installation* Reflections / Refractions in BlaQ *(2017) using footage by Riggs in the artist's archive in the Special Collections at Stanford University. Williams appropriates Riggs's footage of the Black, trans, feminine, gender-nonconforming artist Jessie Harris—the only femme-presenting person in the film—most of which did not make Riggs's final cut.*

◄
Kiyan Williams, *Reflections / Refractions in BlaQ*, 2017. Installation with projected moving image on hanging mirror fragments, dimensions variable. Shown in the exhibition *Nobody Promised You Tomorrow: Art 50 Years After Stonewall*, Brooklyn Museum, 2019

1. José Esteban Muñoz, *Cruising Utopia: The Then and There of Queer Futurity* (New York: New York University Press, 2009), 189.
2. Marquis Bey, *Black Trans Feminism* (Durham, NC: Duke University Press, 2022), 66.
3. Gayle Salamon, *Assuming a Body: Transgender and Rhetorics of Materiality* (New York: Columbia University Press, 2010), 64.

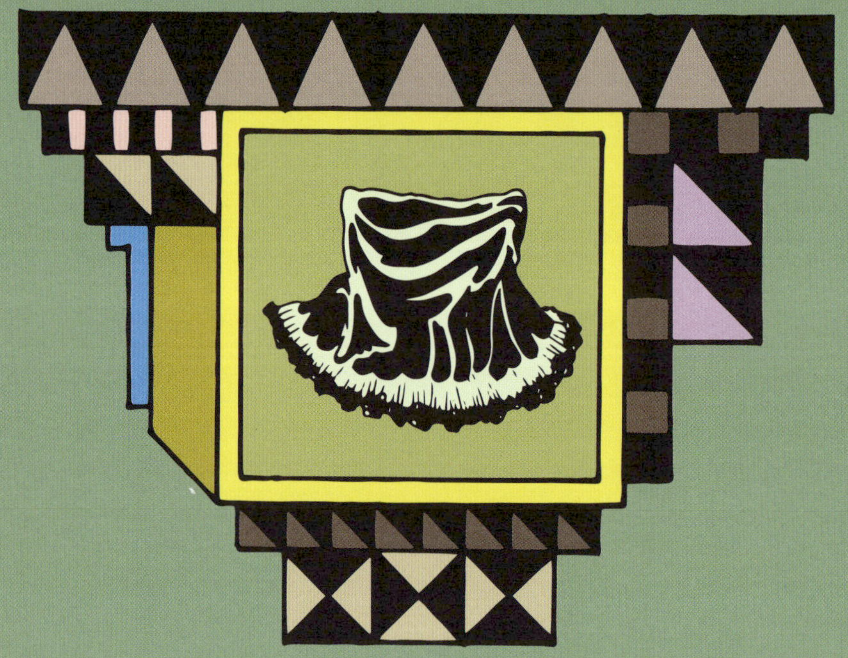

RESTAGE

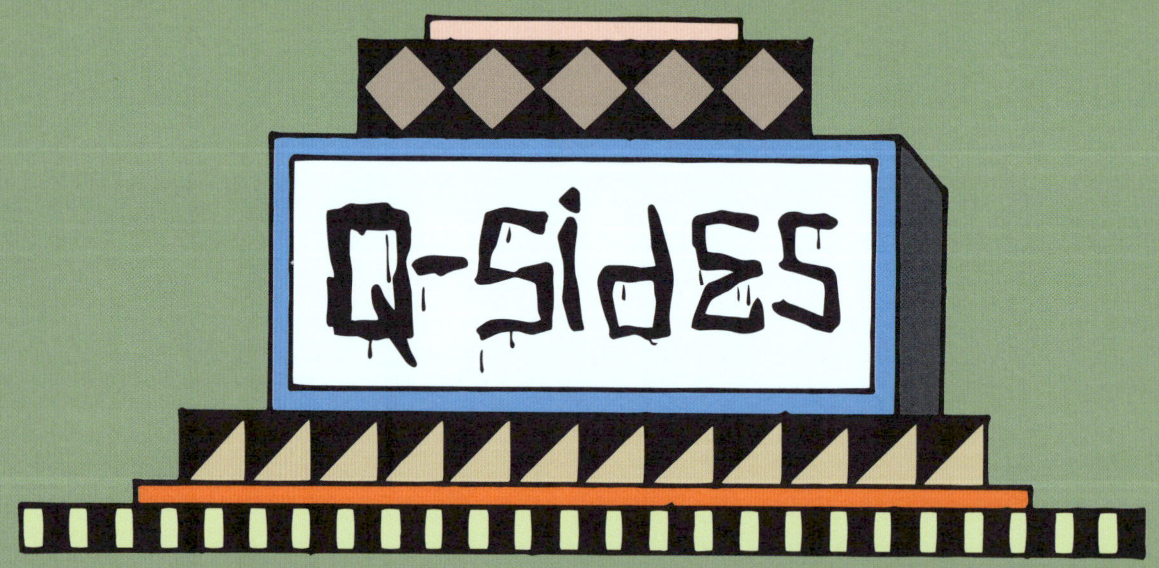

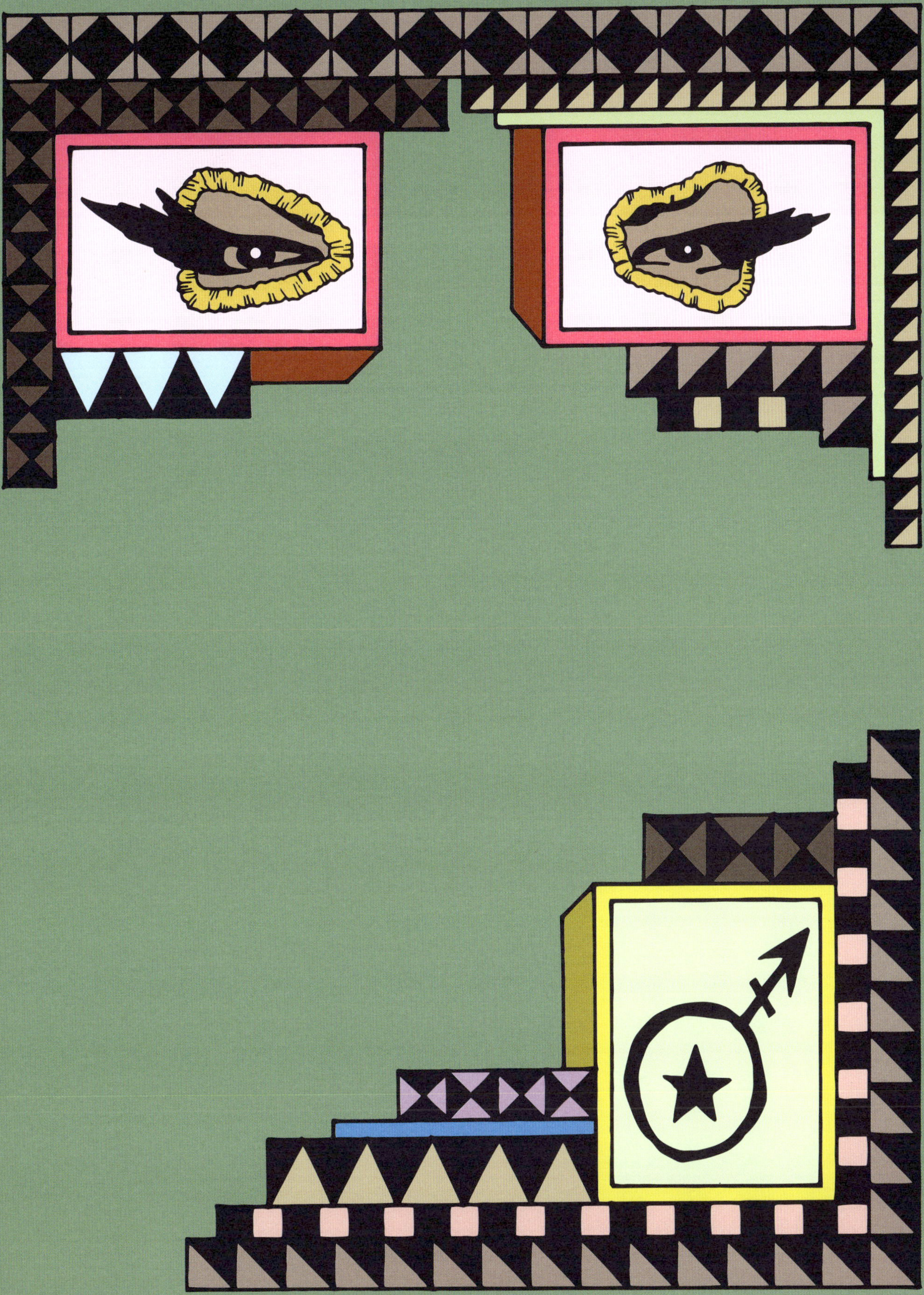

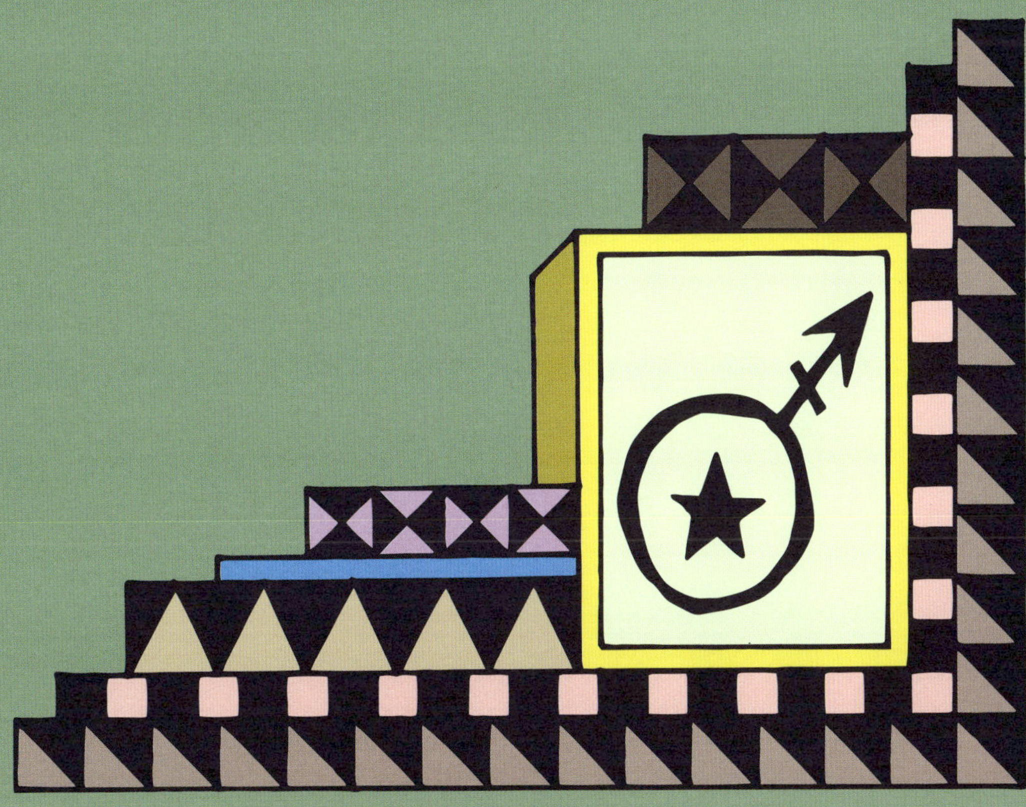

69 TUESDAY SMILLIE, *STREET TRANSVESTITES 1973*, 2015

It's almost impossible for me to imagine the Christopher Street Liberation Day Parade of 1973 in sharp Technicolor. The charging bodies and catchy slogans are forever caught in the grainy black-and-white of photographs and handheld film. In one photograph, Saints Sylvia Rivera (1951–2002), in a form-fitting jumpsuit, and Bebe Scarpinato (1951–2019), in a dark flowing dress, raise their fists to the sky as they frame a large billowing banner. These mothers of the revolution are only minutes away from a moment now seared into our collective memory. In a rally held in Washington Square Park, Rivera literally fought her way past Vito Russo and others to take the stage that she and other transvestites had been denied by respectable gay activists who had no time for trans revolutionists, or at least no patience for a group that had gained a reputation for being difficult and rowdy: the Street Transvestite Action Revolutionaries (STAR).[1]

In the photograph, we're reminded that STAR was not just Rivera and Marsha P. Johnson (1945–1992). Lost in today's discussions are the many other mothers of the movement. Scarpinato was a high school teacher and stripper who fought for what we might today call trans inclusion in nascent gay liberation groups like Gay Activist Alliance, where she met Rivera. And on the other side of the photo stands an unidentified Black trans woman next to Rivera. Is she Zazu Nova, a Stonewall veteran who later joined the famous STAR House, or Bambi L'Amour, a fellow sex worker Rivera met during a stint at Riker's Island in 1966? It's these queens I think about when I look at Tuesday Smillie's *Street Transvestites, 1973* (2015).

The billowing banner from the black-and-white photograph is reproduced forty-two years later, in the midst of another moment of trans cultural revolt, not just in full color but undulating still, moving in a wind that has long passed or perhaps returned. The canvas or burlap banner, announcing the Street Transvestite Action Revolutionaries, is slashed with strips of black lace

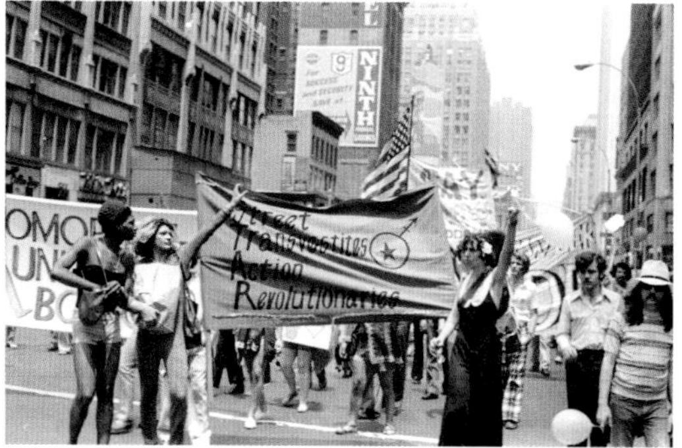

Street Transvestite Action Revolutionaries (STAR) in the Christopher Street Liberation Day Parade, New York, June 24, 1973. Photo by Richard C. Wandel. Richard C. Wandel Photographs, The LGBT Community Center National History Archive, New York

to mimic the folds and shadows of a flag in flight. Looking closer still at this optical and transhistorical illusion, the dark lace sparkles with beads, buttons, sequins, and more. Are these pearls cast off by our collective mothers in the discos, prison cells, and homeless shelters where they forged a politics, a community, and a life for us all across time? Smillie weaves the glitz of these street queens into the object itself, rejecting the harsh machismo that dominates vintage liberation aesthetics, as if to say, "our frivolity will not hurt the cause. If I can't have glamour, I don't want to be in your revolution."

—Morgan M Page

1. Like many, I first became aware of Rivera's powerful speech through the research of artist Tourmaline in 2012. The footage was captured on that day by L.O.V.E. (Lesbians Organized for Video Experience), a collective of lesbian videomakers founded in 1972 and consisting of Betty Brown, Delia Davis, Tracy Fitz, Barbara Jabaily, Doris "Blu" Lunden, and Denise Wong. The video, uploaded by L.O.V.E., can be viewed here: https://www.youtube.com/watch?v=Jb-JIOWUwlo.

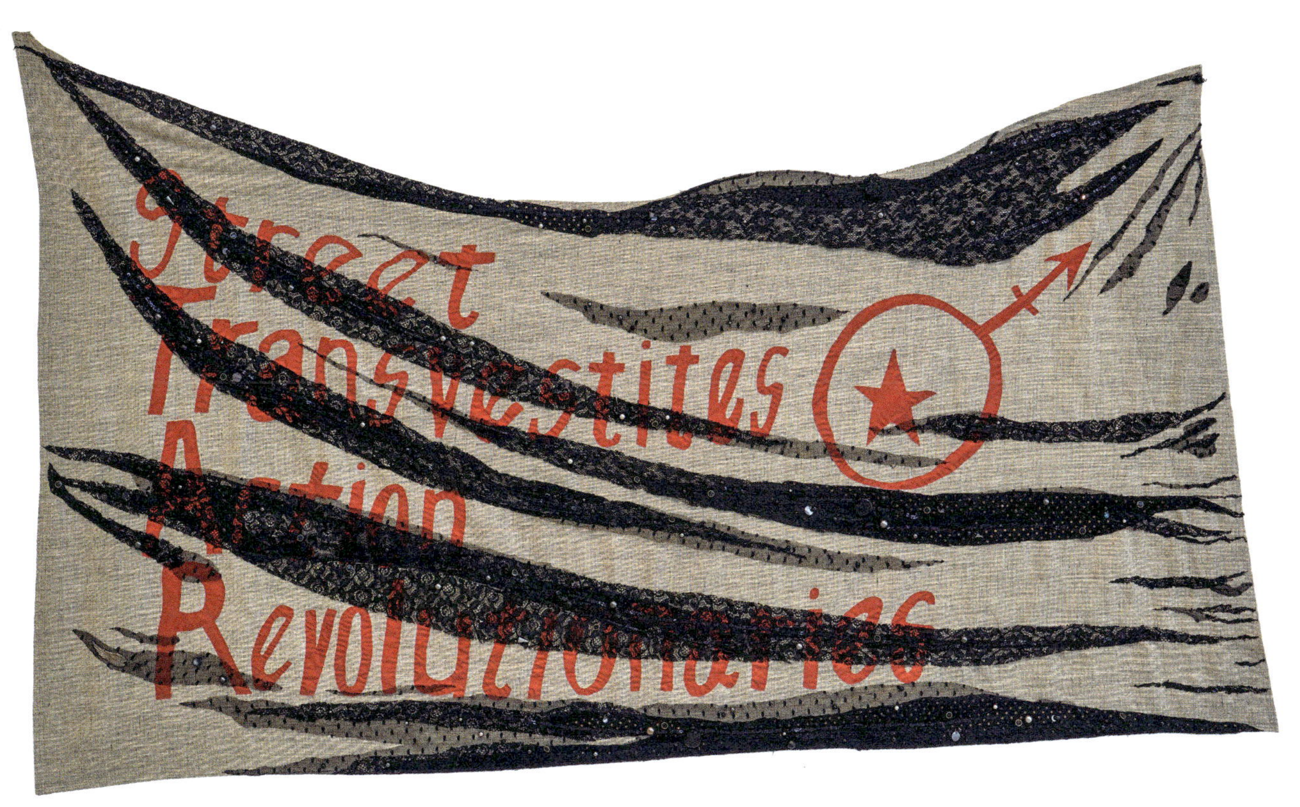

▲
Tuesday Smillie, *Street Transvestites 1973*, 2015. Textile, beads, button, and bits, 48 × 83 in. (121.9 × 210.8 cm). Rose Art Museum, Gift of Lizbeth and George Krupp, 2018.22

70 RÍO SOFIA, *FORCED WOMANHOOD!*, 2017

"Don't you just want to be treated as a 'normal' woman?" the Canadian performance artist Nina Arsenault once rhetorically asked herself in an interview in 2015, slipping on the guise of your average Joe Cispack.[1] "No," she responded, now as herself, "I see the way you treat them, too." And yet so many of us trans women continue gaming the system, that system being the patriarchy, despite knowing full well that among our rewards for succeeding at adjusting our position are the sexism and misogyny to which Arsenault alluded.

So, why do we do it? Why does any woman do it, cis or trans? Río Sofia's *Forced Womanhood!* does not provide an answer, as so much trans-centric media attempts to do so neatly. Rather, her series of self-portraits, a mix of still photography and film, sits with the irreconcilability of it all, capturing the inner monologue of a trans woman as she realizes in horror that going for something she wants will come with so much that she does not.

The imagery found in *Forced Womanhood!*, completed and exhibited in 2017 during Sofia's final year as an undergraduate at New York City's Cooper Union, evoke those that one might find in forced feminization pornography. The Mexican-born visual artist and community organizer was directly inspired by the erotica magazine of the same name, which she encountered while working at a fetish clothing and toy store when she was beginning to transition years prior.

"There was this explosion of representation in that post-'Tipping Point' moment," Sofia says, referring to *Time*'s 2014 "Transgender Tipping Point" cover story featuring Laverne Cox.[2] We're sitting in the crook of her living room's L-shaped sectional in August of 2022, scrolling through images from the series as she reflects on what drove her to make it, "A lot of trans women were pushing through the sort of pre-packaged rhetoric around transness and assuming more control over the narratives we've been relegated to since forever. I remember Janet Mock talking to Piers Morgan on his show and then speaking out against the interview because they had literally framed her face with a 'BORN A BOY' chyron." Despite these breakthrough moments, "a lot of that representation was still being marketed and packaged by cis people." *Forced Womanhood!* gave her a different kind of trans narrative. "I was really repulsed by how the magazine objectified trans people but also was really drawn to the powerlessness and lack of agency."

In her series, Sofia casts herself as both the feminizer domme and the feminized submissive, sometimes within the same frame. A video portrait riffing on Frida Kahlo's *The Two Fridas* (1939) features the artist seated in a demure white nightgown, tugging a pink rope that's attached to the genitals of another seated Sofia, this one bound and gagged in a lacy white bra and matching fishnet thigh-highs. In a different composite, she holds a ruler over another Sofia's bare ass, while a third Sofia plays the role of the viewer, observing this scene as she flips through the pages of the titular porno mag. In a twist on the expected power dynamics, a third image shows Sofia in a frilly pink sissy dress and synthetic blonde wig giggling delightedly at another, decidedly less cartoonishly feminized version of herself whom she has tied up and trapped in the oblong loop of a toy train set.

"Something about transitioning I had a really hard time with was that it felt like self-sabotage—knowingly transitioning further into marginalization," Sofia says. "As I was making changes to the way I looked and dressing a certain way and then later taking hormones, I could feel in real time what the consequences of that were—bottles thrown at you, death threats, all that stuff. I just couldn't not feel like I was edging with violence."

Though her series speaks to coercive elements of transition, Sofia is careful to note that it's not a uniquely trans phenomenon. "Gender is coercive for everyone," cis or trans. "In one way or another, everyone is coerced into making decisions about their gender presentation and their body, and if they're not, they're pushing up against it."

—Harron Walker

1. "TEDxToronto Women: Nina Arsenault, Transsexual Artist," *She Does the City*, October 15, 2015, accessed January 31, 2023, https://www.shedoesthecity.com/tedxtoronto-women-nina-arsenault-artist/.

2. All quotes in this text from Río Sofia, interview with the author, August 26, 2022.

▸ Río Sofia, Still from *Forced Womanhood! (Stay Seated)*, 2017. Digital video, 9 min., 55 sec.

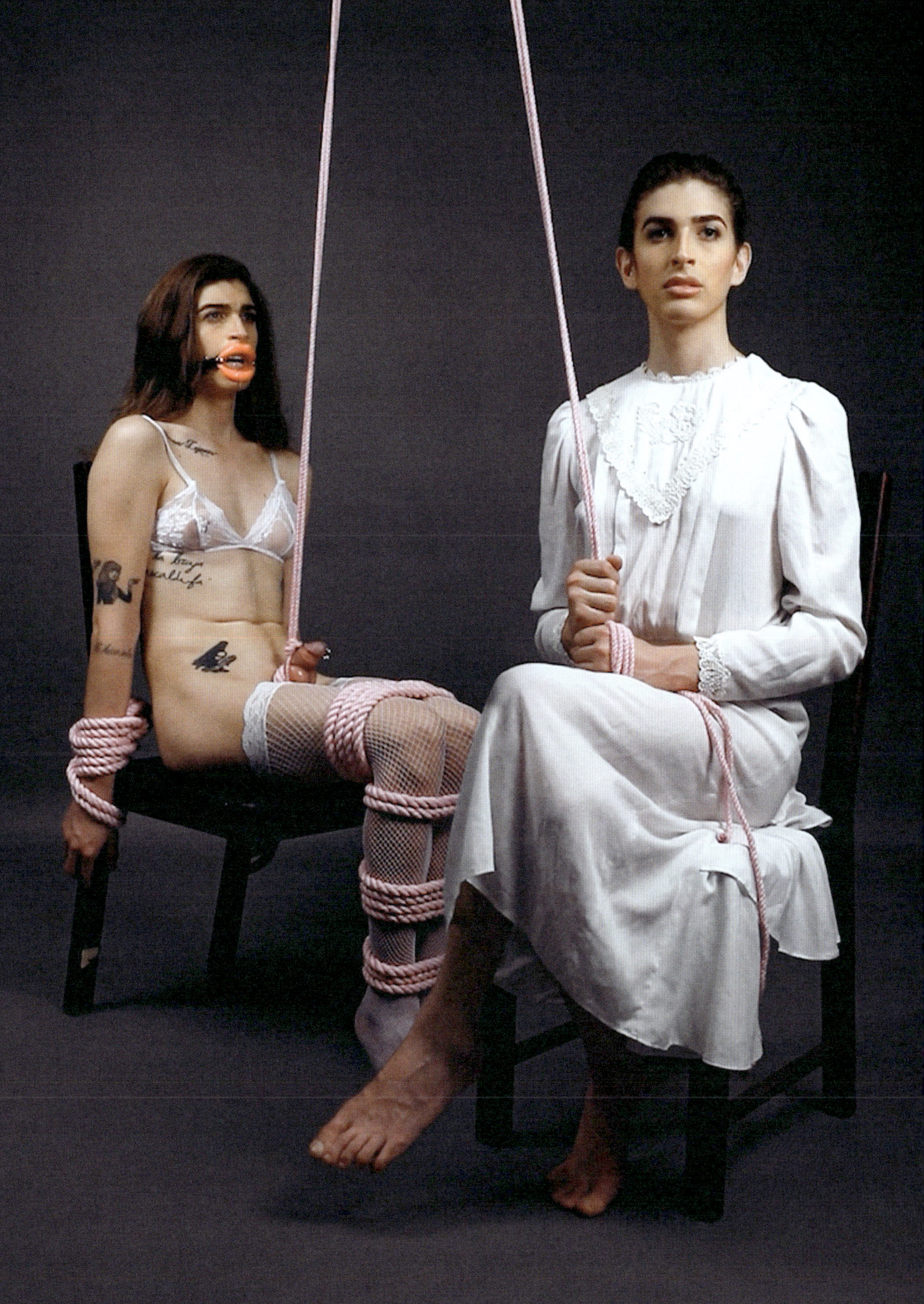

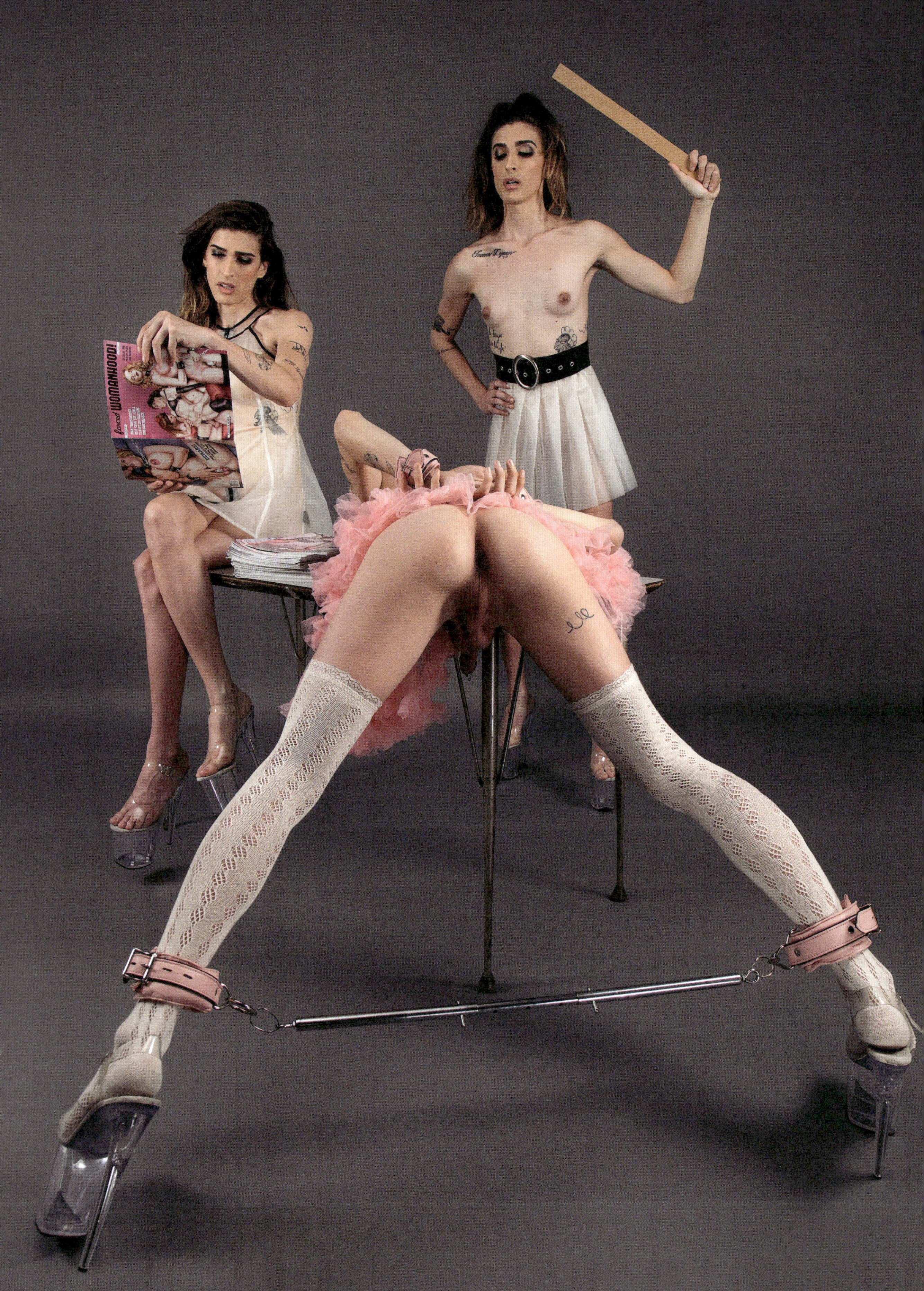

◀
Río Sofia, *Forced Womanhood! (Study Group)*, 2017. Digital photograph

▼
Río Sofia, *Forced Womanhood! (Damsel in Distress)*, 2017. Digital photograph

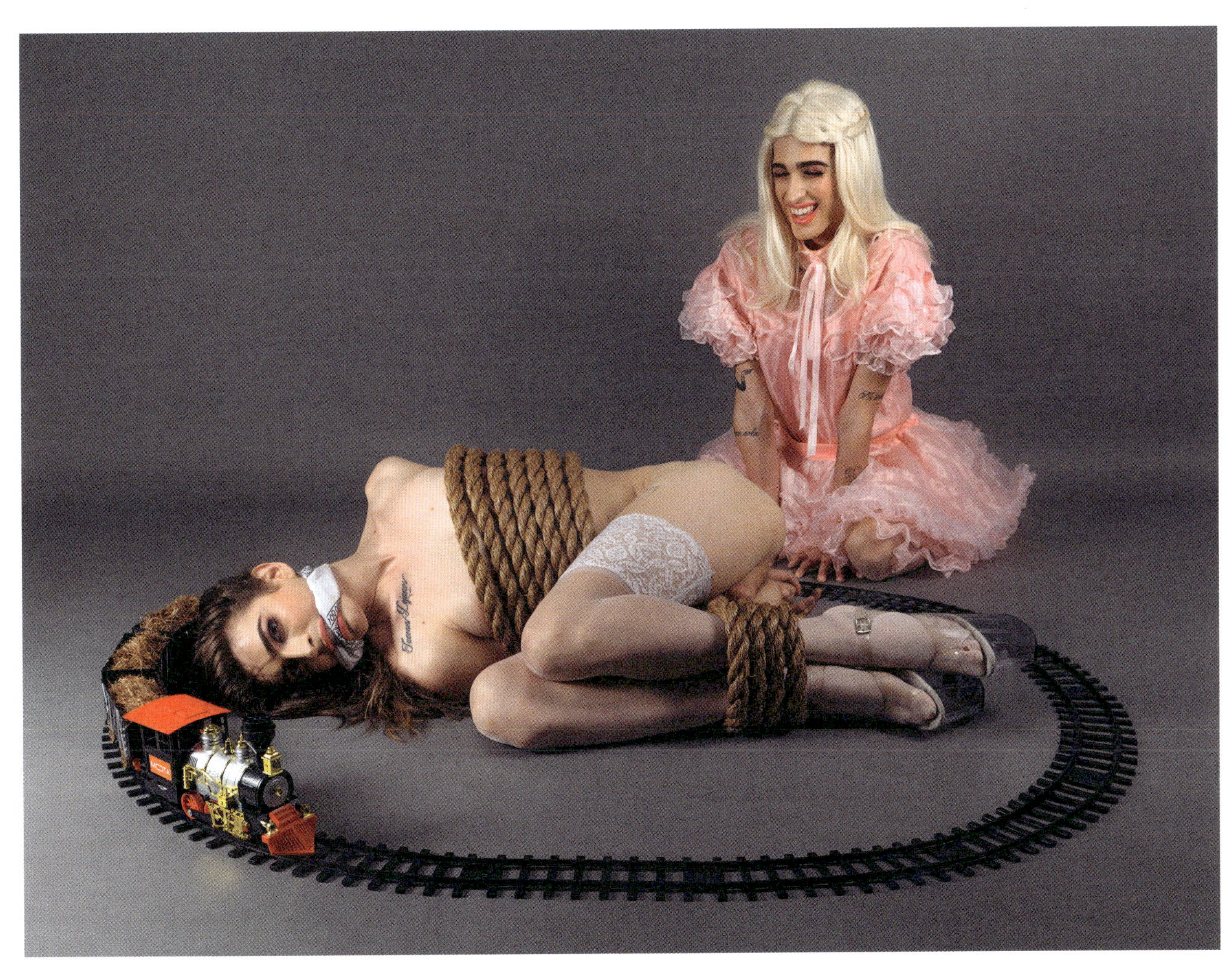

71 VIVEK SHRAYA, *TRISHA*, 2016

My story has always been bound to your prayer to have two boys. Maybe it was because of the ways you felt weighed down as a young girl, or the ways you felt you weighed down your mother by being a girl. Maybe it was because of the ways being a wife changed you. Maybe it was all the above, and also just being a girl in a world that is intent on crushing women. So you prayed to a god you can't remember for two sons and you got me. I was your first and I was soft. Did this ever disappoint you?

You had also prayed for me to look like Dad, but you forgot to pray for the rest of me. It is strange that you would overlook this, as you have always said "Be careful what you pray for." When I take off my clothes and look in the mirror, I see Dad's body, as you wished. But the rest of me has always wished to be you.

I modeled myself—my gestures, my futures, how I love and rage—all after you. Did this worry you and Dad? Did you have the kinds of conversations in bed that parents of genderqueer children on TV have, where the dad scolds the mom—"This is your fault"? No one is to blame. Not you, not the god you prayed to. I was right to worship you. You worked full time, went to school part time, managed a home, raised two children who complained about frozen food and made fun of your accent, and cared for your family in India. Most days in my adult life, I can barely care for myself.

I remember finding these photos of you three years ago and being astonished, even hurt, by your joyfulness, your playfulness. I wish I had known this side of you, before Canada, marriage, and motherhood stripped it from you, and us.

I learned to pray too. My earliest prayers were to be released from my body, believing that this desire was devotion, this was about wanting to be closer to god. I don't believe in god anymore, but sometimes I still have the same prayer. Then I remind myself that the discomfort I feel is less about my body and more about what it means to be feminine in a world that is intent on crushing femininity in any form. Maybe I got my wish to be you after all.

You used to say that if you had a girl, you would have named her Trisha.

—Vivek Shraya

▸ (and following spread) Vivek Shraya, *Trisha*, 2016. Color photographs, dimensions variable. Creative direction: Vivek Shraya; artwork and photography: Michelle Campos Castillo; makeup: Alanna Chelmick; hair: Fabio Persico; clothing: M. Orbe; set and wardrobe assistants: Shemeena Shraya and Adam Holman

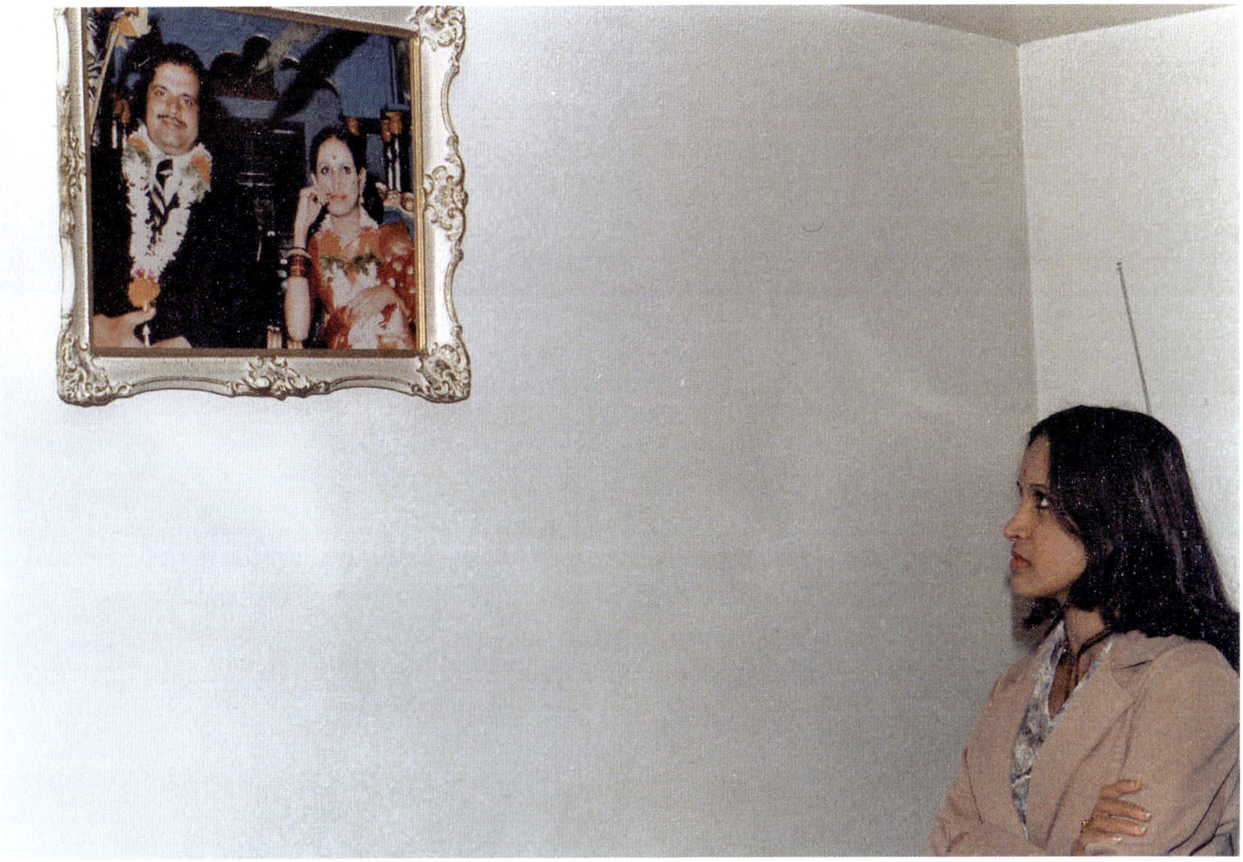

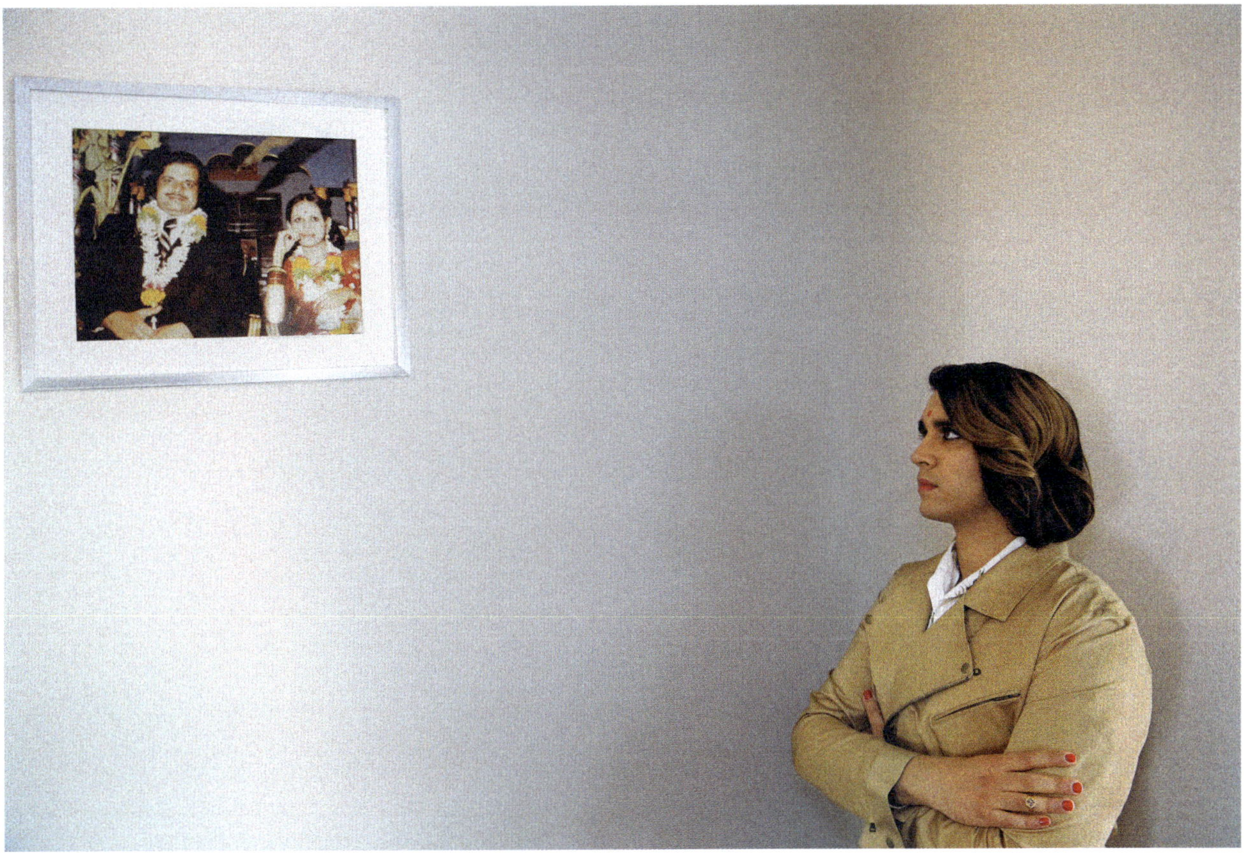

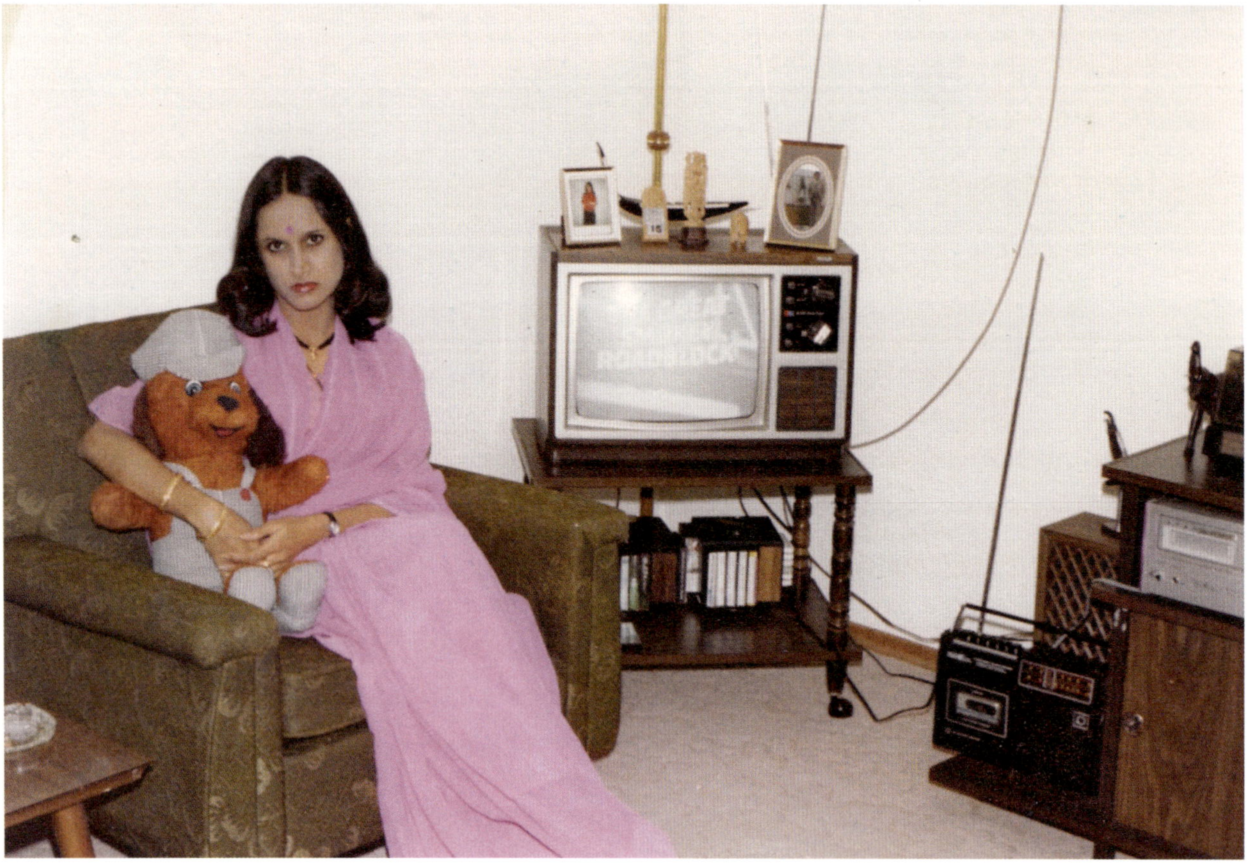

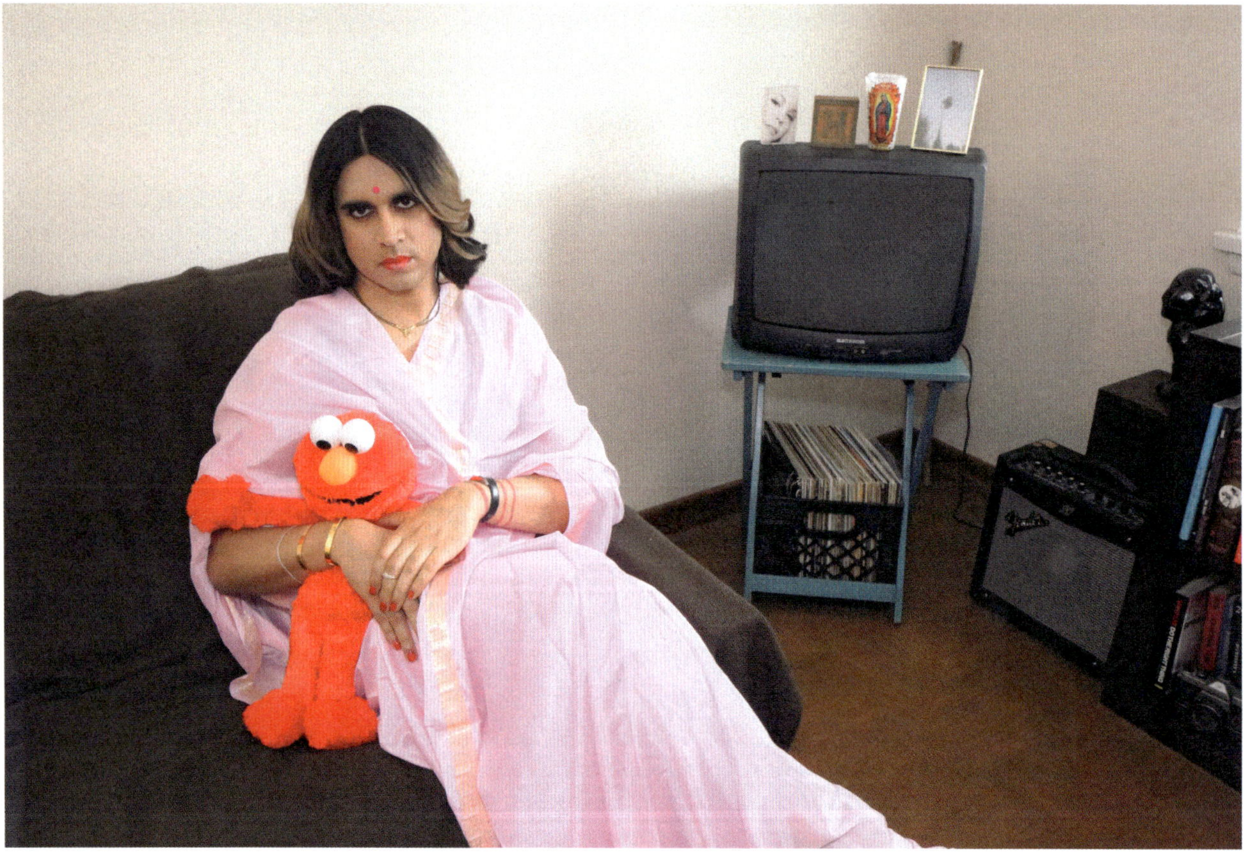

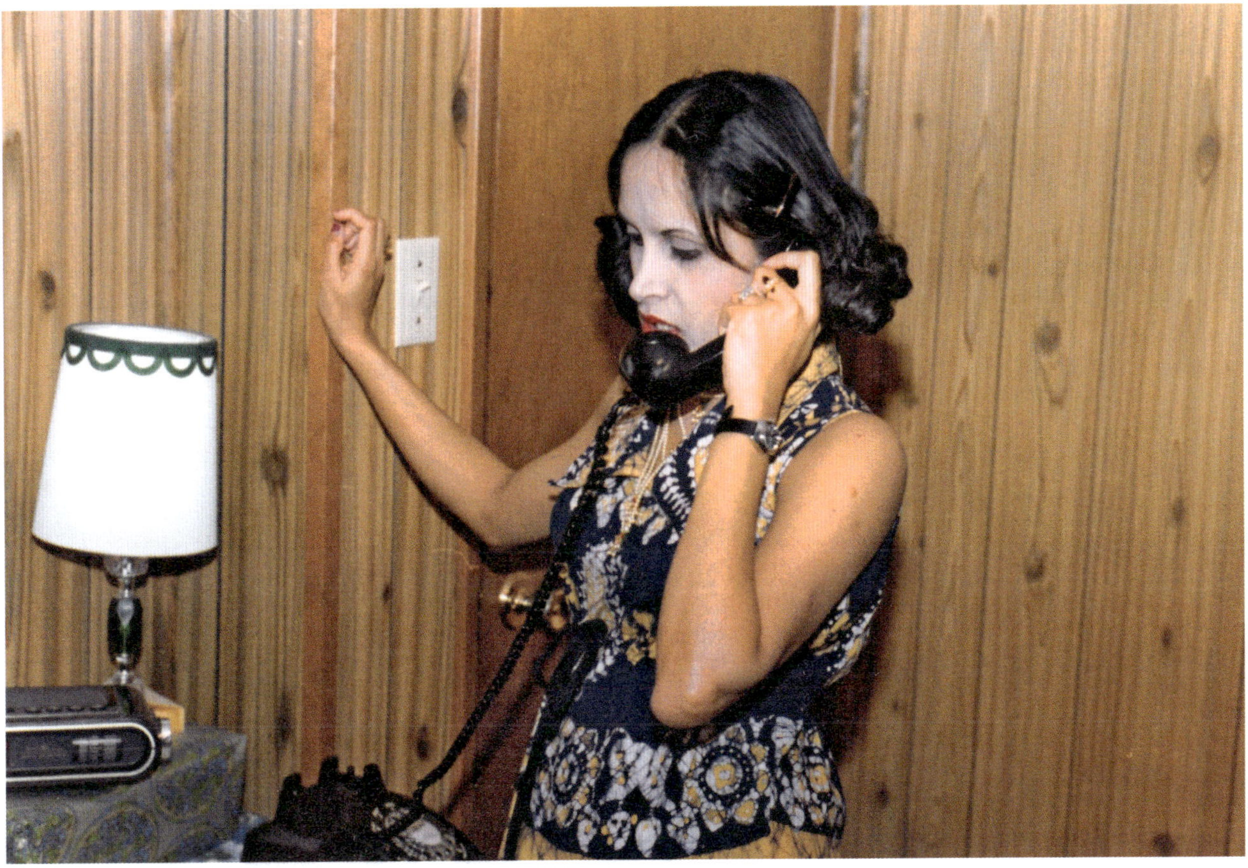

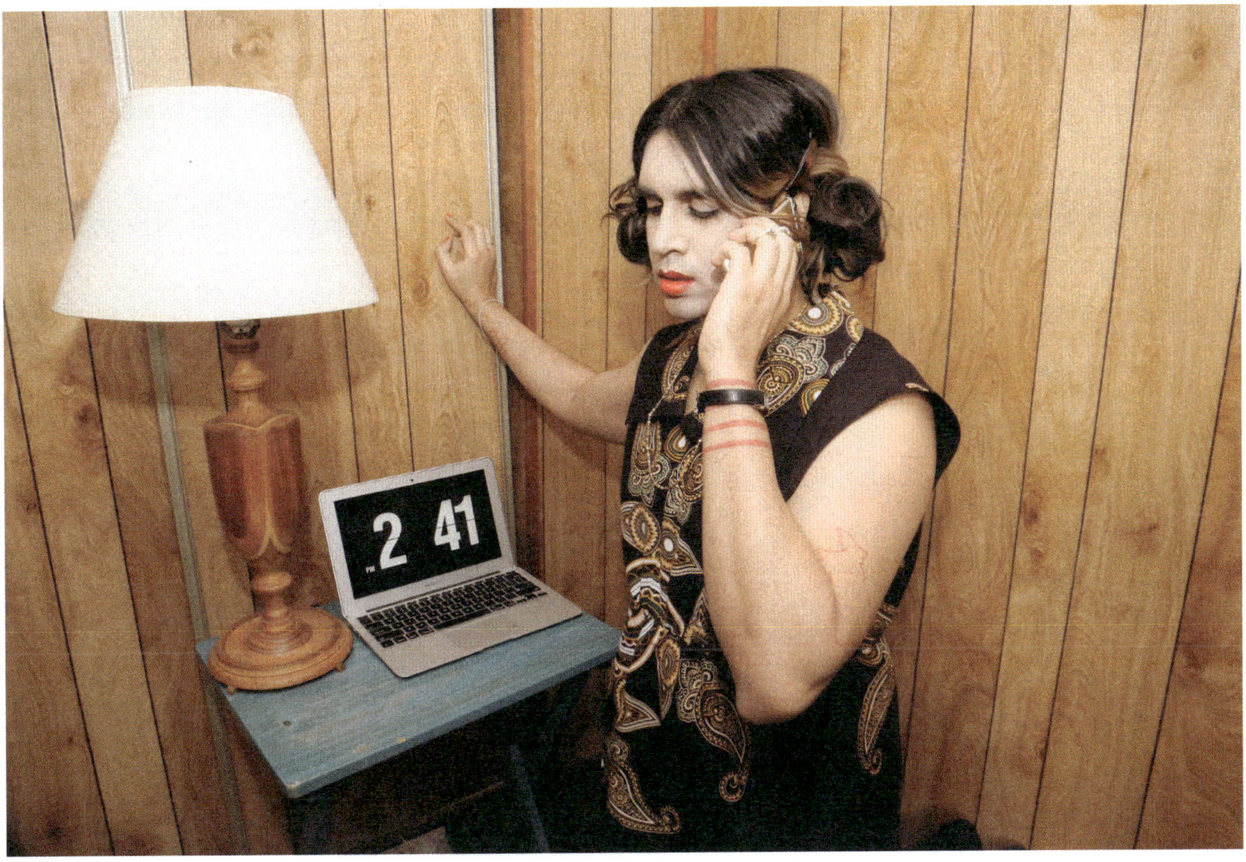

72 KENT MONKMAN, *HONOUR DANCE*, 2020

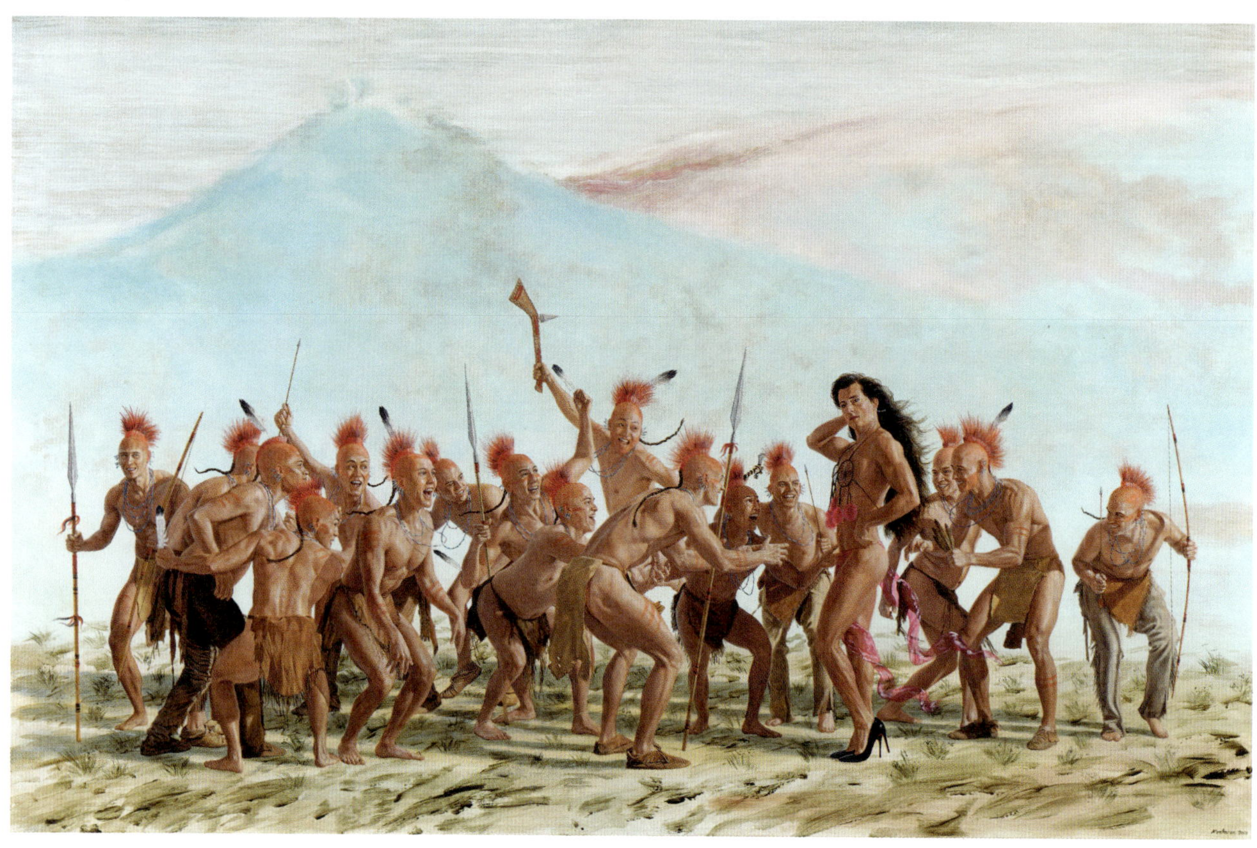

Cree artist Kent Monkman intervenes here to present an Indigenous perspective on a scene depicted in an earlier painting by George Catlin (1796–1872), a white settler in the United States. Born in Pennsylvania, Catlin set out around 1830 on a self-appointed mission to create a visual record of the lives of Indigenous people in North America. He first sketched the scene depicted in this painting at a Sac and Meskwaki (Fox) village in 1835. His notes on the event convey his bias and contempt: "… a very funny and amusing scene … the 'Berdashe,' as he is called in French … is a man dressed in woman's clothes, as he is known to be all his life, and for extraordinary privileges which he is known to possess, he is driven to the most servile and degrading duties, which he is not allowed to escape; and he being the only one of the tribe submitting to this disgraceful degradation, is looked upon as medicine and sacred, and a feast is given to him annually."[1] *Monkman has replaced the Two-spirit figure in Caitlin's original painting with his own alter ego, Miss Chief Eagle Testickle, who poses confidently, suggesting individual and collective Indigenous sovereignty.*

1. George Catlin, *Letters and Notes on the Manners, Customs, and Condition of the North American Indians*, vol. 2, no. 56 (New York: Wiley and Putnam, 1841; reprint 1973), as presented on the collection website for the Smithsonian American Art Museum, accessed December 27, 2022, https://americanart.si.edu/artwork/dance-berdash-4023.

They Are Honored

Peeling off the first layer is often the most difficult. Debris in the fingernails. Tiny cuts, digging down to clean. The resistance to change. In this world, to move forward one must disentangle a thing. Slough off the fat, cut down into bone, and collect marrow. Allow some to seep back into the ground. This opens the portal. You have made the bundle for this. Sun and shadow. Turpentine and oil paint. Sky. Some kind of vessel for water. The old ways are no longer useful here/now. Letting them go makes room for old medicines to reassert their teachings and become known again. Two Spirit. The stone told him to give itself to me. He listened. How many people came and went before it could travel? No wisdom, but a sexuality that burns a *settler binary* to ash. Falling through the hole of it and back to Creation's mud. Dance. Dance. Dance. Let the ceremony begin. Sing the song. Let those you are connected to bear witness. You've been alone and disgusted for far too long. You know they want to skin you alive, leave your flesh to rot while you suffer with the passage of time. They disgust *you*. They want to wear you like hide and believe the story is their own. Box your skeleton to keep the mythos viable. They are honored. You've taken a pale lover or two. You know their ways. They want you to peacock around and be seen in proximity to a hollow whiteness. The museum. The People know who you are. You've given them their names. You've helped their babies come in. These lands know you—the mycelium and the disco ball are one. No time has passed. There is no line. Red ochre has stained your hands. This is not a history you are responding to. You were there. It's you. No inversion or contrast needed. No explanation. It's you. The work is not response, yet how much of the other has invaded your aesthetic? I can count on one hand how many times I have been seen here. Queer still means white and Eagle knows how many of us are missing and where our bodies are. Here. Then. Now.

We are the most beautiful.

—M. Carmen Lane

◂ Kent Monkman, *Honour Dance*, 2020. Acrylic on canvas, 60 × 94¼ in. (152.4 × 239.4 cm). Hirshhorn Museum and Sculpture Garden, Smithsonian Institution, Joseph H. Hirshhorn Purchase Fund, 2020.030

▸ George Catlin, *Dance to the Berdash*, 1835–37. Oil on canvas, 19½ × 27½ in. (49.6 × 70 cm). Smithsonian American Art Museum, Gift of Mrs. Joseph Harrison, Jr., 1985.66.442

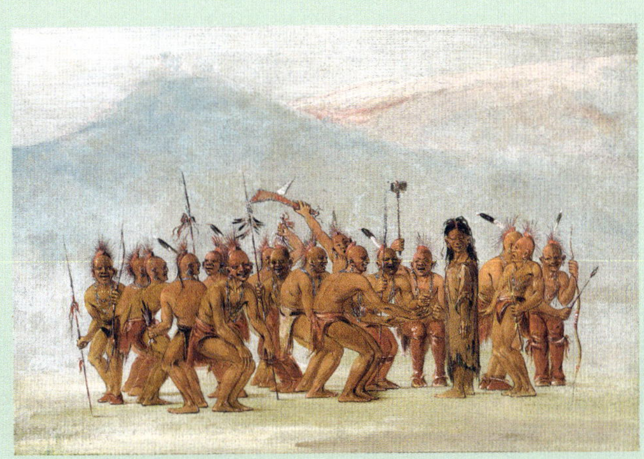

73 TOBARON WAXMAN, *FEAR OF A BEARDED PLANET—COLLECTIVE SEMITIC SELF-PORTRAIT AFTER ROBERT BLANCHON*, 2007–PRESENT

Since 2007, artist Tobaron Waxman has sat for portraits by souvenir artists at tourist and pilgrimage sites across Europe and North America. When Waxman began this project, they were part of the ultra-orthodox Chassidic community in New York and not out as trans. Passing as cisgender and perceived as Jewish, Muslim, and/or Arab, depending on the eye of the beholder, Waxman sought correlations between the shifting perceptions of masculinity, ethnicity, religious identity, and belonging they experienced, particularly following the rise of nationalism and Islamophobia after 9/11.

Waxman pays homage to Robert Blanchon (1965–1999) by invoking Blanchon's work *Untitled (self-portrait)* (1991), a series of fourteen portraits similarly commissioned by various sidewalk artists. Rather than assemble a coherent study of the subject, Blanchon's collection reflects each artists' perception of non-traditional masculinity and the projection of homosexual types: a young sailor, a prissy schoolboy, a rough trade stud. Blanchon explored life as an HIV+ gay man in the 1990s with both wit and vulnerability, and Waxman's reference to this artist points to their long-held commitments to intergenerational queer dialogue and the slipperiness of identity.

Waxman has sat for portraits in Barcelona, Berlin, London, New York, Paris, Toronto, and Vienna. Some images attempt realism—a warm smile, caring eyes, and bushy beard emerge from the various renderings—while others are alternately anti-Semitic and Islamophobic caricatures, exaggerating a perception or bias of the portraitist. Waxman wears the same clothes when sitting for each portrait; their set wardrobe includes black trousers, a white button-down shirt, and a knit Jewish kippah (skullcap). When asked by the artist, "Where are you from?"—a common question for a street portraitist—Waxman consistently responds, "Where do you think I'm from?" sparking conversation around their perception of Waxman, but also the politics of the moment. When Waxman shares that they are Jewish and oppose Israel's occupation of Palestine, another, deeper conversation ensues.

Unlike Blanchon's series, Waxman's project has been drawn out over many years (2007–present) and thus reflects the changing political topography of immigration, racialization, and discontent depending on where and when a portrait was made. In a drawing from New York in 2007, Waxman is caricatured as a dark-eyed rock star with money flying from his pockets wearing a turban. The figure stands before the World Trade Center towers over six years after they were destroyed. The convergence of anti-Semitic and Islamophobic stereotypes and an icon of national trauma is arresting and bizarre. In another portrait from 2010, the artist has colored Waxman's eyes a striking blue while rendering the face with a baby-faced impression of whiteness. In a handful of pictures, the portraitists have shaded Waxman's face to perhaps signal a darker complexion and a racialized perception. In portraits commissioned in Europe during the wave of anti-authoritarian protests across the Arab world known as the Arab Spring, Waxman, when presumed part of the Arab diaspora, appears confident and hopeful, especially when drawn by Muslim immigrants. In a portrait drawn in Paris in 2015, soon after shootings at a Hypercacher kosher supermarket and the offices of the satirical magazine Charlie Hebdo, Waxman is caricatured as a grinning Salafist.

For Waxman, the series has been a forum to understand the privilege they are afforded, whether presumed cisgender or part of a shared community. As described by the artist: "Privilege means I am the one who gets to decide when the relationship shifts, I determine the reveal, coming out as not having the same set of circumstances as that person; rather, I'm coming to them as an ally with my own set of privileges."[1] The project generates an empathetic forum for coalition building and navigating connections across religious traditions through an intimate exchange when recognition between marginalized people is felt, even if details can be misconstrued. Reflecting on these tender connections in 2016:

> For much of the past decade, I've been moving through the Western world frequently presumed as an ambiguously raced cisgender male Semite. These exchanges begin with a Muslim man looking at my face and seeing something that reminds him of home.... These experiences with men are dimensions of gender that I couldn't have learned from the feminism or queer theory I had been exposed to before masculinizing my own appearance. I didn't understand this male vulnerability until I was in it.[2]

Waxman's portraits provide viewers an opportunity to consider the global trajectories of Muslims and Jews and the human propensity for projecting bias, connection, or expectation onto the face of another. .

—David Evans Frantz

1. Document by Tobaron Waxman about *Fear of a Bearded Planet* shared with the author, December 2022.

2. Document by Tobaron Waxman.

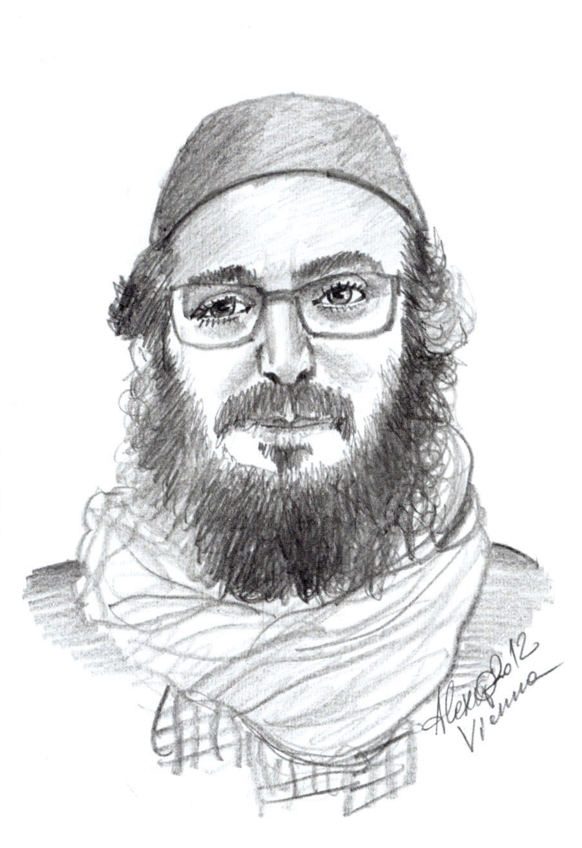

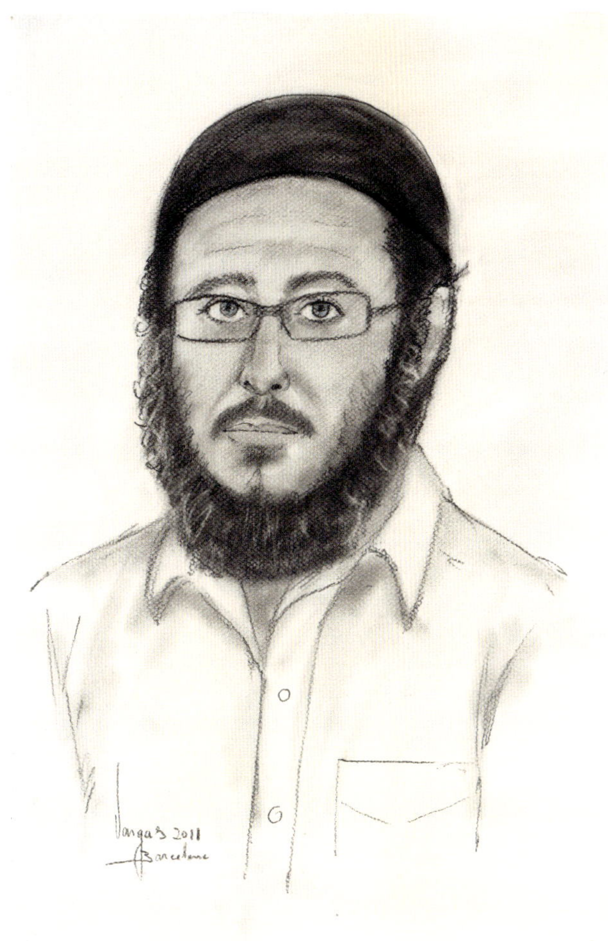

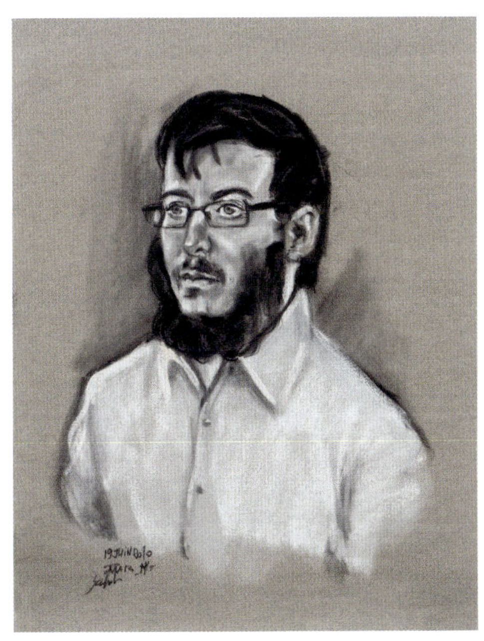

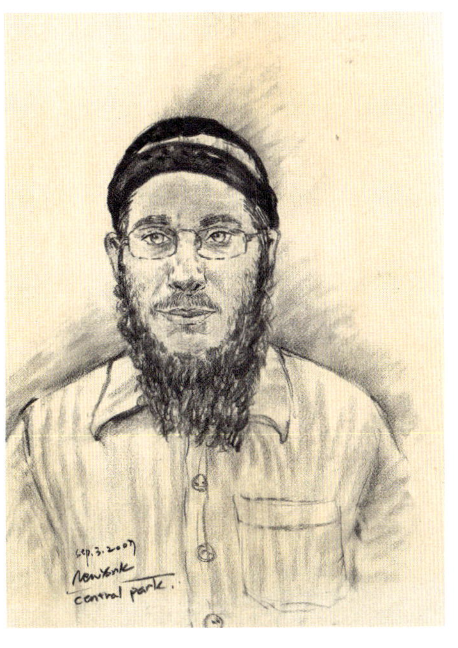

▲
(and following spread) Tobaron Waxman, Selection of portraits from *Fear of a Bearded Planet*, 2007–present. Mixed media on paper, dimensions variable

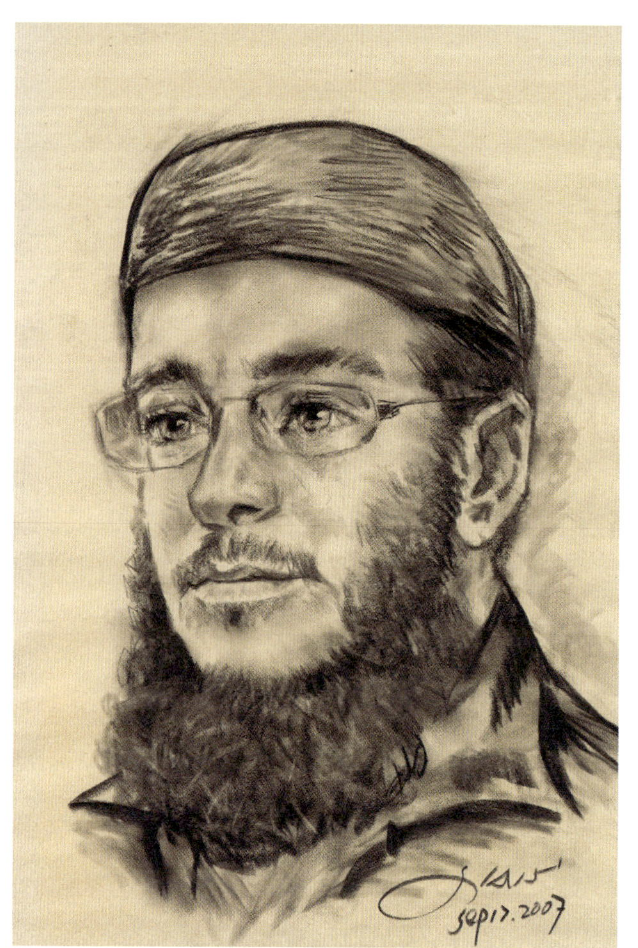
sep17.2007

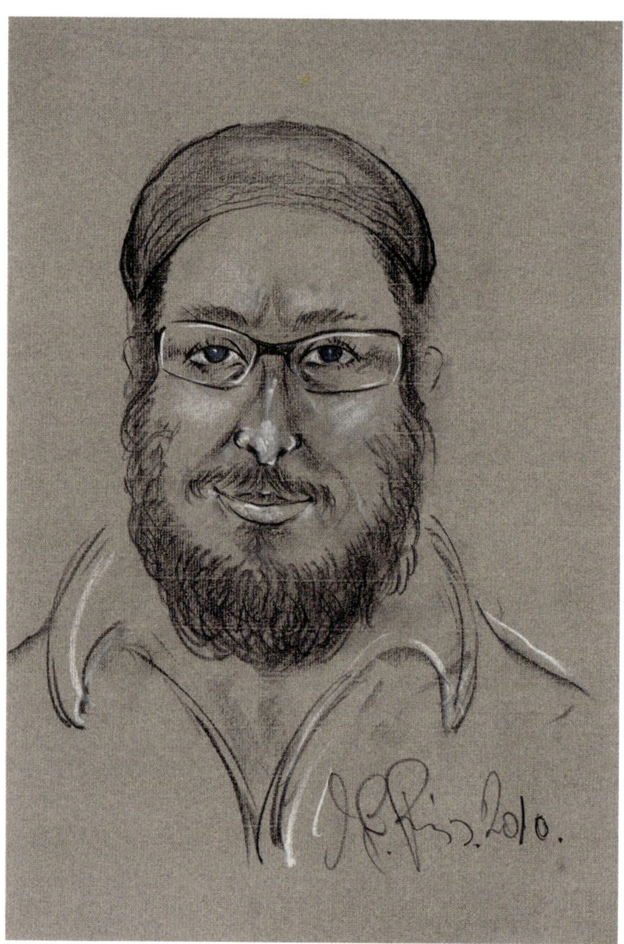
2010.

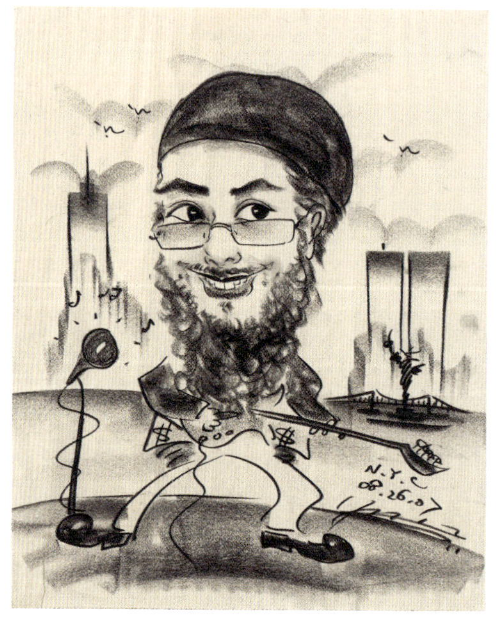
N.Y.C
08.26.07

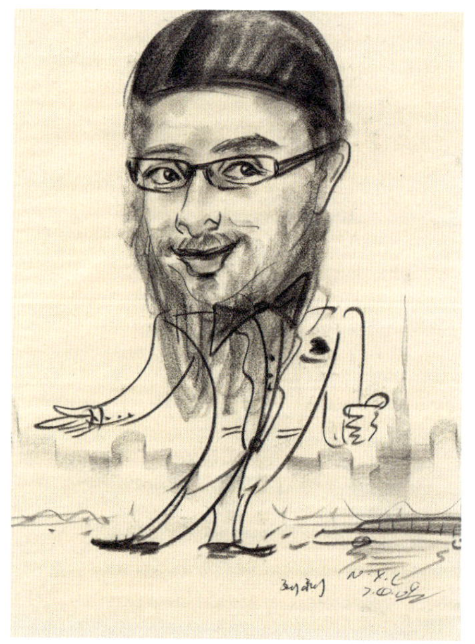

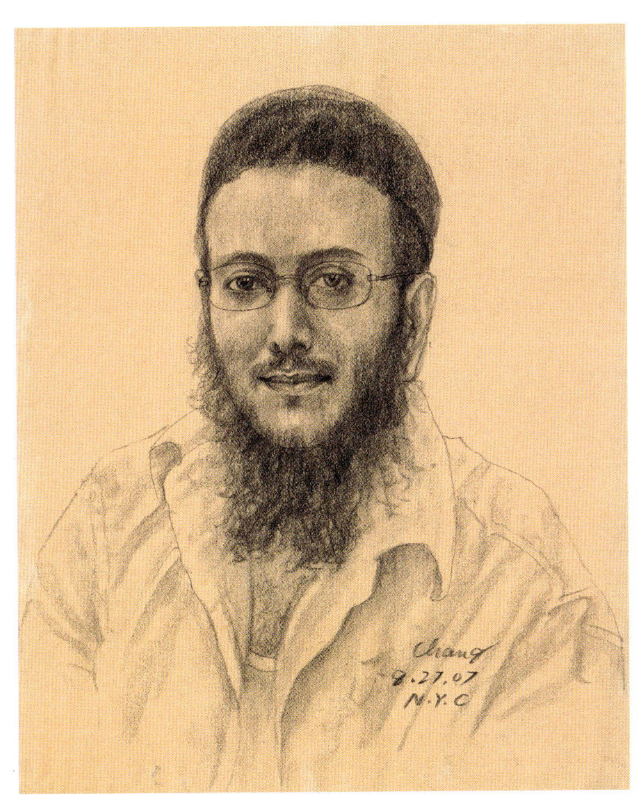
Chang
8.27.07
N.Y.C

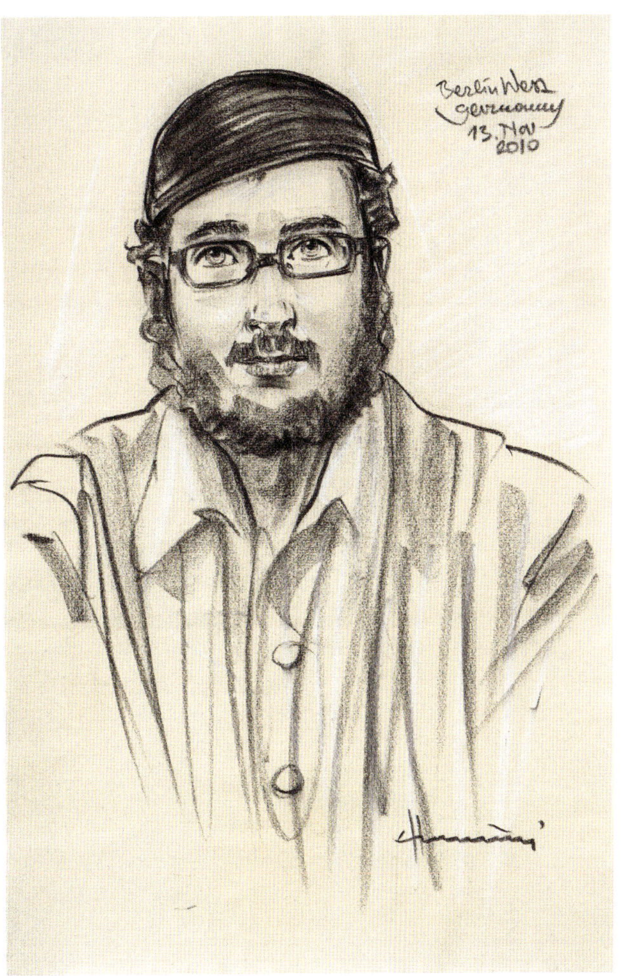
Germany
13. Nov
2010

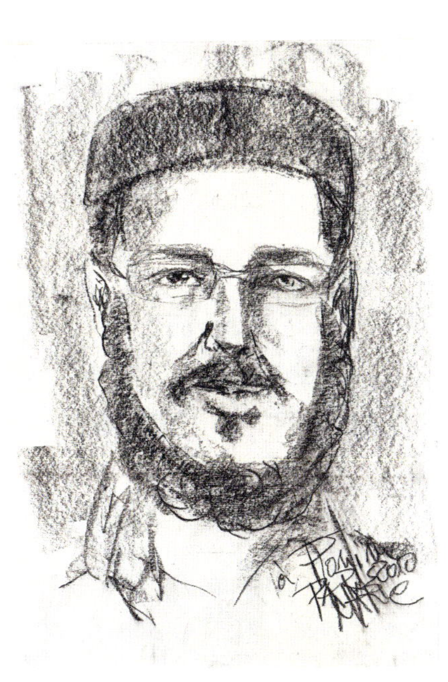

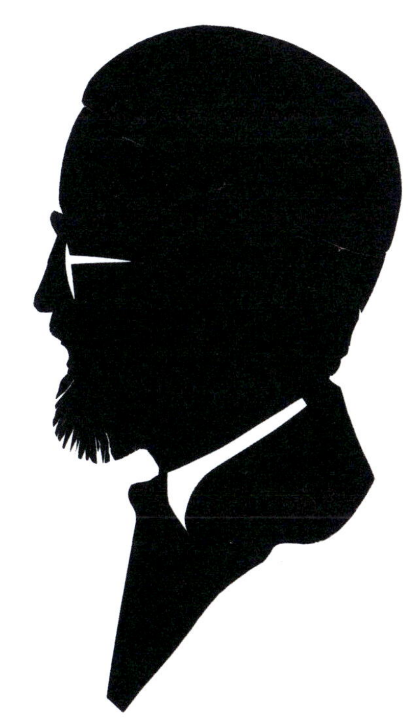

74 VERO MAJANO, BROWN AMY, AND KARI ORVIK, THE Q-SIDES, 2015

Before we start ... please play *East Side Story, Volume 3:* https://archive.org/details/eastsidestory_vol1-12/Vol.3.flac

You hear it? Perfect.
Now we are here. Together.

In 2015 I came into San Francisco's Galería de la Raza and saw striking photographs showing Brown queer and trans folks looking fierce, sharp, and unapologetic, posing next to colorful lowriders. These photos were from The Q-Sides series, a collaboration between filmmaker and San Francisco Mission District native Vero Majano, Amy Martinez (DJ Brown Amy), and photographer Kari Orvik. The project came from a conversation between Amy and Vero on the corner of 16th and Capp Street about making a queer version of the *East Side Story* album covers.

The *East Side Story* albums were compilations of the B-sides of popular records featuring slow-moving soul and doo-wop oldies. These accidentally popular compilations, made by businessman Anthony Boosalis in the late 1980s as a marketing strategy, became a nostalgic cultural phenomenon in lowrider culture. At the time, not too many albums had Brown people on their covers, and these images showed people like our *tíos, primos, y amigues*. The albums, with music made by Black artists such as The Shirelles, Etta James and The Delfonics, became Chicanx lowrider anthems, marking a special cross-cultural blessing.However, lowrider culture felt exclusionary for queer and trans folks. It was filled with toxic masculinity, misogyny, homophobia, and transphobia. Vero and Amy grew up listening to this music, and they had experienced queer love and desire while listening to these albums. The Q-Sides collaboration was the flip side to the B-sides of these records, where queer desire and lowrider culture were not mutually exclusive after all. The Q-Sides became a visual testament to queer and trans folks ingraining themselves in this culture. A sense of possibility that was carefully and consensually materialized in all the images.

There isn't a lowrider in any of *The Q-Sides Volume 3* photographs, but in one we see a pyramid of bodies, a staged photograph of friends and kin sharing a sunny moment together. I enjoy the soft handshake between Yelz Gochez and Prado Gómez, Manuel Rodrigues standing in a casual contrapposto while Al Lujan shows us his iconic Virgin of Guadalupe tattoo. Esteban Rodriguez is staring back at the viewer while Jess Vu smiles back at us, giving us a hint of welcoming familiarity. I love seeing trans masculine shirtless bodies in the sun because to this day I still don't see many Brown trans bodies in visual culture.

The opening night of the original exhibition of The Q-Sides at Galería de la Raza was on June 5, 2015. The place was packed; there were lowriders outside the gallery; there was music playing and folks cruising. The Q-Sides had created a beautiful container that hadn't been explored in this way before. A space for all the pluralities of the Mission District to exist together, from the highly palpable tensions of Latinx masculinity to the flamboyant and extravagant queer and trans aesthetics. And, of course, San Francisco's nightlife icon and drag mother Juanita MORE! was there too.

The photos remain a testament of existing in community, of looking out for each other and collectively making space for us in the cultural narratives we didn't see ourselves in while growing up.

—Marcel Pardo Ariza

▸ Vero Majano, Brown Amy, and Kari Orvik, *The Q-Sides Volume 3 (Album Cover)*, 2015. Color photograph, 24 × 24 in. (61 × 61 cm)

THE Q-SIDES

VOL. 3

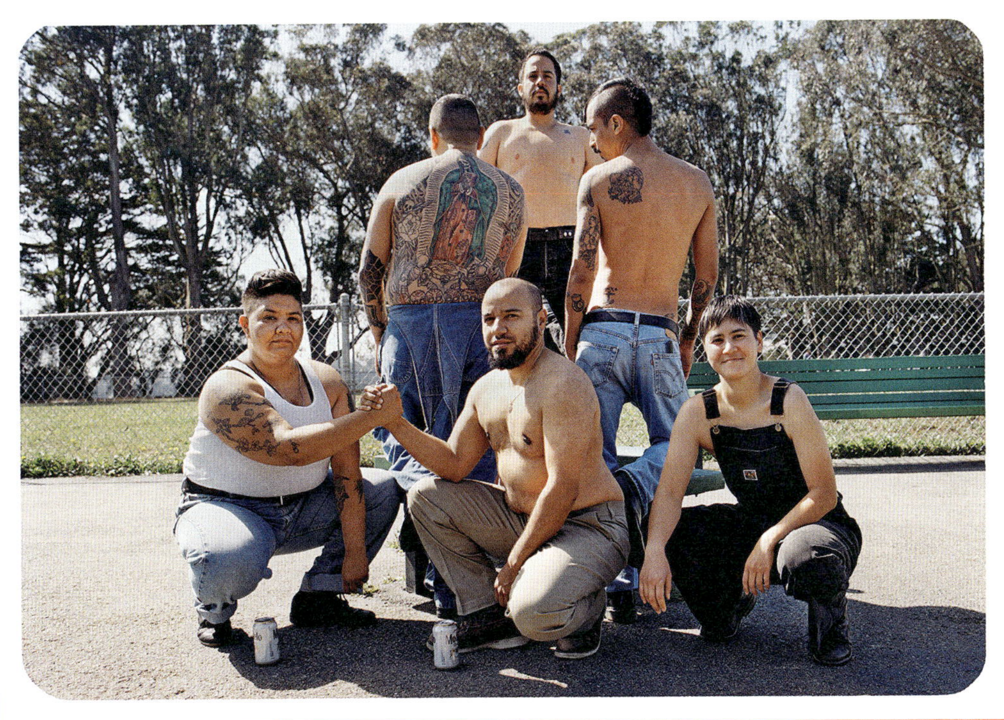

STEREO

75 CARMEN SELAM, *SWITCH DANCE*, 2022

Sensitive content warning: grief, suicide.

Carmen remembers cruising on the Yakama rez, making turns that hugged along the Cascade Mountain range. There was nothing to do besides pick up a burger, and meander like the Columbia River with her younger brother, Eric. They would take turns sharing stories, laughing, and ragging on each other, talking about their rodeo studs and rez-bian lovers. It was their time to be their whole selves in the safety and comfort of their blood, talking about things they couldn't talk about at home.

In a Switch Dance, competitors dress themselves in the opposite regalia of what is the "traditional" gender norm. It's a community staple, a part of the powwow competition but also a break in the order of things for laughs. Carmen would Switch Dance, but Eric never did; he participated in ceremonial gourd dances. When Eric was young, he was primed as a spiritual leader. He learned all the songs, revered the longhouse, and participated in the Shaker Church. Carmen never felt called to participate in gourd dances. The women stand well behind the men, encircling the songs and swaying their bodies to the consistently scattered beat of hollow rattles. The siblings danced together each season, though, in step at many powwows.

While conceptualizing the transdisciplinary artwork *Switch Dance* (2022), Carmen saw the act of putting on her brother's regalia as documenting a moment in queer *Yakamanche* history. Yakama and Comanche are the nations Carmen and Eric share through matrilineal lines. Wearing Eric's regalia became a way to bring him back to this realm. Her artistic style abruptly matured from bright and playful portraits to embodying the reality of navigating life without him, forced into intimacy with mortality and its shadows.

In this work Carmen has channeled her disoriented feelings of grief. Her tribe's mourning protocol is lonesome and detached out of reverence for the relative's transition of realms. The audio component of *Switch Dance* is a recording from the last time she heard Eric perform at the Spilyay-Mi art show. The work's sonic atmosphere resembles what Carmen hears at powwows now, but with Eric singing amidst echoed emcee announcements and laughter. Her soundtrack evokes the feeling of dancing in the middle of the arena during Intertribal: vulnerable and small, lost in a sea of dancers with the resonant sounds of bells, beadwork, and shells. Her suppressed grief mirrors the thundering of drums and the rhythmic escalating anxiety when momentarily estranged from kin. Sometimes Carmen can't hear Eric's guiding voice when she goes to powwows without him, but because of him she considers the arena a safe place to be lost. They danced together in the arena and the arena is where he is now and forever.

Eric's regalia had remained untouched since his walk into the woods a short and long three years ago, until Carmen resurrected their secret Switch Dance. Eric was tall with long black hair that didn't always want to be braided. He wore cute glasses and danced Top Hat specials adorned in red, yellow, and blue. When Eric sang his poetry and played his guitar, he was feminine and soft. He was beautiful and fluid. And he decided to end his life.

Portraiture by queer Native artists is a decolonial defiance, an act of Survivance. Indigenous people are still posed as muses: romanticized, commodified, static, and monolithic. Queer Indigeneity can be many beings at once and it lives within different lifetimes. We can be anywhere at any moment with anyone—if we need to be.

Over the last few years since Eric's death, Carmen intentionally grew her hair long and wore it down. In the photographs displayed in *Switch Dance,* she has her head turned, hair whipping to the past in frustration, confusion, and ambivalence all at once; emotions embodied in thick black hair carried by the weight of "why?" with few answers. When she duplicated the blackest of black paint Eric used on his face, she saw herself looking at him looking at her.

In this *Switch Dance*, siblings step together again in the secret arena.

—Hank Cooper

▸ Carmen Selam, *Switch Dance*, 2022. Digital photographs, video, and sound, 38 sec.

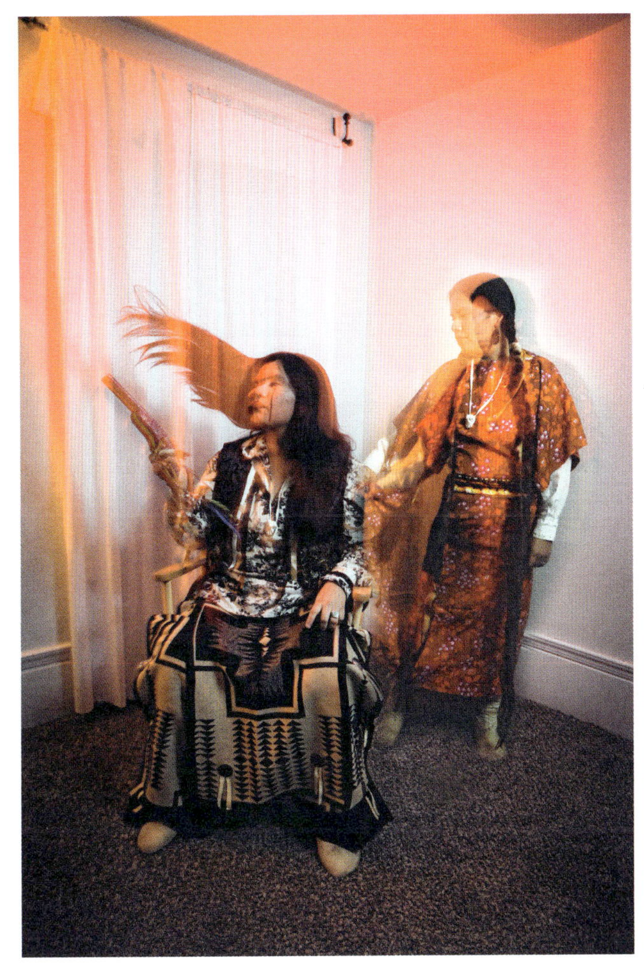

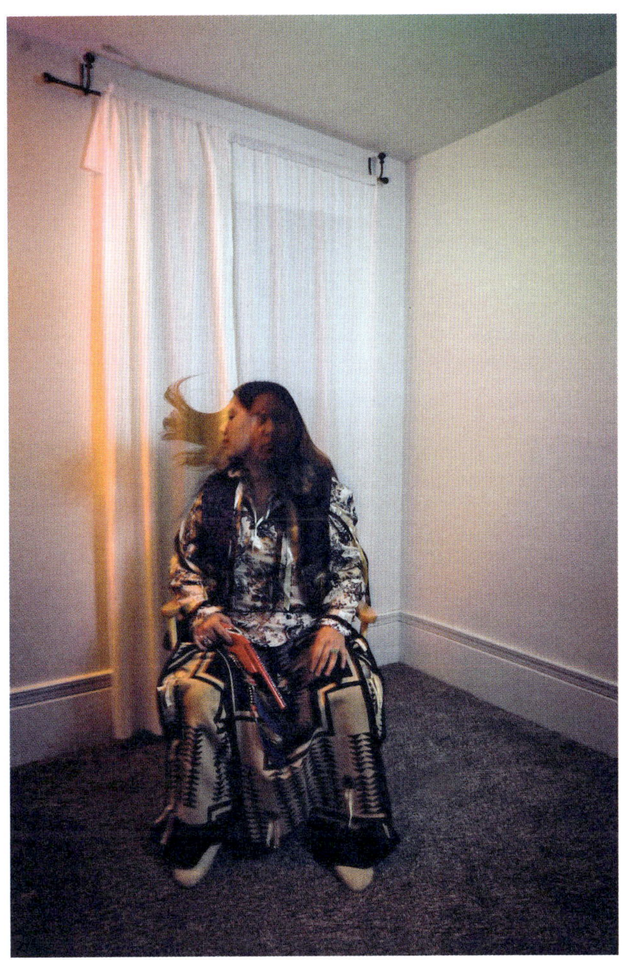

76 YOUNG JOON KWAK, *HERMAPHRODITUS'S REVEAL II*, 2017

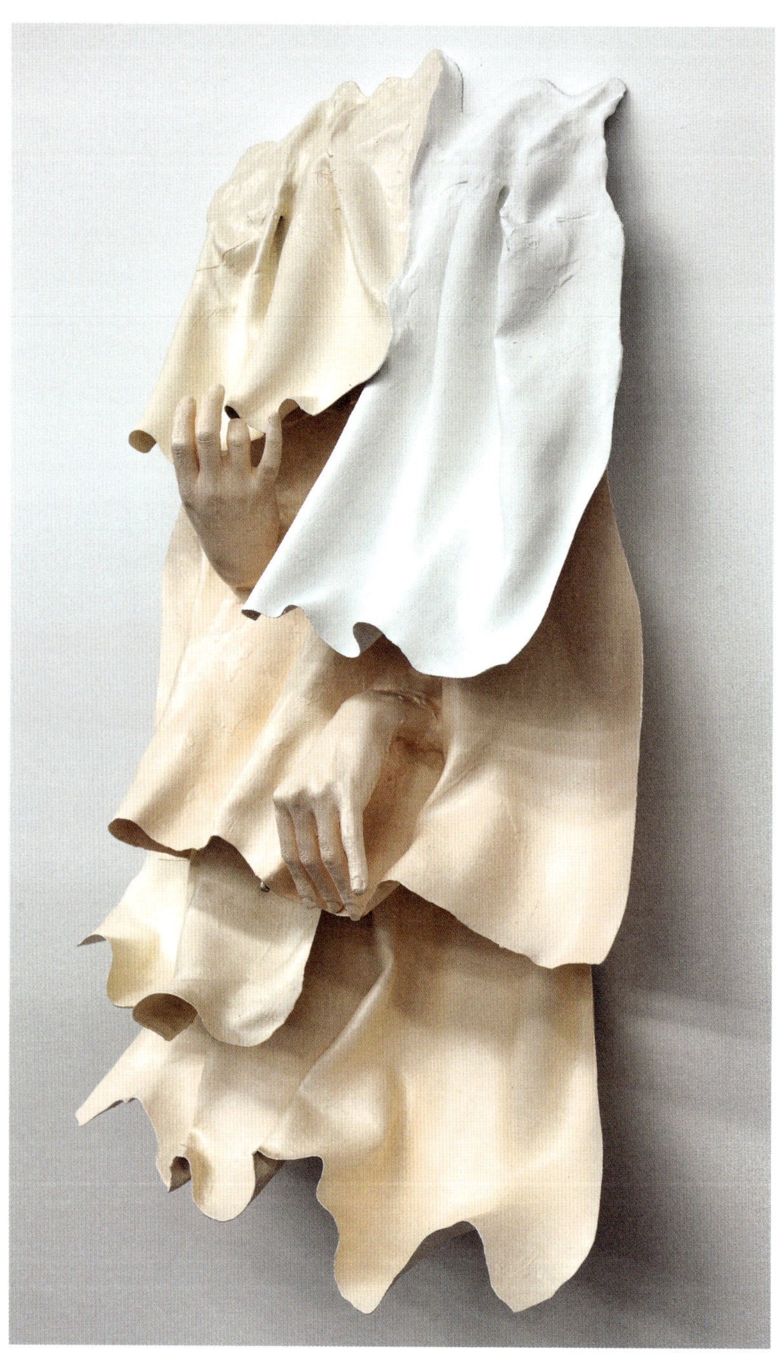

▲
Young Joon Kwak, *Hermaphroditus's Reveal II*, 2017. Fiberglass cloth, resin, silver leaf, and paint, 39 × 24 × 7 in. (99.1 × 61 × 17.8 cm)

A famous legend about the ancient Greco-Roman intersex deity, Hermaphroditus, goes like this: a female nymph named Salmacis falls head over heels for the young beauty Hermaphroditus (in this version of the story, he's the son of the Greek gods Hermes and Aphrodite). Hermaphroditus rejects the flirting nymph's advances, but she hides herself in a nearby bush and watches him undress to bathe. Hermaphroditus, believing himself alone, "thr[ows] aside [his] thin garments," revealing his naked body. Upon seeing it, Salmacis flings herself upon him and begs the gods to unite them forever. Answering her prayers, the gods fuse the two of them into a single intersex body that has the shape, the poet Ovid tells us, of "neither [sex], and yet both."[1]

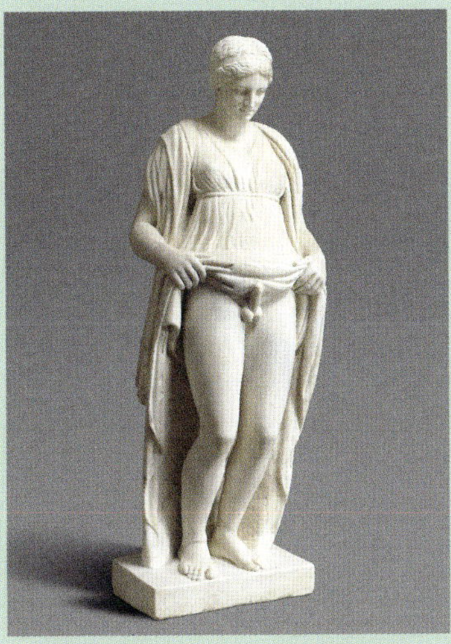

Hermaphroditus anasyromenos, Roman, c. 100–200 CE. Marble, 59 × 23⅝ × 18 in. (150 × 60 × 46 cm). Louvre Museum, Ma 4866, MR 221

The Hermaphroditus story turns on acts of voyeurism and revelation, tropes that also haunt the visual history of intersex.[2] We see them in the ancient Roman sculpture *Sleeping Hermaphroditus* (with Gian Lorenzo Bernini's early modern addition), now on display in the Louvre Museum. The famous sculpture depicts a feminine figure lying on a mattress, with bedding pulled aside to expose a nude body. Displayed in the round, the sculpture invites the viewer to discover that the reclining figure has "male" genitals, which become visible when one has circled the sculpture. The impact of the work rests on a dramatic moment, when the viewer realizes that the feminine form is more complex than initially meets the eye.[3] We might also think of Nadar's famous nineteenth-century medical photographs of an anonymous, reclining intersex person, body exposed from the waist down. The French surgeon Jacques-Gilles Maisonneuve's hand enters the photographic frame: it seizes our attention and directs it toward the intersex person's genitals.[4] The revelation of the nonbinary body is the point here, but the "reveal" is never on the subject's own terms.

Young Joon Kwak's powerful sculpture *Hermaphroditus's Reveal II* (2017) takes this long visual history and queers it, reasserting agency and placing the power of exposure right into Hermaphroditus's own hands.[5] In fact, hands are the only visible body parts in Kwak's sculpture. They part and lift draped skirts in a gesture that harkens back to the *hermaphroditos anasyromenos*, an ancient Greek sculptural tradition that pictures a standing, feminine figure who lifts skirts to show a penis and testicles.[6] In *Hermaphroditus's Reveal II*, hands redirect and obscure as much as they reveal. Secured to the wall, Kwak's sculpture controls the viewing area, as well as the grounds upon which it might be viewed: there are to be no stolen glances, no simple categorizations. Instead, Kwak repurposes the visual vocabulary of Greco-Roman antiquity to new and reparative ends. Building on work by artists such as Del LaGrace Volcano (whose "Visibly Intersex" also resists voyeurism by presenting photographs of fully clothed members of the intersex community), *Hermaphroditus's Reveal II* refuses spectacular revelation and invites complex engagement.[7] (And very close engagement yields a surprise in the form of a gilded silver "secret" hidden underneath the sculpted fabric). Kwak's work also evokes the classical Hermaphroditus tradition in another way. For ancient viewers, Hermaphroditus's nonbinary sex was a visionary means of transcending male–female dichotomies, a process associated with healing and protection. We might read Kwak's work in this register too, offering a protective votive for modern-day queer, trans, and intersex viewers—and an act of visual and historical transcendence.

—Leah DeVun

1. Ovid, *Metamorphoses*, trans. Frank Justus Miller, 2 vols. (Cambridge, MA: Loeb Classical Library, Harvard University Press, 1971), 4.375–9 (I: 203–5).
2. Ruth Evans, "The Intersex Look," *Postmedieval: A Journal of Medieval Cultural Studies* 9 (2018), 117–19.
3. Aileen Ajootian, "The Only Happy Couple: Hermaphrodites and Gender," in *Naked Truths: Women, Sexuality, and Gender in Classical Art and Archaeology*, eds. A. O. Koloski-Ostrow and C. L. Lyons (New York: Routledge, 1997), 231–35; Katharine T. Von Stackelberg, "Garden Hybrids: Hermaphrodite Images in the Roman House," *Classical Antiquity* 33, no. 2 (2014): 395–426.
4. Anne E. Linton, "The Dangers of Looking for 'True Sex' in Nadar's 'Hermaphrodite' Series," *Yale French Studies* 139 (2021): 153–70; *Unmaking Sex: The Gender Outlaws of Nineteenth-Century France* (Cambridge: Cambridge University Press, 2022); A. Blume, "Mesh: The Tale of the Hermaphrodite," *LTTR* 4: section III (2005), accessed on August 15, 2022, http://www.lttr.org/journal/4/mesh-the-tale-of-the-hermaphrodite.
5. On agency, see Linnea Åshede, "Desiring Hermaphrodites: The Relationships of Hermaphroditus in Roman Group Scenes," PhD diss, Department of Historical Studies, University of Gothenburg, 2015. On quotation, Mieke Bal, *Quoting Caravaggio: Contemporary Art, Preposterous Play* (Chicago: University of Chicago Press, 1999), 8.
6. Ajootian, "The Only Happy Couple," 221–30, and Diana M. Swancutt, "*Still* Before Sexuality: 'Greek' Androgyny, the Roman Imperial Politics of Masculinity and the Roman Invention of the *Tribas*," in *Mapping Gender in Ancient Religious Discourses*, eds. Tom Penner and Caroline Vander Stichele (Leiden: Brill, 2007), 11–61.
7. Del LaGrace Volcano, "Visibly Intersex," accessed August 15, 2022, https://www.dellagracevolcano.se/gallery/visibly-intersex-35548944.

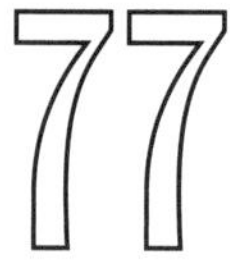

BRANDY BASURTO, EMMA YESICA DUVALI, CÉSAR GONZÁLEZ-AGUIRRE, TERRY HOLIDAY, ERICK MOLINA, SAMUEL NICOLLE, AND MARÍA PONCE, *CLOTHING HOSPITAL*, 2022

The "Clothing Hospital" is a symbolic, nomadic space. It has no fixed address and can't be located in any specific Mexico City neighborhood. It exists when Brandy Basurto, Emma Yesica Duvali, Terry Holiday, Erick Molina, Samuel Nicolle, María Ponce, and I get together in any one of our homes. In 2022, we started stitching together stories told by Emma, Brandy, and Terry, using fabric to illustrate them. This collaborative work is meant to embody memory and to recognize trans women and gender-nonconforming individuals who have died of AIDS in Mexico since the 1980s.

The project's title is derived from a story told by Emma—a Mexican trans activist and ex-showgirl—about Yaco, a choreographer in Mexico City in the 1980s who had what he called a "Clothing Hospital." This site of material and symbolic transformation—where a *quinceañera* gown could be turned into a wedding dress or where second-hand garments were bedazzled and given a new lease on life—serves as a simile, referring to the emotional power contained in one's personal world but also in collective desire: a power that survives and manifests itself in the residual. Scraps of fabric, clothes that once belonged to loved ones, costume jewelry, and other hand-me-downs formed the bulk of the materials we amassed to create imagery that dealt specifically with experiences of remembrance and grief, with identities shaped by the AIDS epidemic.

For the artistic project *Clothing Hospital*, we designed textiles for six people who were important to Emma, Brandy, and Terry to prompt processes of remembrance and reconstruct a diffuse ancestry. Meeting periodically provided us time to identify and describe emotional relationships with the convictions, life experiences, and disputes of a generation whose artistic careers began around the 1980s and '90s.

Clothing Hospital aims to further the work begun in 1987 by the NAMES Project AIDS Memorial Quilt in San Francisco, and by Colectivo Sol in Mexico City as of 1990. Our goal is to keep compiling a visual trans/queer history using autobiographical storytelling, embroidery, and patchwork as characteristic tools of artivism and transfeminism.

The project involves three creative duos consisting of individuals from different generations who share a history in terms of how they went about constructing their own rebellious identities. One group consists of trans women over the age of fifty and the other, of nonbinary people under thirty. Bringing together these diverse crowds was meant to go against the grain of contemporary practice defined by individualism and profitability. In this sense, we see collaboration as a means of perceiving the other's inner world within the outer world we share, and we conceive of art as a hub to address the past from the perspective of desire, fiction, and ambiguity.

—César González-Aguirre

Clothing Hospital is a project of the Archivo Memoria Trans México. The project was first exhibited in *Bewitched Clothing* at Outsiderland, Amsterdam, August 2022.

▶
Terry Holiday, *Gil Cardiel (Hidalgo, 1953–Monterrey, 1988)*, 2022. Textile and mixed media, 59 × 39 in. (149.9 × 99.1 cm). Courtesy of Archivo Memoria Trans México

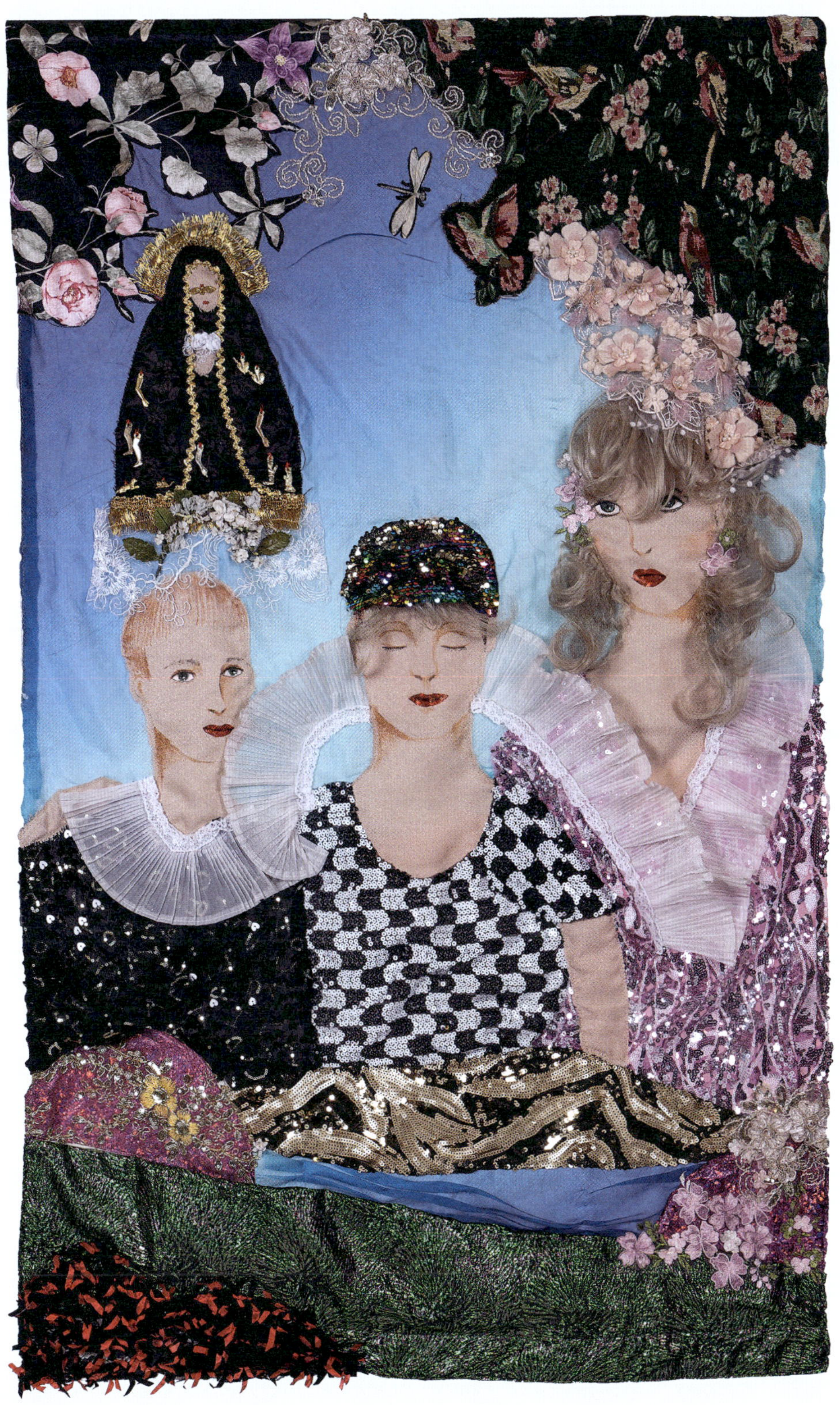

▼
Emma Yesica Duvali and Erick Molina, *Gabriela Martell (Durango, c. 1959–Mexico City, November 20, 2001)*, 2022. Textile, kimono, and mixed media, dimensions variable. Courtesy of Archivo Memoria Trans México

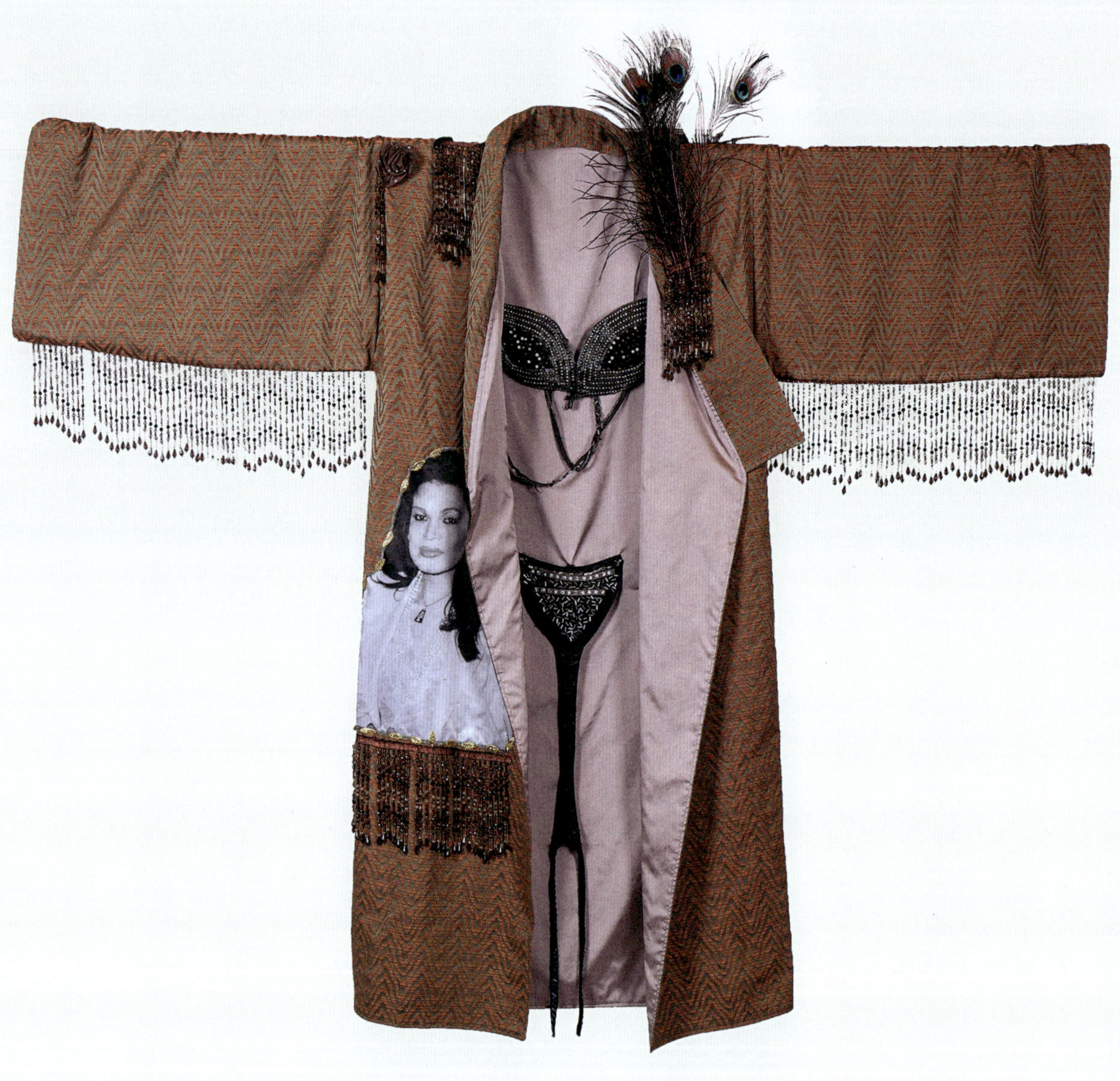

▶
Basurto and Samuel Nicolle, *Roshell—Rafael (Mexico City, 1977–2005)*, 2022. Textile and mixed media, 75 × 39 in. (190.5 × 99.1 cm). Courtesy of Archivo Memoria Trans México

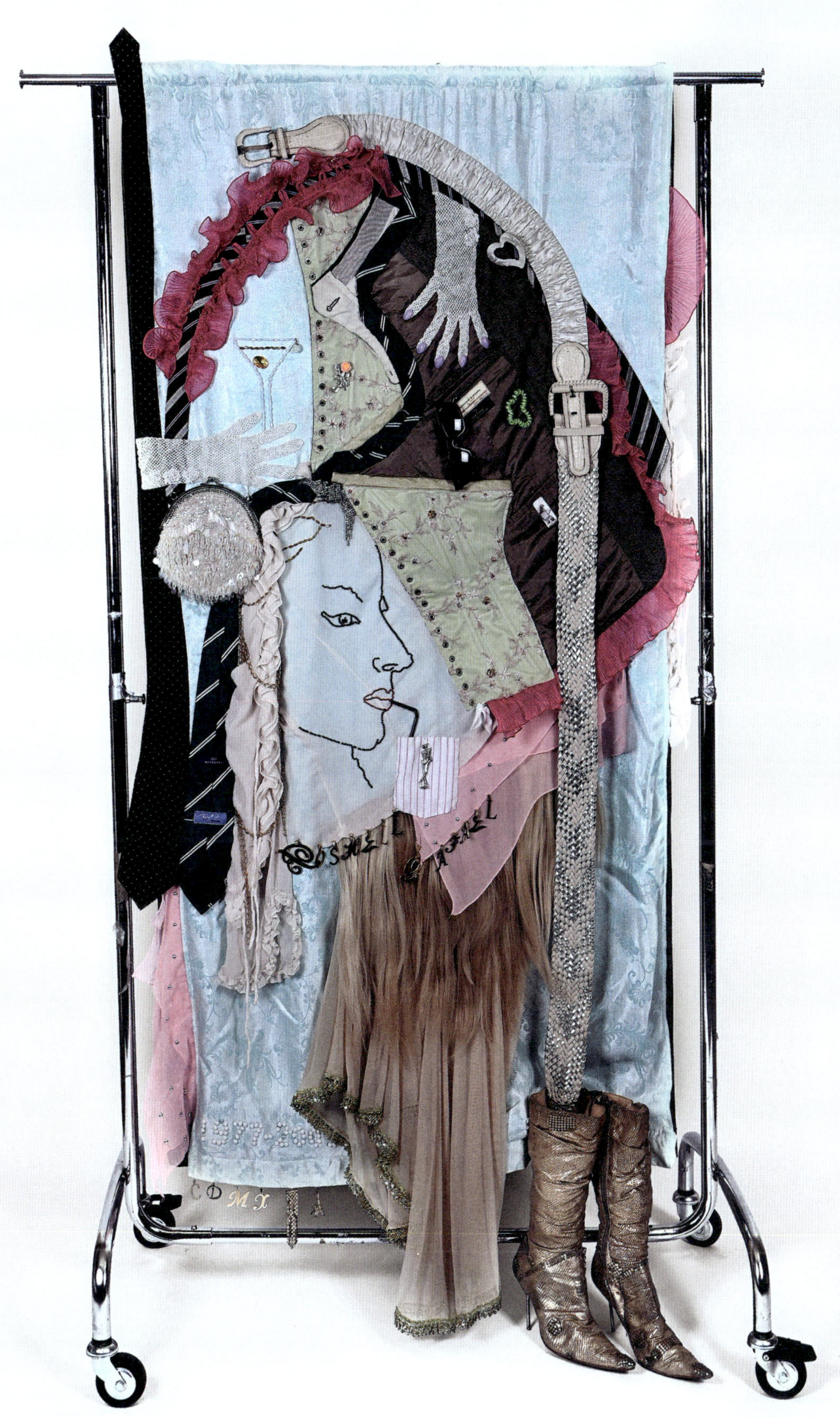
CDMX

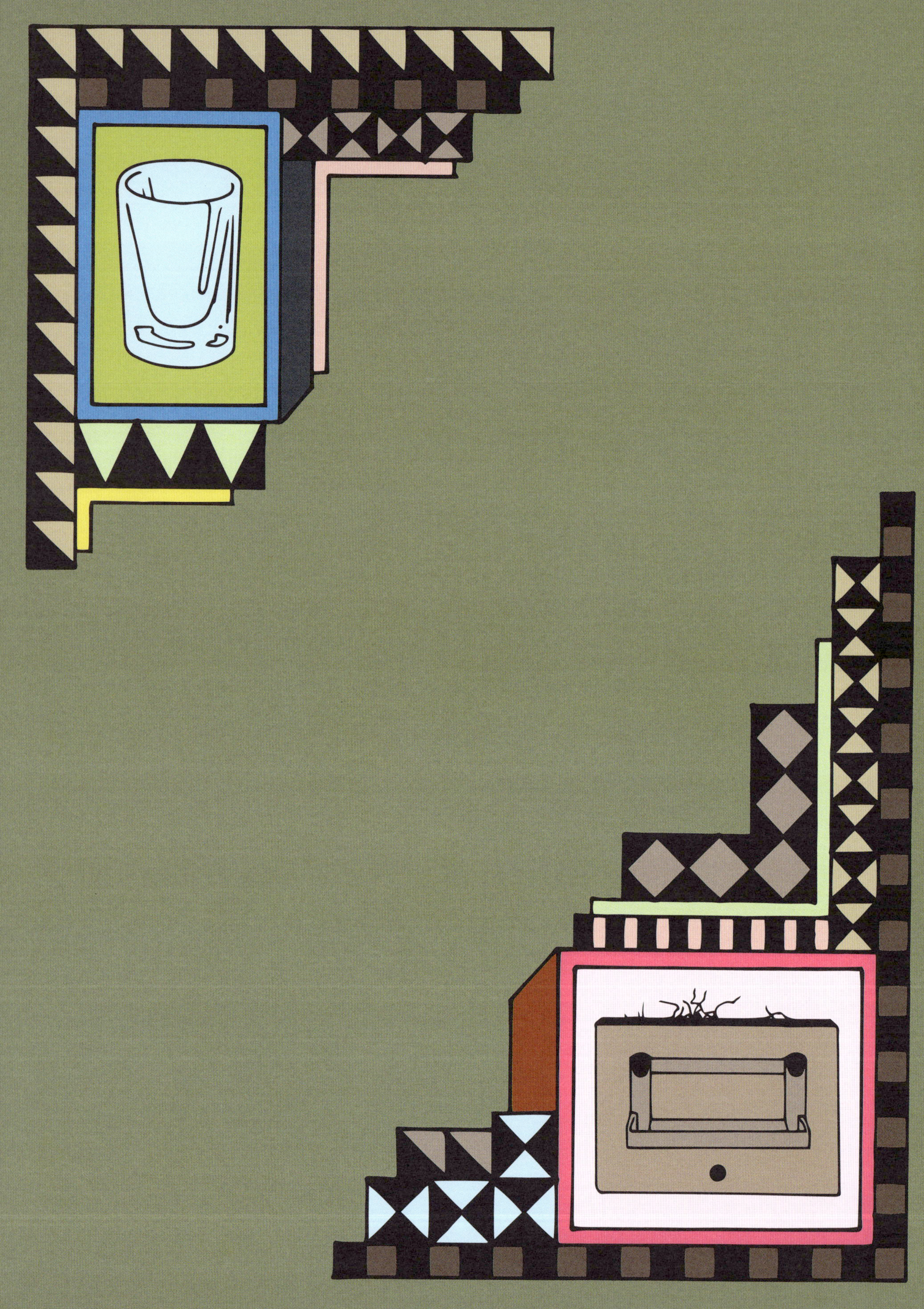

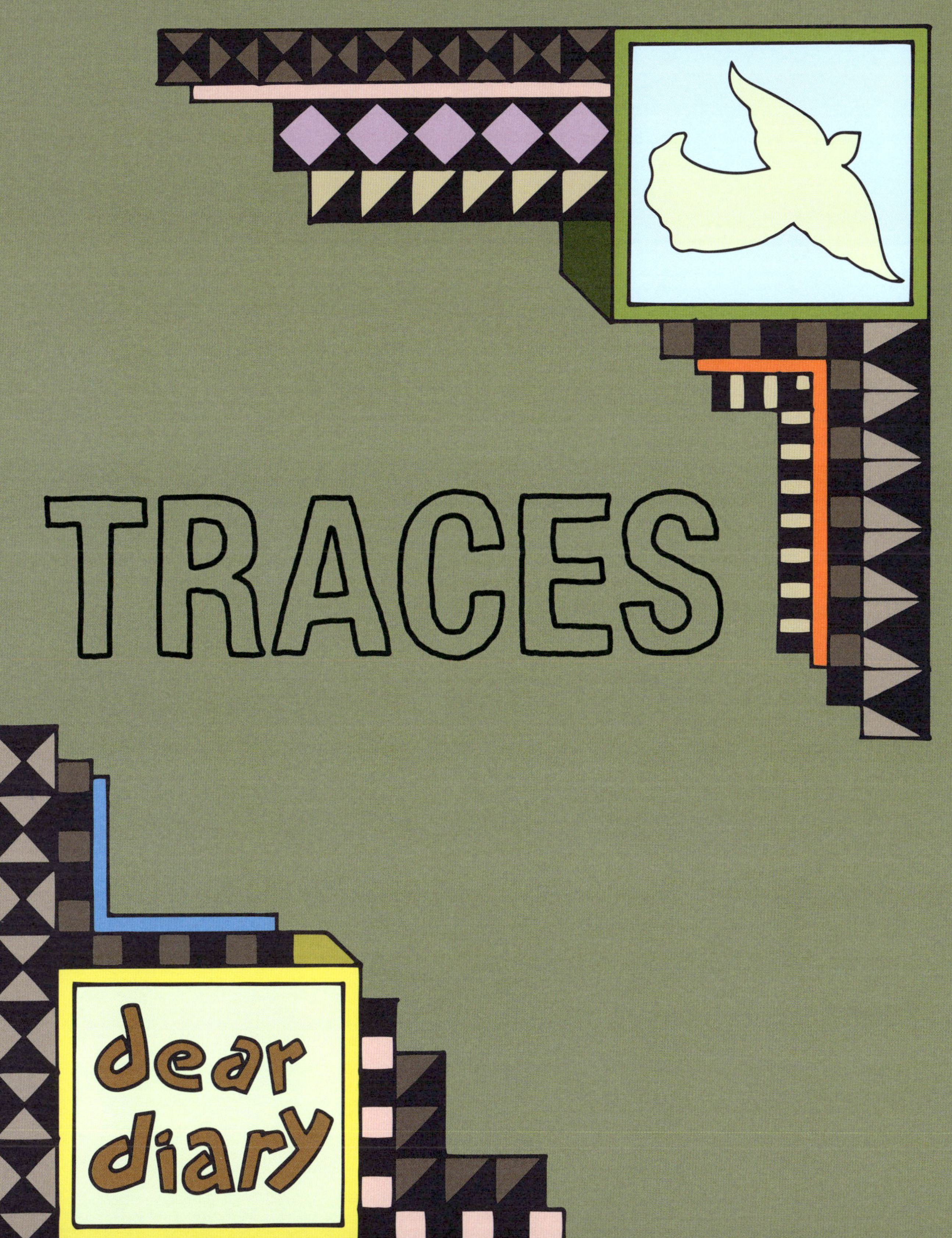
TRACES
dear diary

78 "ARTIFACTS" FROM THE STONEWALL RIOTS, n.d.

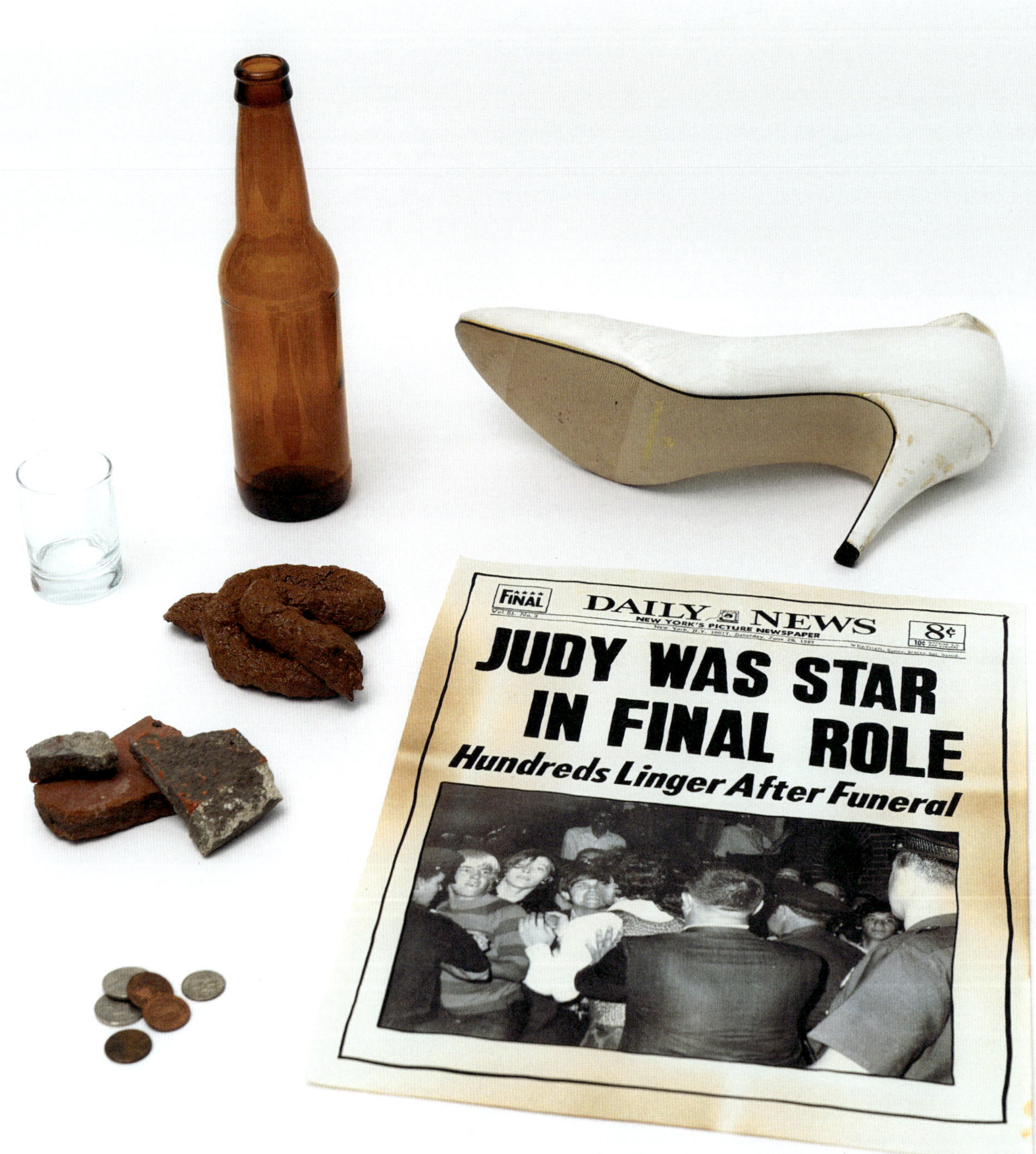

What exactly was it that sparked the collective act of queer resistance in the early morning hours of June 28, 1969, at the Stonewall Inn bar in New York City's Greenwich Village? The event has long been commemorated as the origin of the modern LGBTQIA+ rights movement. Because it was an instance of queer people standing together against police harassment and brutality (the cops were there that night to conduct a routine raid), it has often been looked back on as a symbol of what Gay Liberation once stood for, and perhaps could stand for again.

There are conflicting accounts about what object was thrown first at the cops. Was it a shot glass hurled by Marsha P. ("Pay It No Mind") Johnson? Or did patrons toss coins to goad the police about the payola they had come there to collect? Others insist it was a high heel shoe bursting out of the back of a paddy wagon and into the chest of an arresting officer. Perhaps it was a Molotov cocktail—Sylvia Rivera asserted she threw the second one that night, but not the first. Still others say it was a brick, or even dog excrement, found on the sidewalk outside. Some say it wasn't an object at all, but a punch thrown by Stormé DeLarverie, the famous singer and the MC of the renowned drag touring show, the Jewel Box Revue. Or perhaps it was Judy Garland who got things started. It's been said the patrons' heightened emotions were residue from the gay icon's funeral earlier that day. According to Martin Duberman's account of Stonewall, for which he interviewed Rivera, she attributed that night's events to herself and the community being particularly moved by hearing news of the actress's funeral earlier that day.[1] Though Rivera later denied this.[2] Even how to characterize what happened that night is up in the air. Was it an "uprising," a "rebellion," or a "riot"?

Generations later, queer and trans people continue to debate and struggle over how to commemorate the mythic event. Important reparative work has been done especially to wrest the story of Stonewall from white cis gay men and instead center the experiences of trans women of color. There has also been a lot of work to displace Stonewall as the origin point of queer resistance to police repression. Before it happened, there was already the riot at Los Angeles's Cooper Do-nuts in 1959, another at Philadelphia's Dewey's Famous in 1965, another at San Francisco's Compton's Cafeteria in 1966, and yet another, again in LA, at the Black Cat Tavern in 1967. Still, New York City's 1969 Stonewall uprising—or uprisings, plural, because the resistance continued over six days—is the most widely known. Maybe it was just the right place and the right time for an event to catch and set fire to the collective queer imagination: the first gay pride marches took place the following year on Stonewall's anniversary. Or perhaps New York City simply has a stranglehold on US cultural awareness: unless something happened there, it's not worth noting.

Understandably, queer and trans people want our history to be legitimized and archived. This often takes the form of objects preserved in climate-controlled storage and occasionally put on display under museum plexi. In this way history survives, but at what cost? One agreed-upon narrative cast in cement only serves to dispel and disregard conflicting and shifting truths. Stonewall erupted out of the anger and frustration built up over time by continual social marginalization and police harassment. Burgeoning gay political activism aligned itself with and was galvanized by contemporary intersecting movements like Black Power, Third World Liberation, and feminism. We've become too preoccupied with locating one singular object, moment, person, or place at the origin of major events and turning points, and we conflate locating that singular source with getting history right. Let us instead focus on collective affect, mobilization, and action. Let's find a different way to historicize and to archive: a way that accounts for conflicting experiences and even an archive of conflicting feelings.[3] As queers, we get to choose our lineages and *hir*stories.

—Chris E. Vargas

◄
Recreation of objects rumored to have initiated the Stonewall riots, 2023. Previously shown in the exhibition *MOTHA and Chris E. Vargas: Consciousness Razing—The Stonewall Re-Memorialization Project*, New Museum, 2018–19. Collection of MOTHA

1. Martin Duberman, *Stonewall* (New York: Plume, 1993), 190–91.
2. Sylvia Rivera, "Queens in Exile: The Forgotten Ones," in *Street Transvestite Action Revolutionaries: Survival, Revolt, and Queer Antagonist Struggle* (Untorelli Press, 2012), 48, https://files.libcom.org/files/STAR.pdf.
3. See Ann Cvetkovich, *An Archive of Feelings: Trauma, Sexuality, and Lesbian Public Cultures* (Durham, NC: Duke University Press, 2003).

79 KEIOUI KEIJAUN THOMAS, *MEMORIES ON COTTON AND SUGAR CANE RECEIPTS*, 2022

Flour. Honey. Heineken beer. Lube. Yaki hair braids. Crackers. Sugar. Vaseline. A tree stump burned at 550 degrees Fahrenheit for twenty-four hours until completely carbonized into a source of energy. Black bodies. Is a history of Black trans life a story of edible objects, coded commodities, and pliant flesh? One where slippage, conjecture, trespass, opacity, and objecthood are historical givens? The acumen of Brooklyn-based artist Keioui Keijaun Thomas is apparent in her ability to fold these queries and others into her deeply poetic and ruminative performance works that collapse the past and present while juxtaposing mourning alongside celebration. Thomas—who identifies as Black, trans, and femme—continually tries to stretch and break the taut containers around identities in her multidisciplinary practice. In her live performances and multimedia installations, Thomas repeatedly wields her own variously adorned (and oft-semi-nude) body as a pliant medium and an instrument of transcription, "a new language," in her words.[1] *Hands Up, Ass Out*, a collection of seven years of work (2014–2020) shown at Participant, Inc. in New York in 2021, circumnavigated through loaded concepts—visibility, passing, disposable labor, chattel slavery, and Black femme caretaking—in bold and experimental works that were quietly powerful. Meanwhile, Thomas's 2022 performance at Perrotin Gallery, also in New York, entitled *Come Hell or High Femmes: Act 2. The Last Trans Femmes on Earth: Dripping Doll Energy* radically imagined a postapocalyptic future solely inhabited by Black femmes. Alternatively doused in water or resplendent in glitter, Thomas created a communal space of affirmation while writhing to a soundtrack of brash hip-hop and contemplative ballads blended with a voiceover of her own poetry.

Thomas's impulse to imagine a transhistorical poetics of Black trans life also informs her response to a shocking 1771 fugitive slave advertisement in a Boston newspaper for a "Negro man servant, named Cato" who was also known by the name of "Miss Betty Copper."[2] The seemingly quotidian non-binarism openly alluded to in the

RAN away from his Mafter *John Sober*, Efq; on Monday the 8th of *April* Inft. a Negro Man Servant, named Cato, formerly owned by Mr. William Cooper of Bofton, and well known by the Name of Mifs Betty Cooper ;—— Whoever takes up faid Negro, and will bring him to the Subfcriber fhall have TWELVE DOLLARS Reward, and all neceffary Charges paid.

Bofton, April 12, 1771. JOHN SOBER.

Fugitive slave advertisement for Miss Betty Cooper in *The Massachusetts Gazette, and the Boston Post-Boy and Advertiser*, April 15, 1771. Massachusetts Historical Society

wanted ad is suggestive of the sly subversion of historical figures like Ellen Craft, who cleverly manipulated multiple disguises (racial *and* gender passing, feigned disability, and class performance) in the name of fugitivity, rendering seemingly static identity markers remarkably elastic.[3] And as William Wells Brown documented, such inventive and performative scrambles of identity were, in fact, common ploys for staging the art of escape. At first glance, Thomas's *Memories on Cotton and Sugar Cane Receipts* (2022) may seem a perplexing *response* to this history. Resembling a provisional monument of sorts, it recalls sculptor Barbara Chase Riboud's bronze, wax, and braided sculptures on a decidedly smaller and lo-fi scale. At approximately fifty inches tall, the assemblage is also the average human eye-height. Composed of a cacophony of heterogeneous materials—including cotton yarn, a blackened tree stump, bubble wrap, a hairbrush, black balloons, cardboard, ceramic snakes, and three years' worth of the artist's hair—it, alternatively, is suggestive of an altar or, vaguely, an elusive, even mythic, personage. And yet, in my mind, this conceptual opacity seems purposeful, an object-based homage to our magnificent ancestors whose artfully designed camouflage was often in full view while imperceptible to most except, perhaps, those whose mutability was also a necessary given.[4]

—Uri McMillan

1. Laura Zornosa, "For Keioui Keijaun Thomas, the Body Becomes a Vessel," *New York Times*, July 13, 2021, accessed January 10, 2023, https://www.nytimes.com/2021/07/13/arts/design/keioui-keijaun-thomas-participant-gallery.html.
2. *The Massachusetts Gazette, and the Boston Post-Boy and Advertiser* X, no. X (April 15, 1771): PAGE
3. For more on Craft's passing performances, see Uri McMillan, *Embodied Avatars: Genealogies of Black Feminist Art and Performance* (New York: New York University Press, 2015).
4. Thomas's thinking on the imperative of the fugitive slave to camouflage, shape-shift, and transform is informed by the work of scholar Joy Priest, specifically her article "Toward a Black Feminist Fugitive Poetics" in *Crosscurrents* 68, no. 4 (December 2018): 472–87. Keioui Keijaun Thomas, correspondence with the author, January 12, 2023.

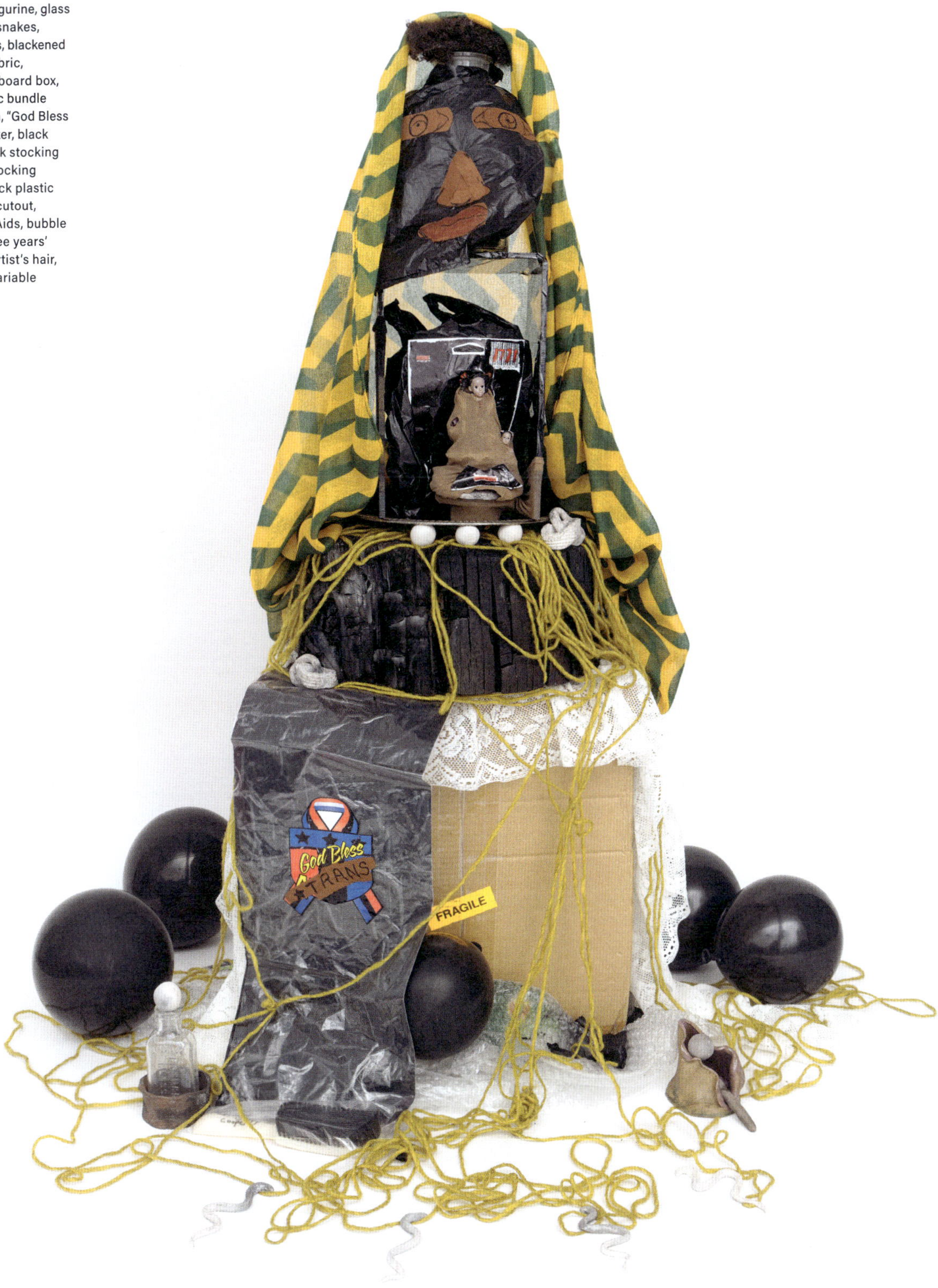

▼
Keioui Keijaun Thomas, *Memories on Cotton and Sugar Cane Receipts*, 2022. Black packaging tape, plexiglass pedestal, cotton yarn, vintage serving tray, figurine, glass jars, ceramic snakes, ceramic jewels, blackened tree stump, fabric, recycled cardboard box, 30-inch plastic bundle bag, hairbrush, "God Bless America" sticker, black balloons, black stocking cap, brown stocking cap, small black plastic bags, sticker cutout, brown Band-Aids, bubble wrap, and three years' worthof the artist's hair, dimensions variable

80 BAPTISMAL REGISTER OF MISSION SAN JOSÉ, SEPTEMBER 2, 1797–NOVEMBER 17, 1830

Entry #3681, Yoñequichs

Another man of 22 years, Joya bad name and worst role. Homines et jumenta salvabit Dominus. May it be done! I gave the name Luis Antonio. Before that he was called Yoñequichs.

The priest who entered this baptismal information left behind these extra notations that illuminate how *joyas* (a Spanish interpretation of an Indigenous term for third-gender people, meaning "jewels") were perceived and treated by Spanish colonizers. He reports that Yoñequichs is a *joya*, which is "a bad name and the worst role." In other words, Yoñequichs was a biological male who lived as a woman, a third-gender role that was well established and well regarded by Indigenous peoples who had lived for many thousands of years in the area currently known as California. For the Spanish, this was the *pecado nefando*, the heinous sin of sodomy.

Immediately after this judgment, the priest writes, *Homines et jumenta salvabit Dominus*, or "The Lord will save men and beasts/animals," from Psalms 35.[1] A Latin commentator notes that this Psalm is interpreted as God's generous mercy towards both mankind and animals, "not only [toward] men, rational beings, but even beasts; that is, men who, like beasts, are led by their appetites and sensuality only."[2] Spaniards are *gente de razon*, or people of reason, while (in this priest's view) *joyas* are beasts or animals without control over their "appetites and sensuality"; still, they might be saved. "May it be done!" the priest concludes, then (only because this is protocol that valorizes this "conversion"), records "Yoñequichs" as the person's former, pagan name. In naming, or renaming, resides great power.

Like most Indigenous people taken into missions, Yoñequichs lived only a short time after baptism: records show Yoñequichs was buried five years later on March 2, 1824, at the age of about twenty-eight.[3]

Mission San José's book of burials notes Yoñequichs's marital status as *soltero*—single, never married—an indication that for five years Yoñequichs avoided the priests' insistence that all adult Indians enter into a Church-sanctioned, heterosexual marriage. Such avoidance was an accomplishment, as even widows and widowers were required to remarry (often multiple times, as death of a spouse was the norm). While a cause of death for Yoñequichs is not recorded, the high level of mission mortalities is known to be the result of an unrelenting barrage of unfamiliar diseases, inaccessibility of Indigenous medicines and spiritual nurturance, malnutrition, forced labor, beatings, imprisonment, sexual assault by priests and soldiers, depression, and overwhelming trauma. *Add to this* being forcibly regendered and made to live and work as a man without the company and support of Indigenous women companions, and we must wonder at the strength required to, somehow, also resist intense pressure from one's oppressors to marry outside of one's sexuality and contribute to the mission labor force by fathering children. Perhaps, too, Yoñequichs's contemporaries within the mission also resistëd the priests' efforts (and maintained cultural integrity) by avoiding arranged marriages with third-gender people.

Because of this, I read Yoñequichs's story, and that of other California Indians experiencing the same violent regendering in the missions, as one of unimaginable courage and fierce sovereignty.

—Deborah A. Miranda
(Ohlone/Costanoan Esselen Nation,
Santa Ynez Chumash)

1. Latin translation provided by Dr. Daniel Conner, Ohlone/Costanoan Esselen Nation and Santa Ynez Chumash, at Purdue University.
2. Robert Bellarmine, *A Commentary on the Book of Psalms* (Dublin & London: James Duffy & Co., 1866), https://www.ecatholic2000.com/bell/psalms.shtml#_toc417747136.
3. The Early California Population Project (ECPP) is a database developed by the Huntington Library providing public access to all the information contained in the California mission registers from 1769 to 1850. It includes baptism, marriage, and burial records of each of the California missions, providing historical information on the Indians, soldiers, and settlers of Alta California: https://huntington.org/early-california-population-project.

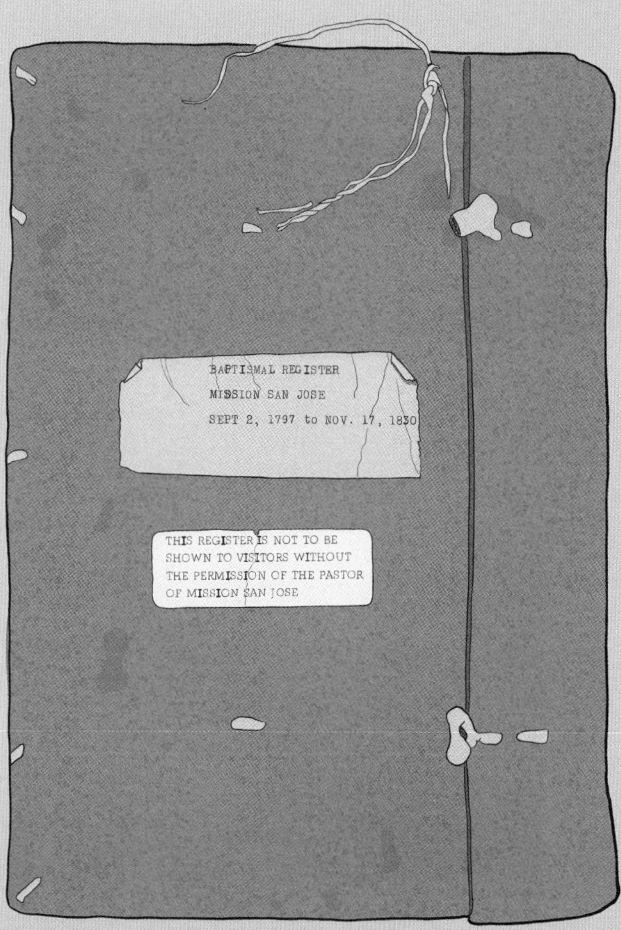

▲ Drawing of Entry #3681 (Yoñequichs, baptized as "Luis Antonio") based on the Baptismal Register of Mission San José, September 2, 1797–November 17, 1830. The Archives of the Archdiocese of San Francisco denied permission to reproduce the original records in this book

81 LYNN EDWARD HARRIS'S DRIVER'S LICENSES, 1977 AND 1981

I didn't know Lynn. (He was born in 1950 in Orange, California. He died in 2023 in Los Angeles.) You and I meet him now through whichever details the state of California decided were most important. This portrait is, after all, government property.

I don't know which songs lit up Lynn's face, what he took in his coffee, whose voice made his heart flutter. I do know that, just like me, Lynn was 5'8" tall. He had brown hair and problems with his driver's license's "sex" field.

Lynn went up against state bureaucracy. And he won.

As an intersex child, Lynn escaped the infant genital surgeries so many of us are subjected to. He avoided surgeries once more as an adult by petitioning California to change his driver's license without "medical evidence" of "sex change" surgery—which, at the time, anyone who hoped to change their documents needed. This victory was unprecedented.

Lynn leveraged his intersex status to do what he had to do. This is a move that today's intersex trans people are surely familiar with: playing up or down one's anatomical differences to please colonial systems that demand "proof" the eye can see. Lynn did what he had to do, and he did what we've always done.

Several prominent white transgender people who posed early challenges to state and medical control were only able to do so by the (un)luck of their birth. Lili Elbe, a Danish trans woman and the subject of a controversial 2015 film adaptation, accessed medical and surgical transition care in the 1930s. Though rarely discussed, some accounts credit this with her speculated intersex status.[1]

It's no surprise to me, in my work in today's intersex movements, how many transgender people still hope they are intersex. Many countries still require medical documentation or major genital surgeries of anyone seeking to change their government-issued sex or gender marker. My heart aches for this continued, false legacy of proof.

The courage of people like Lynn fuels today's intersex and transgender resistance. Each generation's work supports the next in splintering into the surveillance of our bodies.

As destroying transgender people becomes a load-bearing pillar of right-wing politics, and as doctors sit in courtrooms arguing that XX chromosomes "prove" intersex infants should want their clitorises trimmed like hedges, I wonder what Lynn might have done with his time if he hadn't had to keep proving himself to fascists and bureaucrats. I guess that's why we keep going.

Lynn's struggle enabled countless others to bring similar challenges over sex and gender markers. In 2021, Lambda Legal client and intersex Navy veteran Dana Zzyym won an X gender marker for their US passport after spending over six years in court.[2]

While these are certainly hard-won legal victories, intersex and transgender people know that court rulings alone will never support our material safety. Until we achieve the complete removal of gender markers from government documents, we'll be the ones to bear bureaucracy, surveillance, and persecution.

I like to think Lynn knew that he was so much more than a single letter that belonged to his government. I like to think he rested, reveled, danced, and loved furiously—in ways the state will never know.

—Hans Lindahl

1. Karin, "Lili Elbe's Autobiography, Man into Woman," Intersex Human Rights Australia, April 17, 2009, accessed January 16, 2023, https://ihra.org.au/789/book-review-man-woman/.
2. "Dana Zzyym receives first U.S. passport with 'X' gender marker," *Weekend Edition Saturday*, NPR, October 30, 2021, accessed January 16, 2023, https://www.npr.org/2021/10/30/1050782672/dana-zzyym-receives-first-u-s-passport-with-x-gender-marker.

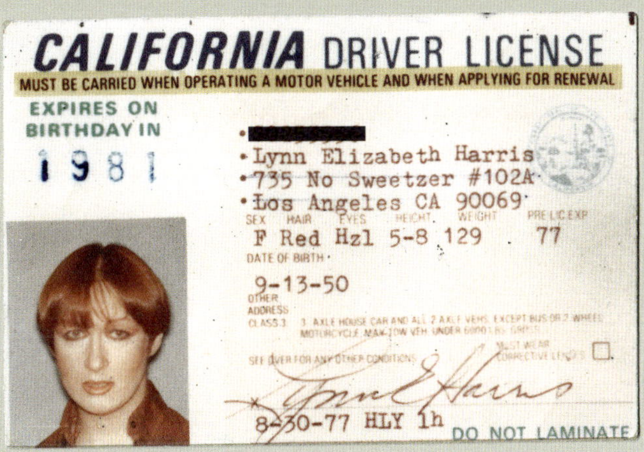

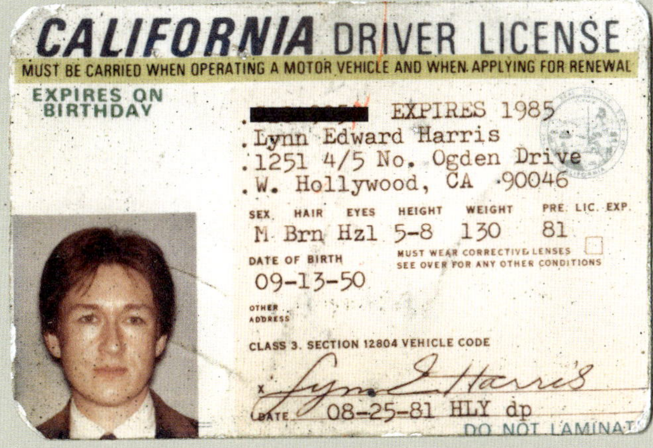

▲ Lynn Edward Harris's California Driver's Licenses issued August 30, 1977, and August 25, 1981. Lynn Edward Harris Papers, ONE National Gay & Lesbian Archives at the USC Libraries

82 EMMETT RAMSTAD, *PUBE FILE*, 2012–22

With his installation *File*, sculptor, participatory artist, and former hairdresser Emmett Ramstad smuggles pubes into the sanctified halls of museums, galleries, and now, onto the pages of a prestigious art catalogue. In 2012 he began soliciting donations through correspondence, face-to-face hand-off, public ritual (on a beach, in a gallery), and private shave. A meditation on collecting and collectivizing, *Pube File* (2012–22) approaches preservation by remixing gay sexual practices within the contemporary trans-queer commons.

Pube File references Samuel Steward's iconic Stud File, a metal box full of index cards documenting thousands of sexual encounters across fifty years of life. Steward's cult following drools over his meticulous, unabashed presentation of queer sexual conquest. The Stud File's clinical kink showcases midcentury personalities ("the one-eyed sadist") and celebrities (Hudson, Wilder, and Lord Alfred Douglas), including details of each sexual encounter (size, time, acts, quirks) and, on the card for Rudolf Valentino, a lock of pubic hair. Pointedly, Ramstad's citation of Stud File is not about identification, nostalgia, or mediating the schisms between gay sexual culture and transfag desire; it emerges from his drive to locate traces of the body in the archive, to touch back and commingle for a spell.

The artist also engages one of the prize holdings of the GLBT Historical Society in San Francisco: a box of spice jars formerly known as Robert Chesley's pubic hair collection. Ramstad has discovered the collection didn't originate with Chesley but was entrusted to him by the collection's gatherer, John Pfleiderer, in a quick bequest during the early AIDS epidemic. Of course pubic hair can cover and reveal. In this case, Ramstad's pubic assemblage revels in a material reperformance of Pfleiderer's collectivizing queer impulse.

Pube File's imaginings of trans rites position sexual legacy as a mobile and malleable set of communal practices. In repurposing Steward and Chesley Pfleiderer, Ramstad builds a more inclusive file—one that insists on a queer trans world where sex inspires and animates community bonds.

A mound of pubic hair is the opposite of a mirror, it is a nest space for resting, dreaming, hatching. In 2019 Ramstad and I return to Chesley's archive, where the pube jars spawn a new project we call HOLD. Drawn to Chesley's 1986 AIDS play about love, sex, and community, *Jerker, Or The Helping Hand: A Pornographic Elegy with Redeeming Social Value and a Hymn to the Queer Men of San Francisco in Twenty Telephone Calls, Many of Them Dirty*, we decide to stage trans *Jerkers* as free shows with local collaborators around the country in archives, community centers, and sex clubs. During the tour launch at Chicago's Leather Archives & Museum, we run *Jerker* through our bodies before an audience so knowledgeable about generations of queer sex cultures, AIDS art, and trans life that performing feels like being held.

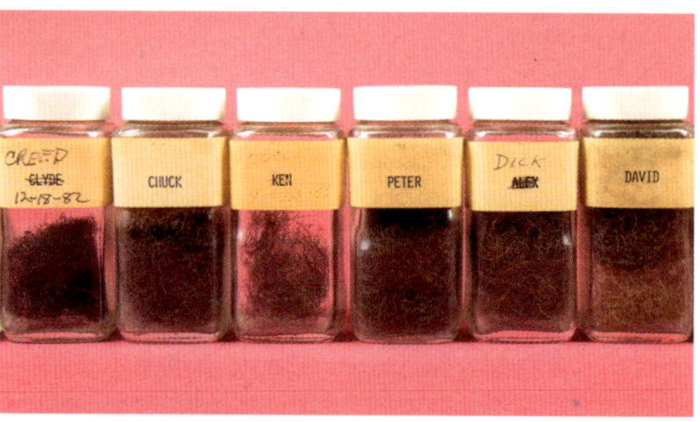

Robert Chesley's collection of pubic hair clippings in repurposed spice jars, c. 1976–89. Robert Chesley Papers (1993-06), Gay, Lesbian, Bisexual, Transgender Historical Society. Photo by Marcel Pardo Ariza

Across his archival works, Ramstad finds intimacy in accumulation, tending to the unexpected spirals of personal belongings. *Pube File* indexes a distinctly sexual queer artistic lineage, and contextualizes that legacy within present and future trans/missions. In preserving and revising rituals of the past, Ramstad fantasizes for trans-queer togetherness—our shared potential for sexual community action.

—Maxe Crandall

A version of this text previously appeared in the brochure accompanying the exhibition *Transgender Hirstory in 99 Objects: Legends & Mythologies* at ONE National Gay & Lesbian Archives at the USC Libraries, 2015.

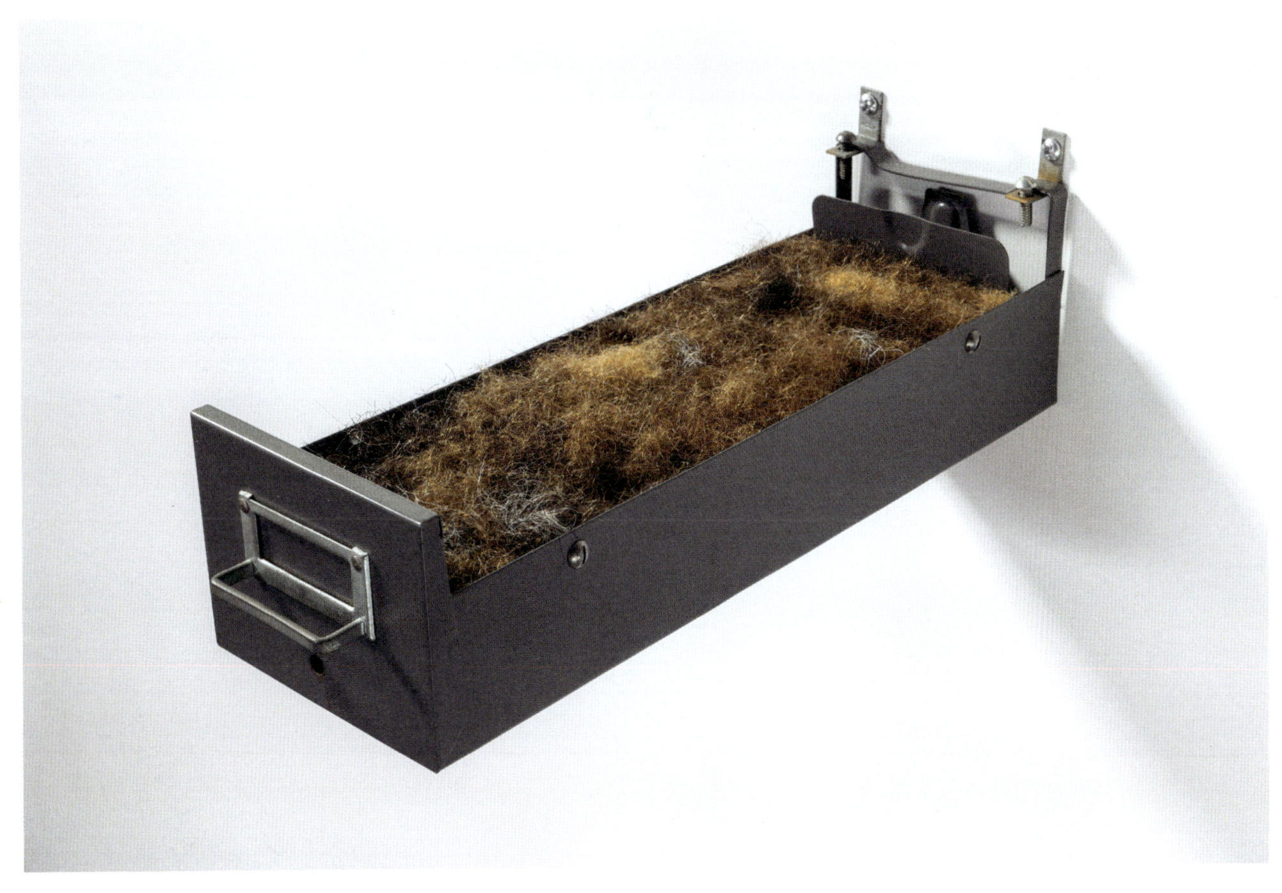

▲
Emmett Ramstad,
Pube File, 2012–22.
Intermingled pubic hair,
file drawer, and plexi-
glass, 5½ × 4 × 16 in.
(14 × 10.2 × 40.6 cm)

83 LOU SULLIVAN'S JOURNALS, c. 1960s–91

Lou Sullivan (1951–1991) kept journals throughout his life. In the entry reproduced on the following spread, a twenty-one-year-old Lou is living "as a woman," in Milwaukee, watching his lover kiss another man and longing to be, in his words, "a man among men."[1] Here, Lou is uncertain and unseen, with a "growing sense of being kinky and trans and having no language for it."[2] In three years, Lou will move to San Francisco, begin transitioning hormonally, get top surgery, a semi-botched bottom surgery, and begin identifying as a gay man. Between contracting HIV and dying of AIDS-related complications at age thirty-nine, he will author *Information for the Female to Male: Crossdresser and Transsexual* (1985) and *From Female to Male: The Life of Jack Bee Garland* (1990), an early-twentieth-century proto-trans man. His interviews with psychiatrist Dr. Ira Pauly will shift the medical community's understanding that trans people can be gay, and he will cofound the GLBT Historical Society, where his diaries will lie in obscurity until Susan Stryker processes them as a young archivist, writing "Portrait of a Transfag Drag Hag as a Young Man" in 1999, which catapults Lou into public awareness.

Salacious, quotidian details punctuate his diaries: his jewelry fetish, his fangirl tendencies, his luxurious pettiness, quick wit, and his inscrutable, unyielding optimism. These fragments implicate a before/after, a promise of temporal coherence that Lou's writing, in contrast to so many contemporary trans tropes, manages to hold. *It's too much for my mirror,* my lover said, after I read this excerpt aloud to them. *It's too close.* For the accompanying poem, I collaged language from Lou's interviews and trans-feminization vocal training YouTube videos.[3] This layering embodies a convoluted trans temporality, one that allows for shifting, redaction. A space of potential in which transitioning is not only a future crossing, but a past *we write ourselves / layering into / onto.*

—Emji Saint Spero

▲ Lou Sullivan's journal, 1972. Louis Graydon Sullivan Papers (1991–07), Gay, Lesbian, Bisexual, and Transgender Historical Society. Photo by Marcel Pardo Ariza

1. Lou Sullivan, *We Both Laughed in Pleasure: The Select Diaries of Lou Sullivan, 1961–1991*, eds. Ellis Martin and Zach Ozma (Brooklyn/Oakland: Nightboat Books/Timeless, Infinite Light, 2019), 90, 97, 377.
2. Susan Stryker, "My Own Interpretation of Happiness: An Introduction to the Journals of Lou Sullivan," *We Both Laughed in Pleasure*, 9.
3. A longer version of this poem, "autocorrect is just another word for," was published in *OUT!spoken*, ed. Caroline Gasparini, June 30, 2022, accessed January 23, 2023, https://simplebooklet.com/unnamedsimplebooklet3898.

his wrists...]

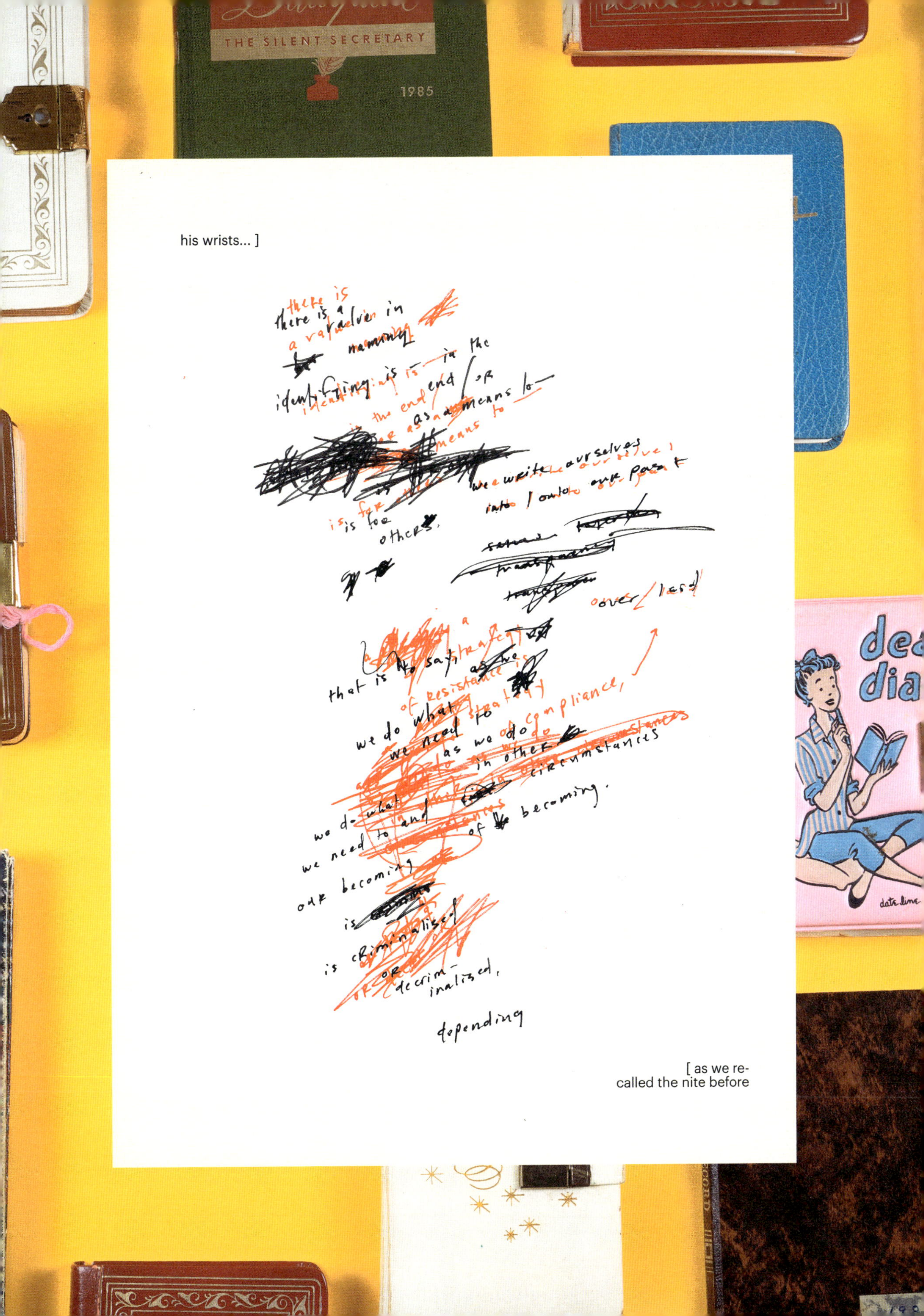

[as we re-
called the nite before

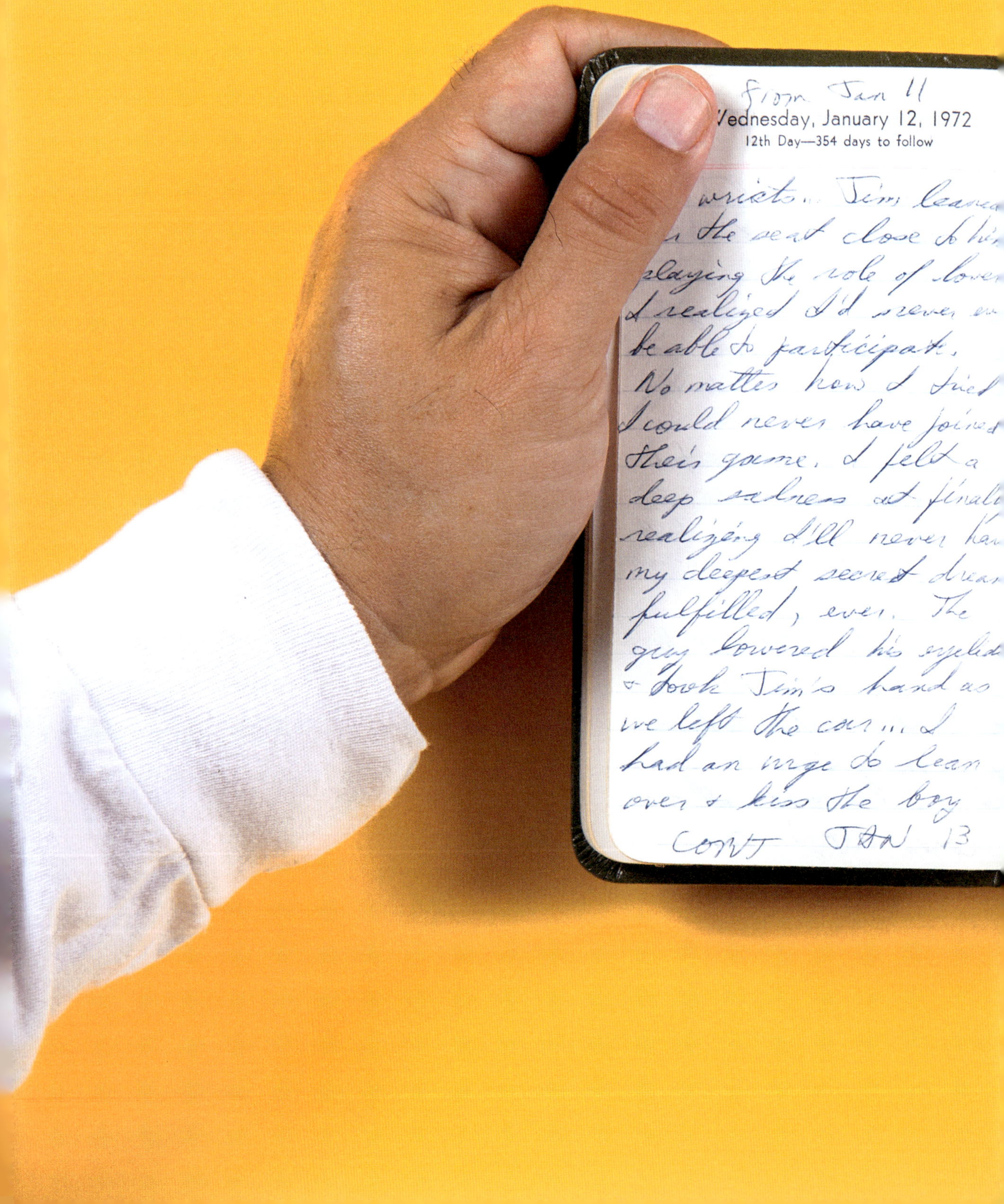

▸
Lou Sullivan's journal entry from Wednesday, January 12, 1972. Louis Graydon Sullivan Papers (1991–07), Gay, Lesbian, Bisexual, and Transgender Historical Society. Photo by Marcel Pardo Ariza

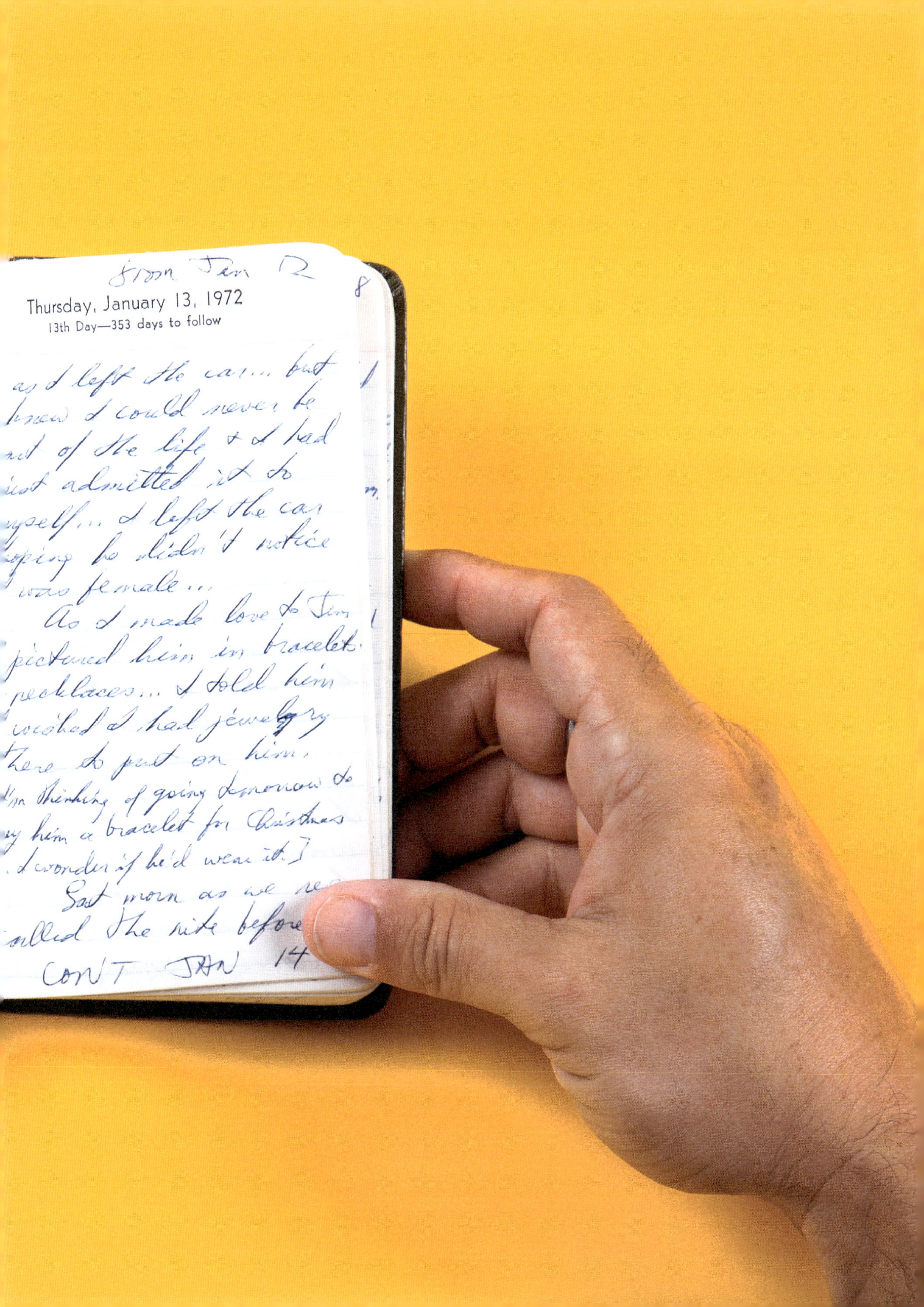

from Jan 12 8

Thursday, January 13, 1972
13th Day—353 days to follow

as I left the car... but
knew I could never be
out of the life & I had
just admitted it to
myself... I left the car
hoping he didn't notice
I was female...
As I made love to Jim
pictured him in bracelets
necklaces... I told him
wished I had jewelry
here to put on him.
I'm thinking of going tomorrow to
buy him a bracelet for Christmas
I wonder if he'd wear it.]
Sat morn as we re
called the nite before
CONT JAN 14

84 JAMIE DIAZ, *THE NAKED TRUTH*, JUNE 27, 2020

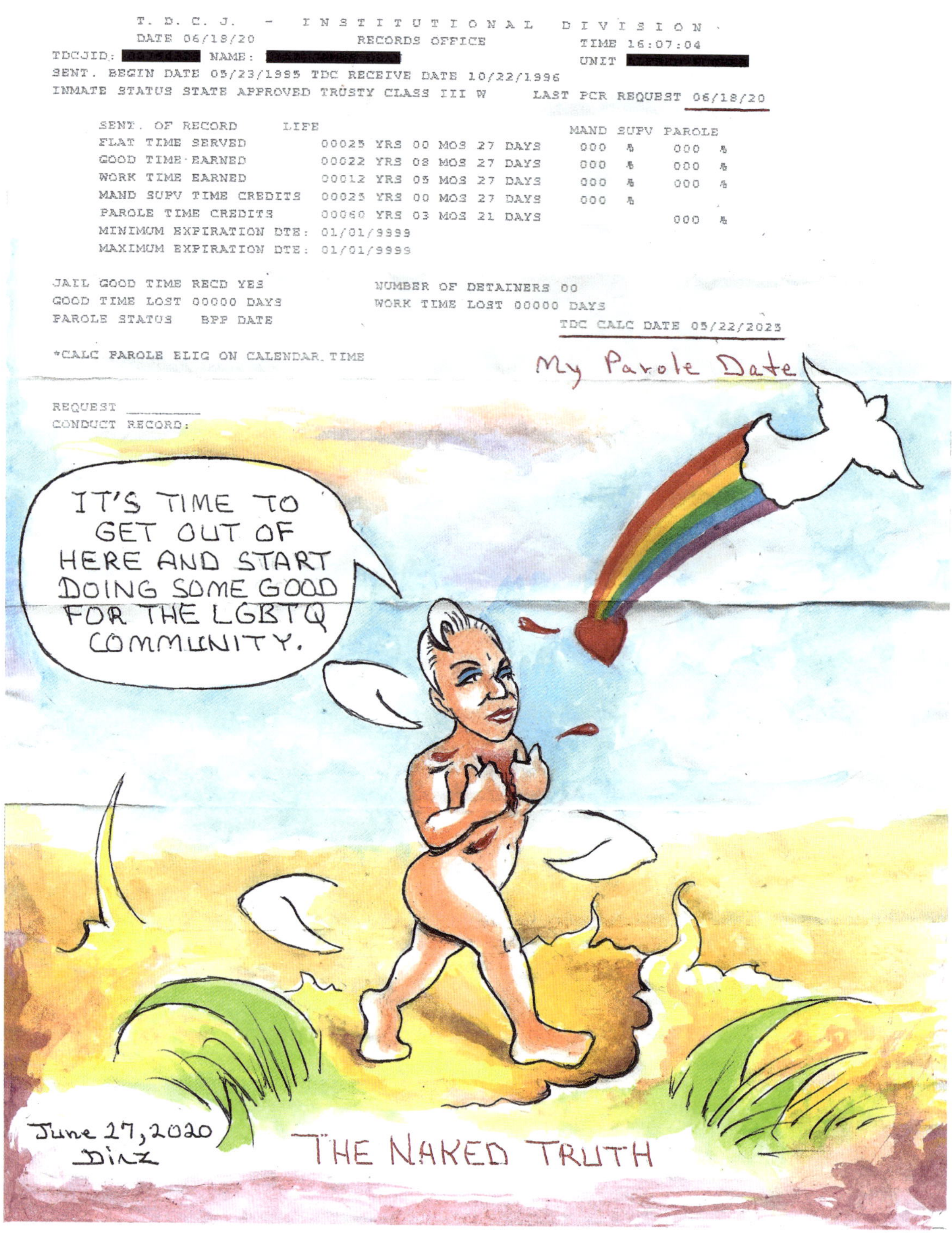

T. D. C. J. - INSTITUTIONAL DIVISION
DATE 06/18/20 RECORDS OFFICE TIME 16:07:04
TDCJID: ████ NAME: ████ UNIT ████
SENT. BEGIN DATE 05/23/1995 TDC RECEIVE DATE 10/22/1996
INMATE STATUS STATE APPROVED TRUSTY CLASS III W LAST PCR REQUEST 06/18/20

SENT. OF RECORD	LIFE	MAND SUPV	PAROLE
FLAT TIME SERVED	00025 YRS 00 MOS 27 DAYS	000 %	000 %
GOOD TIME EARNED	00022 YRS 08 MOS 27 DAYS	000 %	000 %
WORK TIME EARNED	00012 YRS 05 MOS 27 DAYS	000 %	000 %
MAND SUPV TIME CREDITS	00025 YRS 00 MOS 27 DAYS	000 %	
PAROLE TIME CREDITS	00060 YRS 03 MOS 21 DAYS		000 %
MINIMUM EXPIRATION DTE:	01/01/9999		
MAXIMUM EXPIRATION DTE:	01/01/9999		

JAIL GOOD TIME RECD YES NUMBER OF DETAINERS 00
GOOD TIME LOST 00000 DAYS WORK TIME LOST 00000 DAYS
PAROLE STATUS BPP DATE TDC CALC DATE 05/22/2025

*CALC PAROLE ELIG ON CALENDAR TIME

REQUEST ________
CONDUCT RECORD:

Jamie Diaz
Interviewed by Gabriel Joffe

Jamie Diaz is a Mexican American trans woman and self-taught artist whose work has inspired many in the LGBTQ+ community by conveying the resilience of the human spirit through a message of love, hope, and beauty. Born in the Midwest in the late 1950s, Jamie grew up in Houston and started drawing and painting at the age of fifteen. Jamie primarily creates from her imagination and describes experiencing new ideas like an endless stream of imagery in her mind. Her art has garnered a following in the art world, and she had her debut solo show in 2022 at Daniel Cooney Fine Art in New York City.

Jamie is currently incarcerated in a men's prison in Texas. In 2013, she connected with Gabriel Joffe, who would become a close friend and supporter, through the pen pal program of Black and Pink, a grassroots organization dedicated to abolishing the criminal punishment system and liberating queer people. Jamie is eligible for parole in 2025 after thirty years of confinement.

GABRIEL JOFFE (GJ) When you imagine the future and the next three hundred years of trans life, what do you see?

JAMIE DIAZ (JD) When I imagine the future of transgender life, you know what I see? I think that three hundred years from now we'll still know what we are, and people will still recognize us, but it won't be a big deal like it is today. We're just gonna be creations... living beings. It won't matter whether you're straight, trans, gay, bi... people won't even be talking about that. We'll just be recognized as who we are.

I think by then if humans are still living on earth, people in general are not going to be just human. I think they are also going to be part cyborg, and that's going to be a bigger deal than being trans. To have parts of your body that are electronic and robotic and still be human.

GJ When I think of how MOTHA blurs the line between the real and the imaginary, your comic book *Queer Angels & Devils: Table of Immortals* (2023) comes to mind. As the protagonist, what's your encounter at the Table like?

JD The artists—actors, painters, photographers, writers—that I put at the "Table of Immortals" are all real people who have lived before and left a legacy. They are immortalized through the work that they left behind. Artists like Oscar Wilde, James Baldwin, Audre Lorde, William S. Burroughs, Robert Mapplethorpe, etc.

In the comic book, I'm seeking a seat at the Table, and there's a scene where the artists I just mentioned are all seated behind the Table watching me. I'm standing and Burroughs is speaking to me.

He asks me if I wish to proceed, then he says, "Okay, disrobe."

"Disrobe?" I reply.

He responds, "You heard correctly, naked as the day you were born." And he continues, "Nothing shall be concealed... from the moment of your birth to the present, everything shall be revealed."

I drop my robe and hear a loud clap of thunder and fall to the ground. And that's when the interrogation starts. They start confronting me with my history of being deceitful, doing drugs, being selfish, things like that. I am laying on the floor sobbing, crying, and hitting the floor with my first. "Stop, please, why are you doing this? It's true. I did all those things, but I never do that again. I swear."

Then it ends and Burroughs tells me to stand up and put on my clothes. And then he asks, "What do you desire more than anything in the world?"

I reply, "To continue with my work and to have a seat at the Table."

◄
Jamie Diaz, *The Naked Truth*, June 27, 2020. Watercolor and ink on the artist's timesheet, 11 × 8½ in. (27.9 × 21.6 cm)

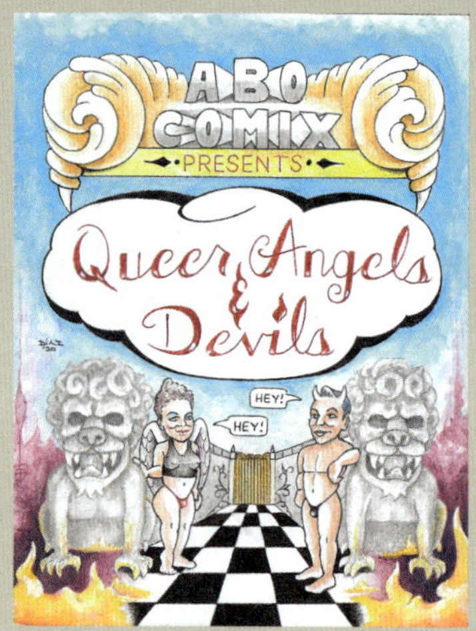

Jamie Diaz, Cover for *Queer Angels & Devils: Table of Immortals*, 2020 (published 2023). Watercolor and ink on paper, 11 × 8½ in. (27.9 × 21.6 cm). Published by A.B.O. Comix, 2023

And he goes, "Yeah, that's what we all wanted. You would have traded your soul for a seat at the Table. Oh, we know all about that. That isn't necessary." He continues, "Go and continue with your work. When the time comes, you will have your seat at the Table."

So right there, that's it. That's my destiny. To get a seat at the Table when my time here on Earth is over.

What gave me the idea for the comic book was my own mortality and desire to create a legacy of my own. As a trans artist, it means a lot to me to get as much queer art done as I can in my lifetime. I still got some years left, I'm sure. But most of it's over. I'm just happy knowing that my history is sealed already, my legacy. To be immortalized through my art.

GJ What does time and history mean to you as an artist? Why is the history of transgender communities important?

JD I think the history of trans life should all be documented, so we can be more understood by society in general. Not only to document a history to leave behind but start building it for the future.

I always say that queer people are some of the most wonderful people I've ever known in my life—full of love. And I believe that to be true. I do my art for queer people and hope people get a lot of joy, love, and hope from what I do. We've been brutalized so much, that I want to present a positive image of being queer and trans to convey happiness. And a real flamboyant way of saying to the people that don't like it, "Go to hell."

Time is important to me because I know I'm running out of time. But the door has been opened for us and I know we're gonna have something to leave behind.

▸
Jamie Diaz, Page from *Queer Angels & Devils: Table of Immortals*, 2020 (published 2023). Watercolor and ink on paper, 11 × 8½ in. (27.9 × 21.6 cm). Published by A.B.O. Comix, 2023

3

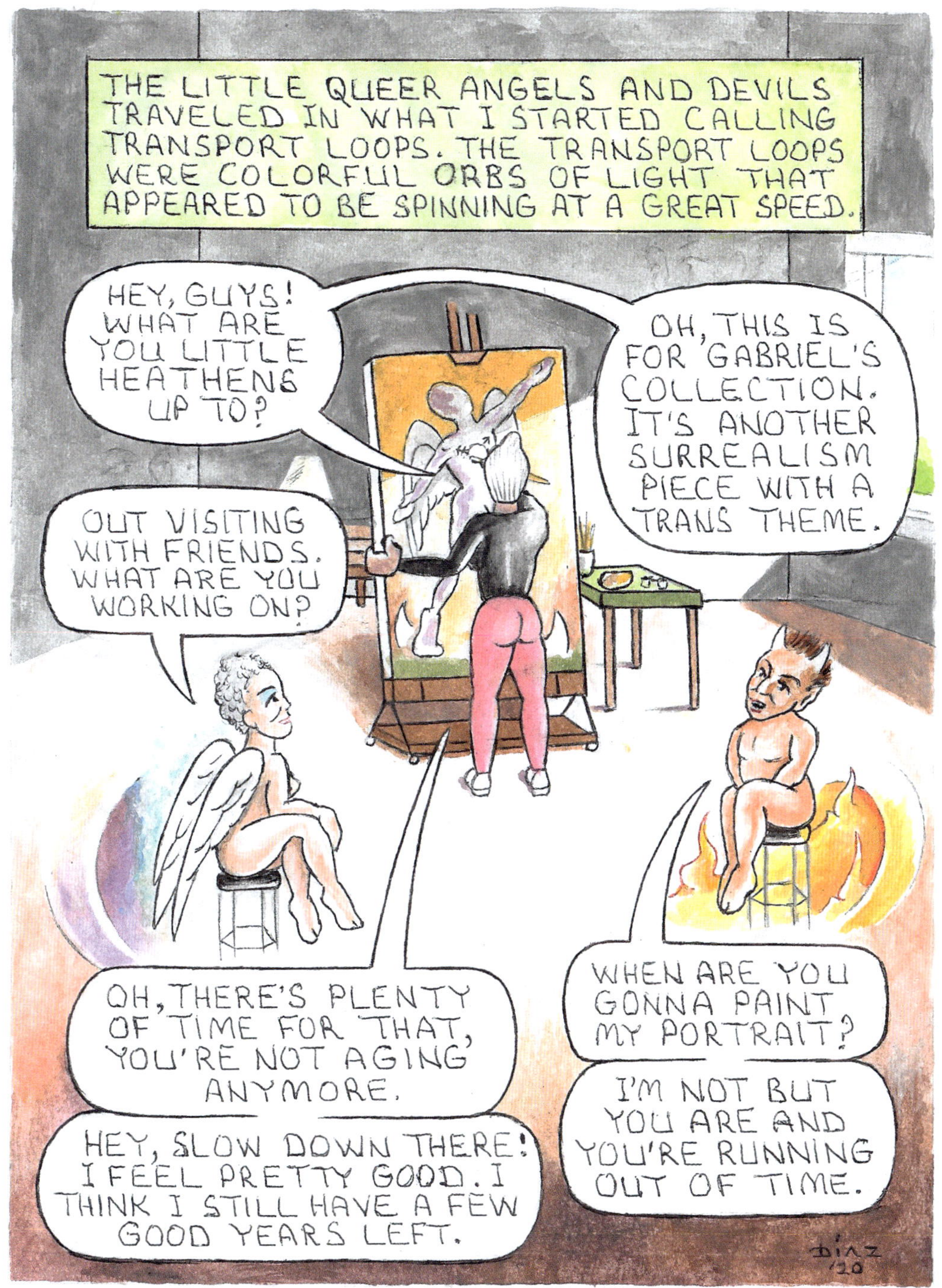
THE LITTLE QUEER ANGELS AND DEVILS TRAVELED IN WHAT I STARTED CALLING TRANSPORT LOOPS. THE TRANSPORT LOOPS WERE COLORFUL ORBS OF LIGHT THAT APPEARED TO BE SPINNING AT A GREAT SPEED.
HEY, GUYS! WHAT ARE YOU LITTLE HEATHENS UP TO?
OUT VISITING WITH FRIENDS. WHAT ARE YOU WORKING ON?
OH, THIS IS FOR GABRIEL'S COLLECTION. IT'S ANOTHER SURREALISM PIECE WITH A TRANS THEME.
WHEN ARE YOU GONNA PAINT MY PORTRAIT?
OH, THERE'S PLENTY OF TIME FOR THAT, YOU'RE NOT AGING ANYMORE.
I'M NOT BUT YOU ARE AND YOU'RE RUNNING OUT OF TIME.
HEY, SLOW DOWN THERE! I FEEL PRETTY GOOD. I THINK I STILL HAVE A FEW GOOD YEARS LEFT.
DÍAZ '20

85 STERILIZATION RECOMMENDATION LETTER FOR MARIA RAMIREZ, JULY 1, 1940

More than 60,000 people underwent compulsory sterilizations in the United States in the twentieth century. From 1907 to 1937, thirty-two states passed eugenic laws that authorized the sterilization of people deemed "unfit" and "undesirable." Most were poor and labeled as disabled. Initially the majority of those sterilized were white men, but over time, women, especially women of color, were targeted for the procedure.

In 1940 Maria Ramirez was one of the approximately 20,000 persons sterilized in California, the most aggressive sterilizing state in the nation. She was one of 4,389 patients in the Stockton State Hospital, one of the 1,001 recommended for sterilization in California in 1940, and one of 209 in that facility subjected to reproductive surgery that year.

Maria was sterilized in a hospital for the "insane" and labeled as abnormal based on her gender nonconformity. She was not alone. In all the states that passed sterilization laws, concerns about sexual deviance, promiscuity, and homosexuality—all seen as largely hereditary in origin—spurred reproductive coercion. Young girls fond of trysts with neighborhood boys were hauled in by juvenile authorities, given IQ tests, and often sent to homes for the "feebleminded" where sterilization awaited. Men who engaged in what doctors viewed as excessive masturbation troubled white middle class heteronormativity and were candidates for state-directed vasectomy.

Authorities expressed both bewilderment and scorn for those, like Maria, who challenged cisgendered binaries and exhibited queer sexualities and sensibilities.

There are two pieces of documentation related to Maria's sterilization and they reveal insights about her pathway into the institution and the disdain with which she was treated.

Maria was thirty years old, single, and originally from Arizona. Although she had never been hospitalized before being committed to Stockton, she was diagnosed with "psychopathic personality with psychosis." This alliterative yet convoluted diagnosis marked Maria as mentally ill, delusional, and potentially a danger to others if not herself. The box checked on the state form to deprive her of reproductive liberty was "perversion or marked departure from normal mentality."

Racialized as "Mexican-Indian," Maria had two years of schooling and had worked as a dishwasher and farm laborer in Arizona, and probably also in central California. Clearly poor and trying to make ends meet, at times with sex work, she had been jailed four times for vagrancy. The catalyst for her commitment to Stockton was her appearance in the yard of someone (perhaps a neighbor), where she walked "around with a bunch of flowers" and was derided as confused.

The person offended by Maria's benign infraction likely contacted the authorities who made the initial psychiatric diagnosis and eventually labeled Maria a "passive sodomist," noting that she wore "feminine clothing" and used "lipstick and other feminine devices." In the homophobic and eugenic logic of the time, Maria was viewed as an effeminate sexual invert with a fixed psychological and genetic constitution who required state and medical management.

Sterilization was one of the state's harshest punishments for being poor, Brown, and queer in mid-twentieth-century California. Notably, Maria was sterilized not because she desired permanent birth control or even because a relative requested the operation, but because Stockton's medical superintendent, Dr. Margaret Smyth, wanted to apply the full force of the state's legal and medical authority on Maria's sexual-reproductive body and future.

Maria was not sterilized because of her reproductive past, but because her trans-ness was seen as undesirable and threatening. A vasectomy not only would shutter the possibility of passing deleterious genes to her children, but, in accordance with some doctors' beliefs about the therapeutic benefits of "asexualization," the surgery also might quell her queer predilections.

Although the letter Dr. Smyth sent to Sacramento asking the director of the Department of Institutions for approval refers to Maria as him/his and a "man," it is striking that Maria is the only name used in the documents. Thus, there is a wisp of onomastic justice for Maria in these harrowing documents.

We don't know what happened to Maria while she was incarcerated in Stockton, if she was released, or if she was able to find queer or trans community in subsequent decades. I'd like to imagine a future for her, outside the clutches of the state's eugenic program, where she presented as she desired, bedecked with lipstick and flowers.

—Alexandra Minna Stern

▸ Letter recommending the sterilization of Maria Ramirez/Ramierez, Stockton State Hospital, California, July 1, 1940. Reproduction from microfilm held at the Sterilization and Social Justice Lab, University of California, Los Angeles. Original document housed in the Department of Mental Hygiene, Sterilization Records, 1925–1954, California State Archives, Office of the Secretary of State, Sacramento

AARON J. ROSANOFF, M.D.
DIRECTOR OF INSTITUTIONS

CULBERT L. OLSON
GOVERNOR OF CALIFORNIA

MARGARET H. SMYTH, M.D.
MEDICAL DIRECTOR
AND SUPERINTENDENT

STATE OF CALIFORNIA
DEPARTMENT OF INSTITUTIONS

STOCKTON STATE HOSPITAL
STOCKTON, CALIFORNIA

July 1, 1940

Aaron J. Rosanoff, M.D., Director
Department of Institutions
Sacramento, California

Re: MARIA RAMIREZ

Dear Dr. Rosanoff:

The above named was committed to this hospital May 31, 1940 upon the following complaint: "Entered the yard of petitioner and walked around with a bunch of flowers in his hand; appeared to be confused." He was found to be suffering from Psychopathic Personality with Psychosis.

This patient is a Mexican-Indian born in Arizona, on May 10, 1910. Two years schooling. Dishwasher and farm laborer. Denies liquor and drugs. Arrested and jailed four times for vagrancy. No previous hospital record.

This man admits being a passive sodomist, wearing feminine clothing, using lipstick and other feminine devices. He accepts his homosexuality and is resigned to it. Admits accepting money for his sexual activity.

It is the opinion of the staff that this patient should be sterilized. We have been unable to locate any relative of whom to obtain permission for the operation. Enclosed is Recommendation and Approval for Vasectomy for the purpose of Sterilization which I ask that you kindly sign and return, so we may proceed.

Very truly yours,

Margaret Smyth

MARGARET H. SMYTH, M.D.
MEDICAL DIRECTOR AND
SUPERINTENDENT

MHS:MF

86 CASSILS, *PISSED*, 2017

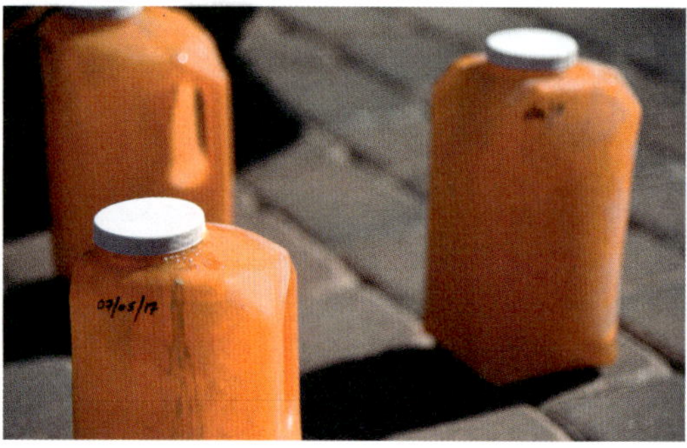

Cassils, *PISSED: Collection Day Image No. 50* (Various Locations, Los Angeles), 2017

Cassils's *PISSED* is a sculpture, an endurance performance, a sound installation, and (most of all) a protest. It was created in response to the Trump administration's spiteful, reactionary decision in 2017 to rescind an Obama-era executive order that endorsed the rights of transgender students to use the bathroom of the gender they know themselves to be. As an immediate and visceral reply, Cassils resolved to hold their urine, publicly: for 200 days, they retained and stored all of it. Cassils's daily labor over this half-year involved the conversations (some curious, some sympathetic, some antagonistic) that resulted from them carrying a bright orange medical bottle for this purpose. In the end, Cassils retained 255 bottles, each of them having served as a highly visual disruption of the public realm and a reminder of the privacy and dignity that trans people were denied. That is, *PISSED* is also a social endurance performance of having the awkward and impassioned dialogues about why only some people had the right to privacy while others had their bodily functions policed and outlawed. This grew to be a communal effort, as friends and collaborators loaned their refrigerators to store bottles and (when the artist had to leave the country and was unable to carry liquids) contributed their own urine in Cassils's stead.

The dispersed yet vital political work of those conversations with friends and strangers became confrontationally materialized in the final sculpture and installation, the center of which is an imposing acrylic cube containing 200 gallons of urine. It takes the austere and simplified Minimalist form of the cube as a means to activate that movement's association with "theatricality" in which the reductive art object waits for the viewer's interaction to activate it. *PISSED*, too, waits; it retains waste until it has become too colossal to be ignored. Cassils exhibits this cubic sculpture against a backdrop of the 255 medical containers that they had used over the previous months (each meticulously dated). A sound installation accompanies these visual components. In it, recorded testimony from the Virginia School Board and the Fourth US Circuit Court of Appeals plays from speakers in the corners of the room. The testimony, much of it injuriously negative, is drawn from then high school student Gavin Grimm's lawsuit for his right to use his appropriate bathroom. This two-hour sonic component, with its disembodied voices, ensured that it is impossible to see Cassils's installation as a merely formal exercise—*PISSED* stands defiant against the hateful and ignorant opinions that swirled around it. Even though it employs abstraction, *PISSED* insists on the political and personal urgencies at stake. Human waste is obsessively evacuated, yet this work makes it monumental and emblematic. The experience of holding oneself when one cannot find a bathroom became, in Cassils's work, a mutinous act of resistance. From the hundreds of conversations that accompanied Cassils's daily lifework to the massive cube that makes visible the bodily processes we are told to hide, *PISSED* refuses to be out of sight.

—David J. Getsy

▸ Cassils, *PISSED, Installation Image No. 9* (Monumental, Ronald Feldman Gallery, NYC), 2017. 200 gallons of urine, 18,000 grams of boric acid, and acrylic, 38 × 38 × 38 in. (96.5 × 96.5 × 96.5 cm). Leslie-Lohman Museum of Art

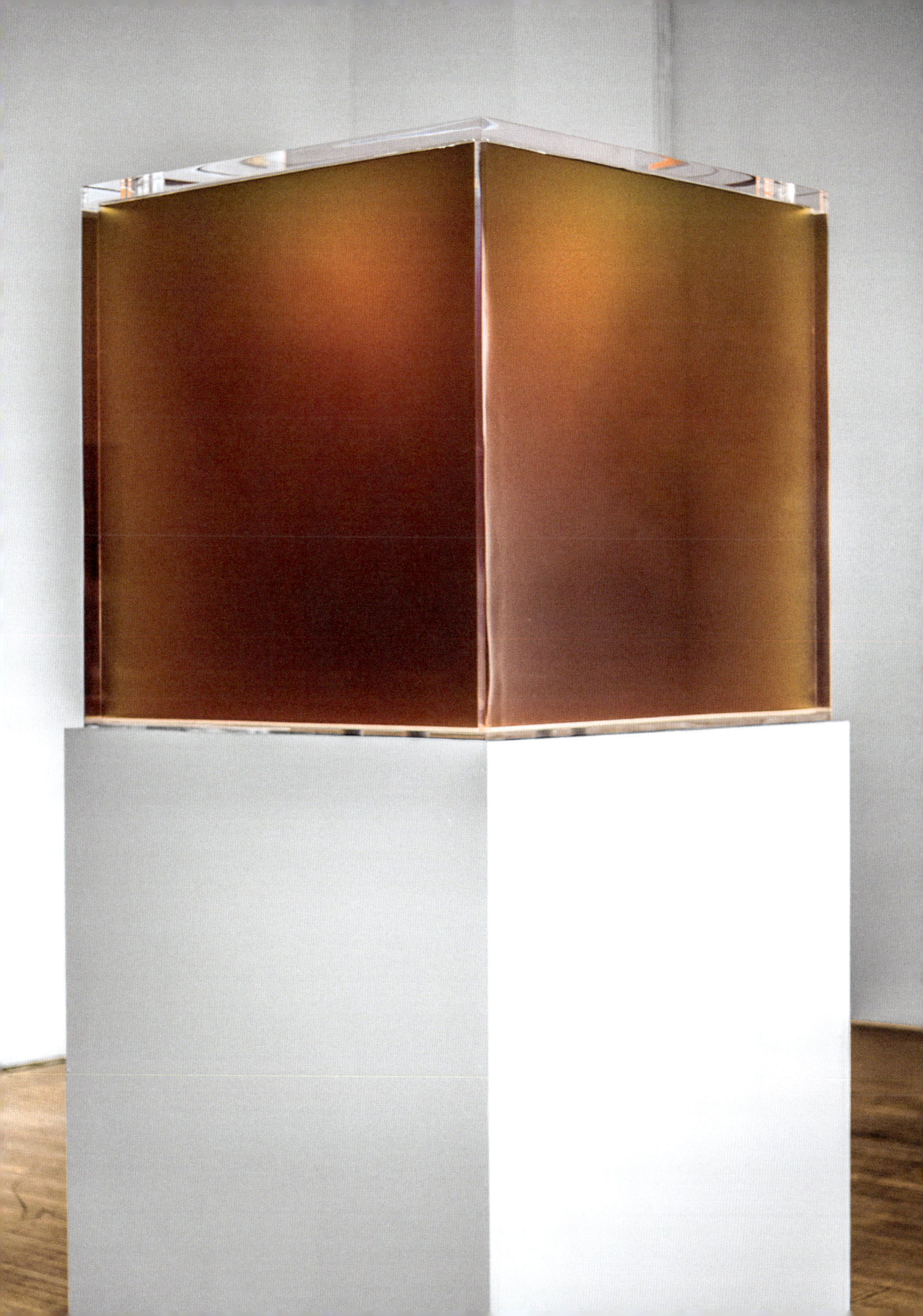

87 MILLIE WILSON, *FAUVE SEMBLANT: PETER (A YOUNG ENGLISH GIRL)*, 1989

She was a woman. She dressed as a man. She was authoritative and uncompromising. She was romantic and domestic. She was born working class. She was acclaimed in stylish circles. She became famous. She withdrew from the public. She was a mannish renegade. She wanted to marry the love of her life. She was a flawless technician. She neglected to paint for years at a time. She risked everything to be an artist. She gave up her art for love. She flaunted her sexuality. She accepted various inversion theories. She was scornful of art schools. She was generous in her support of genuine talent. She was a misfit. She continually sought to be recognized. She was dangerous in her intentions. She was a favorite of the wives of distinguished men. She longed for nature. She could live only in the city. She wanted autonomy. She was haunted by family ties. She generated excitement. She secretly wished for tranquility. She was flagrantly promiscuous. She insisted on integrity in the most mundane transactions. She worked very quickly. She painted with exquisite precision. She had a reckless temper and was arrogant. She was deeply moved by the plight of the unfortunate.

She was a disaffected expatriate. She found that certain neighborhoods allowed for refuge in unconventional salons. She was subject to the anxiety that her alienation from art history instilled. She was engaged by the central debates of the period. She was concerned with the invention of a lesbian aesthetic. She was irrelevant to the male avant-garde's nostalgia for the women of antiquity. She endured a loneliness particular to those erased from history. She devised aesthetic strategies grounded in mutuality. She could never match the devasting wit of the intelligentsia. She displayed on occasion the gift of retort. She was described by male critics as the heroine of modernism. She was all but absent from the accounts of the period. She espoused the rhetoric of collectivity. She demanded that each of her lovers be all things to her. She escaped abroad to anonymous adventures. She longed for delight in love and the perfect union. She was the target of sexual speculation. She did not resemble case studies of the consequences of unnatural attachments. She was accused by her male contemporaries of displaying a morbid desire. She found the courts of law would not acknowledge the existence of a desire like hers.

—Millie Wilson

This text appeared as the introductory text panel for Wilson's installation *Fauve Semblant: Peter (A Young English Girl)*, presented at LACE (Los Angeles Contemporary Exhibitions), 1989.

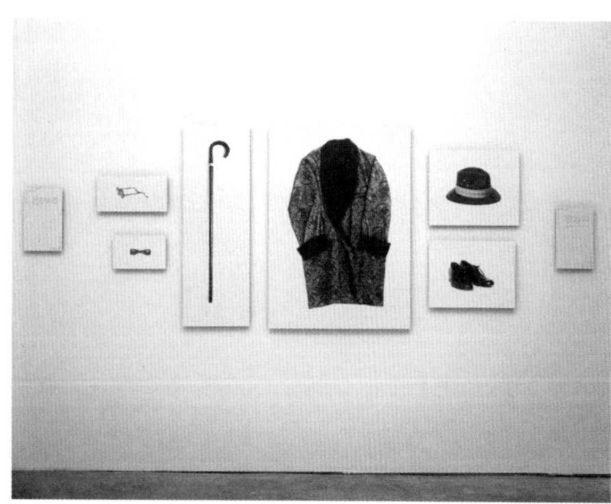

▲
Millie Wilson, *Cross-dressing*, 1989. Gelatin silver prints and text, dimensions variable

Millie Wilson's artistic practice is rooted in imagining queer futures through fictive extrapolation and (purposeful) historical misinterpretation. For her 1989 installation Fauve Semblant: Peter (A Young English Girl)*, she invented the persona of an early-twentieth century lesbian painter in the mold of artists Romaine Brooks and Gluck. The installation's subtitle is a direct allusion to Brooks's 1923–24 portrait of Gluck, a gender-nonconforming British artist known within avant-garde artistic and literary circles in the 1920s as Peter. Both Brooks and Gluck inspired the backstory, predilection for crossdressing, and uncompromising demeanor of Wilson's Peter. Using the conventions of museological display, Wilson's installation purported to rediscover Peter's life and work, presenting her only surviving painting alongside archival images and photographs of her clothes. Wilson appeared at the exhibition's entrance dressed dapperly in an aggrandizing photographic portrait as Peter, reproduced here. While Wilson uses the female pronoun repeatedly in this text, numerous components of the exhibition's didactics and installation alluded to Peter's gender transgressions. In one of the faux-exhibition wall texts, Wilson's Peter reflected on their masculine attire, "I am thriving in this new attire. Incredibly exciting. Everyone loves it."*

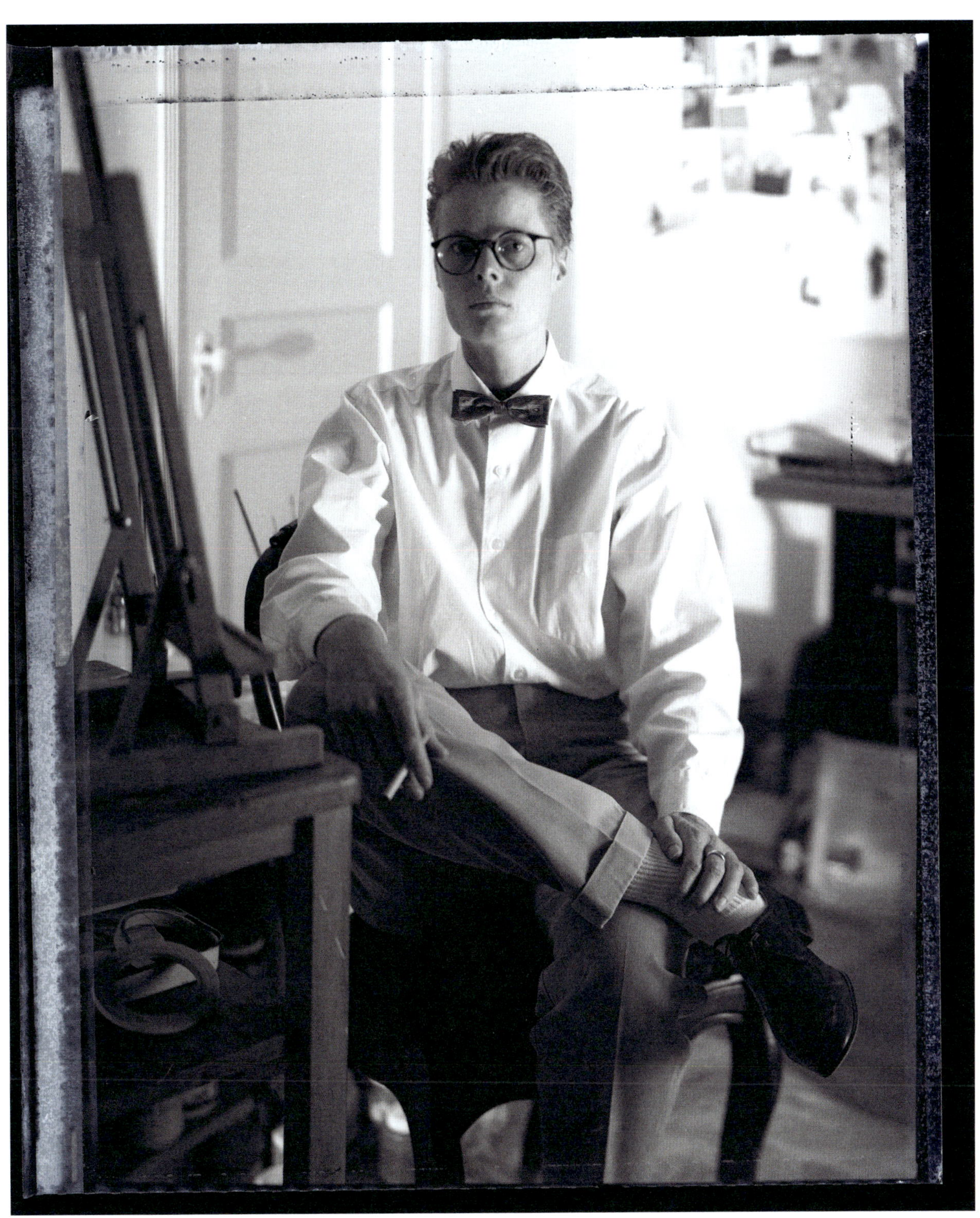

▼
Portrait of Millie Wilson as Peter for *Fauve Semblant: Peter (A Young English Girl)*, 1989. Photo by Catherine Opie

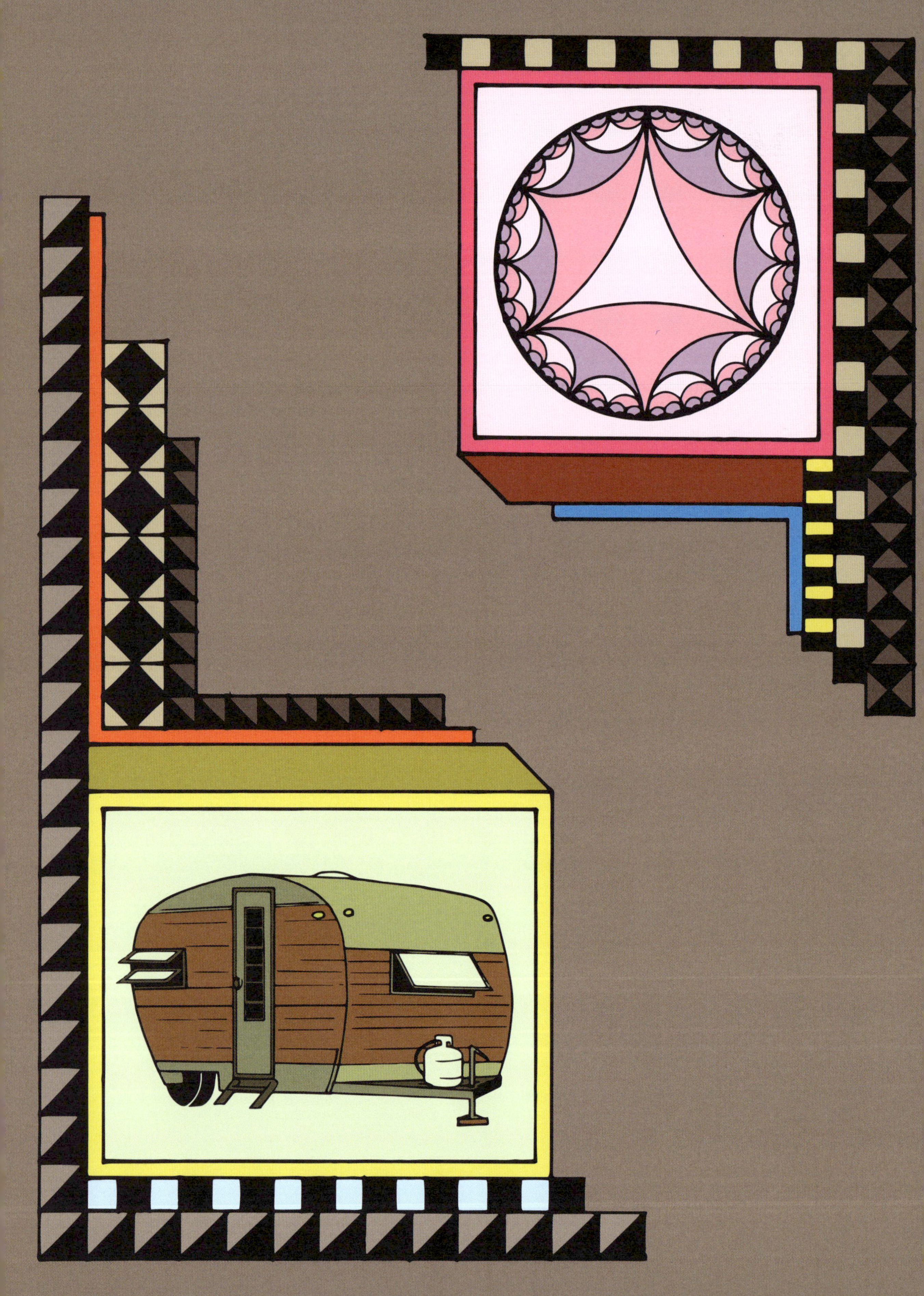

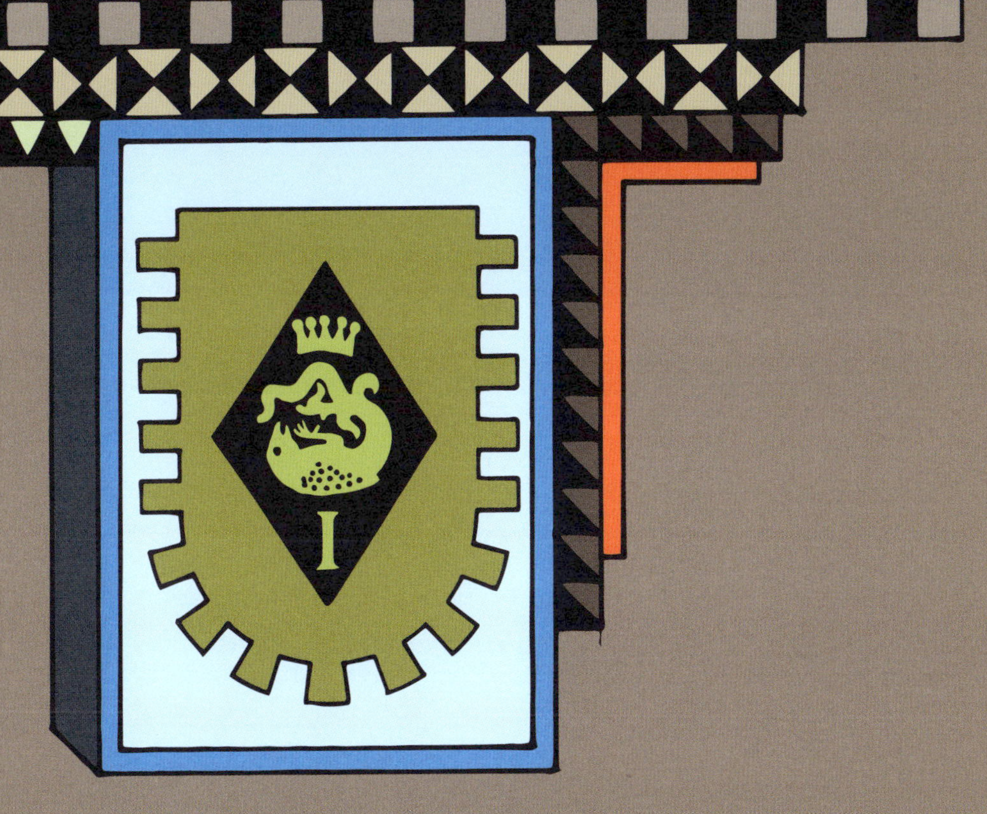

SPACES

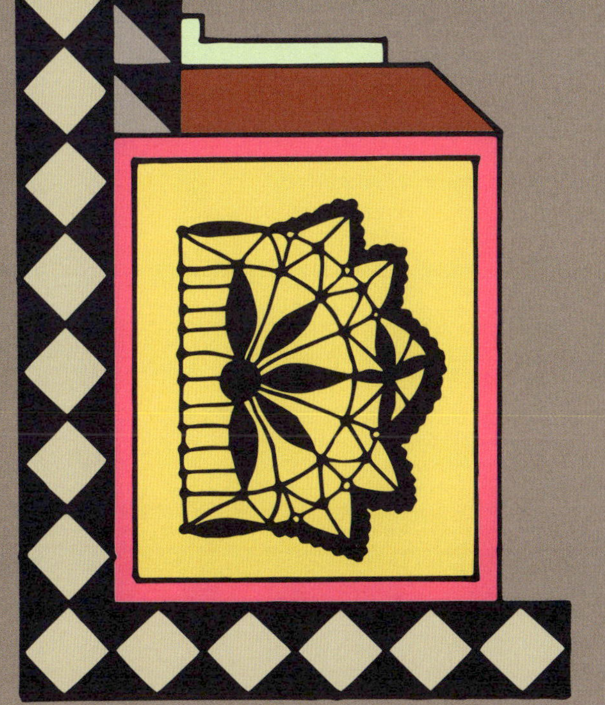

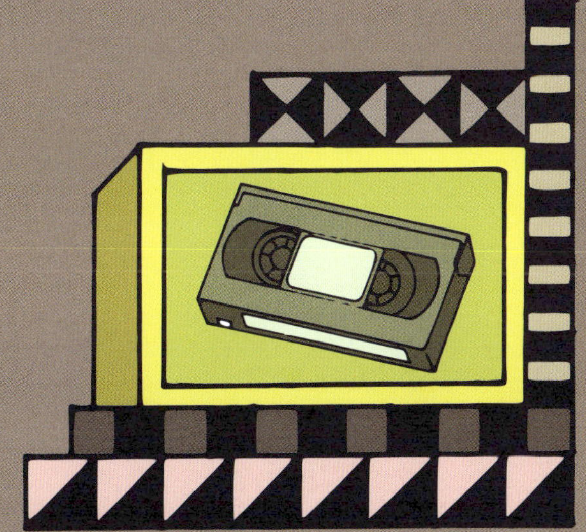

88 GLITS 1 SOUTH, 2020–PRESENT

Standing three stories tall in a tree-filled section of Queens just south of sprawling Forest Park, GLITS 1 South is, in many ways, like nothing that came before it. The residential apartment building—opened by GLITS, or Gays and Lesbians Living in a Transgender Society, towards the end of 2020—is the first Black trans-owned housing community in New York City.[1] The crowd-funding campaign that led to its purchase was also quite notable, as it inarguably exceeded expectations as to what is and is not possible when it comes to organized digital fundraising for Black trans-led initiatives. GLITS managed to clear its lofty $1 million goal in only one week back in June of 2020[2]—a moment in time concurrent with both the early weeks of the George Floyd rebellion and the first Pride month of the ongoing COVID-19 pandemic—allowing the grassroots organization to make a down payment on the $2 million property the following month.[3]

Yet, GLITS 1 South is not without precedent. It exists within a storied lineage of trans people devising ways to keep members of their communities housed and safe—a history that spans all of STAR House's many iterations in 1970s Manhattan, Brooklyn's Transy House in the 1990s and 2000s, as well as countless contemporaneous efforts, including but not limited to: My Sistah's House in Memphis, Trans Housing Atlanta Program, House of Tulip in New Orleans, Our Trans Home SF, For the Gworls' rent fundraiser parties in New York, House of Rebirth in Dallas, and so on. "They aren't taking care of us, so we have to take care of us," GLITS founder and executive director Ceyenne Doroshow, a legendary figure in New York's trans and sex worker organizing circles, once told me in an interview for *Teen Vogue*.[4] "We are all that we have."

The GLITS house is made up of twelve apartments plus an additional non-residential unit used for social events and educational courses. Unlike many of the aforementioned housing programs, residency is not strictly based on need and available resources. "This is not a shelter," Doroshow clarified in a 2021 interview with *Time*.[5] "This is not emergency housing." Prospective residents must fill out an application for GLITS's Leadership Academy in which they are asked about goals they have for themselves, goals they have for their communities, and how stable housing at GLITS 1 South would help them be able to meet those goals. "This is about building leaders," Doroshow told *Time*, "creating people that can take the lead, can take charge, and when I'm gone they can do this work."

In the future, GLITS hopes to expand even further by opening a community-designed, patient-centered health clinic somewhere in the five boroughs. Doroshow has even considered buying property in Upstate New York to start a farm. "I would love to see a trans-owned farmers market, a distillery run by trans girls," she told me in a 2020 interview for *GQ*.[6] "They're all just dreams, but the dreams are starting to manifest and happen." The importance of dedicated community space is evident in Doroshow's work, from GLITS's half-decade of securing housing for trans people in need to the organization's most recent efforts to preserve Riis Beach, a vital cultural and historical place for queer New Yorkers.[7] For now, though, there is GLITS 1 South with its red-brick exterior, green roof, and purple door.

—Harron Walker

1. Max Parrot, "LGBTQ+ Activist Buys Woodhaven Building," *Queens Chronicle*, December 3, 2020, accessed January 31, 2023, https://www.qchron.com/editions/south/lgbtq-activist-buys-woodhaven-building/article_17e48859-6c6d-51d3-a86c-72ead4cc84e8.html.
2. Río Sofia, "We Raised $1,000,000 in Week One," Instagram, June 15, 2020, accessed January 31, 2023, https://www.instagram.com/p/CBeMulgjf9m/?hl=en.
3. Harron Walker, "The Godmother of the Moment," *GQ*, August 27, 2020, accessed January 31, 2023, https://www.gq.com/story/ceyenne-doroshow-glits-founder-profile.
4. Ceyenne Doroshow, as told to Harron Walker, "Black Trans Lives Matter March: Ceyenne Doroshow Reflects," *Teen Vogue*, June 17, 2020, accessed January 31, 2023, https://www.teenvogue.com/story/black-trans-lives-matter-march-ceyenne-doroshow.
5. Cady Lang, "'This Is Not a Shelter.' Ceyenne Doroshow on Providing Free, Safe Space for LGBTQ People in Need," *Time*, March 3, 2021, accessed January 31, 2023, https://time.com/5942121/ceyenne-doroshow-interview/.
6. Harron Walker, "The Godmother of the Moment."
7. Learn more about preserving Riis Beach from The Audrey Lorde Project at https://alp.org/we-keep-riis-beach.

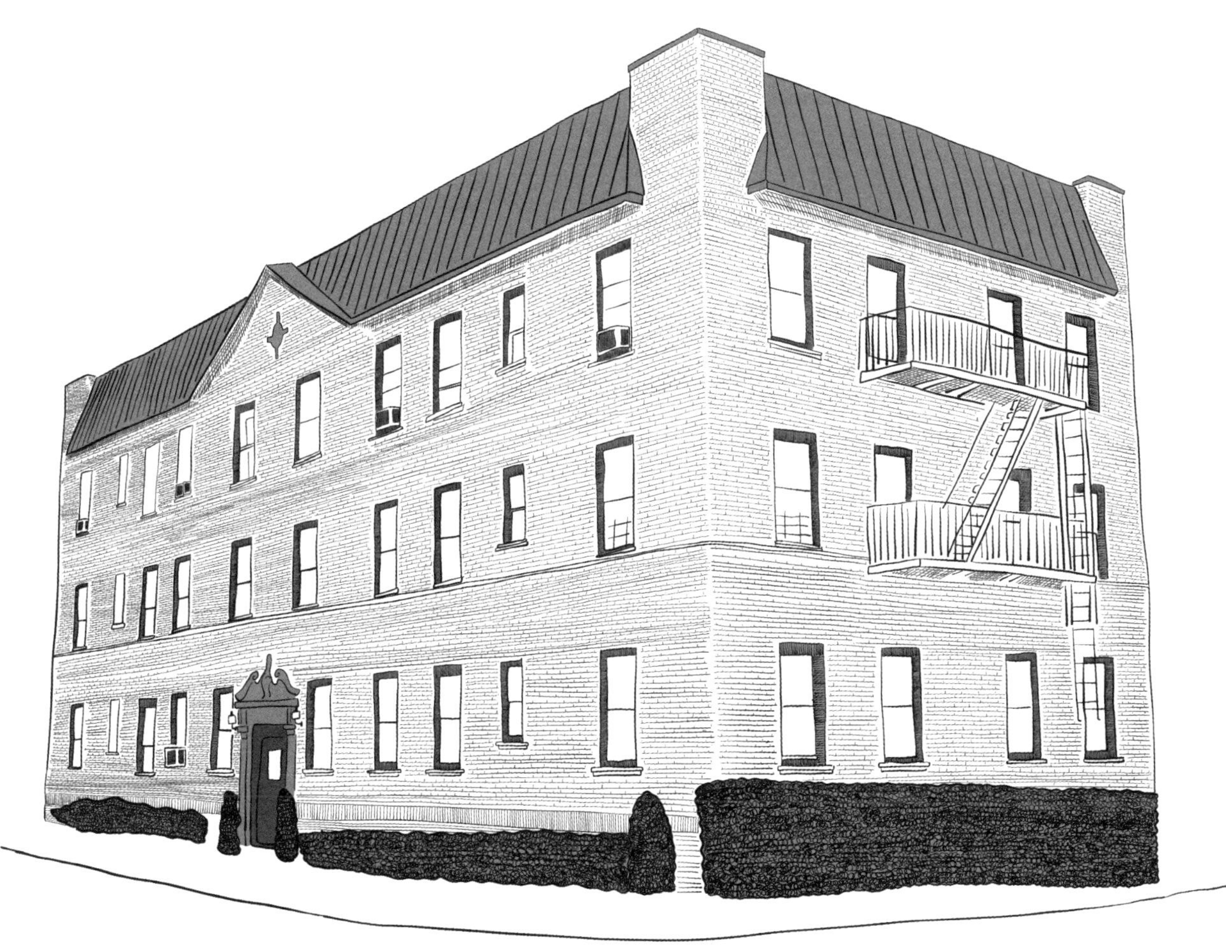

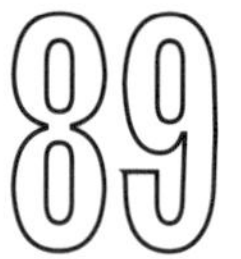

MARK AGUHAR, *LITANIES TO MY HEAVENLY BROWN BODY*, 2011

FUCK YOUR WHITENESS
FUCK YOUR BEAUTY
FUCK YOUR CHEST HAIR
FUCK YOUR BEARD
FUCK YOUR PRIVILEGE
FUCK THAT YOU AREN'T MADE TO FEEL
SHAME ALWAYS
FUCK YOUR THINNESS
FUCK YOUR MUSCLES
FUCK YOUR ATTRACTIVE FATNESS
FUCK YOUR SHAMING ME FOR NOTHING
FUCK YOUR ACCUSATIONS THAT I
PRODUCE SHAME
FUCK YOUR READING ME AS A
CARICATURE
FUCK YOUR DESTRUCTION OF MY
PERSONHOOD
FUCK YOUR MARGINALIZATION OF MY
IDENTITY
FUCK YOUR JUDGING ME FOR SELF CARE
FUCK YOUR ABILITY TO BE ASSERTIVE
FUCK YOUR LACK OF SOCIALIZATION TO
BE A SUBMISSIVE
FUCK YOUR ASKING ME TO PRODUCE
SAFETY FOR YOU AND NOT MYSELF
FUCK THE AMOUNT OF EFFORT I EXERT
TO GET LESS THAN ENOUGH
CONSIDERATION
FUCK THAT THE AMOUNT OF SPACE I
TAKE UP IN THE WORLD IS
CONSTANTLY QUESTIONED
FUCK THAT PEOPLE THINK I'M A SLUT
FUCK THAT YOU CAN DEMAND
ATTENTION
FUCK THAT I'M WILLING TO GIVE YOU
WHAT I CAN'T HAVE
FUCK THAT YOUR VALUES AND YOUR
ACTIONS NEVER MATCH UP
WHEN IT COMES TO ME
FUCK THAT I CAN'T EXPECT ANYTHING
FROM ANYONE
FUCK THAT THE AMOUNT OF WORK I
PUT INTO THE BEAUTY OF MY
INTELLECT AND MY TALENT IS
STILL NEVER ENOUGH

AMEN

▸
Bishakh Som, *Litany for Mark*, 2022. Watercolor and ink on paper, 10 × 7½ in. (25.4 × 19.1 cm)

BLESSED ARE THE SISSIES
BLESSED ARE THE BOI DYKES
BLESSED ARE THE PEOPLE OF COLOR
MY BELOVED KITH AND KIN
BLESSED ARE THE TRANS
BLESSED ARE THE HIGH FEMMES
BLESSED ARE THE SEX WORKERS
BLESSED ARE THE AUTHENTIC
BLESSED ARE THE DIS-IDENTIFIERS
BLESSED ARE THE GENDER ILLUSIONISTS
BLESSED ARE THE NON-NORMATIVE
BLESSED ARE THE GENDERQUEERS
BLESSED ARE THE KINKSTERS
BLESSED ARE THE DISABLED
BLESSED ARE THE HOT FAT GIRLS
BLESSED ARE THE WEIRDO-QUEERS
BLESSED IS THE SPECTRUM
BLESSED IS CONSENT
BLESSED IS RESPECT
BLESSED ARE THE BELOVED WHO I
DIDN'T DESCRIBE, I COULDN'T
DESCRIBE, WILL LEARN TO
DESCRIBE AND RESPECT AND LOVE

AMEN

—Mark Aguhar

Transcription of Mark Aguhar's *Litanies to my heavenly brown body*, originally posted in two parts to the artist's Tumblr "Blogging for Brown Gurls," January 15 and 17, 2011, https://calloutqueen-blog.tumblr.com.

Mark Aguhar (1987–2012) was a transgender Filipinx American visual artist, activist, and writer. She was widely recognized in the early 2010s as the Tumblr and YouTuber user "calloutqueen," known for her sharp, and often humorous, takes on beauty ideals, fat shaming, racism, and femmephobia. Many of Aguhar's Tumblr posts were concise and reflective, a strategy she also explored in her visual art; her frequently reposted work Making Looks *(2011) presents the handwritten declaration "I'd Rather Be Beautiful Than Male" in a gradient of bright blue, purple, and pink. In this artwork, comic artist Bishakh Som pays loving tribute to Aguhar and her legacy.*

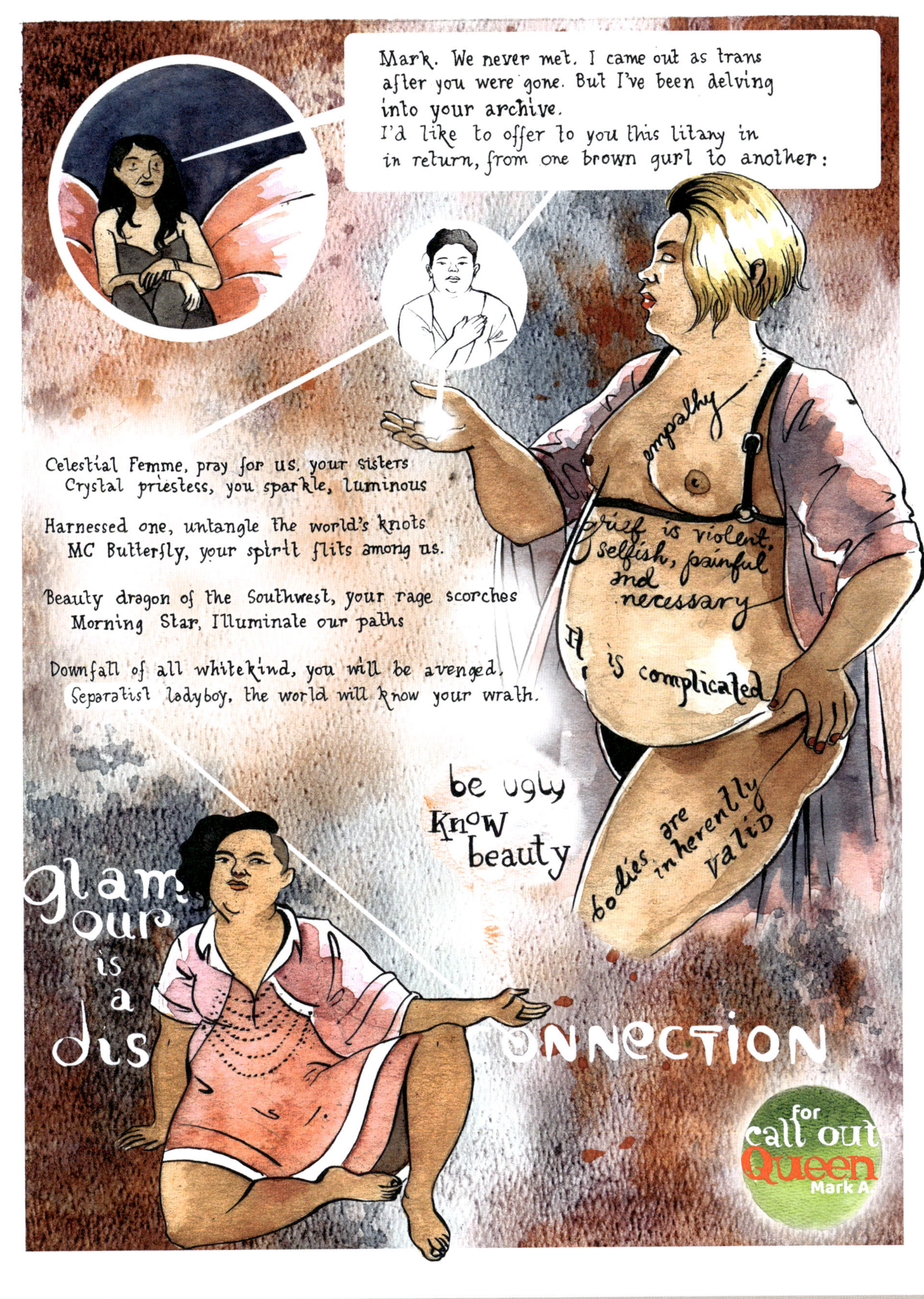
Mark. We never met. I came out as trans after you were gone. But I've been delving into your archive.
I'd like to offer to you this litany in in return, from one brown gurl to another:
Celestial Femme, pray for us, your sisters
Crystal priestess, you sparkle, luminous
Harnessed one, untangle the world's knots
MC Butterfly, your spirit flits among us.
Beauty dragon of the Southwest, your rage scorches
Morning Star, Illuminate our paths
Downfall of all whitekind, you will be avenged.
Separatist ladyboy, the world will know your wrath.
empathy
grief is violent, selfish, painful and necessary
It is complicated
be ugly
Know beauty
bodies are inherently valid
glamour is a dis
onnection
for call out Queen
Mark A.

90 "CAMP TRANS: FOR HUMYN-BORN HUMYNS" SIGN, 1994

Raised for the first time at the 1994 gathering of Camp Trans, the hand-painted "CAMP TRANS: For Humyn-Born Humyns" sign helped solidify the annual summer gathering convened to protest the prohibition of trans women attendees at the Michigan Womyn's Music Festival (MWMF); the slogan on the sign became the protest's tag line for some time. Then in its third year, the camp had originated as a small action in the wake of the 1991 harassment and eviction of trans camper Nancy Jean Burkholder from the festival. It was the first time that the festival's "womyn-born womyn-only" policy was enforced; indeed, many festivalgoers had no idea that such a policy even existed and that trans women were not welcome on the festival grounds. Burkholder herself had attended in the past and her time had been pleasurable and without incident. After the traumatizing experience of a blindsiding interrogation about her gender, followed by being abruptly removed from the festival, Burkholder and some close friends decided to return the following year. Camping outside the festival gates, they distributed flyers to the attendees with information about the obscure policy while providing truthful information to counteract the myths and lies that propped it up.

This small action garnered much support from women attending the festival; Burkholder and her friends returned the following year to again challenge the festival's anti-trans policy while demystifying gender and transsexuality for the cisgendered, feminist attendees. It was in 1994, under the leadership of activist and author Riki Wilchins, that this small and somewhat earnest response transformed into Camp Trans, a formidable, organized resistance, provocatively stationed directly across from the MWMF gates. And now they had an elegant sign, the letters in a stylized font with a slightly hippie vibe, not polished enough to look slick, but far more artful than a simple, homemade protest sign. The sign asserted beyond a doubt that something was *happening* there on the other side of the road, that people were organizing; this was more than the grievance of a single person. An injustice had been done to a community, and the community had arrived to condemn, protest, and educate. Along with the sign and official name, the 1994 Camp Trans boasted nearly thirty attendees ranging in age from four years old to seventy and included author/activist Leslie Feinberg and their poet/activist partner Minnie Bruce Pratt.

Clearly a riff on MWMF's "womyn-born womyn" clause—a phrase which blasts a gender essentialist philosophy while simultaneously making a fuss about having to share the m-a-n with m-e-n—Camp Trans's "humyn-born humyns" motto worked in multiple ways. By lampooning the festival's language, it one-upped the so-called "radicalness" of this radical feminist stance, showing that the urge towards separatism had clearly gone too far, entering discrimination territory. The womyn of MWMF had lost their "humynity," and were now pushing oppression on people with even less cultural power than themselves. Barring trans women, who arguably needed the safety of a women-only nature bath more than anyone, was inhumane.

With its call to recognize a common humanity, the Camp Trans sign positioned support for trans people as part of a basic regimen of progressive, humanistic ethics—antiwar, antinuke, pro-whale, etc. The lettering also recalls the typefaces of the Arts and Crafts movement, giving the sign a classical flair. It no doubt called out to the very many lesbian craftspeople who flooded the festival each year to sell their wares, for whom such an aesthetic was perennial, shifting only slightly to accommodate the 1970s, 1980s, and the 1990s.

At the time of my own trip to Camp Trans, in 2003, the protest had grown so large that it had to be relocated a bit down the road to accommodate the numerous campers. The "CAMP TRANS: For Humyn-Born Humyns" sign had been retired—maybe damaged from its years flying in the dirt and dust, maybe leaving with the older guard of activists who'd made it, as a newer group of organizers with a different aesthetic took over. In 2003 the T-shirts for sale to benefit the effort were designed by comic artist and writer Ariel Schrag. I imagine the sign, lovingly mended and unavoidably dingy, rolled into itself and sitting in an attic, waiting for its eventual discovery as an iconic piece of trans history.

—Michelle Tea

▼
Group photograph of members of Camp Trans across the street from the Michigan Womyn's Music Festival, 1994. Photo by Mariette Pathy Allen

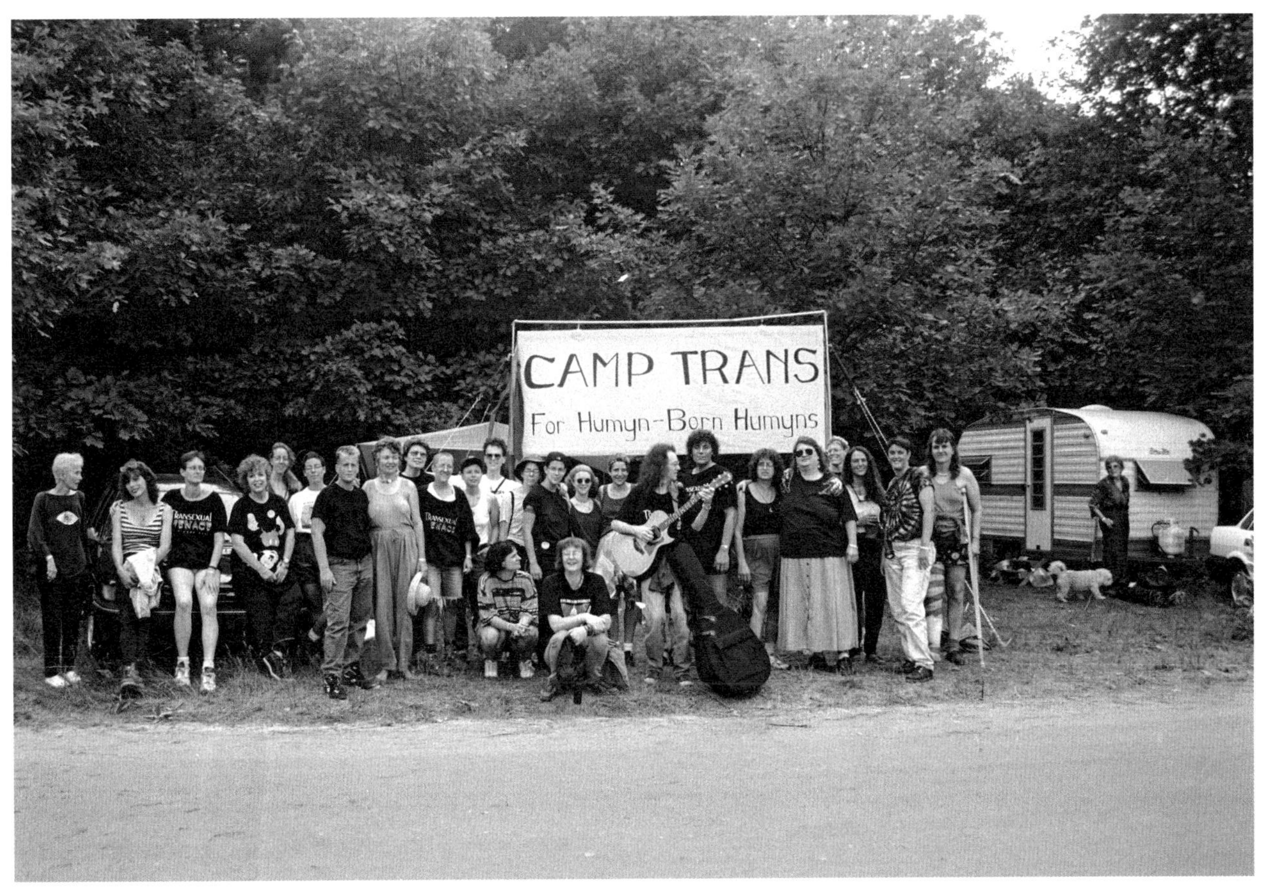

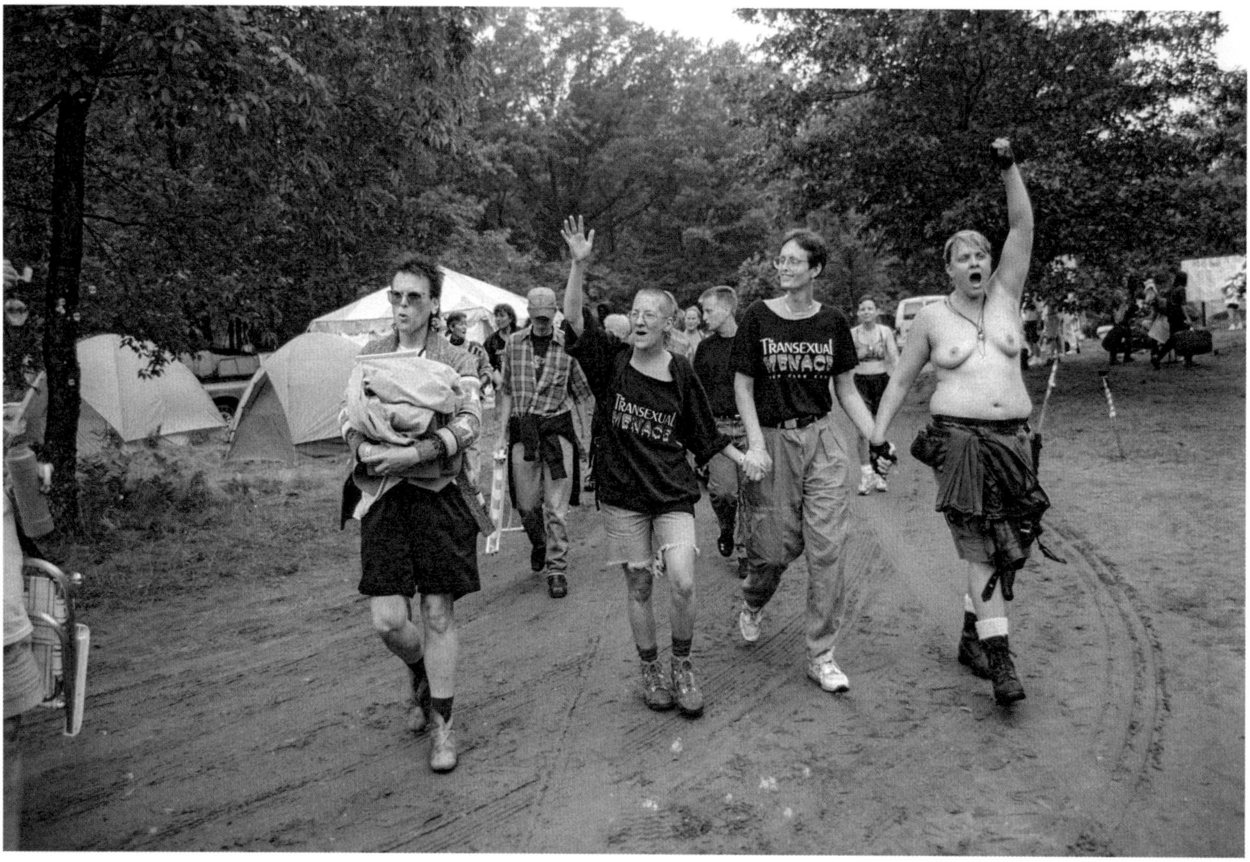
TRANSEXUAL MENACE
TRANSEXUAL MENACE

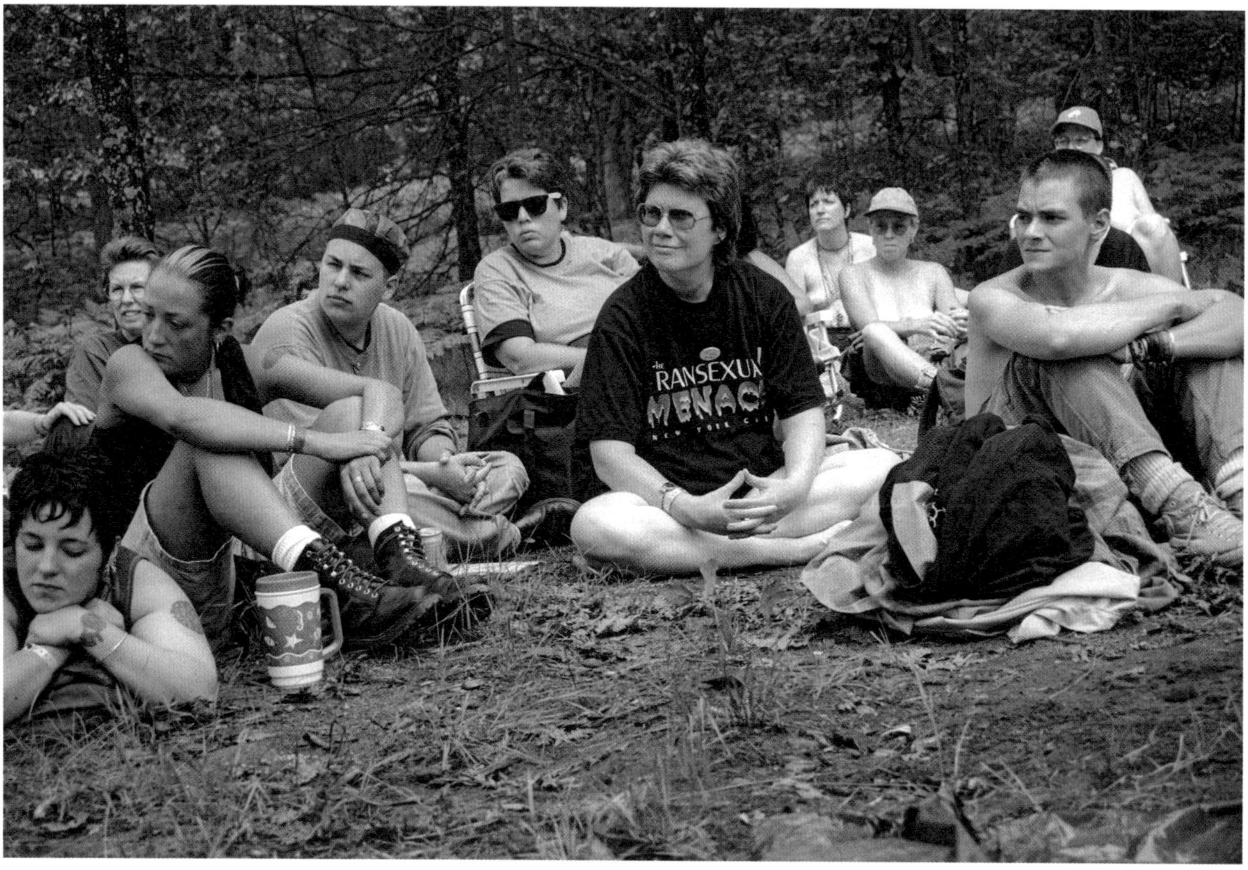
THE TRANSEXUAL MENACE
NEW YORK CITY

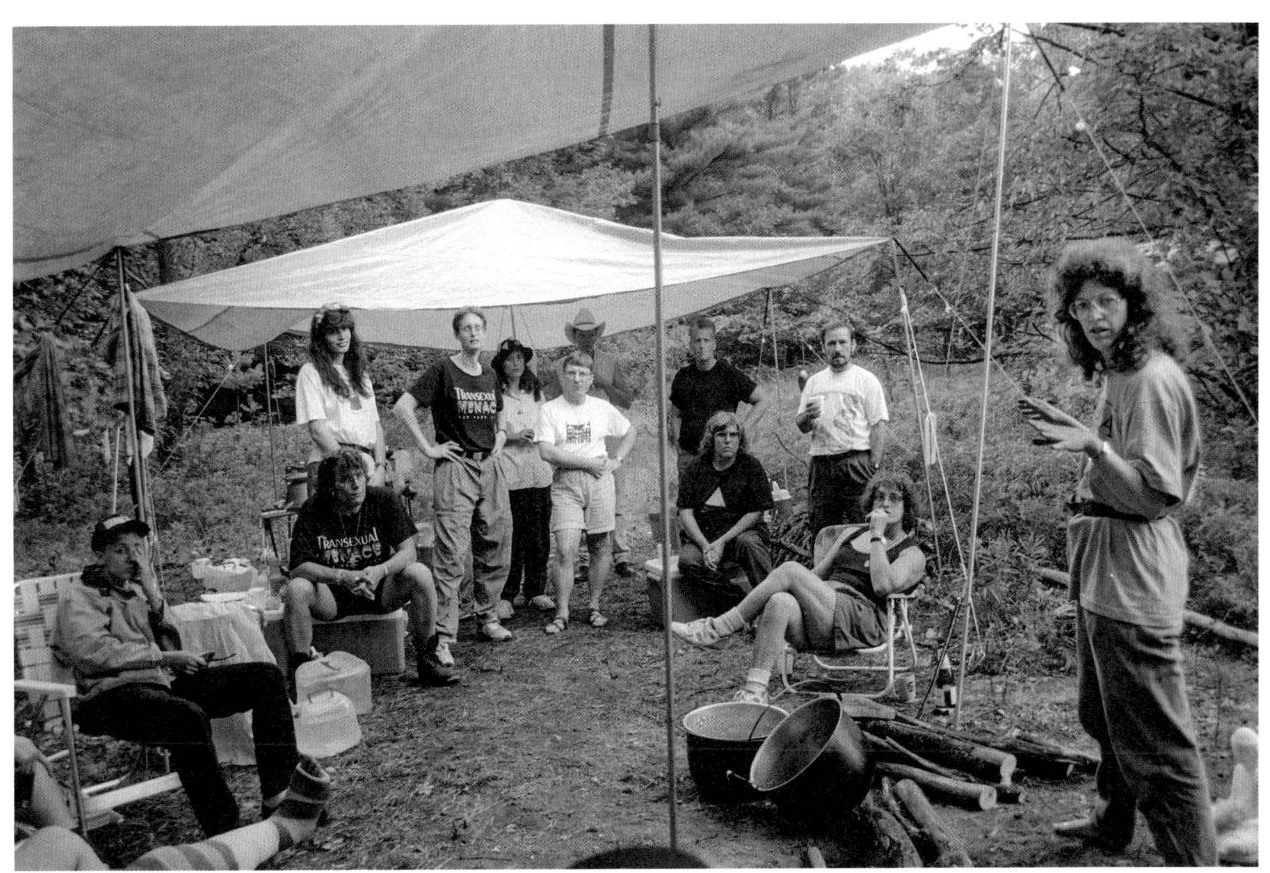

◄
(top) Riki Wilchins and others from Camp Trans at the Michigan Womyn's Music Festival, 1994. Photo by Mariette Pathy Allen

(bottom) The Michigan Womyn's Music Festival denied transgender women entry to the festival—only "womyn-born womyn" were allowed inside—however this rule was briefly suspended for a talk by Leslie Feinberg, 1994. Photo by Mariette Pathy Allen

▲
Discussion at Camp Trans, 1994. Photo by Mariette Pathy Allen

91 BEVERLY SHAW'S STAR SIGN, c. 1950s

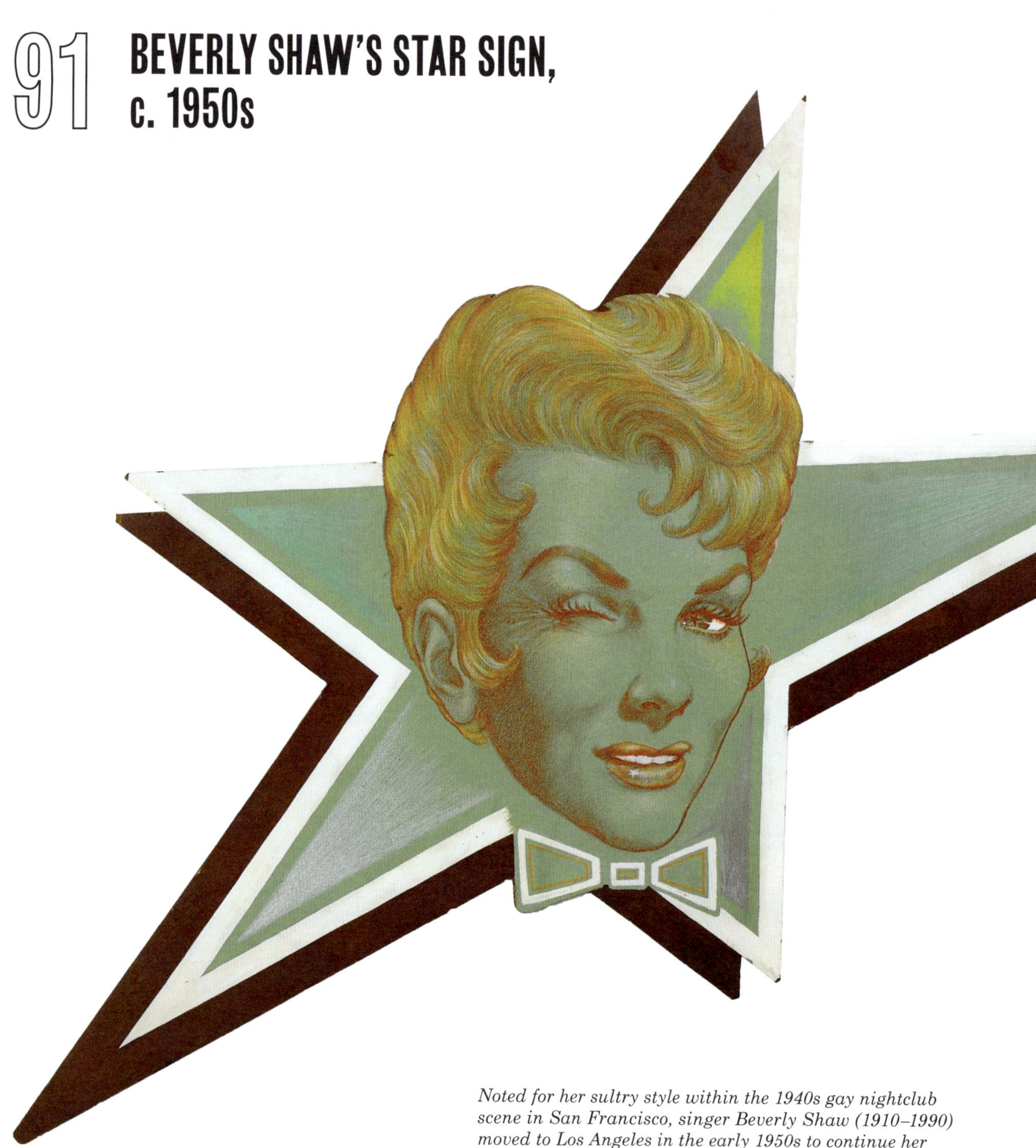

▲
Sign from Beverly Shaw's nightclub, Club Laurel, in Studio City, California, c. 1950s. Oil and conté on board, 39 × 79 in. (15.4 × 31.1 cm). ONE National Gay & Lesbian Archives at the USC Libraries

Noted for her sultry style within the 1940s gay nightclub scene in San Francisco, singer Beverly Shaw (1910–1990) moved to Los Angeles in the early 1950s to continue her musical career. She performed at The Flamingo, a lesbian bar in Hollywood, and later at Club Laurel in Studio City, which she eventually bought and operated for over fourteen years. During this time Shaw adopted the moniker "Beverly Shaw, Sir!" after hearing Groucho Marx refer to Tallulah Bankhead as "sir" in an interview. In the late 1950s or early 1960s, Shaw started her own record label, Club Laurel Records, and recorded her only full-length album, Songs "Tailored to Your Taste." *Shaw continued to perform into the 1960s at Joani Presents, a lesbian nightclub in North Hollywood, and Larry Potter's Supper Club in the San Fernando Valley.*

The Club Laurel

There is a club where I hang out,
Where the oddest people are about.
Some are alright, but others—well,
I'm not in a position to tell!

The owner is an infamous dame—
Beverly Shaw, sir, is her name.
Nightly, she sings up a real good show
And there's nothing this lady don't know!

Cute waitresses, anxious to pour—
Will grab you as you enter the door.

As you sit down in drunken repoire,
She smiles, We have no hard liquor.
And recites the familiar refrain...
We serve beer, wine, champale & champaign!

Soon you are enjoying the atmosphere.
Only to find your lap full of beer.
You may sip your drink slowly and stall
But you're in for more before last call!

Witty remarks fly through the air!—
People are cruising—everywhere!!
What's your home sweetie!—suffer bitch!!—
The marijuana corner for you—witch!

The phone ring brings the cry, I'm not here,
—The receiver gets sequence in my ear!
Someone is always bound to insist—
You must try Beverly's mystery twist!

Many muffled voices—as you leave,
Whisper stories you won't believe.
Fantastic tales that deceive—
Fill the room with intrigue—intrigue!

For this intimate club you will yearn,
And time after time you will return.
You can't escape—the gay—the sublime.
The Laurel, each night, at twilight time!

—Bobbie Hughes

Bobbie Hughes, "The Club Laurel," c. 1950s, transcribed from a poster in the Beverly Shaw Collection, ONE National Gay & Lesbian Archives at the USC Libraries.

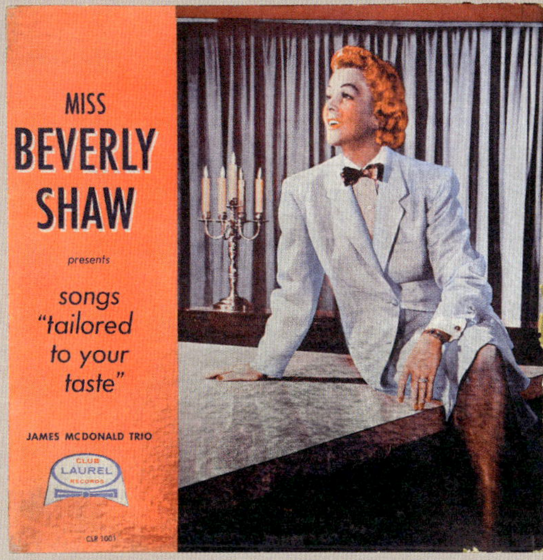

Beverly Shaw, *Songs "Tailored to Your Taste,"* c. 1960. Released by Club Laurel Records, Studio City, CA. ONE National Gay & Lesbian Archives at the USC Libraries

92 VIRGINIA PRINCE, *TRANSVESTIA*, 1960–86

If you speak to transgender people of a certain age, most will tell you about early lives spent in quiet desperation, wondering if perhaps they were the only person on the planet who felt as they did. There were isolated pockets, usually in gay and lesbian clubs, where people could go in relative safety and meet others, but for the most part, transgender people were alone and bereft on information that wasn't derogatory or libelous. Most had no name for themselves, other than transvestite.

True community began to form at an unlikely place: the apartment of Louise Lawrence, in the San Francisco Bay Area. Louise began correspondence with sexologists Alfred Kinsey and Harry Benjamin and put them in touch with the few "transvestites" who had contacted her after reading about her or seeing her present at medical schools. One of these was Arnold Lowman, who would eventually become known as Virginia Prince. Soon, a few people we might today call transgender were meeting in private.

In 1952 four crossdressers—Virginia Prince, Louise Lawrence, Edith Ferguson, and Joan Thornton—banded together to produce and disseminate sheets of news clippings about crossdressing; it was called *Transvestia*.[1] The enterprise folded after two issues.

Eight years later, Virginia Prince resurrected the project and began publishing a magazine with the same name. The issues were filled with editorials by Prince and others, fanciful stories about crossdressing, cartoons, photographs, and contact ads. The identities and even the chosen feminine names of those placing the ads were never revealed in print. Instead, each individual who placed a contact ad was assigned a coded number. Those wishing to correspond were required to send their message and a blank stamped envelope to a central authority (a post office box maintained by Prince), who would fill in the name and address of the intended recipient (usually, the address was also a post office box, as most early crossdressers were concerned about possible arrest and disastrous repercussions to their relationships, families, and jobs). This method of communication, while slow and cumbersome, was reassuring to subscribers to the new *Transvestia*. Regular correspondents would, of course, often eventually exchange their feminine names and mailbox addresses.

Transvestia lasted for 108 issues, the first 100 edited by Prince and the last eight by Carol Beecroft. The list of subscribers formed the basis for Prince's subsequent launch of social and support groups in the United States, Europe, New Zealand, and Australia.[2] We have been able to trace almost all transgender organizing in the United Sates back to these organizations. Other organizations were eventually formed in response to Prince's autocratic leadership style and her insistence that transsexuals and gay crossdressers not be permitted to join her organizations.[3] Similarly, other publications arose to compete with and counteract *Transvestia*.

—Ms. Bob Davis and Dallas Denny

1. Crossdresser, versus the Latin term transvestite, was perceived at the time as a less clinical and more descriptive category.
2. Quite a few of these are still in existence.
3. Transsexualism is a now outdated term for those transgender people who seek to change their bodies through hormones and/or surgery. Prince's exclusion of transsexuals from her groups resulted in a needless separation of crossdressers and transsexuals and ultimately hampered the very community she worked so hard to create.

▸
Selection of *Transvestia*, c. 1960s. ONE National Gay & Lesbian Archives at the USC Libraries

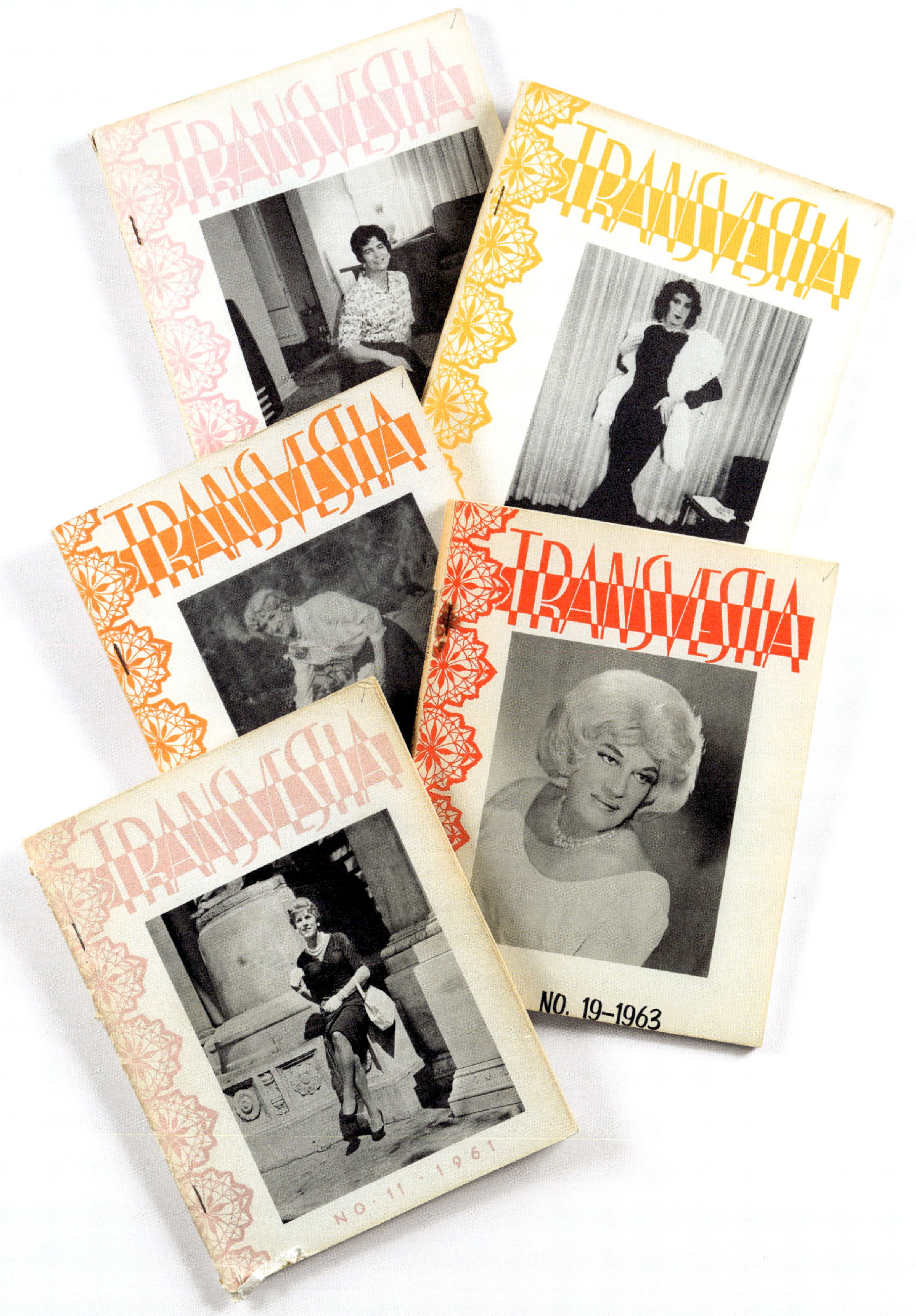
TRANSVESTIA
TRANSVESTIA
TRANSVESTIA
TRANSVESTIA
NO. 19–1963
TRANSVESTIA
NO. 11 · 1961

93 AMOS MAC AND ROCCO KAYIATOS, *ORIGINAL PLUMBING*, 2009–19

In 2009, two young men in San Francisco—creative, entrepreneurial, talented, and driven to express themselves—from a new generation of trans guys, seized an opportunity—almost on impulse—to create a quarterly print magazine targeting the invisible global community of trans guys who they felt had been starving for connection. Amos Mac and Rocco Kayiatos created *Original Plumbing* as a statement: there are many ways to be a trans man.

Just as the internet was becoming more accessible to more people, Mac and Kayiatos recognized that as much as it made content available, the internet encouraged isolation. And the marginalized world of trans men needed something physical, something to hold onto. Previous generations of trans men had produced newsletters and a few one-off zines, always on a shoestring and in a near vacuum, building each issue on whatever was close at hand, whatever came in through the mail or over the telephone. Mac and Kayiatos committed to something more constructed, more intentional. By curating every issue according to a theme, *OP*—as it was called colloquially—was less haphazard. And the sensibility of transmasculine culture was born, though the beating heart at the core of the Mac and Kayiatos effort rested consciously on the shoulders of those who came before. These energetic young men reached outward to draw in even more voices, from every corner of the globe.

OP reflected the concerns, fantasies, fears, and fascinations of the men whose images and words were featured in its pages. The fact that it was so committed to showing us images, reflections, and dreams of who we are in all our diversity, was the strength of its enterprise. Earlier publications didn't have the technologies or the budgets that *OP* managed to secure. Mac and Kayiatos were able to travel around the country to promote their work, and they used events to draw people out, let us gather together, and experience each other in creative spaces with a constant focus on the celebration of who we were in the moment, with no requirement to be anything other than ourselves as trans male-embodied hearts and souls, no matter what those bodies looked like.

The name *Original Plumbing* came from the recognition that trans men all had original plumbing: some of us kept it, remodeling around it, and some of us altered it along with other components of ourselves, and some of us replaced it with new designs. But we all had original plumbing... that's what made us a community within the masculine genre.

For ten years, *OP* accompanied the expanding transmasculine American spirit as we tried to sort ourselves out against the external backdrop of a world turning more politically reactionary than ever. In 2019, Mac and Kayiatos had already moved in different directions in their own artistic endeavors and careers. Knowing that what they had accomplished in those ten years was deserving of preservation so that it could be discovered by future generations of transmasculine people and studied by scholars of culture, sexuality, queerness, and masculinity, they collaborated with the Feminist Press to produce a single-volume book entitled *Original Plumbing: The Best of Ten Years of Trans Male Culture*, a big, fat four hundred pages long. That's not going to disappear anytime soon!

—Jamison Green

▸ Selection of *Original Plumbing*, 2009–19. ONE National Gay & Lesbian Archives at the USC Libraries

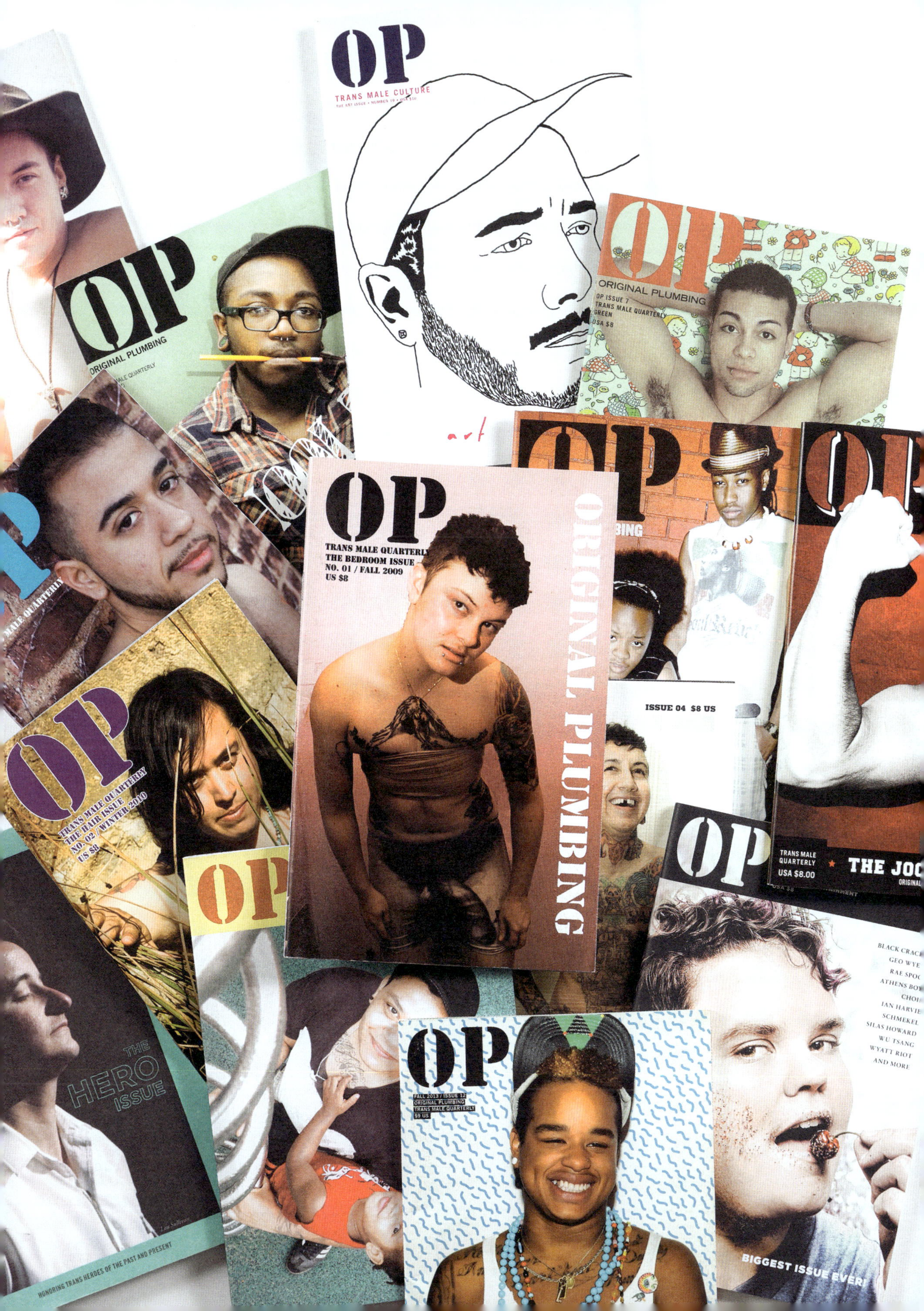

OP
TRANS MALE CULTURE
art
OP
ORIGINAL PLUMBING
OP
ORIGINAL PLUMBING
OP ISSUE 7
TRANS MALE QUARTERLY
GREEN
USA $8
OP
TRANS MALE QUARTERLY
THE BEDROOM ISSUE
NO. 01 / FALL 2009
US $8
ORIGINAL PLUMBING
ISSUE 04 $8 US
OP
TRANS MALE QUARTERLY
THE HAIR ISSUE
NO. 02 / WINTER 2010
US $8
OP
THE HERO ISSUE
HONORING TRANS HEROES OF THE PAST AND PRESENT
OP
TRANS MALE QUARTERLY
USA $8.00
OP
FALL 2013 / ISSUE 12
ORIGINAL PLUMBING
TRANS MALE QUARTERLY
$9 US
BIGGEST ISSUE EVER!

94 CHRISTOPHER LEE, *ALLEY OF THE TRANNY BOYS*, 1998

Like many transmasculine people in our thirties and forties, I transitioned because of the moving image. Between 2006 and 2009 I was glued to YouTube, voraciously consuming long-form video entries of trans men as they documented the effects of testosterone and surgery. Watching their faces change, their voices drop, their bodies transform—they became men in front of my eyes, a kind of processual magic I had never previously witnessed. On YouTube it seemed like a wholly new visual language of trans masculinity *in motion* was being developed.

One foggy midafternoon several years after I moved to the Bay Area, I found myself at El Rio on Mission Street. As I sat down at the bar and ordered a beer, I realized I had stumbled into a funeral: the community was holding a service for trans filmmaker and activist Christopher Lee (1964–2012), whose documentaries and pornographic films are some of the first trans-of-color-produced cinema ever created. Lee was a cofounder of Trannyfest (now the San Francisco Transgender Film Festival), the first transgender film festival in the world. His work pioneered new cinematic approaches to documenting trans masculinity and trans male eroticism, establishing on video what YouTube would attempt later in digital form. At the time, I had no idea who Lee had been, or about his incredible influence at the intersection of transgender embodiment and the moving image—an intersection I would end up studying professionally.

Lee's best-known work, *Alley of the Tranny Boys* (1998), was the first pornographic film ever made by a transgender man. The film consists of six erotic scenarios exploring gay sex, mutual masturbation, group sex, cruising, BDSM, fetishism, and fisting between and among trans men. Flouting the cissexist fascination with the "bonus hole" that overdetermines trans men's role in today's mainstream gay porn, *Alley* explores the diversity of trans masculine erotic expression and fantasy with a tongue-in-cheekness (in one scene trans men gangbang a cop named "Officer Swallow") that never devolves into exploitation or camp. Rather, it serves up a trans masculine body politics that illustrates the diversity of trans men's sexualities, visually documenting how our bodies work while taking our differently economized yet nonetheless phallic power seriously. From its opening shots of an ecstatic trans man's face as he bottoms for another trans man, the film presents trans masculinity as an integrated, materially erotic mode of unmistakably male subjectivity. Although it cites the standard tropes of gay porn, *Alley* expands on these familiar codes by intercutting them with unprecedented shots of trans masculine sexual practice and pleasure. The result is an entirely new FTM4FTM erotic repertoire.

While academic works from the 1990s tended to theorize trans masculinity as a form of drag or a feminist appropriation of male roles, *Alley of the Trannyboys* uses filmic space to enflesh trans men, to make us real in space *together*. Across the film's scenes, there are always at least two trans men present on screen at once. *Alley* therefore documents one way that trans masculinity has historically taken place: between trans men engaged in witnessing each other as materially and sexually real. The film presents audiences with mutually sexualizing forms of admiration between trans men that today we would describe as a "T4T" mode of erotic care. While the transgender community lost Christopher Lee at far too young an age, *Alley* lives on—articulating a vision of trans masculine erotic relationality that remains far too unfamiliar, and utterly electric.

—Cáel M. Keegan

▶
VHS case for *Alley of the Tranny Boys*, 1998. Directed by Christopher Lee

ALLEY OF THE TRANNY BOYS

TRANSSEXUAL MEN
DIRECTED BY CHRISTOPHER LEE
EDITOR J ZAPATA

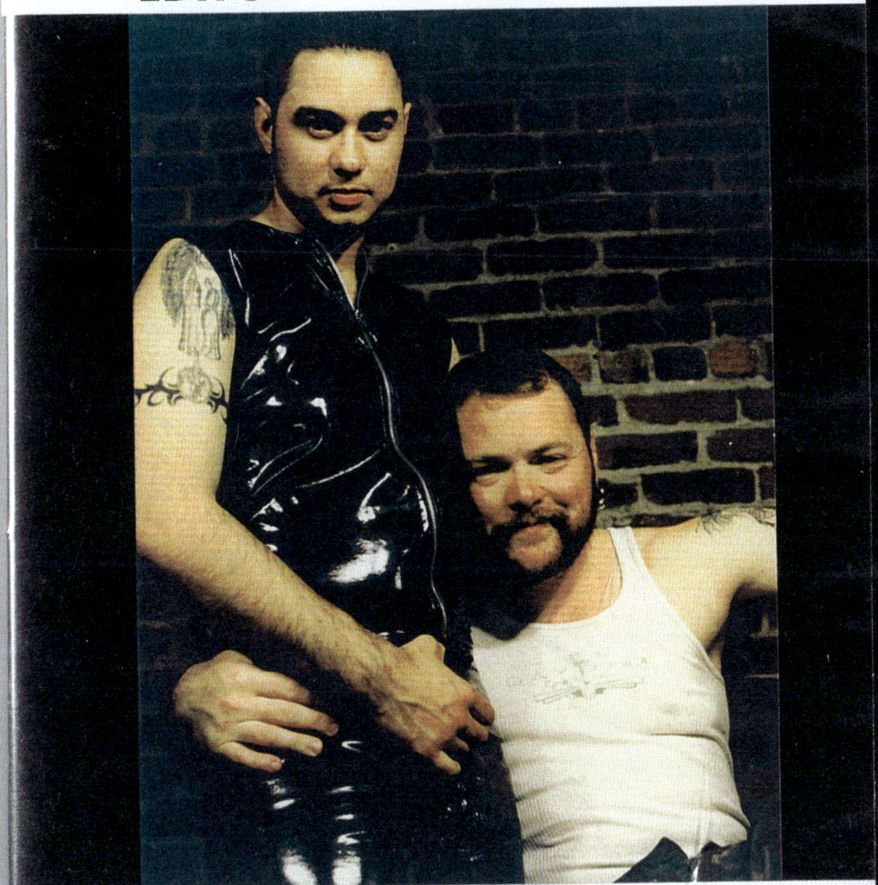

PHOTO: P. WISE

STARRING
ANGEL **BUCK DAVIS**
JADE-BLUE ECLIPSE

95 GIUSEPPE CAMPUZANO, MUSEO TRAVESTI DEL PERÚ, 2003–13

More than twenty years ago, while Peruvian philosopher and drag queen GiuCamp (aka Giuseppe Campuzano, 1969–2013) was dressing up in sequined costumes and high heels, he began to wonder about the lost ancestors of her joyful cross-dressed body. This question was also a performance, and a portable revolution about to explode. Out of her silver bag, Campuzano took a series of writings, images, and objects that he had been accumulating since his childhood: this was the album of becoming-transvestite. This collection of recycled fictions was the beginning of an unstoppable vampire journey constituted by activism, theoretical writing, sexual practices, and cultural production. It was a vital journey on the road to subversion, with no return ticket, and it would lead her to gather a collection of queer images and create the extraordinary archive, warehouse, and arsenal of disobedient bodies that she called Museo Travesti del Perú—the Transvestite Museum of Peru.

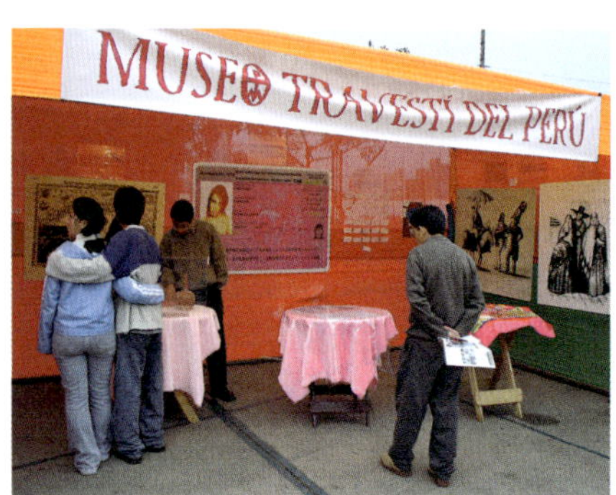

Giuseppe Campuzano, Museo Travesti del Perú public intervention in Lima, Peru, 2004

Before founding the Transvestite Museum in Lima in 2003–04, Campuzano had already been intensely exploring the political possibilities of his transgender body at parties, discos, street fairs, protests, and art galleries. It was her personal questioning of the public role of the drag queen in the context of a misogynistic dictatorship in Peru in the 1990s that brought Campuzano to initiate this visual, historical, and philosophical archeology of cross-dressing origins. "I see transvestism (cross-gender) as a ritual, like a priest performing a liturgy, or a shaman of the native cultures," she said in 2008. Understood as an analogy for the mask—the false, the copy, the camouflage—transvestism became a useful analytical concept capable of visualizing and philosophizing the processes of colonization, resistance, hybridization, and *mestizaje*.

Campuzano founded the Museo Travesti to advance corrosive and discontinuous fictions that visualized unrealized pasts and alternative bodies, antagonists to the seeming social facts of realist historiography. GiuCamp understood that, in order to fracture the centrality of heteronormative narratives that were presented as History, she had to cannibalize the museum, one of modernity's most effective apparatuses of political discipline, one of the most sophisticated Western promises of truth. Its anachronistic methodology and queer strategies of display—the museum used as a Trojan horse—envisioned a different relationship with history that denaturalized the expectations of scientific truth and legibility, deploying forms of belonging beyond nation-state accounts and reclaiming social models that puncture and disengage from the demands of national identity.

The Museo Travesti never existed physically as a building; it was an invented space that cannibalized the form of the museum to question the normative process of the preservation of history in a racist, homophobic society. However, the museum did have a collection. Since its founding, the project called for an assembly of photographic representations, objects (textiles, replicas of Pre-Columbian ceramics, Andean costumes, artworks), press clippings, oral histories, and recycled fictions culled from the sewers of the heterosexual gaze's regime of representation, collected with the help of Campuzano's transgender friends and family. It wasn't a collection of "queer objects"—like the results of an investigation tracking down the still-unfound remains of queer bodies in history—but an operation of *queering* the historiographic methods, forms of display, and the systems of normative meanings that were passed on as truth. By juxtaposing elements not necessarily previously reclaimed by queer history, this strategy avoids falling easily into community formation based on identification and recognition. The project's promiscuous trans-temporal readings defied Western scientific knowledge systems by taking the drag Indigenous body as a locus of enunciation—a prosthetic body "whose nature is uncertainty," as GiuCamp said.

—Miguel A. López

▸ Giuseppe Campuzano, *ID: Pictures for Identification*, 2011. Digital inkjet on paper, 18⅜ × 14 in. (46.6 × 35.5 cm)

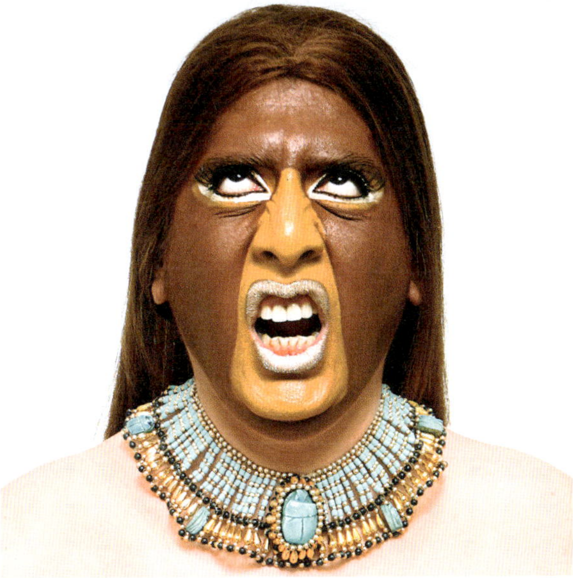

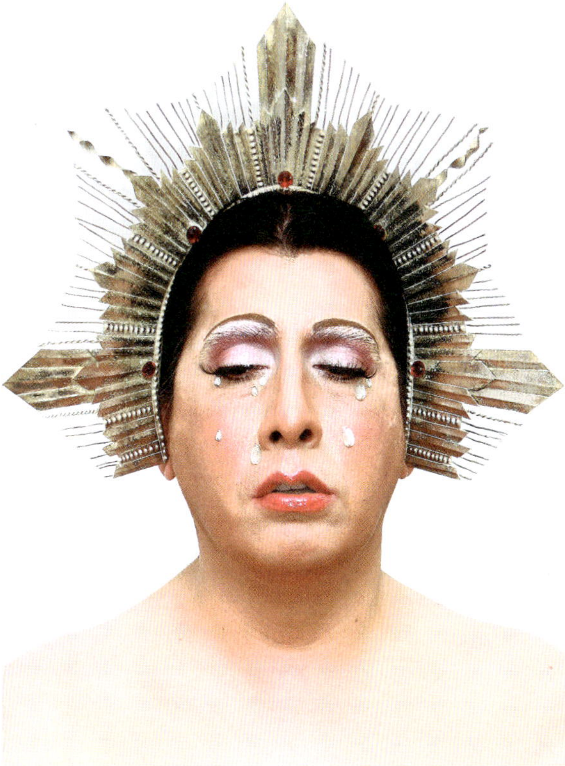

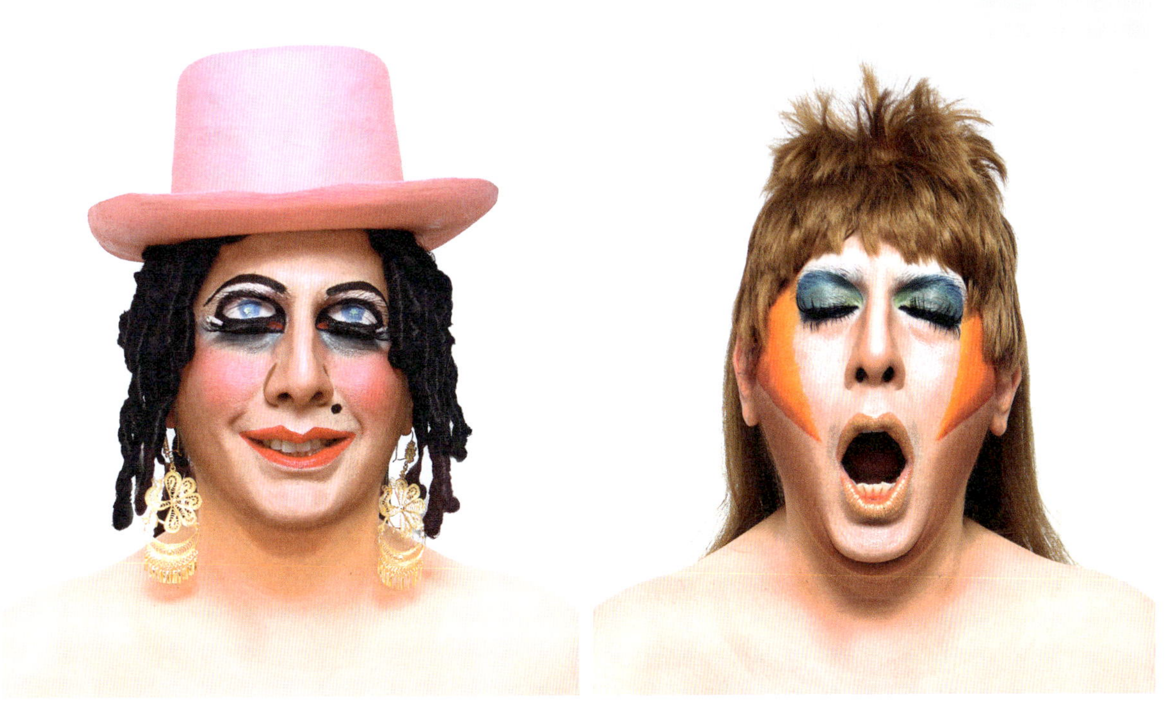

96 ABSOLUTE EMPRESS III SHIRLEY, FELT BANNER USED TO REPRESENT THE GRAND MERE, ABSOLUTE EMPRESS I DE SAN FRANCISCO AND THE WIDOW NORTON, JOSÉ JULIO SARRIA, THE NIGHTINGALE EMPRESS, c. 1965

This banner commemorates the reign of The Grand Mere, Absolute Empress I de San Francisco, the Widow Norton, José Julio Sarria, The Nightingale Empress (1922–2013). It was created by Absolute Empress III Shirley in about 1965. Mama José, as she was known, was a femme drag performer, singer, and community organizer. She recognized that our freedom and rights as LGBTQ people depend on us uniting to fight for social justice.

Today, Mama José is remembered by the emperors, empresses, dukes, duchesses, and royal members of the Imperial and Ducal courts around the world. I remember José as a fixture in San Francisco who was quick to pick up a mic to school us on queer and trans hirstory, often while spilling some serious tea along the way.

This banner represents the tenacity of a Latinx femme-presenting person who created her own source of power during the 1960s, when power was held almost exclusively by men who did not want to share it with women, transgender individuals, or drag performers. Instead of cowering, José brought us together with great style, urging us to support one another via grassroots fundraising and organizing. Often, this is done one dollar at a time in bar fundraisers and mobilizing campaigns that highlight both our power and fabulosity as queer and transgender people.

My own transgender mother, Teresita La Campesina, was a singer with an operatic voice like Mama José's. They both used their voices, seduction skills, and storytelling to enthrall audiences of all genders and races. Teresita regularly sang in bars in North Beach and the Mission. Mama José sang in Union Square where the Black Cat operated initially as a bohemian hangout bar and later as one of the first openly gay bars. Teresita's and Mama José's singing were lures to make us fall in love with them, while their commentaries instigated us to become activists with them. The world is a better place because of their Brown femme magic.

I love that Mama José's legacy is commemorated by José Sarria Court on 16th Street (a transgender and queer Latinx corridor from the 1970s through the 2010s) in the Castro LGBTQ Cultural District of San Francisco. Children and adults can go to the neighborhood branch of the library at 1 José Sarria Court to connect with the idea that we are all a part of a movement built by our trailblazing transgender and queer ancestors. This banner represents not only Mama José's reign as the first Empress, it represents a throwing down of the gauntlet for us to stand up, fight for our rights, and do it with style and flair. *¡Que Viva José Sarria!*

—Mx. Tina Valentin Aguirre

In 1965, José Sarria founded the Imperial Court System, a pageant organization that remains active with chapters across North America. Each year the chapters elect their empresses and emperors, who take elaborate titles and make regalia like the banner shown here. They also lead charitable fundraising efforts for a variety of local causes. In addition to their influence on the Imperial Court, Sarria is remembered as political activist; in 1961 they ran for the San Francisco Board of Supervisors, becoming the first openly gay candidate to run for public office in the United States.

▸ Absolute Empress III Shirley, Felt banner used to represent The Grand Mere, Absolute Empress I de San Francisco and the Widow Norton, José Julio Sarria, The Nightingale Empress, c. 1965. Felt, glue, and sequins, 38¾ × 28½ (98.4 × 72.4 cm). José Sarria Papers (1996-01), Gay, Lesbian, Bisexual, Transgender Historical Society. Photo by Marcel Pardo Ariza

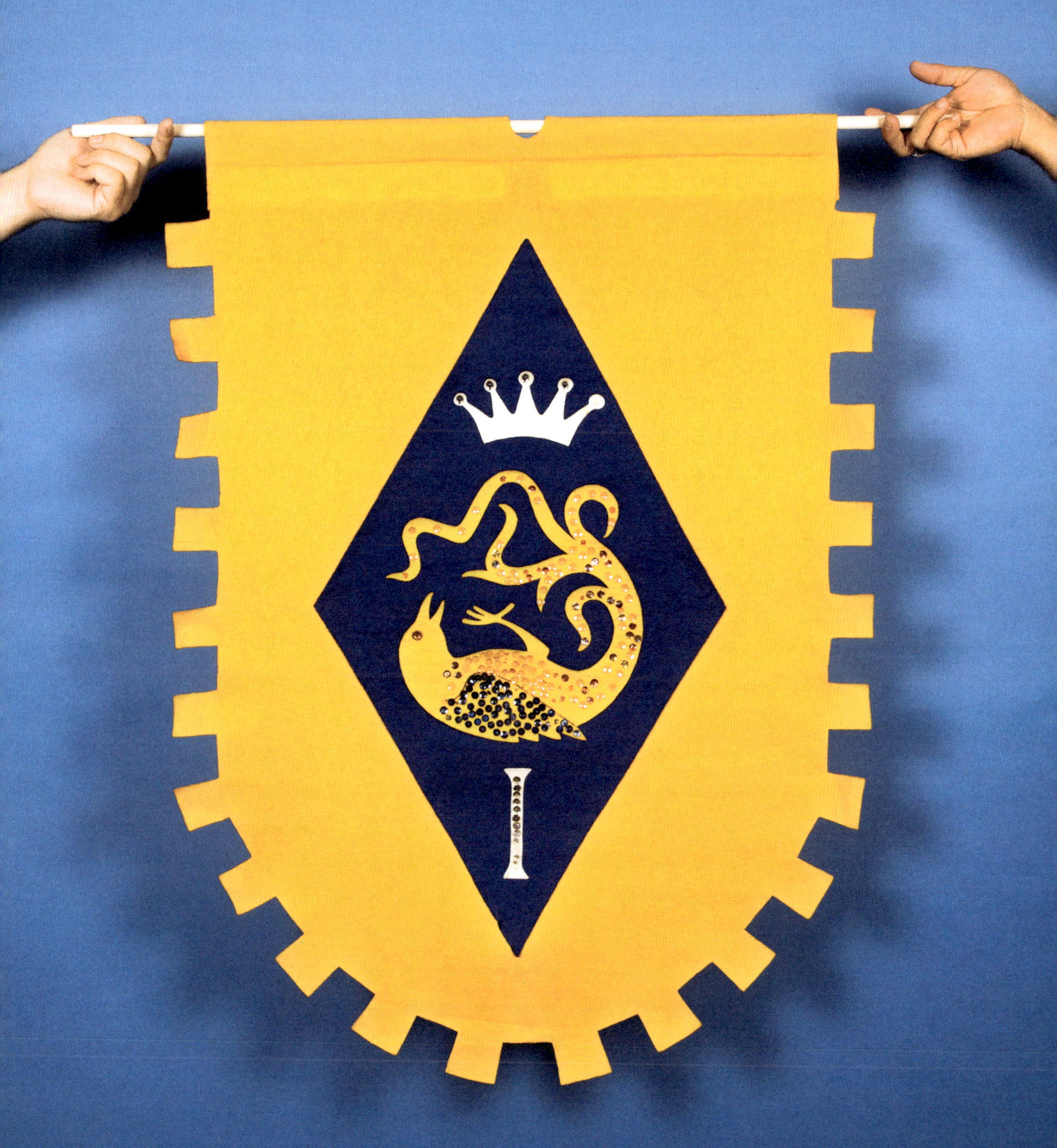

97 ARCHIVO DE LA MEMORIA TRANS ARGENTINA, 2012–PRESENT

Argentinian trans activist Claudia Pía Baudracco (1970–2012) began collecting photographs of friends and activists in the 2000s to document the lives and struggles of her nation's transgender communities. After she died suddenly, her collection passed to fellow activist María Belén Correa, then living in Germany, who launched a private Facebook group for other trans individuals to share anecdotes, photos, testimonies, and letters. Since 2014, with the support of the photographer Cecilia Estalles, this project has gradually transformed from a digital platform into a physical archive—the Archivo de la Memoria Trans Argentina (AMT)—which holds over 15,000 images and objects. AMT remains a community-initiated and supported enterprise, sustained through the efforts of numerous individuals, including Luisa Paz, Beatriz Evelyn Silva, and Kouka Garcia de Mesureur, who reflect here on the importance of the archive.

What does the Archivo de la Memoria Trans Argentina (AMT) mean for the trans community?

At first, the AMT meant our memory, everything we might forget as time passes, but we need to store it somewhere. But later, I began to understand that it is essential, not just for our memory, but also for those who come after. I think the past is everything. If we don't ask ourselves where we come from, we won't find where we are going. What is happening at the AMT is fundamental. There is a large part of society that does not know our history. There are also many trans people, especially the younger ones, who do not know our history. Many of them will have a better life because of the efforts of those before, but they should not forget that this road is made with our memory.

—Luisa Paz

In 2012, our compañera María Belén Correa created this wonderful group on Facebook called Archivo de la Memoria Trans to gather the survivors, their memories, and their images. To preserve, first in virtual space and later in physical space, the memory of the girlfriends who suffered the injustices of the police, the abandonment of the state, and the hostility of society. A sort of collective construction of trans memory by the few of them who survived. The group's description stated: "It [the archive] is the collection and protection of trans memory in photos, clippings, videos, magazines, films, and interviews, but above all, the stories told by the survivors." This archive is focused on the period from the seventies to the end of the nineties when many compañeras went into exile. But not all of them were able to do so. The situation during the nineties in Argentina was difficult. One of the main sources of revenue for the police was to charge trans women for simply walking on public streets. HIV was wreaking havoc, there were no public policies for prevention and health care, and society was a silent accomplice in the deaths of one after another. Some who could go into exile discovered that freedom in Europe was bittersweet, while others had a better time. Many returned several years later—others died abroad and could never return. Some were imprisoned, and others married. Those who made it past the age of forty are survivors.

—Beatriz Evelyn Silva

For me, the AMT is the documents that provide the evidence to construct a history. Let us understand the document in its broadest sense—as a source of information, recorded in any medium, which serves as testimony and proof of human activity, the memory of an era, of a community. In this case, the forgotten trans people of Argentina.

It is imperative that this archive serves society by furnishing information about trans rights, providing a space to communicate about gender identity—especially for a new trans generation—and preserving documents so that archivists can preserve democratic and social advances.

—Kouka Garcia de Mesureur

▸ Claudia Pía Baudracco's collection that began the Archivo de la Memoria Trans Argentina, Buenos Aires, 2022. Photos by Luis Juárez, a member of the AMT

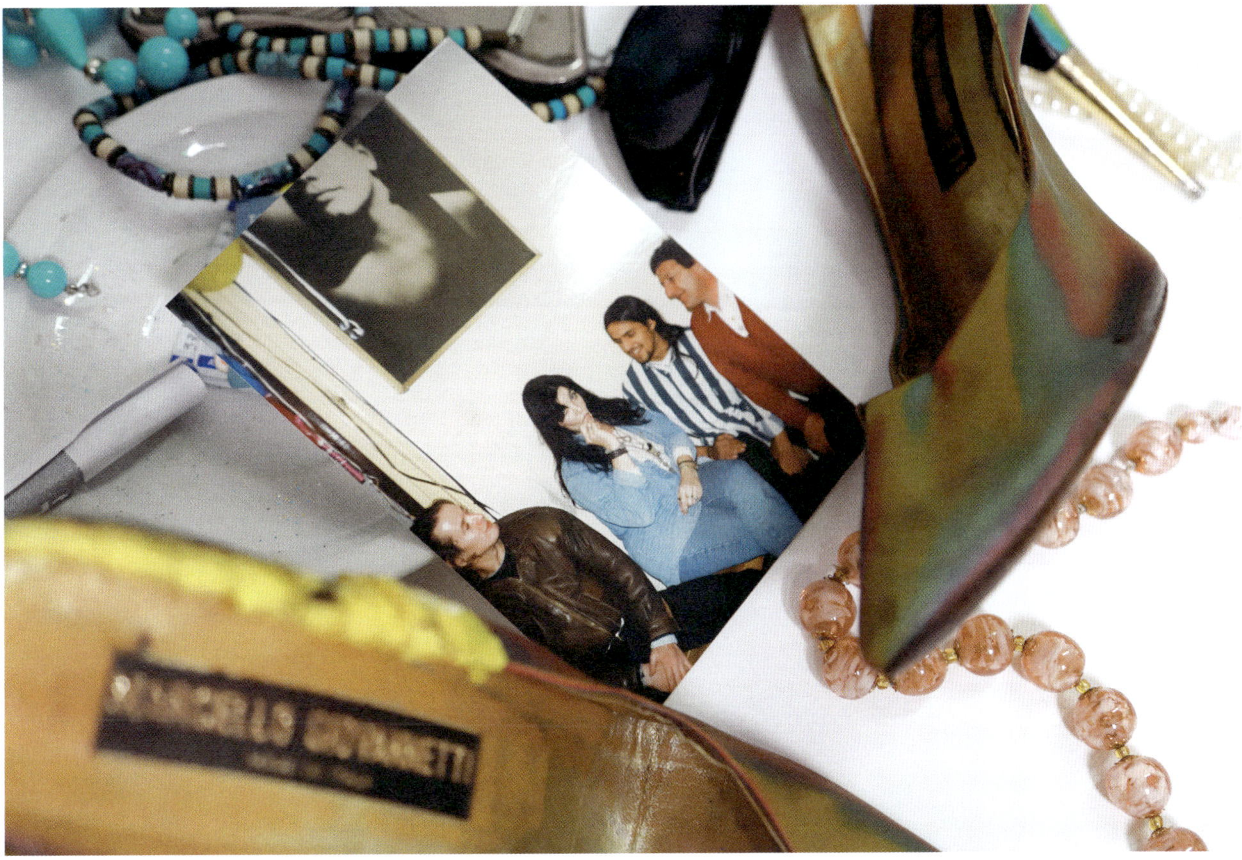

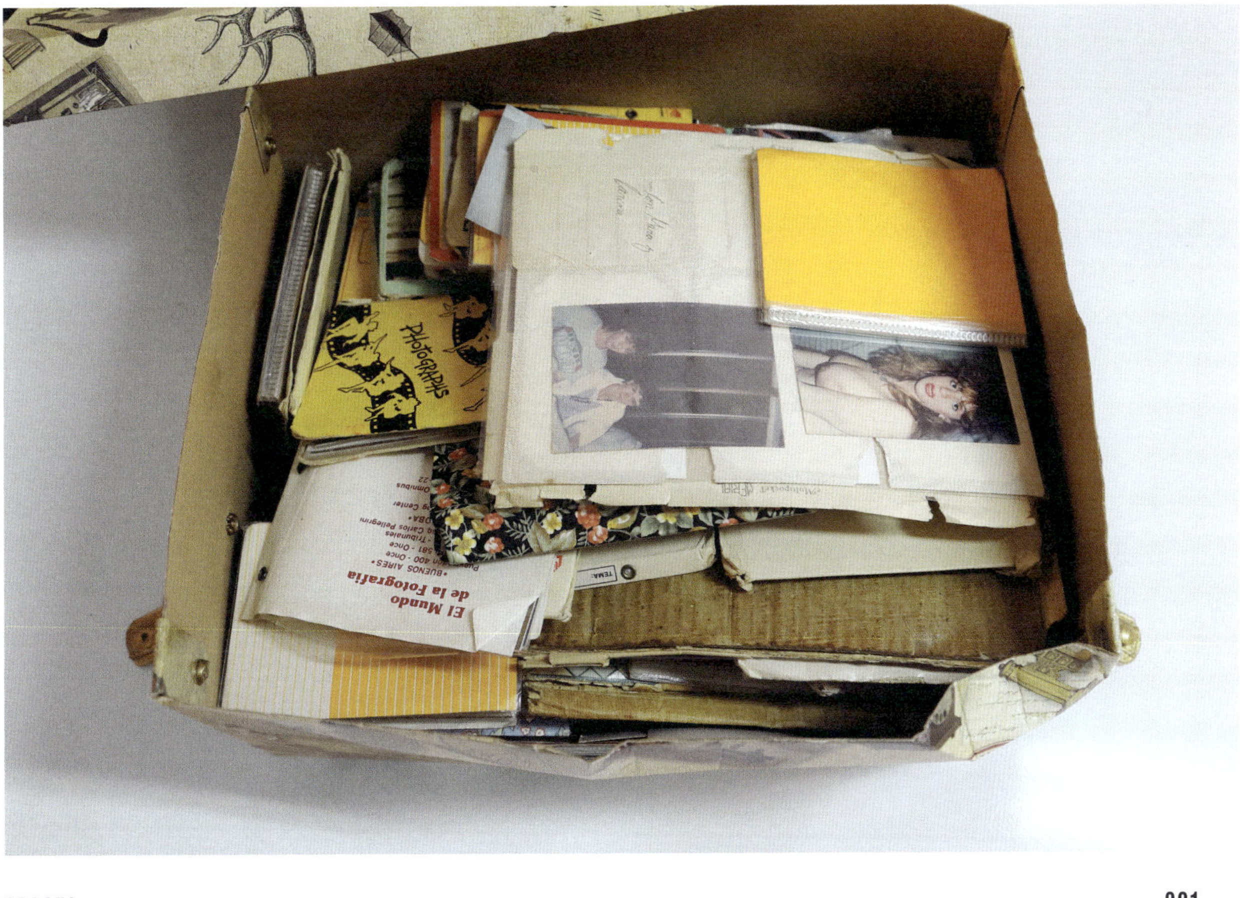
PHOTOGRAPHS
El Mundo
de la Fotografia
•BUENOS AIRES•

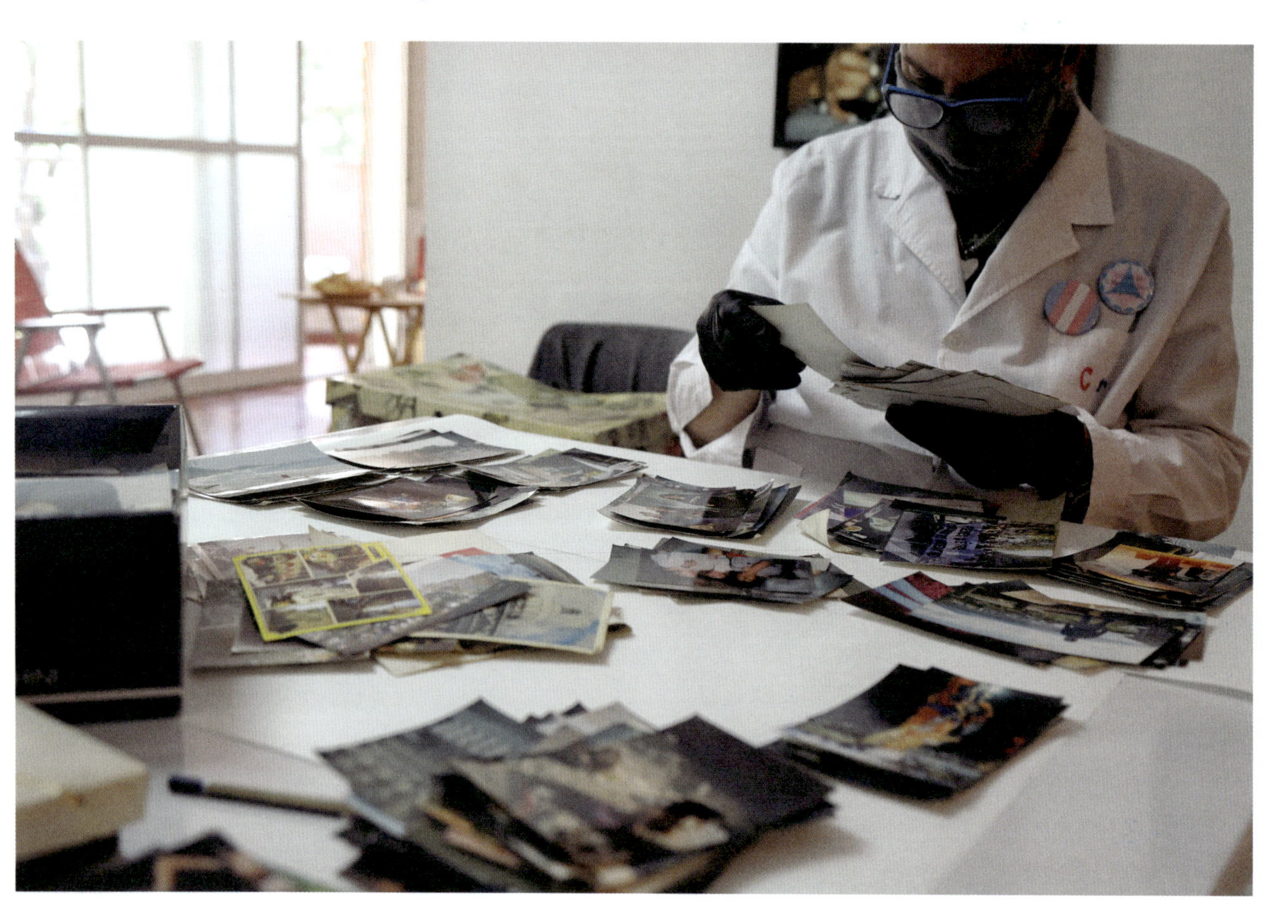

▼
Volunteers organizing materials at the Archivo de la Memoria Trans Argentina, Buenos Aires, 2022. Photos by Luis Juárez, a member of the AMT

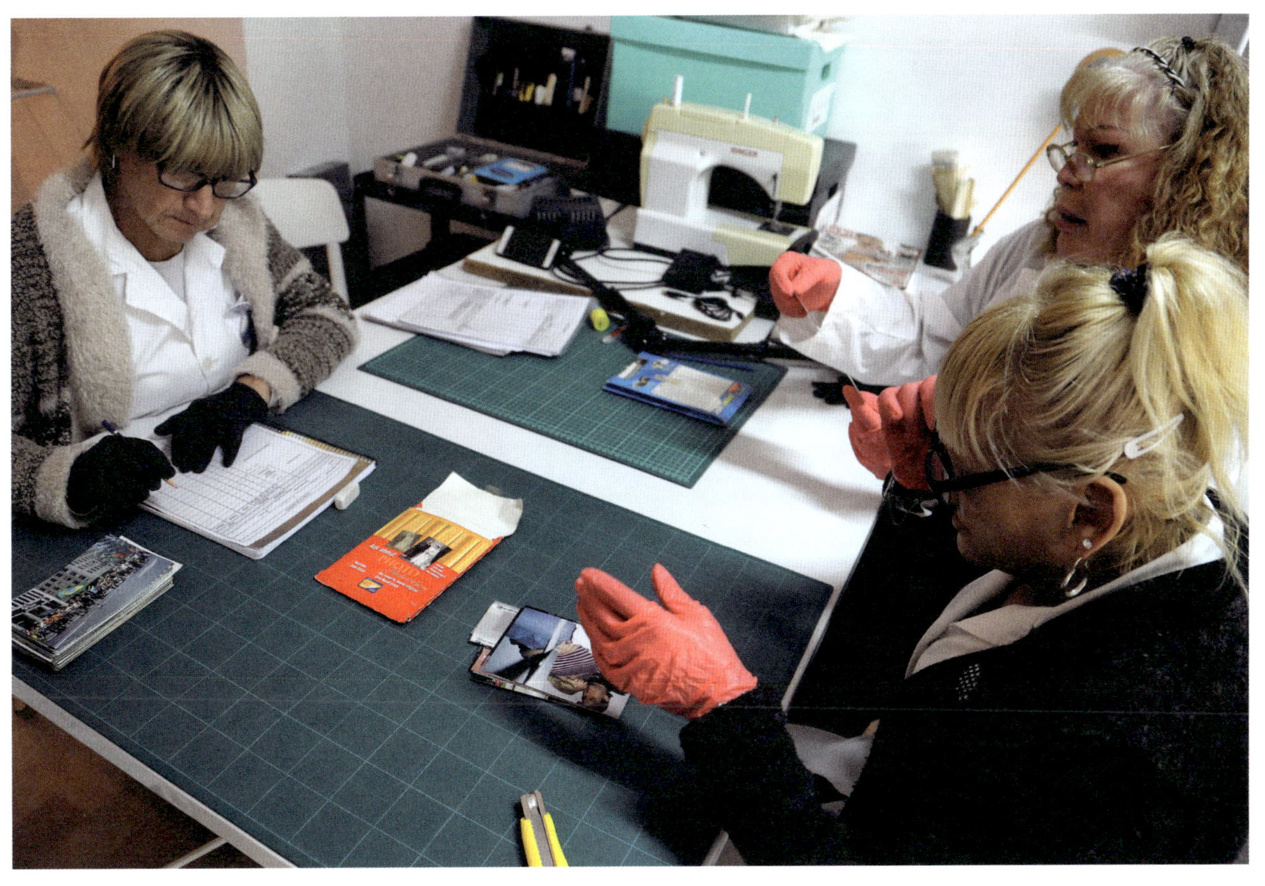

98 IMPERIAL LODGE OF ELKS IN *PARIS IS BURNING*, 1990

Nothing embodies the meaning of Black queer space quite like the Imperial Lodge of Elks, often referred to as the Elks Lodge. This venue was made famous as a main location for the balls on display in the documentary *Paris is Burning* (1990), directed by Jennie Livingston. Located at 160 West 129th Street in Harlem, the hall is recognizable in the film for its red walls with gold molding—as seen in this photograph taken before Livingston began shooting the documentary. A taxidermy deer's head is visible in this image, harkening back to the venue's original usage as a fraternal lodge. Today the Elks Lodge is the Faith Mission Christian Fellowship Church.

Balls have a long tradition in New York City. They began in the nineteenth century as masquerade ball fundraisers for middle-class fraternal organizations. In Harlem, the Hamilton Lodge, a Black fraternal organization, became known in the late nineteenth and early twentieth century for balls at the Rockland Palace which drew thousands of people. As the 1920s and '30s rolled around, these events became known as "Faggot Balls" during New York City's Pansy Craze as many openly gay, lesbian, bisexual, gender-nonconforming, and trans people would attend, bedecked in their finest outfits. As a space for glamour, freedom of expression, and unbridled fun, the balls became a hub for female impersonators. This tradition carried on at other venues in New York as female impersonators began hosting their own balls, such as Phil Black who put on the Funmakers Ball at the Rockland Palace in the 1940s and '50s. It is fitting that the mothers of the ballroom scene—Dorian Corey, Paris Dupree, Pepper LaBeija, Avis Pendavis, and the first mother of ballroom, Crystal LaBeija—emerged from this tradition of competition. As they hosted their first balls in the 1970s, they brought their knowledge of these earlier balls to spaces like the Elks Lodge to form the foundation of ballroom culture.

As described by Marlon M. Bailey in his work on ballroom and Black queer space, Black and Brown LGBTQ+ people create new spaces and sites of creativity with our bodies and with the way we occupy and appropriate space. Ballroom's ability to transform any location into a ball is part of the magic of the culture. The floor of the Imperial Lodge of Elks was more than just a floor, it was a runway, a ceremonial cypher. It was our church. Our space for breaking bread, coming together, praising and worshipping each other's artistry and hard work. Unlike our straight, cis siblings, the places and spaces for people like us come at night in the wee hours. This is where the magic happens. This is where our community comes together to celebrate ourselves. For a lot of the femqueens, butchqueens, butches, straight, gay, and bisexual cis women, and trans men of ballroom, places like the Elks Lodge and other makeshift runways like Washington Square Park or the Christopher Street Pier, were—and for some, continue to be—places for ball competition and ingenuity as well as refuges from discrimination and violence.

In reflecting on the Elks Lodge and its unique history for the ballroom scene, its usage as a place of worship for Harlem residents reiterates the purpose of the space today. A different congregation may be there, but ultimately, its uses are the same today as they were then: a place for folks to come together, share in communion, and connect on a human level in a celebration of life.

—Sydney Baloue

1. Marlon M. Bailey, "Engendering Space: Ballroom Culture and the Spatial Practice of Possibility in Detroit," *Gender, Place & Culture* 21, no. 4 (2014): 489–507.

▸
Unidentified ballgoer at the Imperial Lodge of Elks, c. 1986. Black and white work print, 4 × 6¼ in. (10.2 × 15.9 cm). Photo by Jennie Livingston

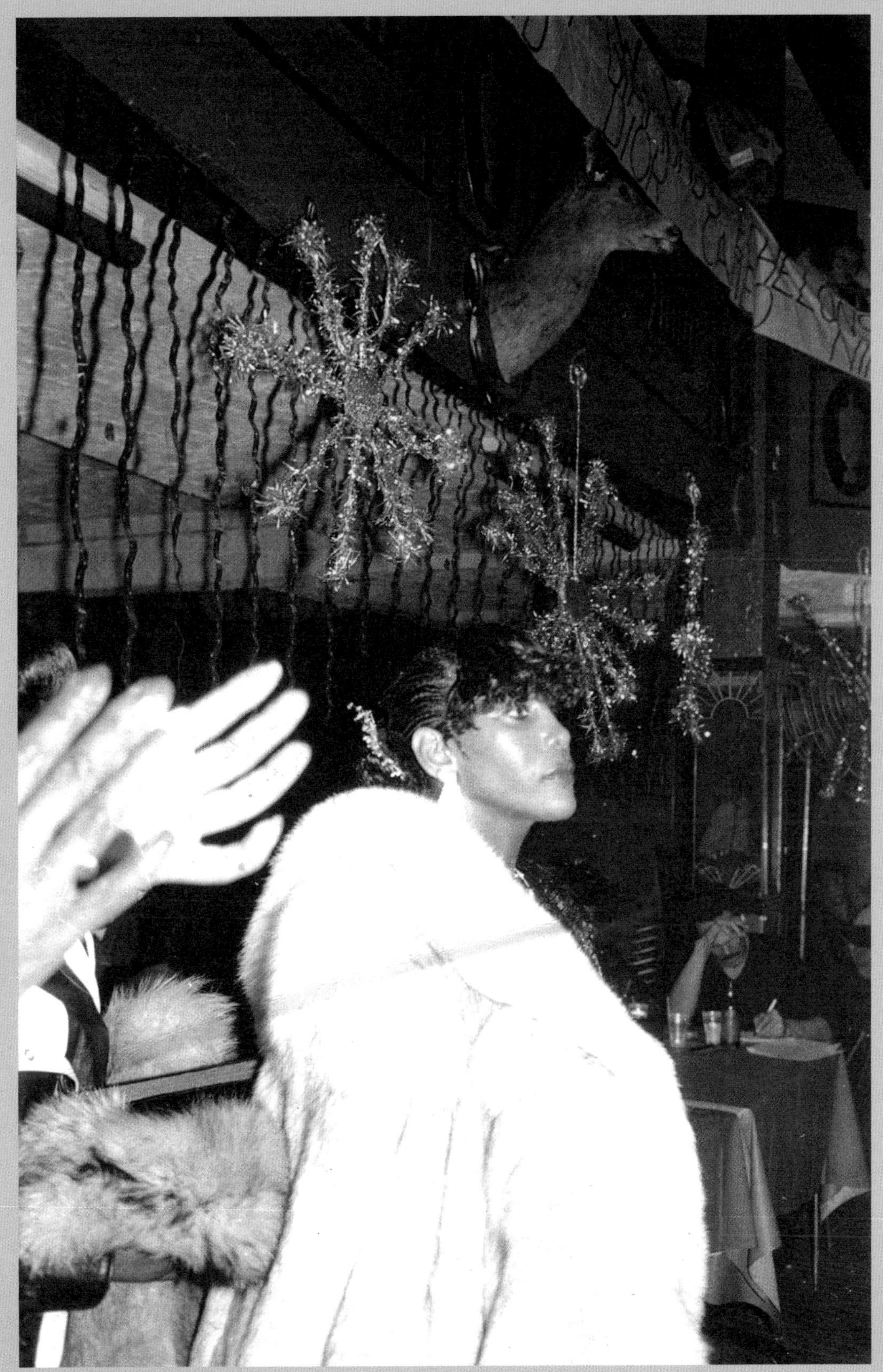

99 WU TSANG, *THE FIST IS STILL UP*, 2010

Overlooking the crossroads of politics and pleasure, aesthetics and commitment, *The Fist Is Still Up* (2010) is a radical alteration made in the image of the neon sign above the entrance to the Silver Platter, a queer bar located in the Westlake neighborhood of Los Angeles. One of Wu Tsang's earliest works, it brought the club to the gallery in a vehicle of revolutionary alterity and economic glamour, then back again.

From 2008 to 2010, Tsang founded and ran a legendary club called Wildness on Tuesdays at the Silver Platter with DJs Ashland Mines, Daniel Pineda, and Asma Maroof (the latter two performing under the moniker Nguzunguzu). Prior to 2008, the Silver Platter had predominantly served as a nonromantic refuge for immigrant transgender women to gather safely in the name of earning a living. Tsang's club brought in new blood from the city's artistic ecosystems, including many recently arrived New York City transplants.

Tsang's genre-shaking documentary *Wildness* (2012) centers around the Silver Platter and the Tuesday parties. There is a short scene in the film focusing on a visit to the club by the late Mother Flawless Sabrina (1939–2017), a legendary New York drag queen. Divinity personified, in her performance she softly and subtly pivots an open palm in several directions within the Silver Platter. She scans the ether through the string of lights, a pointillistic study in neon candy glowing in the background, the camera angle pointed up at her in prayerful worship. She pauses, interrupted by the hauntings that permeate the fabled walls.

Mother tells the crowd that she's happy to return to the Silver Platter. The air is thick with sweat and crackling with electricity. She is easily the oldest and fiercest person in the small barroom with its stamp-sized dance floor and thumbnail stage, her winking belly peeking out from under the festive frills falling from her stunning firetruck-red ruched top. (Was it the holidays? Were we drowning our newfound recession realities in cheap champagne and cans of Modelo? Wishing for coal instead of the mortgage crisis in our holiday stockings?)

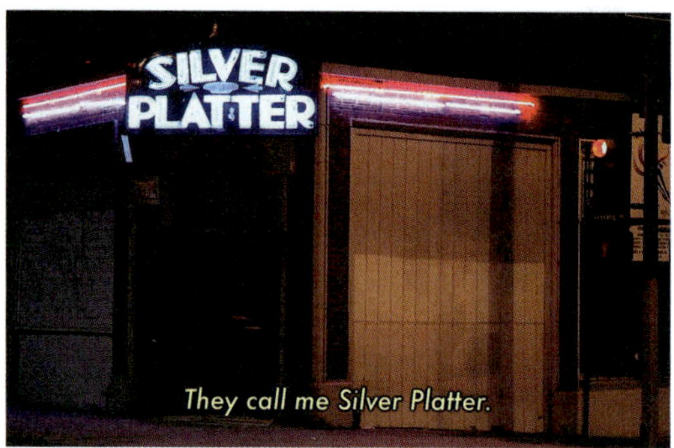

Wu Tsang, Still from *Wildness*, 2012. HD video, color, and sound, 76 min.

Mother's presence is hallowed for the lot of us there that night because she starred (alongside the indomitable Ms. Crystal LaBeija) in the 1968 documentary *The Queen*. That film is a gorgeous visual text that takes back stage at a drag competition Mother Flawless organized.

She dazzles on the occasion of her return to the Silver Platter and marvels at the space that attracts "intelligent young people." Upon seeing the convergence of various communities coming together inside the Silver Platter, seemingly healing whatever rifts—real and imagined—that stood between New York and Los Angeles, between different generations and backgrounds, between the art school and school of hard knocks, Flawless Sabrina offered this blessing to the assembly of transgressive artists demanding new modes for self-expression: "the fist is still up."

—Raquel Gutiérrez

▸
Wu Tsang, *The Fist Is Still Up*, 2010. Neon and acrylic on wood panel, 40 × 70 × 10 in. (101.6 × 177.8 × 25.4 cm)

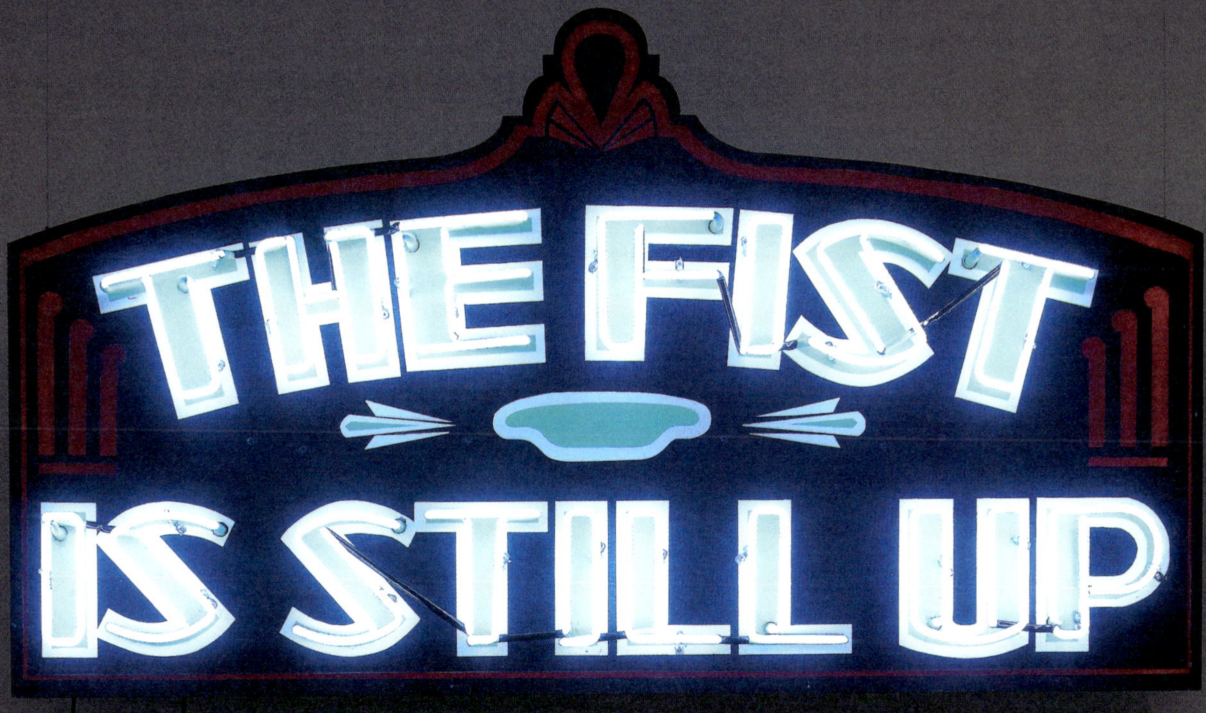
THE FIST
IS STILL UP

MOTHA CHRONOLOGY: 2013–PRESENT —Sage Ballard de la Bastida

2013

POSTER

***Transgender Hiroes*, 2013**
Broadside
33 × 22¾ in. (83.8 × 57.8 cm)

MOTHA's promotional broadside introduced this imminently eminent arts and hirstory institution. The collage featured over 280 individuals: hiroes and trancestors; artists and activists; the famous and the infamous; the real and the fictional; the living and the passed; those who self-identify as trans and those who predate the category altogether.

RESIDENCY

Community Engagement Artist-in-Residence
Yerba Buena Center for the Arts
San Francisco
April 1–June 30, 2013

YBCA's interdisciplinary residency program supported the development of MOTHA as it launched to the public.

Curator: Patricia Maloney

Related Programs:

MOTHA Ribbon-Cutting Ceremony and Inaugural Celebration
June 21, 2013

This event marked the introduction of MOTHA as an autonomous and amorphous institution. The ribbon-cutting ceremony took place in the YBCA atrium, and the event featured performances by local legends.[Fig. 1]

Performers: Gina LaDivina, DJ Lil' Sumo (Toshio Meronek), LOVEWARZ (Zara Thustra and Siobahn Aluvalot), and Honey Mahogany

Necessary Disguise: The Temporary Transvestite Film
June 23, 2013

A reception and panel discussion accompanied this non-existent film series. The panel featured film critics, art historians, and queer academics who presented on films ranging from *Queen Christina* (1933) to *White Chicks* (2004) to investigate the radical, reactionary, and recuperable aspects of this Hollywood film sub-genre.[Fig. 2]

Co-presented by MOTHA and Art Practical
Moderator: Matt Sussman
Panelists: Ralowe Trinitrotoluene Ampu, Annie Danger, Morty Diamond, Irene Gustafson, and Matt Sussman

PROGRAM

MOTHA Art Awards
December 10, 2013

The first annual 2013 MOTHA Art Awards sought to highlight the trans contributions to the cultural landscape while highlighting the inherent structural and societal limitations impacting transgender folks. The democratic nomination and voting process took place from September to November 2013, receiving approximately 2,700 voluntary participant votes across four hundred nominees, whittled down to fifty award winners across twelve voting categories.

Awardees:

Artists of the Year: Laverne Cox, Caldwell Linker, and Amos Mac
Performers of the Year: Ivan Coyote and Red Durkin
Stage Productions of the Year: *F. A. G. G. O. T. S. The Musical!* and *The Fully Functional Cabaret*
Transition Vlogs of the Year: Red Durkin and We Happy Trans
Writers of the Year, Literary: Imogen Binnie, Kate Bornstein, and Ivan Coyote
Writers of the Year, Critical: Janet Mock and Dean Spade
Artist Books/Publications of the Year: *Nevada* by Imogen Binnie and *Original Plumbing* by Amos Mac and Rocco Kayiatos
Musicians of the Year: Big Freedia, KOKUMO, and Rae Spoon
Historians of the Year: Susan Stryker and Transgriot.blogspot.com
Archives of the Year: Center for Sex and Culture and the NYC Trans Oral History Project
Solo Exhibitions of the Year: *Body of Work* by Cassils and *HAG—small, contemporary, haggard* by Vaginal Davis
Group Exhibitions of the Year: *Queers in Exile: The Unforgotten Legacies of LGBTQ Homeless Youth* curated by Alexis Heller and *TWAT/fest: Trans Women's Arts Festival*, Toronto
Art Film/Video of the Year: *MAJOR!* by Annalise Ophelian, *She Gone Rogue* by Zackary Drucker and Rhys Ernst, and *Wildness* by Wu Tsang
New Upcoming Artists of the Year: Hannah Barrett, Erika Bijeljic, Imogen Binnie, KOKUMO, and Morgan M Page
Unrecognized Artists of the Year, Hermit: Malic Amalya, Elliott DeLine, Raphaële Frigon, Nicki Green, Dalice Malice, H. Melt, Mirha-Soleil Ross, Thu Ha Vu, Tobaron Waxman, and Quito Ziegler
Unrecognized Artists of the Year, Too Busy Surviving: Ben McCoy, Chelsea Manning, and Morgan Sea

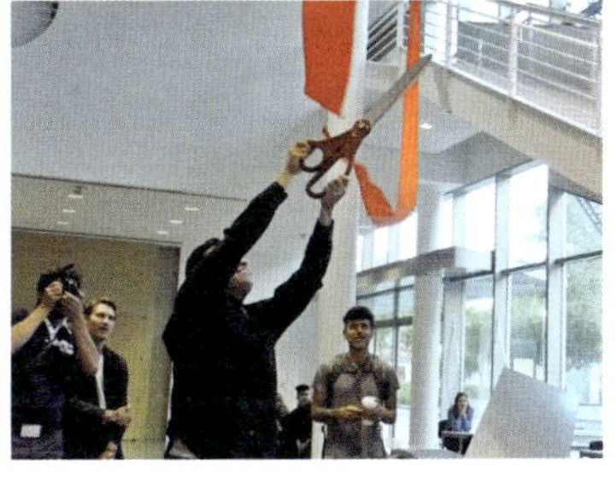
Fig. 1

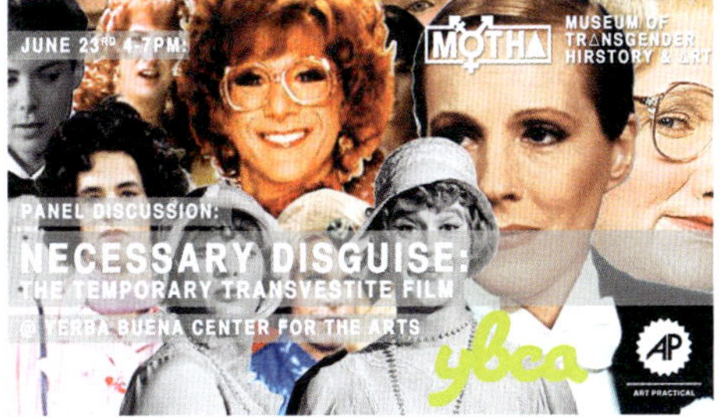

Fig. 2

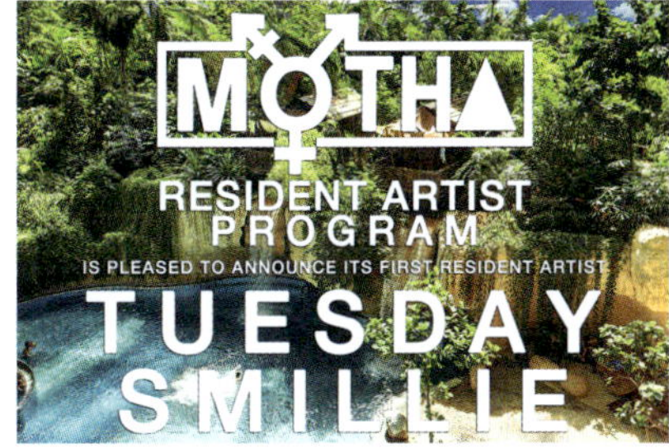

Fig. 3

2014

PROGRAM

MOTHA Resident Artist Program: Tuesday Smillie
2014

The MOTHA Resident Artist Program is an amorphous initiative that seeks to support the work of contemporary trans artists, freeing the artist to create or not create work during the duration of the program. Tuesday Smillie was the inaugural artist-in-residence. She is a multidisciplinary artist working primarily in watercolor, collage, and textiles.[Fig. 3]

PUBLICATION

Transgender Art & Culture in 2014
Buzzfeed
December 29, 2014
https://www.buzzfeed.com/motha/transgender-art-culture-in-2014-15ig3

In lieu of soliciting another round of awards, MOTHA highlighted forty-one trans artists and projects that had any sizable spritz of success in 2014. Notable projects included, but were not limited to: Janet Mock's autobiography *Redefining Realness* (2014); Rhys Ernst's *Dear Lou Sullivan* (2014); *Greer Lankton: LOVE ME* retrospective curated by Lia Gantiano at Participant Inc.; the University of Victoria, British Columbia conference Moving Trans* History Forward (March 21–23, 2014); and the album *Rich Kitchen* (2015) by Geo Wyeth.

2015

EXHIBITION

Transgender Hirstory in 99 Objects: Legends & Mythologies
Organized by MOTHA
ONE National Gay & Lesbian Archives at the USC Libraries
Los Angeles
March 21–August 1, 2015

MOTHA's first exhibition examined the cultural history of trans folks through the material culture of trans hirstory. By blurring the lines of the real and imagined, *Transgender Hirstory in 99 Objects* examined the role of legitimacy and legitimizing arts and history for marginalized and erased histories, such as those of trans people.

Curator: David Evans Frantz

Contributors: Ari Banias, Ezra Berkley Nepon, Kelly Besser, Craig Calderwood, Maxe Crandall, Aaron H. Devor, Angela Douglas, Cyrus Dunham, Reed Erickson, Nicki Green, Raquel Gutiérrez, Monica Helms, Onya Hogan-Finlay, Abram J. Lewis, Sam Lopes, RJ Messineo, Emmett Ramstad, Sir Lady Java, Tuesday Smillie, Tourmaline [fka Reina Gossett], Wu Tsang, and Chris E. Vargas

EXHIBITION

Bring Your Own Body: Transgender Between Archives and Aesthetics
41 Cooper Gallery,
Cooper Union School of Art
New York
October 13–November 14, 2015

Presenting the work of transgender artists and archives, varying from the institutional to personal experience, the exhibition historicized the sexological and cultural imaginary of transgender through a curatorial exploration of collections. While transgender is "neither new nor finished," *Bring Your Own Body* presented contemporary art and world-making practices that move beyond the category of identity politics and existing historical narratives and move towards new historical genealogies of transgender history and culture. MOTHA contributed the poster *Transvestism in the News* (2015) to the exhibition, a collaged poster composed from mid-twentieth-century newspaper clippings collected by Louise Lawrence in the scrapbook "Transvestism in the News," now held at the Kinsey Institute at Indiana University.

Curators: Jeanne Vaccaro with Stamatina Gregory

Exhibition traveled to Glass Curtain Gallery, Columbia College, Chicago, IL, December 10, 2015–January 13, 2016

POSTER

***PRONOUN SHOWDOWN*, 2015/19**
Poster and digital graphic
11 × 17 in. (27.9 × 43.2 cm)

PRONOUN SHOWDOWN humorously intervenes on the inherently patriarchal word HISTORY with various trans, gender neutral, feminist, and "nounself" pronouns. It was created first as a digital graphic and later printed and sold at the Oakland Museum of California's gift shop in conjunction with the exhibition *Queer California: Untold Stories.*

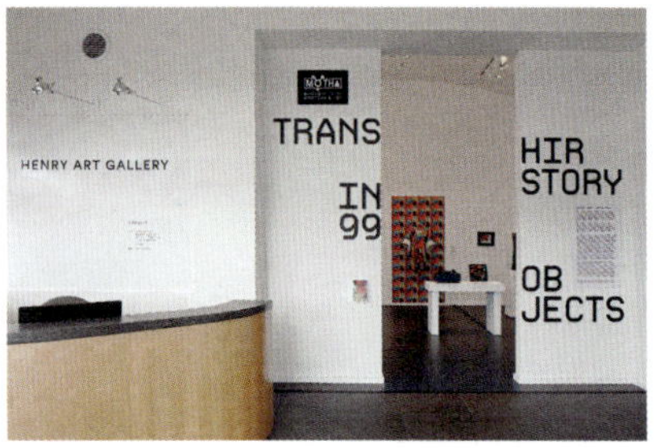

Fig. 4

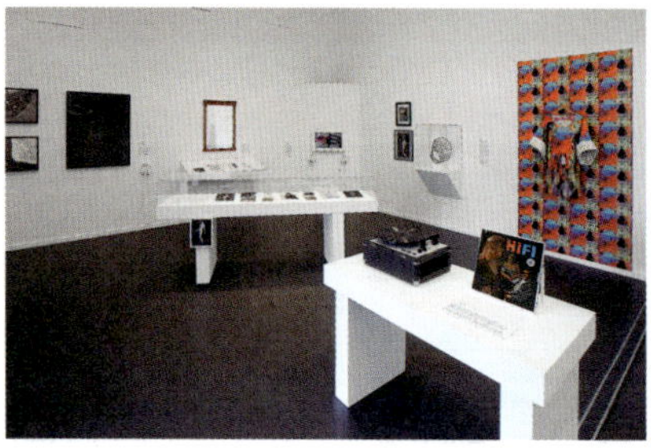

Fig. 5

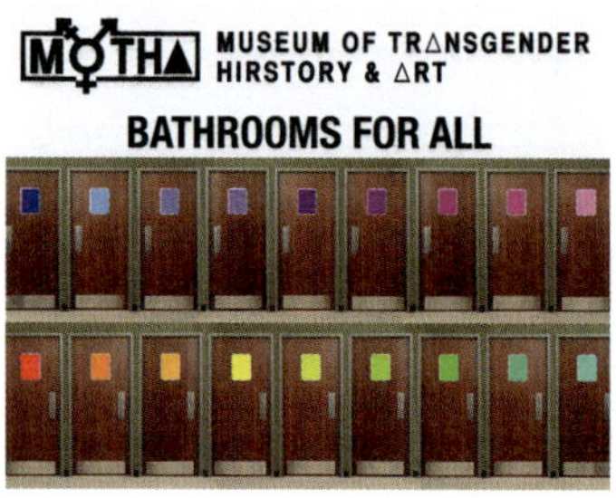

Fig. 6

2016

EXHIBITION

MOTHA and Chris E. Vargas present: Trans Hirstory in 99 Objects
Organized by MOTHA
Henry Art Gallery
Seattle, WA
August 3, 2016–June 4, 2017

This second presentation of *Trans Hirstory in 99 Objects* focuses on the trans lives and experiences of the Pacific Northwest. Taking an expansive approach to transgender, nonbinary, and gender-transgressive identities and expressions, the exhibition explores the histories of community making and activism, historical figures, and legacies of violence and resilience. Figs. 4–5

Curator: Nina Bozicnik

Contributors: Harry Allen, Ria Brodell, Marsha Botzer, micha cárdenas, Darius X, Rhys Ernst, Assunta Femia, Garden of Allah, Francis Hill, Imperial Sovereign Court of Seattle, Ingersoll Gender Center, Aleksa Manila, Dominique Ste. Laurent, *The Transfused Rock Opera* (Freddie Fagula, Nomy Lamm, and The Need), Billy Tipton, *Third Antenna: A Documentary About the Radical Nature of Drag* (Reno Durham, Freddie Perry, and E.T. Russian), Lorenzo Triburgo, Molly Vaughan, and Storm Webber

2017

EXHIBITION

Occupancies
808 Gallery, Boston University
Boston, MA
February 3–March 26, 2017

In response to the political climate in regards to personal resistance against systemic injustices, this group exhibition featured emerging and mid-career artists who use the body as the grounds for political and institutional critique and ideas of agency and visibility. MOTHA contributed a number of posters and videos: the promotional broadside *Transgender Hiroes* (2013); the broadside and video compilation, both titled *Transvestism in the News* (2015), of headlines taken from Louis Lawrence's scrapbooks archived at the Kinsey Institute at Indiana University; *Nell Pickerell (aka Harry Allen, Harry Lingston)* (2016), a video compilation of archival news articles; and *Transgender Alerts: New York Times* (2016), a video compilation of alerts about trans topics received by an email inbox in 2016.

Curators: Kimber Chewning and Lynne Cooney

EXHIBITION

Wild—Transgender and the Communities of Desire
Edith-Russ-Haus for Media Art
Oldenburg, Germany
April 6–June 18, 2017

Inspired by scholar Jack Halberstam's concept of "wild," this international group exhibition drew together artworks dealing with questions and challenges of transgender life and communities. By framing current societal conditions within transgender perspectives, the exhibition looked at how gender complexities challenge the pervasive and entangled role of heteronormativity in societal organization. MOTHA contributed the broadsides *Transgender Hiroes* (2013) and *Transvestism in the News* (2015), as well as three video works of Chris E. Vargas performing as Executive Director of MOTHA.

Curators: Edit Molnár and Marcel Schwierin

PUBLICATION

***Bathrooms For All*, 2017**
For the article by Hugh Ryan, "We Asked Five Artists to Design All-Gender Restroom Signs," *Vice*, April 7, 2017, https://www.vice.com/en/article/d7qnwm/we-asked-five-artists-to-design-all-gender-restroom-signs.

As an uptick of anti-transgender bathroom legislation swept across the country, Ryan invited Vargas, along with four other artists, to imagine all-gender bathroom signage. Fig. 6

EXHIBITION

Trigger: Gender as a Tool and a Weapon
New Museum of Contemporary Art
New York
September 17, 2017–January 1, 2018

Trigger: Gender as a Tool and a Weapon investigated gender's place in contemporary art and culture at a moment of political upheaval and renewed culture wars. The exhibition featured an intergenerational group of artists who explore gender beyond the binary to usher in more fluid and inclusive expressions of identity. MOTHA presented the broadside *Transgender Hiroes* (2013) in the elevator of the museum.

Curators: Johanna Burton, Sara O'Keeffe, and Natalie Bell

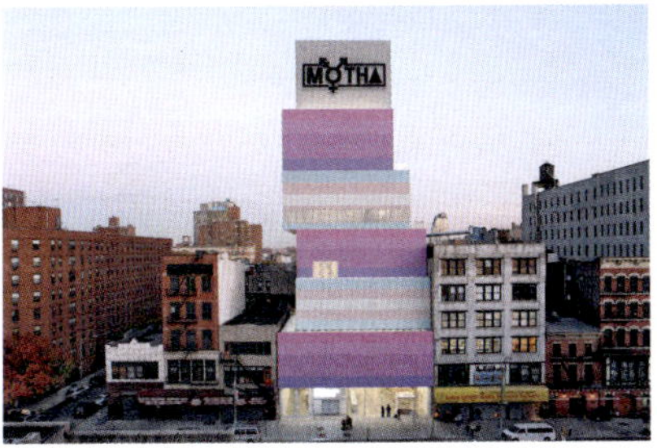

Fig. 7

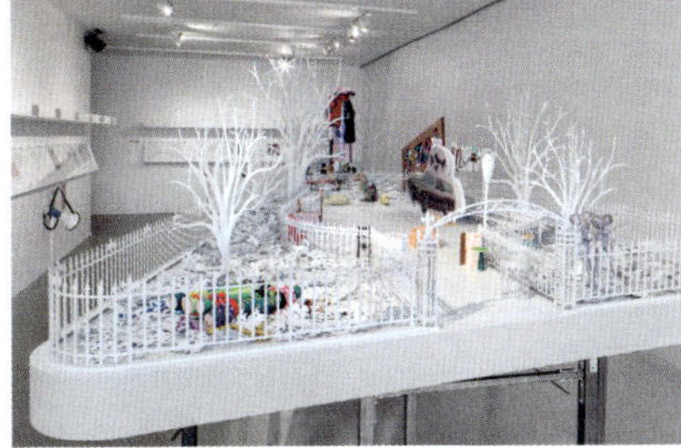
Fig. 8

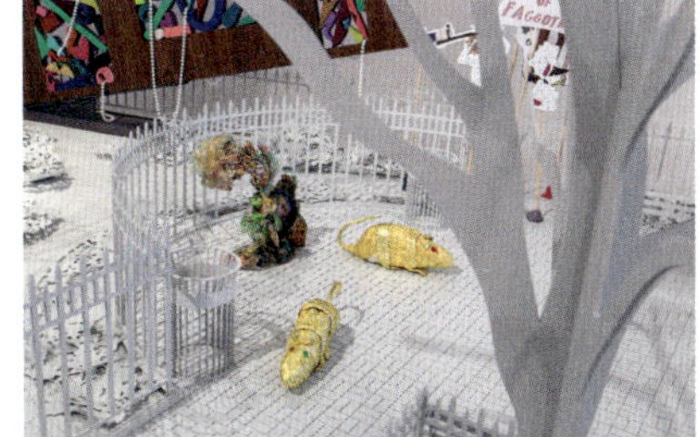
Fig. 9

2018

EXHIBITION

Trans Hirstory in 99 Objects: The University of Victoria Transgender Archives Meets the Museum of Transgender Hirstory & Art (MOTHA)
Organized by MOTHA
Legacy Art Gallery,
Transgender Archives at UVIC
Victoria, BC
January 13–March 29, 2018

The third iteration of *Trans Hirstory in 99 Objects*, presented archival materials from the University of Victoria's Transgender Archives alongside work by contemporary artists from both inside and outside the collection. In addition to documents and publications, the Transgender Archives also has an immense collection of visual art, including work by artists and art made by, and featuring, important trans historical figures.

Contributors: Harry Benjamin, BJ (Barbara Jean), Jayne County, Cassils, Reed Erickson, Garbage Pail Kids, Nan Goldin, Debbie Humphry, Christine Jorgensen, Betty Anne Lind, Aiyyana Maracle, Virginia Prince, Vivek Shraya, Del LaGrace Volcano, and various objects from the Transgender Archives, including T-shirts, buttons, and VHS tapes

EXHIBITION

We. Construct. Marvels. Between. Monuments.
Part of the iteration *Between.*
Portland Art Museum
Portland, OR
July 20–October 14, 2018

This series of five exhibitions developed in partnership with artists and art collectives invited a range of emerging and established voices to ask questions about how the Museum can become more artist-centered and inclusive in its practices and become more critically engaged with a broader array of emerging and established artists in the region.

MOTHA was included in the fourth iteration, *Between.*, which showcased the curatorial processes of folks between or beyond the binary. Through the work of LGBTQIA2S+ artists primarily showcasing video-based work they challenge normative art world conventions accounting for the contemporary conversations of visibility politics. MOTHA contributed *Trans Video Store* (2018), a broadside containing black-and-white digital drawings of VHS and DVD covers as the third continuation to *Trans Hirstory in 99 Objects.*

Curators: Libby Werbel with Sara Krajewski, Grace Kook-Anderson, and Stephanie Parrish

RESIDENCY AND EXHIBITION

MOTHA and Chris E. Vargas: Consciousness Razing—The Stonewall Re-Memorialization Project
Organized by MOTHA
New Museum of Contemporary Art
New York
September 26, 2018–February 3, 2019

For the fifth iteration of *Trans Hirstory in 99 Objects*, Vargas expands on the complex history of memorializing the Stonewall riots by exploring it as a geographically, demographically, and historically contested site. By inviting an intergenerational group of artists to propose new monuments for the riots, Vargas interrogated history as a singular or fixed narrative. Presenting a 1:17 scaled maquette of Christopher Park, the project explores the notion that the history of Stonewall is generative, perpetually unfolding with space for many histories, memories, or concerns. [Figs 7–9]

Contributors: Chris Bogia, Jibz Cameron, Nicki Green, Martine Gutierrez, Sharon Hayes, Thomas Lanigan-Schmidt, Catherine Lord, Devin N. Morris, D'hana Perry, Keijaun Thomas, Geo Wyeth, and Sarah Zapata

2019

EXHIBITION

Trans Hirstory in 99 Objects: Trans Hirstories of the Bay Area
Part of the exhibition *Queer California: Untold Stories*
Oakland Museum of California
Oakland, CA
April 13, –August 11, 2019

Powerful examples of social activism through contemporary artworks and historical materials go beyond the mainstream of queer history in this exhibition. With stories focusing on transgender communities, people of color, women, and other folks at the margins of history, this exhibition deepens and expands the understanding of California's queer history. A physical incarnation of MOTHA installed within the gallery walls was decked out with artwork, archival materials, and ephemera with walls covered in black-and-white digital drawings of California's iconic queer historical figures and landmarks. [Figs. 10–11]

Contributors: Absolute Empress III Shirley, Tina Valentin Aguirre, Jerome Caja, Pat Campano, Willy Chavarria, The Cockettes, DJ Brown Amy (Amy Martinez), Rhys Ernst, Nicki Green, Vero Majano, Miss Major, Toshio Meronek, Kari Orvik, Augie Robles, José Sarria, and Sylvester

Curator: Christina Linden

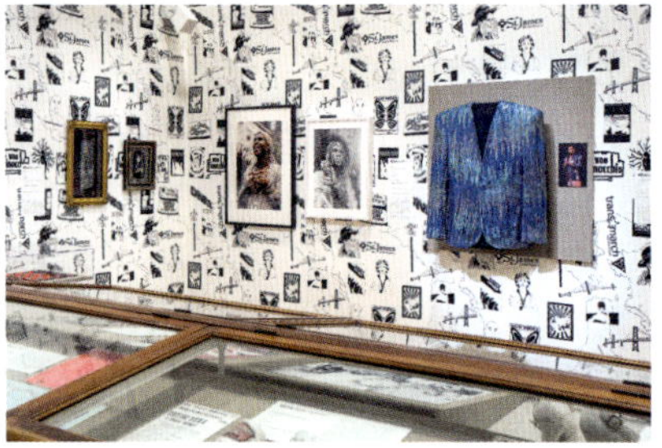

Fig. 10

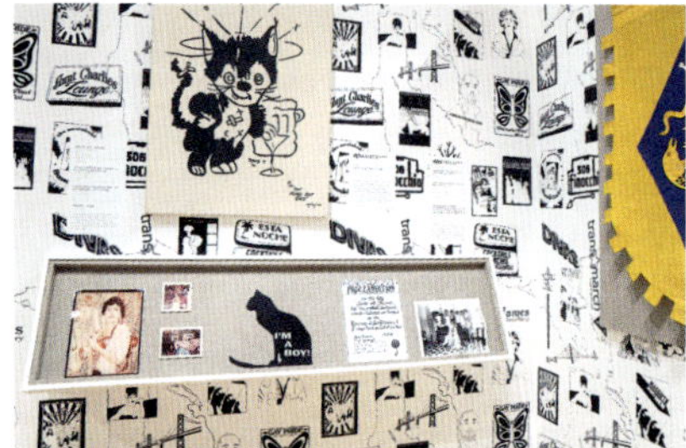

Fig. 11

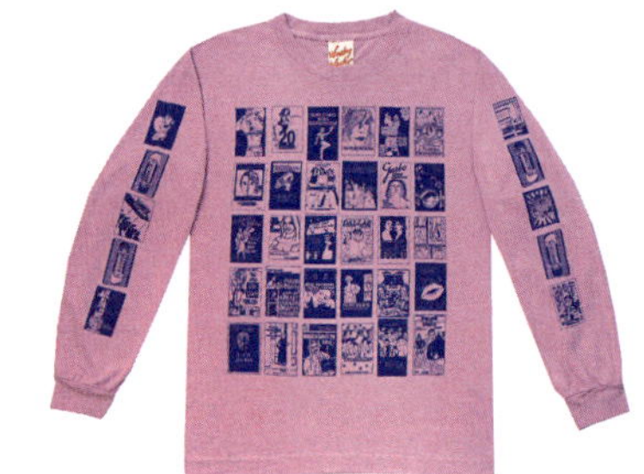

Fig. 12

EXHIBITION

Y'all Better Quiet Down
Leslie Lohman Museum of Art
New York
June 14, 2019–September 15, 2019

On the fiftieth anniversary of the Stonewall uprising, *Y'all Better Quiet Down* recalled Rivera's impassioned demand to show up and commit to the collective struggle. What showing up looks like takes many forms—rage, protest, care, community, and introspection. This exhibition presented contemporary works, protest banners, archival ephemera, and stories from the NYC Trans Oral History Project, *Y'all Better Quiet Down*, centering the everyday and enduring legacies of liberation movements. MOTHA contributed the broadside *Transvestism in the News* (2015).

Curators: Nelson Santos and Jeanne Vaccaro

PROJECT

Merchandise with Wacky Wacko, 2019–23
Los Angeles

In collaboration with Wacky Wacko, a queer Los Angeles-based shop and record label, MOTHA released a *Trans Video Store* (2018) merch line including a long sleeve T-shirt, short sleeve collared shirt, and a tote bag. A portion of proceeds were donated to LGBT Books to Prisoners: A trans-affirming, racial justice-focused, prison abolitionist project sending books to incarcerated LGBTQ-identified people across the United States.Fig. 12

2022

EXHIBITION

***Museum of Transgender Hirstory & Art: Coming Soon Forever*, 2022**
Art on Sunset Digital Billboard
Sunset Spectacular
West Hollywood, CA
October 28, 2022–February 28, 2023

A digital billboard on Sunset Boulevard of an animated video collage of over 280 individuals, many of whom first appeared in the broadside *Transgender Hiroes* (2013). The billboard was a part of an exhibition series, *Art on the Outside*, under the City of West Hollywood's Moving Image Media Art Program (MIMA).

Curator: Jeanne Vaccaro

PROGRAM

MOTHA Resident Artist Program: Jamie Diaz
October 2022

The second MOTHA artist-in-residence, Jamie Diaz is a Mexican American trans woman and artist currently incarcerated in Texas, chosen in recognition of her service to the community, accomplishments as a contemporary artist, and to join her support network on the outside. Through her unique and recognizable style, she weaves motifs representing themes of love, queerness, and human suffering throughout her paintings.

2023

EXHIBITION

Unschöne Museen
gta Exhibitions, ETH Zurich
Zurich, Switzerland
March 1–May 19, 2023

The Museum—capital T, capital M—is the site for contentious debate about the historicization of objects. There is perhaps no other institution whose mere designation so effectively increases the value of what it houses. Drawing on Benedicte Savoy's expression "Unschöne Museen," literally unbeautiful museums, this exhibition presented a selection of works that emphasized the museum as a custodian of power while undoing its camouflage. MOTHA contributed the broadside *Transgender Hiroes* (2013) and videos of Vargas performing as the museum's Executive Director.

Curators: Fredi Fischli, Niels Olsen, and Geraldine Tedder

POSTER

***Hiroes and Transcestors (Transgender Hiroes 2)*, 2023**
Broadside
33 × 22¾ in. (83.8 × 57.8 cm)

A tenth anniversary update to the original *Transgender Hiroes* promotional broadside that visualizes the explosion of gender expansiveness and transgression over the past ten years! Features all new (no repeats) trans, nonbinary, gender-nonconforming artists, public figures, and historical icons not pictured on the first poster.

Bajko, Matthew S. "Political Notebook: Oakland Museum Shines a Light on LGBT History." *Bay Area Reporter*. April 17, 2019. https://www.ebar.com/story.php?274995.

Ballard de la Bastida, Sage. "Trans Like Me: The Museum of Transgender Hirstory & Art and Transgender Approaches to Museum Practice and Historiography." MA thesis. New York University, 2021.

Bryan-Wilson, Julia. "Impermanent Collections: Julia Bryan-Wilson on Queer and Trans Artists' Museums." *Artforum* 60, no. 1 (September 2021): 228–33.

deLire, Luce. "You Are Compensated in Exposure and Nothing More: A Roundtable Discussion with Kübra Uzun, Chris E. Vargas, and Vidisha-Fadescha." *Text Zur Kunst*, no. 129 (March 2023): 98–121.

Earnest, Jarrett. "Does NYC's 'Gay Liberation' Monument Whitewash Stonewall? The New Museum Proposes Replacements." *Vulture*. November 28, 2018. https://www.vulture.com/2018/11/is-nycs-gay-liberation-monument-too-white.html.

Flash, Wesley. "Chris E. Vargas + Trans Representations." Interview with Chris E. Vargas. *How's Your Gender?*. Podcast audio. December 22, 2021. https://podcasts.apple.com/us/podcast/chris-e-vargas-trans-representations/id1560872537?i=1000545886322.

Graves, Jen. "MOTHA Faces the Challenges of Building a Trans Museum." *The Stranger*. September 7, 2016. https://www.thestranger.com/visual-art/2016/09/07/24541297/motha-faces-the-challenges-of-building-a-trans-museum-jen-graves.

Gregory, Stamatina and Jeanne Vaccaro. "Canonical Undoings." In *Trap Door: Trans Cultural Production and the Politics of Visibility*, eds. Johanna Burton, Eric A. Stanley, and Tourmaline [fka Reina Gossett], 349–62. Cambridge, MA: MIT Press, 2017.

Harris, Gareth. "Out and Proud: Stonewall at 50." *The Art Newspaper*. May 2, 2019. https://www.theartnewspaper.com/2019/05/02/out-and-proud-stonewall-at-50.

Hernández, Sarita. "Resisting the Museum: Archiving Trans* Presence and Queer Futures with Chris E. Vargas." *American Quarterly* 71, no. 2 (June 2019): 371–78.

Hotchkiss, Sarah. "Oakland Museum's 'Queer California' Brings Lesser-Known Narratives to Life." *KQED*. April 12, 2019. https://www.kqed.org/arts/13854867/at-omca-californias-past-present-and-future-is-queer.

Kenney, Nancy. "New Museum Hosts Artists & Proposed Monuments to Stonewall Uprising." *The Art Newspaper*. October 24, 2018. https://www.theartnewspaper.com/2018/10/24/new-museum-hosts-artists-proposed-monuments-to-stonewall-uprising.

Kuwabara Blanchard, Sessi. "How Should We Remember the Stonewall Uprising?" *Vice*. October 20, 2018. https://www.vice.com/en/article/a3pxme/stonewall-transgender-history-motha-chris-vargas-new-museum.

Morley, Jack Balderrama. "The Museum of Trans Hirstory & Art (MOTHA) Queers Monument Design." *The Architects Newspaper*. October 31, 2018. https://www.archpaper.com/2018/10/motha-stonewall-memorial-new-museum/.

Posner, Jessica. "Remembering 'Consciousness Razing—The Stonewall Re-Memorialization Project': Chris E. Vargas in Conversation with Jessica Posner." *QED: A Journal in GLBTQ Worldmaking* 6, no. 2 (Summer 2019): 133–54.

Radin, Sara. "Queer Stories Reign Supreme at the Oakland Museum of California." *Vice*. March 22, 2019. https://www.vice.com/en/article/nexg9z/oakland-museum-of-california-2019-queer-art-exhibit.

Ryan, Hugh. "We Asked Five Artists to Design All-Gender Restroom Signs." *Vice*. April 7, 2017. https://www.vice.com/en/article/d7qnwm/we-asked-five-artists-to-design-all-gender-restroom-signs.

Sargent, Antwaun. "99 Objects Embody the 'Hirstory' of Trans Art." *Vice*. August 26, 2016. https://www.vice.com/en/article/4xqzyp/museum-of-transgender-hirstory-art.

Sussman, Matt. "'Queer California: Untold Stories': A Confetti Shower of the Overlooked." *48Hills*. May 10, 2019. https://48hills.org/2019/05/queer-california-oakland-museum/.

Talusan, Meredith. "These Beautiful Pieces of Trans Artwork Offer Glimpses into Diverse Trans Experiences." *Buzzfeed*. November 9, 2015. https://www.buzzfeed.com/meredithtalusan/these-beautiful-pieces-of-trans-artwork.

Tang, Jeannine. "Contemporary Art and Critical Transgender Infrastructures." *In Trap Door: Trans Cultural Production and the Politics of Visibility*, eds. Johanna Burton, Eric A. Stanley, and Tourmaline [fka Reina Gossett], 363–92. Cambridge, MA: MIT Press, 2017.

Vargas, Chris E. "Disembodied States: Press Release." *SFMOMA's Open Space* blog. April 27, 2016. https://openspace.sfmoma.org/2016/04/disembodied-states-press-release/.

Vargas, Chris E. "Introducing the Museum of Transgender Hirstory and Art." In *Trap Door: Trans Cultural Production and the Politics of Visibility*, eds. Johanna Burton, Eric A. Stanley, and Tourmaline [fka Reina Gossett], 121–34. Cambridge, MA: MIT Press, 2017.

Vargas, Chris E. "Selected Objects from the Museum of Trans Hirstory's 'Trans Hirstory in 99 Objects.'" *Girls Like Us*, no. 12 (2019): 22–31.

Visual AIDS. "Interview with Chris Vargas, Executive Director of the Museum of Transgender Hirstory and Art." *Visual AIDS* blog. November 12, 2013. https://visualaids.org/blog/interview-with-chris-vargas-executive-director-of-the-museum-of-transgender.

Walker, Benjamin. "Institutionalized." Interview with Anand Giridharadas and Chris E. Vargas. *Benjamin Walker's Theory of Everything*. Podcast audio. February 28, 2019. https://theoryofeverythingpodcast.com/2019/02/institutionalized/.

Willis, Raquel. "MOTHA Is Preserving Transgender Hirstory One City at a Time." *Out*. April 29, 2019. https://www.out.com/art/2019/4/29/motha-preserving-transgender-hirstory-one-city-time.

Wright, Eric. "Fifty Years after Stonewall, How Do We Commemorate Its Radical History?" *Xtra Magazine*. June 6, 2019. https://xtramagazine.com/power/fifty-years-after-stonewall-how-do-we-commemorate-its-radical-history-156991.

ACKNOWLEDGMENTS

First and foremost, we thank the numerous artists, writers, poets, activists, and other contributors to this book who have generously shared their work with us. Their trust and support have been energizing and gratifying. This project is indebted to the numerous transcestors—some profiled in the book—who came before us and with whom we cannot meet. Their tenacity and resilience created a world for this book and MOTHA to exist in.

Hank Cooper, Qwo-Li Driskill, Che Gossett, Miguel Lopez, Amos Mac, Cyle Metzger, Susan Stryker, Jeannine Tang, and Jeanne Vaccaro all provided expert thoughts and guidance in assembling the 99 objects in this book. Additionally, we thank the following individuals for their assistance, permissions, and support with the works in this publication: Michael Aguhar; Tyler Blackwell; Jacob Breedlove; Anthony Cianciolo and the Jerome Project; Emperor 28 After Norton John Carrillo, The Millennium Emperor, Chairman of the Imperial Council of San Francisco and the late Ron Ross, Mr. Gay San Francisco 1974–1975, Founder of the San Francisco History Association; Jemma DeCristo; eBay user eastsidewarrior; Courtenay Finn; Michael Fox; Christina Frank; Patrick Hill and Julianna Jones; Alexandra Grant and X Artists' Books; Gabriel Joffe; Andrea Joki, Cara Levine, Cybele Lyle, and hannah rubin; Curtis Quam; Mallery Quetawki; Veronica Roberts; Mark Scala; Chino Scott-Chung, Maya Scott-Chung, and Shivaun Nestor; Vivian Sming and Sming Sming Books; T.T. Takemoto; and Jerome Woods and the Black LGBT Project, Los Angeles. A special thanks go to Mariette Pathy Allen, Demetrius Freeman, Jennie Livingston, Javier Romero, and Del LaGrace Volcano for allowing us to reproduce their work in relation to objects within the book.

As editors, we have been supported in our lives and with this project by many folks. Chris would like to thank Fernando Aguilar, Charles Anderson, Jibz Cameron, Eric Cho, Elizabeth Colen, Elaina Ellis, Nicole J. Georges, Barbara Hammer, Christopher Hartshorne, Ryan Kelly, Mom, Beth Pickens, Silky Shah, Milo Smiley, Eric A. Stanley, Jeanne Vaccaro, Amanda Verway, and Greg Youmans for both emotional and creative support. David is indebted to the continued love and encouragement of Jon-erik Mendez. Christina is grateful to Sunny A. Smith and Claude Linden Smith for their patience and love.

Book projects are always a team effort, and we have been privileged to work with stellar colleagues on this publication. Addy Rabinovitch has been fundamental to overseeing permissions, and we thank her for her administrative know-how, managerial excellence, and enthusiasm for this project. Sage Ballard de la Bastida was eager to assemble the chronology of MOTHA's activities to date. We are grateful to have worked with two terrific copyeditors, Nina Lewallen Hufford and Bryne Rasmussen, and we thank them for their thorough and nuanced review of the many texts. Working with ELLA to design this rather complex publication has been especially gratifying. Thanks to partners River Jukes-Hudson and Stephen Serrato, as well as V.E. Chen, Gabrielle Pulgar, and Emma Sutton. We thank Hirmer Publishers, especially Rainer Arnold and Elisabeth Rochau-Shalem, for publishing and distributing this book. *Trans Hirstory in 99 Objects* is a project of Fulcrum Arts' Emerge Program, and we recognize Robert Takahashi Crouch and Patrick J. Reed for their administrative support. Acknowledgments also go to the photographers we worked directly with to document selected objects in this book: John Berens, Ian Byers-Gamber, John Schweikert, and Andreas Michael Velten.

A handful of artists were commissioned to realize new work for this book, and we are incredibly grateful for these dynamic contributions. Edie Fake's ecstatic section dividers and endpapers tease at the objects to come in the book and provide moments for reflection and discovery. Marcel Pardo Ariza photographed several objects and individuals in this book—shown on Ariza's signature vibrant backgrounds. Special thanks to Beth Elliott, Patricio Manuel, Autumn Sandeen, and Sunny A. Smith for appearing in Ariza's photographs with their objects, as well as Matti Bautista, Eugenio Contreras Castillo, and Rainey Korang for modeling in other images by the artist. Finally, we thank Vincent Chong, Sirene Martin, Sunny A. Smith, Bishakh Som, and Keioui Keijaun Thomas for realizing new artworks specifically for this book.

This project would not have been possible without many generous funders. We thank the Ford Foundation, especially Rocío Aranda-Alvarado; Creative Capital; the John Simon Guggenheim Memorial Foundation; the Michael Asher Foundation, especially Karen Dunbar, Roxy Gonzalez, Mathieu Gregoire, and Kate Rouhandeh; and Western Washington University's Research and Sponsored Programs for their recognition and support of this project.

Many museums, archives, and other institutions have kindly shared their collections with us. Special thanks are due to the Archivo Memoria Trans México, especially César González-Aguirre; Archivo Memoria Trans Argentina, especially Luis Juárez; Lambda Archives of San Diego; Louise Lawrence Transgender Archive; Kinsey

Institute at Indiana University; Magnus-Hirschfeld-Gesellschaft, Berlin, especially Ralf Dose; Royal Danish Library, especially Laurids Nielsen; Transgender Archives at the University of Victoria, especially Aaron H. Devor and Lara Wilson; and Yates County History Center, Penn Yan, New York, especially Jonathan Monfiletto. Chapter NY, Commonwealth and Council, Daniel Cooney Fine Art, François Ghebaly, Galerie Isabella Bortolozzi, Hannah Hoffman Gallery, Lyles & King, Ryan Lee Gallery, and STARS Gallery all assisted with obtaining images and permissions from artists. Special thanks to the GLBT Historical Society, especially Isaac Fellman and Ramon Silvestre, and ONE National Gay & Lesbian Archives at the USC Libraries, especially Joseph Hawkins, Alexis Bard Johnson, Michael C. Oliveira, Loni Shibuyama, and Bud Thomas, for providing exceptional support to this project, including access to their collections, the opportunity to photograph objects, and space to meet to plan the book.

MOTHA has organized six exhibitions in the *Trans Hirstory in 99 Objects* series. We thank the hosting institutions and their staffs for realizing these projects, including ONE National Gay & Lesbian Archives at the USC Libraries (curated by David Evans Frantz); the Henry Art Gallery at the University of Washington (curated by Nina Bozicnik); the Legacy Gallery, in collaboration with the Transgender Archives, University of Victoria (curated by Gillian Booth); the New Museum (curated by Johanna Burton, Sara O'Keefe, and Kate Wiener); the Portland Art Museum (curated by Libby Werbel); and the Oakland Museum of California (curated by Christina Linden).

Throughout its decade in existence, MOTHA has been nurtured and supported by numerous advocates, including Lou Barcott, Julia Bryan-Wilson, Gonzalo Casals, E.G. Crichton, Kiersten Fellrath, Stamatina Gregory, Sarita Hernández, Vera Hofmann, Faythe Levine, Katya Min, Bradford Nordeen, Noam Parness, Jessica Posner, Jordan Reznick, Kirstin Ringelberg, Rox Samer, and Raquel Willis, among others.

MOTHA's activities over the past decade have been supported through the enthusiasm and efforts of many artists, writers, educators, organizers, and curators, among others, too numerous to name. MOTHA was initiated as a collective exploration of trans history and identity, and the project has always strived to exceed the bounds of what is possible within institutional structures as well as be something beyond the work of a single creator. We thank you, reader, for your attention, care, and efforts to realize a better future for us all.

—David Evans Frantz,
Christina Linden,
and Chris E. Vargas

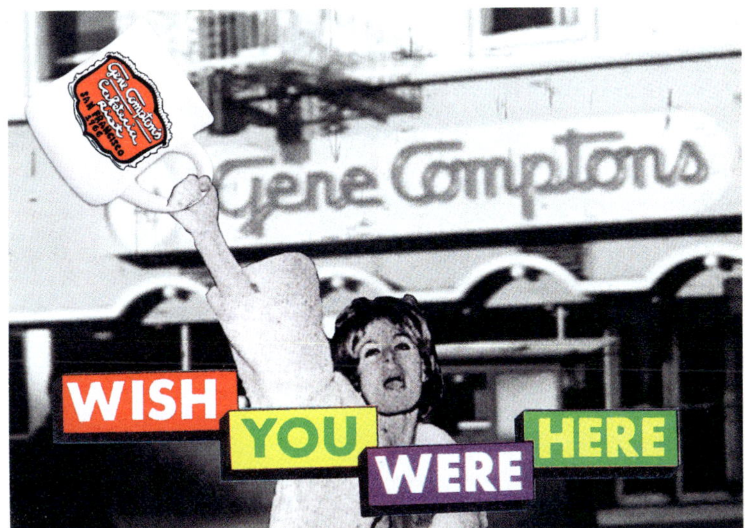

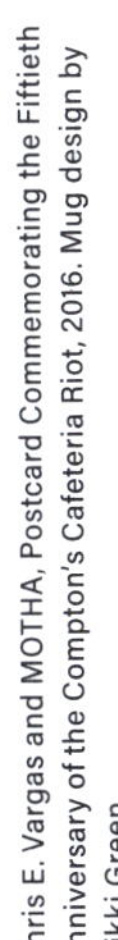
Chris E. Vargas and MOTHA, Postcard Commemorating the Fiftieth Anniversary of the Compton's Cafeteria Riot, 2016. Mug design by Nikki Green

CONTRIBUTOR BIOGRAPHIES

Numerous individuals contributed to this publication. The following individuals wrote texts or contributed works of contemporary art that appear in this book.

A

Tina Valentin Aguirre (they/them) makes movies, writes poetry and prose, and produces art shows and artistic performances. They are the Director of the Castro LGBTQ Cultural District, which centers LGBTQ people, culture, and places in the Castro. Tina holds a BA in Communication from Stanford University.

Dante Alencastre's grassroots dedication and consistent commitment to advancing the LGBT community is reflected in his filmmaking and work on the boards of regional LGBTQ+ arts organizations and political and community groups. His film and activist work has focused particularly on the overlapping Latino/a, transgender, and gender nonconforming sub-tribes within our community, supporting and purposely working with young filmmakers, artists, and activists.

Mariette Pathy Allen is a fine art photographer who focuses on transgender, genderfluid, and the range of people who can be identified as gender variant. Since 1978, she has photographed, interviewed, and advocated on behalf of gender nonconforming people.

Ms. **Ralowe T. Ampu** has been a noted keynote of San Francisco's Lesbians and Straight Corporate Allies Who Tech both 2018 and 2021. Ampu worked hand in hand with the State Department to develop the encryption protocol for Tur, a popular, secure activist messaging app to help the CIA flag Bay Area insurgents.

Archivo de la Memoria Trans Argentina (AMT), located in Buenos Aires, is a space for the protection, construction, and celebration of trans memory. Originating from a collection assembled by Claudia Pía Baudracco, the archive contains more than 15,000 historical items. The archive's team is currently made up of María Belén Correa, Cecilia Estalles, Carmen Ibarra, Cecilia Saurí, Magalí Muñiz, Carola Figueredo, Teté Vega, Luis Juárez, Julieta Gonzalez, Sonia Beatriz Torrese, Carolina Nastri, Guade Bongiovanni, Marina Cisneros, Katiana Villagra, and Paola Guerrero.

Marcel Pardo Ariza (they/them) is a trans visual artist, educator, and curator whose work explores the relationship between queer and trans kinship through constructed photographs, site-specific installations, and public programming. Born in Bogotá, Colombia, and based in San Francisco, their work has been exhibited at the McEvoy Foundation for the Arts, SFMOMA, YBCA, and Palm Springs Art Museum.

B

Sydney Baloue is a TV writer/producer, dancer, archivist, and journalist. He is part of the House of Xtravaganza and was Co-Executive Producer on HBOMax's *Legendary* seasons one and two. Sydney is the author of the forthcoming book *Undeniable: A History of Voguing, Ballroom and How it Changed My Life (and the World).*

Sage Ballard de la Bastida is a transdisciplinary musician, artist, and scholar. Their research focuses on MOTHA's curatorial practices, materiality and collections, and trans art and cultural history. Through their creative work, they aim to uplift the experiences of trans, queer, Latinx, and immigrant voices.

Kelly Besser is the UCLA Library Special Collections Archivist. Besser has processed collections for the African American Firefighter Museum, the Mayme A. Clayton Library and Museum, the Yosemite National Park Service Archives, the Los Angeles County Museum of Art, and the Tom of Finland Foundation. Besser holds an MLIS with an archival studies specialization from UCLA.

Kate Bornstein is an author, actor, and performance artist. She has toured her solo shows worldwide for over thirty years and has appeared on Broadway and NBC's *The Blacklist.* She's well known for her pioneering books on nonbinary gender, such as *Gender Outlaw* and *My New Gender Workbook*, as well as her life-saving book *Hello Cruel World: 101 Alternatives to Suicide for Teens, Freaks, and Other Outlaws.*

Ria Brodell is an artist, educator, and author. Their work explores gender, sexuality, and identity within the context of history, society, and religion. Brodell has exhibited internationally and throughout the United States. Their work has appeared in numerous publications. Their first book, *Butch Heroes*, was released in 2018, and volume two is forthcoming from MIT Press.

Brown Amy (they/them) is a queer Chicanx musician and DJ based in the Bay Area. They are a co-founder/DJ of the award-winning event Hard French in San Francisco and are a collective member/mentor of the queer/female-identified vinyl collective Chulita Vinyl Club. Their style of DJing ranges from lowrider oldies to current house tracks. They have played with some of the most respected DJs in the world, including Honey Dijon, Lakuti, and Egyptian Lover.

C

Cabello/Carceller started their collaboration in the early nineties to examine hegemonic constructions of gender and sexuality in visual practices and propose critical alternatives from queer positions. Their artistic projects combine research, writing, curating, and teaching. Their work was selected for the Spanish Pavilion at the 56th Venice Biennale and has been exhibited in Madrid, Barcelona, Philadelphia, Mexico City, and New York, among others.

Craig Calderwood is a self-taught artist working with drawing and low craft. Their work pushes against the expectations of their chosen materials, creating opaque narratives that explore desire, communities of otherness, and personal biography.

micha cárdenas, PhD, is an artist, and Associate Chair and Associate Professor of Performance, Play & Design, and Associate Professor of Critical Race & Ethnic Studies, at the University of California, Santa Cruz, where she directs the Critical Realities Studio.

Cassils is a transgender artist who makes their own body the material and protagonist of their performances. Cassils's art contemplates the history(s) of LGBTQI+ violence, representation, struggle, and survival. They have had recent solo exhibitions at HOME, Manchester; Station Museum of Contemporary Art; PICA (Perth Institute for Contemporary Arts); and Ronald Feldman Fine Arts, New York.

KJ Cerankowski is an interdisciplinary scholar and writer. His poetry and prose appear in *Entropy*, *DIAGRAM*, *Pleiades*, and *Sinister Wisdom*, among others. He is the author of *Suture: Trauma and Trans Becoming,* a critical lyric memoir published by punctum books. He teaches at Oberlin College.

Susana Vargas Cervantes is a transdisciplinary scholar, internationally recognized for her artistic and academic work at the intersections of alternative criminology, visual studies, and queer studies, both in Anglo North America and Latin America. Her research mines the connections between gender, sexuality, class, and skin tonalities to reconceptualize pigmentocracy as a system of perception.

Shu Lea Cheang is an artist and filmmaker whose genre-bending, gender-hacking practices challenge the existing operating mechanisms and the boundaries imposed on society, geography, politics, and economic structures. From homesteading cyber-space in the 1990s to her current retreat to the post-netcrash BioNet zone, Cheang takes on viral love and biohacking in her current cycle of works.

Vincent Chong (莊志明) is a Queer mixed-race Chinese American artist working in Chinese calligraphy, seal carving, painting, drawing, and performance. Their work centers their QTAPI and QTBIPOC community and chosen family. They have shown their work at SoMad, Skånes Konstförening, Center for Book Arts, Bodeguita 718, the Museum of Chinese in America, and Site Brooklyn.

Clothing Hospital is a nomadic symbolic space created by Archivo Memoria Trans México. As a collaborative project, it attempts to use textiles to embody memory to celebrate the lives of trans women and gender nonconforming people who have died of AIDS in Mexico since the 1980s. The project involves two-person teams; each creative duo features individuals from different generations who nonetheless share a history of how they constructed their own rebellious identities.

Hank Cooper is a Two-Spirit citizen of the Cherokee Nation of Oklahoma and holds an MA in Museology from the University of Washington. As Exhibitions Coordinator at SITE Santa Fe, Hank develops exhibitions that center living contemporary artists and vital community voices rooted in the southwest.

Jayne County moved to New York City in 1968, where she participated in the Stonewall Riots and began a career in underground theater alongside Jackie Curtis. County is best known as the vocalist in her bands Queen Elizabeth (1972), Wayne County and the Backstreet Boys (1974), and Wayne County and the Electric Chairs (1977), and for her multiple studio albums. Her autobiography, *Man Enough to Be a Woman*, was released in 1995.

Maxe Crandall is a poet, playwright, and director. His performance novel about AIDS archives and intergenerational memory *The Nancy Reagan Collection* made the New York Public Library's Best 10 Poetry Books of 2020. Crandall is Associate Director of the Program in Feminist, Gender, and Sexuality Studies at Stanford University.

D

Ms. **Bob Davis** is the founder and director of the Louise Lawrence Transgender Archive. She previously served on the GLBT Historical Society Board of Directors and has presented papers at the University of Victoria's Moving Trans History Forward conference and the ALMS conference in Berlin. Her articles have appeared in *TSQ: Transgender Studies Quarterly* and *Glimmerings* (TransGender Publishing, 2019).

Vaginal Davis is the internationally revered intersexed doyenne of intermedia arts and sciences. She takes public discourse to Dementia 13 levels as she spells out the queer and blatino experience in her own inimitable fashion creating new words out of thin air and crashing bull-in-a-Madame Mau China-Shop style over notions of propriety and reality.

Dr. **Kate Davison** is Lecturer in the History of Sexuality at the University of Edinburgh. She has worked extensively in the LGBTQ archives and museum sector and community activism. Her first book, *Aversion Therapy: Sex, Psychiatry and the Cold War,* will be published by Cambridge University Press.

Dallas Denny edited *Gender Dysphoria: A Guide to Research*, *Current Concepts in Transgender Identity* and the journals *Chrysalis* and *Transgender Tapestry.* She founded American Educational Gender Information Service (AEGIS), was instrumental in creating the Southern Comfort Transgender Conference and FTM Conference of the Americas, and has served as director of Fantasia Fair.

Dr. **Aaron H. Devor**, PhD, FSSSS, FSTLHE, has been studying and teaching about transgender topics since the early 1980s. He established and holds the world's first Chair in Transgender Studies; initiated and hosts the international, interdisciplinary Moving Trans History Forward conferences; and founded and serves as subject matter expert for the world's largest Transgender Archives.

Leah DeVun is Professor of History and Women's, Gender, and Sexuality Studies at Rutgers University. DeVun is the author of *The Shape of Sex: Nonbinary Gender from Genesis to the Renaissance* and co-editor (with Zeb Tortorici) of *Trans*historicities*, a special issue of *TSQ: Transgender Studies Quarterly* devoted to transgender history.

Dr. **Heather Dewey-Hagborg** is an artist and biohacker interested in art as research and technological critique. Her biopolitical art practice includes the project *Stranger Visions*, in which she created portrait sculptures from analyses of genetic material (hair, cigarette butts, chewed-up gum) collected in public places.

Jamie Diaz is a Mexican American trans woman and self-taught artist whose art has inspired many in the LGBTQ+ community by conveying the resilience of the human spirit with a message of love, hope, and beauty. Her work has also garnered a following in the art world and acclaim in publications such as *Artforum*, *Them*, *Xtra*, and *NBC OUT*. Jamie is currently incarcerated in Texas and will be eligible for parole in 2025 after 30 years of confinement in a men's prison.

Mo B. Dick—MC, performer, producer, and historian—is a Drag King Legend. Cited as one of the founding fathers of the modern-day Drag King movement, Mr. Dick has been the subject of books, documentaries, articles, periodicals, podcasts, and more on Drag Kings, proving he is a force to reckon with.

Zackary Drucker is an independent artist, filmmaker, and cultural producer. She has performed and exhibited her work internationally in museums, galleries, and film festivals, including the Whitney Biennial 2014, MoMA PS1, Hammer Museum, Art Gallery of Ontario, and SFMOMA. Drucker was a producer on the Golden Globe and Emmy Award-winning show *Transparent*. *The Lady and The Dale*, her directorial debut for television, premiered on HBO in early 2021.

F

Edie Fake is a painter and visual artist whose work examines issues of trans identity and "queer space" through the lens of architecture and ornamentation.

Bree Fram is an astronautical engineer and Lieutenant Colonel in the US Space Force. She is one of the highest-ranking transgender officers in the US military. Bree is also president of SPARTA, a transgender military education and advocacy non-profit, and writes about LGBTQ+ leadership development.

David Evans Frantz is a curator based in Los Angeles. He began his curatorial career at ONE National Gay & Lesbian Archives at the USC Libraries, where he first worked with Chris E. Vargas and MOTHA and met Christina Linden.

Edgar Fabián Frías works in installation, photography, video art, sound, sculpture, printed textiles, GIFs, performance, social practice, and community organizing, among other forms. Their art addresses historical legacies and acts of resistance, resiliency, and radical imagination within the context of Indigenous Futurism, spirituality, play, pedagogy, animism, and queer aesthetics.

A native of Los Angeles, **Anthony Friedkin** has been documenting the social landscape through photo essays for over fifty years. By using his camera as a means of personal discovery, his full-frame, black-and-white photographs explore the many layers of reality. His work is included in the permanent collections of the J. Paul Getty Museum, Museum of Modern Art, Los Angeles County Museum of Art, and the George Eastman House in Rochester.

G

Pippa Garner is a transdisciplinary American artist pushing back against systems of consumerism, marketing, and waste. For over five decades, her uncompromising approach to life and practice has allowed her to interact with the worlds of illustration, editorial, television, and art without ever becoming beholden to them.

David J. Getsy's books include *Queer Behavior: Scott Burton and Performance Art* (University of Chicago Press, 2022), *Abstract Bodies: Sixties Sculpture in the Expanded Field of Gender* (Yale University Press, 2015/23), and the anthology of artists' writings, *Queer* (MIT Press, 2016). He teaches at the University of Virginia, where he is the Eleanor Shea Professor of Art History.

Jamison Green is an accomplished activist, community leader, and author whose work has focused on trans rights, health, and visibility, especially for trans male/masculine individuals. He hails from Oakland, California, and he transitioned in 1988. His best-known work is *Becoming a Visible Man* (Vanderbilt University Press, 2004/20).

Nicki Green is a transdisciplinary artist working primarily in clay. Her sculptures, ritual objects, and various flat works explore topics of historical preservation, conceptual ornamentation, and the aesthetics of otherness. She has exhibited internationally, notably at the New Museum, New York, and the Musée d'Art Moderne, Paris. She received a BFA from San Francisco Art Institute (2009) and an MFA from UC Berkeley (2018).

César González-Aguirre is an independent curator based in Mexico City. He was chief curator of Centro de la Imagen from 2018 to 2021, where he curated *Agustín Martínez Castro: Piratas en el boulevard. Irrupciones públicas, 1978–1988* (2018) and *Positivo negativo: Adherencias culturales en la lucha contra el sida en México,* 1978–2022 (2023). He is a co-founder and member of the Archivo Memoria Trans México.

Martine Gutierrez is a transdisciplinary artist who creates elaborate narrative scenes to subvert pop-cultural tropes in the exploration of identity. Her work includes billboards, episodic films, music videos, and the renowned magazine *Indigenous Woman*. Her malleable, ever-evolving self-image catalogs the confluence of seemingly disparate modes, conveying limitless potential for reinvention and reinterpretation.

Raquel Gutiérrez is an award-winning critic, essayist, poet, and educator based in Southern Arizona. Gutiérrez's first book *Brown Neon* (Coffee House Press) was named one of the best books of 2022 by *The New Yorker* and listed in the Best Art Books of 2022 by *Hyperallergic*.

H

Justin Hall is an award-winning cartoonist whose work has appeared in *The Best American Comics*, *Best Erotic Comics*, and *SF Weekly*. He is the Chair of the MFA in Comics program at California College of the Arts, the first Fulbright Scholar of Comics, and the Producer of the documentary *No Straight Lines*, inspired by his Lambda-Award-winning book.

Gabby Omoni Hartemann (they/them) is Afro Guianese, Omo Òrìṣà in the Ilê Axé Iyaba Omi community (Brazil), and a PhD candidate in Anthropology and Archaeology at the Federal University of Minas Gerais, Brazil. Their research is rooted in anti-colonial and Afro-centered re-understandings of archaeology in order to tell the stories of silenced existences.

Monica Helms is an American transgender activist, author, and veteran of the United States Navy. She is the creator of the transgender flag.

Murray Hill (aka "Mr. Showbiz") is a comedian, host, and international entertainment phenomenon. When he's not on stage, he's on *TV in Life & Beth* (Hulu), *Somebody Somewhere* (HBO), and *Drag Me to Dinner* (Hulu). *New York Magazine* named him one of the "Fifty Most Iconic Gender Benders of All Time."

Banyi Huang is an artist and writer who navigates identity, gender, and bodily orientation through 3D-printed sculptures and animation. A diasporic drifter, Huang locates their belonging in mythologies, the non-human, and personal rituals, within a process of queer worldbuilding. Born in Bejing, they are based in Brooklyn, New York.

Bobbie Hughes was a poet who visited Beverly Shaw's Club Laurel in Studio City, California, sometime in the 1950s.

J

Andrea Jenkins is a soulful poet, educator, artist, respected historian, and political powerhouse. In 2017, she became the first out Black Trans woman elected to public office in the United States. She is President of the Minneapolis City Council. She holds an MA in Community Development from Southern New Hampshire University and an MFA in Creative Writing from Hamline University.

Gabriel Joffe is a Denver-based communications worker who met Jamie Diaz in 2013 while volunteering with Black & Pink in Boston. They are honored to work alongside Jamie and organizations such as A.B.O. Comix, Justice Arts Coalition, and Trans Pride Initiative. Gabriel is passionate about the role of art and imagination in movements for prison abolition and trans liberation.

John Johnston is a documentary filmmaker and an accomplished multidisciplinary artist and designer. He has collaborated with director Dante Alencastre on three award-winning documentary films, crafting stories of exemplary, untold activism within the Los Angeles Trans and LGBTQ communities as the team's producer, researcher, writer, and designer.

K

Rocco Kayiatos is an artist, educator, and organizer who released four albums as Katastrophe, the first openly trans man to release an LP. He co-founded *Original Plumbing* magazine, created award-winning content for BuzzFeed, Grindr, Spotify, and FOLX Health, and founded the Intentional Man Project, Camp Lost Boys (the first sleep-away summer camp exclusively for adult men of trans experience), and authored the *Mindful Masculinity Workbook*.

Cáel M. Keegan is an Associate Professor at Concordia University whose research and writing analyze the histories and theoretical implications of queer and transgender media representation, aesthetic figuration, and cultural production. He has written extensively on how trans/queer affects and phenomenologies are articulated through popular media formats, platforms, and genres.

Young Joon Kwak (they/she) is an LA-based multidisciplinary artist whose work spans sculpture, performance, video, sound, and community-based collaborations. Kwak is also the founder of Mutant Salon, a roving beauty salon/platform for collaborative performances and installations with their community of queer/trans/POC artists and performers, and the lead performer in the electronic-dance-noise band Xina Xurner.

L

Greta LaFleur is Associate Professor of American Studies at Yale University, the author of *The Natural History of Sexuality in Early America* (2018), and the editor of *Trans Historical: Gender Plurality Before the Modern* (2021) and a special issue of *TSQ: Transgender Studies Quarterly* on "Trans Exclusionary Feminisms and the Global New Right" (2022).

Lawrence La Fountain-Stokes is Professor and Chair of the Department of American Culture at the University of Michigan. He is the author of *Queer Ricans: Cultures and Sexualities in the Diaspora* and *Translocas: The Politics of Puerto Rican Drag and Trans Performance.* He has performed as Lola von Miramar since 2010.

M. Carmen Lane (African American, Mohawk, Tuscarora) is a two-spirit artist, writer, doula, and facilitator based in Cleveland, Ohio. Carmen is the founder and director of ATNSC: Center for Healing and Creative Leadership, an artist-led, socially engaged, urban retreat, residency, research, and exhibition space sited in a residential home.

Scott Larson is a Lecturer in the Department of American Culture at the University of Michigan. He holds a PhD in American Studies from George Washington University. His work on transgender history has been published in *Early American Studies* and *TSQ: Transgender Studies Quarterly* as well as edited volumes.

Thomas (T.) Jean Lax is a curator, writer, and scholar specializing in Black art and performance. At the Museum of Modern Art, they recently organized the exhibition *Just Above Midtown: Changing Spaces* with Lilia Rocio Taboada in collaboration with JAM's founder Linda Goode Bryant.

Abram J. Lewis is a public historian-activist interested in intersectional feminist, queer, trans, and disability social movements, and is a co-founder of the New York City Trans Oral History Project. As a day job, Lewis teaches in Women's, Gender, and Sexuality Studies at Williams College, with a research focus on uses of madness and magic in 1970s queer and trans activism.

Candice Lin and **P Staff** live and work in Los Angeles and have collaborated since 2010. Their practice focuses on the queer potential of herbal practices, hacked technologies, and cross-species interactions. Solo presentations include *Lesbian Gulls, Dead Zones, Sweat and T.*, Human Resources, Los Angeles (2017), and *Stressed Herms, Sweat, & Period Gas.*, ICA Shanghai (2020). Their work has been included in significant group exhibitions internationally, including *Trigger: Gender as a Tool and a Weapon*, New Museum (2017), *Between Bodies*, Henry Art Gallery (2018), *I, I, I, I, I, I, Kathy Acker*, ICA, London (2019), and *The Body Electric*, Walker Art Center (2019).

Hans Lindahl is a writer bringing intersex community perspectives to medicine and popular media. As the former Communications Director of interACT, Hans was part of the team that passed the first US legislation denouncing intersex infant genital surgeries. Hans's resources on intersex topics have been translated into four languages.

Christina Linden met Chris E. Vargas through friends. She met David Evans Frantz while conducting research for the exhibition *Queer California: Untold Stories*, which she curated at the Oakland Museum of California, and in which MOTHA had an installation. She is the Director of Academic and Public Programs at the Cantor Arts Center at Stanford University.

Jennie Livingston's film *Paris is Burning*, which won the Sundance Film Festival Grand Jury Prize in 1991, was added to the Film Registry at the Library of Congress in 2016. In 2022, *New York Times* critic A.O. Scott named it one of the ten best films of all time. Other films by Livingston include the shorts *Hotheads* (1996), *Through the Ice* (2005), and *Who's the Top?* (2005).

Miguel A. López is a writer and curator whose work focuses on the role of art in politics and public life, collective practice, and queer and feminist rewritings of history. He worked as chief curator and later co-director at *TEOR/éTica* (Costa Rica) from 2015 to 2020. He recently curated the retrospective exhibition *Cecilia Vicuña: Seehearing the Enlightened Failure.*

M

Amos Mac is an out trans artist, writer, and co-founder of *Original Plumbing* magazine. Amos has written and produced for television on shows including *Gossip Girl*, *Clean Slate*, and *Gaycation* and co-wrote *No Ordinary Man*, a documentary about the complicated jazz man and trans icon Billy Tipton.

Vero Majano is a multidisciplinary artist born and raised in San Francisco's Mission District. As a storyteller and curator, her practice includes live cinema, archival film, performance, and collage, to preserve and include untold queer Latinx narratives in a greater San Francisco history.

Miss Major is a living legend in trans/queer circles around the world. She is currently based in Little Rock, Arkansas, where she runs the House of GG-TILIFI retreat center.

Kameelah L. Martin is Professor of African American Studies and English at the College of Charleston. Her research sits at the crossroads of African Diaspora literatures and Folklore Studies. Her interdisciplinary reach spans such topics as African-derived spiritualities, African American genealogy, Beyoncé, and Black popular culture.

Sirene Martin is a multimedia artist from Kentucky. She holds a BA in Pan-African Studies from the University of Louisville. Her art elevates the rich Root culture and religions of the Black folks that made Kentucky their home.

A graduate of Goldsmiths, University of London, Montreal-based multidisciplinary artist **Manuel Mathieu** is known for his works, which explore themes of historical violence, erasure, and the physicality of Haitian visual culture and legacy. His research invites us to consider different possible futures by revisiting the past.

Uri McMillan is a writer based in Los Angeles. He has published essays in *Women & Performance: a journal of feminist theory*, *GLQ: A Journal of Lesbian and Gay Studies*, *ASAP/Journal*, and museum/gallery-based publications for the Studio Museum in Harlem, Aperture Foundation, MCA Chicago, and the Brooklyn Museum.

Freddie Mercado Velázquez is a Puerto Rican visual and performance artist who focuses on the crossings between painting, sculpture, installation, and performance art. A graduate of the Escuela de Artes Plásticas y Diseño de Puerto Rico, he has been exploring drag and androgyny for over thirty years.

Toshio Meronek is a San Francisco-based journalist, host of the podcast Sad Francisco, and co-author of *Miss Major Speaks: Conversations with a Black Trans Revolutionary* (Verso Books, 2023).

Cyle Metzger is an Assistant Professor of Art History in the Department of Art at Bradley University. His current manuscript, *Deep Cuts: Transgender History in American Art after World War II*, engages histories of gender transformation in American art since the end of the Second World War.

Deborah A. Miranda is an enrolled member of the Ohlone-Costanoan Esselen Nation with Santa Ynez Chumash ancestry. She is the author of *Bad Indians: A Tribal Memoir*, four poetry collections, and essays exploring California Indian experiences of missionization. She is co-editor of *Sovereign Erotics: An Anthology of Two-Spirit Literature.*

Kent Monkman is an interdisciplinary Cree artist practicing in Canada. Known for provocative interventions into Western art history, Monkman explores the complexities of Indigenous experiences. His gender-fluid alter-ego Miss Chief Eagle Testickle often appears in his work as a legendary being who reverses the colonial gaze to challenge received notions of Indigenous peoples.

N

Annalee Newitz (they/them) writes science fiction and nonfiction. Their latest novel is *The Terraformers*, and their latest nonfiction book is *Four Lost Cities: A Secret History of the Urban Age.*

O

Kari Orvik is a photo-based artist and educator. She engages ideas of presence and absence through portraiture and site-specific narratives. She has been in residence at Headlands Center for the Arts and RecologySF. Her work has been shown at the SFO Airport Museum and the Oakland Museum of California. She teaches at Stanford University.

P

Morgan M Page is a writer, artist, and historian in London, UK. She hosts the trans history podcast *One From the Vaults* and co-wrote the feature film *Framing Agnes.*

Eric Darnell Pritchard is an award-winning writer, cultural critic, and the Brown Chair in English Literacy and Associate Professor of English at the University of Arkansas. They are the author of *Fashioning Lives: Black Queers and the Politics of Literacy* (Southern Illinois University Press, 2016) and numerous publications on fashion, beauty, popular culture, and its intersections with rhetoric, language, and literacy.

Puppies Puppies (Jade Guanaro Kuriki-Olivo) lives and works in New York. She recently received the Toby's Award, given every two years by the Museum of Contemporary Art in Cleveland, Ohio. Recent exhibitions include *Transcendence*, Performance Space, New York (2022); *TRANNY*, Galerie Barbara Weiss, Berlin (2022); and *Nothing New*, New Museum, New York (2023).

Brontez Purnell is an American writer, musician, dancer, and director based out of Oakland, California. He is the author of several award-winning books, including the punk zine *Fag School* (c. 2000s), *Since I Laid My Burden Down* (2017), and *100 Boyfriends* (2022), which won a Lambda Literary Award for Gay Fiction. Purnell is the frontman for the punk band *The Younger Lovers* and founded the Brontez Purnell Dance Company.

R

Emmett Ramstad is a transdisciplinary sculptor living in Minneapolis, Minnesota. His work explores body maintenance and the intimate collectivity of public space. Recent achievements include a McKnight Visual Artist Fellowship, a Franconia Sculpture Park Fellowship, and a Forecast Public Art Research and Development Grant.

Richard T. Rodríguez is Professor of English at the University of California, Riverside. He is the author of *Next of Kin: The Family in Chicano/a Cultural Politics* and *A Kiss across the Ocean: Transatlantic Intimacies of British Post-Punk and US Latinidad*, both published by Duke University Press.

Liz Rosenfeld is an interdisciplinary artist and writer. Rooted in the corporeal, Liz focuses on the sustainability of emotional and political ecologies, cruising methodologies, hypocritical desire, and past/future histories regarding how memory is queered. Liz lives and works in Berlin, Germany.

S

Dorothy R. Santos (she/they) is a Filipino American writer, artist, and educator. She is a PhD candidate in Film and Digital Media at the University of California, Santa Cruz. Her writing appears in *art21*, *Art in America*, *Ars Technica*, *Hyperallergic*, *Rhizome*, *Slate*, and *Vice Motherboard*.

Carmen Selam's work is a reflection of living in contemporary society as a queer Yakama-Comanche woman. She is a multidisciplinary artist working in printmaking, painting, and installations, in addition to being a traditional tribal artist in weaving and beadwork. She was born and raised on the Yakama Reservation located in Washington State. She is an enrolled member of the Yakama Nation and is also of Comanche descent.

Vivek Shraya is an artist whose body of work crosses the boundaries of music, literature, visual art, theatre, and film. Her album *Part-Time Woman* was nominated for the Polaris Music Prize, and her best-selling book *I'm Afraid of Men* was heralded by *Vanity Fair* as "cultural rocket fuel." She is a director on the board of the Tegan and Sara Foundation, and is currently adapting her debut play, *How to Fail as a Popstar*, for television with the support of CBC.

Tuesday Smillie is a visual artist working with textiles, collage, printmaking, and watercolor. At the core of her work is a question about the individual and the group: the binary of inclusion and exclusion and the porous membrane between the two.

Sunny A. Smith is a queer, non-binary artist, time traveler, and practical animist based in the San Francisco Bay Area. Their activism takes form in a queered materiality that summons the ghosts of history/herstory/hxstory, tracing alternate lineages, transmitting different storylines, offering hopeful re-workings.

Dr. **SA Smythe** is a poet, transdisciplinary artist, translator, and critical theorist committed to Black trans thrival and Black belonging beyond all borders. They are Assistant Professor of Black Studies and the Archive at the University of Toronto and are based between Europe and Turtle Island (Tkaronto and Tongva land).

C. Riley Snorton is a scholar and author of *Black on Both Sides: A Racial History of Trans Identity* (2017) and *Nobody is Supposed to Know: Black Sexuality on the Down Low* (2014).

Río Sofia is a visual artist, arts worker, and organizer. Her recent body of artwork explores forced feminization porn, a genre that fantasizes about experiencing gender transformation through coercion and loss of control. In June 2020, Río joined a small team of volunteers to organize a viral fundraising campaign with GLITS, an organization founded by trans and sex worker advocate Ceyenne Doroshow.

Bishakh Som is an Indian American trans femme artist and author. Her graphic novel *Apsara Engine* won a 2020 Los Angeles Times Book Prize for Best Graphic Novel and a 2021 Lambda Literary Award for Best LGBTQ Comics. Her graphic memoir *Spellbound* was also a 2021 Lambda Literary Award finalist.

Dean Spade has been working to build queer and trans liberation based in racial and economic justice for the past two decades. Dean is the author of *Normal Life: Administrative Violence, Critical Trans Politics and the Limits of Law* (South End Press, 2011) and *Mutual Aid: Building Solidarity During This Crisis (and the next)* (Verso Books, 2020).

Emji Saint Spero is a transqueer performer, pervert, and the author of *disgust* and *almost any shit will do*. They co-founded the Oakland-based small press Timeless, Infinite Light with Joel Gregory, and they were co-developmental editor for *We Both Laughed in Pleasure: The Selected Diaries of Lou Sullivan* with Lauren Levin.

Eric A. Stanley is the author of *Atmospheres of Violence: Structuring Antagonism and the Trans/Queer Ungovernable*. They organize and teach in the San Francisco Bay Area.

Alexandra Minna Stern is the Dean of Humanities and Professor of English, History, and in the Institute for Society and Genetics at the University of California, Los Angeles. She is the author of the award-winning *Eugenic Nation: Faults and Frontiers of Better Breeding in Modern America* and the founder and co-director of the Sterilization and Social Justice Lab.

Allucquére Rosanne (Sandy) Stone is Professor Emerita and founder of the ACTLab at the University of Texas at Austin, Senior Artist at the Banff Centre for the Arts, and a Fellow of the University of California Humanities Research Institute. She has been a filmmaker, rock 'n roll music engineer, neurologist, social scientist, science fiction author, cultural theorist, and performer.

Chris Straayer is an Associate Professor of Cinema Studies at New York University and the author of *Deviant Eyes, Deviant Bodies* (Columbia University Press, 1996). His current research combines trans/queer studies with interests in medical science, social science, the arts, and cultural studies.

Dr. **Jonathan Michael Square** is the Assistant Professor at Parsons School of Design. He was previously a lecturer in the Committee on Degree in History and Literature at Harvard University and a fellow in the Costume Institute at the Metropolitan Museum of Art. The recipient of numerous fellowships and grants, Dr. Square's work considers histories of enslavement through the lens of fashion, and his research has appeared in numerous scholarly and public-facing venues.

T

Jeannine Tang is an art historian and Assistant Professor in the Department of Performance Studies at NYU. She writes about contemporary art in such venues as *Art Journal*, *Artforum*, and *GLQ: A Journal of Lesbian and Gay Studies*, among others, and is completing the monograph *Living Legends: Contemporary Art and Transgender History*.

Michelle Tea is the author of over twenty books, including Valencia, the PEN-award-winning *Against Memoir*, and the memoir *Knocking Myself Up*. She is the brainstormer of Drag Queen Story Hour, Sister Spit, and other literary interventions.

Joey Terrill is an artist who lives and works in Los Angeles. As a young person, Terrill was active in both the Chicano Movement and Gay Liberation, through which he learned the grassroots activism and skills he used a decade later during the AIDS crisis. His work is held by the Museum of Contemporary Art, Los Angeles; the Museum of Modern Art; and the Whitney Museum of American Art, among others.

Keioui Keijaun Thomas is based in Brooklyn, New York. She earned her MA from the School of the Art Institute of Chicago and her BFA with honors from the School of Visual Arts in New York City. Thomas is the inaugural winner of the Queer | Art 2020 Illuminations Grant for Black Trans Women Visual Artists and a 2018 Franklin Furnace Fund recipient.

Chelsea Thompto (she/her) is a transdisciplinary artist and educator working at the intersections of art, trans studies, and technology. Her research-based studio practice is strongly rooted in her experience as a transwoman and spans a variety of media which often includes code, video, sound, writing, and sculpture.

Tourmaline is an artist, filmmaker, activist, editor, and writer. Her work was recently included in *The Milk of Dreams* at the 59th Venice Biennale and she was the subject of a solo exhibition at the Mudam Luxembourg. Tourmaline's work is in major public and private collections such as the Brooklyn Museum, New York; Metropolitan Museum of Art, New York; MoMA, New York; National Gallery of Victoria, Melbourne; and Tate Modern, London.

Wu Tsang is an award-winning filmmaker and visual artist who combines documentary and narrative techniques with fantastical detours into the imaginary. Tsang is a 2018 MacArthur Fellow, and her projects have been presented at museums, biennials, and film festivals internationally. Tsang received a BFA (2004) from the Art Institute of Chicago (SAIC) and an MFA (2010) from the University of California, Los Angeles (UCLA).

V

Jeanne Vaccaro is an Assistant Professor of Transgender and Museum Studies at the University of Kansas. She curated *Bring Your Own Body: transgender between archives and aesthetics* and is co-founder of the New York City Trans Oral History Project, a community archive partnership with the New York Public Library.

Chris E. Vargas is an artist, the founder of the Museum of Trans Hirstory & Art, and co-editor of this book you're holding.

Dan Vena is an Assistant Adjunct Professor in the Department of Film and Media at Queen's University. He is radically invested in horror cinema, spirituality, and death positivity as part of his pedagogical and research practices.

W

Harron Walker is a writer and freelance journalist who lives in Brooklyn. Her work has appeared in the *New York Times*, *New York Magazine*, *GQ*, *Out*, and other publications. She is writing her first book, an essay collection, for Random House.

McKenzie Wark is the author of *Reverse Cowgirl* (Semiotexte, 2020), *Capital is Dead* (Verso Books, 2021), and *Raving* (Duke University Press, 2023), among other things. Her correspondence with Kathy Acker was published as *I'm Very into You* (Semiotexte, 2015). She lives and teaches in New York City.

Tobaron Waxman is a visual artist who sings. Based in New York, Toronto, and Warsaw, Waxman composes performances for photographs, video, and site-specific installations, and is a trained vocalist in Jewish liturgical music. Waxman also produces curatorial projects internationally, including the Intergenerational LGBT Artist Residency as a combined curatorial, relational/live art, and sociopolitical praxis. Since 2017, Tobaron has developed the Trans Collections at the ArQuives in Toronto.

Karleigh Webb wears a lot of hats. This out transgender woman has worked as a reporter, anchor, sportscaster, and videographer, and for nearly twenty years as a TV network producer. In addition to being a dynamic, versatile journalist, she's an activist and advocate for intersectional justice across her work and in her life. She is currently a contributor to the LGBTQ sports website Outsports.

Leila Weefur (he/they/she) is an artist, writer, and curator. Their interdisciplinary practice examines the performative elements connected to systems of belonging present in Black, queer, gender-variant life. This work brings together concepts of sensorial memory, abject Blackness, hyper surveillance, and the erotic.

Riki Wilchins is an American activist and author of seven books on gender theory and politics. Wilchins founded the first national transgender protest group, The Transexual Menace, and the first transgender advocacy group, GenderPAC. Her analysis eventually broadened to include the harms a rigid gender system does to all people.

Kiyan Williams is a visual artist based in New York City. They are attracted to quotidian materials and methods that subvert dominant narratives of history and American identity.

Millie Wilson's work utilizes the frame of the museum to propose a secret history of modernity informed by queer sexuality, femininity, race, and class. From 1985 to 2014, she was on faculty in the Program of Art at the California Institute of the Arts. Her work is in numerous collections, including the Hammer Museum, Orange County Museum of Art, and San Francisco Museum of Modern Art.

Credits and Permissions

Every reasonable attempt has been made to identify the copyright holders, photographers, and sources of images contained in this publication. If errors or omissions are identified, please contact the Museum of Trans Hirstory & Art so that corrections can be made in subsequent editions. Unless otherwise noted all reproductions are © the listed artist(s) and/or provided courtesy of the institution or individual in the image caption. The following applies to images for which additional acknowledgment is due. Numbers refer to the page on which an image appears.

Courtesy of Alamy Stock Photo: 133.
© Mariette Pathy Allen: 265, 266, 267.
Photo by Claudia Alva: 276.
Photo by Daniel Ballesteros: 73.
© Estate of Harry Benjamin: 68–69.
Photo by John Berens: 98, 155, 219, 220, 221, 237.
Photo by Ian Byers-Gamber: 64, 66, 83, 90, 100, 102, 104, 105, 127, 128, 164–65, 234, 271, 273, 275.
© micha cárdenas: 70 (top).
© Cassils; photo by Robyn Beck: 254; photo by Cassils with Vince Ruvolo: 255.
Courtesy of Susana Vargas Cervantes: 117, 118, 119.
© Shu Lea Cheang; courtesy of the Solomon R. Guggenheim Foundation / Art Resource, New York: 110.
© Vaginal Davis; courtesy of the artist and Galerie Isabella Bortolozzi, Berlin: 144, 146, 147.
© Heather Dewey-Hagborg; photos by Paula Abreu Pita; courtesy of the artist and Fridman Gallery, New York: 60.
Courtesy of the Division of Cultural and Community Life, National Museum of American History, Smithsonian Institution: 136.
Photo by Jonathan Dorado: 202.
Photo by Katherine Du Tiel: 161.
Courtesy of Monica Erickson: 149, 151.
© Edie Fake: Interior of cover, 26–27, 56–57, 88–89, 114–15, 152–53, 184–85, 204–05, 232–33, 258–59.
© Demetrius Freeman/The New York Times/Redux: 32.
© Pippa Garner; courtesy of the artist and STARS, Los Angeles: 75, 76–77.
© Grove Press/Photofest: 49.
© Guerrilla Girls, courtesy of guerrillagirls.com: 18.
© Martine Gutierrez; courtesy of the artist and RYAN LEE Gallery, New York: 102, 104, 105.
Photo by Houston Hickey-Robertson: 81.
Courtesy of Italian Ministry for Cultural Heritage and Activities and Tourism, Gallerie Estensi, Biblioteca Estense Universitaria: 175.
© Young Joon Kwak; courtesy of the artist and Commonwealth and Council, Los Angeles: 226
Photo by Guy L'Heureux: 37.
Photo by No Limits! Art Castle (Founder/Director: Jan Hoek; Chief Photographer: Mirthe Beerling): 229, 230, 231.
© Candice Lin and P Staff; courtesy the artists, François Ghebaly, Los Angeles, and Commonwealth and Council, Los Angeles: 62.
© Jennie Livingston: 285.
Photo by Felipe Luna: 178.
© Estate of Jeffrey Catherine Jones: 73.
Photo by Luis Juárez: 281, 282, 283.
Courtesy of the Maryland Center for History and Culture, Item ID # 4637: 18.
Courtesy of Mattress Factory Museum, Pittsburgh, PA: 139.
Photo by Elle Mehrmand: 70 (bottom).
Photo by Howard Morehead: 31 (foreground).
Courtesy of Oakland Museum of California: 17, 20, 292 (left and middle).
© Marcel Pardo Ariza: 35, 44, 55, 79, 93, 112, 135, 156, 173, 181, 242, 244, 245 (background), 246–47, 279,
© Puppies Puppies (Jade Guanaro Kuriki-Olivo); courtesy of the artist and Hannah Hoffman, Los Angeles: 85, 86, 87.
Photo by Javier Romero: 177.
Courtesy of Autumn Sandeen and Lambda Archives of San Diego: 93.
Courtesy of SF Camerawork, photo by Henrik Kam: 22.
Photo by Rik Sferra: 141, 243.
Photo by John Schweikert: 41.
Courtesy of the Smithsonian Institution, Creative Commons Zero (CC0) license: 47, 121, 217.
Courtesy of the Sterilization and Social Justice Lab based at the University of California, Los Angeles, and reproduced in accordance with California State code: 253.
© 2014 TIME USA LLC, All rights reserved, Used under license: 101.
Courtesy of Billy Tipton Jr.: 127.
© Tourmaline; courtesy of the artist and Chapter NY, New York: 120, 122, 123.
Tranvestia © Transgender Archives, University of Victoria Libraries: 271.
© Wu Tsang; courtesy of the artist and Galerie Isabella Bortolozzi, Berlin: 286, 287.
© Chris E. Vargas: Cover, spine, back cover, 8–9, 24–25, 29, 38, 43, 82, 94, 125, 191, 197, 239, 261.
Photo by Andreas Michael Velten: 198, 199.
© Del LaGrace Volcano: 97 (bottom).
Courtesy of the Yates County History Center, Penn Yan, NY: 182, 183.

Published by:
Museum of Trans Hirstory & Art (MOTHA)
Pasadena, CA
www.motha.net

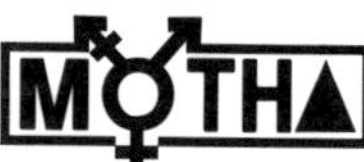

Hirmer Publishers
Bayerstrasse 57–59
80335 Munich
Germany
www.hirmerpublishers.com

HIRMER

Edited by:
David Evans Frantz, Christina Linden, and Chris E. Vargas

Editorial and permissions assistance:
Addy Rabinovitch

Design and visual editing:
ELLA with V.E. Chen and Gabrielle Pulgar

Senior Editor Hirmer Publishers:
Elisabeth Rochau-Shalem

Project Manager Hirmer Publishers:
Rainer Arnold

Copy editing:
Nina Lewallen Hufford and Bryne Rasmussen

Proofreading:
James Copeland

Pre-press:
Reproline Mediateam, Munich

Printing & binding:
Printer Trento

Printed in Italy

Paper: Tauro Offset 140 g/m2
Typefaces: Griott, Century Schoolbook,
Acumin Variable Concept

2nd edition:

Library of Congress Control Number: 2023913529

ISBN: 978-3-7774-4293-8

Trans Hirstory in 99 Objects is made with the generous support of the Ford Foundation, Creative Capital, the John Simon Guggenheim Memorial Foundation, the Michael Asher Foundation, and the Western Washington University's Research and Sponsored Programs.

Ford
Foundation

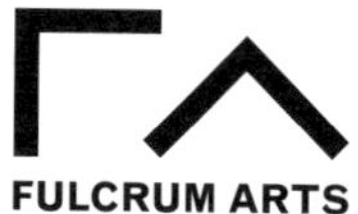

Trans Hirstory in 99 Objects is a project of the Fulcrum Arts' Emerge Fiscal Sponsorship Program.

FULCRUM ARTS